SOCIAL PROBLEMS

Alex Thio
Ohio University, Athens

Jim D. Taylor
Ohio University, Zanesville

JONES & BARTLETT
LEARNING

World Headquarters

Jones & Bartlett Learning
40 Tall Pine Drive
Sudbury, MA 01776
978-443-5000
info@jblearning.com
www.jblearning.com

Jones & Bartlett Learning
Canada
6339 Ormindale Way
Mississauga, Ontario L5V 1J2
Canada

Jones & Bartlett Learning
International
Barb House, Barb Mews
London W6 7PA
United Kingdom

Jones & Bartlett Learning books and products are available through most bookstores and online booksellers. To contact Jones & Bartlett Learning directly, call 800-832-0034, fax 978-443-8000, or visit our website, www.jblearning.com.

Production Credits
Publisher, Higher Education: Cathleen Sether
Acquisitions Editor: Sean Connelly
Editorial Assistant: Caitlin Murphy
Production Manager: Jenny L. Corriveau
Associate Production Editor: Jessica deMartin
Associate Marketing Manager: Lindsay White
Manufacturing and Inventory Control Supervisor: Amy Bacus
Cover Design: Kristin E. Parker
Photo Research and Permissions Supervisor: Christine Myaskovsky
Photo Research Assistant: Elise Gilbert
Composition: diacriTech
Cover Image: © Monkey Business Images/Dreamstime.com
Printing and Binding: Malloy, Inc.
Cover Printing: Malloy, Inc.

Library of Congress Cataloging-in-Publication Data
Thio, Alex.
    Social problems / Alex Thio and Jimmy Taylor.
        p.   cm.
    ISBN-13: 978-0-7637-9309-8 (pbk.)
    ISBN-10: 0-7637-9309-4 (pbk.)
    1. Social problems.   2. Social problems—United States.   I. Taylor, Jimmy.   II. Title.
    HN18.3.T45 2011
    306.0973—dc22
                                                                                    2010047195

6048

Printed in the United States of America
15 14 13 12 11   10 9 8 7 6 5 4 3 2

Brief Contents

Contents

8   Sexual Behavior 178

14 Healthcare Problems 326

Part V — Problems of Globalization 353

15 — Urbanization, Population, and Environment 354

Box Contents

Preface

Today we are swamped with numerous social problems in our lives. Everywhere we look we can see in person or through the media various kinds of social inequality, such as that between rich and poor and between men and women. We can also see a variety of social deviances such as crimes and drug abuse. We can further see the problems that bedevil our families, healthcare, and other social institutions. Finally, we can see how our lives are affected by problems that exist all over the world, including environmental pollution, war, and terrorism. In this textbook, we use the latest sociological research and insight not only to understand all these social problems but also to solve them in some ways. As a result, we produce a book that is different and better than other texts.

How Our Book Differs from Others

Correct application of theories   Many other texts misapply sociological theories to social problems, incorrectly using the theories about *nonproblematic* social phenomena to explain social *problems*. Consider how other texts typically use the functionalist theory about educational functions to explain educational problems. But instead of showing how the theory could explain educational *problems* such as incompetent teachers, school violence, and poor academic performance, they merely demonstrate how the theory is capable of pointing out the *functions* of education, such as teaching young people knowledge and skills, offering them employment opportunities, and enabling them to achieve upward social mobility. Aware of such a misapplication of theories, we take care to avoid it, and use sociological theories to explain specific social problems rather than describe nonproblematic events.

Free of popular stereotypes   Many other texts tend to use popular stereotypes to explain social problems. According to one of these texts, for example, prostitution exists because it serves the sexual needs of unattractive men and others who cannot attract a conventional woman to marry them. Such an explanation may make sense but it is not supported by facts. For sociological literature on prostitution suggests that prostitution performs a much more important, though ironical, function. It serves to strengthen the sexual morality of society by encouraging men to go to prostitutes for premarital sex, extramarital sex, and other "immoral" sex so that they would not entice conventional women to engage in the same "immoral" sex. This may explain why societies where prostitution is legal, such as some Asian countries, have lower rates of premarital and other "immoral" sex acts than some Western societies that ban prostitution. In discussing sociological theories, then, we avoid the use of popular stereotypes about social problems like prostitution.

The relevance of boxed readings   Other texts are typically embellished with many boxes that do not seem relevant to the text. After all, the boxes are not even mentioned in the summary as though they do not exist in the text. Students are thus inclined to assume that the boxes are not as important as the narrative material in the body of the text. They often ask their professors, "Do we have to read them? Will they be on the test?" In our text, however, we make sure that the boxes we use not only illustrate and reinforce the ideas in the text but also are interesting to read.

Constructionist views   Seen through the sociological eye, a social problem is a dual phenomenon for having both an objective and subjective component. But other texts tend to present it only as an objective entity made up of some negative qualities such as racial conflict as opposed to social harmony. It is our belief that students need to know also the subjective aspect of social problems as viewed through the constructionist perspective. Thus, in each of the chapters ahead, we present in the form of a box two divergent constructionist views on a given social problem.

The global perspective   Nowadays it is important to know as much about people in faraway lands as about ourselves because what happens to them affects us in some way. Such a global perspective not only enhances and deepens our understanding of other societies' social problems. But, more importantly, it helps us gain special insight into our own problems by looking at them more objectively. Other texts do not adequately present this global perspective, but it is provided in every chapter in this book.

Improving our everyday lives   Our text is more innovative and thought-provoking than the rest. It is often suggested in other texts that students can learn from the study of social problems that personal troubles are caused by society along with the way individual social actors react to social forces. But we take a step further to show how this insight can be extremely useful for the student's everyday life. Suppose someone insults us. We know from the study of social problems that the insult is largely a product of the individual's social circumstances, such as joblessness, broken relationships, or simply having had a bad day. Armed with this knowledge, it does not make sense for us to get upset or angry at the individual for insulting us. In fact, we should feel lucky or grateful—in effect, happy—for not having those bad experiences that weigh heavily on that "nasty" person. Throughout this text we present many thought-provoking insights like this one to show how they can be used to improve our everyday lives.

A unique blend of style and substance In this text we offer a substantive analysis of various social problems, backed up with the latest sociological theories and data. It is presented with a simple, straightforward, and lively style of writing. This book should thus be not only easy but also fun to read, similar to co-author Alex Thio's other texts, excerpts of which have appeared as pedagogical exemplars in a number of textbooks on writing techniques.

■ Supplements

INSTRUCTOR RESOURCES

Instructor's Manual

- Offers tips to create the course syllabus along with both in-class and online student activities
- Contains answers to the questions in the student study guide and lecture outlines

Complete TestBank

- Includes multiple-choice, true or false questions, and short-answer questions and essays, all with answers and page references

Microsoft® PowerPoint lecture slides®

- Supply ready-to-use presentations that are both engaging and educational. Slides can be modified to suit your own preferences and needs.

STUDENT RESOURCES

Fundamental elements to the learning process include additional resources available on a Companion Website. Students are able to reinforce their knowledge of the key concepts of social problems. Some available resources include:

- Practice quizzes
- Chapter outlines & summaries
- Interactive flashcards
- Links to relevant research databases
- Newsfeed updates

Acknowledgments

We would like to express our profound gratitude to the reviewers of *Social Problems*, for their valuable insight and helpful suggestions.

Toni Calasanti, Virginia Tech

Brenda Chappell, University of Central Oklahoma

Lisa A. Eargle, Francis Marion University

Michael L. Hirsch, Huston-Tillotson University

Kristin Holster, Dean College

Hua-Lun Huang, University of Louisiana, Lafayette

Peter Remender, University of Wisconsin Oshkosh

We would also like to thank Sean Connelly, Megan Turner, Caitlin Murphy, Elise Gilbert, Christine Myaskovsky, and Jenny Corriveau at Jones & Bartlett Learning for their dedication to this project.

About the Authors

Alex Thio, PhD - Professor Emeritus of Sociology, Ohio University, Athens, Ohio

Alex Thio was born of Chinese parentage in Penang, Malaysia. He grew up in a multicultural environment. He acquired fluency in Mandarin Chinese, Malay, and Indonesian. He also studied English, French, and German.

Professor Thio went to Central Methodist University in Missouri, where he majored in social sciences. Later, he studied sociology as a graduate student at the State University of New York at Buffalo, where he completed his doctorate while working as a research and teaching assistant.

Professor Thio regularly teaches courses in deviance, introductory sociology, social problems, and criminology. In addition to teaching, he enjoys writing. Aside from this book, he is the author of the popular texts *Deviant Behavior* (2010), and *Society: Myths and Realities* (2009), and has written many articles. The author is grateful for the feedback he often receives from faculty and students, which he believes improves the quality of his books. If you have any comments, suggestions, or questions, please write to him at the Department of Sociology, Ohio University, Athens, OH 45701, or via e-mail at thio@ohio.edu.

Jim D. Taylor, PhD - Professor, Ohio University Zanesville

Jim D. Taylor, PhD, is a Professor of Sociology and Criminology at Ohio University - Zanesville. A lifelong motorcycle rider and enthusiast, hack songwriter/guitarist and former skydiver, Dr. Taylor specializes in the sociology of masculinity, deviant behavior and race relations. Dr. Taylor has published a book on American Gun Culture, and scholarly articles on the topics of stigma management and self-injury. His current research focuses on the noble struggle of the rodeo cowboy and the intersections of rodeo sports and honky tonk music. He currently lives in Ohio with his wife and two young sons.

Introduction to Social Problems

PART

I

CHAPTER 1 The Sociological Study of Social Problems

The Sociological Study of Social Problems

In the summer of 2000, actor George Clooney starred in the hit Warner Brothers movie *The Perfect Storm*. The movie was based on the true story of a fishing crew from Gloucester, Massachusetts, who lost their lives when their boat, the Andrea Gail, sank during a hurricane of unprecedented strength. The National Weather Service had labeled the hurricane "the perfect storm" because the climate conditions that created the storm had been such a prefect recipe for natural disaster. On June 18, 2008, in a *Time* magazine article titled "Pregnancy Boom at Gloucester High," Kathleen Kingsbury reported on a different kind of perfect storm. Gloucester, like many other towns in the United States, is reeling from a long-lasting economic downturn, job loss, underemployment, and increased instances of homelessness. Christopher Farmer, Gloucester's superintendant of schools, blames these troublesome social conditions for leaving so many local people "directionless," "with broken families," and confronted with an "epidemic" of teen pregnancies.

As many as 17 high school girls in Gloucester participated in a "pregnancy pact." This was more than four times the number of teen pregnancies at the school the previous year. Many students went to the school clinic several times to get pregnancy tests. According to Kingsbury's article, "On hearing the results, some girls seemed more upset when they weren't pregnant than when they were. . . . Some of the girls reacted to news of being pregnant with high fives." As part of the pact, the unmarried girls not only became pregnant intentionally but also agreed to help support each other as members of a new, extended family. When asked how she felt about girls getting pregnant on purpose, Gloucester High School student Karia Lowe said that at least for now "no one's offered them a better deal." Whatever the reasons these girls had for getting pregnant, it was clear that teen pregnancy had risen sharply in Gloucester amid a perfect storm of negative social conditions.

For these girls and their families, the pregnancy presents a challenge and undeniable trouble. But is this simply a personal problem for which the girls are to blame? Are they wild and reckless, incapable of planning for the future and making good, responsible decisions? On the contrary, they are responding to faltering support networks and weakening national and local economies with what they believe to be rational survival strategies. Other likely contributing factors are religious beliefs that discourage the use of contraceptives and the pervasive portrayal in the U.S. culture of sexuality as free and thrilling, ideas that saturate the daily life of young individuals like these. In fact, these cultural influences are so powerful that there are now about 1 million teen pregnancies every year. American adolescents are also far more likely to get pregnant and have babies than their peers in other developed countries. Given this prevalence of premarital pregnancies, the girls in this story no longer can be said to have a personal problem, or to have some difficulty besetting only them and perhaps a few others. What they have, instead, is a part in a serious social problem that afflicts many young people.

What has just been discussed implies that there are two ways to tell whether a problem is personal or social. One way has to do with numbers, whether the problem at hand involves a few people or many. If few, it is a personal problem; if many, a social problem. Another way to tell the difference between the two kinds of problems has to do with causation. If the causes of a problem are psychological in nature, such as recklessness and irresponsibility, it is a personal problem. But if the causes are sociological in the form of some larger social forces, such as the widespread media depiction of sexuality, we are faced with a social problem. To sociologists, however, many problems that appear personal are actually social, because personal experiences are in one way or another influenced by some social forces. C. Wright Mills (1916–1962) uses the term **sociological imagination** to refer to this ability to see the impact of social forces on individuals, especially on their private lives.

■ The Sociological Imagination

To understand social problems, sociologists stand back and look "from the outside" at individuals as members of society, rather than looking "inside them" to examine their thoughts, personalities, and motivations. Sociologists use this approach because they have long found that no matter how personal our experiences are, they are influenced by **social forces**—forces that arise from the society of which we are a part. Social forces exist outside the individual in the form of social relationships, such as those we have with relatives, friends, and people in familial, educational, economic, religious, and other institutions. Through these social forces, which may be positive or negative, society exercises so much power over individuals that observers can effectively see it through their behaviors, such as treating others merely as sex objects after being constantly exposed to pornography in the media. See **Box 1.1** to learn how this sociological imagination can be used to improve your life.

We have briefly observed how U.S. society influences premarital pregnancies among teenagers with its freewheeling media depiction of sexuality. This is an example of a social force. Let's take a closer look at how a social force influences another social problem that appears to be personal only: suicide. It is reasonable to assume that those who kill themselves have terrible personal troubles. They are deeply frustrated and unhappy. But suicide cannot be explained that simply. After all, most people who are deeply frustrated and unhappy do not commit suicide. More importantly, individual unhappiness cannot tell us why, for example, people who live in wide-open areas, such as the prairies in Montana and Wyoming, have much higher suicide rates than those who live in crowded areas, such as the cities in New York and New Jersey. There is no evidence that those who live in the wide-open areas are more frustrated and unhappy. How, then, can we account for the difference in suicide rates?

The sociological imagination leads us to look not at the individual feelings of those who commit suicide but at social forces. When French sociologist Emile Durkheim (1858–1917) examined suicide in the late 19th century, he discovered variations in the rates of suicide among different countries and groups. For example, suicide rates are higher in Protestant than in Catholic countries, and higher among men than women. These different rates between religion and sex constitute social, not individual, facts; to explain them, Durkheim turned to social forces. One force that he found to have a great impact on suicide was social isolation. Divorced and widowed individuals, for example, are more likely than married people to be isolated from others and to receive little affection or moral support when they have problems. As a result, they are more likely than married people to commit suicide. Similarly, people who live in sparsely populated states, such as Montana and Wyoming, are more isolated from others than those who live in densely populated states, such as New York and

Sociological imagination Mills's term for the ability to see the impact of social forces on individuals, especially on their private lives.

Social forces Forces that arise from the society of which we are a part.

BOX 1.1   USING SOCIOLOGICAL INSIGHTS

If someone is nasty to you, you are likely to feel upset. But sociological insights can make you feel better.

Why Be Nice to Others Who Are Nasty to You?

How would you react if somebody behaved badly toward you? Suppose you are driving on a highway and someone suddenly comes from behind to cut you off. When you glance at the person, he gives you the finger. Would you get angry, irritated, or react in some negative way? Or would you instead smile at the person and wish him a good day? What if somebody insulted you, calling you all kinds of names in front of your friends? Would you respond negatively or positively? What a silly question to ask, you may say. Of course, a common reaction would be to react negatively. You would probably feel bad about it later, but you just couldn't help it. You believe that the person was clearly at fault for ruining your day. Unfortunately, your negative reaction to the person's bad treatment of you doesn't do any good. You still feel awful. But the study of social problems can provide sociological insights that you can use to make you feel better—and even improve the quality of your life and the lives of those around you.

As discussed earlier, the sociological imagination suggests that many personal troubles, such as getting laid off, feeling frustrated, and driving recklessly, arise from social forces. These social forces may include the poor conditions of the society, the economy, and other social institutions. Because these social forces significantly cause the individuals to suffer from personal troubles, the individuals are largely the victims. They are thus mostly not to blame for their troubles. The social forces are to blame. According to the sociological imagination, then, if someone behaves badly toward us, that person is already a victim of the social circumstances beyond his or her control. Therefore, it doesn't make much sense to blame the victim by getting upset or angry at that person. To blame the victim for causing us pain makes as much sense as blaming a whip that strikes us. Armed with this knowledge, the next time somebody mistreats you, instead of responding negatively, you should react positively, feeling *grateful* or *lucky* for not having those personal troubles yourself that weigh so heavily on the "nasty" person. You could also feel *sympathetic* and *compassionate* toward the person for having the problem. That's why it makes sense to smile at the offensive driver and wish him a good day.

New Jersey (U.S. Census Bureau, 2010). Greater isolation tends to make people more individualistic, more dependent on themselves than on others. This individualism may underlie the higher rate of suicide in the wide-open areas. By relying on themselves to solve their personal problems, people tend to be too subjective and too emotional to find viable solutions and are hence more likely to commit suicide. But why is suicide a social problem in the first place?

■ The Sociological Definition of Social Problems

Social problem
A social condition that is perceived to be harmful to more than just a few people.

To sociologists, suicide is a social problem because it is a social condition that is perceived to be harmful to more than just a few people. This definition suggests that a social problem is both an objective reality and a subjective perception. As an objective reality, a social problem is absolutely or intrinsically real in that it possesses a harmful quality that can be verified by the experience of some people. The harmful nature of this experience is universal, existing all over the world. Suicide, poverty, violence, alcoholism, terrorism, human trafficking, and many other social problems are harmful wherever they take place (see **Box 1.2**). However, a social problem is also a matter of personal perception; that is, whether something constitutes a social problem depends on how people see it. If people perceive something as a social problem, it is a social problem; if they view it as something else, it will be something else. In fact, the same thing can be both a social problem and its exact opposite. Take abortion as an example. To people who oppose it, abortion is murder and thereby a problem. But to those who support it, abortion is a solution to being pregnant with an unwanted child for whom the pregnant individual cannot provide care. Premarital pregnancy, too, may or may not be considered a social problem: It is widely considered a social problem if it involves teenagers but not as often if it involves adults. Even suicide can be perceived both ways. Some people may consider it a social problem for bringing

BOX 1.2 GLOBAL PERSPECTIVE

Human Trafficking

Human trafficking involves the involuntary movement of people across and within borders through the use of coercion, deception, or violence. It is an objective reality in that it is a universal problem that can be found all around the world. The United Nations estimates that there are globally at least 4 million people falling victim to human trafficking every year, which generates annual revenues of $7 billion to $10 billion for the traffickers. Deregulation, open borders, entwined economies, and the ease of international banking have all facilitated the trafficking of human beings. Many victims are turned into some form of human slavery, serving as sex, farm, factory, or domestic slaves. One of the largest exporters of sex slaves is Southeast Asia, where an abundant supply of these sex slaves is available to serve wealthy customers in Japan, China, Australia, Europe, and the United States (Aguilar-Millan et al., 2008).

In human trafficking, people such as this woman are moved across and within borders through the use of coercion, deception, and violence.

Another large exporter of sex slaves is the former Soviet bloc countries in Central and Eastern Europe. Most of these sex slaves are transported to Western Europe, and roughly a quarter end up in the United States. The rise of the sex slave trade can be traced to the fall of the Soviet Union. The borders that were once heavily guarded by the Red Army became porous when the former Soviet satellites saw their industries and subsidies collapse. Millions of young women tried to escape this economic misery by seeking a better life in the West. But they soon afforded a golden opportunity to the human traffickers, who promised the women good jobs but turned them into enslaved prostitutes. These sex slaves are usually kept under lock and key in the back rooms of bars that double as brothels. When a customer arrives, the slaves are told by their owners to parade in skimpy lingerie before him so that he may pick one to have sex with. Every day the women are forced to have sex with as many as 10 men (Mendenhall, 2009).

so much grief to its survivors, but others may regard it as a compassionate act for allowing the terminally ill to die with dignity.

Conflicting Constructionist Views

We have observed how sociologists see a social problem as a dual phenomenon with its objective and subjective components. This view reflects the influence of two general perspectives in sociology. One is the positivist perspective, and the other the constructionist. According to the positivist, a social problem is absolutely or intrinsically real in that it possesses some negative qualities as opposed to the positive qualities of a social well-being. Thus poverty is a social problem as opposed to prosperity as a social well-being, racial hatred as opposed to racial harmony, mental illness as opposed to mental health, war as opposed to peace, and so on. On the other hand, according to the constructionist perspective, a social problem is an idea that people use to define a certain condition as a problem. The so-called intrinsically negative characteristics of a social problem do not come from the problem itself. They are, instead, socially constructed, originating from some people's minds. Although a socially constructed problem is not intrinsically real, it has the potential to have very real consequences for those involved.

While the objective component stays the same when different people look at it, the subjective component often varies from one person to another. This is particularly true in our multicultural society. **Box 1.3** considers how the same thing—the status of morality in the United States—appears different to two observers through the subjective lens of their own constructionist perspectives.

Sociological Theories of Social Problems

Sociologists approach the study of human society in different ways. They can look at the "big picture" of society to see how it operates. This is a macroview, focusing on the large social phenomena of society, such as culture, institutions, and inequality. Sociologists can also take a microview, zeroing in on the immediate social situations in which people interact with one another. From these two views, sociologists have developed various perspectives, each with a set of general assumptions about the nature of society. There are three well-known perspectives in sociology: The functionalist perspective assumes that society is stable and orderly, the conflict perspective sees society as always changing and always marked by conflict, and the symbolic interaction perspective views society as being made up of countless social interactions, therefore focusing on the details of any specific situation and the interaction between individuals in that situation. Thus the functionalist and conflict perspectives reflect the macroview of society, while the symbolic interaction perspective represents the microview. In the study of social problems rather than society in general, however, sociologists derive more specific theories from the three perspectives to explain the causes of social problems.

Functionalist Theory

According to functionalist theory, every part of society—the family, the school, the economy, the government, and other social institutions and groups—performs certain functions for the society as a whole. The family raises children, the school teaches knowledge, the economy provides jobs, the government offers security, and so on.

BOX 1.3 DIVERGENT VIEWS

Is the United States in Moral Decline?

The answer is "yes" according to Robert Bork, a conservative, but "no" according to Kay Hymowitz, a liberal. According to Bork, the signs of the U.S. moral decline include high rates of crime, low rates of punishment, high rates of illegitimate births, and high rates of divorce. For example, as Bork points out, the proportion of illegitimate births was only about 5% in 1960 but shot up to 30% in 1991. Bork further sees the moral decline in popular culture. In his view, for example, a popular song of the 1930s titled "The Way You Look Tonight" is sweet and innocent, but today the song "Horny" sung by Snoop Dogg is downright decadent and obscene. The first, older song contains these words:

According to one view, the United States suffers a moral decline as suggested by the song "Horny" sung by Snoop Dogg. But another view sees a moral regeneration.

> Oh, but you're lovely,
> With your smile so warm,
> And your cheek so soft,
> There is nothing for me but to love you,
> Just the way you look tonight.

But the second, more recent song includes the following:

> I called you up for some sexual healing.
> I'm callin' again so let me come get it.
> Bring the lotion so I can rub you.
> Assume the position so I can f—— you.

Bork blames this moral decline on modern self-centered liberalism, excessive liberty, and the pursuit of happiness being pushed too far. He also argues that the constant denigration of such institutions as the family, church, school, neighborhood, and old morality has necessarily weakened the restraints on individuals (Bork, 1996; Fukuyama, 2009).

However, Hymowitz does not see a moral decline but instead observes a moral regeneration. She notes that since 1965 most of the growing trends in juvenile delinquency, adult crime, divorce, illegitimacy, drug use, and the like have turned around today. "What is emerging," she says, "is a vital, optimistic, family-centered, entrepreneurial, and yes, morally thoughtful, citizenry." To support her observation, she offers statistical evidence on the decline of those various indicators of "immoral" activities. In regard to juvenile crime, for example, she notes that the juvenile murder rate has sunk 70% since the early 1990s, the arrest rate for all violent crime among teenagers has dropped 44% since its peak in 1994, and juvenile arrest rate for burglary has gone down 56% since the early 1990s (Fukuyama, 2009; Hymowitz, 2004).

Moreover, all parts of society depend on each other to bring about a stable social order. Thus the family depends on the school to educate its children, and the school, in turn, depends on the family to provide emotional support, and both the school and the family depend on the government to offer a safe environment. If some parts of

Dysfunction
The failure of some parts of society to perform their functions and the resulting disruption of the network of interdependence among all parts.

Manifest function
A function that is intended and widely recognized.

Latent function
A function that is unintended and unrecognized.

society fail to perform their functions so as to disrupt the network of interdependence among all parts, we have a case of **dysfunction**. As dysfunctions occur, social disorder will take place in the form of social problems, such as high rates of delinquency, crime, unemployment, and poverty.

There are two kinds of functions. **Manifest functions** are those that are intended and widely recognized, while **latent functions** are unintended and unrecognized. The manifest function of attending college, for example, is to acquire knowledge, but attending college also has the latent function of enabling many students to find their future spouses. Often, however, the manifest function is carried too far because some social institutions, groups, and other parts of society are too successful in performing their functions. Sometimes this may cause their latent function to become *negative* in nature, which is popularly known as "unintended consequences." If this occurs, it is known as a social problem. Thus, by focusing too much on acquiring knowledge, students may neglect to pick up social skills. Also consider the excessive pursuit of the American Dream. It is widely believed to have the manifest function of making us rich by encouraging us to work hard. But it may also have the latent function of causing widespread deviance by encouraging people to adopt an "anything goes" mentality in the relentless pursuit of material success. The relentless pursuit of the American Dream may cause deviance because it induces a strong *self*-interest with little or no *social* interest. Self-interests focus on personal success, while social interests emphasize concern for the welfare of others. People tend to engage in deviance if they have strong self-interests while lacking social interests (Konty, 2005; Messner and Rosenfeld, 2007).

Conflict Theory

According to conflict theory, social problems arise from various kinds of social conflict. The most important and common are class conflict, racial or ethnic conflict, and gender conflict. Each conflict stems from the inequality between the powerful and the weak. As observed by Karl Marx (1818–1883), a German economist who spent much of his life writing in England, **class conflict** involves the struggle between the **bourgeoisie** (capitalists), who own the means of production such as factories and machineries, and the **proletariat** (laborers), who do not. These two classes are inevitably locked in conflict, with the capitalists successfully maximizing profit by paying their workers as little as possible and the laborers failing to get as high a wage as they desire. This exploitative nature of capitalism causes many social problems, such as crime and deviance, by generating poverty among the lower classes. Capitalism further causes social problems by bringing about widespread unemployment. To increase profit, capitalists must find ways to enhance productivity at low labor costs, including introduction of automation and other labor-saving devices; relocation of industries to cheap-labor places, such as nonunionized areas in the southern United States or in labor-rich developing countries; and hiring of workers from poor countries. These measures inevitably throw some of the existing labor force out of work. The workers' inability to maintain a decent living pressures them toward crime and deviance.

Capitalism produces not only property crimes such as theft and robbery among the unemployed lower-class people; it also causes personal crimes such as assault, rape, and homicide in addition to various other forms of deviance such as alcoholism,

Class conflict
Marx's term for the struggle between capitalists, who own the means of production such as factories and machineries, and laborers, who do not.

Bourgeoisie
The capitalists who own the means of production such as factories and machineries.

Proletariat
The laborers who do not own the means of production.

suicide, and mental illness. As Sheila Balkan, Ronald Berger, and Janet Schmidt (1980) explain, "Economic marginality leads to a lack of self-esteem and a sense of power-lessness and alienation, which create intense pressures on individuals. Many people turn to violence to vent their frustrations and strike out against symbols of authority, and others turn this frustration inward and experience severe emotional difficulties." By this reasoning, capitalism pressures people to commit crimes and become deviant by making them poor in the first place.

The capitalistic pressure to commit crime and other forms of deviance is not confined to the lower classes, but reaches upward to affect the higher classes as well. By making possible the constant accumulation of profit, capitalism inevitably creates powerful empires of monopoly and oligopoly in the economy. These economic char-acteristics bring about corporate misconduct. By dominating a sector of the economy, a few firms "can more easily collude to fix prices, divide up the market, and eliminate competitors" (Greenberg, 1981). Smaller companies, unable to compete with giant corporations and earn enough profits, also are tempted to shore up their sagging profits by illegal means, such as resorting to tax evasion.

Racial or ethnic conflict can further be a source of social problems. Racial conflict typically appears in the form of prejudice and discrimination held and practiced by the dominant group, namely whites, against the minorities, which include African Americans, Hispanics, Asians, and other racial or ethnic groups. Deprived of equal treatment, these minorities end up being saddled with higher rates of unemployment and poverty. Generally, the more a minority group suffers from prejudice and discrimi-nation (and consequently unemployment and poverty), the more likely its members are to commit crime than are other minorities. African Americans, for example, suffer more than Asian Americans and are therefore more likely to commit crime.

Gender conflict can also be a source of social problems. Gender conflict appears in the form of prejudice and discrimination by men against women. Thus women's posi-tion in most social situations is unequal to that of men. Compared with men, women have less power, freedom, respect, and money. This gender inequality goes hand in hand with the widely held sexist belief that women are inferior to men. Women are further oppressed—restrained, subordinated, controlled, molded, or abused—by a male-dominated society. This is the essence of **patriarchy**, a system of domination in which men exercise power over women. The oppression may involve overt physical violence against women, such as rape, wife beating, and incest. It may assume more subtle forms such as unpaid household work, underpaid wage work, sexual harassment in the workplace, and standards of fashion and beauty that reduce women to men's sexual playthings. Not surprisingly, women earn less than men, and unmarried women are poorer than their male counterparts. Nevertheless, women are still less likely to commit crimes, a finding that also seems to have something to do with patriarchy. Females are socialized to be less aggressive and violent than males, and females are subjected to greater parental supervision and social control.

Patriarchy
A system of domination in which men exercise power over women.

Symbolic Interaction Theory

Both functionalist and conflict theories assume that a social problem is a *product* of society. In contrast, symbolic interaction theory views a social problem as a *symbolic interaction* between individuals without the problem and others with the problem, leading the former to behave like the latter. Generally, symbolic interaction is the interaction between a person and others that is governed by the meanings that they impute to each other's actions and reactions. The interaction would be a pleasant one if the two parties interpret each other's behavior as friendly, but unpleasant if the two parties regard each other's behavior as unfriendly. This is because people react to others not in accordance with the others' behavior but instead with their own interpretation of the others' behavior. Thus even if your boyfriend or girlfriend treats you badly, you would still react to him or her with kindness if you define his or her behavior positively, with understanding or affection. To symbolic interaction theory, then, the meaning (variously referred to by symbolic interactionists as a symbol, significant gesture, interpretation, definition, or label) that people attach to an act in a given interaction is much more important than the act itself, because our reaction to others depends on the meanings we ascribe to their behavior rather than the behavior itself.

In symbolic interaction theory there are at least two ways a social problem can arise from the attachment of positive meanings to some deviant, criminal, or delinquent behavior. One way involves *differential association*, the process of acquiring, through association with others, "an excess of definitions favorable to violation of law over definitions unfavorable to violation of law" (Sutherland, 1939). This means that an individual is likely to commit a crime if the individual interacts more frequently with people who define the crime positively ("it's okay") than with those who define it negatively ("it's wrong"). Another way for a social problem to emerge is through *labeling* individuals as deviants, usually by convicting and imprisoning them as criminals or treating them as disreputable characters. Once a person has been labeled a thief or a robber or a drunk, he or she may be stuck with that label for life and rejected and isolated as a result. Finding a job and making friends may become extremely difficult. Consequently, the person may be forced to continue committing such acts or may commit increasingly deviant acts. Being labeled a deviant, then, can push the individual toward further and greater deviance. Being labeled a deviant involves, in effect, the individual being caught up in a symbolic interaction with the authorities or hostile others.

Evaluating the Theories

Functionalist theory has been criticized for portraying society as stable. Consequently, it focuses on the positive functions of social institutions and ignores the negative ones. It has also drawn fire for being inherently conservative, effectively justifying the status quo. Such criticisms seem valid if the functionalist theory is used here to show *society* as an orderly entity. But the theory is employed here to deal with *social problems* as a disorderly phenomenon—for the purpose of seeking out the causes of the problems.

Conflict theory has been faulted for going too far in blaming inequalities for the prevalence of social problems. Advocates of the theory seem to hold the *unconvincing* assumption that in a utopian, classless society, such nasty human acts as killing, robbing, raping, and otherwise hurting one another will disappear. It may be more realistic to assume, as Durkheim did, that social problems are inevitable, even in a society of saints, although the type of misconduct committed by saints can be expected to be mostly unserious or even trivial.

The symbolic interaction theory offers a close-up view of social problems and consequently tends to ignore how the larger social forces may have influenced it. Suppose we want to study the interaction between whites and blacks through the eye of symbolic interactionism only. We can get a rich, detailed understanding of the racial interaction, but this understanding is likely to be limited or even distorted if we do not know how the interaction is affected by such larger social forces as the popular belief in democracy and equality and the election of Barack Obama to the presidency. These larger forces can be better understood through the lens of the functionalist and conflict theories. For a quick review of these three sociological theories, see Box 1.4.

BOX 1.4   THEORETICAL THUMBNAIL

Explaining Social Problems

Theory	Focus	Insights
Functionalist Theory	Threat to social order	Social problems arise from failure of social institutions, groups, and other parts of society to perform their functions properly. But these functions if carried too far may turn into negative, unintended consequences.
Conflict Theory	Contribution to social conflict	Social problems originate from the exploitative nature of capitalism along with class, racial, ethnic, gender, and other inequalities.
Symbolic Interaction Theory	Negative interaction between individuals	Social problems result from associating to a greater extent with law violators than abiders and from being labeled as unsavory characters.

QUESTIONS TO EXPLORE

1. Which of the theories would be the most useful for understanding human trafficking as a social problem? Why do you feel that this theory is best suited for this particular problem? Are there any limitations to using this theory? If so, what are they?

2. If you were a member of a special task force to study the possible effects of television viewing on divorce, what theoretical perspective would you use to guide your study? Explain your answer.

3. Students and researchers alike have a tendency to pick their "pet theories" to make sense of the social world around them. Of the three theories, which one do you favor? Why?

■ Research Methods: Seeking Facts

From those sociological theories, we can draw many ideas about how certain social forces bring about social problems. Yet these ideas are merely idle guesswork unless they are backed up by scientific facts. The need for facts is one important reason sociologists conduct research. There are four methods for researching social problems: survey, observation, experiment, and secondary analysis.

Survey

Survey
A research method that involves asking people questions about their opinions, beliefs, or behaviors.

Population
The entire group of people to be studied.

Sample
A relatively small number of people selected from a large population.

Random sample
A sample drawn in such a way that all members of a population must have the same chance of being selected.

Structured interview
An interview in which the researcher asks standardized questions that require respondents to choose from several standardized options.

Unstructured interview
An interview in which open-ended questions are asked and respondents are allowed to answer freely, in their own words.

Of the four methods, the **survey** is most frequently used by sociologists. It involves asking people questions about their opinions, beliefs, or behaviors. To take a survey, we first select a **population**, the entire group of people to be studied. We can choose a population of any size, but all of its members must have something in common. Thus, a population may consist, for example, of all U.S. citizens aged 30 to 40 years, all U.S. congresswomen, all of the students at a large university, or all the people in the world.

If a population is relatively small, all of its members can be approached and interviewed. If a population is very large, it would cost too much time and money to contact all of its members. In such a case, we need a **sample**, a relatively small number of people selected from a large population. The sample, however, must accurately represent the entire population from which it is drawn. Otherwise, the information obtained from the sample cannot be generalized to the population. If a sample is to be representative, all members of the population must have the same chance of being selected for the sample. Selection, in effect, must be random, which is why a representative sample is often called a **random sample**.

Given a representative or random sample, we can ask its members about their opinions, attitudes, or behaviors. This is usually done by using self-administered questionnaires, personal interviews, and telephone interviews. In using *self-administered questionnaires*, the researcher simply gives or sends the people in the sample a list of questions and asks them to fill in the answers themselves. Usually the list consists of true/false or multiple-choice questions. The respondents are asked to answer "yes," "no," or "don't know" or to check one of the answers, such as "single," "married," "divorced," or "widowed." Today the questionnaires can be answered on the Web by people who have a very high rate of Internet use, such as professionals and college students (Schutt, 2009).

Personal interviews may be either structured or unstructured. In a **structured interview**, the researcher asks standardized questions that require respondents to choose from several standardized options on a list, comparable to those in self-administered questionnaires. In contrast, in an **unstructured interview**, open-ended questions are asked and respondents are allowed to answer freely, in their own words, and typically with no restrictions. The interviewer, however, must be friendly and respectful to the respondents (Schutt, 2009; Weiss, 2004).

Telephone interviews have nowadays become popular in survey research and are routinely used in many public opinion polls. A recent *Time* poll, for example, was conducted by telephone and asked a representative national sample of Americans how the 2009 severe economic problem of recession has affected their belief in the American Dream. Although most (57%) said they believed the American Dream would be harder to achieve in 10 years, a surprising majority (56%) also said they believed

America's best days were still ahead, a testament to the enduring American optimism (Gibbs, 2009). A similar survey method is used to find out whether Americans trust others less today (see Box 1.5).

Observation

In surveys, we depend on others to tell us what has happened. By contrast, in observation, we rely on ourselves to go where the action is—and to watch what is happening. One way of observing an ongoing activity is through **detached observation**, whereby we

Detached observation A method of observation in which the researcher observes as an outsider, from a distance, without getting involved.

BOX 1.5   WHAT RESEARCH REVEALS

Declining Trust in Others Today

Every year since 1964 the General Social Survey has asked a random sample of Americans about their trust in others with questions such as "Generally speaking, would you say that most people can be trusted or that you can't be too careful in dealing with people." The survey indicates that over the last 40 years the proportion of Americans who trust other individuals has declined significantly. In the early 1970s, more than 65% of Americans said that most people were trustworthy, but by the 2000s only about half said the same. This decline in trust is largely a result of what sociologists call "generational replacement," the highly trusting older generation being replaced by the less trusting younger generation. Why this generational difference? The generation of the past was more trusting because their shared experience of World War II brought them a sense of solidarity and an increased desire to join organizations. But today's generation is more

Research shows that Americans trust others much less today than in the past. An important reason is the prevalence of corporate scandals.

socially isolated—less likely to join clubs, attend civic meetings, play card games, go to dinner parties, or have close friends to discuss important matters with. The September 11, 2001, terrorist attacks did initially bring them together so as to ramp up their trust in others, but the unpopular war in Iraq has subsequently diminished their solidarity and trust (Paxton, 2005; Putnam, 2006).

Of the same generation, however, some people are more trusting than others. Poor people and racial minorities are less likely to trust others, more likely to believe that others will take advantage of them in some ways. In contrast, people with more education have more trust in others. People with more contacts with others are also more trusting. Such people can thus be easily found in voluntary organizations like a church choir or bird-watching group (Paxton, 2005).

The decline in trust does not only involve others as individuals. Over the last 40 years, the trust in various institutions such as business and religion has also gone down. These declines are mostly triggered by scandals. In the 2000s, for example, the Enron and other corporate scandals caused a big drop in the percentage of Americans saying that they had a great deal of confidence in major companies. Similarly, the sex scandals involving Catholic priests caused Americans' confidence in religious institutions to plummet. Once the scandals fade, however, the public's trust in the institutions returns (Paxton, 2005). Still, the general pattern of decline in trust remains, with the trust in institutions as well as individuals being lower today than in the past.

observe as outsiders, from a distance, without getting involved. As detached observers, we may, for example, watch children playing in a schoolyard or bring them into a room and watch from behind a one-way mirror. Detached observation has the advantage of making it less likely that the subjects will be affected by the observer. But it has at least one disadvantage: The detached observer has difficulty perceiving and understanding subtle communication among the subjects. The detached observer behind a one-way mirror might not see some important facial expressions or understand the emotions attached to some unconventional symbols.

Participant observation
A method of observation in which the researcher takes part in the activities of the group being studied.

This problem can be avoided with **participant observation**, in which researchers take part in the activities of the group they are studying. Sometimes they conceal their identity as researchers when they join the group, thus enhancing the chances that the unknowing subjects will act naturally. If the subjects know they are being observed, they might change their behavior. As members of the group, researchers have the opportunity to observe practically everything, including whatever secret activities are hidden from outsiders. As a result, researchers can discover some surprising acts about their subjects. Consider, for example, the following classic case of participant observation involving a researcher with a concealed identity.

If you assume that men must be gay if they engage in same-sex practices, the results of Laud Humphreys's (1970) research may surprise you. Humphreys concealed his identity as a researcher by offering to serve as a lookout for men engaging in same-sex activities in public restrooms, which was against the law. Without being suspected of being an outsider, Humphreys also succeeded in secretly jotting down his subjects' automobile license plate numbers, which he used to trace their addresses. A year later, he disguised himself, visited those men at their homes, and found that they were mostly conservative working-class married men who were seeking the same-sex experience as a means of releasing tension. They considered themselves straight and masculine. Humphreys has been severely criticized for being unethical in deceiving his subjects. He has argued, though, that had he not concealed his identity, it would have been impossible to get scientifically accurate information because his subjects would have behaved differently or would have refused to be studied.

Ethnography
An analysis of people's lives from their own perspectives.

Many sociologists do identify themselves as researchers to the people they study. In fact, they live with them as friends, engaging in **ethnography**, an analysis of people's lives from their own perspectives. In ethnography, the researcher focuses more on *meanings* (what subjects think, believe, or ponder) than on *activities* (what subjects do or how they behave). The use of ethnography has produced interesting insights. In their ethnographic study of people who were homeless in Austin, Texas, for example, David Snow and Leon Anderson (2003) made a startling discovery. Conventional people often associate disabilities—such as a drinking problem, drug abuse, or mental disorder—with homeless individuals. But Snow and Anderson found that the disabilities usually do not inhere in homeless persons but instead stem from the disabling situation called *homelessness.* Thus, if the presumably disabled people are removed from homelessness, their disabilities often disappear.

Experiment

A theory can be tested only indirectly, not directly. It must be translated into a hypothesis or a series of hypotheses that can be tested directly, because hypotheses are more specific statements that can be demonstrated to be either true or false. Testing a theory, then, effectively means testing a hypothesis. To do so, researchers first specify what they assume to be the *independent variable* (cause) and the *dependent variable* (effect). Then they create a situation in which they can determine whether the independent variable indeed causes the dependent variable. They are, in effect, conducting an **experiment**, a research operation in which the researcher manipulates variables so that their influence can be determined.

Consider an experiment conducted by Matthew McGlone (1998). He wanted to test the hypothesis that nice-sounding statements make even dubious notions more believable. He gave students a list of rhyming sentences, such as "Woes unite foes," and asked them how accurately the sentences described human behavior. Then he asked the same students to judge the accuracy of nonrhyming statements, such as "Misfortunes unite foes." The result was that the students considered the rhyming statements more accurate. Later, when asked whether they agreed that financial success makes people healthier, nearly all of the students said no. But they regarded "Wealth makes health" as somehow more plausible. All this confirmed the hypothesis that nice-sounding sentences are more convincing. Not surprisingly, the researcher concludes, at the football star O. J. Simpson's 1995 murder trial, his defense lawyer's repeated intonation of "If the glove doesn't fit, you must acquit" may have had the desired impact on the jurors.

In another, more current experiment, Devah Pager (2003, 2007) tested the effects of a prior criminal record on employment. She gave fictitious criminal records to some black and white subjects and noncriminal records to others. She then sent out all these subjects to apply for jobs. The experiment showed that not only were people with a criminal record less likely to be called back for a second job interview, black subjects with noncriminal backgrounds were also less likely to be called back for interviews than whites with a criminal record.

Secondary Analysis

The methods we have discussed so far involve collecting data from scratch, but this is not always necessary because of the availability of information collected previously by someone else. Besides, it is simply impossible to conduct an interview, observation, or experiment when the people we want to study are long dead. Thus, sociologists often turn to **secondary analysis**, searching for new knowledge in the data collected earlier by another researcher. Usually, the original investigator had gathered the data for a specific purpose but the secondary analyst uses them for something else.

Suppose we want to study religious behavior by means of secondary analysis. We might get our data from an existing study of voting behavior conducted by a political scientist. This kind of research typically provides information on each voter's religion, along with his or her education, income, gender, and other social characteristics. The political scientist may try to find out from research whether, among other things, men are more likely than women to vote in a presidential election and whether the more religious are more politically active than the less religious. As secondary analysts, however, we can find out from the same data whether women attend church more often than men.

Experiment
A research operation in which the researcher manipulates variables so their influence can be determined.

Secondary analysis
Searching for new knowledge in the data collected earlier by another researcher.

Content analysis
Searching for specific words or ideas and then turning them into numbers.

These data for secondary analysis are usually quantitative, presented in the form of numbers, percentages, and other statistics, such as the percentage of women compared to the percentage of men attending church once a week. What if the existing information is qualitative, in the form of words or ideas? Such information can be found in virtually all kinds of human communication—books, magazines, newspapers, movies, TV programs, speeches, letters, songs, laws, and so on. To study human behavior from these materials, sociologists often do a **content analysis**, searching for specific words or ideas and then turning them into numbers by counting the frequency of these words or ideas.

Suppose we want to know whether public attitudes toward sex have changed significantly in the last 20 years. We may find the answer by comparing popular novels of today with those of the past to see if one set is more erotic than the other. We would first decide what words will reflect the nature of eroticism. After we settle on a list of words, such as *love, kiss,* and *embrace,* to serve as indicators of eroticism, we will look for them in a novel. We will then count the number of times those words appear on an average page and use the number as the measure of how erotic the novel is. In repeating the same process with other novels, we will see which ones are more erotic. Similarly, we can analyze media advertisements for products such as music, movies, and new technology in order to find out the frequency of various forms of gender relations such as sexual violence, sexual tolerance, and workplace equality (Carter and Steiner, 2003).

Review

SUMMARY

1. As used by C. Wright Mills, the term *sociological imagination* refers to the impact of social forces on individuals, especially on their private lives. This means that people with personal troubles are victims of larger social forces. They are therefore not to blame for their troubles. So, when they behave badly toward you, it doesn't make sense for you to get upset. It makes more sense to feel grateful or lucky for not having their troubles—as well as sympathetic and compassionate toward them for their suffering.

2. Sociologists define a *social problem* as a social condition that is perceived to be harmful to more than just a few people. It is both an objective reality because it harms large numbers of people and a subjective reality because it is perceived by some people as harmful but as something else by others. Human trafficking exemplifies an objective reality for being universal, because it exists all over the world.

3. The sociological definition of a *social problem* reflects the influence of two major perspectives in sociology: positivism and constructionism. From the positivist perspective, social problems remain the same to different people, but from the constructionist perspective, social problems differ, as illustrated by the divergent views on the moral status of the United States.

4. Three major sociological theories point out different causes of social problems. According to functionalist theory, social problems will arise if some parts of society—the family, the school, the economy, the government, and other social institutions and groups—fail to perform their functions properly or if they carry their performance of the functions too far. According to conflict theory, the causes of social problems stem from the exploitative nature of capitalism along with racial, ethnic, and sexual inequalities. According to symbolic interaction theory, social problems occur if individuals interact more frequently with criminals than with law-abiding citizens and therefore become criminals themselves. Social problems also occur if people are labeled (through conviction, imprisonment, or mistreatment) as criminals or unsavory characters so much that they end up repeatedly engaging in deviant activities.

5. There are four research methods for the sociological study of social problems. The first is the *survey*, which asks people, usually a random sample of them, about their opinions, beliefs, or behaviors. This can be done with self-administered questionnaires or interviews. An example of using a survey indicates that Americans are trusting others less today than before. The second is *observation*, which may be detached, observing subjects from a distance, or participant, joining the subjects in their activities. Observation may also include *ethnography*, analyzing the subjects' lives from their own perspective. The third method is *experiment*, in which

the researcher manipulates variables in order to determine their influence on the subjects. The fourth is *secondary analysis*, searching for new knowledge in the data that have been collected by somebody else.

CRITICAL THINKING QUESTIONS

1. Identify a social problem that you consider to be a relevant concern in your own community and address the following:
   a. Describe the problem and explain how you know this is a true "social" and not a "personal" problem.
   b. What are the primary "social forces" that you see at work behind this problem?
   c. Do you see any potential solutions for coping with this social problem?
2. Do you favor the positivist or constructionist view of social problems? Discuss what you consider to be the strengths and weaknesses of each approach to studying social problems.

INTERNET RESOURCES

The SSSP (Society for the Study of Social Problems): http://www.sssp1.org/. This official site for the SSSP includes current scholarship on global social problems as well as event schedules. You may find it beneficial to peruse this site and familiarize yourself with the breadth of current research projects on social problems and emerging concerns in the United States and abroad.

The *Social Problems* journal, which is published by the University of California Press, can be reviewed at http://caliber.ucpress.net. This journal is one of the primary collections of scholarly research on social problems. You can look at article abstracts and titles dating all the way back to June of 1953. This will allow you to get an idea of different social problems that have come into focus in the past 50 years and imagine ways in which some key social problems have worsened or lessened in terms of impact and severity.

U.S. Bureau of Labor Statistics: http://www.bls.gov/. With unemployment at the forefront of today's global economic news coverage and growing public concern, this site is a valuable source of current, up-to-date statistics on national and international comparative employment trends and other economic trends.

The Willie Nelson Peace Research Institute (http://willienelsonpri.com/) offers an attempt to take on social problems in an innovative manner: through the free and open use of music with the sole intention of addressing social problems pertaining to armed conflicts and other forms of violence.

Problems of Inequality

PART II

Economic Inequality

O nly 5 weeks old, Anastasia Garcia shares a cramped room in a homeless shelter with her young mother and father and two sisters, ages 2 and 6 years. They have moved into the shelter since the father lost his construction job half a year ago. He has recently found a job at a Home Depot warehouse and will soon move with his family to transitional housing, where they can stay rent-free for up to 18 months. His wife also plans to look for a job if she can find day care for her two youngest children. Their caseworker says that "they are really trying, highly motivated." Also trying is another young woman, a single mother living with her two sons, ages 4 months and 3 years, at another shelter. She says, "I'm saving all the money I can." Every day she catches a 7 a.m. bus so she can drop her kids off at a day-care center and get to work by 8 (Clary, 2009).

The extreme poverty of these two young families cracks the popularly held image of the United States as a rich nation where there are opportunities galore for everybody to realize the American Dream. The reality is that some Americans enjoy more and better opportunities than others for achieving success. That's why some get rich and others turn poor. In this chapter, we will take a close look at this economic inequality.

Income
The amount of money one earns from employment, business, investments, and other economic activities.

■ Economic Inequality

One indicator of economic inequality in the United States is its unequal distribution of **income**, the amount of money one earns from employment, business, investments, and other economic activities. Rich families, who are in the top 3%, have an annual income of above $200,000, but poor families, who are in the bottom 13%, make less than $20,000 a year (U.S. Census Bureau, 2009a). The unequal distribution of income can further be seen in **Figure 2.1**. Nearly half of the nation's entire income goes to

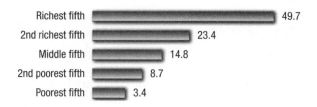

FIGURE 2.1 Unequal Income Distribution in the United States

The income of the richest Americans far exceeds that of the poorest. Almost half of the nation's income goes to the richest fifth of the population, but less than 4% goes to the poorest fifth.

Critical Thinking: *Considering the extreme income inequality that exists in the United States today between the top and bottom income earners, what could be done to move the country toward greater equality?*

Source: U.S. Census Bureau, Current Population Survey, 2008 and 2009 Annual Social and Economic Supplements.

the richest one-fifth of families, but less than 4% of all the income ends up with the poorest one-fifth of families.

The gap between rich and poor is even greater in **wealth**, the value of all the assets one owns subtracted by the debts one owes. As **Figure 2.2** shows, the richest 1% of families own 42% of the nation's wealth while the enormous poorer 90% of families account for only 19% of the wealth.

Wealth
The value of all assets one owns subtracted by the debts one owes.

■ The Very Rich

There are two kinds of the very rich: the old and the new. The *old rich* are families that have been wealthy for generations. They can be considered an aristocracy of birth and wealth. Examples are the Rockefellers, the Vanderbilts, and the DuPonts.

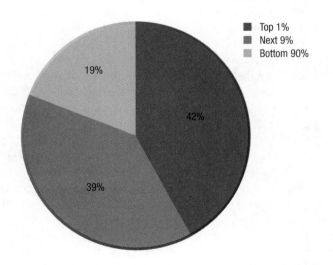

FIGURE 2.2 Unequal Wealth Distribution in the United States

The wealthiest 1% of households in the United States own much more wealth than the poorer 90% of all families.

Critical Thinking: *Does the division of wealth in the United States tell us more about inequality than the division of income?*

Source: Modified from Lawrence Mishel, Jared Bernstein, and Heidi Shierholz, *The State of Working America 2008–2009*. New York: Cornell University Press, 2009.

By contrast, the *new rich* are self-made individuals who have created their own wealth. They include Bill Gates of Microsoft, the investor Warren Buffet, and TV talk show host Oprah Winfrey. The new rich outnumber the old rich by more than two to one (Thibault, 2009).

However their wealth is acquired, the very rich are indeed different from most of us. They live in exclusive areas, belong to private social clubs, rub elbows with one another, marry their own kind, and try very hard to keep their private lives private—all of which make them so aloof from the masses that they have been called the *out-of-sight class* (Barron, 2009; Fussell, 1992). But their lifestyles, such as going to parties in elegant clothes, are so often portrayed in the media that the masses try to emulate the rich by spending more than they can afford. More than most other Americans, the rich tend to be conscious of being members of a class. They also command an enormous amount of power and influence in government and business, affecting the lives of millions (for a more in-depth look, see Box 2.1). These are, however, the richest Americans, whose average net worth is above $3 billion (Thibault, 2009). The majority of wealthy Americans have far less than that, possessing an average of $2 million (see Box 2.2).

BOX 2.1   WHAT RESEARCH REVEALS

A Social Profile of the Super Rich

Sociologist Sean Elias (2008) used the two principal tools of ethnography—participant observation and interviewing—to investigate the super rich at their favorite resort town of Aspen, Colorado. He found that this elite group maintains their power in society by "hiding from the public, cutting deals behind closed doors and on gondolas that most people can't afford to ride."

The elite can be divided into different ranks. The top dogs are the ultra elite, multibillionaires who own, among other highly expensive properties, a ranch on the outskirts of town. Their homes in Aspen are used only for vacation, so they are vacant most of the year. They travel on their private jets worth $30 million to $300 million, build homes for their pilots and chefs, routinely spend a grand or two for wine, and purchase jewelry that equals the life wages and savings of several upper-middle class families.

The second rank consists of multibillionaires who own somewhat less expensive homes and jets. They include huge real estate developers, entertainment industry tycoons, and highly successful corporate executives. Below them are the multimillionaires, who have been effectively forced by the multibillionaires to move to less expensive areas. Finally, at the fourth rank, are supermodels, star athletes, actors, musicians, and other entertainers, along with the newly arrived business people who have acquired multiple millions. These diverse groups, however, do interact frequently, associating or doing business with each other.

In talking with the super rich, Elias often spoke of their outlawry, the fact that to hang on to their riches, they needed to be an outlaw, to play outside society's rules and laws. They "knowingly smiled and responded in agreement." He concludes that most of the Aspen elite "appear to be motivated primarily by profit and accumulation of resources and power at the expense of others. . . . They are focused wealth generators with blinders to the social evils of no-limit materialism and unfettered capitalism."

BOX 2.2   USING SOCIOLOGICAL INSIGHTS

How to Become a Millionaire

Contrary to popular myth, the majority of millionaires are far different from the super rich. As we have pointed out, they do not possess billions of dollars. They have accumulated only a few million. They are not high-powered lawyers, doctors, business executives, celebrities, and others with sky-high incomes and lavish lifestyles. They do not live in upscale neighborhoods, own private jets, drive foreign luxury cars, wear expensive clothes and jewelry, attend fancy parties, eat gourmet food, and join country clubs. Instead, they are the kind of people whom you, with a college education, can emulate while having an excellent chance of becoming a millionaire yourself. Here are some key facts about them from a study by Thomas Stanley and William Danko (1998) that may enhance your hope of making it big:

- Their annual median income is only $131,000 and their accumulated wealth totals about $2 million.
- Two-thirds are self-employed, mostly in such unglamorous businesses as welding contracting, auctioneering, rice farming, pest control, scrap metal, and paving contracting.
- They work very hard; about two-thirds put in 45 to 55 hours a week. But they are extremely enthusiastic, and they can't wait to go to work in the morning.
- About half live in the same modest home for more than 20 years, which they bought long before they got rich.
- They live well below their means: Most drive inexpensive, older-model cars, rarely dine out, and spend very little on leisure pursuits.
- They are fastidious savers and investors. They sock away nearly 20% of their income every year, which is mostly invested in stocks and mutual funds.

The most striking thing about the millionaires is their frugality. Most lawyers, doctors, and other high-income people do not become millionaires because they live above their means with a high-consumption lifestyle. By contrast, most millionaires live far below their means. So, if you want to get rich, you can start now by being as frugal as possible. As the millionaire Mark Cuban says, "Instead of coffee, drink water. Instead of going to McDonald's, eat macaroni and cheese" (Fried, 2008).

■ What Is Poverty?

For individuals, poverty can be a temporary condition. But for societies, poverty is a constant reality, as it can be seen even in the midst of the most prosperous areas. What, then, exactly is poverty? To be specific, what if an American family of four has an annual income of $22,100? Would you consider them poor? The U.S. government says that they are not poor because their income exceeds the poverty line of $22,025. But according to supporters of poor people, the family is definitely poor. Most of us would probably agree. Who is right? The answer depends on which definition of poverty we choose to accept.

Absolute Poverty

To determine whether we are poor or not, the U.S. government asks if we are experiencing **absolute poverty**, the lack of minimum food and shelter necessary for

Absolute poverty
The lack of minimal food and shelter necessary for maintaining life.

maintaining life. The government, then, decides what income is needed to sustain that minimum standard of living. If our income is lower than that, we are said to be absolutely poor, falling below the poverty line. To find out what that income is, the government multiplies the cost of food by three because the average family is assumed to spend *one-third* of its income on food. Thus, for 2009, the poverty line for a four-person family was $22,025. About 13% of U.S. families had income less than that amount (U.S. Census Bureau, 2010). They were therefore defined as poor.

Those figures have stirred controversy. Conservatives contend that the figures *overestimate* the extent of poverty because they do not count as income the many *noncash benefits* such as food stamps, school lunches, housing subsidies, and medical assistance that the so-called poor receive from the government. These noncash benefits are highly significant because they account for two-thirds of government programs for the poor. If these benefits were added to cash incomes, many people would rise above the poverty line—and thus would no longer be poor.

Liberals, on the other hand, argue that the official rate *underestimates* the extent of poverty. This is because it is based on the erroneous assumption that the average U.S. family today spends one-third of its income on food, as it did in the early 1960s, when the government's formula for determining poverty was first used. Actually, nowadays the typical family spends only one-fifth of its income on food, largely due to increases in *nonfood costs* such as taxes, medical expenses, and child care. What all this means is that the family today needs a much higher income than the family of 50 years ago in order to stay out of poverty. Failing to take this into account, the government excludes from its poverty statistics many families that are actually poor.

Poverty experts at the National Academy of Sciences have suggested that both the liberal and conservative criticisms be taken into account. This involves *deducting* nonfood costs from family income as well as *adding* noncash benefits to the income. Such a calculation, though, is likely to increase the official poverty rate—with more people falling below the poverty line—because the nonfood costs are higher than the noncash benefits.

Relative Poverty

Poverty can further be found to be even more prevalent than officially reported if it is defined as having a lower standard of living than the majority of the population. More specifically, people who earn less than half of the nation's median income are said to be poor because they lack what is considered to be needed by most people to live a decent life. By this definition, for more than 40 years, the percentage of the U.S. population living in poverty has usually been twice as high as what has been reported by the government. These people are defined as living in **relative poverty**, a state of deprivation resulting from having less than the majority of the people in their society.

Relative poverty
A state of deprivation resulting from an individual having less than the majority of the people in their society.

To determine the extent of poverty in the United States, the government pays attention only to absolute poverty. But if we want to know the extent of both absolute and relative poverty, we will find that only a minority of Americans are poor in any given year. Over the last four decades, 11–15% have become absolutely poor while 22–30% have been relatively poor. However, according to an analysis of how many American adults are absolutely poor throughout their lifetimes, a *majority* (nearly 70%)

will have spent at least a year below the poverty line by the time they turn 75 years old. This spell of poverty may result from a job loss, divorce, disability, or old age. Poverty, then, doesn't strike just a few Americans but most of them (Rank, 2003).

■ The Faces of Poverty

According to the U.S. Census Bureau (2010), a little over 13%, or nearly 40 million Americans, live in poverty today. On the heels of President Lyndon Johnson's "war on poverty" policy and a host of new federal programs and services for the poor, there was a notable drop in poverty from the early 1960s and 1970s. Unfortunately, as Figure 2.3 illustrates, over the past 40 years, the poverty rate has remained relatively unchanged, hovering between 12% and 15%. However, it is important to note that certain groups of Americans are more likely than others to fall into poverty. They include children under 18 years of age, single mothers, the less educated, the unemployed, low-wage workers, racial/ethnic minorities, women, the homeless, and rural and inner city residents.

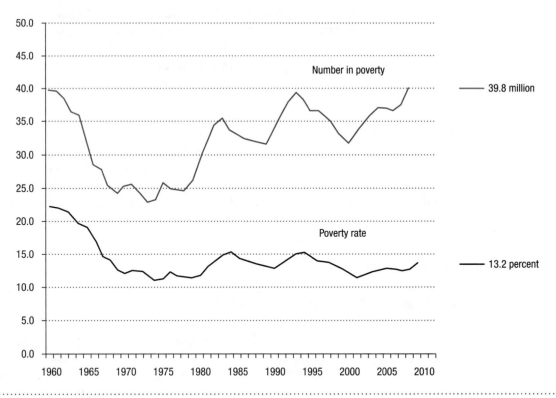

FIGURE 2.3 Poverty Number and Rate: 1960–2009

In the 1960s and 1970s, the poverty rate in the United States fell substantially as a result of many government programs for the poor. However, from then until now, over the last 40 years, the poverty rate has remained largely the same, hovering between 12% and 15%, while the number of people falling into poverty has gone up.

Critical Thinking: *Drawing on both the material in this chapter and other observations that you have made, what do you think has caused the number of poor Americans to increase over the last 30 years while the rate of poverty has remained largely unchanged?*

Source: U.S. Census Bureau, Current Population Survey, 1960 to 2009 Annual Social and Economic Supplements. Numbers are in millions; rates in percentages.

Children

Of all age groups, children 17 years old and younger are most likely to be poor. About 19% of the children are poor, while the poverty rate of all the other age groups falls below the national average of 13%. Fifty years ago it was the elderly—age 65 years or older—who had the highest rate of poverty. Since then they have become less and less poor. Today, they have the lowest poverty rate of all age groups, largely thanks to the substantial increase in government support of Medicare and Social Security benefits. Similar assistance to poor children could reverse their fortunes, but it is still lacking (U.S. Census Bureau, 2009b).

Single mothers are much more likely than married couples to be poor, largely because they are unemployed due to having to care for their children.

Single Mothers

Single mothers are much more likely than married couples to be poor. The poverty rate of single mothers is 29%, nearly five times higher than the rate (6%) for married parents. Single mothers have such a high poverty rate largely because they are usually unemployed as a result of having to care for their children. Poor single mothers tend to have children who have difficulties growing up. But the problem is not the mother being unmarried. It is her poverty. After all, the majority of children raised by a single mother are doing well, because she has adequate financial resources and is able to provide a harmonious home environment (Jayson, 2008a).

The Less Educated

The less educated are more likely than the more educated to be poor. Those who have not completed high school are twice as likely as high school graduates to be poor, and five times as likely as college graduates to be poor. The importance of education for avoiding poverty has increased tremendously in today's more technologically advanced society. Before 1970 it was relatively easy for a high school dropout to find employment and earn a decent wage, but much less so today.

The Unemployed

As many as half of all poor adults do not work. They include the disabled, welfare recipients, and individuals with little skill and education. Some of the unemployed were once skilled workers in mechanized industry. They later became unskilled workers in electronically run factories, where they initially served as assistants, then became occasional workers, and finally became chronically unemployed. Compared to the employed, the unemployed are less likely to be married and more likely to live alone or with relatives (Stewart, 2006). Jobless and poor, they suffer the indignity of living in rundown houses, wearing old clothes, eating cheap food, and lacking proper medical care. They are often stigmatized as the *underclass*, a term conjuring up images of them not only as the down-and-out but also as violent criminals, drug addicts, welfare mothers who cannot stop having babies, or able-bodied men on welfare who are too lazy to work.

Low-Wage Workers

Workers who are paid low wages are generally unskilled, such as migrant workers, janitors, and dishwashers. They also include many women working as domestics, cleaners, and waitresses. Because they are underpaid, they often have to hold two jobs. They still find it hard just to get by. Every now and then, they also are faced with a critical hardship, such as having their utilities shut off and doing without needed medical care. They are called the **working poor**, because they work for a wage that makes them fall below the official poverty line.

They could have escaped poverty if they were paid a *living wage* (above $10 an hour) rather than the *minimum wage* ($7.25 an hour). Employers frown on such a wage increase because they believe it will drive up the cost of doing business. In cities and counties that have passed a living-wage law, though, the higher wages have spurred gains in productivity, lowered job turnover, and stimulated greater loyalty to employers, all of which helps offset the cost.

Working poor
Individuals who are poor because they work for a wage that makes them fall below the official poverty line.

Racial/Ethnic Minorities

African Americans and Hispanics are twice as likely to be poor as whites. While the poverty rate of whites is 11%, the rate for African Americans is 25% and the rate for Hispanics is 23%. The greater prevalence of poverty among these minorities can be attributed to discrimination against them. It can also be attributed to the massive loss of manufacturing jobs in the inner city, which typically has a high concentration of African Americans and Hispanics (U.S. Census Bureau, 2009b).

Women

There is more poverty among women than men. For many years, since 1970, while about 9% of men have lived below the poverty line, 13% of women have done so. The persistent and pervasive phenomenon of women living in poverty at higher rates than men is what sociologists call the **feminization of poverty**. It can be attributed to certain changes in U.S. society. Increases in the rates of divorce, separation, and out-of-wedlock birth have caused many women to become single mothers or heads of poor households. The increase in divorced fathers not paying child support, along with the reduction in government support for welfare, also has caused many more female-headed households to sink into poverty. The fact that women live longer than men has further contributed to a growing number of older women living alone in poverty (Hartmann, 2009).

Feminization of poverty
The persistent and pervasive phenomenon of women experiencing poverty at higher rates than men.

The Homeless

The homeless are so poor that they sleep in streets, parks, shelters, and places not intended as dwellings, such as bus stations, lobbies, and abandoned buildings. Many of the homeless are families with children, alcohol and drug abusers, and the mentally ill.

There are about 672,000 homeless people. Why are there so many homeless individuals in the supposedly richest country in the world? One reason is the increased shortage of inexpensive housing for the poor, which has resulted from the diminishing government subsidization of such housing. Another reason is the declining demand for unskilled labor that has occurred since the 1980s, causing widespread unemployment among the poor. A third reason is the erosion of public welfare benefits that has taken place over the last two decades (Deam, 2009; HUD, 2009).

Rural and Inner-City Residents

The rate of poverty varies from one place to another. Globally, developing countries have higher poverty rates than do developed ones (see Box 2.3). Among the developed countries, however, the United States has the highest rate. Inside the United States, the South has the highest poverty rate and the Northeast the lowest, with the West ranking second in poverty and the Midwest third (see Figure 2.4). The Southwest has the highest percentage of poor people primarily because it has proportionately more rural people than do other regions; people who live in the rural areas are more likely than those in the urban areas to fall below the poverty line. Within the urban areas, though, the inner city has an exceptionally high poverty rate because of the scarcity of jobs (U.S. Census Bureau, 2009b).

BOX 2.3   GLOBAL PERSPECTIVE

The Inequality Among Nations

The economic inequality between rich and poor countries is extreme. While they constitute only about 20% of the world's population, rich countries possess well over 85% of global income. The global inequality looks even worse through other economic indicators: The poorest fifth has less than 1% of world trade, domestic savings, and domestic investment, far below the over 84% enjoyed by the richest fifth. Moreover, 40% of the people in developing countries live in absolute poverty, unable to meet their most basic needs, in sharp contrast to the 9% in developed countries (Porter, 2006).

Poverty is most widespread in African countries, where 18 of the world's 20 poorest nations are located. Nearly half of the African population is poor compared with about 30% for all developing countries. To realize how difficult it is for the Africans to meet their basic needs, consider this fact: The gross national product of all African countries combined (excluding South Africa), home to 600 million people, is about the same as the gross national product of Belgium, which has a population of only 10 million (Porter, 2006).

In the developed world, however, the extent of poverty varies from one country to another. The United States has the highest rate of poverty, and the Scandinavian countries have the lowest. Similarly, the United States has the largest income inequality. Generally, countries with greater inequality have more health problems and other social problems. Their rates of mental illness, drug and alcohol abuse, obesity, and teenage pregnancy are higher; their homicide rate is higher; their life expectancy is shorter; and their children's educational performance is worse. Not only the poor suffer from these problems; the rest of the population does, too. One survey of the world's richest 20 nations reveals that the rate of mental illness, for example, is five times higher across the whole population in the most unequal countries (such as the United States, Britain, and Portugal) than in the least unequal countries (Japan, Sweden, and Denmark). Apparently, inequality increases stress, which is likely to cause depression, anxiety, and other mental problems in most people (Wilkinson and Pickett, 2009).

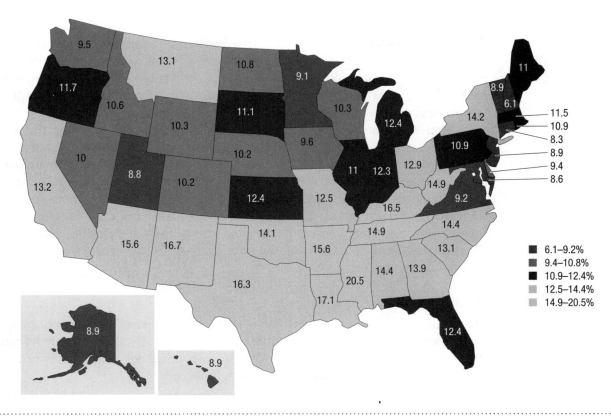

FIGURE 2.4 Percent of Persons in Poverty, by State: 2006, 2007, 2008

Poverty rates are highest in the South and lowest in the Northeast. Poverty rates are more than three times higher in Mississippi, which has the highest rates of poverty in the United States, than in New Hampshire, which boasts the lowest.

Critical Thinking: *What social factors would you attribute to the relatively high levels of poverty in the Southwest?*

Source: U.S. Census Bureau, Current Population Survey, 2006–2008 Annual Social and Economic Supplements.

■ Explanations of Poverty

There are two kinds of explanation for the existence of poverty. One is based on the popular belief that the poor are to blame for their poverty. The other is sociological in nature, attributing poverty to the positive functions it performs for society.

Blaming the Poor

The general public assumes that the United States is a land of opportunity. Individuals who become poor, then, have themselves to blame for their poverty because they have failed to grab the opportunity by not working hard.

Some social scientists have sought to find the source of this self-defeating behavior. Political scientist Edward Banfield (1974) claimed to have found it in the present-oriented outlook among the poor, who, he said, live for the moment, unconcerned about the future. Earlier, anthropologist Oscar Lewis (1961) had discovered the same lifestyle among the poor families he studied. He found the poor to be fatalistic, resigning themselves to poverty or seeing no way out of poverty. They were said to have developed a "culture of poverty," characterized by a sense of hopelessness and passivity, low aspirations, feelings of powerlessness and inferiority, and present-time orientation. According to Lewis, this culture of poverty is passed on from one generation to another. The poor are therefore discouraged from working hard, which keeps them poor.

But there are holes in the blame-the-poor explanation. For one thing, the poor are not necessarily averse to working hard. In fact, most are willing to work if given the opportunity. The problem is that if they work, they are still likely to remain poor because of extremely low wages. Low wages are why the working poor account for half of the people who fall below the poverty line. Also, in 60% of all poor families, at least one person works (Ehrenreich, 2001). In addition, the blame-the-poor explanation may have confused cause and effect. The self-defeating values that Banfield and Lewis found among the poor may well be the effect rather than the cause of poverty.

Defending the Poor

According to sociologist Herbert Gans (1971), poverty exists because poor people serve useful functions for society. This explanation for poverty effectively refrains from blaming the poor for their poverty. Instead, it defends them for performing some specific functions, which include the following:

- The poor make it possible for society's dirty work to be done. Many boring, underpaid, and unpleasant jobs—such as washing dishes, scrubbing floors, and hauling garbage—would be left undone if poor people did not do them.
- By working as maids and servants, poor people make it easier for the affluent to pursue their business and professional careers.
- Poor people create jobs for social workers and other professionals who serve the poor. Poor people also produce jobs for police and other law enforcers, because the majority of criminals they deal with come from the ranks of the poor.

By emphasizing the functions of poverty, however, we still do not know how society creates poverty in the first place. To know the answer, we may have to turn to conflict theory, which suggests that the inegalitarian nature of society makes inevitable the unequal distribution of economic opportunities. Receiving few or no opportunities, some people are bound to be poor. As Barbara Ehrenreich (2001) has found, even when these people with few opportunities hold two jobs, their wages are so low and their housing and other living expenses are so high that they cannot help becoming poor.

■ Sociological Theories of Economic Inequality

Functionalist theory attributes economic inequality to the positive functions it performs for society, but conflict theory blames the inequality on the exploitation of the powerless by the powerful. While these two theories deal with the causes of inequality, symbolic interaction theory focuses on how inequality influences the interaction between the powerful and the powerless that reinforces the gulf between rich and poor.

Functionalist Theory

According to functionalist theory, inequality arises from the fact that, like poverty, it serves a very important positive function for society. Inequality and poverty differ, though, in the specific functions they perform. Poverty ensures, for example, that dirty, unpleasant work is done, that the affluent can advance their careers, and that certain professionals are employed. On the other hand, inequality serves a much more useful function—in effect, a function without which no society can survive.

But what is this function? According to Kingsley Davis and Wilbert Moore (1945), inequality motivates people to work hard by promising them such rewards as money, power, and prestige. The amount of reward one gets depends on two things: how important a job is to society and how much training and skill are required to perform that job. A physician, for example, must receive more rewards than a garbage collector, not only because the physician's job is more important but also because it requires more training and skill.

Without this system of unequal rewards, many jobs important to society would never be performed. If future physicians believed that they would be paid and respected just as little as garbage collectors, they would not bother to spend years studying for long hours at medical school.

In short, inequality is necessary for society because it ensures that "the most important positions are conscientiously filled by the most qualified persons" (Davis and Moore, 1945).

Conflict Theory

To conflict theorists, it is difficult to see why large inequalities are necessary to fulfill the function of motivating people to work (Tumin, 1953). Why is it functional, for example, to pay a corporate executive two or three times more than the president of the United States? Functionalist theory suggests that the corporate executive's job is more important. But is it really? Even the physician's job is not necessarily more important than the garbage collector's because uncollected refuse can pose a serious problem to society. The intrinsic satisfaction of being a doctor far outweighs that of being a garbage collector. Why, then, should the doctor be given more rewards?

All this suggests that inequality is an unfair system of differential rewards, which harms rather than benefits society. Because inequality limits the opportunities of those who are poor, it leads to a failure to take advantage of the full range of talent in society. Thus, if intelligent teenagers are too poor to stay in school, society loses. It is therefore wrong for functionalist theory to suggest that inequality is functional or beneficial. But if inequality is dysfunctional or harmful, as conflict theory suggests, what causes it to appear in the first place? The answer can be found in the classic theory by Karl Marx (1818–1883). According to Marx, inequality originates from the conflict between capitalists and workers. As discussed in Chapter 1, the capitalists, who own the means of production, are driven to maximize profit, which leads them to pay their workers as low a wage as possible. The capitalists' desire for profit further leads them to cut the cost of running a business by moving their factories to labor-cheap countries, thereby causing many Americans to lose their jobs.

Symbolic Interaction Theory

According to symbolic interaction theory, inequality influences how people of different statuses interact with each other, which in turn reinforces the inequality. In the interaction, higher-status persons tend to show off their power and superiority, while lower-status persons are likely to feel humiliated, resentful, or inferior.

One common example involves a higher-status person calling lower-status people by their first names. At work, our bosses call us by our first names, but we do not call them by their first names. By readily using lower-status persons' first names, higher-status persons apparently try to be personal and friendly, but in doing so, they disregard whether the lower-status persons may prefer to be shown respect instead. As a result, the lower-status persons may feel humiliated or resentful (Karp and Yoels, 1998).

Even if the interaction between unequals involves only sitting next to each other in a hospital or some other public place, without uttering a single word, the higher-status persons are likely to feel superior and the lower-status persons inferior. In one study of inequality, a higher-status woman said she felt like telling a lower-status man, "Listen, low-life, don't even come near me. We pay to get away from scum like you." The lower-status man felt ashamed and resentful for having to sit next to her, thinking, "This stuck-up cow, you know, slim, attractive." He felt so ashamed for being overweight that he started sweating. Such a bluntly antagonistic interaction is more common in highly unequal societies such as Great Britain and the United States than in more equal societies such as Japan and the Scandinavian countries (Wilkinson and Pickett, 2009).

In short, higher-status persons tend to show and feel their superiority, and lower-status persons their inferiority. This difference in behavior and feeling between superiors and inferiors not only demonstrates the nature of inequality but also reinforces it. For a summary of this theory and the other two theories, see Box 2.4.

BOX 2.4   THEORETICAL THUMBNAIL

Explaining Economic Inequality

Theory	Focus	Insights
Functionalist Theory	How inequality benefits society	Inequality motivates people to work hard.
Conflict Theory	Why inequality is harmful to society	Inequality involves the exploitation of the workers by the capitalists.
Symbolic Interaction Theory	How inequality influences interaction	Inequality causes some people to act and feel superior and others to act and feel inferior.

QUESTIONS TO EXPLORE

1. Consider the most impoverished members of your own community. Applying a functionalist perspective, state the overall benefit to your community that might result from the poverty endured by these citizens.

2. The authors indicate that one of the primary arguments made by functionalists regarding poverty is that without this system of unequal rewards, many jobs important to society would never be performed. Do you believe this claim? Why or why not?

3. Conflict theorists argue that certain members of society benefit financially from the prevalence of inequality. Consider again the most impoverished members of your own community. Who might benefit financially from their poverty? How do they benefit?

■ Social Policies

The U.S. government tries to reduce economic inequality by taxing the rich more than the poor, which is called **progressive taxation**. The government also attempts to decrease inequality by providing the poor with more financial benefits, popularly known as welfare.

Progressive Taxation

If you look at how much taxes the rich and the poor pay for their incomes, you may think that the rich pay more than the poor. People who annually earn over $1,000,000, for example, are supposed to pay about 30% of their incomes in federal taxes, but those who make less than $5,000 pay only 3%. Does this mean that the rich really pay 30% and the poor 3%? For a number reasons, this is not the case.

One reason is the common practice for the rich to take advantage of various tax loopholes, which reduces their tax burden to a minimum. Another reason is that while low-income people have to pay taxes for the interest they earn from a savings account, the rich often use their surplus cash to buy state and city bonds from which they can earn interest without having to pay taxes for them. A third reason is that while everybody has to pay a sales tax to the state and city every time they purchase something, the poor end up shouldering a heavier tax burden. This is because the poor spend a much larger proportion of their income on consumer goods than do the rich. The sales tax is effectively regressive, rather than progressive.

On top of those three causes of increased tax burden suffered by the poor, there is the regressive payroll tax, which funds Social Security and Medicare. Most people, including the poor, are required to pay a flat rate of about 8% of their incomes, but the rich, who

Progressive taxation Government's attempt to reduce economic inequality by taxing the rich more than the poor.

It may appear that the rich pay more taxes than the poor, but through various tax loopholes the rich are able to reduce their tax burden to a minimum.

earn more than $102,000, are exempt from the payroll tax. If we take into account how the poor actually have to carry a heavier tax burden in those four different ways, the effective tax rate is roughly the same for people with different income levels. According to a study by the nonpartisan educational nonprofit Tax Foundation, those whose income is in the highest 20% pay, on average, 30% in taxes, while those whose income is in the lowest 20% pay 31% (Kenworthy, 2009). It is thus clear that the official policy of progressive taxation does not reduce income inequality.

Welfare Programs

Another program the government uses to reduce economic inequality is welfare, which is supposed to offer more benefits to the poor than to the rich. Contrary to popular belief, however, most of the poor in the United States are not on welfare. Only about one-third are. Of those welfare recipients, the overwhelming majority are single mothers and their children. Still, these people are generally reluctant to sign up for welfare. The reasons include the stigma of receiving welfare, the mountains of paperwork required for obtaining benefits, and the official requirement of working for non-living, poverty-level wages.

If you believe that poverty results mostly from social forces beyond the control of poor people, you would support welfare, wanting the government to give them financial support. If, however, you believe that the poor are primarily responsible for their plight, you would oppose welfare and want the government to prod them to clean up their act. Most Americans hold the second belief. To them, poor people bear children irresponsibly and lack the drive to work hard. The poor on welfare, then, are widely assumed to get so dependent on it that they will never leave it (Block, Korteweg, and Woodward, 2006).

The rich such as these corporate executives at a congressional hearing can get low-interest loans, subsidies, and bailouts, in addition to enjoying such benefits as special tax breaks, tax credits, and tax deductions.

Because of this perception of poor individuals abusing the welfare system, a law was passed in 1996 to end welfare dependency in the United States. Its key provisions were that the head of every family on welfare must work in order to receive benefits and that the benefits are limited to a total of 5 years throughout the recipient's lifetime. Today, many welfare recipients have found employment and consequently left the welfare rolls, but most are still stuck in poverty because their jobs pay very low wages without benefits and they have few opportunities to advance. As a result, while welfare caseloads have plunged, antipoverty programs such as Medicaid, food stamps, and disability benefits are bursting with new recipients (Ohlemacher, 2007).

While there is welfare for the poor, there is also welfare for the rich, though it is not widely known as such. Of these two kinds of welfare, the one for the rich is much more generous. Thus the rich enjoy enormous benefits in the forms of special tax breaks, tax credits, and tax deductions, so that many rich people end up paying little or no taxes. The large corporations that they own or operate also receive low-interest loans, subsidies, and bailouts (Brasch, 2008; Newman, 2008). During the recession in 2009, when soaring numbers of poor workers lost their jobs, many troubled huge banks were bailed out by the government with $370 billion (Calmes, 2009). Thus, the welfare for the rich enables its beneficiaries to fly high, while the welfare for the poor lets its recipients fall below the poverty line. Liberals see this rising inequality as a serious social problem, but conservatives view it otherwise (see Box 2.5).

BOX 2.5 DIVERGENT VIEWS

How Bad Is Rising Inequality?

Liberals like to emphasize that the economic gap between rich and poor has grown dramatically in the United States in the last 30 years. The gap, they further emphasize, is now much wider than in any other affluent society. The purchasing power of the richest 1% of Americans has soared 157% from 1979 to today, while the average American's purchasing power has risen only 10%. It is true that the United States is far from being as unequal as Russia, Mexico, many other Latin American countries, and other developing countries, but the United States is the most unequal among advanced countries, more unequal than Scandinavian and European countries and Japan (Jencks, 2002; Kotkin, 2009).

Liberals like to emphasize the huge increase in economic inequality between rich and poor over the last 30 years, but conservatives regard the liberals' claim as greatly exaggerated.

Liberals regard the huge rise in inequality as a serious problem because it hurts human welfare. For example, it lowers life expectancy (i.e., shortens people's lives). This is because increased inequality breaks social bonds that make people care about one another, which is crucial for being able to live a long life. Thus, life expectancy is lower in the United States, which has a large gap between rich and poor, than in Japan and European countries, which have a smaller gap. Additionally, economic inequality makes educational opportunities more unequal (Jencks, 2002).

Conservatives argue that the liberals' claim about rising inequality and its negative impact on people is greatly exaggerated. First, they point out that the rise in inequality is far from dramatic. They cite Census figures indicating that the income of the top quintile (20% of the population) went up 22% between 1993 and 2003, the income of the middle quintile increased 17%, and the income of the bottom quintile rose 13%. Conservatives emphasize that the poorest quintile are also getting richer along with the top quintile and that although the richest quintile are getting richer faster, their rise in income is not as high as liberals make it out to be (Brooks, 2007).

Conservatives further question the liberals' argument that increased inequality is socially undesirable because it makes people miserable. If this argument is correct, the happiness levels should have fallen for years when inequality rose. But this is not the case. As shown by the National Opinion Research Center's General Social Survey, the proportion of Americans saying they were "very happy" with their lives was 30% in 1972, 31% in 1982, 32% in 1993, and 31% in 2004. In other words, no significant change in reported happiness occurred even though income inequality has increased. In fact, the majority of Americans are not concerned about the enormous incomes of multibillionaires, because they hope that their kids might become the next Bill Gates or Warren Buffett. Apparently, most Americans still believe in the American Dream—that is, if you work hard, you can make tons of money, even though you may start out poor (Brooks, 2007).

Review

SUMMARY

1. Income and wealth are common indicators of economic inequality in the United States. Nearly half of the nation's entire income goes to the richest one-fifth of families, but only 4% of all income is distributed to the poorest one-fifth of families. The gap between rich and poor is even greater in wealth than income. Over 80% of the nation's wealth belongs to the richest one-fifth of families, but less than 1% of this wealth belongs to the poorest families.

2. There are two kinds of the "very rich": the old and the new. The *old rich* are families that have been wealthy for generations. They can be considered an aristocracy of birth and wealth. Examples are the Rockefellers, the Vanderbilts, and the DuPonts. By contrast, the *new rich* are self-made individuals, who have created their own wealth. They include Bill Gates of Microsoft, the investor Warren Buffet, and TV talk show host Oprah Winfrey. The new rich outnumber the old rich by more than two to one.

3. The "very rich" are different from most of us. They live in exclusive areas, hold exclusive club memberships, and have high-profile associates. They further command enormous power and influence in government and business. More so than other social classes, the rich tend to be conscious of being members of a class. The "very rich" are the richest Americans. They are the super rich, whose average net worth is above $3 billion, but most millionaires have an average net worth of $2 million. An example of the super rich is those who own expensive homes for vacation in the exclusive resort town of Aspen, Colorado.

4. The lifestyle of the majority of millionaires is far different from that of the super rich. They do not live in upscale neighborhoods, own private jets, drive foreign luxury cars, wear expensive clothes and jewelry, attend fancy parties, eat gourmet food, and join country clubs. Instead, they are the kind of people whom all college-educated people can realistically emulate. Most are extremely frugal, hard working, and self-employed in nonglamorous occupations, with annual incomes far below $1 million.

5. The U.S. government defines an American family of four with an annual income of $22,025 or less as living in poverty. Conservatives contend that the official poverty rate *overestimates* the extent of poverty rates, but liberals argue that the official rate *underestimates* the poverty. Regardless of which estimate is right, the government finds the rate of *absolute* poverty to be about 13%, while the rate of *relative* poverty is twice as high.

6. Certain groups of Americans are more likely than others to be poor. They are the faces of poverty, including children under age 18 years, single mothers, the less

educated, the unemployed, low-wage workers, racial/ethnic minorities, women, the homeless, and rural people.

7. The economic inequality between rich and poor nations is extremely great, with African countries suffering the most widespread poverty. Among rich countries, however, the United States has the highest rate of poverty and the Scandinavian countries the lowest. There are two kinds of explanation for the existence of poverty. One is based on the popular belief that the poor are to blame for their poverty. The other is sociological in nature, attributing poverty to the positive functions poor people perform for society.

8. Functionalist theory attributes inequality to its positive function of motivating people to work hard to contribute to society, but conflict theory blames inequality on the exploitation of the powerless by the powerful. While these two theories deal with the causes of inequality, symbolic interaction theory focuses on how inequality influences the interaction between powerful and powerless that reinforces the gulf between rich and poor.

9. The government tries to reduce inequality with progressive taxation, which is supposed to tax the rich more than the poor. But the rich end up paying about the same amount as the poor thanks to tax loopholes, tax-free bonds, and regressive sales and payroll taxes. The government also attempts to decrease inequality by providing the poor with more financial benefits than the rich, but welfare benefits for the poor are limited and the recipients are forced to work for poverty-level wages. On the other hand, welfare for the rich, including tax breaks and subsidies, is far more generous.

10. Liberals and conservatives hold divergent views on the rising inequality in the United States. To liberals, rising inequality is a serious problem because it hurts human welfare, such as by lowering life expectancy and increasing inequality in educational opportunities. Conservatives argue that while the income of the rich rises so does the poor's and that increasing inequality does not make the less well-off unhappy.

CRITICAL THINKING QUESTIONS

1. Prior to taking this course and reading the textbook, what was your own definition of poverty? What dollar amount or annual income did you associate with being poor? After reading this chapter, has your view of poverty changed in any way? How so?

2. If you were king for a day, what is the first thing that you would do to combat inequality? Why would you do this first? What do you imagine the immediate and long-term benefits would be?

3. Which social institution has had the most dramatic impact on poverty during your lifetime (family, media, etc.)? Please explain.

INTERNET RESOURCES

The U.S. Census Bureau: http://www.census.gov. This official site for U.S. Census data provides a variety of current and historic reports, tables, and statistics related to trends in poverty, wealth, and income distribution.

Heifer International (http://www.heifer.org) is unique in its approach to fighting poverty. Founded in 1944, the organization seeks to pass along "gifts" to impoverished citizens throughout the world. This is not accomplished only through monetary donations, but the gifts include very specific livestock and agricultural needs unique to the region, as well as the technical and medical training to maintain these resources once received. The organization is based on the simple principle that a starving child doesn't really need the temporary gift of a cup of milk; the child needs the cow that produces the milk and the skills to work and maintain the cow.

The Poverty Action Lab (http://www.povertyactionlab.org/index.php) was founded in 2003 as a research center to combat global poverty by a group of professors in the Department of Economics of the Massachusetts Institute of Technology. The site includes information on current projects, research efforts, publications, and data.

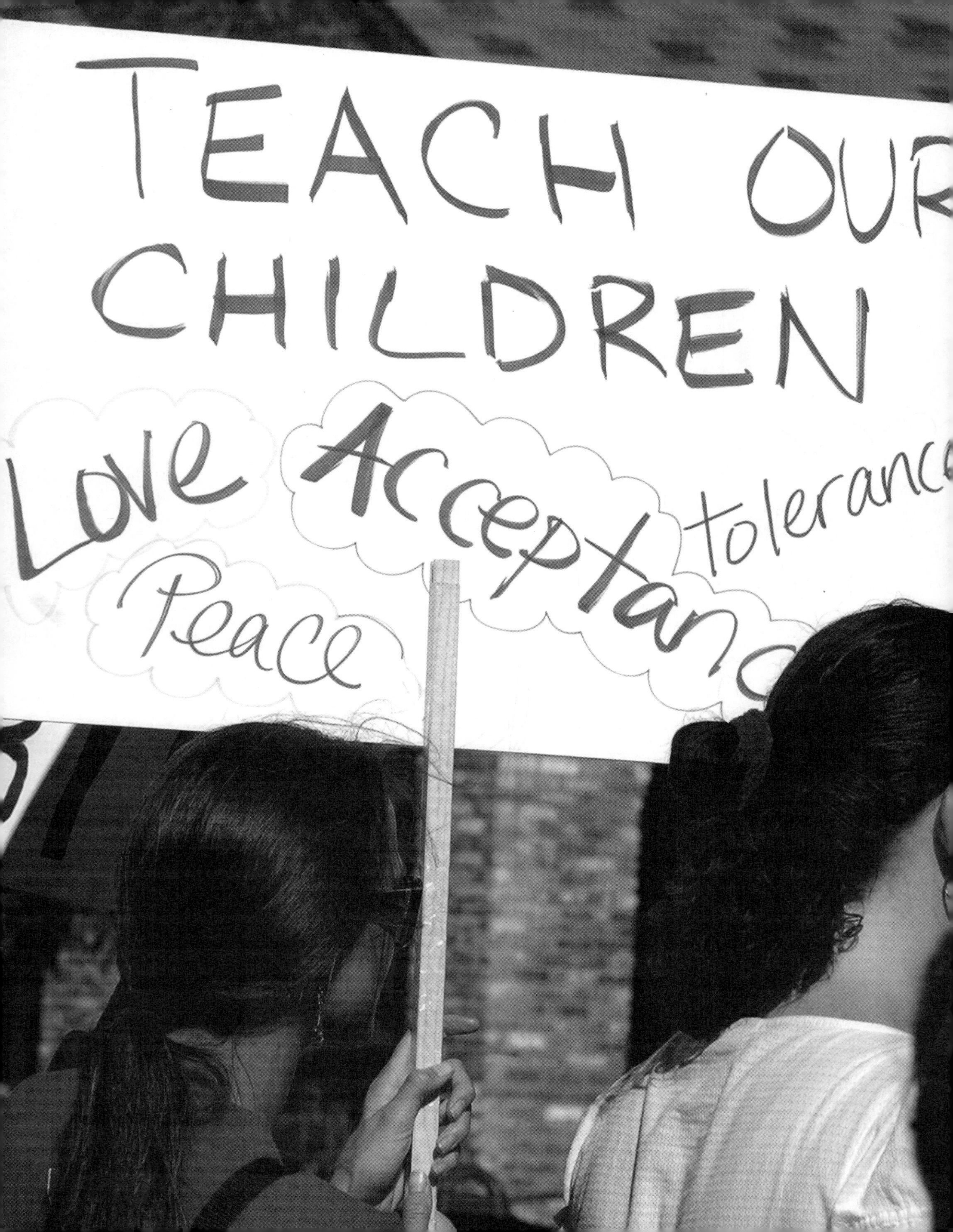
TEACH OUR
CHILDREN
Love
Peace

Racial and Ethnic Inequality

CHAPTER 3

One morning in 2007 the famous radio talk-show host Don Imus was talking about the NCAA women's basketball game between Rutgers University and the University of Tennessee. At one point he said, "That's some rough girls from Rutgers. . . . That's some nappy-headed hos there." Then he let out a belly laugh, apparently considering his racist remark to be amusing. In his career as a shock jock, he had insulted others in a similar fashion, calling Arabs "towelheads," a Jewish reporter a "boner-nosed, beanie-wearing Jewboy," an African American NBA star a "knuckle-dragging moron," and an African American woman correspondent covering the White House "the cleaning lady [at] the White House." But this time, through *YouTube*, the outrage over the racial slur spread like wildfire, causing Imus to lose his multimillion-dollar job a week later (Kosova, 2007).

Imus's behavior reflects the continuing existence of prejudice against racial and ethnic minorities not only in the United States but also in many other countries. Racial and ethnic prejudice is part of the inequality between the minorities and the dominant group, with the former having a worse life than the latter. In this chapter, we will analyze various aspects of this social problem throughout the world.

■ Sociological Views

The general public thinks of a *minority* as a category of people who are physically different from others and who make up a small percentage of a country's population. But this is not the way sociologists define a minority. Consider the Jews in China. They do not "look Jewish"; they look like other Chinese. Similarly, the Jews in the United States do not "look Jewish"; they look like other white Americans. Jews cannot be differentiated from the dominant group on the basis of their physical characteristics, but sociologically, they are considered a minority. In South Africa, blacks are also sociologically a minority, although they make up a majority of the population. Neither physical traits nor numbers alone determine whether people constitute a minority. To understand the sociological views of minority, we need first to look at race and ethnicity.

Race

If used as a biological concept, *race* refers to a large category of people who share certain inherited physical characteristics. These may include a particular skin color, nasal shape, or lip form. Human races are popularly divided into three groups: Caucasoid, Mongoloid, and Negroid. Caucasoids have light skin, Mongoloids yellowish skin, and Negroids dark skin, along with other physical differences among the three groups.

There are at least two problems with this classification of races. First, some groups fit into none of these categories. Natives of India and Pakistan have Caucasoid facial features but dark skin. The Ainu of Japan have Mongoloid faces but white skin. The Vogul of Siberia have Caucasoid faces but yellowish skin. Some aboriginal groups in Australia have dark skin and other Negroid features but blond hair. The Polynesians of Pacific islands have a mixture of Caucasoid, Mongoloid, and Negroid characteristics.

Another problem with the biological classification of races is its assumption that there are pure races. The reality is that there are no pure races because people in various races have been interbreeding for centuries. In the United States, for example, about 70% of blacks have some white ancestry, and approximately 20% of whites have at least one black ancestor. Biologists have also determined that all the current populations of the world originated from one common genetic pool—one single group of humans that evolved some 100,000 years ago in Africa. Today, 99.9% of the DNA molecules (which make up the genome) are the same for all humans, and only the remaining 0.1% are responsible for all the differences in appearance (Angier, 2000). Even these outward differences are meaningless because the differences among members of the same race are greater than the average differences between two racial groups. Some American blacks, for example, have lighter skin than many whites, and some whites are darker than many blacks.

Since there are no clear-cut biological distinctions between racial groups—in physical characteristics or genetic makeup—sociologists define race as a social rather than a biological phenomenon. Defined sociologically, a race is a group of people who are *perceived* by a given society to be biologically different from others. People are assigned to one race or another not necessarily on the basis of logic or fact but by public opinion, which, in turn, is molded by society's dominant group (Morning, 2005).

Consider a boy in the United States whose father has 100% white ancestry and whose mother is the daughter of a white man and a black woman. This youngster is considered black in U.S. society, although he is actually more white than black because 75% of his ancestry is white. In many Latin American countries, however, this same child would be considered white. In fact, according to Brazil's popular perception, a black is a person of African descent who has no white ancestry at all; by this definition, about three-fourths of all U.S. blacks would *not* be considered blacks.

Race
A group of people who are *perceived* by a given society to be biologically different from others.

The definition of race, then, varies from one society to another. Sociologists use this societal definition to identify races because it is the racial status assigned to people by their society, rather than their real biological characteristics, that has profound significance for their social lives.

Ethnicity

The Jews have often been called a race. But are they really? Actually they have the same racial origins as Arabs—both are Semites—and throughout the centuries, Jews and non-Jews have interbred extensively. As a result, as noted earlier, Jews are often physically indistinguishable from non-Jews. Besides, any person can become a Jew by conversion to Judaism. Thus, the Jews do not constitute a race but instead are a religious group or, more broadly, an ethnic group.

Ethnic group
A collection of people who share a distinctive cultural heritage.

While race is based on popularly perceived physical traits, ethnicity is based on cultural characteristics. An **ethnic group** is a collection of people who share a distinctive cultural heritage. Members of an ethnic group may share a language, religion, history, or national origin. They identify with each other as members of a distinct group. In the United States, members of an ethnic group typically have the same national origin. As a result, they are named after the countries from which they or their ancestors came. Examples are Polish Americans, Italian Americans, and Irish Americans.

For the most part, ethnicity is culturally learned. People learn the language, values, and other characteristics of their ethnic group. Members of an ethnic group may be born into it, but the cultural traits of the group are taught by one generation to the next.

Minority

Minority
A racial or ethnic group that is victimized by prejudice and discrimination.

Prejudice
A negative attitude toward a certain category of people.

Discrimination
An unfavorable action against individuals that is taken because they are members of a certain category.

A **minority** is a racial or ethnic group that is victimized by prejudice and discrimination. **Prejudice** is a negative attitude toward a certain category of people. It includes negative ideas, beliefs, and feelings, and predispositions to act in a negative way. For example, whites who are prejudiced against blacks might fear meeting a black man on the street at night. They might resent blacks who achieve a high position in their field of endeavor. They might sell their house if a black family moved into the neighborhood.

While prejudice is an attitude, discrimination is an act. More specifically, **discrimination** is an unfavorable action against individuals that is taken because they are members of a certain category. It is discrimination, for instance, when a landlord refuses to rent an apartment to a family because the family is Hispanic or African American.

A minority does not necessarily make up a small percentage of the population. Blacks are considered a minority in South Africa, even though they constitute about 70% of the population, because they are the subordinate group. Similarly, the dominant group need not comprise a large part of the population. People of English descent in the United States today represent only about 13% of the population. But because of their continuing social and cultural influence, they are still considered the dominant group, as they were more than 200 years ago. Although less influential than the dominant group, minorities still can find ways to succeed in achieving their goals (see Box 3.1).

BOX 3.1   USING SOCIOLOGICAL INSIGHTS

How to Climb the Corporate Ladder

Whether you are a minority or not, the insights from analyses of how minority people succeed in corporations can be useful for anybody in a highly diverse society such as the United States. Kenneth Roldan, a Hispanic CEO of a leading executive search firm that specializes in recruiting and placing minorities, shows how minorities can reach the summit of corporate America. Among the steps that lead to that perch are, according to Roldan, the following (Roldan and Stern, 2006):

Although you are different in some way from the majority of employees in a corporation, you should avoid being a lone wolf and become a team player in order to be successful.

- *Don't get stuck in the ethnic trap.* Minority members tend to interact with only their own group, with African Americans joining the African American network, Hispanics the Hispanic network, and so on. This is a bad move because it will cut off many networking opportunities with white colleagues, opportunities that make it easier to move up the corporate ladder, because whites occupy most of the high positions.
- *Capitalize on your ethnic background.* Too often, minorities avoid sharing with whites their ethnic heritage for fear of being seen as less talented. Instead, minorities should use their ethnic background as an asset, seeking out ways for their company to sell products with their knowledge of what African American, Hispanic, or Asian consumers want.
- *Avoid being a lone wolf; be a team player.* Bright and hardworking Latinos, African Americans, Asians, and other minorities often stand out in high school and college. These talented ethnic minorities usually operate as loners, diligently making their way through with little interaction with others. But working at Xerox, Wells Fargo, or some other corporations, they will find that everything is about the team. To succeed, they must cooperate and listen to colleagues and be responsive to their teammates.

■ Racial and Ethnic Minorities

The United States is a nation of immigrants. More than 20,000 years ago, before the United States turned into a nation, the American Indians arrived from Asia and settled as Native Americans. Long after that time, numerous immigrants began to pour in from Europe and later from Africa, Asia, and Latin America. They came as explorers, adventurers, slaves, and refugees, mostly hoping to fulfill a dream of success and happiness. The English were the earliest of these immigrants and, on the whole, the most successful in fulfilling that dream. They became the dominant group. Eventually, they founded a government dedicated to the democratic ideal of equality, but they kept African Americans as slaves and discriminated against other racial and ethnic groups. This **American dilemma**—the discrepancy between the ideal of equality and the reality of inequality in the United States—still exists today, though to a much lesser degree than in the past. Next, we will take a close look at how various racial and ethnic minorities have fared under the burden of the American dilemma.

American dilemma
The discrepancy between the ideal of equality and the reality of inequality in the United States.

Native Americans

After more than two centuries of colonial subjugation, Native Americans end up being the poorest minority in the United States today.

Native Americans have long been called *Indians* as a result of Columbus's mistaken belief that he had landed in India. The explorer's successors passed down many other distorted views of the Native Americans. They were called savages, although it was whites who slaughtered hundreds of thousands of them. They were portrayed as scalp hunters, although it was the white government that offered large sums to whites for the scalps of natives. They were stereotyped as lazy, although it was whites who forced them to give up their traditional occupations. These false conceptions of Native Americans were reinforced by the contrasting pictures whites painted of themselves. The white settlers were known as pioneers rather than invaders and marauders; their conquest of the Native Americans' land was referred to as homesteading, not theft.

Ironically, when Columbus discovered the land that would later become the United States, the natives he encountered were very friendly. He wrote: "Of anything they have, if it be asked for, they never say no, but do rather invite the person to accept it, and show as much lovingness as though they would give their hearts" (Hraba, 1979).

But as the white settlers grew in number and moved west, Native Americans resisted them. As a result, the native population was decimated by outright killing, by destruction of their food sources, and by diseases brought by the whites, such as smallpox and influenza. With their greater numbers and superior military technology, the whites prevailed. Sometimes, they took land by treaty rather than by outright force, but they often violated the treaties. Consequently, some 75% of the U.S. land mass that Native Americans controlled two centuries ago has shrunk to only 2% today (van Biema, 1995).

Native Americans have also suffered a huge loss of population, from 10 million at the time of Columbus's arrival to 4.4 million today. About one-third now live on the reservations, mostly in the Southwest and Northwest, and the other two-thirds live in urban areas. After more than two centuries of colonial subjugation, Native Americans today find themselves at the bottom of the socioeconomic ladder—the poorest minority in the United States. Their unemployment and poverty rates are much higher than those of other Americans, and their average family income is also considerably lower (see **Figure 3.1**). Moreover, they have much higher rates of pneumonia, influenza, diabetes, tuberculosis, suicide, alcoholism, and car accidents compared with the general U.S. population (Hayden, 2004; Martin, 2009).

African Americans

African Americans represent the second-largest minority in the United States. They number about 39 million, constituting about 12% of the U.S. population. They are concentrated in the South and Southeast (see **Figure 3.2**).

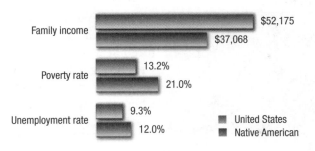

FIGURE 3.1 Native Americans as the Poorest Minority

Native Americans are at the bottom of the U.S. socioeconomic ladder. Compared to the national average rate of poverty for all races combined (13.2%), we can see the Native American rate of poverty is almost twice the national average. Native American family incomes are also about $15,000 less than the national average, and they have a much higher unemployment rate.

Critical Thinking: *What unique challenges face Native Americans that must be addressed in order to ease their extreme burden of poverty?*

Source: U.S. Census Bureau, Community Survey, 2006–2008.

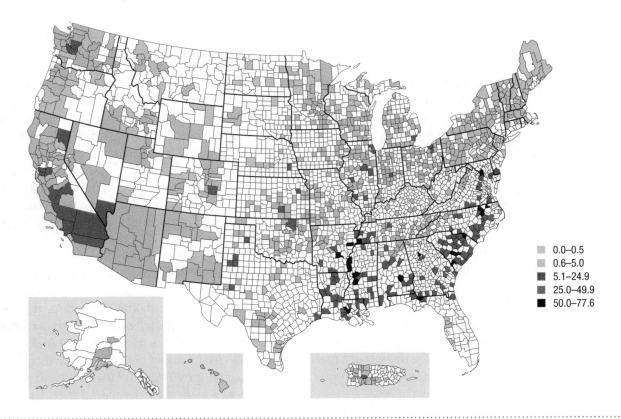

Legend:
- 0.0–0.5
- 0.6–5.0
- 5.1–24.9
- 25.0–49.9
- 50.0–77.6

FIGURE 3.2 Geographic Distribution of African Americans

Of the approximately 39 million blacks in the United States, the majority are concentrated in the southern and southeastern states. Washington, DC, and Mississippi account for the highest concentrations, at 54.4% and 37.1%, respectively, compared to Idaho and Vermont, at only 0.6% and 0.8%, respectively.

Critical Thinking: *Why do you suppose the majority of blacks live in areas more closely associated with race-related prejudice and discrimination, historically, than other areas presumed to be more racial-tolerant?*

Source: U.S. Census Bureau, 2006–2008 American Community Survey.

More than one hundred years ago, many laws were enacted to segregate blacks from whites in all kinds of public and private facilities, from restrooms to schools.

Jim Crow laws
A set of laws that segregated blacks from whites in all kinds of public and private facilities, from restrooms to schools.

African Americans first started coming from Africa to North America as indentured servants in 1619. Soon after, they were brought as slaves. Most lived in what would become the southern United States, where they worked on cotton, tobacco, or sugar-cane plantations. Slavery ended during the Civil War in 1865, but soon after federal troops withdrew from the South, white supremacy returned. Many so-called Jim Crow laws (the name was a derogatory term for blacks) were enacted to segregate blacks from whites in all kinds of public and private facilities, from restrooms to schools. A more basic control tactic was terror. If an African American man was suspected of killing a white person or of raping a white woman, he might be lynched, beaten to death, or burned at the stake.

The North offered more opportunities for African Americans, though. Beginning in the early 1900s, as southern farms were mechanized and the demand for workers in northern industrial centers rose during the two world wars, many southern African Americans migrated north. When the wars ended and the demand for workers declined, however, they were often the first to be fired. Even in the North, where there were no Jim Crow laws, African Americans faced discrimination and segregation.

A turning point in U.S. race relations came in 1954, when the U.S. Supreme Court ordered that the public schools be desegregated. The order boosted the long-standing campaign against racial discrimination. In the late 1950s and throughout the 1960s, the civil rights movement launched marches, sit-ins, and boycotts. The price was high: Many civil rights workers were beaten and jailed; some were killed. Eventually, Congress passed the landmark Civil Rights Act of 1964, prohibiting segregation and discrimination in virtually all areas of social life, such as public facilities, schools, housing, and employment.

In the last 30-plus years, the Civil Rights Act has put an end to many forms of segregation and paved the way for some improvement in the position of African Americans. Various studies have shown a significant decline in white opposition to such issues as school integration, integrated housing, interracial marriage, and voting for an African American president. The number of African Americans elected to various public offices has increased sharply since 1980, with the greatest achievement being the election of Barack Obama as the U.S. president in 2008. The proportion of African Americans with college degrees has also grown significantly. An affluent middle class has emerged among African Americans.

But full equality is still far from being achieved. Most evident is the continuing large economic gap between blacks and whites. The latest figures on median family income are $29,026 for blacks and $46,900 for whites—with blacks earning only about 62% of the amount earned by whites (U.S. Census Bureau, 2009b). Job discrimination against blacks is still prevalent. More than twice as many blacks live in poverty as whites. Even more glaring racial inequalities show up in housing. Over the last decade, there has been some decline in residential segregation. Nonetheless, most blacks continue to reside in segregated neighborhoods and are more likely than whites with similar incomes to live in overcrowded and substandard housing.

In short, progress has been significant in education and politics but not in housing and economic conditions. Unemployment and poverty have soared in the black working class, primarily the result of numerous plant shutdowns caused by the shift from a manufacturing to a service economy in the face of increased global competition. On the other hand, the black middle class has become more prosperous, largely because they have attained an advanced education and the skills required by the technological changes in the U.S. economy. However, African Americans still perceive racism as a greater problem than do other Americans, particularly whites (see Box 3.2).

Hispanic Americans

In 1848 the United States acquired through wars or purchases from Mexico the lands that would become Texas, California, Nevada, Utah, Arizona, New Mexico, and Colorado. Many Mexicans consequently found themselves living in the United States as American citizens. The vast majority of today's Mexican Americans, however, have immigrated into the United States from Mexico since 1900. At first, the immigrants came largely to work in the farmlands of California and to build the railroads of the Southwest. Later, a steady stream of Mexicans began to pour into the United States, driven by Mexico's population pressures and economic problems and attracted by U.S. industry's need for low-paid, unskilled labor.

In 1898 the United States added Puerto Rico to its territory by defeating Spain in the Spanish-American War. In 1917 Congress granted all Puerto Ricans citizenship, but because Puerto Rico is not a state, Puerto Ricans may not vote in presidential and congressional elections. Over the years, especially since the early 1950s, many Puerto Ricans, lured by job opportunities and the cheap plane service between San Juan and New York City, have migrated to the mainland.

BOX 3.2   DIVERGENT VIEWS

How Bad Is Racism in America?

Blacks and whites do not see eye to eye on the problem of racism in the United States. According to a Gallup poll, two-thirds of whites say they are *satisfied* with the way blacks are treated in the United States, but two-thirds of blacks say they are *dissatisfied*. Most whites consider racism a minor factor or not a factor at all in such problems as blacks having a shorter life expectancy than whites and a higher likelihood of ending up in prison. Most blacks, however, identify racial discrimination as a major factor in these problems. Seventy-five percent of whites say that black–white relations are good, but only 55% of blacks agree. There is one bright spot when it comes to improvement in race relations. On this issue there is only a slight difference between blacks and whites: 80% of whites and 70% of blacks say civil rights for blacks have improved in the past decade.

As a 52-year-old medical receptionist from Port Charlotte, Florida, who is white, says about race relations, "They're better than they used to be, that's for sure. It's the younger people who are doing this." Similarly, a 30-year-old retail sales manager from Oak Park, Michigan, who is black, says, "I don't believe we've totally overcome everything that's necessary for equality, but I do believe things are getting better" (Page and Risser, 2008).

Nowadays, besides Mexican Americans and Puerto Ricans, there are Cuban immigrants who began to flock to the Miami area when their country became communist in 1959. There are also immigrants from other Central and South American countries who have come as political refugees and job seekers. By 2007, the members of all these groups, collectively called Hispanic Americans or Latinos, totaled about 46 million, constituting more than 15% of the U.S. population. Hispanics have surpassed blacks as the largest minority (see Figure 3.3).

The Spanish language is the unifying force among Hispanic Americans. Another source of their common identity is religion: At least 85% are Roman Catholic. There are, however, significant differences within the Hispanic community. Mexican Americans are by far the largest group, accounting for 64% of Hispanics. They are heavily concentrated in the Southwest. Puerto Ricans make up 11% and live mostly in the Northeast, especially in New York City. As a group, they are the poorest among the Hispanics. The Cubans, who constitute 5% of the U.S. Hispanic population and live mostly in Florida, are the most affluent and therefore have the greatest tendency toward integration with Anglos (white Americans). The remaining Hispanics are a diverse group from Central and South America, ranging from uneducated, unskilled laborers to highly trained professionals.

Hispanics lag behind both whites and blacks in educational attainment. Among those age 25 years or older, only 9% have completed college compared with 25% of whites and 12% of blacks. But some Hispanic groups are more educated than others. Cubans are the best educated, primarily because most of the early refugees fleeing communist Cuba were middle-class professional people. Mexican Americans and

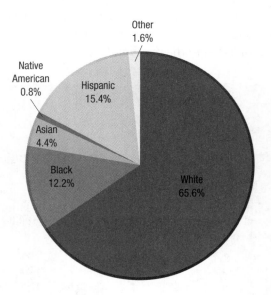

FIGURE 3.3 Hispanics as the Largest Minority

Census data revealed as far back as 2004 that Hispanics have surpassed blacks as the largest racial minority group in the Unites States. This trend has not yet changed, with Hispanic population growth outpacing that of blacks by more than 3% between 2004 and 2008 reports.

Critical Thinking: *With the increased growth of the Hispanic population, what special problems would you anticipate plaguing this group (other than lagging behind other Americans in education, income, and employment opportunities)?*

Source: U.S. Census Bureau, 2008 Population Estimates.

Puerto Ricans are less educated because they consist of many recent immigrants with much less schooling. Young U.S.-born Hispanics usually have more education. Lack of proficiency in English has slowed recent Hispanic immigrants' educational progress. As many as 25% of Hispanics in public schools speak little or no English, which has resulted in higher dropout rates than among non-Hispanic students.

Hispanics are mostly clustered in lower-paying jobs, earning far less than whites. They also have higher rates of unemployment and poverty. However, the higher educational achievement of young Hispanics provides hope that more will join the higher-paid white-collar workforce in the future. Research has shown that if Hispanics speak English fluently and have at least graduated from high school, their occupational achievement is close to that of non-Hispanics with similar English fluency and schooling. Nationwide, Hispanics are also a growing force in politics, gaining representation as members of Congress, state governors, and mayors of large cities.

Asian Americans

There is tremendous diversity among Asian Americans, whose ancestry can be traced to more than 20 different countries. The larger groups are Chinese, Japanese, Filipinos, Koreans, and Vietnamese. The first two have the longest history in the United States.

The Chinese first came in 1849 during the gold rush on the West Coast, pulled by better economic conditions in the United States and pushed by economic problems and local rebellions in China. Soon, huge numbers of Chinese were imported to work for low wages, digging mines and building railroads. After these projects were completed, jobs became scarce and white workers feared competition from the Chinese. As a result, special taxes were imposed on the Chinese, and they were prohibited from attending school, seeking employment, owning property, and bearing witness in court. In 1882 the Chinese Exclusion Act restricted immigration to the United States, and it stopped all Chinese immigration. Many Chinese returned to their homeland.

Emigrants from Japan ran into similar hostility. They began to come to the West Coast somewhat later than the Chinese, also in search of better economic opportunities. At first they were welcomed as a source of cheap labor. But soon they began to operate small shops, and anti-Japanese activity grew. In 1906 San Francisco forbade Asian children to attend white schools. In response, the Japanese government negotiated an agreement with the United States: The Japanese would stop immigrating to the United States, and President Theodore Roosevelt would end harassment of the Japanese who were already here. But when the Japanese began to buy their own farms, they met new opposition. In 1913 California prohibited foreign-born Japanese from owning or leasing lands; other Western states followed suit. In 1922 the U.S. Supreme Court ruled that foreign-born Japanese could not become U.S. citizens.

Treatment of Japanese Americans became worse during World War II. All the Japanese from the West Coast—both aliens and U.S. citizens—were rounded up and confined in concentration camps in isolated areas. They were forced to sell their homes and properties. The action was condoned even by the Supreme Court as a legitimate way of ensuring that Japanese Americans would not help Japan defeat the United States. Racism, however, was the real source of such treatment. There was no evidence of any espionage or sabotage by a Japanese American. Besides, German Americans were not sent to concentration camps, although Germany also was at war with the United States and there were instances of subversion by German Americans. In 1987, when the survivors sued the U.S. government for billions of dollars in compensation, the solicitor general acknowledged that the detention was "frankly racist" and "deplorable." In 1988 the Senate voted overwhelmingly to give $20,000 and an apology to each of the surviving internees.

Despite this history of discrimination, Asians have shown signs of success in the United States today. When compared with whites, Asians are more likely to graduate from college and to have a higher income, and they have a lower poverty rate.

Discrimination against Asians is subtle, however. Many well-educated Asian Americans can get work as professionals and technicians, but they rarely become officials and managers. White bosses often cite language deficiencies as an excuse for denying promotions. Privately, they stereotype Asians as weak and incapable of handling people, although Japanese-managed companies are well known for outperforming U.S. companies. It is assumed that Asian talent can flourish in the classroom or laboratory but not in senior management. The Asians are, in effect, victims of the **glass ceiling**, the prejudiced belief that keeps minority professionals from holding leadership positions.

Glass ceiling
The prejudiced belief that keeps minority professionals from holding leadership positions.

There is also another stereotype of Asians being a model minority. It implies that virtually all Asians do well, which, of course, is not true. There is still much poverty among, for example, Filipinos and Chinatown residents. By suggesting that Asian Americans are not victims of discrimination, the model minority stereotype further shuts Asians out of affirmative action programs. The stereotype is similarly used against Hispanics and African Americans, who are told that they do not need racial preferences because "the Asians have made it, so why can't you?" This flawed reasoning provokes resentment and even hostility against Asians, as African Americans have shown at Korean stores in some cities. Finally, the model minority stereotype puts undue pressure on young Asian Americans to succeed in school, particularly in mathematics and science classes, which may lead to mental health problems.

Muslim Americans

Contrary to popular belief, most U.S. Muslims are not Arabs. Arab Americans make up only about 12% of all Muslims in the United States, far outnumbered by African American Muslims and even Muslims from South Asian countries such as Pakistan and Bangladesh. Most Arab Americans are not Muslim, either. They are instead Christian because emigrants from Arab countries are mostly Christian rather than Muslim. Only 23% of Arab Americans are Muslim (see **Figure 3.4**).

Devout Muslim Americans follow a strict code of ethics and diet. They stay away from alcohol, illicit drugs, and pork. They refrain from premarital and extramarital sex and dating. They are forbidden to gamble and to pay or accept interest on loans or savings accounts. These religious rules bring Muslims into conflict with the dominant U.S. culture, which is based largely on credit purchases and payment of interests for such activities as buying homes and cars. Devout Muslims find U.S. society shockingly permissive, riddled with what they consider moral problems such as sexual freedom, drug use, crime, and lack of respect for authority. Immigrant Muslim parents often clash with their teenage children over dating and drinking.

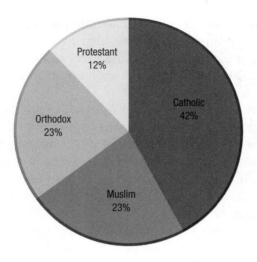

FIGURE 3.4 Arab Americans by Religious Faith

Contrary to popular belief, most Arab Americans are not Muslim. Only a minority (23%) of them are Muslim.

Critical Thinking: *Which social institutions are primarily responsible for the inaccurate view of Arabs as most likely to be Muslim? What purpose, if any, is served by this false perception?*

Source: The Prejudice Institute, 2010. Fact Sheet 5: Arab Americans.

However, Muslim Americans are not equally devout. Some are deeply religious, others are religiously moderate, and still others are secular, being Muslim only in name. The religious diversity of Muslim Americans is similar to that of U.S. Christians. Muslim Americans also share similar socioeconomic characteristics with the general U.S. population, having similar education and income (Read, 2008).

In many ways, U.S. mosques function more like Christian churches than traditional mosques in Islamic countries. The Toledo Center—the largest U.S. mosque— has 22 nationality groups among its members. Weddings and funerals are held in the mosque. There are Sunday classes for children and teenagers as well as lectures for adults. After the afternoon prayer service, the faithful get together for a meal in a lower-level dining room. In contrast, traditional mosques in Islamic countries are more likely to be used only for praying and other strictly religious activities.

Also distinctively American is the fact that U.S. Muslims are generally more tolerant of religious differences, more resistant to fundamentalism, more at home in a secular society, and more ethnically diverse than their counterparts in other societies. American Muslim women attend mosque as often as Muslim men, in sharp contrast with many Muslim countries where the mosques are primarily for men.

Despite the Americanization of these Muslims, most Americans have a negative view of Islam, believing that Muslims are likely to commit terrorist acts because many of the terrorist attacks against the United States are carried out by Muslims. This stereotype has generated hate crimes against Muslim Americans as well as ethnic profiling that defines them as terror suspects (Audi, 2006; Goodstein, 2009).

Jewish Americans

After they were expelled from Spain in 1492 and Portugal in 1496, the Jews eventually went to Brazil and then came to the United States. Other Jews later came directly from Europe. Their numbers were very small until the 1880s, when large numbers began to arrive—first from Germany and then from Russia and other Eastern European countries. In the United States, they were safe from the *pogroms* (massacres) they had faced in Europe but not from prejudice and discrimination (Schreiber, Schiff, and Klenicki, 2003).

In the 1870s many colleges in the United States refused to admit Jewish Americans. At the turn of the century, Jews often encountered discrimination when they applied for white-collar jobs. During the 1920s and 1930s, they were accused of being part of an international conspiracy to overtake U.S. business and government, and anti-Semitism—prejudice or discrimination against Jews—became more widespread and overt. Many country clubs and other social and business organizations barred Jewish Americans from membership.

Anti-Semitism
Prejudice or discrimination against Jews.

Since the late 1940s, anti-Semitism has declined sharply, but in recent decades there has been an increase in anti-Semitic acts—including verbal slurs, vandalism, and physical violence. Understandably, most Jewish Americans see anti-Semitism as a problem (Cohen, 2009). But Jewish Americans face less prejudice and discrimination than other minority groups, such as African Americans and Hispanics. In fact, Jewish Americans are widely recognized as hardworking, family-oriented, religious, and friendly. Their contributions to U.S. culture are appreciated. And a growing number of Jews are regularly elected to high public office by non-Jews.

Jewish Americans are so highly regarded largely because as a minority they are the most successful. Their levels of education, occupation, and income are higher than those of any other group. Their success may stem from the emphasis Jewish culture gives to education, from a self-image as God's chosen people, and from parental pressure to succeed. Not all Jews are successful, though. There is still significant poverty in their midst. Being rich or poor has much to do with how recently they arrived in the United States. Most of the poor are Orthodox Jews, who are the most recent immigrants. More successful are Conservative Jews, who have been in this country longer. The wealthiest are Reform Jews, who have been in the United States the longest.

Although Jewish Americans as a whole are highly prosperous, they are not conservative nor inclined to vote Republican, as other prosperous Americans are. Instead, they tend to be liberal—supporting welfare, civil rights, same-sex marriage, women's rights, civil liberties, and the like—and to vote Democrat. Perhaps this reflects their ability to identify with the dispossessed and oppressed. It also reflects the influence of Jewish norms underlying *tzedakah* (pronounced *si-DOCK-ah*, meaning "righteousness"), which requires the fortunate and the well-to-do to help individuals and communities in difficulty. Many Jewish Americans, however, have lost their traditional identity. About half of Jewish Americans are no longer affiliated with a synagogue; only a small minority (about 20%) still attend synagogue regularly. Marriage with non-Jews has increased greatly, with over half of all Jewish marriages involving a non-Jew.

■ Dimensions of Racism

Racism
The belief that one's own race or ethnicity is superior to that of others.

All the minorities we have discussed are subjected to racism by the dominant group of a given society. Racism is the belief that one's own race or ethnicity is superior to that of others. Considering themselves superior to the minorities, the dominant group can abuse the minorities in various ways.

Extermination

The most horrific action against minorities is to kill them on a massive scale. This is called genocide, the wholesale killing of members of a specific racial or ethnic group. It has been carried out in various countries. In the early 19th century, on the island of Tasmania, near Australia, British settlers killed the entire native population, whom they hunted like wild animals. From 1915 to 1923, the Turks massacred more than 1 million Armenians. Between 1933 and 1945, the Nazis systematically murdered 6 million Jews. More recently, in 1992, the Serbs in Bosnia killed and tortured numerous Muslims and Croats as part of their campaign of ethnic cleansing. From 1993 to 1996, thousands of minority members were slaughtered in Rwanda and eastern Zaire. In 2004 the ethnic Arab government in Sudan killed at least 30,000 of its non-Arab citizens in the Darfur region (Noonan, 2008; Siegel, 2006; Tolson, 2007).

Genocide
The wholesale killing of members of a specific racial or ethnic group.

Expulsion

Expulsion involves the dominant group expelling a minority from certain areas or even from the country entirely. During the 19th century, Czarist Russia drove out millions of Jews, and the U.S. government forced the Cherokee nation to travel from their homes in Georgia and the Carolinas to reservations in Oklahoma. About 4,000 Cherokee died on this "Trail of Tears." In the mid-20th century, China took over Tibet, driving tens of thousands of independence-seeking Tibetans into India (see Box 3.3). During the 1970s, Uganda expelled more than 40,000 Asians—many of them Uganda citizens—and Vietnam forced 700,000 Chinese to leave the country (Schaefer, 2008).

Expulsion
An act that involves the dominant group expelling a minority from certain areas or even from the country entirely.

BOX 3.3   GLOBAL PERSPECTIVE

Tibet Through Chinese Eyes

Tibetans are one of the many different ethnic minorities in China, living mostly in the southwestern part of the country. They have long sought independence from China without success. In 1959 the independence-seeking Tibetans were forced to flee into neighboring India. Since then they have been campaigning all over the world to demand that their homeland be freed from China. They have gained support from all Western countries, which criticize China for violating human rights by taking over Tibet. They feel that it is entirely justifiable to free the poor Tibetans from the oppressive communist government.

But virtually all the Chinese, including liberal Western-educated intellectuals, think that the Western protests have little to do with human rights. Instead, the Chinese think the West's real motivation is to deny China the triumph it is expected to enjoy for its enormous economic successes. According to this Chinese view, Westerners cannot stomach the thought of Chinese succeeding. More importantly, the Chinese believe that China has exercised sovereignty over Tibet as a part of China for 700 years now, ever since the Yuan dynasty, founded by the Mongol Empire. To the Chinese it doesn't make sense for Tibet to become independent of China. It is therefore doubtful that Tibet will ever be taken away from China.

The Chinese further believe that they have not committed human rights abuses against the Tibetans but have instead provided them with special treatment. For example, their ruined religious sites have been repaired, monasteries have been reopened, new monks have been allowed to join orders, and the Tibetan language has been permitted to be used more extensively than before (Mahbubani, 2008).

Segregation

Segregation means more than spatial and social separation of the minorities from the dominant group. It means that minorities, because they are believed to be inferior, are compelled to live not only separately but in inferior conditions. Their neighborhoods, schools, and other public facilities, for example, are both separate and inferior to those of the dominant group.

De jure segregation
Segregation sanctioned by law.

De facto segregation
Segregation that results from tradition and custom.

Segregation can be legal. If so, it is called **de jure segregation**, which is sanctioned by law. De jure segregation no longer exists in the United States, because segregation is already officially outlawed. However, we still have **de facto segregation**, which results from tradition and custom. This type of segregation is particularly evident with regard to housing for African Americans.

Like the United States, most nations no longer practice de jure segregation. Even South Africa finally ended its official policy of *apartheid*—racial separation in housing, jobs, and political opportunities—in 1992. But apartheid has become so entrenched that it will persist in the form of de facto segregation for many years to come.

Prejudice and Discrimination

As has been suggested, discrimination is unfair treatment of individuals just because they are members of a minority. Usually, discrimination is an expression of prejudice, the negative attitude toward minorities. Thus, when dominant group members discriminate against a minority person, they are very likely to be prejudiced too. The Ku Klux Klan and neo-Nazis, for example, are both prejudiced and discriminating against minorities. They practice what they believe; they are out-and-out racists.

However, prejudice and discrimination do not always go together. Some people are not prejudiced but do practice discrimination because of social pressure. Unprejudiced homeowners, for example, discriminate by refusing to sell their homes to minority families for fear of offending the neighbors. Unprejudiced executives may also hesitate to promote minority employees lest other employees be resentful. On the other hand, some people are prejudiced but refrain from practicing discrimination, because their friends frown on discrimination or because it is against the law to discriminate.

Institutionalized discrimination
The persistence of discrimination in social institutions that is not necessarily recognized by everyone as discrimination.

Even if every single white person in the United States were no longer prejudiced and discriminating, discrimination would still exist for some time. This is because over the years it has been built into various social institutions so that discrimination can occur even when no one is aware of it. If employers prefer to hire people who graduated from their own universities, which have long denied entrance to blacks, then blacks will not have much chance of being hired. When fire and police departments continue to use the height requirements in hiring that were originally intended for evaluating white applicants, then many otherwise qualified Mexican and Asian Americans—who are generally shorter than whites—will not get the jobs. These minorities are effectively subjected to **institutionalized discrimination**, the persistence of discrimination in social institutions that is not necessarily recognized by everyone as discrimination.

Public Policy: Affirmative Action

In the 1960s, under the pressure of the civil rights movement, federal legislators passed a series of antidiscrimination laws. However, because of institutionalized discrimination, Congress further instituted the policy of **affirmative action**, which requires employers and colleges to make special efforts to recruit qualified minorities and women for jobs, promotions, and educational opportunities. Given equal qualifications, the opportunity must be given to the minority or woman. Sometimes, a less qualified black may have to be chosen over a more qualified white. President Lyndon Johnson provided the reasoning behind special opportunities for African Americans in a 1965 speech: "You do not take a person who for years has been hobbled by chains, and liberate him, bring him up to the starting line, and then say, 'You are free to compete with all the others'" (Hacker, 1992).

Since then, affirmative action has helped many qualified African Americans to enter higher education and to gain professional and managerial positions. This has partly contributed to the rise of a significant black middle class. Affirmative action has nonetheless sparked racial tensions. Many whites, especially conservatives, see it as reverse discrimination against them. They argue that equal opportunities should be open to all people, without regard to race. Still, most Americans consider it important for a college to have a racially diverse student body.

The support for diversity has come from the U.S. Supreme Court. In 2003 the Court ruled that it was legal for the University of Michigan's law school to achieve diversity by considering race as a factor in admissions. The Court also said that race should be only one of many considerations, along with such factors as grades, test scores, special talents, extracurricular activities, work experiences, and family background.

The Supreme Court has effectively sent a double message: It is legal to consider race for attaining diversity (a general mix of different races) but not for seeking a quota (a specific number of minority persons). Most colleges and corporations have already heeded that message by focusing on diversity efforts and rejecting quotas. The search for diversity includes not only considering race but also using outreach programs to find qualified minority students and workers. These diversity efforts avoid reverse discrimination and rigid quotas while considering *only* qualified minorities for college admission, employment, and promotion. In the few states that have banned affirmative action, there has been yet another attempt to achieve diversity. In Texas, for example, the top 10% of students from all high schools, which includes schools with mostly minority students, are automatically granted admission to the state university of their choice. In the larger society, diversity has apparently reduced discrimination, which makes Americans more color-blind today (see **Box 3.4**).

◼ Sociological Theories of Racial and Ethnic Inequality

We have seen that racial and ethnic minorities are unequal to the dominant group, with the former having lower income, more poverty, less education, or otherwise getting the short end of the stick. What causes this inequality? There are three sociological theories to explain it.

Functionalist Theory

According to functionalist theory, three kinds of social practices can serve to eliminate racial and ethnic inequality. The first is **assimilation**, which involves the minorities

Affirmative action
A policy that requires employers and colleges to make special efforts to recruit qualified minorities and women for jobs, promotions, and educational opportunities.

Assimilation
The process by which a minority adopts the culture of the larger society.

BOX 3.4   WHAT RESEARCH REVEALS

More Color-blind Today

A large majority of young Americans are now very open-minded about interracial dating, with 95% of them approving of blacks and whites dating.

There are more Americans today who do not judge each other on the basis of their skin color. This is particularly true among the new generation; individuals 14 to 24 years of age are much more likely to approve of and engage in interracial dating than are the older generations. In fact, the large majority of U.S. youth are now very open-minded about interracial dating. According to a Gallup poll, 95% of young people approve of blacks and whites dating and about 60% have dated someone of a different race. As a college student says, referring to his peers, "People are finding people with common interests and common perspectives and are putting race aside" (Jayson, 2006; Joyner and Kao, 2005).

A major factor behind the emergence of this color blindness is the increase in racial diversity. Nowadays, many Americans younger than 18 years of age are racial minorities, representing about 33% of the whole U.S. population of their age. Much of this increased diversity has resulted from a huge influx of immigrants. Over the last two decades, more than 35 million have entered the United States, representing the largest wave of immigration in American history (Jayson, 2006).

Another factor behind the emergence of color blindness comes from the culture of diversity. The young people of today have grown up with "diversity," "multicultural," and "inclusion" as buzzwords. Many college courses include discussions of social diversity. The media such as movies, television, and advertising fuel color blindness by portraying interracial friendship and romance (Jayson, 2006).

Amalgamation The process by which various groups blend their subcultures to form a new culture.

Cultural pluralism The peaceful coexistence among various racial and ethnic groups while allowing each group to retain its own subculture.

adopting the culture of the larger society. The second is **amalgamation**, which involves various groups blending their subcultures to form a new culture. And the third is **cultural pluralism**, also known as multiculturalism, which involves a peaceful coexistence among various racial and ethnic groups while allowing each group to retain its own subculture. These three social practices can ultimately improve the lives of the minorities and end racial and ethnic inequality.

On the other hand, *failure* to carry out those social practices is likely to create and reinforce racial and ethnic inequality, with the minorities falling behind the dominant group in education, income, and other social conditions. Thus, if immigrants fail to assimilate to the U.S. mainstream culture by learning English, they will find it hard to get ahead, economically and socially. Similarly, if minorities refuse to get amalgamated into the new, emerging culture of the larger society by sharing their subcultures with each other, they will likely become socially isolated, losing contacts for obtaining employment and other opportunities of moving up in the world. Finally, if various groups do not live peacefully with each other, social chaos will likely ensue, making it difficult or impossible for minorities to improve their living conditions.

Conflict Theory

While functionalist theory in effect blames the minorities for failing to catch up with the dominant group, conflict theory points to larger social forces that cause racial and ethnic inequality through prejudice and discrimination. One is *sociological*, involving socialization. If our parents, teachers, and peers are prejudiced, we are likely to follow their lead. If minorities are often presented in the media as inferior or violent, we are likely to be prejudiced and to discriminate against them. A second cause is *economic*, involving the desire for job security and business profits. Widespread prejudice and discrimination against minorities ensure job security for the dominant group's middle and working classes. Prejudice and discrimination also bring profits to the dominant group's upper class, because racism can create a huge supply of cheap labor from among oppressed minorities. A third cause is *political*, involving the retention of governmental power. This is why many state and local governments have used various means to prevent minorities from voting, which include charging a poll tax, requiring a literacy test, or printing ballots only in English in areas where many minority people do not know the language.

Symbolic Interaction Theory

According to this theory, if members of the dominant group perceive minorities as inferior, undesirable, dangerous, or in some other negative way, the interaction between them is likely to be one between unequals—tense or superficial. The inequality between the dominant group and the minorities, then, can be said to originate from the former's negative perception of the latter.

That perception is seldom based on reality. Instead, it is a **stereotype**, an oversimplified, inaccurate mental picture of others. Consider, for example, the stereotype of poor blacks as dangerous. Many whites seem to carry this picture in their minds after having been repeatedly fed images of black violence and criminality by the media. The reality is that the vast majority of poor blacks are law-abiding people; most are young children and single mothers. Besides, the small minority that commit violence rarely target whites; most of their victims are fellow blacks. Still, many whites are fearful of blacks.

The stereotype of them as dangerous often causes blacks—including those who are highly successful and middle class—to suffer legal harassment at the hands of white police officers. The stereotype can also bring about grotesque consequences for whites themselves. As a white man said:

> My wife was driving down the street in a black neighborhood. The people at the corners were all gesticulating at her. She was very frightened, turned up the windows, and drove determinedly. She discovered, after several blocks, she was going the wrong way on a one-way street and they were trying to help her. Her assumption was they were blacks and were out to get her. (Terkel, 1992)

For a summary of the three theories of racial and ethnic inequality, see **Box 3.5**.

Stereotype
An oversimplified, inaccurate mental picture of others.

■ Global Variations of Racial/Ethnic Problems

Racial or ethnic problems seem to be universal, existing all over the world. Apparently, wherever there is a minority, there is a racial or ethnic problem. Extremely few countries are free of racial problems. Iceland is one such country, but this is because its population is homogeneous in race or ethnicity. The nature and amount of racial problems around the world, however, vary from one society to another.

Developing Countries

Ethnic antagonism can be found in many African countries, the most violent being in Rwanda, where hundreds of thousands of lives were lost as a result in the mid-1990s.

BOX 3.5   THEORETICAL THUMBNAIL

Explaining Racial and Ethnic Inequality

Theory	Focus	Insights
Functionalist Theory	Three social practices that keep inequality in check	Failure to improve life through assimilation, amalgamation, and cultural pluralism creates inequality.
Conflict Theory	Social forces that create inequality through prejudice and discrimination	Sociological, economic, and political factors bring about inequality.
Symbolic Interaction Theory	The influence of perception on social interaction	The dominant group's negative perception of minorities leads to unequal interactions.

QUESTIONS TO EXPLORE

1. Identify one way in which cultural pluralism has influenced race relations in your own school or community? Has pluralism moved your community toward greater racial equality or not? Explain your response.

2. Cite one racial problem you would consider to be the most relevant to your own life. According to conflict theorists, racial and ethnic inequality often operates through prejudice and discrimination as part of socialization. Which "agents of socialization" (e.g., parents, teachers, media figures, peers) do you feel contribute the most to the racial problem that you identified? Explain how they do so.

3. Visit the Bureau of Indian Affairs Web site at http://www.bia.gov/ After reading the mission of this organization within the U.S. Department of the Interior, which theory do you feel is best represented by it? Explain your response.

Similarly, many Asian countries are no strangers to racial or ethnic problems, which occasionally erupt into violent clashes. In the 1980s, for example, a full-scale civil war broke out in Sri Lanka, where the majority Buddhist population killed numerous minority Hindus. Generally, ethnic problems are much more severe in Africa and Asia than in other parts of the world. In the 1992 Los Angeles race riot, the most destructive in recent U.S. history, 44 people died, but some 250,000 were killed in the ethnic conflict in Rwanda in 1994 alone (Rosenblatt, 1994).

Many Latin American scholars have argued that their societies are not racist, but the U.S. State Department has reported racial discrimination in Bolivia, Brazil, Ecuador, Guatemala, and Peru. In these countries, blacks generally receive less education and income than whites and experience discrimination in housing and services. In nearly all Latin American countries, the privileged classes are largely European in origin.

Western Europe

Before the 1970s, few countries in Western Europe had serious ethnic problems. The exception was the genocidal slaughter of Jews by the Nazis during World War II. Another well-known ethnic clash took place between the majority Protestants and the minority Catholics in Northern Ireland. The Catholics wanted to join the predominantly Catholic Republic of Ireland because they had long felt that they were discriminated against by the dominant Protestants, but the Protestants preferred to remain a part of predominantly Protestant Britain. Britain, in turn, sought to suppress the nationalist aspirations of the Catholics. A similar problem has long existed in Spain, which tries to control the restless minorities Basques and Catalans, and in France, which attempts to subdue the Bretons, Corsicans, and Basques.

Since the 1970s, new sources of ethnic conflict have emerged throughout Western Europe. They have stemmed from the significant numbers of guest workers and immigrants pouring into virtually every Western European country from North Africa and other developing countries and most recently from Eastern Europe. Racial attacks on foreign workers and their descendants occur often, and extreme right-wing political groups routinely campaign against immigrants. Such ethnic hostilities are most prevalent in France and Germany and least common in Sweden and Luxembourg.

Eastern Europe

Since the collapse of communism in the early 1990s, ethnic problems have exploded throughout Eastern Europe. The most devastating conflict took place in the former Yugoslavia. Ethnic conflict split this country into five independent republics—Serbia, Bosnia, Croatia, Slovenia, and Macedonia—but all except Slovenia have remained ethnically diverse and continue to experience interethnic hostilities. Especially in Bosnia and Croatia, violence continues to break out among the Serbs, Muslims, and Croats.

Ethnic problems have also led the Czechs and Slovaks to split their former country, Czechoslovakia, into two independent republics, although they did not experience the same kind of violence as in Bosnia. In other Eastern European countries, minorities continue to face discrimination. Examples include the Hungarian minority in Romania, the Turkish minority in Bulgaria, and the Jews, Gypsies, and foreigners in other Eastern European countries.

Russia

Before the demise of the Soviet Union in the early 1990s, the Russians forced various minorities to become "Russified" by, for example, sending minority children to Russian schools. Sometimes, whole ethnic groups—such as the Tartars of the Crimea, the Germans of the Volga, and the Chechens of the Caucasus—were deported. All the republics under the control of non-Russians became independent. But since many of these republics contain minorities, tensions have risen between the new dominant group and minorities.

Review

SUMMARY

1. One problem with the biological classification of races is that some groups such as the natives of India and Pakistan fit into none of the racial categories. Another problem is the assumption that there are pure races. The reality is that there are no pure races because people in various races have been interbreeding for centuries. Since there are no clear-cut biological distinctions between racial groups—in physical characteristics or genetic makeup—sociologists define race as a social rather than a biological phenomenon.

2. While race is based on popularly perceived physical traits, ethnicity is based on cultural characteristics. An ethnic group, then, is a collection of people who share a distinctive cultural heritage, such as a language, religion, history, or national origin.

3. Racial and ethnic groups become minorities when they are subjected to prejudice and discrimination by the dominant group. Minority members tend to interact with only their own group. This is a bad career move because it will cut off many networking opportunities with white colleagues, opportunities that make it easier to move up the corporate ladder, because the whites occupy most of the high positions.

4. About one-third of Native Americans live on the reservations, mostly in the Southwest and Northwest, and the other two-thirds live primarily in urban areas. Native Americans represent the poorest minority in the United States, having the highest unemployment and poverty rates, and the lowest average family income. They also have much higher rates of alcoholism, suicide, and several health problems compared to the general U.S. population.

5. In the last 30-plus years, the Civil Rights Act has put an end to many forms of segregation. White opposition to racial equality has declined and a higher percentage of African Americans have risen to high positions of political power and made gains in both education and career attainment. However, blacks still earn only about 62% of the amount earned by whites, more than twice as many blacks live in poverty as whites, most blacks continue to reside in segregated neighborhoods, and blacks are more likely than whites with similar incomes to live in overcrowded and substandard housing. Seventy-five percent of whites say that black–white relations are good, but only 55% of blacks agree. However, there is only a slight difference between blacks and whites in how they perceive the impact of civil rights: 80% of whites and 70% of blacks say that civil rights for blacks have improved in the past decade.

6. Hispanics are mostly clustered in lower-paying jobs, earning far less than whites, and experiencing higher rates of unemployment and poverty. However, the higher educational achievement of young Hispanics provides hope that more will join

the higher-paid white-collar workforce in the future. Hispanics are also a growing force in politics, gaining representation as members of Congress, state governors, and mayors of large cities.

7. Although they have long suffered discrimination, Asians have shown signs of success in the United States today. When compared with whites, Asians are more likely to graduate from college and to have a higher income, and they have a lower poverty rate. But subtle discrimination against Asians remains. Asians can get work as professionals and technicians, but rarely become officials and managers. Asians are, in effect, victims of the glass ceiling, the prejudiced belief that keeps minority professionals from holding leadership positions.

8. In many ways, U.S. mosques function more like Christian churches than traditional mosques in Islamic countries. Also distinctively American is the fact that U.S. Muslims are generally more tolerant of religious differences, more resistant to fundamentalism, more at home in a secular society, and more ethnically diverse than their counterparts in other societies.

9. Jewish Americans' educational, occupational, and economic statuses are very high. Their affluence, however, has not weakened their traditionally liberal stand on social and political issues.

10. Racism appears in a variety of ways. It may take place as genocide, the extermination of a whole racial or ethnic group. It may involve expelling an entire minority from certain areas or even from an entire country. Regarding the expulsion of Tibetans from their homeland, it is regarded by the whole world as a violation of human rights, but the Chinese insist that it is justifiable. Racism may also involve segregating a minority from the dominant group, while subjecting the minority to prejudice and discrimination. Public policy in the United States has called for outlawing school segregation, enacting antidiscrimination laws, and instituting affirmative action.

11. About 95% of young people in the United States approve of blacks and whites dating, and about 60% have dated someone of a different race. A major factor behind the emergence of this color blindness is the increase in racial diversity. Nowadays about 33% of Americans younger than 18 years of age are racial minorities.

12. Functionalist theory attributes racial inequality to failure to improve life through assimilation, amalgamation, and cultural pluralism. According to conflict theory, sociological, political, and economic factors create inequality through prejudice and discrimination. Symbolic interaction theory focuses on how the dominant group's negative perception of minorities influences unequal interactions and social exchanges.

13. Racial and ethnic problems vary from one society to another. The problems are most severe in Africa and Asia. But they also take place in Latin America, Western Europe, Eastern Europe, and Russia—virtually in every country in the world.

CRITICAL THINKING QUESTIONS

1. What forms of prejudice and discrimination do you see most often in the community in which you live?

2. List at least two forms of de facto discrimination that you have seen in your lifetime. What purpose do they serve? Can you identify a likely cause? Please explain.

3. What race-related changes have you seen in your lifetime?

INTERNET RESOURCES

The Anti-Defamation League (ADL) (http://www.adl.org/about.asp) was founded in 1913 "to stop the defamation of the Jewish people and to secure justice and fair treatment for all." Now the ADL fights anti-Semitism and all forms of bigotry, in the United States and abroad.

The Black Collegian Online (http://www.black-collegian.com/) is an online version of a magazine and resource management center originally launched in 1970. The Black Collegian is a career and self-development magazine catering to African American students and other students of color seeking information on careers, job opportunities, graduate/professional schools, internships/co-ops, and study abroad programs. The online version was launched in November of 1995 to reach an even larger audience. The site also offers an online career center and job bank for searching and applying for jobs with employers who are interested in recruiting a diverse workforce.

The Bureau of Indian Affairs (http://wwwbia.gov/ is responsible for the administration and management of land held in trust by the United States for American Indians, Indian tribes, and Alaska Natives. Developing forestlands, leasing assets on these lands, directing agricultural programs, protecting water and land rights, developing and maintaining the infrastructure, and creating economic development are all part of the agency's responsibility. In addition, the Bureau of Indian Affairs provides education services to approximately 48,000 Indian students.

The U.S. Census Bureau: http://www.census.gov. This official site for U.S. Census data provides a variety of current and historic reports, tables, and statistics related to trends in poverty, wealth, and income distribution.

The U.S. Commission on Civil Rights (http://www.usccr.gov/) investigates complaints and collects information on claims alleging injustices that are in violation of civil rights (e.g., discrimination, being deprived of the right to vote by reason of race, color, religion, sex, age, disability, or national origin, or by reason of fraudulent practices). The committee also seeks to appraise federal laws and policies with respect to discrimination or denial of equal protection of the laws because of race, color, religion, sex, age, disability, or national origin, or in the administration of justice. Finally the committee submits reports, findings, and recommendations to the president and Congress and issues public service announcements to discourage discrimination or denial of equal protection of the laws.

Gender Inequality

J ennifer James Soto is a 37-year-old attorney and a mother of two small children. Recently she spent a weekend at a college campus in Georgia, participating in a White House conference designed to encourage women to run for high office. Jennifer and the other women spent 2 days listening to women who held elected office and women whose job was to prepare other women to run. Then she gave a speech expressing her political ambition, saying, "Good afternoon; thank you so much for coming. My name is Jennifer James Soto, and I hope to have the opportunity to be your next governor" (Gezari, 2009).

Jennifer was inspired by Barack Obama's election, a dramatic reminder that the United States can transcend its past and present discrimination against minorities. But for women, the highest executive offices—the president and vice president—are still out of reach. So are the top positions in other areas of life, although women are making great progress everywhere. Women now make up 57% of college students but less than 20% of college presidents. Women constitute more than 40% of MBA candidates but only 2% of the chief executive officers (CEOs) of the nation's largest 500 corporations. Women account for nearly half of law school students but less than one-fifth of law firm partners (Gezari, 2009). It is clear that women are still far from achieving gender equality in American society. **Gender inequality** refers to the difference in the amount of rewards that males and females are socially expected to get.

Gender inequality The difference in the amount of rewards that males and females are socially expected to get.

■ Gender Roles as the Source of Gender Inequality

Gender inequality can be traced to **gender roles**, the patterns of attitude and behavior that a society expects of its members as females and males. Generally, the roles females are expected to play are regarded by society as somehow negative, and the roles males are expected to play are regarded as positive. The two sexes are thus regarded as unequal, with women being considered inferior to men. (For a contradictory belief, though, see **Box 4.1**.) Let's take a close look at the nature of gender roles in the United States and other societies. We will also find out where the roles come from.

Gender roles
The patterns of attitude and behavior that a society expects of its members as females and males.

Gender Roles in the United States

In the United States, women are traditionally assigned the role of homemaker and men the role of breadwinner. The woman's world is the home; her job is to comfort and care for her husband and children, maintain harmony, and raise her children to conform to society's norms. The man is expected to work in the outside world,

---

BOX 4.1   DIVERGENT VIEWS

Are Women the Fairer Sex?

For many years all the members of the U.S. Supreme Court were men. In 1981 Sandra Day O'Connor became the first woman appointed to the court. Since then only three women have been appointed, while the rest (six) of the justices have continued to be men. The traditional view is that women are not as competent as men to serve in the Supreme Court. Recently, however, there has emerged the popular view that women can do a better job as judges.

In 2005 O'Connor learned that John Roberts would take her place after she retired. She then declared to the press that he was "good in every way, except he's not a woman." Most Americans agreed. According to a public opinion poll, 80% of respondents said that it was a good idea for a woman to replace O'Connor. In fact, over the last two decades, many feminist scholars have argued that female judges are fairer than their male peers in rendering judgment. For example, the feminists found from one study that female judges were significantly more likely to rule in favor of sexual discrimination victims. The explanation is that women prefer to look at the totality of the circumstances, favor an "ethic of care" (being compassionate toward others) over an "ethic of rights" (sticking to impersonal rules), and choose a more "relational" approach to the law. But men prefer their law with rigid rules, clear lines, and neutral principles—emphasizing unchanging rules and crisp legal principles.

Critics point out that it is unclear whether female judges are more likely than their male counterparts to rule in favor of the victims in cases other than those involving sexual discrimination. Therefore, critics still insist that there is no convincing evidence that female judges rule differently—more fairly—than male judges (Lithwick, 2009).

competing with other men in order to provide for his family. The man's world outside the home is viewed as a harsh and heartless jungle in which men need to be strong, ambitious, and aggressive. The problem is that society treats woman's role as less valuable than man's. Thus, unlike men, who are paid for their role as breadwinners, women who elect to stay home instead of entering the workforce work much longer hours at home without pay (U.S. Census Bureau, 2010).

There are many popular stereotypes about how males differ from females, such as the belief that women are emotional while men hold back their emotions.

That gender division of labor is accompanied by many popular stereotypes—oversimplified mental images—of what women and men are supposed to be, and again the stereotypes portray women as inferior to men. Women are supposed to be shy, easily intimidated, and passive; men, bold, ambitious, and aggressive. Women should be weak and dainty; men, strong and athletic. Women are expected to be emotional, even to cry easily, but men should hold back their emotions and never cry. Women are expected to be sexually passive and naïve; men, active and experienced. Women are believed to be dependent, in need of male protection; men are supposed to be independent, fit to be leaders. Women are expected to be intuitive and inconsistent; men, logical, rational, and objective.

Some groups are more likely than others to accept or reject those stereotypes about how men and women should behave. Among women, those who are relatively young, not married, well educated, and gainfully employed—or who have strong feelings of personal competence—tend to reject the traditional gender-role attitudes. Among men, the working and lower classes are more receptive to the traditional gender-role outlook than are the middle and upper classes. Today's women and men, regardless of their social class and other demographic characteristics, are more likely than their counterparts of 10 or 20 years ago to reject traditional gender roles (Jayson, 2009).

Nevertheless, people who consciously reject the traditional gender roles may behave otherwise. Research has shown that women are more likely to be passive and men aggressive in a number of ways despite their conscious rejection of the gender stereotypes. Thus, in interactions between the sexes, the male is more likely to initiate interactions and the female to respond. During a conversation, men are more likely to touch women than vice versa. When a man opens the door for a woman, most women would say "thank you" or smile in appreciation. But men tend to look confused if a woman opens the door for them because they are not accustomed to being women's passive beneficiaries. Women are also more likely than men to express feelings of sympathy, sadness, and distress but are more inhibited in expressing anger and sexual desire. All these behaviors reflect the powerful influence of traditional gender roles, which reinforces and perpetuates the inequality between men and women.

Gender Roles in Other Countries

The traditional gender roles in the United States appear virtually the same in all societies. But there are exceptions. Many years ago, anthropologist Margaret Mead (1935) found striking differences among three tribes in the Southwest Pacific island of New Guinea. One of them, the Arapesh, practiced gender equality, with both women and men behaving in what many North Americans would consider a *feminine* way. They were passive, gentle, and home loving. The men were just as enthusiastic as the women about taking care of babies and bringing up children. The second tribe, the Mundugumor, also practiced gender equality but in the opposite way, with both sexes showing what many in our society would consider *masculine* traits. Both women and men were competitive, aggressive, and violent. In the third tribe, the Tchambuli, the norm was gender inequality with female and male roles being sharply different; however, they were the *opposite* of those traditional in the West. Tchambuli women were the bosses at home; they were the economic providers, doing the hunting, farming, and fishing. Tchambuli men were emotional, passive, and dependent; they took care of children, did housework, and used cosmetics.

Despite these exceptions, the traditional U.S. gender roles can be found in virtually all societies, with men assigned the primary role of breadwinner and women the secondary role of homemaker. The public world is considered a man's domain and the private world a woman's. Men's work is more highly valued than women's work. Even in most of the egalitarian hunting-gathering societies, where women often contribute more than half of the food supply by gathering nuts, fruits, and plants, men dominate women. In short, male dominance over females is practically universal. As anthropologists Kay Martin and Barbara Voorhies (1975) have observed, "A survey of human societies shows that positions of authority are almost always occupied by males." Because this gender inequality appears to be universal, it may be attributed to biological differences between females and males that exist all over the world.

The Biological Influence

What makes a person female and another male has to do with *chromosomes*, the materials in a cell that transmit hereditary traits to the individual from his or her parents. Females have two similar chromosomes, XX, each X inherited from each parent. Men have two different chromosomes, XY, the X inherited from the mother and the Y from the father.

Whether a person will develop the appropriate sex characteristics—say, breasts or facial hair—depends on the proportion of female and male sex *hormones*, chemical substances that stimulate or inhibit vital biological processes. If a woman has more male than female hormones, she will have facial hair rather than breasts. If a man has more female than male hormones, he will end up with breasts instead of a beard. In most females, the proportion of female hormones is greater, and in most males, the proportion of male hormones is greater. It is clear that women and men differ both chromosomally and hormonally.

The chromosomal and hormonal differences underlie other biological differences between the sexes. Stimulated by the greater amount of male sex hormones, men are on average bigger and stronger than women. Yet because of their lack of a second X chromosome, men are less healthy. Men are susceptible to more than 30 types of genetic defects, such as hemophilia and color blindness, which are very rare in women. At birth, males are more likely to die. Throughout life, males tend to mature more slowly. They are more physiologically vulnerable to stress. They are stricken with heart disease at a younger age. And they have a shorter life than females (Gorman, 1992b).

There are also sex differences in brain structure. Neuroscience research has long established that the left hemisphere, or half, of the brain controls speech, and the right hemisphere directs spatial tasks such as object manipulation. There is less specialization in the female's brain, so that she tends to use both hemispheres for a given task at the same time, whereas the male tends to use only one hemisphere. That's why, for example, women are more likely to listen with both ears and men with the right ear. Moreover, the female experiences greater cell growth in her language-dominated hemisphere, while the male's greater growth is in his spatial perception-dominated hemisphere (Gorman, 1992b).

The differences in brain structure and hormonal production may contribute to some behavioral differences between the sexes. Female babies are more sensitive than male babies to certain sounds, particularly their mother's voices, and are more easily startled by loud noises. Female infants are also quieter, while males are more vigorous and inclined to explore, shout, and bang in their play. Female infants talk sooner, have larger vocabularies, and are less likely to develop speech problems such as stuttering. Girls are superior not only in verbal abilities but also in overall intelligence, but boys excel in spatial performances such as mental manipulation of objects and map reading. When asked how they have mentally folded an object, boys tend to say simply, "I folded it in my mind," while girls are more likely to produce elaborate verbal descriptions (Trotter, 1987).

In sum, nature makes women and men different, but these differences do not add up to female inferiority or male superiority. On some measures, such as physical health and early verbal ability, females as a group seem superior to males, and by other measures, especially size and strength, males as a group seem superior. Regardless of these biological facts, however, society still defines women as inferior to men simply because of their gender.

The Cultural Influence

The biological differences between males and females seem logically related to the division of labor between the sexes. If men are bigger and stronger, then it makes sense for them to do the work that requires strength. Likewise, assigning women the care of the home and children may be a logical extension of their biological ability to bear and nurse children.

However, there are limitations to biological constraints on gender roles. Because women generally have smaller hands and greater finger agility than men, they are logically more fit to be dentists and neurosurgeons. Yet men dominate these high-paying professions because American culture has long defined them as men's work. Indeed, the cultural definition of gender roles exercises awesome power. Because U.S. culture has defined being a physician as men's work, the majority of our doctors are males, and they are among the highest-paid professionals. By contrast, in the former Soviet Union, where medicine was defined as a feminine profession, most of the doctors were women, and they were generally paid women's wages—less than what skilled blue-collar male workers earned.

Undeniably, biology sets females and males apart, but it can only predispose— not force—us to behave in certain ways. Society does much to accentuate gender differences. As Alice Rossi (1984) points out, women may have the natural tendency to handle an infant with tactile gentleness and a soothing voice, and men may have the natural tendency to play with an older child in a rough-and-tumble way, but these tendencies are often exaggerated through socialization—under the guidance of culture. Also, boys may have been born with *slightly* greater spatial ability than girls, but as adults, men can perform *much* better on spatial tasks, largely due to socialization. As Beryl Benderly (1989) explains, "Most boys, but few girls, grow up throwing baseballs, passing footballs, building models, breaking down engines—activities that teach about space." In brief, we are born female or male, but we learn to become women or men (Ripley, 2005). In the next section, we will take a closer look at how various agents of socialization lead us to develop our gender roles.

■ Agents of Gender Socialization

No matter how a society defines gender roles, its socializing agents pass that definition from generation to generation. The family, peer group, school, and mass media all teach important lessons about these roles.

Families

Newborn babies don't even know their sex as female or male, much less their genders in terms of how to behave like girls or boys. Yet, as they are influenced by parents, children quickly develop a sexual identity and learn their gender roles. Right from birth, babies are usually treated according to their gender. At birth, girls tend to be wrapped in pink blankets and boys in blue ones. Baby girls are handled more gently than boys; girls are cuddled and cooed over, but boys are bounced around and lifted high in the air. Girls are given dolls, whereas boys are given action figures. Mothers tend to fuss about how pretty their little girls should look, but they are less concerned about their little boys' appearance.

When they learn to talk, children become more aware of the gender difference. They are taught to differentiate *he* and *his* from *she* and *hers.* Gender cues are also available. Both parents use more words about feelings and emotions with girls than with boys, so that by 2 years of age, girls use more emotion words than boys do. Mothers also tend to talk more politely ("Could you turn off the TV, please?"), but fathers use more commanding or threatening language ("Turn off the TV!"). By 4 years of age, girls and boys have learned to imitate those conversational styles: When talking among themselves, girls emphasize agreement and mutuality, and boys use more threatening, dominating language.

Mothers tend to talk politely to their children ("Could you turn off the TV, please?"), but fathers use more commanding or threatening language ("Turn off the TV!").

Girls are taught to be ladylike, polite, and gentle and to rely on others—especially males—for help. They are allowed to express their emotions freely. Observing their mothers' relative interest in fashion and cosmetics, they learn the importance of being pretty, and they may even learn that they must rely more on their beauty than their intelligence to attract men. They also learn to run the home by doing such chores as cooking and dishwashing (Shellenbarger, 2006).

On the other hand, boys are taught to behave like men and to avoid being sissies. They are told that boys don't cry. If they put on makeup and wear dresses, though done in play, their parents are horrified. Growing up with a fear of being feminine, young men learn to maintain a macho image, as well as an exploitative attitude toward women. Boys are also encouraged to be self-reliant and assertive, to avoid being "mama's boys" (Shellenbarger, 2006).

Gender-neutral socialization
The socialization of children into egalitarian gender roles.

In recent years, there has been a trend toward more **gender-neutral socialization**. Young parents, female professionals, and well-educated parents are particularly inclined to socialize their children into egalitarian gender roles. Still, across the country, most parents carry out the traditional unequal socialization for boys and girls. One nation-wide study shows that boys ages 10 through 18 years are told more often than girls to mow the lawn, take out the garbage, clean the garage, and handle household repairs, for which they are likely to get paid because their parents consider their work a job that should be paid. Girls are more likely to do such chores as dishwashing and cooking, which are often regarded by their parents as routine and are done without pay. In addition, girls do 2 hours more housework each week than boys (Shellenbarger, 2006).

Peer Groups

The socialization of girls and boys into their traditional gender roles gets a boost from their same-sex peers. First, girls engage more often in cooperative kinds of play. They jump rope and count in unison, swing around jungle gym bars one after another, or practice dance steps in a synchronized fashion. Girls further tend to say "Let's . . ." or "We gotta' . . ." to generate collaborative action. By contrast, boys engage more in competitive rough-and-tumble play and physical fighting. Older boys like to play competitive sports. They also like to appear tough by issuing verbal threats: "Shut up or I'll bust your head" or "I'm gonna punch you." Such threats are sometimes made in annoyance or anger but also in a spirit of play. These characteristics tend to remain when the boys grow into adulthood in their twenties (see Box 4.2).

Second, girls like to spend time with only one or two best friends, but boys tend to hang around with a larger group of casual friends. With best friends, girls often show gestures of intimacy, such as combing each other's hair or borrowing each other's sweaters. On the other hand, boys express their solidarity in a rough way—through high fives, friendly teasing, or mock violence such as pushing or poking. This gender difference may explain why friendships among young women are much more likely than friendships among young men to endure far into adulthood, remaining strong more than 20 years later (Thorne, 1993; Zaslow, 2003a).

Third, far from being "sugar and spice and everything nice," girls do occasionally suffer breakdowns in group harmony, experiencing considerable tension and conflict. However, girls are not as direct and confrontational as boys in expressing their conflict. The offenses of others are usually talked about behind their backs rather than to their faces. A dispute among girls is consequently more protracted, much of it carried out through reports to and by third parties (Thorne, 1993).

BOX 4.2 USING SOCIOLOGICAL INSIGHTS

It's Time to Leave Guyland

Several years ago sociologist Michael Kimmel (2008) interviewed 400 college-educated men in their twenties. He found many of them living in what he called "Guyland," a subculture in which single young men continue to behave like adolescents. They can be found in college fraternities and post-college sports bars. They wallow in heavy drinking, video games, sports on television, pornography, and predatory heterosexual sex. Their code of behavior calls for showing off toughness, which includes "Boys don't cry," "It's better to be mad than sad," and "Take it like a man." Thus, as women often told Kimmel, those young men would be very nice when alone, but in the presence of other males, they would take on an attitude of toughness, talking about "bitches" and "hos."

However, the young men merely project the image of a band of backslapping buddies. In actuality they are most often socially isolated. According to the General Social Survey, twenty-something guys are more likely than the rest of society to bowl alone, spending more time by themselves than with others. They are also less likely to "attend church, vote for president, and believe that people are basically trustworthy, helpful, and fair" (Dokoupil, 2008). More significantly, since they are stuck in perpetual adolescence, they are reluctant to assume the adult responsibilities of marriage and fatherhood.

Many studies have suggested that married men are happier and more sexually satisfied than their single counterparts. They also earn more and are more likely to own a home. As one researcher says, "Men benefit from just being married, regardless of the quality of the relationship. It makes them healthier, wealthier, and more generous with their relatives. It further enhances their stability and security. In general, those are the things that lead to happiness" (Dokoupil, 2008). In view of these benefits of becoming an adult, you may want to leave Guyland if you have joined it—or avoid it if you haven't.

Schools

Until recently, schools usually segregated courses and sports on the basis of gender. Secretarial courses and home economics were for girls; business and mechanics courses were for boys. Girls played softball; boys, baseball. High school counselors were less likely to encourage girls to go on to college because they were expected to get married and stay home to raise children. If a girl was going to college, counselors tended to steer her toward traditionally feminine careers, such as teaching, nursing, and social work. While these overtly differential treatments are no longer prevalent, more subtle practices of gender inequalities are still common.

One practice involves buying into the stereotype of math as a male domain so that boys benefit more than girls from math classes. They are spoken to more often, are called on more often, and receive more corrective feedback, social interaction, individual instruction, and encouragement. They learn more than what is in the textbook. By contrast, girls are often led to believe that they are not as proficient in math as boys. They are thus likely to learn math anxiety from their female teachers. They are also mostly consigned to learning by rote the math in the text, with little exposure to extracurricular math and science. Consequently, girls usually score lower on standardized math tests, though they may receive better grades on classroom exams—which largely require memorization of course material (Kimball, 1989; Schmid, 2010).

Another subtle lesson of gender inequality is rooted in the structure of the school. In virtually all elementary and secondary schools, men hold positions of authority (principals and superintendents), and women hold positions of subservience (teachers and aides). In such a male-dominant atmosphere, children are led to believe that women are subordinate, needing the leadership of men. As Laurel Richardson (1988) observes, "Children learn that although their teacher, usually female, is in charge of the room, the school is run by a male without whose strength she could not cope."

Mass Media

The media are pervasive sources of gender-role socialization. In such traditional magazines as *Good Housekeeping* and *Family Circle*, until recently, the tendency has been to talk down to women as if they were children needing endless reiterations of basics on how to take care of the family. Today, the publications are more sophisticated, but they still tend to define the female role in terms of homemaking and motherhood and to offer numerous beauty tips to help attract men or please husbands. *Cosmopolitan*, for example, featured such articles as "Be the Best Sex of His Life" and "Ten Make-Him-Throb Moves So Hot You'll Need a Firehose to Cool Down the Bed" (Kuczynski, 1999).

Women's magazines are not alone in perpetuating gender stereotypes. Traditionally, television commercials presented women as sex objects and as dedicated housewives. Young bikini-clad women were shown strolling on the beach in front of ogling, beer-drinking men. Housewives were presented as being in ecstasy over their shiny waxed floors or stricken with guilt for not using the right detergent to remove stains from their children's clothes. Prime-time television programs also often typecast women as lovers, as mothers, or as weak, passive sidekicks to powerful, effective men.

Today, the media are more likely to present the image of women as successful and able to support themselves and their families, but the traditional stereotypes of women still exist. On television and in movies, women are still too often depicted as sex objects, even when they are successful professionals. In women's as well as general-interest magazines, women are told that it's all right to be successful in the workplace but that they shouldn't forget that they must also be sexy because "looks are crucial." Even in coloring books for children, gender stereotypes are prevalent, portraying women as passive and weak, and men as superheroes (*Birmingham Post*, 2009; Comiteau, 2005; Fitzpatrick and McPherson, 2010).

■ Sites of Gender Inequality

For a long time, laws have denied women "the right to hold property, to vote, to go to school, to travel, to borrow money, and to enter certain occupations" (Epstein, 1976). Today, there has been significant movement toward gender equality, but large inequalities remain. They are evident in such areas of life as education, workplace, politics, religion, and the military. Underlying these inequalities is **sexism**—prejudice and discrimination based on one's sex.

Sexism
Prejudice and discrimination based on one's sex.

Sexism

A fundamental characteristic of sexism is the belief that women are inferior to men. Even when a man and a woman have the same personalities or are equally competent in performing the same task, the woman is still likely to be considered inferior to the man. We can see this sexist attitude even in psychiatry, a profession that is supposed to be scientific and objective in analyzing human traits. Psychiatrists tend to describe normal men positively—as independent, courageous, and the like—but are more likely to describe normal women negatively as having sexual timidity and social anxiety. What if women lose their sexual timidity and become sexually active—a trait typically considered normal for men? Then they are likely to be diagnosed as abnormal (Goleman, 1990; Leslie, 1996).

This negative attitude toward women has come through clearly in a classic study of college students who were asked to evaluate the social desirability of men and women with various characteristics. Women with supposedly feminine traits, such as compassion and sensitivity to others' needs, were rated more poorly than men with supposedly masculine characteristics, such as assertiveness. But women with masculine traits were also rated less favorably than men with feminine traits (Gerber, 1989).

Sexism produces gender inequality in two ways. When sexism takes the active form of discrimination against women, it obviously creates inequality. At each level of occupational skill, for example, men receive higher pay than women. Sexism also fosters inequality in a less direct way. If women have been socialized to feel inferior or abnormal, they may lower their expectations, aiming to achieve less than they otherwise might. Whether through overt discrimination or traditional gender-role socialization, sexism has brought about gender inequalities in education, workplace, politics, religion, and the military.

Education

About 100 years ago, it was widely believed that "schoolwork would make women sick, diverting blood from their wombs to their brains" (Manegold, 1994). U.S. schools began to offer elementary and high school education to girls and young women in the second half of the 19th century, but women were long deprived of the opportunities for higher education. Although some women's colleges were founded in the 1800s, women were barred from many colleges and universities until the mid-1900s. Many graduate and professional schools did not admit female students until the 1960s. In general, the more prestigious the educational institution, the more strongly it discriminated against women. Harvard's graduate business school, for example, was one of the last to admit women, doing so in 1963.

In 1973, the federal government, under pressure from the women's movement, began to pass laws against sex discrimination in schools. As a result, American women have made impressive gains in education. As **Figure 4.1** shows, more women than men are now attending and graduating from college. Women in many other rich nations are also attending universities in greater numbers than men. In the United States, still fewer women than men receive medical and law degrees, but the proportion of women earning these degrees has increased enormously since 1970. Women are expected to equal or surpass men in receiving these and other advanced degrees in the near future. Apparently, education has become the institution with the most equal opportunity for both sexes.

Nonetheless, substantial inequality still exists in other aspects of education. From preschool through high school, girls are given less attention than boys. Teachers call on boys more often, offer boys more detailed and constructive criticism, and allow boys to shout out answers but reprimand girls for doing so, especially in math and

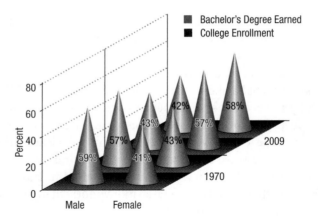

FIGURE 4.1 Moving Toward Gender Equality in Education

More than any other social institution, education has provided the most impressive gains for women. Since 1970, women have achieved so much in education that nowadays more women than men attend and graduate from college.

Critical Thinking: *What social factors may be involved in women achieving more in education than men?*

Source: Data from U.S. National Center for Education Statistics, 2009.

science classes. Receiving less attention from teachers, girls suffer a drop in self-esteem when they reach high school. At 9 years of age, a majority of girls are confident and assertive and feel positive about themselves, but by age 14, less than one-third feel that way (Sadker and Sadker, 1995). Some conservatives argue that boys are doing worse than girls in school because of reverse discrimination against them (Sommers, 2000). Liberals and feminists, however, disagree, citing the evidence that men continue to outearn women in the workplace (Lewin, 2008).

Significant inequalities also persist on the faculties of numerous colleges and universities. Women make up less than 30% of full-time college faculty. The figures are even lower in the higher ranks of faculty and at prestigious universities. Various studies have consistently shown that compared with their male colleagues, female academics are less likely to be hired, less likely to be promoted, and more concentrated in the lower ranks of institutions. They are also paid substantially less. This gender inequality can be attributed to gender discrimination because there is no evidence that women faculty are less competent in teaching or doing research (Toumanoff, 2005).

Workplace

Since laws were passed to prohibit sexual discrimination in employment more than 40 years ago, women have seen significant gains in the workplace. Only a minority of women used to be gainfully employed, but now a majority are. By late 2009, women already held 49.9% of the nation's jobs, and very soon they will outnumber men in the workplace. This trend is largely because the recent recession has caused many men to lose their jobs and many women who previously didn't work to seek employment. Still, women are far from economically equal to men (Evans, 2009).

Women typically hold lower-status, lower-paying jobs such as nursing, public school teaching, and secretarial work. These traditionally female occupations are subordinate to positions usually held by men. Thus, nurses are subordinate to doctors, teachers to principals, and secretaries to executives.

Moreover, when women hold the same jobs as men and have comparable skills, training, and education, they tend to earn less. Even in predominantly female occupations, such as nursing and hairdressing, women generally earn less than men. Not surprisingly, although Washington and other states have instituted the policy of *comparable worth* by paying women the same as men for doing different but equally demanding work, such as office cleaning and truck driving, the gender gap in earnings persists. Today women earn only about 77% of what men earn (Budig, 2002; Evans, 2009).

Increasing numbers of American women have been climbing the corporate ladder, but the *glass ceiling*—the prejudiced belief that keeps minority professionals from holding leadership positions—has kept most of them out of the top jobs. According to several studies, women represent less than half of the officials and managers in various industries as a whole. As mentioned earlier, women represent only 2% of CEOs at the largest corporations. The situation is worse in most other countries, with far fewer women in the top positions of organizations (Gezari, 2009; Jacobs, 2003; Seager, 2003).

Politics

It seems easy for women to acquire more political power than men. After all, female voters outnumber male voters, and most of the volunteer workers in political campaigns are women. Yet until recently, most women felt that politics was a male activity and that women should not plunge into that dirty world. Sexism also tended to trap women in a double bind to squash their political ambition: If a woman campaigned vigorously, she was likely regarded as a neglectful wife and mother. If she was an attentive wife and mother, she was apt to be judged incapable of devoting energy to public office. However, in a man, comparable qualities—a vigorous campaigner or a devoted husband—have always been considered great political assets.

In recent years, more and more women have assumed political leadership, but they still have a long way to go. Although they make up over 50% of the voting population in the United States, women capture only 17% of the senate seats, and only 9 of the 50 states have female governors. The United States further lags behind many other countries in female political leadership. No American woman has ever been elected president, but women have served as heads of government in at least 40 other countries, including key U.S. allies such as Canada, France, Germany, Great Britain, and Israel (Jost, 2008). Moreover, in 14 countries women represent more than one-third of the national legislative bodies, which is twice the proportion in the United States (see **Figure 4.2**).

No American woman has ever been elected president, but women have served as heads of government in at least 40 other countries, including Canada, France, Germany, Great Britain, and Israel.

Why are U.S. women so severely underrepresented in political leadership? One reason is that women generally have less personal wealth than men and therefore do not have the start-up money for a campaign. Another reason is that many voters harbor doubts about women running for high office. They wonder how a woman can be soft and warm and yet be tough and commander in chief. The third reason is the

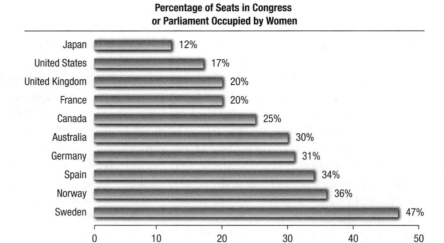

Percentage of Seats in Congress or Parliament Occupied by Women

Country	Percentage
Japan	12%
United States	17%
United Kingdom	20%
France	20%
Canada	25%
Australia	30%
Germany	31%
Spain	34%
Norway	36%
Sweden	47%

FIGURE 4.2 The Sex of Politics: A Global View

Although more women in the United States continue to gain positions of power, they still have a long way to go in the world of political leadership. Women in the United States constitute more than 50% of the voting population but occupy only 17% of the seats in Congress. The United States still lags behind many industrialized nations in female representation in political leadership.

Critical Thinking: *Why have women in the United States advanced more slowly in political influence than in educational achievement?*

Source: The United Nations, Human Development Report, 2009.

sexist bias against women in politics. If a female politician like Hillary Clinton is seen as competent, she is put down as masculine so that many voters will not support her candidacy for president. If a female politician like Sarah Palin is considered feminine, she will not get many votes either, because she is looked down on as incompetent (Jost, 2008).

Religion

Long used to justify male dominance, the sexist notion of female inferiority can be found in the sacred texts of all the world's major religions. Buddhism and Confucianism instruct wives to obey their husbands. The Muslim Koran states, "Men are superior to women on account of the qualities in which God has given them preeminence." The Christian Bible says that after Eve ate the forbidden fruit and gave it to Adam, God told her, "In pain you shall bring forth children, yet your desire shall be for your husband, and he shall rule over you" (Genesis 3:16). The daily Orthodox Jewish prayer for men includes this sentence: "I thank Thee, O Lord, that Thou have not made me a woman."

All this should *not* be taken to suggest that religion *always* puts down women. In the four Gospels of the New Testament, for example, "there are a total of 633 verses in which Jesus refers to women, and almost none of these is negative in tone" (van Leeuwen, 1990). But sexist ideas can be found in other parts of the Bible. Even the most central concept of religion—God—is spoken and thought of as being male. To some feminists, the notion of the Supreme Being as male is the quintessence of sexism. For this reason, some liberal church leaders have begun purging hymnals and liturgies of references to God as male (such as "God the Father") and preaching about a genderless deity (called the *Creator* or *Great Spirit*). However, many bishops, pastors, and laypeople have resisted these changes (Götz, 1999; Niebuhr, 1992).

Sexism is hardly confined to sacred historic texts. It also shapes contemporary religious organizations and practices. For the past 20 years in the United States, under the increasing influence of the women's movement, more women have been enrolling in theological seminaries and becoming ordained ministers. But they are still a small minority and have limited career opportunities. Compared with their male counterparts, female clergy are more likely to be underemployed, to be paid low salaries, to serve merely as assistant or associate pastors, and to be relegated to small congregations. Moreover, Conservative and Orthodox Judaism and the Missouri Synod Lutherans are still opposed to ordaining women. The Roman Catholic and Eastern Orthodox churches, which represent over half of all Christians, also continue to prohibit ordination for women (Götz, 1999; Gray, 1995).

The Military

There has been a tremendous increase of women in the U.S. armed forces. In 1970 women comprised less than 2% of the military, but today their presence has soared to 14%—a sevenfold increase over the last 40 years. While women often complain about bumping against barriers in the civilian workforce, they are the most satisfied working as soldiers because they believe that the military has leveled the playing field (Clemmitt, 2009; Kliff, 2008).

But gender inequality still prevails in the military. Although the proportion of women in the military has jumped to 14%, it nonetheless is a very small figure in view of women being 50% of the general population. More seriously, many female soldiers have been sexually harassed by their male comrades. As one woman told a researcher, "You just expect it. That's why we go to the latrine in pairs," and another woman said, "That's why we create a brother–sister relationship with a male soldier."

There is also opposition to integrating women into the military. They are thus banned from ground combat. The reason offered is that women are not as strong as men, and therefore when a male comrade is injured in combat a female soldier cannot carry him to safety. Moreover, there is the stereotypical assumption that women, being feminine and in need of protection, should not be expected to kill and be killed like a macho man (Clemmitt, 2009). That's why female soldiers are generally limited to combat-support roles in the war rather than being directly involved in killing the enemy. However, the distinction between combat units and support units in the military has blurred in Iraq and Afghanistan. The women in support units are just as exposed as the men in combat units to violence from roadside bombs and blind ambushes. As one male soldier says, "One of the most dangerous things you can do in Iraq is drive a truck, and that's considered a combat-support role. You've got women that are in harm's way right up there with the men" (Corbett, 2007).

▪ The Perils of Gender Inequality

There are at least two ways for gender inequality to seriously hurt women. One involves sexually harassing women and the other inflicting violence on women.

Sexual Harassment

Sexual harassment
An unwelcome act
of a sexual nature.

Most sociologists define **sexual harassment** as an unwelcome act of a sexual nature. In 1993, the U.S. Supreme Court came out with a more precise legal definition: Sexual harassment is any sexual conduct that makes the workplace environment so hostile or abusive that people find it hard to perform their jobs.

The Supreme Court's definition came with its ruling on the suit that Teresa Harris filed against her former boss, Charles Hardy. In 1987, Harris quit her job in despair because she felt she had been sexually harassed by Hardy. According to Harris, Hardy often asked her—and other female employees—to retrieve coins from the front pockets of his pants. He once asked her to go with him to a hotel room to negotiate her raise. And he routinely made such remarks to her as, "You're a woman, what do you know?" She spent 6 years trying to convince judges that she was sexually harassed in violation of federal law but to no avail. The judges found Hardy's conduct was not severe enough to "seriously affect her psychological well-being." But Harris persisted, and finally the Supreme Court ruled that sexual harassment does not have to inflict "severe psychological injury" on the victim. As the Court says, federal law "comes into play before the harassing conduct leads to a nervous breakdown."

The Harris case was the second one on sexual harassment to reach the Supreme Court. In the first, in 1986, the Court ruled that sexual harassment was a form of gender discrimination prohibited by the Civil Rights Act of 1964. Since that first ruling, the number of harassment charges has increased substantially, including the one filed by Harris, which led to the Court's second ruling in 1993. In the late 1990s, two more cases led the Court to rule that employers are liable for their supervisor's harassment of a subordinate. To avoid being sued, many companies, as well as universities and colleges, have instituted antiharassment policies, guidelines, and educational programs (Das, 2009; Strate et al., 2009).

Despite these landmark Supreme Court cases, it is still not easy for victims of harassment to win in court. The problem is that to many judges there is no sexual harassment unless it occurs *repeatedly*, as happened to Teresa Harris. For this reason, the judge in Paula Jones's case against former President Clinton dismissed her case, as Clinton allegedly asked her for oral sex *only once*—despite the fact that to most women, "even one unwelcome sexual advance is too many." Even if the law were completely on the side of harassment victims, the problem of harassment is too prevalent to disappear. According to various studies, about half of all working women have been sexually harassed at some point in their careers. Examples of harassment range from unwanted sexual remarks to actual rape. Also, among high school students, some 67% of girls and 42% of boys have been touched, groped, or pinched while on school grounds (Gregory, 2004; Hendrie, 2004).

Generally, sexual harassment reflects men's attempt to preserve their traditional dominance over women. Men are therefore more likely to harass a woman if they feel threatened by her supposed invasion of their male-dominated world. This may explain why sexual harassment seems to occur most frequently in heavily male-dominated occupations such as the U.S. military. In essence, sexual harassment is an expression of power, involving a more powerful person victimizing a less powerful one. Although it is possible for a female boss to sexually harass a male employee, because of the prevalence of men in positions of power over women, men are the offenders in most cases (Lewis, 2001; Uggen and Blackstone, 2004).

Violence Against Women

There are different kinds of violence against women. The most widely known is rape. According to a survey, some 22% of women have been forced to have sex at least once since age 18 years. Date or acquaintance rape is especially prevalent. More than half of all college women have been sexually assaulted in some way, and about 15% have been forcibly raped by a date at some point (Elliott et al., 2004; Thio, 2010). Given the sexist culture that defines women as sex objects that men can exploit for their own pleasure, it should not be surprising that rape is a common problem.

Even more common is the violence against women that takes place at home. As will be discussed in Chapter 10 ("Family Problems"), the family is the most violent institution in American society, except the military in time of war. The law does not adequately protect women against family violence, because many husbands who strike their wives to keep them under control are not arrested, prosecuted, or imprisoned. Nonetheless, many women remain in abusive relationships because they are afraid that their husbands will stalk and kill them if they leave. Yet by staying, the abused women are likely to end up getting killed by their husbands or being forced to survive by killing their husbands. The violence against wives stems largely from the sexist, patriarchal nature of society, which treats women as if they are their husbands' property.

■ Variations in Gender Discrimination

Discrimination against women is not the same for whites and blacks or other groups within the United States. It varies instead from one group to another. Discrimination against women also varies from society to society. We will discuss these two kinds of gender discrimination next.

Domestic Diversity

In the United States, a multicultural society, the impact of gender inequality varies with race and class. Middle- and upper-class white women may feel oppressed by gender discrimination, but they enjoy advantages made possible by their favorable economic and racial status. Working-class white women are subject to both gender and economic exploitation. And African American, Hispanic, and other minority women face either a combination of two social injustices (gender and racial discrimination) or a convergence of all three (gender, racial, and economic oppression).

Gender inequality is burdensome to all women, but it is more so to those who are already racially or economically oppressed. Most white women from affluent families traditionally raised their children and took care of their homes while their husbands went to work. By contrast, poor, African American, and Hispanic women generally had to do more than household work; they also had to work in low-paying jobs to help support their families. Since the early 1970s, thanks to the women's movement, many white women have entered relatively well-paying professions. Yet the poor among them, as well as minority women, are more likely to have remained at the bottom of the occupational hierarchy (Young and Dickerson, 1994).

It is not only poverty and racism that compound the effects of gender discrimination on many minority women. Culture also plays a role, especially for women in recent immigrant families. Japanese parents, for example, usually treat boys better than girls, as in the case of the mother of 6-year-old twins Peggy and Henry. Peggy is expected to be her mother's helper. If Henry leaves his sweater at school, Peggy has to go back and get it. She has to carry both her own and her brother's lunch boxes. Difficulty in treating female workers as equal to male workers is also more likely to exist in companies where managers and executives of Asian, Middle Eastern, or Latin American descent have been steeped in old-world paternalistic cultures (Dresser, 2005).

Global Diversity

Discrimination against women is also a universal problem. Every country in the world today still treats its women less well than its men. The problem seems more serious and widespread in developing countries than in affluent societies. More specifically, the gender gaps in literacy, education, employment, income, and health are significantly larger in developing countries. Consequently, gender inequality hurts women in poor countries much more. Among affluent societies, however, some nations, such as Japan and Italy, are more gender-inegalitarian (with men having greater political and economic power than women) than others, such as Sweden and Norway (see Box 4.3).

The ways these women suffer from gender inequality may appear unique to certain countries. Many women in China, for instance, are forced to undergo sterilization and abortion so that they will not have more than one child; young village girls in

---

BOX 4.3   GLOBAL PERSPECTIVE

Sexist Behavior in Italy

Italy's Prime Minister Silvio Berlusconi is notorious for treating women as sex objects. When a female student asked him for advice about her financial problems, he said she should marry a man who was rich like his son. He has bragged about the beauty of his party's female parliamentary candidates. He has put former starlets into his government. He has appointed a model as his Minister of Equal Opportunity. His wife has accused him of playing around with young women. Italians have put up with all this because of their famously patriarchal culture.

In addition, Italy has a greater gender inequality than many other countries. According to a report of the World Economic Forum, Italy ranks 67th out of 130 nations in gender equality, lower even than such poor ones as Uganda, Namibia, Kazakhstan, and Sri Lanka. Less than half of Italian women have jobs, compared with two out of three in most other countries. Italian men enjoy 80 more minutes of leisure time per day than do women, thanks to the time women devote to unpaid work, such as cleaning the house. The Italian media often broadcast images of women who are skimpily dressed and silent female beauties serving as decoration with older, fully dressed men running the show. Young Italian women and girls are taught that their bodies, not their abilities and knowledge, hold the key to success.

Recently, feminists have begun to denounce Berlusconi's sexist behavior. They have complained to the European Court of Human Rights and have made a documentary about the objectification of the female body. Before the 2009 G-8 meeting in Italy, a small group of Italian academic women asked the first ladies of the participating countries to boycott the event as a sign of protest. A few days later, some 15,000 Italian women and men signed the petition for the first ladies to boycott. This appeal to the first ladies received great attention from the international news media, but it was largely ignored by the Italian media (Volpato, 2009).

Thailand are sold by their parents to brothel owners; women in the Arab world are killed for sexual misconduct, such as committing adultery; and girls in some African countries are ritually subjected to genital cutting. The tradition of female infanticide continues in small pockets of China and India, and the availability of ultrasound machines that can detect the sex of a fetus has resulted in widespread abortions of female fetuses. Business etiquette in Russia often calls for female secretaries to sleep with their bosses. Such practices of gender discrimination continue to provoke condemnation by people around the world (Dugger, 1996; Greenhouse, 1994; Jehl, 1999; Pope, 1994; Reuters, 2009).

■ Sociological Theories of Gender Inequality

We have seen how gender inequality manifests itself in various ways throughout the United States and other societies. But where does it originate? Functionalists suggest that gender inequality originates from the fact that men and women have to perform different roles to help society function well. But conflict theorists argue that gender inequality stems from men's desire to exploit women economically and sexually. Symbolic interactionists contend that the interaction between men and women often sustains or reinforces gender inequality.

Functionalist Theory: Complementary Roles

According to functionalists, it is functional for society to assign different tasks to men and women. This division of labor was originally based on the physical differences between the sexes. For thousands of years when hunting-gathering societies predominated, men were more likely to roam far from home to hunt animals because men were larger and stronger, and women were more likely to stay near home to gather plant foods, cook, and take care of children because only they could bear and nurse babies. Today, in industrial societies, muscle power is not as important as human brain and machine power. Contraceptives, baby formula, child-care centers, and convenience foods further weaken the constraints that the childbearing role places on women. Yet the notion and practice of traditional gender roles persist.

The reason for this persistence, functionalists assume, is that those two dominant gender roles continue to be functional to modern societies. How? According to Talcott Parsons and Robert Bales (1953), men play the **instrumental role**, which requires performance of a task, and women the **expressive role**, which requires taking care of personal relationships. The instrumental role involves going out to work and making money; playing this role well requires competence, assertiveness, and dominance. The expressive role requires offering love and affection, as in child care, and it is best filled by someone warm, emotional, and nonassertive. When men are socialized into the instrumental role and women are socialized into the expressive role, the family is likely to function smoothly. The reason is that, though different, those two roles complement each other, working together for the same goal of ensuring success in marriage and family. It is thus the complementarity of the two gender roles that leads to lower divorce rates among traditional families than modern, two-career families.

Instrumental role
A role that requires performance of a task.

Expressive role
A role that requires taking care of personal relationships.

But critics argue that the complementarity of gender roles may be functional to a traditional family, but dysfunctional to a modern, two-career family. What works for the modern family, critics continue, is increased gender equality. As one study shows, when men take on more housework and women earn more outside the home, which effectively increases gender equality, modern couples tend to have lower divorce rates (Parker-Pope, 2010).

Conflict Theory: Economic and Sexual Exploitation

Conflict theories argue that gender inequality arose from the exploitation of women by men. According to the classic Marxist view, gender inequality is part of the larger economic stratification. By restricting women to childbearing and household chores, men have ensured their own freedom to acquire property and amass wealth. They have also used their power over women to obtain heirs and thus guarantee their continued hold on their economic power.

In addition, men have directly exploited women by getting them to do a great deal of work with little or no pay. Thus, married women are not paid for housework and child care, which would cost about half of most husbands' incomes if these tasks had to be purchased from others. Gainfully employed wives also do most of the housework and child care, although they work as much as their husbands outside the home. Moreover, as we have seen, they are usually paid less than men for their work outside the home. In sum, according to the conflict theorist, the economic exploitation of women helps bring about gender inequality.

Some conflict theorists give greater weight to sexual exploitation as the source of gender inequality. Randall Collins (1975) argues that "the fundamental motive is the desire for sexual gratification, rather than for labor per se; men have appropriated women primarily for their beds rather than their kitchens and fields, although they could certainly be pressed into service in the daytime too." More recently, according to some feminists, surrogate motherhood has emerged as the ultimate exploitation of women by men because it turns women into mere breeding machines. To conflict theorists, then, female exploitation of one type or another contributes greatly to the development of gender inequality.

Symbolic Interaction Theory: Interaction Between the Sexes

According to symbolic interaction theory, interaction between men and women often sustains or reinforces gender inequality.

When women interact with men, the interaction tends to reflect their inequality. Suppose a group of women and men discuss issues at a meeting. Men usually talk more often than women, and they tend to interrupt women more than the other way around. Men are also more likely to boast about their accomplishments and take credit for those of others. By contrast, women tend to speak more softly and politely and to say "please," "thank you," and "I'm sorry" more often. Such interaction between men and women, while reflecting gender inequality, sustains or reinforces it. Because of their verbal aggression, men are more likely to end up being considered highly competent, having their arguments and decisions accepted, and getting promotions or larger raises. By contrast, the less verbally aggressive women tend to lose out, even if they are actually more competent, are the ones who actually get the job done, or contribute more to the company (Tannen, 2001).

Nonverbal interactions between the sexes also sustain or reinforce gender inequality. Women talking to men typically give such low-status signals as smiling, nodding, holding their arms to their bodies, and keeping their legs together. Men are more likely to use such high-status gestures as smiling only occasionally, holding their heads still, and standing with legs spread apart, taking up substantial space around them. Because of such an unequal interaction, a mutually aggravated spiral is likely to occur: The women's conciliatory and nonaggressive gestures lead the man to see her as weak, which makes him more overbearing and aggressive, which intimidates her and makes her more conciliatory. All this helps to sustain gender inequality by enhancing the man's power at the woman's expense. For a summary of the three theories of gender inequality, see Box 4.4.

BOX 4.4 THEORETICAL THUMBNAIL

Explaining Gender Inequality

Theory	Focus	Insights
Functionalist Theory	The complementary roles of men and women	The complementarity of the gender roles makes the family function smoothly.
Conflict Theory	Men's desire to exploit women economically and sexually	Gender inequality stems from men's economic and sexual exploitation of women.
Symbolic Interaction Theory	Interaction between men and women	In interaction between the sexes, men gain more than women, thereby sustaining or reinforcing gender inequality.

QUESTIONS TO EXPLORE

1. According to the functionalist perspective, what purposes are served by gender inequality? Try to think of examples from within both family structures and work/occupational environments.

2. What types of interactions between men and women in your own community do you see as directly reinforcing gender inequality? Please explain.

3. Visit http://www.nps.gov/wori/index.htm and read about the Women's Rights National Park in Seneca Falls, New York. How might the presence of this park specifically serve to combat gender inequality? Consider your response and indicate whether it is more closely aligned with the functionalist, conflict, or symbolic interactionist perspective? Why?

■ Fighting for Gender Equality

Over the last 50 years there has been significant progress toward gender equality, because of the efforts by women to liberate themselves from the constraints of female-role stereotypes. This liberation movement by women has further induced many men to free themselves from male-role stereotypes.

Feminist Movement

Feminism
The belief that women and men should be equal in various aspects of their lives.

Confronted with gender inequality, many women have fought back by advocating feminism—the belief that women and men should be equal in various aspects of their lives—and joining the social movement for greater equality. This feminist or women's movement can be divided historically into three waves. *The first wave* began in the 19th century, developing out of the larger social movement to abolish slavery. The women who participated in the abolitionist movement came to realize that they were also deprived of freedom. Initially, they attempted to eradicate all forms of sexual discrimination, but gradually, they focused their attention on winning the right for women to vote. When women's suffrage finally became a reality in 1920, the feminist movement came to a complete halt.

In the mid-1960s, the women's movement was revived, and thus began *the second wave* of feminism. Two factors seem to have brought it on. First, after World War II, more and more women went to college. After receiving so much education, they were unhappy to be only housewives or to hold low-status, low-paying jobs outside the home. Second, many young women participating in various social movements (including the civil rights movement, the student movement, and the anti-Vietnam War movement), supposedly fighting for the freedom of the oppressed, found themselves oppressed by the male freedom fighters. These women, wrote Annie Gottlieb (1971), "found themselves *serving* as secretary, mother, and concubine, while men did all the speaking, writing, and negotiating—and these were men who professed to reject the 'oppressive' ritual machinery of their society."

Out of this background emerged a number of women-only organizations. Some were considered radical because they hated men, rejected marriage, and vowed to tear down the whole gender-role system. They gave their organizations such names as Society for Cutting Up Men and Women's International Terrorist Conspiracy from Hell. Other feminist groups were more moderate, the most well known being NOW (National Organization for Women). NOW has been the most successful feminist organization and continues to have a strong influence on women's positions today. NOW's aim is to end sexual discrimination in education, work, politics, religion, and all other social institutions. Consequently, many states have passed laws requiring equal pay for equal work, and government departments have issued affirmative action guidelines to force universities and businesses to hire more women. Also, in many cases, court decisions have supported women's charges of sexual discrimination in hiring, pay, and promotion (Flexner and Fitzpatrick, 1996; Rosen, 2000; Whittier, 1995).

In the 1990s, a new generation of young women in their teens and twenties started *the third wave* of feminism. These women grew up taking equality for granted because of the victories their mothers had won for women's rights. Thus, the third wavers differed from their mothers. They were more inclusive, welcoming men to join them in addressing not only women's concerns but also problems that affect both sexes, such as racism, pollution, and poverty. By being inclusive in organization and concern, these young feminists were able to achieve goals that the older generation largely ignored. Made up largely of highly educated white women, the older feminists made great strides for women in college education, professional schools, and white-collar jobs. But less attention was paid to the plight of poor and minority women, and these issues remain to be addressed by the third wavers.

Today, only about one-third of young females, ages 13 to 20 years, consider themselves feminists, but a large majority of them embrace most of the same feminine values espoused by the women's movement of the last 40 years. Unlike the feminists of the 1960s and 1970s, however, most of the young women today do not see any conflict between being a feminist and being feminine. As 15-year-old Karisa Powers says, "Just because you want to be treated as equal doesn't mean you can't scream when you see a spider." Most of the young women in one survey also agreed that "a man should always open the door for a woman." Older feminists today also tend to support at least one traditional gender role that expects women to look beautiful for men. While they used to burn bras, girdles, and cosmetics in the 1960s, now they are eager to have Botox, enlarged breasts, and other cosmetic surgeries (Kingston, 2010; Schnittker, Freese, and Powell, 2003).

Men's Quiet Revolution

Along with the women's movement, a quiet revolution has been going on among some men who want to free themselves from the demands of the traditional male role. As we have noted, men are expected to be tough, aggressive, and competitive while suppressing their emotions even if they feel like crying when sad. These expectations may explain why men tend to demonstrate their masculinity with violence, such as fighting and binge drinking. It can be difficult for men to relate closely to their wives and children because such close relationships require sensitivity, warmth, and tenderness—the very qualities that are discouraged by the masculine role. It also can be difficult to develop deep friendships with other men because of the pressure to be competitive and to put up a tough, impersonal front.

Understandably, a growing number of men support gender equality. They can see how equality helps reduce the burden of being men. They can also see the benefit of having their wives pursue careers outside the home if that is what they want. Working wives can boost the family income, relieving their husbands of having to work so hard to make a living. The men can work less and spend more time with their family—and enhance their enjoyment of fatherhood. For younger single men, gender equality may mean being as sensitive as women (see Box 4.5).

BOX 4.5   WHAT RESEARCH REVEALS

Young Men's Hidden Love Life

Over the last two decades, the feminist movement seems to have brought about a gender convergence, with young women today behaving more like men and young men more like women. More specifically, while young women have become more assertive and aggressive, young men have become more sensitive and appreciative of relationships. As gender-issues researcher Carol Gilligan (2006) observes, these "emotions and relationships once associated with women and therefore with limitation … have now become desirable attributes of manhood."

Sociologists Peggy Giordano, Monica Longmore, and Wendy Manning (2006) investigated the love life of male adolescents. According to traditional belief, male teenagers are basically cads, who only want sex, with little feelings for their sex partners and no intention to pursue a romance. But these researchers found just the opposite: Teenage boys are just as sensitive and romantic as teenage girls.

When a young man in the study was asked how important his relationship to his girlfriend was, he expressed his emotional commitment this way: "About as important as you get. You know, well, you think of it as this way, you give up your whole life, you know, to save her life, right? That's how I feel."

This young man typified the majority of the male subjects in the study. Some male teenagers did go for "hooking up" with abandon. One 17-year-old estimated that he had had sex with 35 girls, some of whose names he had already forgotten. He had cheated on his girlfriends and had even physically abused them. However, he represented only a minority, fewer than 25% of the male teenagers surveyed.

Ironically, most of the romantic young men were caught up in a "consensual ignorance," assuming that only they themselves were emotionally responsive, not knowing that most of their peers were also responsive, just like themselves. They were thus fearful of being seen as controlled by their girlfriends and thereby being ridiculed by their male friends. They in effect turn themselves into "closet romantics," keeping their loving tenderness toward their girlfriends hidden from others. That's why they tended to make denigrating comments about girls when in the company of their male friends.

Review

SUMMARY

1. It is men's role to be breadwinners, aggressive, and ambitious, while women are expected to be homemakers, passive, and dependent. These gender roles are the same in most societies. The biological differences between the sexes do not make women inferior to men. Men may be biologically superior in some ways but women superior in other ways. Culture defines what the gender differences should be, and through socialization, people develop those differences. One difference is that women are more compassionate toward others, which has led to the controversial argument that women judges rule more fairly than their male counterparts.

2. We learn our gender roles through socialization by the family, peer group, school, and mass media. In recent years young men often get together to engage in heavy drinking and sexual conquests so that they can avoid growing up and assuming the adult responsibilities of marriage and fatherhood.

3. Sexism involves prejudice and discrimination against women based on the belief that they are inferior to men. It can be found in education, workplace, politics, religion, and the military. Today more women than men attend and graduate from college, but most faculty members are still men. At the workplace, women tend to hold lower-status jobs and get paid less than men. In politics, women have fared better than before, but they are still far from achieving parity with men. In religion, women are generally accorded low status and refused ordination in conservative churches. In the military, women are still a minority, subject to sexual harassment by male soldiers and prohibited from ground combat.

4. One peril of gender inequality is sexual harassment, which reflects an attempt by the powerful, such as men, to control the less powerful, such as women. Another peril of gender inequality is violence against women. This violence often involves being sexually assaulted by dates or acquaintances and being physically beaten by husbands.

5. Discrimination against U.S. women varies with their race, class, and cultural background. There is also diversity in gender discrimination around the world, with women in developing countries experiencing more discrimination than their peers in affluent societies. Women in Italy are subjected to greater sexism than those in other European countries.

6. According to functionalists, gender inequality, with men playing the instrumental role and women the expressive role, enables the family to function smoothly. Conflict theorists argue that gender inequality stems from the economic and sexual exploitation of women. Symbolic interactionists show how interaction between women and men sustains or reinforces gender inequality.

7. Before 1920, the feminist movement fought for women's right to vote. Since the 1960s, the aim has been to end all forms of gender discrimination, but the plight

of poor and minority women has largely been ignored. Young feminists of today deal with such issues while inviting men to join them. Under the feminist influence, some men have quietly rejected the traditional masculine role and adopted the feminine role. Thus, teenage boys have been found to be more like girls in being sensitive and romantic.

CRITICAL THINKING QUESTIONS

1. In what ways have you seen gender inequality change in your lifetime?
2. Considering your own experiences, what forms of gender inequality do you see as the most troublesome today?
3. Would you say that there is practically no more gender inequality today? Please explain your response.

INTERNET RESOURCES

The Association for Gender Research, Education, Academia, and Action (AGREAA) (http://www.agreaa.org) seeks to add to the collective understanding of gender and sexuality by encouraging research and providing community space dedicated to the discussion of gender, professional development opportunities, and increased awareness. AGREAA proactively brokers partnerships between and within groups of academics, activists, educators, mental health professionals, policy makers, and researchers interested in furthering gender-related causes.

The Clayman Institute for Gender Research at Stanford University (http://www.stanford.edu/group/gender/) was founded in 1974. With a current focus on gender innovations in science, medicine, and technology, the Clayman Institute seeks to implement change that promotes gender equality at Stanford, nationally, and internationally.

The Center for Women's Health and Gender Research (CWHGR) (http://www.uw-cwhr.org/about.html) facilitates interdisciplinary research related to women's health across the lifespan; promotes research to enhance understanding of the relationship between sociocultural environments, women's health, and gender; and creates opportunities for researchers to study diverse populations of women in culturally relevant ways.

The Office on Violence Against Women (OVW) (http://www.ovw.usdoj.gov/) is a section of the U.S. Department of Justice that offers guidance in developing the nation's capacity to reduce violence against women through the implementation of the Violence Against Women Act (VAWA). OVW administers financial and technical assistance to communities across the country that are developing programs, policies, and practices aimed at ending domestic violence, dating violence, sexual assault, and stalking. Since its inception in 1995, OVW has awarded nearly $4 billion in grants and cooperative agreements, and has launched a multifaceted approach to implementing VAWA. By forging state, local, and tribal partnerships among police, prosecutors, victim advocates, healthcare providers, faith leaders, and others, OVW grant programs help provide victims with the protection and services they need to pursue safe and healthy lives, while simultaneously enabling communities to hold offenders accountable for their violence.

The National Organization for Women (NOW) (http://www.now.org/) is the largest organization of feminist activists in the United States. NOW boasts 500,000 contributing members and 550 chapters in all 50 states and the District of Columbia. Founded in 1966, NOW seeks to take action to bring about equality for all women. NOW works to eliminate discrimination and harassment in the workplace, schools, the justice system, and all other sectors of society by promoting causes such as securing abortion, birth control, and reproductive rights for all women; ending all forms of violence against women; eradicating racism, sexism, and homophobia; and promoting equality and justice in our society.

The Women's Rights National Historical Park (http://www.nps.gov/wori/index.htm), established in 1980, covers 6.83 acres in Seneca Falls, New York. The park consists of four major historic properties, including the Wesleyan Chapel, site of the First Women's Rights Convention.

Age Inequality

Karen told a researcher about her mother being fired from her job of 20 years and replaced by a much younger person. Her mother felt helpless and isolated. She cried at night, even months later, over losing her job, missing her friends from work, and feeling that her employer had violated her trust in getting rewarded for her many years of hard work. Violations of trust, despite a history of hard, dedicated work, hurt older workers the most. Like Karen's mother, Joe, a committed maintenance worker, was let go after 23 years of work. He was angry that his employer simply ignored his employees' dedication and hard work. As Joe said, "They now don't want to pay me my pension. I was a good worker for them and always did everything they asked. I went out of my way to help train people and make everything run smoothly, so everybody was happy and it was a good place to work. And now this is what I get, like I never really mattered to them. It's just not right" (Roscigno, 2010).

Ageism
Prejudice and discrimination against older people.

Karen's mother and Joe can be said to suffer from **ageism**, which is prejudice and discrimination against older people. Various surveys have shown that more than half of older workers have encountered age discrimination on their jobs. This discrimination exists even though older workers often demonstrate greater job commitment, fewer turnovers, and lower rates of absenteeism than do their younger peers. One study at Duke University further reports that when it comes to ageism, not only in the workplace but also in other areas of life, a large majority (84%) of Americans older than 60 years of age say they have experienced age prejudice and discrimination—in the form of insulting jokes, disrespect, patronizing behavior, and stereotypical assumptions about frailty or ailments (Roscigno, 2010).

■ The Aging Process

Ageism reflects the inequality between the old and the young, with the society placing a higher value on the young. This may explain why even older people themselves seem bothered by growing old. The Heinz Company once tried to market dietetic food to older persons under the name "Senior Foods." It turned out to be a flop. A perceptive observer explained, "People didn't want to be seen eating the stuff. It was labeling them old—and in our society, it is still an embarrassment to be old" (Gilman, 1986). The bottom line is that American culture is youth oriented, which makes older people feel bad about their age. This feeling may further be related to the biological and psychological processes of aging. But social forces, such as society's tendency to define older persons as a national burden rather than a national treasure, play an important role, as well. These social forces can aggravate—or diminish—the biological and psychological aging. Moreover, the experience of aging varies within the United States and around the world, entails being subjected to prejudice and discrimination, and is misused to generate the myths of aging.

Biological Aging

Sooner or later, we all gradually lose our energies and ability to fight off diseases. This natural physical process of aging is called **senescence**. Biologists have been trying to crack the mystery of why it occurs but without much success. Some believe that humans are genetically programmed to age; others point to the breakdown of the body's immune system, cells, and endocrine and nervous systems. In any event, it is clear that senescence involves a decline in the body's functioning, which increases the vulnerability to death. It is a gradual process in which the changes come from within the individual, not from the environment. It is also both natural and universal, occurring in all people.

Senescence
The natural physical process of aging.

There are various characteristics of biological aging. The skin becomes wrinkled, rough, dry, and vulnerable to malignancies, bruises, and loss of hair. Aging also causes most older people to lose some muscular strength and 1 to 3 inches in height. Moreover, blood vessels harden as people age, creating circulatory problems in the brain and heart—problems that raise the incidence of stroke and heart disease among older people. Functioning of the kidneys shows the greatest decline with advancing age. However, these deteriorative processes of aging do not cause disability in most older persons.

Aging further affects sensory perceptions. By age 65 years, over 50% of men and 30% of women in the United States suffer hearing losses severe enough to hinder social interaction. Visual acuity also declines with age: 87% of those older than age 45 years wear glasses compared with only 30% of those younger than 45 years. For most people, though, hearing and visual problems are generally inconveniences, not disabilities (Butler, 2001).

Psychological Aging

The psychological process of aging involves changes in psychomotor responses, memory, and personality. Older persons tend to have slower, though more accurate, psychomotor responses—such as being able to type at lower speeds but with fewer errors—than young people. Short-term memory seems to decline with age, although memory of remote events does not. Old age, however, does not inevitably lead to senility, an abnormal condition characterized by serious memory loss, confusion, and loss of the ability to reason. Nor does aging necessarily lead to a decline in intellectual performance. In fact, crystalline intelligence—wisdom and insight into the human condition, as shown by one's skills in language, philosophy, music, or painting—continues to grow with age. However, fluid intelligence—the ability to grasp abstract relationships, as in mathematics, physics, or some other science—tends to decline with age (Begley, 2007b; Rutherford, 2000).

Much of the decline in psychomotor and intellectual performance amounts to a slowing in work, not a falling off in quality. Older people may lose some mental speed, but their accumulated experience more than compensates for their loss of quickness. Contrary to the stereotyped assumption about older people automatically experiencing mental deterioration, many studies have shown the quality of job performance to improve with age. With advancing age, however, people tend to change from an active to a passive orientation to their environment, becoming less inclined to bend the world to their own wishes and more likely to conform to and accommodate it. This apparently works out well for older people, because they are generally satisfied with their lives and enjoy a high level of emotional well-being (Begley, 2007b; Charles and Carstensen, 2010).

Senility
An abnormal condition characterized by serious memory loss, confusion, and loss of the ability to reason.

Crystalline intelligence
Wisdom and insight into the human condition, as shown by one's skills in language, philosophy, music, or painting.

Fluid intelligence
The ability to grasp abstract relationships, as in mathematics, physics, or other sciences.

■ Social Effects on Aging

Biological aging does not affect all people in the same way. In fact, the speed of aging varies greatly from one individual to another. Some people look 60 years old at age 75, and others who are 60 look 75. A number of social factors may determine the disparities. An older appearance, characterized by the sagging and wrinkling of the skin, may stem from too much sun exposure in earlier years, a legacy of an active, outdoor lifestyle. Lack of exercise, another lifestyle, may also speed up the aging process. Thus, those who sit in a rocking chair waiting for the Grim Reaper usually look and feel older than those who are physically active. Social isolation and powerlessness also quicken aging. These largely social and environmental factors suggest that aging can be accelerated.

Psychological aging does not affect all people in the same way either, because of the intervention of social factors. Older people who are well educated, and thus presumably accustomed to flexing their minds, maintain strong mental abilities. So do older persons who have complex and stimulating lifestyles. By contrast, deterioration of the intellect is more likely to occur among the lower classes and those whose lifestyle is marked by lack of mental activity, rigid adherence to routine, and low satisfaction with life.

American Diversity in Aging

In the multicultural U.S. society, the experience of aging varies among people of different social classes, races, and ethnicities, as well as between women and men.

SOCIAL CLASS. Social class exerts a powerful influence on the lives of older people. Compared with older people of the middle and upper classes, those of the working and lower classes have a harder life because they have fewer resources—less education, less money, poorer health, worse housing, and more worries. Not surprisingly, the problems associated with aging are concentrated among the working class and the poor.

SEX. Living longer, women outnumber men in later years. Consequently, a greater number of older women live alone, without a spouse (see **Figure 5.1**). Older women are also more likely to suffer financially as a result of being divorced or widowed. Although gainful employment has increased significantly among women, a substantial number of older women remain completely dependent on their husbands' earnings. Even if they have been gainfully employed, most of these women have been paid much less than men, so their retirement incomes are substantially lower.

Elderly women further face special issues when they divorce or remarry. If an elderly man and his longtime wife want a divorce, their adult children will tend to shake their heads at both of them. (This has inspired a joke about a couple in their late nineties visiting a divorce lawyer. When asked why they have waited so long, they say, "Because our children are all dead now.") However, when it comes to remarriage, adult children tend to be more critical of their father's girlfriend than of their mother's boyfriend. An older woman, then, has to work harder to win approval from the man's children. Also consider that it is already harder for an older woman to find a husband in the first place because there are considerably fewer older men than older women (Fram, 2003; Zaslow, 2003b).

RACE AND ETHNICITY. The experience of aging varies from one race or ethnicity to another. Older Native Americans are the poorest older population, yet the least likely

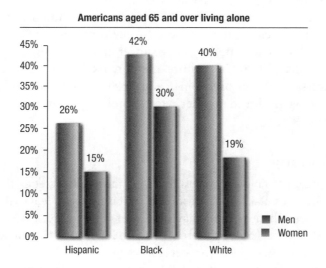

FIGURE 5.1 Elderly Men and Women Living Alone

Because they have a higher life expectancy than men, older women are more likely to find themselves living alone. They also have fewer financial resources, which can make getting by and remarrying more of a challenge.

Critical Thinking: *What can older women do to prepare for the possibility of living alone, and to possibly improve their living conditions in the long run?*

Sources: Department of Health and Human Services—Administration on Aging, *A Profile on Older Americans, 2009*; U.S. Census Bureau, *American Community Survey, 2008.*

to have access to social and government services. Native Americans are also unique in their rejection of the concept of retirement; their elders continue to work in the family or community until they become physically incapable. It is a tradition for them to help support their children and care for their grandchildren.

Older African Americans are more likely than their older white peers to receive assistance from relatives because of their greater prevalence of extended families.

As for older African Americans, they struggle with the problems of having lower Social Security benefits, fewer private pensions, and higher incidences of illness and disability than older whites. Older African Americans are also more likely than older whites to be forced out of the labor market early because of poor health. However, they are more likely than older whites to receive aid from relatives because of their greater prevalence of extended families. Older African Americans also have lower suicide rates than their peers.

Older Hispanic Americans have better health and higher retirement incomes than older African Americans, but they are less healthy and well-off than older Anglo and Asian Americans. They tend to retire because of declining health, but they usually refrain from doing so completely and permanently. Instead, they generally withdraw gradually from the labor force, with intermittent periods of unemployment. The reason is a desire to contribute as long as possible to the system of mutual support among Hispanic family members, which is stronger than among Anglo and African American families.

Financial situations vary among Asian Americans, ranging from relatively high retirement incomes for the Japanese to low incomes for the Filipinos. As a group, though, older Asian Americans have lower incomes than older whites. Those who are less assimilated into U.S. culture are more likely to suffer from depression, emotional distress, and other psychological problems. As a whole, older Asians are likely to be in better health than older whites, probably because of their lower-fat, lower-cholesterol diet.

Global Diversity in Aging

Older people generally enjoy higher status in traditional societies than in modern industrialized societies. Part of the reason is that it is no mean feat to live to old age in traditional societies, which typically have far fewer older people than modern societies, as **Figure 5.2** shows. Thus, by merely living to be old at a time when few survive past middle age, older persons earn a certain respect.

Moreover, because traditional societies change slowly, the knowledge and skills of older persons remain useful. Their experience is greatly valued. They are the community's experts. Not surprisingly, throughout Africa, growing old results in rising status and increased respect.

In many societies, however, the norm changed with the arrival of industrialization. Older people lost their previous role and status. No longer were they regarded

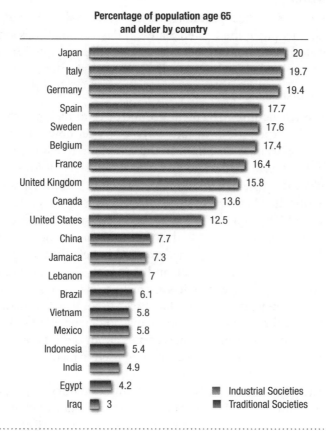

Percentage of population age 65 and older by country

Japan	20
Italy	19.7
Germany	19.4
Spain	17.7
Sweden	17.6
Belgium	17.4
France	16.4
United Kingdom	15.8
Canada	13.6
United States	12.5
China	7.7
Jamaica	7.3
Lebanon	7
Brazil	6.1
Vietnam	5.8
Mexico	5.8
Indonesia	5.4
India	4.9
Egypt	4.2
Iraq	3

■ Industrial Societies
■ Traditional Societies

FIGURE 5.2 Fewer Older People in Traditional Societies

Older people generally enjoy higher status in traditional societies than in modern industrialized societies. Part of the reason is that it is not easy to live to old age in traditional societies, where there are far fewer older people than in modern societies. Thus, by merely living to be old in a society where few survive past middle age, older persons earn a certain respect.

Critical Thinking: *How can traditional societies produce more older people?*

Source: Central Intelligence Agency, *World Factbook*, 2006.

as the storehouses of a community's knowledge or the guardians of its traditions, because the knowledge important to the community changed and the traditions lost their hold. Thus, in many modern societies, older people lose status because their skills become obsolete. The loss of status can also be found in rural areas that have been touched by modernization. In a remote community in the Nepal Himalayas, for example, older people are unhappy with their lot, wishing they were dead, complaining that their children have abandoned them, and trying to drown their sorrows in home-brewed liquor every day. The reason is that many of their young men have gone to India to work on construction projects and have brought back ideas and attitudes that have no room for the traditional value of filial devotion (Chen, 2005; Goldstein and Beall, 1982).

Similarly, the status of older people declined in the United States when the nation was founded on the modern ideology of equality and individualism. With egalitarianism opposing the traditional inequality between old and young, older people began to lose their privileged status when independence was declared in 1776. The emphasis on individualism also helped loosen the sense of obligation between young and old.

Roleless role
Being assigned no
role in society's
division of labor.

Assisted by this ideological background, excessive industrialization has brought down the status of older people in the United States. Today, it sometimes seems as if older people are expected to do nothing but wait to die. Older people can be imprisoned in a roleless role—being assigned no role in society's division of labor.

Age Prejudice and Discrimination

Older people are often victimized by prejudice and discrimination because of their age. The prejudice can be expressed in various ways. Consider how a doctor reacted to an 82-year-old man who went to see him with the complaint that his left knee is stiff and painful. The physician examined it and then said, "Well, what do you expect? After all, it's an 82-year-old knee." The patient retorted, "Sure it is. But my right knee is also 82, and it's not bothering me a bit" (Dychtwald, 1989). In fact, age prejudice, with its underlying stereotype of older people as frail or weak, as shown by that doctor, has become so ingrained in many people's thinking that they are unaware of its existence.

Age prejudice is also evident in the common beliefs that old people are set in their ways, old fashioned, and forgetful, and that they spend their days dozing in a rocking chair. Some of these ageist beliefs are expressed in jokes such as "Old college presidents never die; they just lose their faculties." Prejudice can further be found in the mass media: In prime-time television shows, older people tend to be depicted as cranky, unsuccessful, or unhappy. Stereotypes about older people being accident prone, rigid, dogmatic, or unproductive are often used to justify firing older workers, pressuring them to retire, or refusing to hire them.

Discrimination against elders can be seen in mandatory retirement laws, substandard nursing homes, and the insurance industry's policy of charging older people much more than younger people for the same insurance (Rother, 2009). Older people often lose their jobs or are refused employment because they are said to be *overqualified*—a code word for "too old," or an expression of age bias (Roscigno, 2010). Even people who are well intentioned may unconsciously practice discrimination by patronizing older persons, treating them like children. A 79-year-old man describes how he is patronized:

> Beware of those who are trying to be helpful and too readily flatter you. Second childishness brings you back within range of those kindergarten teachers who exclaim, "But that is very good!" Except that now, instead of saying, "My, you are really growing up!" they will say, "You are not really getting old!" (Skinner, 1983).

The Myths About Aging

From seeing a few older people having difficulty taking care of themselves, many people tend to jump to the conclusion that aging is the cause of their problem. Actually it is diabetes, heart disease, cancer, stroke, osteoporosis, Alzheimer's, and other diseases that leave those older people frail or disabled, not the normal aging of their bodies. The vast majority of people who live to be 100 years old are able to live on their own well into their nineties. Here are some other popular myths about aging (Kotz, 2009; MacArthur Foundation, 2009; *New Internationalist*, 2010):

Myth 1: When you're old, you're bound to get crotchety. Researchers have found that personalities don't change much after 30 years of age. So, if you are a cheerful and gregarious person in your forties, you can expect to be the same in your eighties. If your personality does change dramatically, the cause is not normal aging but some abnormal condition like dementia or stroke.

Myth 2: You will get senile in your old age. Older persons may forget someone's name here or there, but most older people do not have a real impairment in memory that makes it extremely difficult to live normally into old age. The unfortunate ones who do suffer from this problem usually have a memory-losing disease like Alzheimer's.

Myth 3: Physical and mental capacity inevitably decline with aging. Being old does not necessarily make the person frail. Socioeconomic factors such as race, ethnicity, income, and educational attainment have a greater impact on cognitive and functional decline than does age. Income and education in particular play a powerful role in determining the quality of life in old age.

Myth 4: Aging hugely increases healthcare costs. Aging does not determine healthcare costs significantly. For one thing, older persons with a healthy lifestyle make fewer demands on public health than unfit younger people. Chronic health problems do increase with age, but such problems often stem from diseases associated with unhealthy lifestyles rather than old age. Poverty is also a stronger determinant of ill health than old age.

It is a myth that physical and mental capacity inevitably declines with age. Being old does not necessarily make the person frail.

Myth 5: Older people impoverish nations. On the contrary, this statement is clearly untrue if we take into account the value of voluntary work, unpaid child care, and other contributions of older persons. The elders also tend to buy more services, especially care services, which create employment.

Myth 6: Social Security benefits only the elderly—and burdens the young. Social Security payments to older people also make it unnecessary for their middle-aged children to support their parents. In many cases, the elderly are financially able to and do support their children.

Myth 7: In an aging society, the old and young are inevitably pitted against each other. Many pundits and doomsayers have long predicted that the old will vote to increase spending on Social Security, Medicare, and other old-age entitlements while withdrawing support for educational and other programs that benefit the younger generations. In response, young and middle-aged voters are expected to reduce their burden of supporting elders by having their taxes allocated to other purposes. However, evidence has suggested otherwise. Young and middle-aged generations usually show support for, rather than opposition to, benefits for seniors, and the older generation often stands behind educational programs for children.

BOX 5.1   USING SOCIOLOGICAL INSIGHTS

New Ways of Helping the Elderly

Most policy makers seek to help the elderly by focusing too much on the solvency and sustainability of Social Security and Medicare. These issues must be effectively addressed, but they involve seeing older people as only consumers rather than producers of resources. This view of the elderly is based on the widely held stereotype that older people are typically disabled and hence unproductive. The reality is that many elderly people remain fit and highly functional, physically and cognitively. At least 40% of people older than 85 years of age are free of disabilities, and 89% of those between ages 65 and 74 years are not disabled (MacArthur Foundation, 2010).

These older Americans possess considerable capacities that can benefit society and, in doing so, benefit themselves. One example is the ability of older men and women to serve as caretakers and guardians of the young. The use of these untapped resources not only benefits many disadvantaged children but also contributes to the happiness and health of the seniors, as demonstrated by a program called Experience Corps. This program recruits older people to help young children and adolescents in public schools with proven benefit for both groups.

Another way to help older Americans is to avoid focusing on serving only their needs. Doing so can cause young people to see their elders as competitors who consume too much of the "pie." We should therefore invest in both older and younger generations. A policy for helping the elderly can also help the young. Investing in education and health throughout childhood and young adulthood, for example, usually leads to successful aging, because better educated and healthier older adults have been found to live longer and happier lives. On the other hand, investments in programs for the elderly also can benefit younger generations. Thus the Social Security and Medicare benefits that go to elderly Americans relieve their adult children of the burden of taking care of their parents, as well as leaving the adult children with more resources to support their own children (MacArthur Foundation, 2010).

It is important to debunk these widely held myths because they have too often influenced how policy makers and the general public think about how to help our aging population. Knowing the realities about old people can lead us to new and effective ways of improving the lives of not only the aged but also the younger generations (see **Box 5.1**).

Even though they are more likely than younger people to suffer from chronic ailments, most older persons continue to work or manage their own households.

■ The Health of Older Persons

Health plays a special role in the lives of older people. As age increases, so do health problems.

Chronic Ailments

It is widely known that older people are more likely than younger ones to suffer from chronic (long-term) ailments, such as heart disease, cancer, diabetes, arthritis, rheumatism, and hypertension. In fact, a majority of older persons suffer from these problems. But these ailments are usually far from disabling. Most older people with chronic ailments continue to work or manage their own households. Only a small minority are disabled and forced to significantly scale down their everyday activities. Moreover, chronic ailments and disabilities are less likely to afflict older people today than before, largely because today's older people are better educated and thus more likely to exercise and change diets to improve their health. In addition, thanks to advances in medicine, there is a decrease in the prevalence of severe disability but an increase in milder chronic ailments (National Institute on Aging, 2007).

Chronic ailments affect men more severely than women. Men with chronic ailments are three times more likely than their female counterparts to lose their capacity to carry on an active life. This may explain why older men are far more likely than older women to kill themselves. Older white men, in particular, have extremely high suicide rates, far higher than other groups (see Figure 5.3). A major reason is that white men's self-identity tends to derive from performance in the business or professional world. Chronic ailments can threaten such self-identity.

By contrast, the self-identity of older white women and African American men and women is less performance-oriented because sexism and racism have long made it difficult for them to pursue business or professional careers. They are instead more intrinsically oriented, defining their self-worth as a caring family person or a religious individual, and thus less likely to be threatened by the physical decline of old age (Girard, 1993). In short, social forces such as gender and race can aggravate or alleviate the impact of chronic problems on older people.

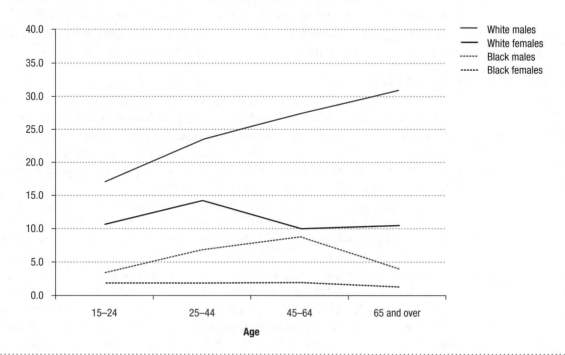

FIGURE 5.3 Suicide Soars Among Older White Males

White males have far higher suicide rates than any other groups. This gap progressively widens after middle age, steadily increasing throughout the remaining stages of life.

Critical Thinking: *What social factors may lead older white men to be more likely than other groups to commit suicide?*

Source: U.S. Department of Health and Human Services, *Health, United States, 2009.*

Mental Problems

If you think it is no fun to get old, you may conclude that older people must be most likely to suffer from mental problems, especially depression. The truth is just the opposite. National surveys have shown that it is the relatively young people who are most likely to become emotionally disturbed (Charles and Carstensen, 2010; Kessler et al., 1994). However, older people are significantly more likely to suffer from brain disorders. The most common of these disorders is senility. As we noted earlier, senility is not a natural part of being old but instead an abnormal condition. In most cases, the symptoms of senility—confusion and forgetfulness—result from nonneurologic problems that can be treated. Malnutrition, fever, and some medications can make a person appear senile. If these underlying problems are not treated, the symptoms of senility may persist.

Alzheimer's disease
A disease of the brain characterized by progressive loss of memory and other mental abilities.

In contrast to these cases of nonneurologic problems, more than 5 million older people in the United States do suffer from neurologic diseases. Most of these people are stricken with **Alzheimer's disease**, a disease of the brain characterized by progressive loss of memory and other mental abilities (Gross, 2007). Scientists suspect that it is hereditary, having found that half the immediate family members of the patient may develop the mental disorder if they live into their nineties. The disease can also strike the middle-aged, but the symptoms usually do not appear before 50 years of age. The victims gradually lose their abilities to remember, think, reason, and count, until, finally, they cannot perform the simple chores of everyday life.

Despite the higher frequency of such serious and other less serious illnesses among older people, old age itself is not a disease. Old people cannot die of old age, just as young people cannot die of young age. There are great differences in the health of older people, just as among younger persons. As gerontologist Matilda Riley (1982) once stated, "Even at the oldest ages there are some who can see as well, run as far, and perform as well on mental tests as younger people can."

Aging and Dying

Older people are more valued and respected in traditional societies than in modern ones. They typically live with their children and grandchildren, are given an honored role, and are often observed dispensing wisdom and advice, so that young people learn to grow old gracefully. Young people also learn to calmly accept death as the natural culmination of life. After all, they often see their old parents and grandparents die at home, handle their corpses, and personally bury them.

In modern societies, we are not adequately socialized for aging and dying. Our old parents and grandparents typically live alone. By not living with them, we fail to learn how to grow old gracefully. Although we may often exchange visits with them, we may not relish the prospect of growing old ourselves because we may believe that older people live unrewarding, lonely, or even degrading lives.

Modern societies also come up short in socializing us for death. We seldom witness a dying scene at home because most deaths occur in hospitals. As Sherwin Nuland (1994) has said, "We have created the method of modern dying. Modern dying takes place in the modern hospital, where it can be hidden, cleansed of its organic blight, and finally packaged for modern burial." The method of modern dying has in effect robbed us of the important realization that death is a natural event. Not surprisingly, many of us find death frightening.

■ Work and Retirement

Americans aged 65 years or older are much less likely than younger Americans to join the labor force. While about 65% of the entire U.S. population was employed in 2010, only 13% of older Americans worked. In many other affluent nations, older people have similarly low rates of employment (U.S. Bureau of Labor Statistics, 2010).

Declining Employment

The drop in employment of older people can be attributed to several factors. First, industrialized economies increasingly demand more and more highly educated workers with the latest skills and knowledge, putting older workers at a competitive disadvantage. Changing technology tends to make older people's skills obsolete, making it difficult for them to retain jobs or find new ones.

Second, older workers are often stereotyped as less efficient and productive than their younger counterparts. Coupled with this myth is employers' reluctance to pay older workers as normally expected because of seniority. Consequently, employers tend to lay off older workers and replace them with younger ones. Age discrimination, then, makes it difficult for older people to get and keep jobs.

Third, employment rates among older people have dropped because retirement has become an established institution. The emergence of private and government-run pension programs allowed workers to retire, and changing attitudes made it socially acceptable to do so. For the majority of U.S. workers, retirement has become financially feasible since Social Security was established in 1935. Later, pension along with programs offering early retirement benefits further encouraged the exodus of older workers from the labor force. Many retirees, though, have tried to return to the work force in order to supplement retirement incomes, especially in recent years because of the deep recession (Ansberry, 2009).

Reasons for Retirement

People may be forced to retire because of poor health, an inability to find a job after being laid off, or a mandatory retirement policy. When retirement is a matter of choice, other factors seem to play an important part in the decision to stop working. According to a study by the National Institute on Aging (2007), the reason most commonly given by older people for their retirement is wanting to spend more time with their family, and the reason least often given is not liking their work. Actually, most retirees have been satisfied with their jobs. This is particularly true of professionals, managers, and others in high-status occupations, who like their work more and are less likely to retire early when compared to those in lower-status occupations. That's why doctors are more likely than nurses and other health-service professionals to keep working past age 65 years, or college professors are more likely than cafeteria employees to continue working into old age. Conversely, people with lower-status, more physically demanding, and less intellectually stimulating work more often retire as soon as they can afford to.

Consequences of Retirement

Compared to people who are still working, retirees are more likely to feel lonely and unhappy. But does this mean that retirement makes people lonely and unhappy, or that people who were lonely and unhappy to begin with are more apt to retire? Research indicates the latter—namely that lonely and unhappy workers are more likely to retire. But another study has shown that when asked how satisfying their retirement had turned out to be, a majority (61%) said "very satisfying." About 33% reported moderate satisfaction, and only 7% indicated that their retirement had not been satisfying at all (National Institute on Aging, 2007).

Retirement can adversely affect some people more than others. For one thing, women and the working class are more likely than men and the middle class to experience poverty and social isolation from retirement. On the other hand, blue-collar workers tend to be less satisfied with retirement than white-collar workers, even though they have been more eager to retire.

In recent years, especially during the recession, surging numbers of retirees have returned to work. The desire to do so arises largely from insufficient pension and Social Security benefits. In fact, more than half of workers in the private sector reach retirement age without any pension from their lifelong work. Many retirees with these problems have been able to find work, but the pay and status are typically low (Ansberry, 2009; Greene, 2009).

■ Economic Challenges

Once out of the labor force, older people are faced with new economic challenges in their lives. Here we focus on two challenges: the uncertainties of getting Social Security and the financial difficulties of older people.

Social Security

While most retirees have three kinds of retirement income (personal savings, employer pensions, and Social Security), working-class or poor people usually depend on Social Security as their only source of income. It is a popular federal program. A widely held myth is that Social Security works like a pension fund: Social Security payroll taxes are deposited in individual accounts in a trust fund, where they earn interest and eventually are used to pay benefits upon retirement. In reality, Social Security is an income transfer operation. As soon as the taxes are collected from workers, they are used as benefits for today's retirees. In other words, the Social Security taxes people pay today do not go toward their *own* future retirement.

This means there is no guarantee that today's workers, upon retirement, will get back from future workers what they are now putting into the system. They will be able to get Social Security benefits only if future workers pay enough taxes. Whether that will happen depends on a number of demographic and economic factors: How many people will retire to claim benefits? How many people will be working and for what wages? How strong will economic growth be? What will the rate of inflation be? If the future workforce is small (because of slow population growth or high unemployment) or if wages are low (because of weak economic growth), Social Security funds will diminish. If, in addition to these unfavorable factors, the number of future retirees or the rate of inflation soars, the Social Security system will go broke and be unable to pay benefits to retirees.

In fact, in 2010 the Congressional Budget Office predicted that in a few years Social Security would be bankrupt because of the deep recession that had brought along low economic growth, high unemployment rates, and other economic problems. Even if the economy recovers, there will be a more basic problem for Social Security beginning in 2016 when the huge baby-boom generation starts to retire because there will be far more retirees than workers (Wolf, 2010). *Each worker* will have to pay a much higher tax to support *more than one retiree*, in sharp contrast to the situation of 50 years ago, when there were 50 workers sharing the cost of supporting 1 retiree.

The Congressional Budget Office has predicted that in 2016, there will be far more retirees than workers, with the latter having to pay Social Security taxes to support the former.

Will young workers of the small baby-bust generation pay the heavy taxes needed to support the hordes of older people? Optimists argue that they will, for the following reasons: First, young adults will realize that government benefits from taxes will go to their own parents and grandparents, whom they might have to support by themselves if the government does not. Second, the baby-bust generation will be in great demand as workers, so they will be well-off enough to accept the tax increases necessary for supporting the elderly. And third, because of improved health, a growing number of older persons will work past normal retirement, and these workers will pay taxes into the Social Security fund rather than draw benefits from it.

But these are mere speculations. In the meantime, some government officials have considered plans to make Social Security run more like an individual retirement account. Part of workers' Social Security taxes would be invested in corporate stocks and bonds, and upon retirement workers would get a pension based on the amount of their contributions and accumulated earnings (Rohter, 2008). A debate has also emerged over whether the government should stop giving Social Security benefits to the wealthy (see Box 5.2).

Financial Difficulties

In some ways older people may appear to be financially better off than younger people. Usually they have fewer expenses. Most do not need to furnish a large new home, raise children, and pay their education expenses. Their expenses for work clothes and transportation are lower. They are also likely to have financial assets that young people do not have. The majority own their homes, free from mortgage payments, have money in the bank, and often own some U.S. savings bonds, stocks, or corporate bonds. However, older people are more likely to pay huge medical bills, beyond what government programs cover. And financial hardship is particularly difficult for those who have been accustomed to a better financial situation in their young days.

The majority of older people are not exactly poor; that is, they do not fall below the poverty line. They receive most of their income from Social Security, personal assets, and private or public pensions. Of these programs, Social Security is by far the most important source of income. For many older persons, this income is supplemented by other government benefits such as Medicare, special property tax exemptions, public

Means testing
The system of determining whether a person is qualified for help from the government, which effectively refuses Social Security benefits to the wealthy.

BOX 5.2   DIVERGENT VIEWS

Cutting Off the Wealthy from Social Security?

Social Security has long provided retirement income to everyone who qualifies, regardless of how much they have earned during their working lives. Now that Social Security may soon go bankrupt, some suggest that the problem can be solved with **means testing**, the system of determining whether a person is qualified for help from the government, which effectively refuses benefits to the wealthy. Others argue that Social Security should remain universal, available to both rich and poor.

To proponents of means testing, it is simply not realistic for individuals to expect to get back all the tax money they have paid into Social Security; nor should they if they are wealthy. This reasoning is well understood for other taxes: The well-off pay more income tax but do not necessarily receive more services from the government. But if individuals are wealthy, they won't miss these services because they don't need them as much as poorer people do. This is how Social Security should work as well: It should go to the poor, not the rich. More importantly, if the well-off do not receive Social Security benefits, enough money will be saved to prevent Social Security from going bankrupt (Twenge, 2010).

Opponents of means testing, however, believe it is unfair to refuse benefits to the affluent. To them, Social Security reflects the insurance nature of the program: All recipients, whether rich or poor, have earned their right to retirement benefits as long as they have paid their payroll taxes while working. Moreover, if the well-off retirees are denied benefits, current young workers who work hard to become affluent will lose the incentive to do so in order to avoid paying considerable payroll taxes. Older people will also be discouraged from continuing to work beyond eligibility age for the same reasons. Besides, it costs very little to rescue Social Security from bankruptcy. According to the Social Security trustees, solvency requires the equivalent of only 2% of payroll (Rother, 2010).

---

housing, and Supplemental Security Income. Thus, older people are not so poor that they are reduced to pilfering food and medicine from a store.

Nevertheless, they still have less income than most of the younger age groups (see **Figure 5.4**). They also suffer from a higher poverty rate. According to the traditional measure of poverty, about 10% of the elderly aged 65 years or older are in poverty, compared to 12% for younger people aged 18 to 64 years. However, according to the new measure of poverty, which takes into account the recent dramatic rise in healthcare expenses paid by the elderly, 19% of older people are in poverty, which is significantly higher than the 14% for younger people (Yen, 2010). Poverty is especially common among older people who live alone, who are women, and who are members of minority groups. Whether poor or not, older Americans as a whole are most likely to find themselves in deep water financially, especially when the nation's economy is faltering (see **Box 5.3**).

■ Family Relations

A large majority of older people say they are not lonely. They often see close relatives, socialize with friends, go to church, and participate in voluntary organizations. Only a few (about 4%) live in a nursing home. About one-third of the elderly—mostly women—live alone, but the majority live with their spouses. For older people as a whole, family relations tend to be far more satisfying than stereotypes suggest. Let us take a closer look.

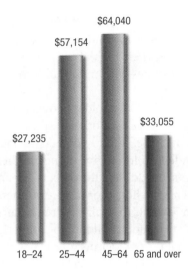

$64,040

$57,154

$33,055

$27,235

18–24　25–44　45–64　65 and over

FIGURE 5.4　Average Annual Income by Age Group

Most people steadily achieve income growth until they reach their early fifties, but as they approach old age, their income declines until it reaches the level of young adults.

Critical Thinking: *The steady drop of income for people in their sixties and older is very problematic in view of their increased need for expensive healthcare and prescription medications. What strategies can the elderly employ to avoid serious financial problems in the midst of a faltering economy?*

Source: U.S. Census Bureau, 2006–2008 American Community Survey.

BOX 5.3　WHAT RESEARCH REVEALS

In Deep Water

Many surveys show that in today's terrible economy many elderly Americans are struggling to pay their bills because the prices of essentials such as food, gasoline, and medical care have gone sky-high. Most Americans feel the sting of inflation, but the pain is particularly severe for the elderly, whose sole means of support comes from small Social Security benefits and, in some cases, a pension that is nonetheless paltry.

According to the Centers for Medicare and Medicaid Services, medical costs gobble up 26% of a senior's typical monthly Social Security check. Because seniors have to pay other bills, more than half of the Social Security recipients are forced to use their credit cards for the healthcare expenses. In fact, as one survey indicates, since 2005 older Americans have ramped up their card debt by 26%, way higher than the increase of only 3% for all card holders. In another survey, a majority (59%) of the elderly reported having trouble paying for food, gasoline, and medicine (Chu, 2009).

In an increasingly typical scene, elderly men and women form a long line in a church parking lot to receive free food from workers at a food bank who have begun distributing the food from the back of a truck. One of these older persons is Jannie Hicks. She says that she is eating more canned vegetables because fresh produce has gotten too expensive. She has also stopped eating frozen food because it is too costly. With the soaring price of gasoline, she has limited her driving to the grocery store, church, and the food bank. She no longer drives to her friends' homes to visit, using the phone instead (O'Shaughnessy, 2008).

Relationships with Children

When their last child leaves home, most American parents do not find the "empty nest" lonely. They have anticipated their children leaving home, and they appreciate their own increased freedom. That's why only a few (about 10%) of older persons in the United States live with their grown children, while most (more than 60%) of their Japanese counterparts live with their children. However, most of the elderly in the United States do maintain close ties with their children, which is much less the case in modern China (see Box 5.4).

In the United States, about 85–90% of older people who have children live less than an hour from them, so they can visit each other easily. Indeed, they do see each other, "maintaining intimacy at a distance." Elderly parents further often give their children advice, gifts, even money. A few children give money to their parents, but many more *receive* cash from their parents. In addition, the parents' generosity involves helping with college tuition, down payment on a house, or furniture. There is a class factor in all this, though. The flow of aid from parents to adult children occurs more often in the middle and upper classes, but the aid from adult children to parents happens more frequently in the working class. The fact that fewer older persons live with their grown children does not reflect an absence of emotional and physical connection (Vassallo et al., 2009).

Although most people in the United States do not like the idea of two or three generations living in the same household, there is increasing support for it. One reason is the rising number of older persons, which has increased sensitivity to their need for social and emotional support. Another reason is the decreased dependence of older persons; improved health and financial status have made them much easier to live with. And a third reason is that young people trying hard to succeed in their careers welcome the benefits of pooled economic resources and the help

BOX 5.4   GLOBAL PERSPECTIVE

Filling the Empty Nest in China

While most elderly American couples do not find their empty nests lonely, many (some 42%) of their counterparts in modern China do. This finding is ironic for China, which has such an enormous number of people, totaling 1.3 billion. Yet many elderly Chinese couples do feel lonely, largely the result of the tremendous change that has swept the entire country in the last three decades: More adult children than ever leave their hometowns—and even the country—looking for jobs. The current generation is the first to grow up under the one-child policy, started in 1979. As a demographer observes, they are more likely to be spoiled and self-centered, many being the only child in the family. As adults now, they are reluctant to support their parents or live and spend time with them.

Consequently, many elderly parents are left to lead a lonely life. One such pair of parents is 75-year-old Wu Shaoqiu and his wife. Their son lives in Canada and their daughter in France. "We need to have someone stay and talk with us from time to time," says Wu. So recently he searched in the local paper for adult women who were willing to be "adopted." Eventually Wu found an executive named Fang Fang and brought her home to meet his wife. Wu and his wife liked Fang Fang instantly, and for a good reason. As Wu says, "She brought a bunch of flowers. . . . She called me 'Papa' and my wife 'Mommy.'"

It didn't take long for Fang Fang to join the family. She later introduced two other women whom the elderly couple took in as well. All three women are in their forties and married. On weekends and holidays, they visit the couple to cook and clean, play cards, or surf the Web. Wu says that he considers them his real daughters now (Liu, 2008).

with child rearing and other domestic tasks. Still, most older people are reluctant to move in with their children, which reflects the importance that American culture attaches to independence and self-reliance.

Sandwich Generation

John and Mary are middle-aged, in their forties. They are still busy raising their children, but they also take care of their elderly parents who need help because of health problems. John and Mary belong to the sandwich generation.

About 25% of Americans younger than 60 years old are members of the sandwich generation. As baby boomers look ahead to old age, with the prospect of living much longer than their parents and grandparents, 67% of Americans younger than 60 years old are expected to care for an aged relative in the next 10 years. There may be some benefits from three generations living under one roof. A family's sense of well-being can increase from members supporting each other, providing younger children with a sense of belonging, helping teenagers grow normally into adulthood, and pitching in with chores (Park, 2005).

However, it is stressful to be squeezed between caring for the younger and older generations. The multigenerational caregivers have to reduce their hours at work or take unpaid leave to maintain their multiple roles. They are also at higher risks of depression, sickness, and financial instability. Not surprisingly, research has suggested that the sandwich generation is less likely than other caregivers to exercise regularly, more likely to smoke, less likely to use seat belts, and less likely to eat healthy foods. These unhealthy behaviors are said to result from the stress of simultaneously caring for two generations (Chassin et al., 2010; Park, 2005).

After Losing a Spouse

After the death of a spouse, women adjust more easily than men do. Although widows are more likely to suffer severe financial setbacks, they usually have a great number of close friends to provide emotional support. In addition, adult children tend to rally around the mother more than the father.

For men, losing a spouse can have serious consequences. When their wives die, men lose the only intimate confidante they may ever have had. That's why, as research has found, they feel disoriented and restless, characterizing their houses as cold places and using such terms as "cavern" and "cave" to describe how they feel. They are overwhelmed with the need to be out of their houses for much of the day. Consequently, older widowers are significantly more likely than married men in the same age bracket to die, get involved in a car accident, commit suicide, and suffer from a heart attack or stroke (Seligmann, 1994; van den Hoonaard, 2009).

For women, too, widowhood brings problems. Although widows have more friends than widowers, the most serious problem for widows is nonetheless loneliness. This is largely because many have been accustomed to the traditional role of being a wife, having derived their identity from being the wife of so-and-so. Widows who have been more independent are better able to cope with their loneliness. Other factors also influence women's reactions to widowhood. Widows who live in large cities are lonelier than those who live in small towns. Working-class widows are more likely than their middle-class counterparts to feel lonely. Younger widows are lonelier than older ones. And white widows suffer more from loneliness than their black peers (Elwert and Christakis, 2006).

Elder Abuse

Elder abuse involves neglect, emotional abuse, physical abuse, or financial exploitation of the elderly. The perpetrators are frequently the victim's adult children who are supposed to care for their elderly parents. Elderly parents are thus more likely to be abused if they live with adult children than if they live alone. The elderly are also more likely to suffer abuses if they are socially isolated, with relatively few contacts with friends and relatives other than the abusive caregiver (Hildreth, 2009).

In physically or emotionally abusing elders, the caregivers often feel stressed out from doing what they consider an unpleasant job. However, when it comes to financial exploitation as a form of elder abuse, the motive has little to do with stress and more to do with greed. Examples include a daughter who uses her power of attorney over her mother's bank accounts to withdraw her life savings, a son caring for his father who pays for substandard care to preserve assets he expects to inherit, and a nephew who coerces his elderly aunt to designate him as the beneficiary of her life insurance policy. Most well known is the case of the wealthy philanthropist Brooke Astor, whose son, who was supposed to be her legal caretaker, not only neglected his mother's care but also enriched himself with millions from her $45 million fortune (Black, 2008).

Elder abusers are usually beset with severe personal problems, including alcoholism, drug addiction, unemployment, antisocial behavior, arrest records, or emotional instability. Moreover, they generally have money problems or are financially dependent on their victims, which may explain why elder abuse often involves financial exploitation and rarely takes the form of physical or emotional abuse (Hildreth, 2009).

■ Sociological Theories of Age Inequality

We have seen how in various ways the elderly are unequal to the young, with the former getting the short end of the stick. The three sociological theories offer different views on how older people end up with a disadvantaged life that reflects age inequality.

Functionalist Theory

Functionalists use the disengagement theory to explain age inequality. According to this theory, age inequality involves being socially disadvantaged and devalued because of old age, which leads the elderly to disengage from others, such as refraining from entertaining in the home, being unconcerned with others' opinions, or avoiding social events with new people (Adams, 2004). Although they do not withdraw like hermits, the amount of their social activities declines significantly. Thus, disengagement occurs when older persons retire; when their grown children leave home; when their spouses, friends, and relatives die; when they lose contact with friends and fellow workers; and when they turn their attention to personal concerns and away from societal ones. They tend to disengage from younger people, which (under the influence of society's ageism) is likely to cause inequality between the old and the young.

According to functionalist theory, the disengagement serves useful functions for society. For one thing, disengagement renders the eventual death of an older person less disruptive to the lives of friends and relatives. For another, disengagement precludes harmful economic effects of the older worker's increasing incompetence or sudden death. All these functions are made possible because younger people have already replaced them in the workplace. However, disengagement also means segregating the elderly from younger people, thereby generating and widening the inequality between the old and the young.

Functionalist theory further argues that the disengagement is also functional for older people themselves because it relieves them of responsibilities, making their lives easier and encouraging them to begin preparing for their own inevitable death. Being well adjusted to old age through disengagement, then, means accepting that one is outside the mainstream of life and coming to terms with one's mortality. However, such disengagement essentially reduces the elderly's contribution to social life, which is likely to create age inequality by making them feel less useful as members of society.

Critics have challenged the assumption that disengagement is universal or inevitable. They point, for example, to many older members of the U.S. Congress who are far from disengaged from society. Critics further contend that disengagement may be harmful to both society and the individual. It may mean losing the talent, energy, and expertise of the disengaged older persons, and may contribute to their poor health, poverty, and loneliness.

Conflict Theory

Conflict theorists use minority theory to explain age inequality. According to this theory, older people are treated in society as an oppressed minority. They are, in effect, victims of ageism, suffering prejudice and discrimination because of their old age. Like race and gender, age is used as the basis for judging and reacting to people regardless of their individual characteristics. The prejudice and discrimination against the elderly produce age inequality.

As we have observed, prejudice against the elderly often manifests as a stereotype of older people as frail, weak, or unproductive, and therefore useless. Prejudice is also evident in the common belief that old people are set in their ways, stubborn, close-minded, and slow. These stereotypes are often used to justify firing older workers, pressuring them to retire, or refusing to hire them. Discrimination against the elderly can further be seen in substandard nursing homes and the domestic neglect and abuse of elders.

Critics argue that in some respects older people are far from oppressed. Especially in politics, many leaders are aged 65 years or older. Also, older people are such a powerful political force that many elected officials are afraid to anger them by cutting Social Security benefits.

Symbolic Interaction Theory

While functionalists argue that old age causes the elderly to disengage from others, symbolic interactionists contend that most older people maintain a great deal of interaction with others by engaging in many age-related activities. This symbolic interactionism is also known as activity theory. Older people may become less socially active when they retire or when their children leave home, but this does not necessarily cause them to disengage. They are likely to make new friends and engage in new activities such as doing volunteer work, socializing with neighbors, and participating in religion (Cornwell et al., 2008). The people with whom they interact are primarily of the same age group, so they can enjoy sharing interests and experiences. However, because the high frequency of interaction among the elderly is age related, it creates separation and thus inequality between older and younger groups.

In fact, there are at least two reasons for the considerable interaction among older people that produces age inequality. First are social and demographic trends, including the increasing size of the older population, the growing concentration of older persons in areas such as retirement communities and public housing for senior citizens, and the proliferation of social services for older people. Second, because of widespread ageism and discomfort with aging, older people may find it difficult to interact with younger adults. If older people want to talk about their impending death, their 40-year-old children are likely to change the subject. That's why older people find it more comfortable to interact with their peers.

Symbolic interactionists also emphasize the benefits of social interaction for older people, while functionalists argue that social disengagement among older people is functional for both society and the aged individuals. As symbolic interactionists see it, keeping socially active helps older people to remain physically and psychologically fit—healthy, happy, and able to live a long life (Charles and Carstensen, 2007).

Critics argue that symbolic interactionists present elders with an unattainable goal by urging them to cling to an active role in life. Because the activities in which they now engage as old people may not seem meaningful in comparison to their previous roles as productive workers or energetic parents, they are likely to feel like failures, useless, and worthless.

For a summary of the three theories, see Box 5.5.

BOX 5.5   THEORETICAL THUMBNAIL

Explaining Age Inequality

Theory	Focus	Insights
Functionalist Theory	How elders' disengagement from others generates age inequality	Disengagement from others is functional for both society and elders.
Conflict Theory	How prejudice and discrimination against the elderly produce age inequality	Prejudice and discrimination against the aged are comparable to those against other minorities.
Symbolic Interaction Theory	How increased interaction among the elderly creates age inequality	The elderly interact much more with each other than with younger groups.

QUESTIONS TO EXPLORE

1. During the 2008 presidential election, Republican Senator John McCain was often portrayed by the media as being too old to hold the office of president. This bias against the senator was based on his age, not his physical or mental state. Which theoretical perspective would you use to explain this treatment of the elderly? Explain your response.

2. Do the elderly people whom you have observed most frequently in your own life fit more closely the functional disengagement view or the symbolic interactionist activity view of the elderly? Explain your response.

3. Read about Tish Sommers and Laurie Shields of the Older Women's League (OWL) at http://www.owl-national.org/Agenda.html. Which sociological theory does their collective philosophy best represent? How so?

Review

SUMMARY

1. Biological aging involves physical changes that accompany old age, such as wrinkled skin and declining visual acuity. These changes are inconveniences, not disabilities. Psychological aging involves slower psychomotor responses, poorer memory, and personality changes. The speed of biological and psychological aging, however, depends on social forces such as lifestyle and education.

2. The experience of aging in the United States varies among people of different social classes, races, and ethnicities, as well as between women and men. Aging also varies globally, with older people in traditional societies enjoying higher status than their counterparts in modern societies.

3. Older people often suffer from prejudice and discrimination because of their age. Prejudice may be expressed in jokes and mass media, and discrimination may involve firing aged workers and charging older people more than younger people for the same insurance. There are also many myths about aging, such as the false belief that senility always occurs in old age or that physical and mental capacity inevitably decline with age.

4. The elderly are more likely than younger people to suffer from chronic ailments. Such ailments affect men more severely than women. Older people are also more likely to have brain disorders. When older people die, their young surviving relatives in modern societies are less able than those in traditional societies to calmly accept death as the natural culmination of life.

5. Older people are likely to be unemployed because of the increasing demand for new skills, the practice of age discrimination, and the popular acceptance of retirement. The most common reason for choosing to retire is spending more time with family. Retirement generally makes older people happier and less lonely.

6. Although most older Americans have three kinds of retirement income, the working class or poor usually depend on Social Security as their only source of income. A debate has erupted over whether the well-off should receive Social Security. In some ways older people are better off because of fewer expenses, compared to younger people. However, their income is relatively low, and poverty is prevalent among women, minorities, and those who live alone. In today's bad economy, many elderly individuals are struggling to pay the high cost of fuel, food, and medical care.

7. Though living apart from them, older Americans often visit their children and give them advice, gifts, and money. In modern China, many elderly parents find their empty nest so lonely that they "adopt" adult women to spend time with them. Many middle-aged Americans are the sandwich generation, caught between raising children and caring for elderly parents. After their spouse dies, women adjust better than men. While the worst problem for widows is loneliness, widowers tend to have even more serious problems, such as suffering from a heart attack and

committing suicide. Elderly parents who live with their adult children are more likely than those who live alone to be abused by the children.

8. According to functionalist theory, the elderly tend to disengage from younger people, which (under the influence of society's ageism) is likely to cause age inequality. Conflict theory attributes age inequality to the oppression of the elderly as a minority. Symbolic interaction theory explains gender inequality as a result of the elderly interacting with their own age group.

CRITICAL THINKING QUESTIONS

1. What issues facing the elderly do you consider to be the most important for U.S. society today? Why?

2. What problems faced by the elderly do you feel could be easily improved? What suggestions would you have for making improvements?

3. What are the issues unique to elderly women? How can the living conditions of elderly women be improved?

INTERNET RESOURCES

AARP (formerly the American Association of Retired Persons) (http://www.aarp .org/) is the largest nonprofit membership organization for adults 50 years of age and older. It offers its members a wide range of information about life transitions, independent living, caregiving, and many other topics, including Alzheimer's disease.

The Administration on Aging (AOA) (http://www.aoa.gov/) is an agency of the U.S. Department of Health and Human Services. This Web site provides extensive information for and about older people and the services they need. It includes a comprehensive directory of state and area agencies on aging with live direct links to their Web sites.

The American Geriatrics Society (AGS) (http://www.americangeriatrics.org/) is a professional society of healthcare providers who specialize in the care of older adults. Their Web site is primarily for professionals, but it does include some consumer information in the Patient Education Forum of their Consumer Education section.

Founded in 1974, the National Institute on Aging (NIA) (http://www.nia.nih.gov/) provides leadership in aging research, training, health information dissemination, and other programs relevant to aging and older people. Currently, the NIA conducts genetic, biological, clinical, behavioral, social, and economic research related to the aging process, diseases and conditions associated with aging, and other special problems and needs of older Americans.

The Older Women's League (OWL) (http://www.owl-national.org/Welcome.html) was founded in 1980. Through the use of research, education, and advocacy, this grassroots membership organization is concerned with issues unique to aging women and improving the quality of life and status of women moving through midlife and beyond. OWL currently boasts over 70 million women 40 years of age and older.

The Red Hat Society (RHS) (http://www.redhatsociety.com/) is a networking society for women older than 50 years of age, with the singular goal of engaging women and pushing them to enjoy life to its fullest, in all that they do! The women of the RHS are part of an extensive network of women approaching 50 years of age or beyond, who are committed to meeting like-minded friends, staying active (or becoming more active than ever), and simply having fun.

Problems of Deviance

PART III

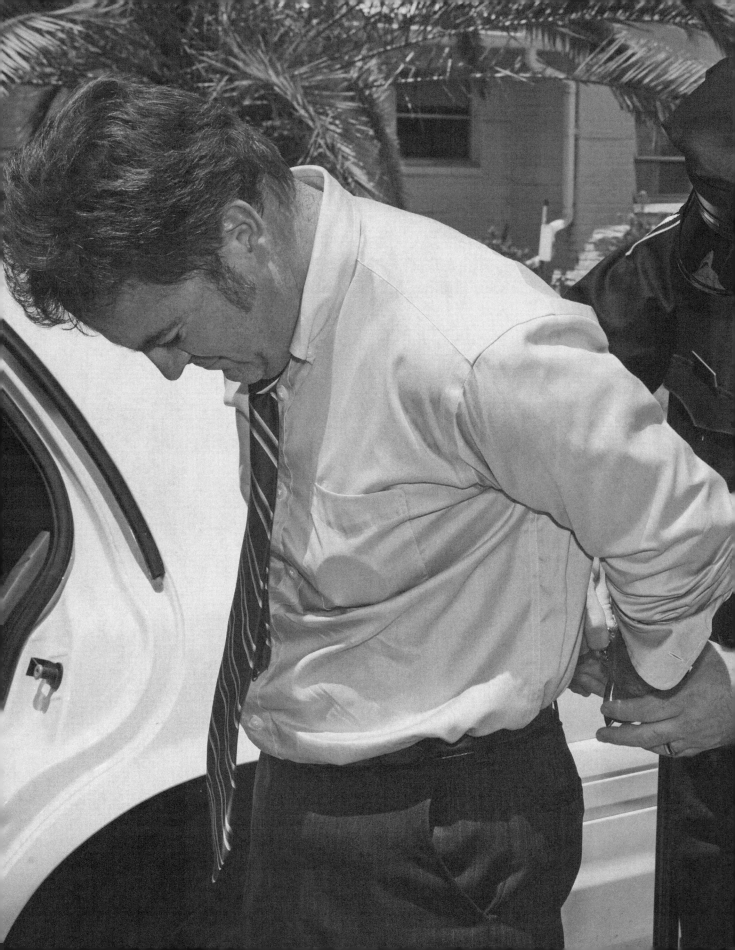

Criminal Behavior

Review

    Summary

    Critical Thinking Questions

    Internet Resources

When Anna Bernanke, the wife of the Federal Reserve Chairman Ben Bernanke, was drinking coffee at a Starbucks, a thief stole her purse from the back of her chair. Inside were her leather wallet, four credit cards, five dollars in cash, and a Wachovia Bank checkbook. The thief was George Reid. A week later, he wrote $900 on his victim's check and deposited it to his account at a Bank of America. Reid was later convicted of identity theft and sentenced to more than 16 years in prison. This old-fashioned way of stealing personal information is still prevalent, accounting for half of all identity theft cases. Today, the other half of identity thefts is committed online, a trend primarily due to the proliferation of computers. We will discuss this modern form of identity theft later in this chapter. Identity theft as a whole is among the fast-growing or serious crimes, which are largely fueled by the recent economic downturn (Markon, 2010; Markon and Irwin, 2009). In this chapter, we will analyze some of these crimes, the social diversity in crime, the criminal justice system, and the sociological theories of crime.

■ Varieties of Crime

Crime appears in many different forms, but when people talk about crimes, they tend to refer to what are widely known as street crimes. Some of these crimes are violent, committed against a person. They include homicide, assault, rape, robbery, and hate crime. Other street crimes are committed against property, such as burglary, shoplifting, arson, and motor vehicle theft. We will discuss some of these street crimes in this chapter—namely, robbery, shoplifting, and hate crime. We will also zero in on other types of crime, such as organized crime, white-collar crime, corporate crime, governmental crime, and online identity theft. These crimes are generally more profitable than street crimes.

Robbery

Robbery is basically a *big-city* crime, with the robbery rate in large cities being many times higher than in small towns and rural areas. Relatedly, the more urbanized a region, the higher its rate of robbery. This is because most of the victims are strangers to the offenders and opportunities abound for encountering strangers in large cities.

Thus, because the northeastern states are more urbanized than the southern states, they have higher robbery rates (U.S. Census Bureau, 2010).

Robbery occurs most frequently in the cold winter months, reaching its peak volume during the holiday season in December, when stores are raking in more money and customers are carrying more cash on the streets. There are additional reasons for the higher frequency of robbery in the winter than in other seasons. The cold weather keeps most people off the streets, which makes it easier for robbers to victimize isolated individuals without the discouragement of having witnesses around. The cold weather also makes it look natural for robbers to wear a heavy coat, which is ideal for hiding a shotgun or other weapon. The increased hours of darkness in the winter further enhance the opportunity for robbing without getting caught. All these factors involve the *opportunity* for committing robbery.

Other factors have to do with the increased *motivation* for committing the crime. One such factor is a higher rate of unemployment in the winter, which largely comes from the loss of seasonal jobs such as construction, tourism, and other outdoor work. Another motivational factor is the economic pressure from the rising cost of living in the winter, because there is greater need to spend on such things as clothing, shelter, and heating. This economic pressure further increases when the economy goes downhill (Joyner, 2008).

Most robberies take place *outdoors*, on the streets. Of those that occur indoors, the general public assumes that many take place in banks. However, *bank robbery is relatively rare*, accounting for only about 5% of indoor robberies (see **Figure 6.1**). Since the early 1990s, though, bank robberies have increased significantly, largely because it is much more convenient to rob banks today. Unlike the fortresslike banks built in the past, many banks today make themselves vulnerable to robbery by having potted plants, subdued lighting, long hours, and open teller stations, all intended to please customers. Moreover, to avoid violence from angry robbers, bank tellers are instructed to quickly hand over the money without a fight, which makes it convenient even for a 12-year-old or an 80-year-old to rob the bank. The road system further makes it easy to pull off a robbery at selected banks, because it takes less than a minute after

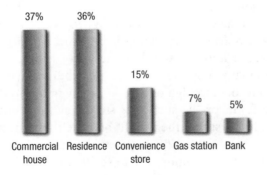

FIGURE 6.1 Locations of Indoor Robberies

It is popularly believed that most robberies that occur indoors take place in banks, but bank robbery is relatively rare. It accounts for only about 5% of indoor robberies.

Critical Thinking: *Why are bank robberies so frequently the subject of movies, TV shows, and news reports, when they occur so infrequently?*

Source: U.S. Census Bureau, *Statistical Abstract of the United States, 2008.*

the heist to zoom away on the freeway. This may explain why California, which has the nation's most extensive network of freeways, has more bank robberies than any other state (Hechinger, 2002; St. John, 2004).

Most robberies today are *armed*. Over the years, armed robberies have increased at a faster rate than unarmed robberies. Most armed robberies involve the use of firearms rather than knives and other cutting instruments, and they are more likely to be committed by adults than teenagers. In contrast, unarmed robberies, which include purse snatching, mugging, and other violent confrontations, involve youngsters more frequently than adults. Unarmed robberies are also more likely than armed ones to take place closer to the offender's home. This is largely because of the spontaneity and predominance of foot travel in unarmed robbery—as opposed to the planned nature of armed robbery and the common use of a vehicle in carrying out the crime (Federal Bureau of Investigation [FBI], 2010).

Shoplifting

Boosters
Professional criminals who shoplift for large profit.

Snitches
Amateurs who steal articles of small value for personal use.

Only a few shoplifters are **boosters**, professional criminals who shoplift for large profit. Most shoplifters are **snitches**, amateurs who steal articles of small value for personal use.

Shoplifting is predominantly a juvenile offense. Individuals younger than 21 years of age are most likely to shoplift. Among these youngsters, those between 11 and 15 years old shoplift the most. This explains the increased incidence of shoplifting on nonschool days, afternoons and evenings, and late in the week, from Wednesday through Saturday. The youth of the common shoplifters further explains why the items most often stolen include beauty products, music CDs and movie videos, and apparel, from athletic shoes to designer clothing. The prevalence of youth shoplifters has led some malls to ban teenagers from entering them during evening hours without adult companions (Lee, 2006).

What, then, causes some teenagers to shoplift? One reason is poverty, suggested by the evidence that poor people are more likely than others to shoplift and that the incidence of shoplifting rises when unemployment is high or when the economy is sluggish. But there are also social psychological reasons for shoplifting. First is the *sense of thrill, excitement, or fun* that shoplifters expect to experience when committing the offense. Another reason is the *desire for peer acceptance*, which makes youngsters, in particular, highly vulnerable to peer pressure. When asked why they shoplift, many would say, "Because my friends are doing it." A third social psychological reason is a cluster of *rationalizations* that the shoplifter can use to justify the crime before committing it. Thus, many shoplifters deny responsibility (saying, for example, "My friends make me do it" or "I'm high or drunk"); deny injury to the victim ("It's only a cheap bottle of perfume" or "It's such a big store they won't miss it"); or argue that the victim deserves it ("It serves them right because they rip us off every time we buy something from them"). Armed with these rationalizations, shoplifters are able to decriminalize their offense, continuing to see themselves as law-abiding citizens rather than criminals (Dugas, 2008; Klemke, 1992).

Hate Crime

Hate crime
An offense committed because of the victim's race, religion, national origin, or sexual orientation.

Every year more than 5,500 Americans fall victim to **hate crime**, an offense committed because of the victim's race, religion, national origin, or sexual orientation.

Slightly more than half of these victims are merely intimidated, nearly half are assaulted, and less than 1% are murdered. Although hate-motivated homicides are comparatively rare, they are obviously the most dangerous and consequently have received considerable attention from the media (Fox, Levin, and Quinet, 2007).

Although hate-motivated homicides are rare among various kinds of hate crime, they are obviously the most dangerous and consequently have received considerable attention from the media.

African Americans and gay Americans are more likely than any other groups to be victims of hate homicide. Such killing is targeted not only at the particular person but also at all the other members of that person's group. In June 1998, when three white men in Jasper, Texas, dragged James Byrd, an African American, behind their pickup truck to his death, they were in effect warning every black person in town to get out or suffer the same fate as Byrd. Similarly, in October 1998, when two young men in Laramie, Wyoming, beat gay college student Matthew Shepard into a coma and left him to die tied to a fence in the desert, they were effectively telling all gay people that they could suffer the same fate.

Hate-filled killers are more likely than perpetrators of other, less serious hate crimes to have joined an organized hate group. James Byrd's three killers, for example, had met each other in prison and joined the Aryan Brotherhood, a white supremacist group. For someone filled with hate, membership in such a group assures them that they are not alone in their bigotry. They are also likely to feel bolder and more willing to take risks when encouraged by the group to attack the victim of their hate.

There are three types of hate killers. First are the *thrill* hate killers, who, being young, bored, and idle, are seized with the idea of going out together to look for someone to attack for the fun of it. As marginalized and alienated youngsters, these offenders feel important and powerful from the thrill attacks. Then, there are the *defensive* hate killers, who feel the need to defend what they consider to be their birthright. A black family moving into a white neighborhood or a gay man attending a predominantly heterosexual party is seen as encroaching on the hatemonger's birthright of being white or straight. Finally, there are the *mission* hate killers, who believe it is their mission to safeguard white supremacy. These are the rarest but the most dangerous of the three types. While the thrill and defensive killers target a single victim, the mission killers seek to destroy all members of a hated group. Thus, they may kill members of a group indiscriminately, target many people simultaneously, and carry on a killing spree in various places (Fox et al., 2007). Such killing is much more widespread in Russia (see Box 6.1).

Organized Crime

There are many different organized crime groups in the United States, each consisting of members of the same race or ethnicity. The best known and most powerful is *the Mafia*, also called *la Casa Nostra*, *the mob*, or *the syndicate*. Composed mostly of Italian Americans, the Mafia is a relatively loose, informal confederation of diverse groups of professional criminals operating independently in large cities around the country.

BOX 6.1   GLOBAL PERSPECTIVE

Hate Killing in Russia

There are many more hate murders in Russia than in the United States. In 2008, for example, as many as 114 immigrant workers were killed by mostly young neo-Nazi skinheads in Russia, compared to just 7 similar hate killings in the United States (Pan, 2008). The typical victims of hate killings are migrant laborers from the impoverished former Soviet republics of Central Asia. The killers are native Russian ultranationalists hell-bent on driving the foreign workers out of the country through intimidation and killing.

Recently, one of these ultranationalist groups sent an e-mail to two organizations that tracked hate crimes in Russia. It carried a disturbing message with an even more disturbing photo. The message accused darker-skinned migrant workers of "an unprecedented wave of criminality that has swamped our capital." It then warned government officials that "If you do not start evicting the blacks, we will begin taking revenge on you for their crimes! Because there is no worse enemy than a traitor who has betrayed his Russian origin." The photo that came with this e-mail showed a man's severed head resting on a wooded chopping block. This was no hoax, as earlier in the day a street cleaner had found a man's head in a grassy area outside a government building. An autopsy confirmed that the head belonged to a native of Tajikistan whose decapitated body was discovered someplace else.

"It's an outrageous crime and very worrying," said Natalia Rykova, executive director of the Moscow Bureau for Human Rights, who was one of those who received the e-mail. "It shows how cruel and inhuman the neo-Nazis can be, and that their ideology is becoming more popular." Indeed, ultranationalist groups have staged rallies, calling on the government to "cleanse" the country of migrant workers, while racist graffiti has proliferated in the neighborhood. A government-controlled youth group also staged a rally urging officials to close the borders to migrants so more jobs are available to Russians. In addition, Prime Minister Vladimir Putin has called for new limits on the number of work permits for migrant laborers, which critics say inflames xenophobic sentiment (Pan, 2008).

Organized crime consists of a hierarchy of positions, ranging from the highest to lowest as follows: boss, underboss, lieutenants, counselor, and "soldiers" such as this person being arrested.

Each group is known to law enforcers as a crime family identified by the name of its founder, such as Genovese, Gambino, or Bonanno. Each family consists of a *hierarchical structure* of positions, ranging from the highest to the lowest as follows: "don" or boss, underboss, lieutenants, counselor, and "soldiers" or button men (so called because they do the bidding of the higher-ranking members when the latter "push the button"). The boss of each family directs the criminal activities of the members of his family.

Members are governed by *a code of conduct*. The most important rules in the code concern *loyalty* ("Be loyal to the family") and *secrecy* ("Don't squeal on fellow members"). If these rules are violated, the individual will be killed. That's why the U.S. government has to spend an enormous sum of money on the witness-protection program for the informers, providing them with new identities, houses in different locations, and new jobs. Various Mafia families engage in the following criminal activities.

SELLING ILLEGAL GOODS AND SERVICES. An example of this crime is *illegal gambling*, which involves betting on horse races, lotteries, and sporting events. It has become less profitable today because of the increasing legalization of lotteries and off-track betting. Far more profitable is *loan sharking*, the lending of money at exorbitantly high interest rates, typically more than 100% a year. In fact, when the economy is bad, hordes of businesspeople and bill payers are forced to borrow money from loan sharks at up to between 200% and 300% annual interest. To ensure repayment, the loan sharks may resort to violence or the threat of violence, but there is hardly any need to threaten violence, let alone actually use it, because they already have a reputation for violence that is enough to scare the borrowers. Another source of revenues is the trade in *illicit drugs*. To maximize profit at minimum risk of interference from law enforcers, members of the Mafia restrict their activities to importing and wholesale distribution. The risky business of selling narcotics on the street is left to independent drug pushers.

ENGAGING IN LARGE-SCALE THEFTS AND RACKETEERING. The Mafia steals in a big way. They make away with huge quantities of negotiable stocks and bonds as well as credit cards; whole carloads of merchandise from docks, railway stations, and international airports; and millions of dollars' worth of automobiles, which they furnish with proper engine identification numbers and registration papers necessary for selling them. To sell these "hot" items, they have *fences* who work like big-time merchandising operators.

Another organized crime activity is racketeering. It may take the simple form of a "protection racket," which involves the extortion of money from legitimate businesspeople. They are given the proverbial offer they cannot refuse: The sale of the mob's "insurance policy" against such "accidents" as the burning of their stores and the breaking of their store windows or their heads—to be carried out by the mobsters if the businesspeople refuse to buy the "insurance."

CORRUPTING PUBLIC OFFICIALS. The mob usually corrupts three kinds of officials: politicians, law enforcers, and bureaucrats in licensing, supervisory, or regulatory agencies. The manner of corruption is outright bribery. The objective is to have the politicians pass laws favoring the mobsters' interests and prevent the passage of laws damaging to their illegal activities, to have the police and other law enforcers ignore the mobsters' criminal activities, and to get regulatory agencies to turn a blind eye to their illegal way of operating legitimate businesses.

INFILTRATING LEGITIMATE BUSINESS. The Mafia has infiltrated numerous businesses, including Las Vegas casinos, nightclubs and restaurants, hotels and motels, trucking companies, wholesale food distributors, as well as the industries of banking and investment, insurance, real estate, electronics, health services, and stock brokerage. The mob's penetration into these legitimate businesses is so deep that many law-abiding citizens routinely deal with the mob. By acquiring any one of these legitimate businesses, the mobsters aim to achieve certain objectives: to gain respectability, to establish a legitimate source of income for paying taxes and thus avoid income tax prosecution, to invest "bad" money (from racketeering and other illegal activities) in a legitimate business for legitimate profit, and to use the legitimate business as a front for carrying out illegitimate schemes.

White-Collar Crime

White-collar crime
A crime that is *occupationally* related, carried out in the course of the offender's occupation, and the occupation involved is *white collar* as opposed to blue collar.

White-collar crime is *occupationally* related, carried out in the course of the offender's occupation, and the occupation involved is *white collar* as opposed to blue collar. Compared with street crimes, which are typically committed by blue-collar persons, white-collar crimes are far more likely to be executed with skill, with sophistication, and, most importantly, with the resources of power, influence, or respectability for avoiding detection, prosecution, or conviction. Examples of white-collar crime include employee theft, embezzlement, tax evasion, and medical malpractice. These crimes are relatively prevalent for at least two reasons.

First, white-collar criminals often see themselves as respectable people rather than common criminals. One way of maintaining their respectable self-image is denying criminal intent. They may admit that they have committed the acts that landed them in prison, but they regard them only as mistakes, not as something motivated by a guilty criminal mind. A convicted tax offender may say, for example, that he or she is not a criminal in the sense of taking a gun to rob somebody, but only in making a serious mistake. Another reason for the prevalence of white-collar crime is the lack of law enforcement for catching the criminals. On the rare occasions when they are caught, they seldom go to jail or, if they are incarcerated, they receive a light sentence. Their pleas for mercy are often accepted after they promise to repay their victims or to cooperate in prosecutions against others. They insist that a long prison term will do no good because their lives are already in ruins. The general public, though, favors punishing white-collar criminals more harshly (Unnever et al., 2008).

Corporate Crime

Corporate crime
A crime that is carried out by the executive of a company for the company's benefit rather than for personal gain.

To some criminologists, corporate crime is practically the same as white-collar crime because both are typically committed by higher-class, professional people. But here we may stress the difference. While white-collar crime is committed for the offender's own gain, **corporate crime** is carried out by the executive of a company for the company's benefit. Corporate crime can be divided into four types in terms of who its victims are.

First is the *crime against employees*. The Occupational Safety and Health Administration, a federal agency, expects corporations to protect their employees against known hazards in the work environment. However, many workers are still exposed to various kinds of pollutants in their workplace, such as coal dust and radiation. Although these substances have been found to cause cancer, leukemia, and other serious illnesses, corporations tend to ignore the problem rather than take corrective action by eliminating the exposure to make their plants safer.

Second is the *crime against customers*. It may involve selling contaminated beef; manufacturing and selling unsafe cars and drugs; fraudulent practices in banking, insurance, real estate, and securities industries; deceptive advertising; and antitrust violations. Consider, for example, how three baby formula companies once violated the antitrust law in order to overcharge their customers. The largest of the three companies, Abbott Laboratories, conspired with the other two to prevent a new competitor, Nestlé, from entering the formula market in the United States. Because they dominated the market, they were able to keep the price of their formulas very high (Wilke, 2004).

Third is the *crime against the government*. The most common example of this crime involves tax evasion by corporations. Yet, even though it is a widely known problem, many corporations are able to get away with it. Because of their pervasive and powerful political influence, large corporations can evade taxes through tax breaks provided by legislation and through tax loopholes made possible by the complexity of tax laws. This is why, according to a congressional study, the top 148 corporations paid less than half of the official tax rate on profits and 10% of these corporations paid no taxes at all (Coleman, 2006; Sloan, 1997).

Fourth is the *crime against the environment*. Most corporations are likely to dump their wastes onto the land and into the air and water, largely because they find it too costly to install antipollution devices. They are also reluctant to clean up the mess or to compensate the public for being affected by it, because to do so would cut into their profits. The most severe polluters of the environment are corporations in the petrochemical, metals, electrical, and transportation industries. In fact, this and the other forms of corporate crime are much more harmful to society than street crimes such as homicide, assault, and robbery, although most people consider street crimes more harmful (see **Box 6.2**).

BOX 6.2   DIVERGENT VIEWS

Which Is More Harmful, Street or Corporate Crime?

To the general public, the typical criminal is a relatively young and poor male who commits street crime such as homicide, assault, rape, robbery, burglary, larceny, or motor vehicle theft. He is not a rich company executive who commits corporate crime such as violating safety laws in the workplace, selling unsafe products, avoiding payment of taxes, and polluting the environment. More importantly, the public believes that the typical street criminal is much more dangerous than the corporate criminal. This is because street crime is widely considered more harmful than corporate crime. However, sociologists disagree, regarding corporate crime as much more harmful.

To the general public, street crime is more dangerous than corporate crime, but research shows corporate crime to be more dangerous.

According to FBI statistics, homicide (a street crime) accounts for about 20,000 deaths every year in the United States. However, government data also suggest that many more Americans die from corporate crime. For example, 60,000 die annually from occupational accidents, diseases, and hazards. About 40,000 die from auto accidents, many of which are preventable. And another 400,000 are killed by tobacco-related diseases. Most of these deaths can be traced to the profit-seeking decisions made in the suite rather than on the street.

The FBI estimates that the annual costs of property crimes committed by street criminals total $3.5 billion for burglary, $4.9 billion for larceny-theft, and $8.6 billion for motor vehicle theft. Similar crimes that can be attributed to the actions of corporate executives cost considerably more. A researcher at American University estimates, for example, that workplace injuries and accidents cost $141.6 billion, air pollution $225.9 billion (paid for health care), and defense contract overcharge $25.9 billion (Burch, 2005).

Governmental Crime

We may expect politicians and governmental officials to break the law every now and then. When seeing one of them get caught, we may remark, "There goes another crook." Mark Twain expressed this popular sentiment well when he said way back in 1894, "It could probably be shown with facts and figures that there is no distinctly American criminal class except Congress." This crime essentially involves the abuse of power. It can be exemplified by political corruption, election improprieties, and official violence.

Political corruption is often associated with bribery, illustrating the abuse of power for personal gain. It may take the form of an outright bribe, in which the public official accepts money from a briber who expects a favor in return. Another type of political corruption involves receiving kickbacks from businesses for purchasing goods and services, for which the government is sent outrageous bills. For example, the U.S. Defense Department is known to have paid hundreds of dollars for a hammer and hundreds more for a toilet seat.

Election improprieties involve the use of political dirty tricks to ensure victory in an election. They include spreading rumors about the opponent's strange character, kinky sex life, or association with drug kingpins, and stealing the opponent's campaign mail. Election improprieties also involve soliciting and receiving huge campaign contributions from large corporations and wealthy individuals, with the latter expecting the politicians to return the favor if elected. Incumbent legislators running *unopposed* can also receive large contributions from the rich with the same expectation.

Official violence involves the government committing violence against various citizens in the United States. The government, for example, drove Native Americans out of their lands and killed many of them in the early period of U.S. history. Today most official violence involves police brutality against citizens, especially African and Hispanic Americans in large cities. As a democracy, however, the United States commits *democide* (the killing of people by their government) to a much smaller extent than many other nations. The vast majority of such killings have been carried out by communist and authoritarian governments.

Why are politicians and government officials likely to engage in those criminal activities? According to power theory, which will be discussed later, there are three reasons: strong criminal motivation, great criminal opportunity, and lax social control. Because of their high position in society, politicians tend to be too ambitious, thereby more likely to experience relative deprivation, which in turn will motivate them to employ illegal means to achieve their high goals. They are further encouraged to abuse their power because they enjoy abundant opportunities for doing so and are not subject to stringent social control, thanks again to their lofty position in society.

Online Identity Theft

Online identity theft involves using a computer to steal credit card numbers, Social Security numbers, and other personal information. The thief can then buy anything online and offline for free by charging the purchases to the owners of those card numbers. This online theft, compared to traditional forms of theft such as burglarizing a store or home, is much more easily carried out and extremely profitable if it is pulled off. Consider computer technician Carlos Salgado. He managed to steal more than

100,000 credit card numbers by using a ready-made computer-intrusion program he found on the Web to hack into several e-commerce databases. Those cards had a combined credit line of more than $1 billion. Unfortunately for Salgado, though, the FBI later caught him, and after pleading guilty he was sentenced to two and a half years in prison (Hansen, 2004).

Hacking into the databases of commercial establishments as Salgado did is one common practice among online identity thieves. Another popular method is called "phishing," which is targeted at individual consumers. Consumers are sent bogus e-mails that appear to come from legitimate banks or e-commerce sites. The recipients are asked to confirm or update their accounts by providing their personal data such as their bank account, Social Security, or credit card numbers. Even longtime Internet users can fall for the phishing trick. Store owner Mark Nichols once received an e-mail from what he thought was eBay. He was told that his account with eBay had been suspended and that he had to supply his new credit card number. Fortunately, though, he did not go through with it because he discovered that the "eBay" site was bogus (Mann, 2006).

A third way for online identity thieves to steal consumers' personal information involves using key-logging programs that copy the computer users' keystrokes and send that information to the crooks. These monitoring programs are secretly planted in certain Web sites, e-mail messages, e-mail attachments, and ordinary software downloads. They are thus known as spyware or Trojans. Thieves use these hidden programs to steal their victims' user names and passwords, and ultimately cash. Such crimes usually cross international borders, putting Internet users everywhere at risk. Joe Lopez, a small company owner in Florida, became a victim when cybercrooks used a key-logging Trojan planted in his business computers to obtain his bank account information and transfer $90,000 to the Eastern European country of Latvia (Zeller, 2006).

Most online identity thefts are inside jobs, carried out by corporate insiders. They are the victimized companies' skilled employees, authorized computer users, and trusted personnel. As one researcher said, "The biggest problem is the workplace, and the biggest problem in the workplace is there's a lack of personal security" (Mann, 2006).

◼ Social Diversity in Crime

Race, class, gender, and age play a significant role in street crime. As research has often shown, large differences in crime rates exist among whites, African Americans, and other racial groups; between higher and lower classes; between men and women; and between younger and older persons.

Race and Crime

According to self-report studies in which teenagers are asked whether they have committed a crime, there are no significant racial differences in the commission of such minor criminal acts as petty theft, vandalism, and disorderly conduct. However, according to the FBI's *Uniform Crime Reports*, African Americans are more likely than whites to commit and be arrested for relatively serious crimes such as homicide and robbery, and Asian Americans have lower crime and arrest rates than whites.

Similarly, according to victimization surveys, crime victims are more likely to identify African Americans than whites as their offenders and are less likely to finger Asian Americans (Harris and Meidlinger, 1995).

Those data, however, do not mean that the biological factor of skin color causes crime. After all, whites in the United States generally have a much higher crime rate than blacks in African countries. Why, then, do U.S. blacks have a higher crime rate than U.S. whites? Major reasons may include a higher incidence of poverty and broken homes, largely the results of racism (Wright and Younts, 2009). But why are Asian Americans, who also experience racism—though to a lesser degree—less likely to commit crimes than whites? A key reason may be the close-knit Asian family, with which its members identify so strongly that they are disinclined to commit crime for fear of bringing shame to the entire family.

Class and Crime

Whether and how social class is associated with crime depends on the type of crime involved. When it comes to nonpredatory victimless criminal acts such as drug use, drunkenness, and truancy, lower-income teenagers are just as likely as their higher-income peers to engage in them. However, lower-income youths tend to commit more serious predatory crimes, such as aggravated assault, robbery, and auto theft, widely known as "street crimes."

Lower-income adults are also more likely than those with higher incomes to commit predatory or street crimes. In contrast, higher-income adults tend to perpetrate more profitable white-collar or corporate crimes, such as price fixing, tax evasion, and fraudulent advertising. This is because higher-income people have greater motivation and opportunity for committing crime and are subjected to weaker social control, as suggested by power theory, which will be discussed later.

Gender and Crime

Crime is mostly a male activity. With the exception of prostitution, men are more likely than women to engage in virtually all kinds of crime. The types of offenses more frequently committed by men range from minor economic crimes (forgery, fraud, and petty theft) to serious economic and violent crimes (burglary, robbery, homicide, and aggravated assault). Over the last decade, there has been a significant increase in female violence, but men still outnumber women in carrying out most criminal acts, especially the serious ones (Lauritsen et al., 2009).

Several factors may explain the lower rates of crime among women. One is socialization: Females are taught to be less aggressive and violent than males. Another is social control: Females are subjected to greater parental supervision and social control than males. A third factor is lack of criminal opportunity. Women are less likely to enjoy criminal opportunities "as a spin-off of legitimate roles or activities." As Darrell Steffensmeier and Emilie Allan (1995) explain, "Women are less likely to hold jobs, such as truck driver, dockworker, or carpenter, that would provide opportunities for theft, drug dealing, fencing, and other illegitimate activities."

Age and Crime

Age is closely related to crime. The young are more likely than the old to engage in crime. The crime rate starts to rise with entry into adolescence and peaks in late teens and early twenties, then drops steadily from early adulthood to old age. Why does crime rise with the young but fall with the old? Before adolescence, children are prevented by parental control from engaging in criminal behavior, but when they become adolescents, the parental control weakens, allowing them to engage in delinquent behavior. When they leave adolescence to become adults, they develop new social controls—employment, marriage, and other adult responsibilities—which make them stay away from criminal activities.

■ The Criminal Justice System

The criminal justice system is a network of police, courts, and prisons for enforcing the law. Let's take a close look at how it operates and whether it is soft or harsh on criminals.

How the Criminal Justice System Operates

The criminal justice system first depends on the *police* to arrest the crime suspect. The police are more likely to make the arrest if the crime is serious, the suspect is antagonistic or uncooperative, the suspect has a prior criminal record, bystanders are present, and the victim insists on having the suspect arrested.

After being arrested, about half of the suspects are released because of lack of evidence. The other half are charged and tried in a *court* of law. The trial is supposed to be an adversarial process, whereby the prosecutor presents the state's case against the defendant, whose attorney responds with a defense. However, most cases do not go through a trial. They are instead settled through plea bargaining, in which the state seeks a guilty plea by offering to reduce the defendant's punishment. By forgoing a trial, plea bargaining saves considerable time and expense, allowing the court to try more serious cases. Plea bargaining essentially takes away the defendant's constitutional right to a trial as well as the presumption that the defendant is innocent until proven guilty.

If found guilty either through plea bargaining or a trial, the defendant is punished in some way, such as being fined, imprisoned, or executed. The punishment is intended to serve the following purposes:

- *Retribution*: seeking revenge against the criminal. Retribution seems to work because many people feel good for getting even with the offender.
- *Incapacitation*: using incarceration or execution to make the offender incapable of committing any more crime. Incapacitation apparently serves its purpose well because an incarcerated or executed criminal cannot commit more crime.
- *Deterrence*: using incarceration to prevent further offense after release from prison. This does not work, as evidenced by the high rate of recidivism; the majority of prisoners commit another crime after being released from prison.
- *Rehabilitation*: using treatment in prison to reform the offender. This works better than deterrence, but the success rate is still relatively low (Conklin, 2007).
- *Probation*: using supervised release to encourage convicted offenders to stay away from crime. This is relatively effective for offenders who have been involved in less serious crimes.

- *Parole*: similar to probation in being supervised release except that while probation is granted to offenders without sending them to prison, parole is given to those who have served time in prison but have not completed their full sentences. Parole is highly effective for reducing prison overcrowding and the cost of incarceration, but less effective for preventing released offenders from committing another crime (Conklin, 2007). Box 6.3 discusses how to cut down on the recidivism of parolees.

Soft on Criminals?

The criminal justice system is supposed to protect society, but it is also a potential threat to an individual's freedom. If it wanted to ensure that not a single criminal could slip away, the police would have to deprive innocent citizens of their rights and liberties. They would restrict our freedom of movement and invade our privacy—by tapping phones, reading mail, searching homes, stopping pedestrians for questioning, and blockading roads. No matter how law abiding we might be, we would always be treated like crime suspects—and some of us would almost certainly fall into the dragnet.

To prevent such abuses, the criminal justice system in the United States is restrained by the U.S. Constitution and laws. We have the right to be presumed innocent until

---

BOX 6.3   USING SOCIOLOGICAL INSIGHTS

How to Stop Ex-cons from Committing More Crime

Every year nearly one-third (700,000) of prison inmates are paroled—released before completing their full sentences. The majority (two-thirds) of these ex-cons commit another crime within 3 years of release. This high rate of recidivism has led community leaders and criminal justice experts to try a new approach to deal with the problem. The old method focused on rehabilitation or release, which assumed that, enjoying freedom like everybody else, the released prisoners could change on their own. By contrast, the new approach entails the process of "coordinated prisoner reintegration," more widely known as "reentry." It concentrates on showing employers, families, and communities how they can help the offenders after they are released.

Reentry programs seek to synchronize such resources as job training, employment searches, stable housing, and health care so that managers of these resources work together to help the released prisoners. Reentry further involves educating communities, families, children, coworkers, and neighbors on how to help the ex-offenders make a healthy return to society. Among these various services for participants of reentry programs, four are most crucial to the successful reintegration of parolees into a normal, crime-free life.

The first is helping the ex-offender secure *employment*. This may involve a case manager looking for job openings and setting up job interviews for former prisoners. A second important service is providing ex-offenders with *education*, helping them finish high school or participate in college-level or postsecondary vocational classes. A third involves strengthening released prisoners' bond to their *family*, which can help reduce strain and negative emotions as well as increase self-control and predictability. Lastly, a fourth important service for ex-convicts involves *community collaboration*, whereby a host of community-based social service agencies collaborate in providing a wide range of services including employment, education, housing, counseling, mental health, medical, dental, clothing, and transportation services (Kingsbury, 2007; Listwan, Cullen, and Latessa, 2006).

proven guilty, the right not to incriminate ourselves, and many other legal protections. The ability of the police to search homes and question suspects is limited. Thus, our freedom, especially from being wrongly convicted and imprisoned, is protected.

In essence, the criminal justice system faces a dilemma. If it does not catch enough criminals, the streets will not be safe; if it tries to apprehend too many, people's freedom will be in danger. Striking a balance between effective protection from criminals and respect for individual freedom is far from easy. This challenge may explain why the criminal justice system is criticized from both the conservatives and the liberals, by the former for coddling criminals and by the latter for being too harsh.

The conservatives seem to be right. Most criminals in the United States are never punished. Of the serious crimes committed, only 20% result in arrest and prosecution. Of the criminals who are convicted, only 25% are sent to prison. Moreover, most of these prisoners do not serve their full terms because they are released on parole. Average prisoners serve only about one-third of their sentences (Anderson, 1994; U.S. Census Bureau, 2010).

Does this mean that the U.S. criminal justice system is soft on criminals? Not necessarily. As liberals would point out, the United States punishes crime more severely than other democracies. It has been for many years the leading jailer in the world (see **Figure 6.2**). Americans are routinely locked up for crimes (such as writing bad checks and using drugs) that rarely land the culprits in prison in other countries. Imprisonment is also generally longer than in other democratic countries. The length of incarceration is measured in weeks and months in Sweden but in years in

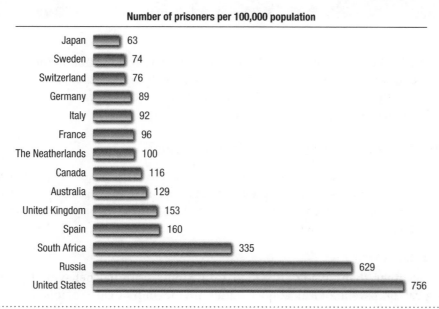

Number of prisoners per 100,000 population

Japan	63
Sweden	74
Switzerland	76
Germany	89
Italy	92
France	96
The Neatherlands	100
Canada	116
Australia	129
United Kingdom	153
Spain	160
South Africa	335
Russia	629
United States	756

FIGURE 6.2 Imprisonment Around the World

The United States reigns supreme as the world's largest jailer. Our country is thrust into this unfortunate role as a result of "get tough" policies toward drug offenders that have proliferated over the past quarter century.

Critical Thinking: *Do more prisoners mean less crime? Why or why not?*

Source: International Center for Prison Studies, World Prison Population List, 8th edition, 2009.

> ### BOX 6.4   WHAT RESEARCH REVEALS
>
> #### Why Crime Fell When Joblessness Rose
>
> As we have suggested, there is a strong connection between class and crime. More specifically, people of the lower classes are more likely than those of higher classes to commit street crime. Thus, the higher the rate of unemployment or poverty (which is more likely to impact the lower classes), the higher the crime rate. It might have been expected, then, that given the recent recession that has caused many millions of Americans to lose their jobs, crime would shoot up. Instead, it fell.
>
> According to the FBI's *Uniform Crime Reports*, various crime rates dropped nationwide in the first 6 months of 2009: Homicide went down 10%, violent crime went down 4.4%, property crime went down 6.1%, and car theft went down 19%, with the sharpest decline in many areas that have been hit the hardest by the housing collapse (MacDonald, 2010). The human dimension of the falling crime rates is extraordinary: In a single year, 2008, lower crime rates meant 40,000 fewer rapes, 380,000 fewer robberies, 500,000 fewer aggravated assaults, and 1.6 million fewer burglaries than if rates had stayed at peak levels. An additional 170,000 Americans would have been murdered since 1992 if the rate had remained the same. That's more U.S. lives than were lost in combat in World War I, Korea, Vietnam, and Iraq combined (Von Drehle and Jewler, 2010).
>
> Why did those crime rates fall in the midst of high unemployment? A major reason is the steep rise in the number of people in prison, from 300,000 in 1977 to 1.6 million in 2008. As sociologist John Conklin (2003) explains, when criminals were treated leniently with only a few being sent to prison in the 1960s and 1970s, the crime rate began to rise. But when the crime wave led to the mandating of tough sentences and construction of numerous prisons in the 1980s and 1990s, the prison population rose, and by the early 1990s, the number of crimes started to fall, which continues today.

the United States. Our country is also the only industrialized nation in the West that still executes convicted murderers (Anderson, 2003; Liptak, 2008; Sutton, 2004). Apparently, this harsh treatment of criminals has in recent decades brought down the crime rates in the United States (see Box 6.4).

■ Sociological Theories of Criminal Behavior

We have so far looked at various characteristics of criminal behavior. Now we may ask what causes criminal behavior. The answer can be found in the three major sociological theories, but there are various versions of each of these theories. Let us see how they explain criminal behavior.

Functionalist Theory

Scholars other than sociologists tend to attribute criminal behavior to certain biological or psychological abnormalities in the individual. Sociologists, however, have long assumed there is nothing physically or mentally wrong with most deviants. This assumption is a legacy of the French sociologist Emile Durkheim (1858–1917), one of the founders of functionalism in the discipline. For him, crime is not only normal but also beneficial to society because, ironically, it contributes to social order. Whereas Durkheim emphasized the functions or benefits of crime, today's functionalists focus on society's dysfunctions or problems as the causes of criminal behavior.

DURKHEIM: FUNCTIONS OF CRIME. According to Durkheim, crime serves a number of functions for society. First, it helps *enhance conformity* in society as a whole. Norms are basically abstract and ambiguous, subject to conflicting interpretations. Even criminal laws, which are far more clear-cut than other norms, can be confusing. The criminal act that an offender commits and is punished for provides other citizens with a concrete example of what constitutes a crime. From criminals, then, we can learn the difference between conformity and criminality, seeing the boundary between right and wrong more clearly. Once aware of this boundary, we are more likely to stay on the side of rightness.

Second, crime *strengthens solidarity* among law-abiding members of society. Differing values and interests may divide them, but collective outrage against criminals as a common enemy can unite them, as it did Americans in the aftermath of the terrorist attacks on September 11, 2001. Because crime promotes social cohesion that decreases crime, Durkheim (1915) described it as "a factor in public health, an integral part of all healthy societies."

Third, crime *provides a safety valve* for discontented people. Through relatively minor forms of crime, they can strike out against the social order without doing serious harm to others. Prostitution, for example, may serve as a safety valve for marriage in a male-dominated society because the customer is unlikely to form an emotional attachment to the prostitute. In contrast, a sexual relationship with a friend is more likely to develop into a love affair that could destroy the marriage.

Fourth, crime can *induce social change*. Martin Luther King, Jr., and other civil rights leaders were jeered and imprisoned for their opposition to segregation, but they moved the United States toward greater racial equality.

There is a limit, however, to the validity of Durkheim's version of functionalist theory. If crime is widespread, it can threaten social order in at least two ways. First, it can wreck interpersonal relations. If a friend were to fly into a rage and try to kill us, it would be difficult to maintain a harmonious relationship with that person. Second, crime can undermine trust. If there were many killers, robbers, and rapists living in our neighborhood, we would find it impossible to welcome neighbors into our home as guests or babysitters.

Durkheim's theory is nonetheless useful for challenging the common-sense belief that crime is always harmful. Crime can bring benefits if it occurs within limits. It is these benefits that ensure the existence of crime.

MERTON: STRAIN THEORY. U.S. sociologist Robert Merton (1938) agreed with Durkheim that crime is "an integral part of all healthy societies." More significantly, Merton drew on Durkheim's concept of *anomie* to develop a theory of crime that later became well known among sociologists for a long time as *anomie theory* but has also been known since the 1980s as *strain theory*. Literally meaning "normlessness," anomie is a social condition in which norms are absent, weak, or in conflict. Anomie may arise, said Merton, when there is an inconsistency in society between the cultural goals and the

Anomie
A social condition in which norms are absent, weak, or in conflict.

institutionalized—socially approved, or legitimate—means of achieving the goals. In the United States, such an inconsistency surrounds the issue of success.

According to Merton, U.S. culture places too much emphasis on success as a valued goal. From kindergarten to college, teachers prod students to achieve the American Dream. Parents and coaches pressure even Little League players not just to play well but to win. The media often glorify winning not only in sports but also in business, politics, and other arenas of life. This emphasis on success motivates hard work, contributing to society's prosperity, but at the same time, people are not equally provided with the legitimate means (such as good jobs and other opportunities) for achieving success. There is, then, an inconsistency between too much emphasis on the success *goal* and too little emphasis on the availability of legitimate *means* for achieving that goal. Such inconsistency produces a *strain* among people in the lower classes, pressuring them to achieve success through what Merton calls *innovation*—using illegitimate means of achieving success, such as committing robbery or theft.

In brief, Merton's theory blames criminal behavior on society's failure to provide all people with legitimate means to achieve success. The theory is useful for explaining the higher rates of robbery, theft, and other property crimes among lower-class people, who are pressured to commit such crimes by their lack of good jobs and other legitimate means for success. However, the theory fails to explain embezzlement, tax fraud, and other white-collar crimes because the people who commit such offenses are typically not deprived of the legitimate means for success, as the lower classes are. Also, as a functionalist, Merton assumes that the same value—belief in *material* success—is shared by everybody throughout society. But this assumption runs counter to the pluralistic and conflicting nature of U.S. society, where many groups differentiated by class, gender, ethnicity, or religion do not share the same values. Some groups, for example, believe in materialism but others in spirituality.

HIRSCHI: CONTROL THEORY.   A functionalist like Merton, U.S. sociologist Travis Hirschi (1969) assumed that the family, school, and other social institutions can greatly contribute to social order by controlling criminal tendencies in all of us. If such control is lacking or weak, in Hirschi's view, people will engage in criminal behavior.

According to Hirschi, the best control mechanism against crime is our bond to others or, by extension, the larger society. He proposed four types of social bond:

1. *Attachment to conventional people and institutions.* Teenagers, for example, may show this attachment by loving and respecting their parents, making friends with conventional peers, liking school, or working hard to develop intellectual skills.

2. *Commitment to conformity.* This commitment can be seen in the time and energy devoted to conventional activities—getting an education, holding a job, learning an occupational skill, improving professional status, building a business, or acquiring a reputation for virtue.

3. *Involvement in conventional activities.* Learning from the maxim "Idleness is the devil's workshop," people keep themselves so busy doing conventional things that they do not have time to take part in criminal activities or even to think about them.

4. *Belief in the moral validity of social rules.* This is the conviction that the rules of conventional society should be obeyed. People show this moral belief by respecting the law.

If society fails to strengthen these four types of social bond, crime is likely to flourish. Indeed, many studies have found that the lack of social bond *causes* crime. However, most of these studies, like the theory, have ignored the fact that the lack of bond can also be the *effect* of crime. Just as the loss of bond can cause people to commit crime, crime can also cause people to lose their bond to society.

Conflict Theory

We have seen how functionalists describe the functions of crime and attribute crime to such dysfunctions of society as anomie and weak social bonds. Now we will look at how conflict theorists regard social conflict—in the form of inequalities or power differentials—as the cause of crime.

MARXIST THEORY. To the followers of Karl Marx (1818–1883), the capitalists' ceaseless drive to increase profits by cutting labor costs has created a large class of poor or unemployed workers. These people become what Marxists call a **marginal surplus population**—superfluous or useless to the economy—and they are compelled to commit property crimes to survive. Marxists argue that the exploitative nature of capitalism also causes violent crimes, such as assault and homicide. As Sheila Balkan and her colleagues (1980) explain, the poverty that results from the capitalist exploitation "leads to a lack of self-esteem and a sense of powerlessness and alienation, which create intense pressures on individuals. Many people turn to violence in order to vent their frustrations and strike out against symbols of authority."

Marginal surplus population
People who are superfluous or useless to the economy.

Marxists further contend that the monopolistic and oligopolistic nature of capitalism encourages corporate crime because "when only a few firms dominate a sector of the economy they can more easily collude to fix prices, divide up the market, and eliminate competitors" (Greenberg, 1981). Smaller companies, unable to compete with giant corporations and earn enough profits, also are motivated to shore up their sagging profits by illegal means.

Marxist theory is useful for explaining why the poor are likely to commit the garden-variety types of violent and property crimes such as assault, homicide, and robbery and why the wealthy who run large and small companies engage in corporate crimes. The theory is also useful for explaining why crime rates soared after the communist countries of the former Soviet Union and Eastern Europe turned to capitalism. However, the theory has been criticized for implying that capitalism is the source of all crimes.

POWER THEORY. It seems obvious that power inequality affects the quality of people's lives. The rich and powerful live better than the poor and powerless. Similarly, power inequality affects the *type* of criminal activities likely to be engaged in. Thus, the powerful are more likely to perpetrate profitable crimes, such as corporate crime, while the powerless are more likely to commit unprofitable crimes, such as assault and homicide. In other words, power—or the lack of it—largely determines the type of crime people are likely to commit.

Power can also be an important *cause* of crime. More precisely, the likelihood of powerful people carrying out profitable crimes is greater than the likelihood of powerless people committing unprofitable crimes. It is, for example, more likely for bank executives to cheat customers quietly than for unemployed persons to rob banks violently. Analysis of the criminological literature suggests three reasons why crime is more common among the powerful (Thio, 2010).

Relative deprivation
The seeming inability to achieve a relatively high aspiration.

First, the powerful have a *stronger criminal motivation*. Much of this motivation stems from **relative deprivation**—feeling unable to achieve a relatively high aspiration. Compared with the powerless, whose aspirations are typically low, the powerful are more likely to raise their aspirations so high that they cannot be realized. The more people experience relative deprivation, the more likely they are to engage in criminal behavior.

Second, the powerful enjoy *greater opportunities for crime*. Obviously, a successful banker enjoys more legitimate opportunities to make money than a poor worker does, but suppose they both want to acquire a large sum of money *illegitimately*. The banker will have access to more and better opportunities that make it easy to defraud customers. The banker also has a good chance of getting away with it because the kinds of skills needed to pull off the crime are similar to the skills required for holding the bank position in the first place. In contrast, the poor worker would find his or her illegitimate opportunity limited to crudely robbing the banker, an opportunity further limited by the high risk of arrest.

Third, the powerful are subjected to *weaker social control*. Generally, the powerful have more influence in the making and enforcement of laws. The laws against higher-status criminals are therefore relatively lenient and seldom enforced, but the laws against lower-status criminals are harsher and more often enforced. Not a single corporate criminal, for example, has ever been sentenced to death for marketing an untested drug that "cleanly" kills many people. Given the lesser control imposed on them, the powerful are likely to feel freer to use illegal means to amass their fortunes and power.

There is evidence to support this theory (presented in greater detail elsewhere (Thio, 2010)). It has been estimated, for example, that in the United States, about six industrial deaths are caused by corporate violation of safe regulations for every one homicide committed by a poor person. It is difficult, though, to get direct data on powerful criminals. Compared with their powerless counterparts, powerful criminals are more able to carry out their criminal activities in a sophisticated and consequently undetectable fashion.

FEMINIST THEORY. There are two parts to feminist theory of crime. First, the theory deals with women as *victims*, mostly of rape and sexual harassment. According to feminists, crime against women reflects the patriarchal society's attempt to put women in their place so as to perpetuate men's dominance. Second, feminist theory looks at women as *offenders*. It argues that the recent increase in female crime has not been great enough to be significant. This is said to reflect continuing gender inequality. Like employment opportunities, criminal opportunities are still much less available to women than to men, making women much less likely to engage in criminal activities. When women do commit a crime, it tends to be the type that reflects their subordinate position in society: minor property crimes such as shoplifting, passing of bad checks, welfare fraud, and petty credit card thefts.

In fact, recent increases in female crime primarily involve those minor crimes, largely reflecting the increasing feminization of poverty—more women falling below the poverty line. It is no wonder that most female criminals are unemployed, school dropouts, and single moms with small children. They hardly fit the popular image of the newly empowered, liberated woman, who benefits from any increase in gender equality. There has been no significant rise in female involvement in more profitable crimes, such as burglary, robbery, embezzlement, and business fraud.

Feminist theory is useful for understanding female crime, but its focus on female crime cannot be easily generalized to male crime.

Symbolic Interaction Theory

Both functionalist and conflict theories portray crime as a *product* of society. In contrast, symbolic interactionists see crime as a *process* of interaction between the supposed criminal and the rest of society. The process of interaction leads the individual to commit crime.

DIFFERENTIAL ASSOCIATION THEORY. According to Edwin Sutherland (1939), people are likely to commit crime if they engage in differential association, the process of acquiring, through association with others, "an *excess* of definitions favorable to violation of law over definitions unfavorable to violation of law." Suppose a father tells his children that "It's all right to steal when you are poor." He is giving them a procriminal definition. On the other hand, if the father tells his children that "It's wrong to steal," he is providing an anticriminal definition. If the youngsters pick up a greater number of procriminal definitions, they are likely to engage in criminal behavior.

While definitions play a crucial role in the process of becoming a criminal, Sutherland emphasized more strongly the importance of social interaction because this is the source of definitions. Thus, Sutherland also stressed that criminal behavior will arise if interactions with those who define criminality positively outweigh interactions with those who define it negatively. Which definitions are most influential depends not just on the frequency and duration of the interactions but also on the strength of the relationship between the interactants.

Sutherland used his theory to explain various forms of crime, including white-collar crimes such as tax evasion, embezzlement, and price fixing. Such misdeeds were assumed to result from some association with groups that viewed the wrongdoings as acceptable. However, it is difficult to determine precisely what differential association is. Most people cannot identify the persons from whom they have learned a procriminal or anticriminal definition, much less whether they have been exposed to one definition more frequently, longer, or more intensely than the other.

LABELING THEORY. According to labeling theory, deviance such as crime or delinquency is not something that a person does but instead a label imposed on that behavior. As Howard Becker (1963) explained, "Deviance is *not* a quality of the act the person commits, but rather a consequence of the application by others of rules and sanctions to an 'offender.' The deviant is one to whom that label has successfully been applied; deviant behavior is behavior that people so label." In other words, if a man robs a bank, he is not a robber unless he is labeled as a robber, for which he is convicted and sent to prison.

Once a person has been labeled a robber or thief or a drunk, the individual may be stuck with that label for life and rejected and isolated as a result. Finding a job and making friends may be extremely difficult. More importantly, the person may come to accept the label, develop a deviant self-image, and commit more deviant acts. Labeling people as deviants, then, can push them toward further deviance.

Frank Tannenbaum (1938) had earlier noted this process of becoming deviant. He observed that children may break windows, annoy people, steal apples, and play hooky—and innocently consider these activities just a way of having fun. Now, suppose parents, teachers, and police regard those acts as a sign of delinquency. They will dramatize the evil by admonishing or scolding the children. They may even go further, hauling the children into juvenile court and labeling the children bad, delinquent, or deviant. This treatment may cause the children to develop a bad self-image and try to live up to this self-image by becoming increasingly involved in deviant behavior. In essence, then, being labeled deviant is the cause of repeated deviance.

Labeling theory is useful for explaining why prisoners are likely to commit more crime after being released from prison. The reason for this recidivism is that being arrested, convicted, and imprisoned is effectively the same as being labeled a criminal. However, labeling theory cannot explain why deviance occurs in the first place—*before* labeling takes place.

The key points of all the theories discussed in this section are provided in **Box 6.5**.

QUESTIONS TO EXPLORE

1. Do you see any limitations to applying labeling theory to dominant social problems in your community? What are they? What are the strengths of taking a labeling approach?

2. Which do you find more compelling, differential association or control theory of deviance? Why so?

3. What are the current crime trends in the largest cities near you? Visit http://www.crimereports.com/ to explore the crimes in your area.

BOX 6.5　THEORETICAL THUMBNAIL

Explaining Criminal Behavior

Theory	Focus	Insights
Functionalist Theory	Functions of crime; dysfunctions of society as causes of crime	*Durkheim*: Crime benefits society by bringing about conformity, social unity, safe release of discontent, and social change.
		Merton's strain theory: Crime results from society's urging people to succeed without giving them the means.
		Hirschi's control theory: Crime stems from society's failure to strengthen social bonds.
Conflict Theory	Crime as a product of social conflict or inequality	*Marxist theory*: Crime is caused by the exploitative nature of capitalism.
		Power theory: The powerful are more likely than the powerless to commit crime because of greater criminal motivation and opportunity plus weak social control.
		Feminist theory: The status of women as crime victims and offenders reflects the continuing subordination of women.
Symbolic Interaction Theory	Crime as a product of social interaction	*Differential association theory*: Crime arises when procriminal interactions outweigh anticriminal interactions.
		Labeling theory: Being labeled criminal in social interaction leads people to see themselves as criminal, which causes them to live up to this self-image by committing more crime.

Review

SUMMARY

1. Robbery is more likely to take place in big cities than small towns and rural areas. It is also more likely to occur in cold winter months, during bad economic times, and on the street. Armed robbery is more likely to be committed by adults and unarmed robbery by youngsters. Shoplifting is mostly a juvenile offense. Some reasons for committing this crime are economic in nature, such as being poor or unemployed. Other reasons are social psychological, which include the thrill of shoplifting, desire for peer acceptance, and rationalizations to justify the crime.

2. Hate crime is committed against someone because of their race, religion, national origin, or sexual orientation. It involves intimidation, assault, and murder. African Americans and gay Americans are more likely than other groups to fall victim to hate-filled killing. Hate killers have usually joined an organized hate group. Some kill for the thrill, others kill to defend what they consider to be their birthright, and still others kill to fulfill their mission of safeguarding white supremacy. Hate killing is more widespread in Russia than in the United States. As for organized crime, it has a well-defined hierarchy of positions and a code of conduct governing the behavior of members. It is involved in selling illegal goods and services, engaging in large-scale thefts and racketeering, corrupting public officials, and infiltrating legitimate businesses.

3. Compared to street crimes, white-collar crimes are far more likely to be executed with skill, sophistication, and the resources of power, influence, or respectability. These crimes are prevalent because the offenders often see themselves as respectable and law enforcement against them is lacking. While white-collar crime is committed for the offender's own gain; corporate crime is carried out for the company's benefit. Corporate crime involves victimizing employees, customers, and the government. While the general public considers street crime very harmful, sociologists find corporate crime to be much more harmful.

4. Politicians and government officials may break the law by engaging in political corruption, election improprieties, and official violence. These governmental crimes can be attributed to three factors: strong criminal motivation, great criminal opportunity, and lax social control. As for online identity theft, it involves the use of a computer to steal credit card numbers, Social Security numbers, or other personal data. It can be carried out by hacking into the databases of business companies, by sending customers bogus e-mails that appear to come from legitimate companies, or by secretly planting key-logging programs into the victim's computer.

5. African Americans are more likely than other groups to be arrested for serious crimes, whereas Asian Americans have the lowest arrest rates. Groups with lower incomes are more likely to commit predatory or street crimes than are their

higher-income peers. Men are more likely than women to engage in practically all kinds of crime. Young people, particularly those in their late teens and early twenties, are more likely to commit crime than are older people.

6. After police arrest crime suspects, half of them will be charged and tried in a court. If found guilty, the defendants will be punished in some way. The purpose of the punishment may be retribution, incapacitation, deterrence, rehabilitation, probation, or parole. To discourage released offenders from committing more crime, they are provided with employment, education, family bonding, and community collaboration. The U.S. criminal justice system appears to treat criminals leniently because extremely few criminals are apprehended and punished; however, compared with other democracies, the United States imprisons proportionately more people and imposes longer prison terms. This has helped reduce the crime rate since the early 1990s.

7. There are different versions of functionalist theory. According to Durkheim, crime benefits society by enhancing conformity, strengthens social solidarity, provides a safe release for discontent, and induces social change. According to Merton, crime arises from U.S. society's emphasizing the importance of success without providing the necessary opportunities for achieving it. And Hirschi theorizes that society's failure to develop social bonds causes crime to flourish.

8. There are various versions of conflict theory. Marxist theory blames crime on the exploitative nature of capitalism. Power theory states that the powerful are more likely to engage in profitable crimes than the powerless committing unprofitable crimes because the powerful have a stronger criminal motivation, greater criminal opportunity, and weaker social control. Feminist theory suggests that women are likely to become victims of rape and sexual harassment as well as more likely than before to commit minor property crimes with little profit, reflecting the continuing subordinate position of women in the patriarchal U.S. society.

9. As a version of symbolic interaction theory, differential association theory states that crime is likely to occur if interactions with people who define crime positively outweigh interactions with those who define crime negatively. As another version of symbolic interaction theory, labeling theory points out that being labeled a criminal causes people to see themselves as a criminal and live up to this self-image by engaging in more criminal behavior.

CRITICAL THINKING QUESTIONS

1. Of the types of crime discussed in this chapter, which do you feel are most relevant to your own community? Are there specific social forces within your community exacerbating these crimes? How so?

2. Which theory discussed in this chapter do you feel is most useful for explaining white-collar crime? What is the greatest strength and weakness of this theory?

3. Which crimes have you seen get worse in your community over the past decade? At the same time, which crimes in your community have decreased? In your opinion, what has contributed to these changes? Please be specific.

🏷 INTERNET RESOURCES

The Federal Bureau of Prisons (http://www.bop.gov/) is an agency within the U.S. Department of Justice. Established in 1930, the Federal Bureau of Prisons is tasked with providing more progressive and humane care for federal inmates, maintaining a professional, centralized authority of all federal prisons, including 115 institutions, 6 regional offices, a central office (headquarters), 2 staff training centers, and 28 community corrections offices. The Bureau is also responsible for the custody and care of about 209,000 federal offenders. About 82% of all federal inmates are confined in the bureau-operated facilities, while the rest are housed in private or community-based facilities and local jails.

Crime Reports (http://www.crimereports.com/) provides detailed online crime mapping for all 50 U.S. states. Crime Reports partners with over 700 law enforcement agencies across North America and also provides sex offender data for all 50 states.

Crime Stoppers International (http://www.c-s-i.org/) seeks to establish local crime prevention and awareness programs around the world. Crime Stoppers International oversees training and organizing forums for information exchange, provides legal services for member programs, and assists in defending any legal challenges related to the organization.

Founded in 1908, the FBI (Federal Bureau of Investigations) (http://www.fbi.gov/) is the principal investigative arm of the U.S. Department of Justice. The FBI also is authorized to provide other law enforcement agencies with cooperative services, such as fingerprint identification, laboratory examinations, and police training. The primary mission of the FBI is to uphold the law through the investigation of violations of federal criminal law.

INTERPOL (http://www.interpol.int/) is the world's largest international police organization, servicing 188 countries around the world. Created in 1923, it facilitates police actions across international borders and supports all organizations, authorities, and services whose mission is to prevent or combat international crime.

CRIME SCENE DO NOT CROSS

Interpersonal Violence

In 2008, three students from a high school in New Jersey were charged with sexually assaulting a 16-year-old special education student at one of their homes. One suspect was 18 years old and the other two were 16. The older youngster invited the girl to come into his house. For the next 4 hours or so, the three young men forced her to perform sex on them and abused her with a broomstick. According to an acquaintance, the oldest boy was a "stand-up kid who played video games and wanted to go to college." A neighbor described him as "a polite teenager who would shovel snow for them" (Fahim and Schweber, 2008).

What those three young men perpetrated is **rape**, the use of force to get a person to do something sexual against his or her will. It is a relatively common and serious form of interpersonal violence, which involves an individual inflicting harm on another or others. Another less common but more serious type of interpersonal violence is **homicide**, the killing of a person by another. We will here discuss these two types of interpersonal violence. Let's start with gang rape, which involves more than one male sexually assaulting a female, as illustrated in the opening vignette.

Rape
The use of force to get a person to do something sexual against his or her will.

Homicide
The killing of a person by another.

Gang Rape

Most of the perpetrators of gang rape are lower-class adolescents who join a street gang. They find their victims in various ways. First, they may cruise an area looking for a female hitchhiker to pick up and drive the unsuspecting victim to a deserted area to rape her. Second, they may use a knife or gun to kidnap a woman from the street at night. Third, a member of the gang may make a date with a woman and then drive her, without her knowledge or consent, to a predetermined location where he and other members will rape her. Once gang rape occurs, it is generally more violent than single rape (Hauffe and Porter, 2009; Zezima, 2004).

Occurring less frequently are gang rapes on college campuses, committed by middle- and upper-class youths. Gang rape takes place at various kinds of schools, from large state universities to small liberal arts colleges, where gang rape is often referred to as "running a train" on the victim. Campus gang rapes often occur at a party, where the men encourage a woman to drink or take drugs and rape her when she gets drunk or high.

Why do those lower-class adolescents and college men participate in gang rapes? Psychiatrists tend to interpret gang rape as an expression of latent homosexuality, arguing that the fellow rapists have an unconscious wish to have sex with each other. To critics, however, such an interpretation makes as much sense as the suggestion that a bunch of guys who go hunting together have a latent wish to kill each other. To sociologists, it seems more convincing to theorize that participation in gang rape fulfills a social need more than a sexual desire, particularly for young boys who feel peer pressure to prove they are not "chicken."

Similarly, college men who share a close relationship may find it hard to resist the pressure to participate in a gang rape because they are afraid of having their masculinity questioned. Moreover, through their camaraderie, they can playfully urge each other to participate in a gang rape without seeing it as a serious crime. This may explain why fraternity brothers and college athletes are more likely than other students to engage in gang rape (Sanday, 2007).

Acquaintance Rape

Compared with those who rape strangers, offenders who rape their acquaintances or dates are more likely to use verbal or psychological coercion and less likely to resort to guns or knives. Verbal coercion may involve pressuring the victim by saying, "C'mon, I know you really want it"; psychological coercion may involve making the victim feel inadequate as an object by ignoring her wishes when she says, "Stop it!" Also, while stranger rapists typically premeditate the rape, acquaintance rapists tend to premeditate only a sexual relation, which leads to rape when the victim refuses and the offender brushes her refusal aside, often assuming that she means yes when saying no.

Acquaintance rape is a relatively common offense. According to a nationwide survey, about 22% of women ages 18 to 90 years reported having been sexually assaulted (Elliott et al., 2004). Most of these victims know their offenders. Acquaintance rape is so common because it appears to be an extension of, rather than a departure from, the conventional pattern of male sexual behavior. In our culture, where men are expected to be aggressive rather than shy in dealing with women, young men can easily go too far and use too much force to execute a sexual conquest. That's why many acquaintance rapists do not regard date rape as real rape. In one survey, about 8% of college men admitted to committing the sexual offenses that can be legally defined as rapes or attempted rapes, but virtually none of these men identified themselves as rapists (Harned, 2005; Koss, 1995).

■ Campus Rape

Rape is relatively prevalent on college campuses. More than half of female students are at risk of being raped (Fisher, Cullen, and Daigle, 2005). Is there something unique about the campus that encourages sexual aggression? The answer is yes. In her study of small tribal societies, Peggy Sanday (1996) found that many are "rape-free" and a few "rape-prone." **Rape-free societies** have a culture that discourages sexual aggression while **rape-prone societies** have a culture that encourages it. Sanday further observed that there are also rape-free campuses and rape-prone ones. On a rape-free campus, sexual assault is treated as a serious offense punishable by expulsion, fraternities discourage heavy drinking, women are respected as friends rather than used as sex objects, and gays and lesbians are accepted in the same way as straights. In contrast, on a rape-prone campus, sexual assault is not seriously dealt with, heavy drinking is encouraged, taking advantage of an intoxicated woman is accepted, bragging about sexual conquests is prevalent, homophobia is rampant, and pornography is a popular guide to female sexuality. Thus we can expect a higher incidence of sexual offense on rape-prone campuses.

Other researchers have made similar observations about what causes the high incidence of campus rape. Patricia Martin and Robert Hummer (1995) conclude from their study of fraternities that such student groups contribute heavily to campus rape through their unique norms and practices. One norm emphasizes the value of maleness and masculinity over femaleness and femininity, causing members to devalue women by using them as sex objects, which can lead to rapes when women resist. Certain fraternity practices that often lead to coercive sex include excessive use of alcohol and pressure from fellow members to prove one's masculinity through sexual conquests. Studies on male athletes have also found them to be more rape-prone than other students. The athletes subscribe to the same norms and practices as the fraternity brothers (Adams-Curtis and Forbes, 2004; Kingsbury, 2006; Testa and Livingston, 2009). Some of these sociological insights can be used to stop rape (see **Box 7.1**).

Rape-free societies Societies that have a culture that discourages sexual aggression.

Rape-prone societies Societies that have a culture that encourages sexual aggression.

■ Marital Rape

Contrary to what you may assume, the majority of marital rapes do not involve vaginal penetration. Vaginal rapes account for less than half of marital rapes, while forced anal intercourse occurs slightly more often. Other forms of extremely degrading rapes in marriage include inserting objects into the wife's private parts, coercing her to have sex in front of children, or forcing sex on her right after she is discharged from a hospital—usually after giving birth (Barnett, Miller-Perrin, and Perrin, 2005).

Most offenders are domineering men who see their wives as "property." When they force their wives to have sex with them, the experience is as traumatic to the

How to Stop Rape

After reading the material on rape, particularly on topics such as campus rape, you may wonder what can be done to help prevent this type of violence. Recall that researchers such as Sanday (1996) have found certain social conditions that help make a campus "rape-prone" as opposed to "rape-free." These dangerous conditions, such as heavy drinking and other recreational drug use, lack of consistent punishment for sexual aggression, tolerance of homophobia, and widespread sexual objectification of women are what Connell (2000) refers to as "the toxic consequences of masculinity." At this point, you may be asking yourself, "What can I do to help?" You could help by supporting or participating in the programs presented by schools and organizations.

To help students reduce sexual violence, some schools, such as Antioch College and Benedict College, have encouraged students to make sure that any sexual contact is based on consent. Many schools have adopted similar policies that are incorporated into their rape prevention handbooks. Although a few colleges call for an extreme measure, such as requiring consent for any physical contact—even hand holding—most schools emphasize the importance of sobriety and safety. They encourage, for example, moderate drinking and having a designated "sober" companion to drink with.

The National Organization for Women has pressured many university administrations to improve prevention-related resources on campus and to enforce reasonable punishment for violations. Many schools have consequently added courses on rape prevention to their core curricula. Another organization, Men Can Stop Rape (www.mencanstoprape.org), mobilizes men to create a culture free from violence, especially men's violence against women. One way to do this is to have men and women engage in more coed, nondrinking social activities that promote cultural diversity and tolerance.

victims as stranger rape, striking tremendous fear into the raped wives. As one victim said, "It was as though he wanted to annihilate me. More than the slapping, or the kicks . . . as though he wanted to tear me apart from the inside out" (Browne, 1987). After the assault, victims who are employed or able to be economically independent tend to get a divorce, while those who are not employed tend to stay married (Barnett, Miller-Perrin, and Perrin, 2005; Bergen, 2006).

A major cause of marital rape seems to be the sexist belief that husbands are *entitled* to have sex in any way they want with their wives. This belief is part of the popular patriarchal myth that wives cannot be raped because they are regarded as "belonging" to their husbands—that is, as their husbands' property (Ferro et al., 2008). Not surprisingly, although all the states have made marital rape a crime, it is still rare for a man to be charged with raping his wife.

◼ Wartime Rape

Historically, when a conquering army destroyed or confiscated the conquered population's property, it also raped the women as if they were part of that property. During World War II, German soldiers raped massive numbers of Jewish and Russian women after occupying many villages and cities in Europe, and the Japanese army systematically raped women and girls as it invaded Korea, China, and various Southeast Asian countries. In 1971, when the Pakistani army marched into Bangladesh, soldiers were first shown pornographic movies and then let loose to rape at least 200,000 women. In 1992 Serbian soldiers in Bosnia raped thousands of Muslim women as part of an "ethnic cleansing" campaign. In 1994 the Hutus in Rwanda, who at that time dominated the country, raped immense numbers of minority Tutsi women. In 1999 when the Serbian forces took over Kosovo, they raped ethnic Albanian women. In 2004 pro-government Arab militias in Sudan used rape as a weapon of war to humiliate black African women in the region where rebels were fighting the government. All these rapes reflect the universally shared attitude that women are men's property (Farwell, 2004; Lacey, 2004; Marino, 2009).

When an army invades a foreign country it tends to rape the women of that country as if they are part of the conquered nation's property. These wartime rapes reflect the universally shared attitude that women are men's property.

Because of that attitude, we could expect wartime rapes to be especially dehumanizing and brutal. In Bosnia, for example, the victims were corralled like cattle in concentration camps where they were repeatedly raped, often in front of family members, neighbors, and other prisoners. The women were not only subjected to extreme humiliation; they were sexually tortured as well. As one victim says, "They would ask women if they had male relatives; I saw them ask this of one woman and they brought her 14-year-old son and forced him to rape her. If a man couldn't rape, he would use a bottle or a gun or he would urinate on me." Worse, many women were killed after being raped. Those who did survive became extremely traumatized from being raped by many men for many months (Carlson, 2006; Diken and Laustsen, 2005; McGirk, 2002).

◼ Female Genital Cutting

Female genital cutting
Female circumcision that involves removing some of the female genitalia such as the clitoris, its foreskin, or the labia.

Often called "female circumcision," female genital cutting involves removing some of the female genitalia such as the clitoris, its foreskin, or the labia. It takes place mostly in Africa, where it has been practiced as part of some African cultures for hundreds of years. The genital cutting is usually performed on girls aged 4 to 14 years. Most of the performers are "ritual leaders," well-respected elderly women in the community who are specially designated for the task (Gruenbaum, 2001; Hassanin et al., 2008).

The cutting has generated a firestorm of outrage in the West. It has been called the worst human rights violation against the female gender. The Western media have portrayed it as extremely cruel, because it is performed without anesthetics. Most Western social scientists have observed how the victims suffer from numerous health problems. Some are physical, such as death, hemorrhage, infection, and severe pain. Some are psychological, such as anxiety, depression, low self-esteem, and recurring memories of the cutting. Some problems are sexual, with the women unable to experience sexual pleasure and orgasm (Barstow, 2004; *Nation's Health*, 2008).

Female genital cutting has been blamed on *patriarchy* with the argument that in societies where the cutting is a common practice, men dominate women in virtually all aspects of social life. The cutting is seen as men's attempt to discourage women from having extramarital sex so as to turn them into obedient and subservient wives. There is also a more specific reason for the cutting: the *cultural belief* that it makes women more desirable. In the societies that practice the cutting, the clitoris and the labia are seen as masculine and unsightly on a woman. They should, therefore, be removed, so that the genitalia will look highly feminine and aesthetically pleasing. Female genital cutting is thus viewed as similar to the use of cosmetic surgery to reshape noses, enlarge breasts, or shrink bellies to make women look more desirable in Western societies (Ahmadu, 2000; Hernlund and Shell-Duncan, 2007).

Men as Rape Victims

We have so far discussed women as victims of rape by men, but men can also be raped by other men.

In Prison

The rape of a man by another man in prison is more prevalent than the rape of a woman by a man outside of prison. About 1 in 5 male inmates in prison have been raped, compared with 1 in 10 females in the larger society. Moreover, while the female rape victims typically get raped only once, the male victims are raped multiple times. Why so many more rapes in prison? There are three basic reasons: (1) The general public has little or no sympathy for convicts. (2) The rapists go unpunished. (3) The "wolves" (rapists) are not segregated from the "punks" (the victims) (Hensley and Tewksbury, 2005; Lehrer, 2001; Young, 2007).

Male rapists and their male victims in prison are comparable to male rapists and their female victims in the larger society in several ways. The rapists within the prison, like the rapists without, are heterosexual. Moreover, the prison rapists are like the men who rape women outside the prison (and the male victims in prison are like the female victims outside) in that both types of rapists are generally older, heavier, taller, and more violent than their victims.

Many people may think that the rape in prison is intended to relieve one's sexual deprivation, but that is not the primary motive for prison rape. If an inmate simply wants to relieve his sexual deprivation, masturbation would be a much more convenient and normal method of relief than same-sex rape. Instead, the primary motive is the need to subjugate and humiliate the victim, as evidenced by the fact that prison rapists often say to victims, "We're going to take away your manhood," "You'll have to give up some face," or "We're gonna make a girl out of you." The drive for power, then, is the primary motive for prison rapes (Lehrer, 2001).

In Larger Society

In the larger society, the risk of a man being raped by another man or by a woman is still far less than the risk of a woman being sexually assaulted by a man. According to a national survey, only 3.8% of men have ever suffered sexual assault compared to 22% of women (Elliot et al., 2004). Most of these male victims are raped by men. Like heterosexual rapes, most same-sex rapes involve acquaintances. Such rapes include attacks by men meeting their victims at parties or bars, gang rapes in the

Navy and other military settings, and seduction with pressure by trusted men, such as doctors, psychotherapists, priests, and teachers. Most victims are in their late teens or early twenties. More than half of the victims are heterosexual, as are more than half of the offenders. The rapist assaults his victim mostly with intent to punish or dominate, rather than for sexual pleasure (Scarce, 1997).

Same-sex rape can be illustrated with two cases of a man being sexually assaulted by another: (1) A heterosexual man became intoxicated at an office party. He let his boss drive him home. He passed out in the car, but he soon woke up to find himself in the backseat, with his pants down, being anally entered by the boss. (2) Three Navy men beat and dragged a shipmate to a secluded area of the ship to rape him, but the victim escaped. Three weeks later the same attackers overpowered the victim, and two of the assailants held him down while the third raped him anally. Victims of male rape such as in these examples are highly unlikely to report their victimization, largely because of the myths that "male rape is a gay crime" and "male rape doesn't happen" (Rumney, 2008; Tewksbury, 2007).

The male victim reacts in about the same way to same-sex rape as the female victim does to heterosexual rape. The reactions include shock, self-blame, anger, and depression. However, these reactions are more distressing to men than women because men are expected to be strong, aggressive, and avoidant of sexual contact with other men. Given this male-role expectation, the male victim is also more likely to control his emotion by denying or minimizing the trauma of rape. Still, unlike the female victim, the male victim tends to feel a loss of masculinity. As one victim said, "Hell, I've got no manhood left. He's made me into a woman" (Elliott et al., 2004; Walker, Archer, and Davies, 2005).

■ What Encourages Rape

Sociologists have discovered that what encourages rape includes the rape culture, sexual permissiveness, and gender inequality.

The Rape Culture

Obviously many societies openly condemn rape as a serious crime. Less obviously, however, those same societies have a hidden culture of rape—a culture that encourages men to sexually assault women. The rape culture does not affect all men in the same way; otherwise, all men would rape. Some men are more inclined than others to rape, although they all live under the influence of the same culture. Research has suggested that those who are immature, irresponsible, and lacking in social conscience are more influenced by the rape culture (Buchwald et al., 2005; Kingsbury, 2006; Sapp et al., 1999). What is, then, the nature of the rape culture? It can be seen through the prevailing attitudes toward women as well as through the popular concept of male and female sex roles.

First, the rape culture treats women like men's property. This can be discerned through the absence of marital-rape laws in some societies and the rarity of husbands being imprisoned for raping their wives in most societies. The assumption in these societies is that in marriage women belong to their husbands who are entitled to use them as a sexual commodity in any way they want. Because women are culturally defined as men's property, men may find it difficult to respect women as human beings. It is through this lack of respect that men are encouraged to rape women.

Second, the rape culture pressures men to use women in their masculinity contests. In a society that places a high premium on competition, men are pressured to engage in what may be called a masculinity contest to prove their male prowess and to earn a macho reputation among peers. To come out a winner, a man must make out with the largest number of women possible. To do so, however, the sexually aggressive man is likely to end up raping some of those women.

The rape culture pressures men to prove their manhood by making out with the largest number of women possible.

Third, the rape culture endorses the popular myth that victims have a secret wish to be raped. The myth is expressed in various ways, often with such sentiments as "She asked for it," "she actually wanted it," "She lied about it," "She earlier consented to sex but later decided to 'cry rape,'" "She wasn't really hurt," and "It was only a form of sex, though without her consent." As a result, many people—particularly men with low income and little education—hold the victim responsible for the rape. They assume that the victim did something that provoked the man to rape her. That "something" involves being in the "wrong" place (going to a bar or walking alone at night), wearing the "wrong" clothes (a miniskirt or some other sexy dress), or turning the man on (letting him kiss or pet her).

Sexual Permissiveness

Sociologists have long observed that the rate of rape is higher in modern, sexually permissive societies such as the United States and Sweden than in traditional, sexually restrictive societies such as Korea and Pakistan. But why?

In a sexually restrictive society, a man is more able to take a woman's rejection in stride. He can protect his ego by rationalizing that she has rejected him not because he is in some way undesirable but because the restrictive society prevents her from accepting his sexual invitation. He may take comfort from the fact that women are too sexually conservative, too afraid to engage in nonmarital sex, that their religion condemns such sex, or that laws against nonmarital sex are too stringent. In a sexually permissive society, however, the rejected man cannot use this kind of rationalization. He is more likely to take the woman's rebuff personally, seeing that it is he himself who is responsible for his failure to win the woman's favors. As a consequence, he is likely to feel hurt, thereby experiencing sexual frustration. This frustration in turn drives many more men in a permissive than a restrictive society to rape women.

Gender Inequality

As the feminists among sociologists argue, rape is primarily an expression of men's dominance over women, which in turn is a reflection of society's gender inequality. Rape, then, serves to intimidate women, keeping them in their place to maintain gender inequality. The evidence on rape as an expression of male dominance exists everywhere. All over the world, the overwhelming majority of rapes involve men raping women rather than women raping men. At the same time, men generally have greater physical, political, or economic power than women. Combined, these two facts suggest that the male power over women, the essence of gender inequality, effectively causes rape. A few radical feminists have drawn fire for exaggerating the influence of male dominance on rape by arguing that rape enables all men to keep all women in a state of fear. Critics have observed that many men do not dominate women by raping them, especially if the women are their mothers and daughters.

Compared with rape of various types that we have so far discussed, homicide is a much less common but much more serious kind of interpersonal violence. Next, we will discuss the social backgrounds of killers, the patterns of killing, the nature of homicide, and what mass and serial killers are like.

■ Social Backgrounds of Killers

The most striking thing about killers is that they are typically poor. African Americans, being generally poorer than whites, are more likely than whites to commit murder. Poor countries have higher rates of homicide than rich nations. Similarly, societies and individuals with violent pasts have relatively high rates of homicide. The South has more homicides than any other region in the United States. Here and abroad, large cities have a higher incidence of killings than smaller cities. Men are far more likely than women to kill, and young men (aged 18 to 24 years) are more likely than other age groups to commit murder. Let us take a closer look at each of these facts.

Class and Race

Homicides are heavily concentrated in the lower class. Over 90% of the murderers in the United States are semiskilled workers, unskilled laborers, and welfare recipients. Poverty is definitely a factor in homicide. As such, poverty crosses racial lines: Poor whites have higher murder rates than better-off whites, and poor blacks have higher rates than richer blacks. There are several reasons for the strong link between poverty and murder. Compared to people of the higher classes, the poor are more likely to have financial, marital, and other stressful problems, which in turn tend to cause interpersonal conflict. The poor are also more likely to resort to physical violence as a way of dealing with interpersonal conflict. Violence is, in effect, a mechanism for getting respect, because the poor generally consider violence a badge of toughness and masculinity (Hannon, 2005; Pridemore, 2008).

Blacks generally have a much higher rate of homicide than whites. This fact makes it appear as if race plays an important role in homicide. Actually, being black has nothing to do with such violence. Instead, African Americans' higher rate of homicide simply reflects their higher rate of poverty, which, along with racial discrimination, generates greater frustration and alienation. In expressing their frustration, however, blacks are more likely to kill their fellow blacks than to kill whites. In fact, most killings are *intra*racial, because whites kill other whites more often than they kill blacks. *Inter*racial murders—in which blacks kill whites and vice versa—are rare because racial discrimination discourages interaction between blacks and white (Strom and MacDonald, 2007).

Regions, Large Cities, and Rural Areas

Usually, the southern region of the United States has the highest murder rate, the western region has the next highest rate, and the northeastern and midwestern states have the lowest rate (FBI, 2010). What accounts for the southern region's leadership in murder rates? Some sociologists attribute it to the "culture of violence," where violent behavior seems more acceptable than in other regions. For example, gun ownership and execution of murderers, along with the history of lynching, which are assumed to reflect a violent culture, are the most common in the South (Lee, Hayes, and Thomas, 2008). Another reason could be the greater prevalence of rurality in the South. A study by Kenneth Wilkinson (1984) shows that the average murder rate in rural areas exceeds the rate in most cities. According to Wilkinson, the dispersion of people in rural areas (as contrasted with the congestion of people in most cities) reduces community integration, thereby forcing family members, friends, and acquaintances to spend too much time with each other. This enhances the opportunity for violent disruption in primary relationships (among relatives and acquaintances), and it is in such relationships that most homicides take place.

The rurality–homicide connection seems to contradict the popular belief that there are more killings in *large* cities. Actually, it does not; large cities do have more killings, which may explain why taxi drivers in large cities are most in danger of getting killed (see **Box 7.2**). The prevalence of murder in rural areas is greater than in urban areas only if we compare the homicide rates of rural areas with those of *most* cities, which are relatively small, having populations of fewer than 50,000 people. Rural areas do have higher homicide rates than these small cities. However, large cities, with populations exceeding 100,000, have significantly higher murder rates than those for small cities as well as rural areas.

BOX 7.2   WHAT RESEARCH REVEALS

"Thank You for Not Killing Me"

Of all the workers in the United States, taxi drivers have the worst occupational hazard. They are saddled with the highest homicide rate of any occupation, being 60 times more likely to be murdered on the job than the average worker. To emphasize the prevalence of this problem, a cartoonist has drawn a picture of a taxi driver with a sign behind him and his passenger staring at it. The sign says, "Thank you for not killing me" (Hamill and Gambetta, 2006).

Taxi drivers are likely to be killed, usually in conjunction with robbery or refusal to pay the fare, because, alone and unarmed, they have to interact with an enormous number of strangers in high-crime urban areas. In New York City, for example, a driver could encounter as many as 20 to 25 strangers every working day, which adds up to more than 7,000 in a year. From these many interactions with strangers, many taxi drivers have learned to single out the harmless passengers from the dangerous ones so that they will pick up only the harmless. But how do they tell those two kinds of strangers apart?

A couple of sociologists found the answer from interviewing taxi drivers in New York City and Northern Ireland's Belfast, two cities where there are many potential criminals who pose as passengers in order to rob or harm the drivers. The researchers found that to differentiate harmless strangers from dangerous ones the drivers look for "trustworthy" characteristics in the strangers such as their age, gender, and race. In regard to age and gender, for example, taxi drivers generally consider older persons and women to be more trustworthy than younger ones and men (Hamill and Gambetta, 2006).

Gender and Age

Men are far more likely than women to kill because men are far more concerned about defending their manhood. Most of these killings involve a man doing away with another man. But if a man and a woman are caught up in a homicidal interaction, he is more likely to be the offender and she the victim. Men who kill their wives or girlfriends do so primarily because they have persistently tried to *keep their victims in an abusive relationship*. Such killing is the culmination of a long series of physically violent acts perpetrated by the men against their female victims. Moreover, men tend to kill in response to their wives' infidelity. Men would also kill their wives as part of a murder–suicide or a family massacre.

In the fewer cases in which women kill, the killers differ from their male counterparts in their choice of victims. Unlike male offenders, who are more likely to kill others of the *same sex*, female offenders are more likely to kill members of the *opposite sex*. In these opposite-sex killings, the female and male murderers usually commit the crime for different reasons. The women rarely kill in response to their husbands' infidelity even if their husbands are extremely adulterous. They usually murder their husbands as a desperate attempt to *get out of an abusive relationship*. The women basically kill for self-preservation or in self-defense. Violence by women, then, is primarily defensive, in contrast to violence by men, which is distinctly offensive. Such defensive killing serves as "self-help social control" against abusive husbands. It often takes place in states where there are no laws mandating arrests for domestic violence (Gauthier and Bankston, 2004).

Males also kill at a younger age than females. When killing, people are more likely to target others of about the same age group than older or younger victims. This is largely because people of about the same age spend more time interacting with one another than with others of a different age. In the few cases in which older persons quarrel with younger ones, the older persons are more likely to end up dead because the younger persons are more impulsive and hence quicker to shoot. While most homicides involve relatives and acquaintances, the younger killers are more likely than their older peers to target strangers and commit murder and robbery together (U.S. Census Bureau, 2009a).

■ Patterns of Killing

Killing does not happen randomly. It follows certain patterns, occurring at a certain time and place, with the offender using a certain method to carry out the killing.

When to Kill

Homicide occurs most frequently during the weekend evenings, particularly on Saturday night. This may explain why the cheap handgun most often used in homicide is popularly called a "Saturday night special." These weekend killings are more likely to involve family members than the homicides occurring during the weekdays; the weekday homicides tend to involve strangers. The reason is that people usually spend more time at home on weekends.

All this does not, however, hold true for the minority of cases involving middle-class and upper-class offenders. These relatively affluent offenders are likely to kill on any day of the week while poor offenders tend to kill during the weekend. Why this class difference? Because murders in the middle and upper classes are more likely to be *calculative* or *premeditated*, while lower-class killings are more often carried out in a burst of rage, usually after heavy drinking during the weekend (Parker, 1995).

Where to Kill

Men are more likely to kill at public places, but women are far more likely to kill in the home. In the past, women most often did the killing in the kitchen, apparently because it was the place where women traditionally were accustomed to handling a knife—which can turn into a dangerous weapon when a quarrel flares up. Nowadays, less likely to be confined to the kitchen as a result of greater gender equality, women tend to kill in the living room. The bedroom is a more dangerous place for women than for men, because women are more frequently killed there by their husbands, boyfriends, or exes. Perhaps, under the lingering influence of gender inequality, men have been socially conditioned to use the bedroom as a place for demonstrating their "manliness" by sexually conquering women and end up using it as a place for physically subjugating them to death (Miethe and Regoeczi, 2004).

Women are more likely to kill or be killed at home. A major reason is simply that they spend more time at home. Other types of people who spend more time at home are also more likely to have the same fate. These include the very young, the very old, minority groups, the married, and the unemployed.

How to Kill

Killing a human is not as mundane as, say, killing a rabbit; rather, it is extremely serious. It consequently fires up the imagination of many mystery writers, who help spread the popular notion that murderers often use mysterious, exotic, ingenious, or superclever methods to get rid of their victims. Yet research shows there is nothing special about the methods of killing. Most objects can be readily turned into murder weapons, as long as they are conveniently accessible when the murderous anger erupts. In our society, firearms are easily available, so they are most often used as murder weapons. Perhaps seeing a gun while embroiled in a heated argument may incite a violent person to murderous action. As Shakespeare has it, "How oft the sight of means to do ill deeds, makes ill deeds done."

Of course, firearms in themselves cannot cause homicide; nor can their absence reduce the motivation to kill. It is true that "guns don't kill people, people do." Still, were guns less available, many heated arguments would have resulted in aggravated assaults rather than murders, thereby reducing the number of fatalities. In fact, the easy availability of guns is one reason why the United States has the highest rate of murder among the developed countries (see Box 7.3).

■ The Nature of Homicide

Most killings are carried out against family members, friends, or acquaintances rather than strangers. Some killings happen as if the victim asks to be put to death. Some involve an attempt to win a seemingly trivial argument. Some serve as an adjunct to suicide. Some end the lives of more than one victim. Let us take a close look at each of these characteristics of murder.

BOX 7.3   GLOBAL PERSPECTIVE

Why Some Societies Kill More Than Others

Homicide is more prevalent in poor, developing countries than in rich, developed ones. In general, developing countries such as those in Latin America, Asia, and Africa have higher rates of homicide than do developed countries such as those in North America and Western Europe.

Among the developed countries, however, the United States has by far the highest rate. This is largely due to the greater amount of poverty in our society compared to the other developed areas like Western Europe and Japan. The easy availability of guns can also explain why the homicide rate in the United States is much higher than in Western Europe and Japan. Within Western Europe, countries such as Finland, where many private citizens own guns, have higher homicide rates than those such as England, where guns are scarcer (Chamlin and Cochran, 2005).

Among the poor, developing countries alone, those in Latin America have unusually high homicide rates, apparently the highest in the world. Some sociologists have attributed these high rates to a "culture of violence," which encourages the use of violence to deal with unbearable interpersonal conflict. This culture seems to have a powerful element of machismo, the belief that men should be concerned about their manhood. In such a culture, men are encouraged to respond aggressively to an insult about their masculinity. If they do not, they are made to feel like cowards. In every country in the world, however, men are much more likely than women to kill, which apparently reflects the influence of machismo, though to a lesser degree than in Latin America. Also in highly patriarchal societies in the Middle East, women are likely to fall victim to "honor killings" by their male relatives, if they engage in premarital or extramarital sex. The woman is considered to have shamed the family, and the killing is intended to bring back the family honor (Baron, 2006).

A Degree of Relationship

Many people are apparently afraid of getting attacked and killed by strangers, particularly in big cities. However, this fear does not reflect reality. Compared with other major crimes, such as robbery, rape, and assault, homicide is the least likely to involve strangers. Of all the murders that occur every year, only a small percentage are committed by strangers (Baker, 2007). In fact, the majority of the homicides involve a degree of relationship between killer and victim as relatives, friends, or acquaintances, as Figure 7.1 indicates. This situation is not unique to our society. It exists in many other countries as well.

It seems incredible that the people we know or even love are more likely to kill us than are total strangers, but spouses, friends, acquaintances, and others whom we know well are a major source of frustration and hurt in our lives, just as they are a major source of pleasure. Few others can anger us so much as the ones we know. Because killing usually requires a great deal of emotion, it may be more difficult to kill a stranger about whom we don't have much feeling—unless we are professional killers, who typically dispatch their victims in a cold-blooded, unemotional manner. Thus we are less likely to become victims of cold-blooded murders carried out by strangers but more likely to die from hot-blooded, emotional murders at the hands of our relatives, friends, or acquaintances.

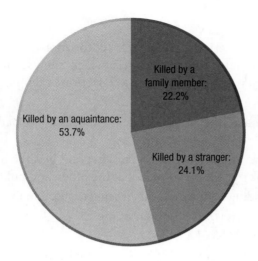

FIGURE 7.1 Most Victims Know Their Killers

Although murder is often portrayed in popular culture as something that typically happens among strangers, it is actually three times more likely to occur at the hands of someone the victim knows.

Critical Thinking: *What social forces influence whether murder victims are more vulnerable to family members or strangers?*

Source: Bureau of Justice Statistics, 2010.

Asking for It

We usually sympathize with the murder victim but not with the offender at all. We assume that the murder victim is weak and meek, helplessly slain by the strong and aggressive offender. However, this assumption is not always correct. In at least one out of four homicides, the victim has first attacked the subsequent slayer, and sociologists have described such murder as *victim-precipitated homicide*. It can be illustrated by this case: A drunken husband, beating his wife in the kitchen, gave her a butcher knife and dared her to use it on him. She warned him that she would use it if he should strike her again. At the very instant he heard this warning, he slapped her in the face—and he was fatally stabbed (Klinger, 2001).

Because they provoke another person to kill them, self-precipitated murder victims may have secretly wanted to kill *themselves*. But if this is the case, why do they not take it on themselves to end their own lives? Perhaps they have been influenced by what may be considered a culture of *showy masculinity*, characteristic of a sexist society. This culture encourages males to show off their toughness and conceal their tenderness, to act like a "man" and avoid acting like a "woman," or to engage in "manly" braggadocio and shun "feminine" quietism. Under the pressure of this culture, suicidal men may not think it right to quietly end their own lives, lest doing so should reveal their "sissy cowardice" or seem a plea for condescending sympathy from others. Instead, they are inclined to display masculine bravado and earn from others some "respect" as the worst person imaginable, by making an ostentatious assault on another person that is secretly designed for their own annihilation—the result being a victim-precipitated murder.

Showy masculinity
A cultural characteristic that encourages males to show off their toughness and conceal their tenderness, to act like a "man" and avoid acting like a "woman."

Killing for Trivia

Murder is an extremely serious human act, yet the motive for committing it often appears downright trivial. Ordinary quarrels, which often seem to be over nothing, are the most common reason for people to kill. Here are examples of why poor killers commit murder:

- A man was fatally shot in front of a tavern because he had refused to lend his assailant $1.
- Two men were arguing over a $5 pool bet and became involved in a scuffle. One then took out a gun, pointed it at the other, and pulled the trigger.
- Two men standing on the sidewalk became engaged in the following argument:

   First man: "Hey, you're lookin' at me."

   Second man: "No, I ain't."

   First man: "Yes, you are. Why you lookin' at me?"

   Moments later one of them lay still in a puddle of blood.

Murder, then, is apparently a quick and effective way for the poor to win an argument—over trifles. Middle-class people usually use a much less drastic means, such as verbal or intellectual ability, to settle an argument. But the poor tend to suffer from lack of such ability and are therefore more often compelled to use their physical strength to end an argument with—and sometimes the life of—another person.

You may note that arguments such as in the preceding examples appear trivial to us. Yet similar arguments are apparently taken by poor males as reasons for defending their dignity or honor as men. A dirty look, a little insult, a jostle would not usually get middle-class people into an argument, let alone impel them to spill another person's blood. The same triviality may be perceived differently by the poor. Why would the poor make such a mountain out of a molehill, and with such deadly consequences for themselves?

The explanation can be found in the economic and social oppression of the poor. The poor man's dignity as a man—or, for that matter, as simply a human being—has been substantially diminished by the frustrating and humiliating forces in his life. Some of these forces are impersonal, such as the general condition of poverty, so that the poor man cannot fight back against them. Other humiliating forces can be found in people, such as the police, bureaucrats in a welfare or unemployment office, and employers—who usually treat him with far less respect than they do the more successful, higher-status persons. Because these people are more powerful, the poor man cannot fight back at them either.

As a consequence, he has extremely little dignity left in him, and in order to live with at least more worth than an animal, he dearly hangs on to it. Although he cannot maintain his fragile dignity in the large society or in the presence of people more powerful than himself, he certainly can at his own home and in his neighborhood, among his equally dignity-deprived family members, friends, and acquaintances. Because his dignity as a man is already extremely limited, the pressure of daily frustration and tension can easily crush it. Thus even a small insult from his relatives, friends, or acquaintances (who are, after all, his last strand of hope for keeping his dignity) can mean, to him, the threat that all his dignity will be taken away. With such a perception, he will very likely fight like mad to defend his dignity, even to the extent of killing the person who has "dissed" him. In fact, as many researchers have found, most murders result from what they call "character contests," in which the offender and victim try to defend their honor after it has been threatened by the other (Mullins, 2006).

Ending with Suicide

We have observed that the so-called victims of victim-precipitated homicide have wanted to die and thus contributed greatly to their own deaths. There is yet a different group of offenders with the same suicidal tendency. They are murder–suicide offenders, who first kill another person and then finish themselves off. The difference between these two types of offenders is obvious. While the "victims" of victim-precipitated murder conceal their suicidal wishes, murder–suicide offenders reveal their wishes.

Virtually all murder–suicides are male and their victims female. The perpetrators are extremely frustrated, depressed, and violent, killing their wives and, often, their children as a way of expressing their dominance or control over them (Harper and Voigt, 2007).

Two conflicting views can be found on the nature of murder–suicide: One is sociological, seeing murder–suicide as a form of *normality*; the other is psychiatric, viewing it as a symptom of *abnormality*. According to the sociological view, the murderer–suicide offender is a normal person because, after killing the loved one, he is able to feel remorse, just as we would expect normal people to feel after they had done such a horrible thing. By contrast, the psychiatrist sees the murderer–suicide offender as psychotic, believing that, instead of feeling remorse, the offender anticipates a reunion with the victim in another world and therefore kills himself to achieve that unreal goal.

Given these various characteristics of murder, you may wonder, does capital punishment deter the crime (see Box 7.4)?

■ Mass and Serial Murder

Mass murder involves killing a number of people at about the same time and place, while serial murder destroys the lives of victims at different times and places. Mass murder usually ends with the murderer dying at the scene of the carnage. The murderer's death results from either committing suicide or forcing the police to take lethal action. Despite the shocking nature of their crime, most mass murderers are not mentally ill. As sociologists James Fox and Jack Levin (2005) conclude after studying mass murderers, "The mass killer appears to be *extraordinarily ordinary*. He is indistinguishable from everyone else. Indeed, he may be the neighbor next door, a coworker at the next desk, or a member of the family."

Some mass murderers are *disgruntled employees* who want to get even with their boss who has wronged them in some way, by firing them, for example. But in the process of killing their boss, they end up murdering their coworkers as well. Other mass murderers are *heads of family* who kill their wives and children after having long felt alone, alienated, helpless, and depressed, aggravated by heavy drinking (Meloy et al., 2004).

BOX 7.4   DIVERGENT VIEWS

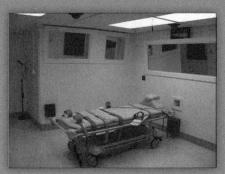

Most Americans believe that the death penalty can effectively deter murder, but research evidence shows otherwise.

Does the Death Penalty Deter Murder?

The United States is among only four countries (along with Iran, Saudi Arabia, and China) that account for nearly all the executions in the world (Quindlen, 2006). Most Americans still believe that the death penalty is an effective deterrent to murder. Some economists back up that belief with studies that purportedly suggest the tendency of the murder rates to fall as executions rise. The economists point out that throughout the 1990s the United States increased the number of executions, and the number of murders dropped sharply; moreover, since 2001, there has been a drop in executions and a rise in murders. The economists further argue that for each convicted killer put to death, 3 to 18 murders are prevented (Adler and Summers, 2007).

Most sociologists, however, argue that many factors other than executions contributed to the decrease in murders. In the 1990s, for example, it might be the improvement of the social and economic conditions rather than the increase in executions that brought down the murder rates along with the general crime rates. More positively, the sociologists offer several pieces of evidence to show that the death penalty does not have its hoped-for effect (Baker, 2007; Liptak, 2007; Zimring et al., 2009).

First is the fact that the homicide rates in *states that have retained* the death penalty are generally much higher than in *states that have abolished* it. This suggests that the death penalty does not deter homicide.

A second piece of evidence indicates that *after* some states abolished the death penalty their homicide rates remained largely the same as before. Moreover, the *restoration* of the death penalty in states that had earlier abolished it has *not* led to any significant decrease in homicides.

A third, final piece of evidence comes from comparing the numbers of homicides *shortly before and shortly after executions* of convicted murderers that have been widely publicized. If the death penalty has a deterrent effect, the execution should so scare potential killers that they would refrain from killing, and the number of homicides in the area should decrease. However, this is not the case, because the number of homicides remains about the same after the publicized executions have taken place (Bailey, 1998).

An important reason for the general failure of the death penalty to deter murder is that murder is essentially a crime of passion. As such, it is carried out under the overwhelming pressure of a volcanic emotion, making it difficult for the individual involved to stop and think that he or she will end up being executed for killing the victim.

While mass murderers are nearly always caught, serial killers are far more elusive because they are practiced and accomplished at what they do. First, they stalk their victims from a distance, studying the victims' routine activities and habits. They then win the victims' confidence by befriending them, or gain entry into the victims' house, which they have staked out for days. Next, they lure the victims into a trap or simply hold them captive by closing off all possibility of escape. Finally, they kill the victims. In the process of killing, they often torture their victims, taking special delight in their agonies. This characteristic should not be surprising.

Most serial killers have in their childhood tortured dogs and cats for the thrill of watching them suffer. They have also been subjected to a lot of physical and emotional abuse by their parents. Such experiences have apparently taught the serial killer to become a sociopath, incapable of feeling remorse or guilt for hurting others. Nonetheless, the vast majority of serial killers are not mentally ill. They appear as normal people who go to school or work, come home, and blend into their immediate neighborhood (Fox, Levin, and Quinet, 2007; Knight, 2006).

Serial killers such as Jeffrey Dahmer (shown here) have often been subjected to physical and emotional abuse by their parents, but the vast majority of them are not mentally ill.

■ Sociological Theories of Interpersonal Violence

The three major sociological theories are useful for explaining the causes of interpersonal violence. According to the functionalist theory, the culture of violence is an important cause of homicide in that people are likely to resort to violence if they live in a society that encourages the use of violence to deal with interpersonal problems. Conflict theory argues that violence can be traced to **external restraint**—deprivation of individual freedom by society. Symbolic interaction theory attributes violence to differential association involving frequent interaction with people who define violence favorably.

External restraint
The social control imposed on people to limit their freedom and range of behaviors.

Functionalist Theory

In his classic study on homicide as a common phenomenon of an anomic, dysfunctional society, Marvin Wolfgang (1958) concludes that it stems from a culture of violence that "does not define personal assaults as wrong or antisocial but instead approves of quick resort to physical aggression." Wolfgang then theorizes that the culture of violence is the basic cause of high homicide rates in poor neighborhoods. According to Wolfgang, the violent culture has such a grip on the poor that they engage in a wider range of violent behavior than the nonpoor. Violence becomes a part of their lifestyles and their way of solving interpersonal problems. They consider the use of violence not only normal but necessary for survival. They do not feel guilty about their aggression against others (Lee et al., 2007).

Conflict Theory

According to conflict theory, the lower classes are more often frustrated in their struggles for a better life when compared to the higher classes. This is primarily because they are subjected to greater external restraint. They are thus more likely to take out their frustration on others in the form of homicide, while their peers in the higher classes, being subjected to less external restraint, tend to express their violence inward—against themselves—in the form of suicide. In fact, not only the lower classes but other socially oppressed groups such as African Americans, are more inclined to commit homicide than suicide because they feel they can legitimately blame others for their frustration (Chamlin and Cochran, 2005; Henry and Short, 1954).

Symbolic Interaction Theory

According to symbolic interaction theory, people are likely to inflict violence on others if they have often gone through a differential association that involves interacting more frequently with individuals who define violence as normal or permissible than with those who define violence as abnormal or objectionable. Thus, children are likely to use violence to settle problems with others if they often observe their parents turn violent against each other, or see themselves physically abused by their parents, or witness their parents use physical punishment to discipline them. Similarly, they are likely to engage in violence if they are members of a peer group that glorifies toughness and violence (Logan, 2009; Sutherland, 1939).

The three theories are summarized in Box 7.5.

QUESTIONS TO EXPLORE

1. Imagine yourself as a social researcher for the mayor's office in an urban environment. Your office has been commissioned to study a recent rise in school violence. Which of the three theoretical perspectives are you likely to use, and why? Which would you be the least likely to use, and why?

2. Are there certain forms of violence that any or all of these major theories are not well suited to explain? How so?

3. What kind of violence impacts the community in which you live? What do you think is the most likely cause? Why?

BOX 7.5   THEORETICAL THUMBNAIL

Explaining Interpersonal Violence

Theory	Focus	Insights
Functionalist Theory	The culture of violence	Violence originates from the cultural definition of violence as a normal way of solving interpersonal problems.
Conflict Theory	External restraint or social oppression	Violence erupts from the external restraint or social oppression suffered by the poor and minorities.
Symbolic Interaction Theory	Differential association or interaction	Violence breaks out when individuals associate or interact with violent individuals more often than nonviolent ones.

Review

SUMMARY

1. Gang rape involves mostly young men pressuring each other to prove their manhood by raping the same woman. Acquaintance rape is an extension of men's socially accepted aggressive sexual behavior. Campus rape is relatively common because of the influence of the rape-prone culture at the school. The sociological insight about campus rape can be used to prevent sexual violence by dealing with the consequences of masculinity.

2. Marital rape involves sexual violence that includes extremely degrading sex acts. Most offenders feel entitled to have sex with their wives regardless of the latter's wishes. In wartime rape, the army that invades a country rapes its women as if they are the conquered country's property. Female genital cutting is practiced in some African societies under the influence of patriarchy and the cultural belief that female genitalia such as the clitoris are masculine and hence unsightly on a woman. Male-against-male rape in prison is comparable to male-against-female rape in the larger society. It involves a more powerful person raping a smaller, weaker person; it is an expression of dominance more than sexual desire. Men can also be raped by other men, and more than half of these offenders and victims are heterosexual.

3. What encourages rape includes the rape culture, sexual permissiveness, and gender inequality.

4. The poor, African Americans, men, and young adults are more likely than the well-off, whites, women, and older adults, respectively, to commit homicide. People who live in the southern region of the United States, large cities, and rural areas are also more likely to kill than those who live in other regions and small towns. To taxi drivers in the city, trustworthy strangers are supposed to be older rather than younger, or female rather than male.

5. Homicides are most likely to occur during the weekend. They tend to take place outside the home if the killers are male, but at home if the offenders are female. Firearms are more often used than any other weapon. Homicide is more common in developing countries than in developed ones, and it is more prevalent in Latin America than other poor regions in the world.

6. Homicide often involves relatives, friends, or acquaintances. It may also involve the victim precipitating the killing, individuals turning a trivial argument into deadly violence, and the killer committing suicide after murdering others. Given the irrational and emotional nature of murder, sociologists generally contend, with evidence, that the death penalty does not deter murder; economists tend to argue otherwise.

7. In mass murder, a number of people are killed at the same time and place, while in serial murder, the victims are killed at different times and places. Most mass murderers are ordinarily people who may be disgruntled employees or lonely

heads of family. Most serial killers are also normal but more clever in eluding the police and more likely to torture their victims before killing them.

8. The three major sociological theories offer different explanations for violence. Functionalist theory attributes violence to living in a culture that encourages the use of violence to deal with interpersonal problems. Conflict theory blames violence on the experience of excessive external restraint, which results from a small, powerful group seeking to protect its own interests. Symbolic interaction theory ascribes violence to people who have learned to develop favorable "definitions" or attitudes about violence through differential association, which involves more frequent interaction with individuals who define violence as normal or permissible than with those who define violence as abnormal or objectionable.

CRITICAL THINKING QUESTIONS

1. Take a position on the capital punishment debate. In Box 7.4 we have presented the conflicting views on whether the death penalty reduces murder. Do you believe the death penalty serves to reduce or increase violent crime? Provide support for your answer.

2. Review the Internet resources at the end of this chapter. Is any information provided that would be useful to you, your community, or your school? How would your community or school benefit directly from this information?

3. In your opinion, considering the forms of violence that are most relevant in your community, do you feel that violent crimes of a sexual and nonsexual nature should carry the same sentence or penalty? Why or why not?

INTERNET RESOURCES

The National Coalition Against Domestic Violence (http://www.ncadv.org/) assists victims of violent crimes and policy makers alike, offering public resources such as fact sheets, support networks, victim success stories, legal assistance, emotional support, and crisis intervention.

The National Organization for Women has developed a detailed "toolkit" for victims of violence and for antiviolence advocates. The toolkit (http://www .now.org/issues/violence/NOW_Sexual_Assault_Toolkit.pdf) includes survival tips for victims of violence, shows how to curb future violence through education, and promotes strict compliance with antiviolence statutes for universities.

The Rape Crisis Center (http://www.rapecrisis.com) provides victims, friends, and family members a variety of free resources including crisis intervention, survivor tips, referrals, educational/awareness training, and counseling services.

How safe is your campus? http://www.ope.ed.gov/security/GetOneInstitution Data.aspx

In compliance with the Jeanne Clery Act, the Office of Postsecondary Education of the U.S. Department of Education reports crime data for all postsecondary institutions that receive Title IV funding (i.e., those that participate in federal student aid programs).

The Office of Violence Against Women (http://www.ovw.usdoj.gov/) offers free access to up-to-date information on victims' rights legislation, grant funding, and a variety of reports on dating violence, stalking, sexual assault, domestic violence, and survival strategies for victims.

The FBI's *Uniform Crime Reports* (http://www.fbi.gov/ucr/ucr.htm) is a list of all official arrests compiled annually by the FBI from arrest data reported by all criminal justice agencies in the United States (which number close to 17,000). Through this site, you can track all forms of violent and property crime.

The *Hate Crime Statistics* report can be viewed at http://www.fbi.gov/ucr/ucr. htm#hate. This report presents crime data regarding reported crimes that were in some way motivated by an established bias against the victim's perceived race, religion, ethnicity, sexual orientation, or disability.

The U.S. Department of Justice houses the official Bureau of Justice Statistics reports online at http://www.ojp.usdoj.gov/bjs/. A variety of reports and statistics on homicide trends, drug crimes, intimate partner violence, and other forms of violent crime for both adults and juveniles can be navigated from this link. The topics covered include a wide range of information pertaining to specific crimes, criminals, and victims. Take some time to explore. If you have any interest in topics pertaining to violence, you will find something of interest at this site.

Sexual Behavior

Sexting
Sending nude or seminude photos electronically.

Sending nude or seminude photos electronically, a social phenomenon known as sexting, is a fast-growing trend among teenagers. In a recent survey of some 1,300 teens aged 13 to 19 years across the United States, 20% say they have sexted, even though most think it could be a crime. Phillip Alpert, who lives in Florida, found out the hard way. When he had just turned 18 years old, he had an argument with his 16-year-old girlfriend and then sent a naked picture of her to dozens of her friends and family members. As Alpert explains, "It was a stupid thing I did because I was upset and tired and it was the middle of the night and I was an immature kid." The law enforcement officials in his city saw it differently. They arrested him and charged him with distributing child pornography, a felony of which he was found guilty. The judge sentenced him to 5 years' probation. Worse yet, he was required by Florida law to register as a sex offender, joining the ranks of pedophiles who have been convicted of sexually molesting children (Feyerick and Steffen, 2009).

But is sexting really a social problem? As observed in Chapter 1, a social problem consists of both an objective reality and a subjective perception. As an objective reality, a social problem possesses some harmful quality. And as a subjective perception, a social problem is perceived as such by some people. Sexting does have these two characteristics of a social problem. First, sexting has some harmful consequences for the girls whose nude photos are disseminated, because they are subjected to ridicule and taunts. Second, sexting is apparently viewed by many people as a social problem. After all, it is treated as child pornography in nearly every state. In this chapter, we will analyze various forms of sexual behavior that fall into the category of social problems in the same way as sexting.

■ The Sociological Nature of Sex

It is widely believed that sex comes naturally, that everybody instinctively knows how to have sex. But this popular belief is false. Only animals are born with a *sex instinct*, an innate biological mechanism that causes its carrier to have sex only in a certain way and at a certain time. All dogs, for example, are instinctively programmed to use the same coital position, with the male mounting and entering the female from behind. They also instinctively copulate for reproduction only. They do not have sex unless the female is in heat—the period when she is ovulating and susceptible to pregnancy.

Humans, in contrast, do not have a sex instinct. This is why we, unlike lower animals, are able to have sex in many different ways and all year round—in fact, most of the time when the female is not ovulating. What we have is only a *sex drive*, a biological potential for, rather than a determinant of, sexual desire or action. Whether, when, where, or how we will turn our sex drive into a certain sexual act depends on the nature of our socialization. The way we are socialized is subject to the influence of social and cultural forces so that human sexuality tends to vary from group to group within a multicultural society such as the United States and from society to society around the globe.

Sexual Diversity in the United States

In the United States, certain sexual practices vary with such social factors as gender, education, race, religion, class, and geography. First, men masturbate more than women of a similar age. Men above age 24 years and mostly married masturbate *more* than those who are younger and mostly unmarried. This fact undermines the popular belief that people are more likely to masturbate if they do not have a sex partner. The general public erroneously assumes that masturbation is only an outlet for sexual tension, a substitute for the sexually deprived. The fact is that masturbation turns out to be a part of being sexually active; the more sex people have, the more likely they will masturbate.

Second, the more educated people are, the more likely they engage in oral sex. Whites are also more likely to do so when compared with Hispanic and African Americans.

Third, the more religiously conservative, the less interest in oral sex. The apparent discomfort with oral sex among the less educated and among Hispanic and African Americans may owe largely to their religious conservatism.

Fourth, the poor segments of the U.S. population tend to use a no-nonsense, quick, silent approach to sex, while those who are richer are more likely to practice an elaborate sexuality. The affluent are inclined to use a larger variety of sexual techniques, such as lengthy foreplay, oral sex, mutual masturbation, and different coital positions.

Fifth, the rate of homosexuality is higher in large cities than in small towns and rural areas. The rate is also higher among the relatively well educated and affluent than among the less educated and less affluent. Moreover, a higher percentage of whites than African Americans identify themselves as gay (Laumann and Michael, 2001; Michael et al., 1994).

Sexual Diversity Around the World

Sexual behavior differs more greatly among societies. In the Western world, some form of kissing accompanies sexual intercourse. The Balinese of Indonesia do not kiss at all, and the Thonga of East Africa, to whom kissing is also unknown, said with disgust when they first saw Europeans kiss: "Look at them—they eat each other's saliva and dirt."

In the United States, most married couples make love about once or twice a week, but the frequency of sex is much higher or lower in other societies. For example, the Mangaians of Polynesia make love and have an orgasm at least once every night, and the Aranda of Australia copulate as often as three times every night. In contrast, the Hindus in India make love less frequently than people in the United States. This relative infrequency relates to the belief of many Hindu men that semen is a source of strength and therefore should not be wasted (Ford and Beach, 1970; Harris, 1995).

In our society, where premature ejaculation is considered a problem, men strive for prolonged intercourse. In more male-dominant societies, however, such as East Bay in Melanesia, where *delayed* ejaculation is considered a hang-up, men try to achieve orgasm as fast as they can—usually in 15 to 30 seconds (Reiss, 1986).

Homosexuality may appear very common in Western societies. But it is even more common in some preindustrial societies, such as the Etoro tribe of Papua New Guinea and people on the Caribbean Island of Carriacou.

Homosexuality is far from prevalent in Western societies, but it is widely practiced in some preindustrial societies, such as the Etoro tribe of Papua New Guinea and the people on the Caribbean island of Carriacou. Male homosexuality flourishes among the Etoro because of their belief that young men can boost their supply of semen by fellating older men. On the other hand, the prevalence of female homosexuality on the island of Carriacou has to do with migration of men in search of work. For most of the year when migrant husbands are away from home, older married women seek sexual favors and emotional support from younger single women (Harris, 1995).

Changes in U.S. Sexual Attitude

Most Americans are more sexually liberal than four decades ago. Today, sex is no longer the hush-hush matter it used to be. Nudity can be seen in theaters, in movies, and on television. Pornographic magazines and films are easily available. Homosexuality has become more open. Cohabitation, oral sex, and the number of sex partners have increased. These changes are the obvious consequences of the sexual revolution that has swept the United States over the last four decades. The revolution has also brought about some basic changes in our sexual attitude that are important to understand because they could explain why what used to be regarded as social problems may no longer be today.

First, there is more tolerance for various forms of sexual behavior. Consider the tolerance for homosexuality. Many more people today believe that homosexual acts between consenting adults should be legal. This reflects the attitude that it is all right for others to do what we may not want to do ourselves. The same kind of tolerance extends to premarital sex. Those who want to postpone sexual relations until they are married do not mind if their friends engage in premarital sex. They may say something like, "Premarital sex

People who want to postpone sexual relations until they are married do not mind if their friends engage in premarital sex.

might work for others. That's fine with me, though I would not do it myself." They may say the same thing about people seeking casual sex through the Internet (see Box 8.1).

BOX 8.1   USING SOCIOLOGICAL INSIGHTS

Beware the Hidden Price of Internet Hookups

On the surface it appears very easy to find an attractive and anonymous person to have casual sex with. You only need to visit the Casual Encounters section of Craigslist.com. However, it harbors certain dangers that you may want to guard against. In 2009 a radio news reporter was stabbed to death in his Brooklyn home by a teenager who answered his Craigslist ad seeking a sexual partner. In the same year, a 26-year-old woman was murdered in a Boston hotel room by a man who answered her ad on Craigslist. People who regularly use Craigslist in search of casual sex have reacted to the violent encounters in ways that ranged from mildly concerned to indifferent. This doesn't mean they throw caution to the wind, as one man who has used Craigslist for casual sex at least a dozen times remarks, "I'm always cautious, always meeting in public." But the seeming acceptance of the crimes is concerning, as another man who has used Craigslist for 5 years says, "In a city of 8 million-plus, this sort of thing was bound to happen statistically."

It is not only the huge size of the population that makes it likely for casual encounters to turn violent; it is also the very nature of the casual encounter that encourages criminal behavior. In catering to the erotic underbelly of society, the Craigslist's Casual Encounter section offers anonymity as a turn-on but at the price of courting danger. As a researcher observes, "We know from basic sex research that anonymity can augment satisfaction in sexual arousal." But anonymity also has a special attraction to dangerous individuals because it makes it easy for them to take risks in harming others in any way they want. As a researcher explains, "A lot of these people have a narcissistic, sociopathic side where they don't have a lot of empathy for other people. . . . The Internet is fabulous for these people."

Not all the Internet hookups are dangerous, however. They run the gamut from the erotic to the bizarre but not necessarily harmful. As one satisfied male client of Craigslist says, "I've met some extraordinarily beautiful women. . . . Craigslist often fulfills its promise of delivering erotic thrills for a minimal effort." In another scenario, a saleswoman posts elegantly written ads seeking a man who will meet her in a public place so she can go to the bathroom, remove her panties, and then hand them to him in an envelope, for which the recipient pays her a small replacement fee. She says she got an erotic thrill from giving men her used underwear, knowing they would use it as a fetish. These people may be narcissistic but apparently far from dangerous. Still we cannot be sure if some may turn out to be sociopathic as well (Quenqua, 2009).

Double sexual standard
The social norm that allows males, but not females, to have certain sexual experiences.

Second, the **double sexual standard**—the social norm that allows males, but not females, to have certain sexual experiences—is not as pervasive as it was in the past. One indication has been the increase in women's premarital experience. Moreover, more women than before expect to enjoy sex and reach orgasm. This means there are now more women who enjoy sexual freedom that has traditionally been "for men only." The double standard has not disappeared completely, though. While women may no longer be condemned for losing their virginity before marriage, they may be ridiculed for having multiple sex partners, often being called "sluts." Men with the same experience, however, are more likely to be called "studs," a term that connotes more approbation than opprobrium.

Third, there is a fundamental change in the perceived purpose of marital sex. In the past, the primary motive for sex in marriage was procreation. Today, most couples want recreation. Thus couples are now much more inclined to engage in a variety of sex acts, such as prolonged foreplay and oral sex, rather than only vaginal intercourse, because the former is aimed at seeking pleasure and the latter reproduction.

Fourth, a new sexual morality has largely replaced the old. In the past, people were more concerned with the marital status of the sexual partners, but today they are more interested in the quality of the partners' relationship. According to the old ethic, a sex act that occurs within marriage is moral, and a sex act that takes place outside marriage is immoral. But according to the new ethic, regardless of whether a sex act is marital or nonmarital, it is moral if the couple love each other and immoral if they sexually exploit each other. Thus, in the old days, premarital sex was widely condemned but marital rape was condoned. Today, marital rape is more likely to be condemned and premarital sex condoned.

Sociologists have referred to supporters of the new sex ethic as *relationalists* for believing in sex as part of a loving relationship, and supporters of the old ethic as *traditionalists* for having long regarded premarital sex as wrong. According to a national survey, relationalists now make up nearly half of the U.S. adult population and traditionalists about a third, with roughly a fifth—the rest of the population— being *recreationalists*, who believe that sex offers only pleasure and has nothing to do with love (Laumann and Michael, 2001; Michael et al., 1994).

■ Teen Sex

Nowadays more than half of U.S. teenagers are sexually active. Compared to their peers of 30 or 40 years ago, teens now have sex younger, have more sexual partners, and have more one-night stands. Further, teens are more likely to get sexually transmitted disease such as herpes, gonorrhea, or human immunodeficiency virus (HIV), and U.S. teens have the highest rate of premarital pregnancy in the industrial world. The sex education that encourages teens to abstain from sex until marriage has worked in some ways, but with some unintended consequences. First, in schools where they have pledged abstinence, teens tend to delay having sex, but they are also less likely to use contraception when having sex. Second, the emphasis on abstinence in sex education has led some teens to maintain "technical virginity" by performing oral sex, which they do not view as real sex because it cannot cause pregnancy. Most of these "virgins" limit their oral sex to just one partner, though, not multiple partners as popularly believed (Guttmacher Institute, 2010; Jayson, 2010b; Yabroff, 2008).

There is, however, a difference between male and female teens in having premarital sex or abstaining from it. As shown by a study of teenagers, males with high self-esteem are more likely to engage in sex, but females with high self-esteem are more likely to abstain. Apparently, the traditional double standard still influences the teen world: Sexually active young men are looked up to as studs, but sexually active young women are looked down on as sluts. Young women are further caught in a double bind: If they maintain their virginity, they risk being stigmatized as a tease. To get around both the "slut" and "tease" stigmas, many teen girls become sexually active within a relationship—by having sex with their boyfriend or somebody they know well rather than a stranger or mere acquaintance (Dunn, 2010; Spencer et al., 2002).

■ Extramarital Sex

Widely known as adultery, infidelity, or an affair, extramarital sex involves a married person having sex with "the other" woman or man. An overwhelming majority of Americans frown on extramarital sex. About 92% of Americans said in a national survey that they consider adultery "morally wrong." Given the widespread disapproval of extramarital sex, it is not surprising that only a relatively small minority engage in it, with 25% of married men and 17% of married women having had at least one affair in their lifetime. Nevertheless, adultery appears very common if the percentages are translated into numbers: At least 19 million American men and 12 million American women have committed adultery. "That's a helluva lot of people being unfaithful," said a sex researcher (Ebenkamp, 2001; Michael et al., 1994; Newport, 2009; Norman, 1998). Moreover, the rate of infidelity has significantly increased among certain groups of people over the last two decades (see **Box 8.2**).

BOX 8.2   WHAT RESEARCH REVEALS

The Changing Landscape of Infidelity

If we just want to know whether the infidelity rate among married couples as a whole is going up, we don't see really impressive changes. However, if we look at specific gender and age groups, we will see some very significant changes.

According to recent surveys, the groups with the greatest increase of infidelity over the last two decades are older men, older women, and young couples. The lifetime rate of infidelity for men older than 60 years of age had increased from 20% in 1991 to 28% in 2006. For women older than 60 years of age, the increase is more striking, up from 5% in 1991 to 15% in 2006. As for relatively young couples (younger than 35 years old), their infidelity rate ramped up to about 18% in 2006 from 14% in 1991.

Why are older men and older women much more likely to cheat on their spouses now than before? Researchers attribute the reason to a host of newer drugs and treatments that enhance sexual performance. These include Viagra and other remedies for erectile dysfunctions for men, and estrogen and testosterone supplements that improve women's sex drive and vaginal health. What about the significant rise in infidelity among young couples? Researchers trace it to the increasing availability of online pornography, along with other electronic gadgets such as cell phones, e-mail, and instant messaging, which make it easier to form intimate relationships. However, surveys also show some positive trends. The most notable one is that married men and women appear to spend more time together—and have sex with their spouse more than once a week (Parker-Pope, 2008).

Popular Myths

Most married men are faithful to their spouses, but they do wish at one time or another to have an extramarital affair. In the late 1940s, sex researcher Alfred Kinsey found that over 70% of married men had such a wish. They apparently believed in the myth that extramarital sex is far more satisfying than marital sex. However, research has shown otherwise. Perhaps because extramarital copulation is mostly carried out in secrecy, and frequently charged with tension and guilt, the experience is far from gratifying. According to one study, two-thirds of married men rated their marital sex "very pleasurable," but fewer than half of the unfaithful husbands gave the same rating to their extramarital coitus. Similarly, while as high as 53% of married women regularly reached orgasm with their husbands, only 39% of the straying wives did so in extramarital intercourse (Katchadourian, 1989).

Another myth about extramarital sex is that people have affairs because they are oversexed. Research suggests, however, that those who engage in adultery are far from oversexed. They generally are much less sexually active—having a lot less sex—than monogamous couples (Adler, 1996; Pittman, 1993). If being oversexed is not the cause of infidelity, what is? The answer can be found in a set of social and cultural factors, as suggested by the fact that the incidence of extramarital sex varies from one group to another in the United States as well as from one culture to another in the world.

Cultural Influences

Adultery is considered legitimate in a few cultures, but illegitimate in most cultures. First, let us take a look at legitimate adultery. It takes place in societies where it is by definition socially approved. Among the Kofyar of Nigeria, for example, a woman who is unhappy with her husband but does not want to divorce may, without seeking his consent, take an extra lover, who lives openly with her in her husband's house. A Kofyar man may do the same for the same reason. In many Italian towns on the Adriatic coast, virtually every married man has an affair with a woman whom he visits regularly. Sometimes younger male servants visit rich men's wives, while rich men occasionally copulate with their maids or cooks. But it is taboo for any married person to ever speak of his or her affair. Boasting, gossiping, or even whispering to others about one's dalliance can expose the extensive network of extramarital relationships, seriously threatening their highly cherished community cohesion and family life (Fisher, 1994). Legitimate adulteries such as these do not exist in American society.

Illegitimate adulteries exist not only in the United States but also in many other societies. They vary in form from one society to another. Among the Lozi of eastern Africa, adultery does not involve sexual intercourse. If a man walks with a married woman he is not related to, or if he gives her a beer, he has committed adultery. By contrast, in most other societies, illegitimate adulteries always involve copulation. To conservative Christians who interpret the Bible literally, even divorce and remarriage, which involves copulation, is condemned as adultery. As Jesus says in Mark 10:11, "Whoever divorces his wife and marries another commits adultery against her; and if she divorces her husband and marries another, she commits adultery." In practically every society, women have historically been punished for adultery more harshly than men. In Muslim societies, unfaithful wives are known to have been whipped, caned, or even stoned to death. Generally, because illegitimate adulteries are socially condemned, they occur less frequently than legitimate ones (Fisher, 1994; Ilesanmi, 2010; Lawson, 1988).

Social Factors

Under the influence of the U.S. culture that discourages infidelity, some groups of Americans are nonetheless more likely than others to cheat on their spouses. As indicated by various studies, men are more likely than women to have an affair; extramarital sex occurs more frequently among those who have had sex before marriage; the less religious generally have a higher incidence of extramarital sex than the more religious; and lower-income people are more likely than their higher-income peers to be unfaithful to their spouses (Duncombe et al., 2004; Janus and Janus, 1993).

Sociobiologists regard the gender difference in adultery as the most significant social factor because it exists in virtually all societies. Sociobiologists trace it to humankind's long evolutionary past when men had to impregnate more women to produce more young so as to ensure the survival of their genes. However, the last thing that today's philandering men want is to produce babies. After all, most people, both male and female, now regard the primary purpose of sex as recreation rather than procreation. The evolutionary theory, then, merely reflects the patriarchal belief that men should prove their manhood by screwing around. It is this widely shared belief that causes men to philander more than women do. Most male philanderers also differ from their affair partners. The men are primarily interested in sex, but the women are looking for love, feeling that they no longer love their husband and that their affair partner is the true love of their life (Allan, 2004; Pittman, 1993).

■ Swinging: The Lifestyle

While most extramarital sex involves having an affair behind the spouse's back, some takes the form of an open sexual activity in which both husband and wife agree to participate. Such extramarital sex is widely known as *swinging* or *the lifestyle*. Swinging involves married couples exchanging spouses for sex only. In the eye of the general public, swinging is much more deviant than traditional infidelity. This perception could explain why swinging is considerably less common. While about 20% of married couples have cheated on their spouses, only about 1% or 2% have engaged in swinging. Still, thanks to the Internet, it is now much easier than before to find swinging couples at any locale. In addition, swinging couples are available in sex clubs in large cities (Gould, 2000; Jenks, 1998; Levy, 1999).

Swinging
The exchange of spouses for sex only by married couples.

Despite their extremely deviant lifestyle, swingers do not stand out as far different from average Americans. Most are middle-class, suburban whites. The majority are between 25 and 45 years old. Politically they are somewhat conservative, particularly if they live in Middle America. They do not attend church regularly, but they often send their children to Sunday school or give them religious instruction. Both the men and women lack outside interests, hobbies, and activities. In general, swingers appear bored, frustrated, and incapable of living a joyful and stimulating life, much like ordinary Americans living lives of "quiet desperation." As one researcher puts it, "Other than their sexual deviance, the most remarkable thing about the swingers is how unremarkable they are." Compared to conventional people, swingers have moved more often, have been living in their communities for fewer years, and are less likely to have a religious identification. Given these experiences, they presumably feel less restricted or controlled by social institutions (Gilmartin, 1975; Jenks, 1998).

Swingers regard their lifestyle as a marital enhancement, believing that "the couple that swings together stays together." For some couples, swinging has indeed been found to improve marital relations. Studies have found a greater amount of intimacy, affection, and communication, as well as a higher frequency of marital sex between swinging couples than between conventional spouses (Gilmartin, 1975; Rubin and Adams, 1986; Wheeler and Kilmann, 1983). Swinging may appear to improve marriage if the swinging couple is able to separate sex from emotion, enjoying sex with the other couples as pure entertainment without getting emotionally involved with them. However, swinging tends to have a negative impact on those who are more sensitive or romantic, unable to completely separate sex from emotion. Having expected to be treated by their swinging partners as *persons*, they are likely to be disappointed when they are used as mere sex *objects*. They are likely to drop out of swinging, often in disgust. In short, swinging goes in two directions: It may swing in the direction of positive consequences or in the opposite direction of negative consequences. The nature of the consequences depends on the individual involved rather than the activity itself (de Visser and McDonald, 2007; Denfeld, 1974).

■ Pornography

Pornography
Sexually explicit material including pictures or words.

It is illegal to distribute **pornography**—sexually explicit material including pictures or words—but the law is not strictly enforced. A large majority of Americans are opposed to the distribution as well as the use of pornography, but it can be found everywhere, and most people, especially men, have used it. We will take a close look at this ubiquity of pornography and its impact on society.

Porn Everywhere

Pornography has become an enormous industry today because the demand for it has soared over the past several decades. The number of hard-core video rentals, for example, skyrocketed from only 75 million in 1985 to 665 million in 1996. Today, the United States has turned into by far the world's leading producer of hard-core videos, churning them out at the astonishing rate of about 150 new titles a week. Also widely disseminated are computer porn, sex magazines, adult cable programming, peep shows, live sex acts, and phone sex. The amount of money spent on all the adult materials is much larger than Hollywood's domestic box office receipts or the entire revenue from rock and country music recordings (Egan, 2000; Schlosser, 1997).

The porn industry's fantastic growth has stemmed mostly from the invasion of pornographic videos into mainstream society. In the past, most people were too embarrassed to go to seedy movie theaters and adult bookstores, but today they can watch porn videos in the privacy of their homes and hotel rooms. That's why cable TV companies profit greatly from pornography videos. Even large, respectable hotel chains such as Hyatt, Holiday Inn, and Marriott reportedly earn millions each year by making their guests feel at home with adult films to watch in their rooms (Ackman, 2004; Egan, 2000).

There is a huge variety of hard-core videos to meet every conceivable consumer demand: videos that feature gay, lesbian, straight, transsexual, interracial, or older couples; "cat fighting" videos that show naked women wrestling each other or joining forces to beat up a naked man; videos for sadomasochists, aficionados of bondage or spanking, or seekers of verbal abuse; and other kinds of videos too numerous to list. Other forms of pornography, particularly computer porn and phone sex, have also proliferated, generating enormous revenues for Internet service providers (Egan, 2000; Koch, 2008; Schlosser, 1997).

The Impact of Porn

Research has produced conflicting findings on the impact of porn. Some studies support the antiporn feminist and conservative view that pornography is harmful, but other studies confirm the anticensorship, liberal view that pornography is harmless. Let us analyze these two views and the studies supporting them.

PORN AS HARMFUL. To some feminists, a woman has the legal right to free expression via pornography even though the material is distasteful. However, many other feminists are opposed to pornography and want it banned because they believe that pornography is harmful to women.

To support this view, antiporn feminists point out many laboratory studies showing that exposure to violent pornography encourages male aggression against women. In one experiment, for example, male subjects were divided into two groups: One watched a film depicting sexual violence against women; the other watched a nonviolent film. After seeing the movies, the subjects who had watched the violent film were more likely to administer electrical shocks to women than were those who had watched the nonviolent film (Donnerstein et al., 1987).

Conservatives also find pornography harmful. They believe that sexually explicit materials can destroy traditional family values and, by extension, the entire society. Often cited to support this belief is the research finding that long exposure to explicit depictions of common sex acts often leads men to seek portrayals of less common, more deviant practices, such as violent, sadomasochistic, or bestial sex. Such men are then more likely to engage in various deviant sexual activities, which they find exciting. At the same time, they become more likely to find conventional, monogamous, or marital sex boring. All this is considered to have "devastating consequences" for traditional monogamy, marriage, family, and society. There is, however, no clear-cut evidence that porn wrecks many marriages, let alone threatens the survival of society (Linz and Malamuth, 1993; Paul, 2004).

PORN AS HARMLESS. Liberals are opposed to the censorship of sexually explicit material not only because it violates the freedom of expression but also because they view pornography as basically harmless.

To support their view, liberals usually cite studies showing that, in the real world outside the laboratory, exposure to sexually explicit material does not cause rape or other sex crimes. For example, the availability of pornography in the United States increased substantially between 1960 and 1969, but the incidence of rape did not go up as much during the same period. Similarly, when the advent of the VCR vastly increased the dissemination of hard-core videos, the rate of rape did not increase to the same extent.

In Denmark, in the late 1960s, after all legal prohibitions on the sale of pornography were removed, sex crimes did not rise but instead dropped sharply. Today most Danes even find hard-core porn beneficial to their lives, which they credit with improving not only their sex lives but their general quality of life. To liberals, then, all these data strongly suggest that pornography is harmless (Diamond, 2009; Hutson, 2008).

We may conclude that pornography may be harmless for the majority of men but harmful for a few men who are already inclined to be sexually violent or deviant. Porn is also more likely to be harmful if it portrays sexual violence, but more likely to be harmless if it merely shows nudity or nonviolent sex acts (Hutson, 2008; Kingston et al., 2008; Procida and Simon, 2003).

■ Nude Dancing

Nude dancing enables the male customer to enjoy the fantasy of sexual intimacy with an attractive woman. At topless bars and lingerie shows, the dancers are scantily clothed and often do not wear panties so they can flash their customers. At nude bars, however, the dancers remove all their clothing. Because they make most or all of their money from tips, dancers do their best to please the customers. Not surprisingly, then, dancers pay hardly any attention to the art and aesthetics of dancing, which they know is not the audience's interest. Instead, maximum effort is made to catch and hold the customers' attention on what they have come to the club to see. Thus, as customers seated near the edge of the stage are prepared with cash in hand to tip her, the dancer may move from one man to another exposing her private parts for their close-up view. She may later lie on her back, spread her legs, and repeatedly stroke her genitalia. If she becomes profusely wet, she may snatch the baseball cap off the head of a client and wipe it between her legs and give it back to him (Schiff, 1999).

At nude bars, most customers fantasize about having an attractive woman treat them like a million bucks, and it is this fantasy the dancer aims to fulfill.

Most customers are working-class men. They are far from loaded. In a patriarchal society where successful or wealthy older men often get trophy wives, it may be difficult or impossible for those working-class men to get a young and attractive woman to be romantically interested in them. In their everyday lives, such a woman might not even look at them or talk to them, let alone expose herself to them. But they can fantasize about having such a woman treat them like a million bucks, and it is this fantasy the nude dancer aims to fulfill (Schiff, 1999).

As for the dancer, she can expect to make as much as $75,000 a year. This could be considered an excellent earning, because most nude dancers have only a high school education and few job skills. Not surprisingly, money is by far the number one reason for becoming a nude dancer. In spite of the high pay, however, nude dancing is still widely regarded as highly disreputable. This does not seem to disturb most dancers, because they do not identify themselves with their stigmatized work. They see themselves instead as wives, single mothers, or some other conventional role, and refrain from telling family, friends, and others what they do. They feel that their dancing job does not reflect their true self, their true values, who they really are. Most find their work empowering, feeling that they can command so much attention and interest from the audience that it is willing to pay them handsomely. They are also confident that they can stop customer antics. If a customer touches their private parts, they may use their hips to bump his head and face, knocking him backward (Reid, Epstein, and Benson, 1995; Schiff, 1999; Spivey, 2005; Wood, 2001).

◾ Prostitution

Prostitution—the selling of sexual services—is legal in many countries in Europe and elsewhere. It is not legal in the United States, except in some counties of Nevada. Nonetheless, prostitution has long been big business in our society. Every year billions of dollars are spent on the sexual favors of prostitutes, whose profit amounts to at least 10 times the annual budget of the U.S. Department of Justice. The number of prostitutes has been estimated to range from 84,000 to 336,000 (Potterat et al., 1990). However, such estimates grossly underrepresent the actual number of prostitutes because they are based almost entirely on sex workers who are known to the police while failing to take into account many who are not.

Prostitution
The selling of sexual services.

Prostitution is not legal in the United States, except in some counties of Nevada. But it has long been big business in our society.

Myths About Prostitutes

It is widely believed that prostitution is the oldest profession in the world. This is a myth; the oldest profession is priesthood. There are many other myths. We will discuss a few (Perkins, 1991; Weitzer, 2005).

First, in folklore and sometimes even in scientific literature, prostitutes are often presented as nymphomaniacs, having an insatiable desire for sex with many men. This idea is male fantasy and is not substantiated by facts. Before going into the sex business, most prostitutes did not have many more sex partners than other, average women. What is true, though, is that prostitutes generally have started having sex at a younger age than other women.

Second, some people believe just the opposite of the first myth, namely that prostitutes are sexually frigid. Actually, when they have sex with their husbands or boyfriends, prostitutes as a group are more responsive than other women—more able to achieve orgasm. The majority of call girls even frequently have orgasms with their clients, primarily because those men tend to treat them like girlfriends. Only streetwalkers are unlikely to experience orgasm with their customers, who are much less friendly than call girls' clientele.

Third, there are two conflicting beliefs about how prostitutes treat their customers. On the one hand, prostitutes are believed to be nasty and hard-hearted—as suggested by the saying "as cold as a whore's heart"; on the other, they are romanticized as sweet and warmhearted—"a hooker with a heart of gold." In reality, however, the average prostitute's attitude toward her customers is quite similar to that of anyone who provides services to a diverse clientele. Some clients she likes, a few others she dislikes, and toward most of them she simply feels neutral. However, being paid more and treated better, call girls, escorts, and brothel prostitutes are more likely than streetwalkers to like their clients.

Fourth, most prostitutes are believed to be drug addicts or to have turned to prostitution to support their drug habits. They are also assumed to have emotional problems. These beliefs may hold true for streetwalkers, because they are more likely than conventional women to be addicted to drugs, but they make up only a minority (10–30%) of prostitutes. The majority of prostitutes, including call girls, escorts, house prostitutes, and others who work indoors rather than on the street, are not drug addicts. They are also relatively free of emotional problems, while streetwalkers are more prone to have psychological issues resulting from the stress and danger of working the streets (Perkins, 1991; Weitzer, 2005).

Similarities of Prostitutes to Conventional Women

Many studies give a distorted view of prostitutes as heavy drug users and victims of low self-esteem, or as being socially immature, emotionally disturbed, or pitifully abnormal in some other way. These studies are biased for having focused mostly on adolescent streetwalkers or prostitutes who have been arrested by police or helped by social agencies. Such prostitutes indeed have more problems in their lives than other sex workers. However, they are a minority, representing only about 10–30% of all prostitutes and differing significantly from most other prostitutes (Perkins, 1991; Weitzer, 2005).

The prostitutes in Roberta Perkins's study are reasonably representative of the women in the sex business. Although they are Australian, they are comparable to their counterparts in the United States and other Western societies (Weitzer, 2005). Perkins found that most prostitutes do not differ significantly from conventional women in their social and sexual backgrounds.

First of all, they have the same desire as conventional women to be married and have a traditional family life. Among those who already have young children, there is a plan to quit turning tricks when the children are old enough to begin catching on to their mothers' stigmatized occupation. As one prostitute says, "My oldest son will be 13 this year, and I don't want to be at work much after that."

Second, prostitutes have about the same level of education as the general population of women. The percentages of prostitutes having been brought up in white-collar and blue-collar families are similar to those of conventional women.

Third, most prostitutes are not friendless, loveless, or particularly "promiscuous" in their private lives. Like most women, they live with their husbands, boyfriends, or children, or share apartments with friends. Because their occupation is highly stigmatized, however, they are significantly more likely than other women to be raped (Perkins, 1991; Weitzer, 2005).

Reasons for Selling Sex

It is widely believed that the common reasons for entering prostitution are drug addiction, severe poverty, low self-esteem, and emotional problems. Such problems have indeed driven most teenage streetwalkers into prostitution, but the large majority of prostitutes are different from these young hustlers. In one study, when prostitutes in a representative sample were asked why they sell sex, a different set of reasons emerged. The most common reasons are economic, such as wanting to make more money, being unemployed, supporting a family, or paying for an education, an overseas trip, a car, or some other specific thing. Money, then, is the most important reason for going into the sex business. This is no different from the reasons that most other people have for working in conventional businesses (Perkins, 1991).

These economic reasons, however, merely serve as a predisposing factor in entering prostitution. They are not enough for a woman to become a prostitute. She usually needs somebody to introduce her to the business of prostitution, as illustrated by the following accounts from two prostitutes (Perkins, 1991):

- I needed some money because I was having legal hassles and my present job wasn't bringing in enough to pay for this. A girlfriend of mine had an escort agency, and this seemed the quickest way to get the amount of money I needed.
- I met an old school friend, and we had lunch together. She told me she was a prostitute and how much money she made. She asked me if I would [go out with] her one night. But the fellows kept asking for me, not her. So, I thought, I must be sitting on a gold mine. And that's how I started.

It should be noted that most prostitutes in the United States *choose* to get into the skin trade, but their counterparts in other countries are more likely to be *coerced* into it (see Box 8.3).

BOX 8.3 GLOBAL PERSPECTIVE

Being Coerced into Prostitution

After the collapse of the Soviet Union in the early 1990s, many unemployed women in Russia and Eastern Europe have migrated to Western Europe and other prosperous countries to sell sex. In Germany today, at least a quarter of the prostitutes originate from the former communist world. In Israel, many newspaper ads offering "entertainment services" boast about "hot new Russians." In Japan, blond and blue-eyed Russian women have become the latest addition to fancy "hostess" bars. Even in profoundly religious Saudi Arabia, many Russian women have arrived to work as prostitutes. Some of these women have freely chosen to enter the skin trade, but most have been forced into it after arriving with phony promises of singing, dancing, modeling, or waitressing jobs (Gearan, 2006; Pristina and Chisinau, 2001).

Many prostitutes in those prosperous countries have also come from Latin America. They also have been tricked and coerced into prostitution. While in their home countries, they were initially offered legitimate-sounding jobs overseas, such as working in a nightclub. Then they were given money for visas and airline tickets as well as cash to present themselves as tourists to immigration authorities. Once abroad, they were forced to work as prostitutes to pay a huge fee. Smuggling women this way has become irresistible to organized criminals, who find it easier and more profitable than trafficking drugs and arms (Pratt, 2001).

Many more women in Asia have also been lured into Western Europe, the United States, and Japan with promises of legitimate jobs only to be sold into brothels. However, most Asian prostitutes remain in their home countries. They have come from poor villages to work mostly as waitresses, servants, barmaids, or other lowly jobs in large cities. They are then forced into prostitution. They cater to not only local men but also Japanese and Western male tourists who come to the poor Asian countries primarily or solely for sex. In fact, prostitution has become a major part of those Asian countries' tourist industry, which represents a significant sector of their national economy (Kuo, 2001; Pristina and Chisinau, 2001).

■ Sociological Theories of Prostitution

Functionalist and conflict theories explain why prostitution as a social phenomenon continues to exist despite efforts to eradicate it. Symbolic interaction theory explains how prostitutes as individuals see themselves, their customers, and the nature of their work.

Functionalist Theory

To functionalists, prostitution exists because it performs two kinds of functions. One is manifest (intended and obvious)—offering what customers want. This includes providing quick and unemotional sexual gratification, a variety of sex partners, and what conventional people may consider kinky sex. Another type of function is latent (unintended and unknown to most people). According to Kingsley Davis (1971), prostitution serves this function by ironically *strengthening the sexual morality* of society. More specifically, prostitution strengthens sexual morality by "keeping the wives and daughters of the respectable citizenry pure" (Davis, 1971). In other words, the sex industry encourages men to go to prostitutes for premarital sex, extramarital sex, and other "immoral" sex so that they do not have to persuade or pressure "respectable" women to engage in the same "immoral" sex. By thus preserving the sexual morality of conventional women, who constitute about half of humankind, the level of a society's morality should be higher than if many ordinary women engage in the same sexual "immoralities" as prostitutes do.

There is some evidence to support Davis's theory. In traditional Asian societies where prostitution is prevalent, "respectable" women are relatively unlikely to engage in "immoral" sex, while in modern Western societies where prostitution is less common, "respectable" women are more likely to get involved in "immoral" sex. Moreover, on many U.S. campuses, male students are more likely than their counterparts in Thailand to persuade or pressure college women to engage in such sexual "immorality" as premarital sex. There is, however, a problem with functionalist theory. It defines sexual morality in sexist terms, implying that only women, particularly prostitutes, are immoral when committing "immoral" sex. Thus, sexually "promiscuous" men, especially those who often patronize prostitutes, are not regarded as a threat to the moral order.

Conflict Theory

In explaining prostitution, conflict theory derives its ideas from feminism. To feminists, functionalist theory merely reflects a sexist society's view that "promiscuous" men are not a threat to the moral order; only "promiscuous" women such as prostitutes are. That's why in a sexist society prostitutes are far more likely to be arrested than their male customers for committing the same sexual act. Why are "promiscuous" men not considered a threat to the moral order in the first place? Because the moral system reflects the larger patriarchal, gender-stratified system in which men dominate and exploit women.

While dominating and exploiting women, the patriarchal system creates prostitution by producing both demand and supply for it. On the demand side, boys are socialized under the influence of patriarchy to be dominant over girls, and when boys become adult, they are expected to desire sexual domination of women, which can be easily realized through sex with prostitutes. If a young man does not want to visit a prostitute, his peers will pressure him to do so. On the supply side, girls are socialized to be submissive to boys and, later as adults, to men in work, play, or sex. At the same time, women are relegated to predominantly low-status employment, including prostitution. Taken together, these factors explain why prostitution is more prevalent in traditional societies marked by great gender inequality, when compared to more modern societies with less gender inequality.

While the patriarchal system with its gender inequality creates prostitution, prostitution in turn reinforces patriarchy. Feminists have often observed that prostitution "serves to perpetuate women's social subordination" (Overall, 1992). Thus, by renting their bodies as a commodity, prostitutes convey the message that men can use women like an object. Learning from this message, many men will continue to support the patriarchal structure of gender inequality, which further encourages prostitution.

Symbolic Interaction Theory

According to symbolic interaction theory, prostitutes see themselves as morally superior to conventional people. They insist that they are honest and others are dishonest. In the eyes of these sex workers, conventional women who marry so they may depend on their husbands for lifelong financial support—especially young women who marry wealthy older men—are, in effect, prostitutes; they simply are not honest enough to regard themselves as such. Prostitutes also see their so-called respectable customers as hypocrites for raising hell against them in public while visiting them in private. If most customers do not publicly condemn prostitutes, they essentially cheat on their wives by patronizing prostitutes. Many prostitutes, therefore, despise their customers, and try to exploit them by maximizing the fee and minimizing the service.

Prostitutes further believe that their sex work is good for society because it performs many important services. One service is believed capable of preventing sex crimes; as one prostitute puts it, "I believe that there should be more prostitution houses and what have you, and then we wouldn't have so many of these perverted idiots, sex maniacs, all sorts of weird people running around." Another service is believed to involve contributing to marital success. According to one prostitute, "I could say that a prostitute has held more marriages together as part of her profession than any divorce counselor. . . . The release of talking about an unhappy home situation may well have saved many a marriage, and possibly even lives, when nerves have been strained to a breaking point." Prostitutes liken themselves not only to marriage counselors but also to humanitarians, social workers, psychologists, or psychiatrists. One prostitute explains, "I don't regret doing it because I feel I help people. A lot of men that come over to see me don't come over for sex. They come over for companionship, someone to talk to" (Bryan, 1966; Hirschi, 1962).

Such a professional self-image has fueled civil rights movements among prostitutes in Western societies. In Great Britain, for example, prostitutes have long campaigned against the law that prohibits public solicitation, as in streets, hotels, and bars, arguing that peaceful soliciting should be as lawful as peaceful picketing. In the United States, prostitutes have formed unions with the aim of decriminalizing prostitution so that their working conditions can be improved and their sex work can be respected like any other legitimate profession. The most famous prostitutes' rights organization is COYOTE (Call Off Your Tired Ethics). It fights for full decriminalization of prostitution and the elimination of all legal restrictions on it. COYOTE argues that prostitutes have the right to sell sex because selling sex is not different from other kinds of work women do:

- A woman has the right to sell sexual services just as much as she has the right to sell her brains to a law firm where she works as a lawyer, or to sell her creative work to a museum when she works as an artist, or to sell her image to a photographer when she works as a model, or to sell her body when she works as a ballerina. (Jenness, 1990)

However, most feminists have rejected COYOTE's crusade to turn prostitution into a legitimate, respectable profession because they consider prostitution a form of sexual slavery—which they want prostitutes to get out of, not into. COYOTE has also failed to get support from most of the general public, legislators, and law enforcers (Weitzer, 1991). This symbolic interaction theory that looks into the prostitutes' subjective world is summarized along with functionalist and conflict theories in Box 8.4.

BOX 8.4   THEORETICAL THUMBNAIL

Explaining Prostitution

Theory	Focus	Insights
Functionalist Theory	The performance of manifest and latent functions creates prostitution	Prostitution offers services demanded by customers while strengthening sexual morality.
Conflict Theory	Patriarchy causes prostitution by producing demand and supply for it	Men are socialized to dominate women, and women are socialized to submit to men.
Symbolic Interaction Theory	Prostitutes' perceptions of themselves, their sex work, and their civil rights	Prostitutes see themselves as honest, their sex work as good for society, and their profession as legitimate.

QUESTIONS TO EXPLORE

1. If you were to conduct a research study on prostitution in your community, which of the three theories would you use as a guide? Why would you favor this theory over the others?

2. After considering each of the three theories, what would you consider to be the major limitations of each in studying prostitution?

3. The following Web site includes a variety of justifications for the legalization of sex work (including prostitution): http://www.sexwork.com/. After visiting the site, select at least one issue and play the devil's advocate by taking the opposing view.

Homosexuality

Although they approve of homosexuality, more than half of Americans are still opposed to gay marriage, with most states having passed new laws banning same-sex marriage. Homosexuality apparently continues to be a social problem but much less so today than before (Corliss, 2006; Leland, 2000; Robison, 2010).

The Myths of Homosexuality

There are many myths about **homosexuality**, sexual attraction to members of the same sex. The first myth stereotypes **gays** (exclusively homosexual men) as feminine, and **lesbians** (exclusively homosexual women) as masculine. Gays are thus believed to walk like women, talk like women, or look like women, and lesbians are believed to walk, talk, and look like men. In reality it is difficult to differentiate most gays and lesbians from **heterosexuals**, who are sexually attracted to members of the opposite sex. Most gays look and behave just like most heterosexual men, and most lesbians look and behave just like most heterosexual women.

The second myth asserts that gays like to molest or seduce young boys. The fact is that the great majority of gay men have no more sexual interest in young boys than the great majority of straight men have in little girls. Actually, most child molesters are heterosexual men.

The third myth views homosexuality as a symptom of mental illness. Some gays and lesbians, particularly those who go to psychiatrists, are perhaps emotionally disturbed, but so are some straights, especially those who go to psychiatrists. Therefore, just as it is wrong to conclude that straights are mentally ill, it is wrong to conclude that gays and lesbians are. This is why the American Psychiatric Association has, since 1973, not included "homosexuality" in its *Diagnostic and Statistical Manual* as a mental illness.

The fourth myth insists that gays and lesbians cannot be expected to have a satisfactory sex life because it is abnormal or unnatural. Research has shown no real difference between gays/lesbians and straights in their physical capacity to enjoy sex. There may, however, be a difference in styles of making love. Same-sex couples tend to treat sex as play, spending much time on foreplay—caressing various parts of the body—before directing attention to the genitals for achieving orgasm. Heterosexual couples are more likely to treat sex as work, bent on a quick attainment of orgasm.

The fifth myth suggests that people are either completely gay or completely straight. In reality, as Alfred Kinsey (1948) explained,

> [People] do not represent two discrete populations, heterosexual and homosexual. The world is not to be divided into sheep and goats. . . . It is a fundamental of taxonomy that nature rarely deals with discrete categories. Only the human mind invents categories and tries to force facts into separate pigeon holes. The living world is a continuum in each and every one of its aspects.

The difference between the sexes, then, is a matter of kind: People are either male or female. But the difference between sexual orientations is a matter of degree: Some people are more, or less, heterosexual (or homosexual) than others. Thus people vary from one another on a scale from one extreme of being exclusively heterosexual to the other extreme of being exclusively homosexual (see **Figure 8.1**). What are usually called gays and lesbians are exclusively homosexual men and women.

Homosexuals
Individuals who are sexually attracted to members of the same sex.

Gays
Exclusively homosexual men.

Lesbians
Exclusively homosexual women.

Heterosexuals
Individuals who are sexually attracted to members of the opposite sex.

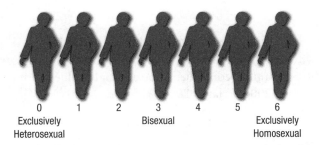

0 – Exclusively heterosexual
1 – Predominantly heterosexual, only incidentally homosexual
2 – Predominantly heterosexual, but more than incidentally homosexual
3 – Equally heterosexual and homosexual
4 – Predominantly homosexual, but more than incidentally heterosexual
5 – Predominantly homosexual, only incidentally heterosexual
6 – Exclusively homosexual

FIGURE 8.1 The Kinsey Heterosexual–Homosexual Continuum

The difference between the sexes is a matter of kind: People are either male or female. But the difference between sexual orientations is a matter of degree: Some people are more, or less, heterosexual (or homosexual) than others. Thus people vary in degrees on a continuum from one extreme of being exclusively heterosexual to the other extreme of being exclusively homosexual. What are usually called gays and lesbians are exclusively homosexual men and women.

Critical Thinking: *Does the continuum imply that most of the people known to themselves and others as straight have some homosexual characteristics? Explain your answer.*

Source: Reproduced from Alfred C. Kinsey, Wardell B. Pomeroy, and Clyde E. Martin. 1948. *Sexual Behavior in the Human Male.* Philadelphia: W. B. Saunders, p. 638. Reproduced by permission of the Kinsey Institute for Research in Sex, Gender, and Reproduction.

The Extent of Homosexuality

How many exclusively homosexuals are there in the United States? The answer depends on the definition of being a homosexual. Various studies have suggested that homosexuality involves one or more of these characteristics: (1) *same-sex feeling*—being attracted to a person of the same gender; (2) *same-sex behavior*—having sex with a same-gender person; and (3) *identifying oneself as gay or lesbian* (Savin-Williams, 2005). Reflecting these different definitions of homosexuality, the following data from a study of a representative sample of the U.S. population show the extent of the three different characteristics of homosexuality (Laumann et al., 1994; Michael et al., 1994):

- Persons with same-sex feeling: 6% of men; 4% of women
- Persons who have ever engaged in same-sex behavior: 9% of men; 4% of women
- Persons with gay or lesbian self-identification: 2.8% of men; 1.4% of women

Most of these numbers fall significantly below the 10% that has been widely cited from Kinsey's classic studies as the proportion of U.S. population being homosexuals. In the late 1940s and early 1950s, Kinsey found that 10% of U.S. adults were "predominantly" or "more or less exclusively homosexual." However, he discovered that only 2.5% were "exclusively homosexual," which is quite similar to the proportion of today's Americans identifying themselves as gay or lesbian (Kinsey et al., 1948, 1953; Voeller, 1990).

The Gay Experience

Compared to straight men, gay men are more "promiscuous" (sexually active). Contrary to popular belief, though, the higher incidence of promiscuity among gay men does not come from being gay itself. It is mainly a product of *heterosexual* society, which socializes men to be more sexually active than women. Through its male-dominated culture, heterosexual society imposes a double standard of sexual behavior on men and women. If a woman is very sexually active, she is likely to be scorned as a "slut," but a man with the same experience is more likely to be praised as a "stud." Men are thus encouraged to be more sexually active. Because they have been brought up in the same heterosexual culture as straight men, gay men equally have learned to be sexually active. Moreover, just as heterosexual men are more sexually active than heterosexual women, gay men are more sexually active than lesbians. But why are *gay men* more sexually active than *heterosexual men*? The prospect of a heterosexual encounter involves only one person (a man) eager for casual sex, while the other person (a woman) is less interested; however, the prospect of a same-sex encounter involves two persons (being men) equally eager for casual sex.

Gay men often engaged in casual sex during the heyday of the sexual revolution in the 1960s and 1970s. However, since the acquired immune deficiency syndrome (AIDS) crisis struck the gay community in the 1980s, there has been a drastic shift from casual to monogamous sex. Afraid to put their lives on the line by playing sexual "Russian roulette," gay men have greatly cut down on the number of partners they have sex with. Today, while gay men are still more likely than straight men to be sexually active, the majority of gay men are involved in a steady, long-term relationship. This kind of relationship is as satisfying to most male couples as it is to most heterosexual couples. In view of the homophobic society's opposition to same-sex marriages, it seems remarkable for male couples to pull off the same level of love and happiness that heterosexual couples enjoy. What's the reason?

Researchers have analyzed gay couples' various personal and social characteristics, such as age, education, income, religion, ethnicity, or living arrangements. None of these was found to be associated with gay couples' happiness. However, researchers did find greater happiness among couples if one partner's income is about equal to the other's. Apparently, the male couples are happier when they perceive their relationships as egalitarian. In such a relationship, both partners make decisions together as equals, which is likely to occur if their incomes are roughly similar rather than widely different. In short, it is equality that helps ensure "marital" happiness among male couples (Peplau and Cochran, 1990; Peplau and Fingerhut, 2007).

The Lesbian Experience

Like heterosexual women, lesbians have been socialized to be less interested in casual sex and more interested in relationships and love. Thus they like to make friends in the context of social gatherings, parties, and school activities. They let the relationship grow slowly, through a long process of knowing the other person, becoming good friends, and cultivating deep affection. Usually, only after a fairly stable, prolonged, and affectionate bond has formed does sexual involvement take place.

Also, like heterosexual women, most lesbians carry on a comfortable relationship with straights by passing as one of them. The posture of heterosexuality is easy to maintain, because they have been socialized to play the conventional female role. Being part of the straight community's social and occupational scene, lesbians can easily slip into its sexual scene as well. In fact, more than one-third of lesbians exhibit a "partial bisexual style" by having sex with men, and about two-thirds are still attracted to men (Rust, 1995).

Finally, like heterosexual women, many lesbians desire to be mothers. They may decide to adopt a child or to bear one through artificial insemination. In fact, about two-thirds of lesbians are already mothers, compared to only 27% of gay men being fathers (LeVay and Nonas, 1995).

However, lesbians differ from straight women in certain ways. For one thing, lesbians are more likely to reject the traditional female role. For example, while the majority of straight women see themselves as "feminine," only a minority of lesbians do so. Moreover, while still in their teens, lesbians are far less likely than their heterosexual peers to know their sexual identity. Virtually all heterosexual youths know they are heterosexual, but most adolescent lesbians are not aware or certain of being lesbian.

Fighting for Gay Rights

For about 70 years now, U.S. gays and lesbians have been fighting for equal rights in a homophobic, antigay society. The gay rights movement began in the late 1940s when many gays and lesbians discovered that they were not alone. This "gay awakening" stemmed from the widely publicized Kinsey report that millions of men and women had engaged in same-sex activities.

At first the gay and lesbian organizations focused on educating the general public about same-sex orientation, counseling gays and lesbians in trouble, and providing them with recreational services. Then, in June 1969, the police raided the Stonewall Inn, a gay bar in New York, simply for serving a gay clientele. The patrons reacted by throwing bottles and stones at the police. This violent reaction against police harassment soon led many young gays and lesbians to form militant organizations. They marched in great numbers, loudly demanding that they be granted equal rights in the same way as African Americans, Hispanics, women, migrant farm workers, and other minorities. By the mid-1970s, the gay movement had enjoyed some victories; the militant fervor cooled, and there was renewed concern with offering counseling and other social services to gays who needed them.

Homophobia
Antihomosexual attitude.

Then, with the outbreak of AIDS in the 1980s, the lesbian and gay rights movement shifted into high gear again. At first, efforts were focused on fighting the disease. Gays and lesbians provided care for the sick and dying, presented AIDS education programs, lobbied for increased government funding for AIDS research, encouraged medical researchers and drug companies to go all out searching for treatments and a cure, and denounced discrimination against people with AIDS or HIV. Then, in the 1990s, after the disease had led to greater **homophobia** (antihomosexual attitude), the gay rights movement adopted confrontational tactics. Giving themselves such militant names as "Queer Nation" and "Queer Action," they shouted their demands for equal rights in the streets, city halls, and suburban shopping malls. They staged gay-pride marches, wearing nipple rings, kissing each other ostentatiously, and exhibiting some other anticonventional behavior. They further organized a massive march on Washington, DC, in 1993, blaring such slogans as "We're here! We're queer! Get used to it!"

Today, the majority of gay-rights activists are far from militant. Consider the Human Rights Campaign, the largest lesbian and gay organization. Its members are moderate, engaging in the same campaigning, fund-raising, and lobbying tactics as conventional interest groups. They further emphasize the importance of equal rights in the same fashion as other minority groups. They have, in effect, mainstreamed.

Thus gays and lesbians have transformed into an important, powerful political force. They can now count on many leaders from both political parties to take their equal rights seriously. Many states and cities have passed laws to protect the sexual minority against discrimination in employment and other areas of social life. Massachusetts and four other states have legalized same-sex marriage. However, homophobia remains throughout society, with 57% of Americans still opposing same-sex marriage and only 40% supporting it (Conant, 2010; Jones, 2009; Lacayo, 2004; Rosenberg, 2004). For the conflicting positions on gay marriage, see Box 8.5.

BOX 8.5   DIVERGENT VIEWS

Should Same-Sex Marriage Be Legal?

Gays and lesbians along with their heterosexual supporters, who are mostly liberals, argue that it should be legal for a person to marry a person of the same sex. They provide many reasons to buttress their view. The most important is that it is unfair and illegal to discriminate against gays and lesbians by denying them the right to marry. They should be treated equally and enjoy the same rights as other Americans. Without being legally married, same-sex couples pay higher taxes than married heterosexual couples and are deprived of rights granted to straight couples. For example, (1) same-sex couples can be denied the right to visit each other when sick or injured in the hospital; (2) gays and lesbians cannot receive Social Security payments upon the death of their partner; and (3) most employers do not provide medical coverage to their gay and lesbian employees' partners.

What about the religious belief that God approves of marriage for men and women only? Doesn't this belief make it impossible to support same-sex marriage? The answer is no because the U.S. Constitution guarantees religious freedom by forbidding government interference in religious activities. This means that there should be separation of church and state. Consider the difference in how the Catholic Church and the U.S. government view divorce and remarriage. Because the church disapproves of divorce, it does not view the second marriage as valid. However, the government does approve of divorce and therefore extends to the remarried couple the same rights as those granted to all other married couples. Similarly, the government can recognize same-sex marriage to uphold equality under law while the church remains free to preach its negative view of same-sex marriage (Human Rights Campaign, 2008; Olson, 2010).

However, opponents of gays and lesbians, who are mostly conservatives, argue that same-sex marriage should not be legal for two key reasons. The first is that gay and lesbian couples fail to meet the minimum necessary condition for marriage, which requires the union of a man and a woman. Even if two homosexuals love each other and want to spend their lives together, just like two heterosexuals, their love and companionship alone are not sufficient to meet the requirement of marriage. If love and companionship were sufficient for marriage, any union of two individuals such as that of a child and an adult (which is prohibited in all of the states) could be defined as marriage.

The second reason for opposing gay marriage is the argument that homosexual relationships do not provide the same benefits to society as heterosexual marriages such as the reproduction of the human race. Instead, homosexual relationships impose substantial costs on society. One example is the fact that AIDS is much more common among men having sex with men than among the general population (Sprigg, 2008).

■ Homosexual Practices Among Nonhomosexuals

As Kinsey suggested, many straights, along with bisexuals, are not exclusively heterosexual. It should therefore not be surprising that they may engage in some homosexual activities. But they may not see themselves as gays or lesbians. They may be called trades, street hustlers, opportunists, and bisexuals.

Trades

Trades are male heterosexuals whose sexual feelings are predominantly heterosexual but who engage in same-sex activities. They are married, or have been married, and seek same-sex experiences as a means of releasing tension. If cheap brothels are easily accessible to them, they would frequent them. They want other men to perform fellatio on them but refuse to reciprocate because they consider themselves straight and masculine. In his classic study on trades, Laud Humphreys (1970) found that most come from lower classes, are Roman Catholic, and feel that they do not get enough sex with their wives.

Street Hustlers

Street hustlers are like trades in having predominantly heterosexual feelings, but they engage in a greater volume of same-sex activities than trades. Like trades, street hustlers are all males. They are also lower-class teenage boys who define themselves as straight and masculine. They make money from letting adults perform oral sex on them, although, like trades, they refuse to reciprocate. Many street hustlers have grown up in broken homes, could not get along with parents, or have run away from home. They generally do not take the initiative to start hustling; they are instead encouraged to do so by some older men. To illustrate, this is how Eddie, a young runaway, got his first trick:

> After arriving in the city by bus, Eddie was standing in the bus terminal, when the customer approached. The man inquired, "Where are you staying?" Eddie responded, "No place. Actually, I'm looking for my uncle." The man suggested that they go to his place so they could look in the telephone book for the uncle's address. Shortly after they arrived at the customer's home, the man asked, "Have you ever had your dick sucked?" Eddie replied, "What? No!" He was shocked by the query. The man said, "Well, how would you like to make $100?" Eddie accepted the offer. (Luckenbill, 1985)

Once youngsters such as Eddie are introduced into prostitution, they search for customers by standing around particular streets, parks, bus stations, or adult bookstore entrances. Because they are basically heterosexual, they are likely to abandon homosexual prostitution when they become adults.

Opportunists

Some heterosexual men and women are **opportunists**, who engage in same-sex acts in situations where the opportunity presents itself. These opportunistic "gays" and "lesbians" are predominantly heterosexual and see themselves as such. They can be found among prison inmates, priests, strippers, and others in one-sex situations.

Opportunities for same-sex involvement are not only available in one-sex situations. Straight married women who find something lacking in their marriage may

---

Trades
Male heterosexuals whose sexual feelings are predominantly heterosexual but who engage in same-sex activities.

Street hustlers
Male heterosexuals whose sexual feelings are predominantly heterosexual but who engage in a greater volume of same-sex activities than trades.

Opportunists
Heterosexuals who engage in same-sex acts in situations where the opportunity presents itself.

have a lesbian lover on the side, although they do not identify themselves as lesbians. As such a woman says, "I don't consider myself gay. I simply can't relate to that for me. I need a romantic involvement in my life and it happens to be with Victoria, but I was with a man before this. I love my husband in a way. I need the kind of anchoring or stability he gives me . . . But I also have a romantic side" (Ponse, 1984).

Opportunistic lesbianism can also be found in some colleges. It involves a straight female student experimenting sexually with a member of the same sex. Such students are known as "LUGs" (lesbians until graduation) or "four-year lesbians" because they stop their same-sex activities when leaving college. As a 25-year-old woman who has been a LUG explains, "It was a real lesbian experience. It was a unique, phenomenal experience. Now it's not an issue anymore. I'm going to marry Richard" (Rimer, 1993).

Bisexuals

Equally straight and gay, bisexuals are sexually attracted to members of both sexes. Most are married to members of the opposite sex, but also have sexual relations with others of the same sex. They do not see themselves as either straight or gay but as totally unique persons with a third kind of sexual identity. As lovers, bisexuals seem more sensitive and empathic than straights and gays because their bisexual orientation enables them to see things from more than one perspective. However, they often feel conflicted. As a bisexual explains, "Your feet are in both camps, but your heart is in neither. You have the opportunity to experience a kind of richness, but you constantly feel you have to make a choice" (Leland, 1995; Rust, 1995; Toufexis, 1992).

This problem is likely to continue because bisexuals usually have sex with either straights or gays rather than with other bisexuals. The problem may diminish if they develop their own bisexual community as gays and lesbians have formed their own. Like the gay community, the bisexual community will be able to strengthen its members' unique sexual identity so that they can enjoy sex with one another without being torn with guilt and other psychological problems. The bisexual community could also bring social harmony to our multicultural society because bisexuals are uniquely qualified to mediate between the homosexual community and the larger heterosexual society (LeVay and Nonas, 1995).

Bisexuals
Individuals who are sexually attracted to members of both sexes.

Review

SUMMARY

1. Human sexuality varies from group to group within a multicultural society such as the United States and from society to society around the globe. Most Americans are more sexually liberal than before. There is, for example, more tolerance for homosexuality and premarital sex. Even casual sex with strangers is now available online, although it can be dangerous. The double sexual standard is less pervasive than in the past. The perceived purpose of marital sex has changed from focus on procreation to recreation. The new sexual morality emphasizes the importance of the quality of relationship between sex partners.

2. Nowadays more than half of U.S. teenagers are sexually active. Compared to their peers of 30 or 40 years ago, teens now have sex younger, have more sexual partners, and have more one-night stands. Teens are more likely to get a sexually transmitted disease, and they have the highest rate of premarital pregnancy in the industrial world. Girls with high self-esteem are less likely to engage in premarital sex, but boys with high self-esteem are more likely.

3. Although extramarital sex remains relatively rare, rates have significantly risen among certain groups, particularly older men, older women, and young couples. According to one myth, sex is more exciting outside marriage than inside, and according to another, people have affairs because they are oversexed. Adultery is socially approved in some societies but not in others. Legitimate adultery varies from one culture to another; so does illegitimate infidelity. Americans who are more likely to have an affair include men, the less religious, and lower-income persons.

4. Swingers are mostly middle-class, white, aged 25 to 45 years, and somewhat conservative. They are not strongly tied to traditional institutions of social control such as religion, family, and community, but they are basically no different from other middle-class couples who do not swing. They claim that swinging improves their marriage, but this may hold true only if they are capable of engaging in sex without any emotion.

5. Pornography has bloated into an enormous industry, considerably more profitable than all the Hollywood movies distributed throughout the United States. To some feminists and most conservatives, pornography is harmful, but to liberals, it is harmless. Evidence suggests that the erotic, nonviolent type of pornography is generally harmless, and the violent type is harmful. As for nude dancing, researchers focus on what it does for the performer and her customers. In nude dancing the performer takes off all her clothes and shows customers her genitalia to encourage them to tip her generously. Most customers are working-class men who expect the nude dancer to fulfill their sexual fantasies. Making a relatively large sum of money, the dancer finds her job disreputable but empowering.

6. The myths about prostitutes portray them as nymphomaniacs, sexually frigid, nasty and hard-hearted or sweet and warmhearted, and addicted to drugs or afflicted with emotional problems. In fact, they have about the same social and sexual backgrounds as conventional women: They desire marriage and traditional family life, have the same amount of education, and are not particularly "promiscuous" in their private lives. Their reasons for selling sex are mostly economic in nature, such as wanting to make more money, being unemployed, or supporting a family, but they are further introduced to the skin trade by their friends or acquaintances. These women in prosperous countries choose to enter prostitution, but their peers in poorer countries are usually forced to sell sex.

7. According to functionalist theory, prostitution stems from its manifest function of offering sexual services demanded by customers as well as from its latent function of strengthening sexual morality. Derived from feminist ideas, conflict theory argues that patriarchy encourages prostitution by creating demand and supply for it. Symbolic interaction theory reveals prostitutes' perceptions of themselves as honest, their sex work as good for society, and their profession as legitimate.

8. One myth of homosexuality is that gays are effeminate while lesbians manly. Another myth claims that gays often molest young children. A third myth insists that homosexuals are emotionally disturbed. A fourth myth is that homosexuals cannot be expected to have a satisfactory sex life. According to a fifth myth, most people are either completely gay or straight.

9. About 2.5% of American adults identify themselves as gay or lesbian. Gays are more likely than straights to be sexually active, but the majority of gays are involved in long-term and satisfactory relationships characterized by equality between the partners. Lesbians are like straight women in having been socialized to desire long-term relationships, in having a comfortable relationship with straights, and in having the desire to be mothers. However, lesbians are likely to reject the traditional female role and to be unaware of their same-sex orientation during adolescence.

10. The gay rights movement began in the late 1940s. Most gay organizations were initially service-oriented, counseling gays in trouble and providing them with recreational activities. Then beginning in the late 1960s, they became militant, aiming to end antigay discrimination in all aspects of life. This brought some victories, cooling the militancy. With the outbreak of the AIDS crisis in the 1980s, gay activists first focused on fighting the disease, but the disease led to greater homophobia in the 1990s, causing some gay activists to become militant again. Today gays and lesbians have turned into a powerful political force, fighting homophobia much like any conventional interest group. However, most Americans are still opposed to same-sex marriage. Many of these people are conservatives, who find same-sex marriage harmful, but liberals argue that it is unfair to discriminate against gays by denying them the right to legally marry.

11. Many heterosexuals are not exclusively heterosexual. Although they usually see themselves as heterosexuals, they may engage in some homosexual activities.

CRITICAL THINKING QUESTIONS

1. Sexual behavior–related topics frequently saturate the news wires and popular culture. What aspect of sexual behavior do you consider to be the most relevant and important today? Explain your response.

2. Given the two divergent views of same-sex marriage, which one do you support and why?

3. During your lifetime, what type of sexual behavior discussed in this chapter have you seen change the most? In your opinion, has the behavior increased or decreased? What has contributed to these changes? Be specific.

📑 INTERNET RESOURCES

The Association for the Treatment of Sexual Abusers (ATSA) (http://www.atsa.com/) is an international, multidisciplinary organization with the mission of reducing and preventing sexual abuse through shared research, education, and awareness.

The Kinsey Institute for Research in Sex, Gender, and Reproduction (http://www.kinseyinstitute.org/) has a long-standing tradition of facilitating interdisciplinary research and scholarship related to human sexuality, gender, and reproduction. The institute also provides the *Continuum Complete International Encyclopedia of Sexuality* for free at http://www.kinseyinstitute.org/ccies/index.php.

The National Sexuality Resource Center (NSRC) (http://nsrc.sfsu.edu/) takes a very liberal approach to sexuality and sex-related research, emphasizing a holistic, social justice approach to promoting sexual literacy. The NSRC is sometimes associated with or known for starting a new sexuality movement.

Sex Addicts Anonymous (http://www.sexaa.org/) is intended to provide a community forum for men and women who share the experience of struggling with sex addictions in an effort to overcome them.

Sexwork Cyber Resource Center (http://www.sexwork.com/) provides information about sexual services that are legal and encouraged outside of the United States, as well as background information on moral and legal oppositions to such enterprises in the United States.

The Society for the Advancement of Sexual Health (SASH) (http://www.sash.net/) provides research studies, lists of available services, and related research links to people seeking information about sexual addiction.

The World Health Organization (WHO) (http://www.who.int/gender/violence/sexual_violence/en/index.html) is a United Nations system responsible for taking a leadership role in determining and setting initiatives pertaining to health research. Their vast umbrella of research responsibilities includes providing policy suggestions to countries and monitoring and assessing sex-related, health-related trends.

Alcohol and Other Drugs

CHAPTER 9

Fifty-year-old Debra Jones had taken the painkiller Percocet safely for 10 years, not to get high but to relieve chronic pain caused by rheumatoid arthritis. Nonetheless, this stay-at-home mother of three became addicted after a friend told her that crushing her pills could bring faster relief. It did work. Besides, she found that the rush of medication gave her more energy. Soon she had to rely on that energy boost to get through the day, so she took six or seven pills a day instead of the three to four prescribed by her doctor. She eventually kicked the habit through a university drug treatment program (Szabo, 2009).

It is not unusual today for people like Jones to get addicted to prescription drugs. In fact, such an addiction has become a largely unknown epidemic. Prescription drugs cause most of the fatal overdoses each year. The number of overdose deaths from painkillers tripled from 1999 to 2006. In the past, most overdoses came from illegal narcotics, such as heroin, but prescription painkillers have surpassed heroin and cocaine as the leading cause of fatal overdoses (Szabo, 2009). In this chapter, we will first take a close look at the abuse of these prescription and other legal drugs, including tobacco cigarettes and alcohol. Then we will zero in on the abuse of illegal drugs such as marijuana, heroin, and cocaine.

◼ Abusing Prescription Drugs

Drugs prescribed by doctors can be used properly—to eliminate the patient's complaints, such as pain, stress, and fatigue. However, these drugs can be abused for the purpose of getting high. This abuse of prescription drugs has soared among both teens and adults over the last two decades, with the abuse of painkillers rising much more sharply than the abuse of tranquilizers, stimulants, and sedatives (see Figure 9.1). Women and whites are more likely than men, African Americans, and Hispanics to abuse prescription drugs. Moreover, people with some college education are more likely than those with less education to abuse these drugs. It therefore appears that the abuse of prescription drugs is mostly a middle-class problem (Kalb, 2001; ONDCP, 2008).

There are three reasons for the increased prevalence of prescription-drug abuse. First, the drug is more easily available today. Doctors are too quick to prescribe the medication, while it is easy to buy the medication online without prescription. Second, it is widely assumed that prescription drugs are safe to take because they are legal and come from the doctor and pharmacy rather than illegal and come from the drug dealer. And third, individuals who abuse prescription drugs are under the influence of such social factors as peer pressure, inadequate social control, and the legal drug culture that encourages people to deal with the stresses of life by using alcohol, tobacco, and various sedatives and tranquilizers (Compton and Volkow, 2006; Schepis and Krishnan-Sarin, 2008).

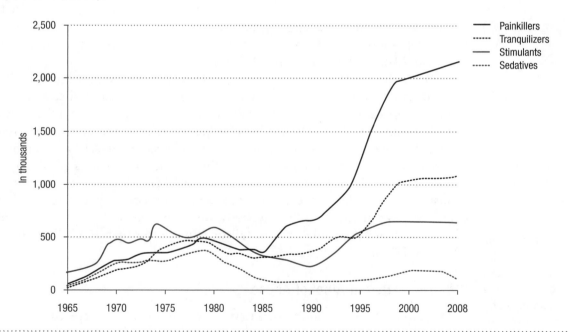

FIGURE 9.1 Rising Numbers of Illicit Prescription Drug Users

The popularity of prescription painkillers and tranquilizers among new illicit drug users has steadily increased since the late 1980s. Among the drugs of choice, prescription painkillers have become the most popular by a margin of more than 1 million new users per year.

Critical Thinking: *Why has the popularity of prescription painkillers and tranquilizers witnessed exponential growth over the past decade, while the abuse of other forms of prescription drugs has remained relatively flat, or even declined by a small margin (as in the case of stimulants and sedatives)?*

Source: National Survey on Drug Use and Health (NSDUH), 2002–2008.

■ Abusing Tobacco Cigarettes

Since the U.S. Surgeon General first announced in 1964 the conclusion of a scientific study that linked smoking to lung cancer, there have been many reports about the serious health hazards of smoking. Still, too many Americans continue to smoke regularly. They represent at least 25% of the U.S. population. Even among the very young (ages 12 to 17 years), about 13% smoke in any given month. Most of these young smokers are very likely to continue smoking in their adult lives, as suggested by the fact that most adult smokers started smoking before 18 years of age (NSDUH, 2006).

Among teenagers, whites are much more likely than blacks to smoke. Among adults, however, African Americans are more likely to smoke.

Among teenagers, whites are much more likely than African Americans to smoke. Among adults, however, African Americans are more likely to smoke. If comparing all the racial or ethnic groups, Native Americans have the highest percentage of smokers and Asian Americans the lowest. These racial differences in smoking may have to do with education: The less educated the groups, the more likely they are to smoke. There is also a gender factor in smoking: Within each ethnic group, men are more likely than women to smoke, the exception being that among white teenagers, females are just as likely to smoke as males (Adler, 2008; McMurray, 2004).

Given the health hazards of smoking, why do smokers continue to smoke? Don't they know the hazards of smoking? Many smokers are already addicted and cannot quit. Others continue to smoke even though they can quit; to them the benefits of smoking outweigh the costs. The benefits include releasing tension, feeling relaxed, and enjoying quiet companionship or lively conversation. It is, however, more than these benefits that cause smokers to continue smoking. Smokers are simply much more inclined to take risks in life than nonsmokers. Contrary to popular belief, most smokers do know the hazards of smoking. In fact, they tend to greatly overrate the risks of smoking. In one study, for example, smokers placed the risk of lung cancer at 38%, while a more realistic risk is lower than 10% (Blizzard, 2004b; Viscusi, 1992).

■ The Extent of Alcohol Abuse

Only about 6% of U.S. adults are **alcoholics**, who by definition have lost control over drinking and consequently have problems with health, work, or personal relationships. About 63% are moderate drinkers. While they drink alcoholic beverages such as liquor, wine, or beer, the men consume no more than two drinks a day and the women no more than one drink. A large minority, 37% of the adult population, are **teetotalers**, who completely abstain from drinking (Blizzard, 2004b; SAMHSA, 2002). Internationally, Americans also appear to be moderate drinkers, ranking neither among the heavy-drinking nations nor among the dry ones. This pattern of moderate drinking has

Alcoholics
Persons who have lost control over drinking and consequently have problems with health, work, or personal relationships.

Teetotalers
Persons who completely abstain from drinking.

become more common since the early 1980s, largely because of increasing concern about the hazard of excessive drinking (Ahlstrom and Osterberg, 2005; Chase, 1996).

Nevertheless, alcohol remains far more widely used than all illegal drugs, and the abuse of alcohol is the most widespread of all legal and illegal drugs. Alcoholism is also one of our nation's biggest health problems, surpassed only by heart disease and cancer, and drunk driving is the number one cause of death among young people (ages 16 to 24 years). The economic cost of alcohol-related problems is enormous, as much as $90 billion a year in reduced industrial production, illness, and traffic accidents (Rivara et al., 2004).

■ Binge Drinking on Campus

Since the late 1980s, many college students have hit the bottle with reckless abandon. They are known as **binge drinkers**, men who gulp down five or more drinks in a row and women who put away four or more. Most college students (about 56%) drink in moderation or abstain from alcohol, but a large minority (44%) engage in binge drinking. Compared to moderate drinkers and abstainers, binge drinkers are more likely to run into trouble with the police, injure themselves or others, have academic and interpersonal problems, and ride in cars with drivers who are drunk. Binge drinkers further cause "secondhand effects," interrupting other students' study or sleep, forcing them to take care of drunken students, and insulting or humiliating them (Seaman, 2005; Wechsler et al., 2002).

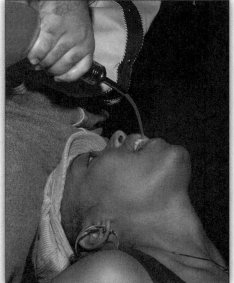

Binge drinkers
Men who consume five or more drinks in a row, and women who consume four or more.

At least four factors lie behind binge drinking: having to study hard, social pressure to get drunk, fondness for partying, and the popular belief that binge drinking is very common.

Binge drinking became a serious problem on many campuses in the late 1980s, about the same time the legal drinking age was raised to 21 throughout the country. Before the enactment of this drinking age law, drinking took place in the open, where it could be supervised by police, security guards, and even healthcare workers. After the drinking age went up, drinking did not stop. It simply moved underground to homes, cars, and frat-house basements where, hidden from adults and authorities, it could get out of hand and lead to binge drinking (see **Box 9.1**).

The problem with binge drinking is that most students today have not learned and practiced moderate drinking as their peers did before the late 1980s. In those years, when all students were allowed to drink, they learned to do so responsibly at college-sponsored events, where alcoholic beverages were served. They also learned to drink in moderation at the homes of professors who invited them to dinners and receptions. However, this kind of drinking experience is no longer available to students. Consequently, when they drink, students tend to do so to get drunk. At least four factors lie behind this binge drinking. One is the stress from having to work hard

BOX 9.1   DIVERGENT VIEWS

Should the Drinking Age Stay at 21?

The drinking age law was passed in the late 1980s, requiring Americans to be at least 21 years old to purchase or consume alcohol. Now the question is, should the drinking age stay at 21? Advocates such as the members of MADD (Mothers Against Drunk Driving) say yes, but a group of college presidents say no, arguing instead for a lower drinking age.

"The Drinking Age Law Saves Lives"

The president of MADD, Laura Dean-Mooney (2008), explains why she believes the drinking age law has saved many lives. The evidence, as she sees it, is overwhelming: More than 50 scientific studies have found that the law saves lives, both on and off the road. Since the age-21 law was widely enacted, the number of young people killed every year in car crashes involving drunk drivers younger than 21 years old has gone down by over half, from more than 5,000 individuals in the early 1980s to about 2,000 in 2005. By the end of 2005, the age-21 law had saved nearly 25,000 young lives, which amounts to approximately 1,000 lives per year. The law saves so many lives because people younger than 21 years old generally drink less—and continue to do so through their early twenties.

Research has further indicated that if the drinking age is lowered to 18, the problems of underage and binge drinking will get far worse, and injury and death rates among the youth will increase. The public also frowns on the lowering of the drinking age: 72% of adults think a lower drinking age would make alcohol more accessible to teenagers, and nearly half believe it would increase binge drinking among the youth.

"The Drinking Age Law Causes Binge Drinking"

Nearly 130 college and university presidents have signed a document declaring that the age-21 law does not work but instead has created a culture of binge drinking on campus. The person who spearheaded this declaration, John McCardell (2008), points out that 5,000 Americans younger than 21 years of age die of alcohol-related causes each year, but only 1,900 of these deaths are traffic fatalities, which means the remaining 3,100 do not occur on the highways. This finding suggests that most underage drinkers do their drinking in private.

In fact, as McCardell sees it, the drinking age law only forces youth drinking into clandestine locations, beyond the sight of adult authority. This is how binge drinking typically takes place. It does not occur in public places, from which the law has effectively banned alcohol consumption. It occurs instead "in locked dorm rooms, off-campus apartments, farmers' fields, and other risky environments." McCardell further argues that the age-21 law does not necessarily reduce alcohol-related traffic deaths. Although the number of these deaths had declined for 10 years or so after the legal drinking age was raised to 21, the decline stopped in the mid-1990s and the number has been inching upward since. Moreover, the evidence that the drinking age has decreased the traffic deaths is underwhelming. One survey of many studies indicated that only about half of the studies found a causal relationship between the age-21 law and declining alcohol-related traffic fatalities; the other half showed no relationship at all. Because the drinking age law doesn't work, McCardell suggests that it is better to lower the drinking age so that young people can be instructed to drink moderately.

for good grades. A second factor is the social pressure to get drunk so as to fit in and not be seen by others as uptight or antisocial. A third factor is the fondness for partying as an important part of college life. A fourth factor is the popular belief that binge drinking is very common on the campus, even if it is actually not so. In other words, the more people are believed to binge, the more likely a student is to follow suit (DeSimone, 2007; Hoover, 2004).

◼ Myths About Alcohol Abuse

Only a small minority of Americans see alcohol abuse as a serious problem. Most would rather consider the use of other, illegal drugs, such as marijuana, cocaine, and heroin, a serious problem. From this relative lack of public concern about drinking, there have emerged a number of misconceptions about alcohol and its abuse. Some popular beliefs (for example, "Drinking on an empty stomach can get you drunk fast") are indeed correct, but many are false.

One commonly held myth is that most alcoholics are homeless. This is probably because most alcoholics have long been widely associated with "skid-row bums," who are homeless. The fact is that homeless alcoholics constitute only a small minority—less than 5%—of the entire alcoholic population in the United States. The overwhelming majority of alcoholics are ordinary people who live with their families.

A second myth is that mixing different kinds of alcoholic drinks can make a person drunk faster. In reality, it is not the mixture of different drinks, but the total amount of alcohol consumed and the length of time taken to consume it that determine the speed of intoxication.

A third myth is that drinking black coffee or dousing one's head with cold water can sober one up. In fact, there is no effective method for getting over intoxication other than waiting for the alcohol to leave the body. The more alcohol in the bloodstream, the more time required to sober up.

A fourth myth is that drinking only beer is unlikely to make one an alcoholic. Actually, beer drinkers are more likely to become alcoholics when compared with drinkers of gin, Scotch, or any other kind of alcoholic beverage. Perhaps because beer is less potent than the other drinks, people drink it for hours on end, and extended, heavy drinking is very likely to lead to alcoholism.

The final myth is a seductive one, namely that sex becomes more exciting after several drinks. Unfortunately for believers of this myth, because alcohol is a depressant rather than a stimulant of the central nervous system, a drinker may find it more difficult to perform sexually even if the drinker feels less inhibited. As Shakespeare says in *Macbeth*, drinking "provokes the desire, but it takes away the performance." A common problem with heavy drinking for men is loss of erections, especially among the middle-aged. Moreover, a drunken man trying to arouse his partner with sensitivity and gentleness is like a gorilla trying to play a violin (Hammond and Jorgensen, 1981).

◼ Social Factors in Alcohol Abuse

Alcohol abuse is more likely to occur among some Americans than others. The difference reflects the influence of certain social factors. Here we will consider the most important ones.

Gender and Age

Getting drunk has long been a predominantly male activity. It has often been found that men are at least four times more likely than women to become alcoholics.

However, this gender difference has been narrowing over the last 40 years, largely thanks to a significant increase in drinking problems among women. Researchers attribute this increase in drinking problems among women to their greater career pressures, their stronger desire for achieving gender equality by behaving like "one of the boys," and the declining social stigma about women getting drunk. Nevertheless, men still have more alcohol problems than women (Blizzard, 2004a; Rowe, 1995).

Apparently more concerned with their masculinity than older men, young men are more likely to drink heavily.

One reason for the gender difference is that drunkenness is more socially acceptable for men than for women. Another reason is that, as a result of gender-role socialization, men are more concerned with their masculinity, such as their need for dominance and emotional control, which is further reinforced by the peer pressure to "drink like a man." In fact, research has long shown a strong link between masculine concerns and alcohol abuse (Huselid and Cooper, 1992).

Apparently more concerned with their masculinity than older men, young men are more likely to drink heavily. The age difference in alcohol consumption among women is not as great as that among men, because women are generally uninterested in being masculine. Younger women, however, are significantly inclined to drink more than older women. This suggests that the age factor can have its own independent influence on heavy drinking, without being affected by the gender factor (Blizzard, 2004a; Breslow and Smothers, 2004).

Race and Ethnicity

In the United States, the rate of alcohol abuse varies from one racial or ethnic group to another.

AFRICAN AMERICANS. Compared to whites, African Americans are less likely to drink but more likely to become alcoholics. Moreover, as they get older, African American heavy drinkers are more likely than their white counterparts to continue drinking heavily. Thus, African Americans suffer from a higher rate of alcohol-related illnesses, such as fatty liver, hepatitis, liver cirrhosis, and esophageal cancer (Herd, 1991).

This racial difference in drinking is largely because African Americans have a much higher rate of poverty, as there is a strong link between poverty and drinking problems. The alcoholism among poor African Americans seems to reflect a futile attempt to use alcohol as a way to escape the stresses of poverty along with racial discrimination. By contrast, blacks from higher social classes benefit more from the traditional Afrocentric values of kinship and spirituality that discourage alcohol abuse. This may explain why black college students, who come mostly from higher social classes, are much less likely to use and abuse alcohol than even their white peers, let alone poor blacks (Peralta, 2005).

HISPANIC AMERICANS. Like African Americans, Hispanic Americans are also more likely than Anglos to drink heavily. This has long been popularly attributed to the Hispanic value of machismo, which emphasizes the importance of masculinity in the form of male dominance, toughness, and honor. However, research has shown that Hispanics who drink heavily do not have greater interest in machismo than those who drink in moderation. A more credible explanation for the higher rate of drinking problems among Hispanics is their higher rate of poverty. In general, more successful Hispanic groups, such as Cubans and Dominicans, are less likely than others, such as Puerto Ricans and Guatemalans, to abuse alcohol (Hanson, 1995).

NATIVE AMERICANS. Of all the minorities in the United States, Native Americans have the highest rate of alcoholism. This problem has been attributed to sociocultural factors, particularly the fact that the life of Native Americans as the poorest minority is full of stress, while their traditional culture that provides them with a sense of pride and dignity has been diminished or destroyed through long years of colonization by Europeans. The same alcohol problems do not, however, plague all of the Native American tribes. Generally, tribes with "an individualistic hunting-gathering tradition" have a higher incidence of alcohol abuse than tribes with "an agricultural tradition stressing communal values and ceremonies" (Hanson, 1995).

ITALIAN AND CHINESE AMERICANS. Although they often drink, Americans of Italian or Chinese ancestry have among the lowest rates of alcoholism in the United States. This is largely because Italian Americans usually drink with meals, discourage solitary drinking as a means of drowning sorrows, and frown on drunkenness. Similarly, Chinese Americans drink a lot but are relatively free from alcoholism. Like the Italians, the Chinese usually drink with meals, particularly on such special occasions as family ceremonies (births, weddings, rites for the dead) and national and religious celebrations. The Chinese do not consider drunken behavior funny or comical. They view it with contempt, believing that drunkenness can seriously disrupt interpersonal relationships and that only moderate, controlled drinking is a social lubricant (Hanson, 1995).

Religion

Jews in the United States begin drinking at a very young age, but they have one of the lowest rates of alcohol problems. The reason has long been assumed to be the culture of Orthodox Judaism, which encourages Jews to use wine only for religious rituals and to consider it sacrilegious to use the alcohol to get drunk.

Conservative Protestants such as Pentecostals and Southern Baptists also prohibit the faithful from using alcohol, and they are therefore more likely to abstain from drinking when compared to Catholics and liberal Protestants. However, if they drink, conservative Protestants are more likely to become problem drinkers. They have been brought up in a religion that preaches total abstinence from liquor but have not learned how to drink in moderation (Galen and Rogers, 2004).

Social Class

People of higher social classes are more likely than those of the lower classes to drink. Paradoxically, there are more problem drinkers and alcoholics among the lower classes. One reason is that drinkers of different classes use alcohol for different purposes. Drinkers

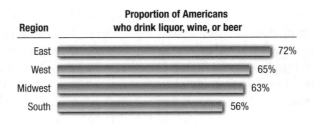

FIGURE 9.2 Prevalence of Drinking by Region

The proportion of U.S. adults who consume alcohol is high. However, a much higher percentage in the East than in any other region report that they consume alcohol.

Critical Thinking: *Why is the percentage of Southerners who consume alcohol so much lower than other U.S. regions?*

Source: "Americans and Alcohol: Drink, Drank, Drunk?" Gallup, 2004.

of higher social classes are more likely to use alcohol *positively* as a means of smoothing social intercourse, but lower-class drinkers tend to drink *negatively* as a futile attempt to drown personal sorrows or problems. This may explain why, when drinking, lower-class persons drink significantly more and faster than higher-class persons. Apparently, a large consumption of alcohol can make the lower-class drinkers lose self-control, which in turn makes it harder to solve problems. They may consequently keep drinking to attempt to achieve a goal that gets progressively harder to achieve the more they drink.

Another reason for the higher rate of alcohol abuse among the lower classes is simply that they suffer from a greater amount of distressful life experiences that are associated with drinking problems. Such experiences include family breakdown (family violence, separation, or divorce) and job loss. Research has consistently found that people with these kinds of experiences suffer from higher rates of alcoholism than those without (Catalano et al., 1993; Mulia et al., 2008).

Region

The rate of alcohol consumption is highest in the Northeast, lowest in the South, and intermediate in the Midwest and West (see Figure 9.2). The states with the highest rates of alcohol use are generally more urbanized, which suggests that cities and suburbs have proportionately more drinkers than rural areas and small towns. One reason for the greater consumption of alcohol in more urbanized regions is the greater stresses and strains of urban life. Another reason is that regions with higher rates of alcohol use probably have more favorable attitudes toward alcohol, fewer legal restrictions, and weaker traditions of temperance or prohibition against alcohol.

Although the South has the lowest rate of alcohol consumption, it has the highest incidence of drunkenness. More specifically, compared to other regions, the South has higher rates of alcoholism and alcohol-related fights, accidents, and problems with work, the police, spouses, and friends (Hilton, 1991). This apparent contradiction between less alcohol consumption and more drinking problems in the South should not be surprising. It is similar to what we have observed in regard to the religiously conservative and the lower classes, who are less likely than others to drink but, if drinking, more likely to abuse alcohol. We have so far compared alcohol consumption in different regions of the United States. For an international comparison of drinking, see Box 9.2.

BOX 9.2   GLOBAL PERSPECTIVE

Russia Tops the World in Drinking

Throughout the world, liquor and beer have, over the last quarter century, become much more popular while wine has gotten less so. The consumption of alcoholic beverages as a whole varies from one society to another. Generally, more affluent societies consume more alcohol than do poorer societies. Thus the prosperous Western European and North American countries consume more alcohol than their less economically developed counterparts in Southeast Asia and the Middle East. Among prosperous countries, France, Germany, and Britain drink more than the United States and Canada. Drinking even more than the Europeans are the Russians, who consume the most alcohol in the world (Ahlstrom and Osterberg, 2005).

The Russians have been burdened with the habit of heavy drinking since they invented vodka, their favorite liquor, 500 years ago. The key reason is apparently the benefits the Russian drinker can obtain from vodka. As a Russian writer explains, "Vodka has provided access to a private life that is closed to the state, a place where it is possible to relax, to forget your troubles, to engage in sex with the illusion of free choice" (Erofeyev, 2002). Heavy drinking has gotten worse since the dissolution of the Soviet Union in the early 1990s, which has brought along severe social and economic problems. Unemployment and poverty have hit more people, the income of the employed has fallen, the prices of goods and services have gone up, and thieves and killers have proliferated. These problems in turn make social life less active. In the past, people often visited friends, patronized cafés and restaurants, went to the movies, attended sports events, or participated in other social activities. But nowadays, people tend to stay home and get drunk (Erofeyev, 2002; Jukkala et al., 2008).

■ Negative Consequences of Alcohol Abuse

Moderate drinking can bring social benefits such as sociability and hospitality. But excessive drinking can bring about negative social consequences. One is the relatively high rate of *automobile accidents*, the leading cause of death among young people in the United States. Over half of each year's automobile deaths and injuries can be traced to excessive drinking. Young people who are especially likely to get involved in auto accidents and deaths are not only inclined to drink excessively but also to use illicit drugs, violate various traffic laws, enjoy taking risks, and exhibit aggressiveness toward others.

Another negative consequence is the high rate of *criminal offenses*. Offenses directly related to excessive drinking include public drunkenness, driving while intoxicated, disorderly conduct, vagrancy, and violation of liquor laws. Such offenses make up the largest arrest category today. Most of the crimes committed by students on college campuses are also related to alcohol. They usually commit multiple crimes, including vandalism, fighting, theft, and alcohol violations (Engs and Hanson, 1994; U.S. Census Bureau, 2010).

Heavy drinking further plays a significant role, though indirectly, in the perpetration of more serious, violent crimes, such as aggravated assault, homicide, and forcible rape. As **Figure 9.3** shows, alcohol is implicated in at least 42% of all violent crimes in the United States. Those who commit these crimes seem to use alcohol as an excuse for expressing their aggression. Alcohol can thus turn into dynamite in the hands of an aggressive person.

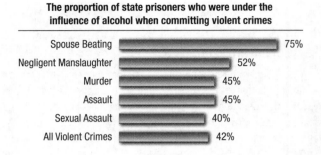

The proportion of state prisoners who were under the influence of alcohol when committing violent crimes

Spouse Beating	75%
Negligent Manslaughter	52%
Murder	45%
Assault	45%
Sexual Assault	40%
All Violent Crimes	42%

FIGURE 9.3 Alcohol and Violent Crime

It is clear that the use of alcohol is a factor in a high percentage of all violent crimes, but its presence is far more visible in cases of domestic abuse. As Figure 9.3 shows, alcohol is most likely to be used in the commission of spousal beating than in other forms of violent crime.

Critical Thinking: *What factors unique to marriage might help to explain why the presence of alcohol is much more prominent in cases of spousal beating than in other forms of violence? What can be done to help reduce the alcohol-related violent crime?*

Source: U.S. Department of Justice, Bureau of Justice Statistics, 2004.

Stages of Becoming an Alcoholic

When people take a drink for the first time in their lives, it doesn't mean they will inevitably become alcoholics. Instead, alcoholics go through a sequence of events that culminate in becoming totally dependent on alcohol. That sequence, according to the influential alcoholism expert E. M. Jellinek (1952), consists of four stages.

In the first stage, prospective alcoholics begin drinking in order to *seek some relief from tension*. But the more they drink, the less their tolerance for tension. The less their tolerance for tension, the more they want to drink to seek relief. At the same time, the more they drink, the greater their tolerance for alcohol, so that they have to consume more and more alcohol to get drunk. At this stage, they can still control their drinking, which enables them to continue to function normally in their occupational and social world.

In the second stage, social drinkers begin to show signs of alcohol abuse by starting to experience **blackouts**. A blackout is an attack of memory loss, but it is different from passing out. If people drink beyond their alcohol-tolerance level, they may pass out on the spot, becoming totally incapable of interacting with others. In contrast, if they experience a blackout, they may be the life of the party, or at least talk with others and move about freely, but the next day they cannot remember what they did. By now they have become *psychologically addicted* to alcohol, having a strong craving for the drug. The craving drives them to drink a lot, drink alone, and drink in the morning, but they still can stop abusing alcohol if they are determined to do so.

In the third stage, the drinkers become *physically addicted* and suffer chills, shakes, and other withdrawal distresses when discontinuing alcohol use. By now they cannot stop drinking even if they want to. Once they start drinking at any time of the day, they will keep doing so until the supply is gone or they get too drunk to continue. Although they cannot control their drinking, they typically insist that they can stop if they really want to. The more they think they can control their drinking, the more they lose control. Then they invent excuses and rationalizations for drinking, blaming, for example, their spouses or bosses for causing so much tension that they need to drink for relief. These rationalizations make them even more attached to liquor, and, as a result, they often skip meals in favor of liquor.

Blackout
An attack of memory loss, different from passing out.

Psychological addiction
Having a strong craving for alcohol or other drugs.

Physical addiction
Having such a strong craving for alcohol or other drugs that the user suffers chills, shakes, and other withdrawal distresses when discontinuing use of the drugs.

BOX 9.3   USING SOCIOLOGICAL INSIGHTS

Applying the AA Method

Founded in 1935, AA (Alcoholics Anonymous) is today the largest and most successful organization for dealing with the problems of alcoholism. The only requirement for joining AA is the desire to stop drinking. After joining the organization, new members may choose another AA member as a sponsor. Sponsors are recovering alcoholics ready to come to a new member's aid whenever needed. The treatment involves attending a series of meetings where any number of alcoholics share their drinking experiences. These meetings may be held in offices, schools, churches, lodges, or private homes. They are open to alcoholics and nonalcoholics alike. At a typical meeting, a volunteer "leader" will begin by saying something like "Hello, I'm John, and I'm an alcoholic." The leader may then introduce some AA members who will discuss their experiences with alcohol as well as their recovery from the drinking problem. Afterward, others may follow suit, relating their own experiences. A crucial part of these sessions is admitting to oneself and others that one is an alcoholic and is powerless in dealing with alcohol alone.

This program is widely considered the most successful method ever devised for coping with alcoholism. Not surprisingly, AA has spawned similar organizations such as Al-Anon (for spouses and other close relatives and friends of alcoholics) and Alateen (for alcoholics' teenage children). Their aim is to help members understand alcoholism and themselves, as well as learn how to live with and help their alcoholic relatives. AA meetings are also available to students in a growing number of colleges. Apparently, the effectiveness of the AA method is attributed the *group support* provided to alcoholics by people who have deep, personal understanding of drinking problems. Group support is particularly important for alcoholics because they are typically "escape drinkers," drinking alone in a futile attempt to solve personal problems. AA offers what these alcoholics have always sought, namely, social acceptance, a more positive identity, and feelings of normalcy and confidence. AA can provide these benefits of group support because it has effectively become its members' family. As a member puts it,

> I lost everything. Family, home, wives, kids, job, everything. Even my parents turned against me. . . . I finally found you people. Now you're my family. Wherever I go, you're there. . . . You give me everything I ever wanted and ever looked for. I feel like I'm needed again. (Denzin, 1991)

In the fourth, final stage, the alcoholics become *isolated and withdrawn* from relatives, friends, and others. They now hit bottom with total dependence on alcohol. They often drink for several days without doing anything else. They are haunted by the tremendous fear that alcohol may be taken away from them. They drink so much that they rarely eat and consequently suffer from malnutrition. They also experience delirium tremens, which can produce terrifying hallucinations, such as seeing millions of little flies chasing, suffocating, or eating them. However, they could successfully deal with these problems by seeking group support from other alcoholics (see Box 9.3).

■ Drug Use in Perspective

As we suggested earlier, *legal* drugs are generally more dangerous than illegal ones. To illustrate, the use of such legal drugs as alcoholic beverages and tobacco cigarettes is considerably more prevalent than the total use of such illegal drugs as marijuana, heroin, and cocaine. Some 125 million Americans drink alcohol and 62 million smoke cigarettes, compared to only 20 million who use illegal drugs. Other legal drugs, such as sedatives, tranquilizers, and stimulants, are less popular than alcohol and tobacco, but they are also more widely used than the illegal drugs heroin and cocaine. Not surprisingly, then, the use of legal drugs causes far more death, sickness, economic loss, and other social problems than the use of illegal drugs. Every year, just those two legal drugs—alcohol and tobacco—kill at least 60 times as many Americans as do all the illegal drugs combined (Caulkins et al., 2005; NSDUH, 2006).

Contrary to popular assumption, then, legal prohibition or societal disapproval of a drug does not necessarily indicate how dangerous the drug really is. Instead, the disapproval reflects more the temper of the time and place. Opium is an illegal drug today, and widely condemned as a panopathogen (a cause of all ills), but in the last two centuries it was a legal drug and widely praised as a panacea (cure for all ills). On the other hand, cigarette smoking is legal in all countries today, but in the 17th century it was illegal in most countries and the smoker was harshly punished in some. The penalty for smoking included death in Turkey and China, removal of noses in Russia, and slitting of lips in Hindustan (Goode, 2005).

In assuming that illegal drugs are more dangerous than legal ones, the general public also believes that people who use illegal drugs typically become addicted, compulsive, or heavy users. In fact, most people who use illicit drugs do so only experimentally, occasionally, or moderately, without sliding down the slippery slope to compulsive and uncontrollable use. This is because the majority of illegal drug users are able to draw the line on what they do. Drugs by themselves do not have the power to pull users down the slippery slope. There are, of course, real horrors in drug use, but they befall only a few rather than most users (Goode, 2005).

■ The Extent of Drug Abuse

Drug abuse, which involves the use of illegal drugs, is relatively common in the United States. Some 12% of the U.S. population age 12 years or older use illicit drugs every year, half of them at least once a month. Of the various age groups, young adults (ages 18 to 25 years) have the highest rate of drug abuse, and teenagers (ages 13 to 17 years) the second highest. The United States as a whole has the highest rate of drug abuse in the world, and U.S. high school seniors have the highest rate among their peers in the industrial world (Lynch, S. N., 2008; NHSDA, 2008).

All these statistics, however, should not be blown out of proportion. It is true that the United States leads the world in drug abuse. It is not true that drug abuse is so pervasive that it invades every nook and cranny of society, enslaving all classes of Americans to the same extent. Most drug problems, especially the most serious ones, such as drug addiction, death from drug overdose, or drug-related homicide, are primarily confined to the lower classes, along with socially and economically oppressed minorities. Drug abuse and overdose among the nonpoor, middle class, or affluent is generally far less common. In fact, for Americans as a whole, the rate of drug abuse has steadily declined over the last three decades. The exception is that the rate has risen slightly for teenagers, driven mostly by white youngsters smoking pot. However, African American students in secondary school are now less likely than their white peers to use drugs because they are more likely to have observed close up how drugs wreck lives in black communities (Bogert, 1994; DEA, 2010).

■ Illegal Drugs

Commonly used illegal drugs are marijuana, heroin, cocaine and crack, meth and roofies, and Ecstasy. Let's take a look at each of these drugs.

Marijuana

Marijuana is the most widely used illegal drug in the United States. It is often smoked in the form of cigarettes, popularly known as "joints" or "reefers." When it was first used in ancient times, marijuana was regarded as a sacred drug, but there has been a great deal of opposition to its use in our society. Many people, particularly government scientists, have argued that it is very harmful to smoke marijuana. Smokers are said to suffer from such short-term effects as memory loss, anxiety, and increased heart rate. Chronic smokers are believed to eventually develop cancer, respiratory diseases, and heart problems. Critics argue that the majority of marijuana users do not suffer lasting harm and that the drug's mild intoxicating effects are no more dangerous than those of alcohol and tobacco (Williams, M. E., 2003).

If used to the point of intoxication, marijuana can create problems in the same way as alcoholic beverages. It can, for example, impair intellectual judgment, short-term memory, and psychomotor function, which can hamper reading or studying. It can also undermine the performance of car drivers and airline pilots. But if used moderately, marijuana can create euphoria, heighten sensitivity, improve perception, and increase appetite. Marijuana can further be used for medical purposes, because it has proved effective for controlling nausea and relieving pain in seriously ill patients with acquired immune deficiency syndrome (AIDS), cancer, and other diseases.

Heroin

Heroin can be smoked, snorted through the nose, taken orally, or injected into the skin, a muscle, or a vein. Injection into a vein, also known as mainlining, produces the quickest and most intense high. Traditionally, mainlining has been by far the most common method of ingestion, but fear of AIDS and the greatly increased potency of today's heroin have made smoking or snorting increasingly popular. Taken in moderate doses, heroin can dull pain as well as diminish anxiety and tension. Most important, heroin can induce euphoria. Many heroin

Most heroin users do not become addicts, as they typically get less and less pleasure from the drug after their early experience of euphoria. But some heroin users do get addicted to the drug.

users claim that the heroin rush is more satisfying than orgasm and the heroin high far more glorious and pleasurable than anything the nonuser could possibly experience. These heroin users can easily become psychologically and physically addicted to the drug.

However, most heroin users do not become addicts; they typically get less and less pleasure from the drug after their early experiences of euphoria. As a former user says,

> Luckily, it was no longer feeling good enough to make it worth getting busted for. Heroin had lost its immense power over me. It simply wasn't worth it. The magic ceased to happen long

ago. There's only the memory . . . Right now I'd rather go out for a good dinner than shoot a bag of heroin. (Goode, 1981)

Nonetheless, some users of heroin do get addicted to the drug.

Cocaine and Crack

Freebasing
Purifying a drug with ether and then smoking it.

Crack
A less pure form of cocaine that is still capable of producing an intense high because users typically smoke rather than snort it.

Before 1900, cocaine was legal, commonly used as a local anesthetic, for offsetting fatigue and depression, and for curing morphine addiction and stomach disorder. By the turn of the 20th century, cocaine had become widely used as a pleasure drug and laws were passed to make it illegal. At that time, most of the users were the powerless, such as African Americans, lower-class whites, and criminals. Since the 1960s, cocaine has transformed into a symbol of wealth and status, mostly used by affluent whites. It is the most expensive drug, known to the cognoscenti as "the champagne of drugs" or "caviar among drugs." Usually snorted, the drug is in the form of white powder. One can seek a greater high by resorting to freebasing, which involves purifying the drug with ether and then smoking it. Since 1986, however, an increasing number of youths, especially those from poor and working-class families, have used crack. It is a less pure form of cocaine but can still produce an intense high because users typically smoke rather than snort it. Crack is much cheaper than pure cocaine.

Most people who use cocaine find their experience exhilarating, but the drug can also be extremely dangerous if taken in large doses or used frequently for an extended time. It can cause insomnia, impotence, extreme irritability, paranoia, and the sensation of bugs crawling under the skin. A single overdose can produce an effect like lighting a fire in the brain, triggering severe headaches, nausea, and convulsions with the potential of total respiratory and cardiovascular collapse. Crack puts its users at even higher risks. Because it swiftly and dramatically increases the blood pressure and heart rate, crack can more easily lead to heart attacks and deaths.

Meth and Roofies

Methamphetamine (meth) is an injectable stimulant known on the street as "speed," "crank," or "crystal." Because it is relatively cheap and easily available, it has supplanted cocaine as the drug of choice for all classes of people. It was initially known as "poor man's cocaine" for being mainly popular among white 18- to 34-year-old working-class and rural men, but today it has found its way into the mainstream, engulfing men and women from various social classes. A major impetus to the popularity of meth stems from the fact that the high from the drug lasts four or five times longer than that from cocaine. When used initially, meth is known to suppress appetite, create euphoria, boost self-confidence, and deliver a burst of energy. After a tolerance for the drug has built up, depression is likely to set in, followed by intense paranoia (Jefferson, 2005; Johnson, 2004).

While meth is a stimulant, what is known on the street as "roofie" is a depressant. It is related to the sedative Valium but is 10 times stronger. Roofies are actually Rohypnol, a prescription drug for severe insomnia. Rohypnol is sold over the counter in some 60 countries, and much of the drug used on the street in the United States is smuggled from Mexico and Columbia. The drug is especially popular with teenagers in the South and Southwest, who like to mix the drug with alcohol for a quick high. Like strong liquor, roofies tend to make users aggressive and fearless, but they often cause blackouts, with a total loss of memory. Because of this effect, some men use roofies to knock women out and then rape them; hence, the drug is also known as "the date-rape drug."

Ecstasy

Ecstasy is relatively popular with high school and college students as well as affluent young adults. It is a psychedelic, a mood-altering drug. Most of its users say they feel happier, their mind gets clearer, and their memory improves. They further feel a stronger desire for human connection and become compassionate and forgiving toward others. They are thus more inclined to embrace people, which leads to Ecstasy's nickname—the "hug drug." In short, at least according to its users, the drug provides a new and better perspective on life.

However, the U.S. government and some scientists insist that the drug is danger-ous. They cite studies showing that rats and monkeys suffer brain damage after being given large doses of Ecstasy. High doses of Ecstasy are indeed dangerous, but so is swallowing a whole bottle of Tylenol, which can wreck a person's liver and cause the person to die. Users of Ecstasy typically take only a small dose of the drug.

Ecstasy does have at least two big problems. One is that the specific doses of Ecstasy may be impure, containing unknown foreign substances that can kill. The other problem is that Ecstasy can cause the body to overheat. If a user does not drink enough water to quench the enormous thirst, he or she may suffer from dehydration, organ failure, or brain damage. But drinking too much water can cause death from thinned-out blood (de Seve, 2006; Klam, 2001).

■ A Class Picture of Illegal Drug Use

Social class—measured in terms of education, occupation, and income—is signifi-cantly related to the type of illicit drug being used. People of high social classes tend to use certain drugs, while people of lower classes usually turn to other drugs. Let's take a closer look.

First, there is a strong connection between higher classes and marijuana: the higher the class, the more likely the use of marijuana. The drug is especially popular among college and high school students; it is by far their number one drug of choice. Marijuana is equally popular with the youth in many other wealthy societies such as Canada, Britain, Switzerland, and Spain. Apparently, pot smoking is the affluent youth's way of pursuing leisure in the developed world (ter Bogt et al., 2006).

Second, heroin is far and away the most popular drug among people of the lower classes, particularly those who live in poor, inner-city neighborhoods. The affluent, including their children of high school or college age, typically stay away from heroin. This has long been the case. Even in the 1960s, when massive numbers of college and high school students experimented with all sorts of drugs, heroin remained at the bottom of their drug choice. However, since the mid-1990s, an increasing number of affluent whites have turned on to heroin, chiefly because the drug is now pure and safe enough to snort or smoke, which avoids the risk of getting AIDS from sharing contaminated needles (Leland, 1996; Wren, 1999).

Third, cocaine has long been associated with affluent people because of its high cost. Today, the drug remains more popular with the affluent than the poor. However, because the drug is much less expensive nowadays, less affluent people have increasingly used it. The cheapest form of cocaine, crack, is especially popular with the poor. In fact, crack has been called "the poor person's drug." Socially marginalized, such as being deprived of social support, financial resources, and good health, the poor continue to be far more likely than the affluent to use crack (Van Der Poel and Van De Mheen, 2006).

Fourth, meth and roofies seem to cast a special allure for working-class and young people. Working-class men tend to use meth to seek euphoria, an enhanced self-confidence, and a burst of energy, while working-class women use the drug to lose weight because it can suppress appetite. Roofie is also popular with the working class and young people, who like to drink alcohol when using the drug, which has the same effect as alcohol but with far more potency. As for Ecstasy, it is often associated with high school and college students and young professionals.

Although we have analyzed users of different drugs separately, most people who use drugs tend to use more than one type. In addition, under the influence of peer groups, they tend to graduate from using relatively soft drugs, such as cigarettes, liquor, or marijuana, to using harder drugs, such as heroin and cocaine. Still, most drug users favor a certain drug over others (Fergusson, 2006).

■ Problems Associated with Drug Abuse

Certain problems are associated with drug abuse. The most important ones are crime and AIDS.

Crime

There is a strong link between drug abuse and crime, as suggested by the fact that people who use illegal drugs generally commit more crime than those who do not. Research has shown that half of the crime suspects arrested in the United States have used illegal drugs in the prior 3 days and that 55% of their counterparts in England have done the same. A review of 30 studies in various countries has further found that drug users are three to four times more likely than nonusers to commit a crime (Bennett et al., 2008; Leinwand, 2009). Because these drug users are typically poor, uneducated, and economically unskilled, they cannot afford to pay for their prohibitively expensive drug habits unless they rob or steal to get the money for their next fix.

AIDS

The connection between drug abuse and AIDS is remarkably strong in the United States. Intravenous (IV) drug users with AIDS make up nearly 10% of the AIDS population in Holland, Sweden, and Canada. It is much worse in the United States, where the figure exceeds 30%. The proportion is much higher in some cities: 40% in New York City and 65% in Newark. Most of these IV drug users have contracted AIDS from sharing used needles, and they have rejected clean needles even if easily available. But why do they take the terrible risk of getting AIDS? One reason is that they are hard-core drug addicts rather than occasional drug users. Their craving for drugs is so overwhelming that they must shoot up right away and cannot be bothered with taking precaution. Another reason is that the essence of the addict's lifestyle is risk taking; as Goode states, "Their habit alone is daily dalliance with mortality. Given a life filled with risks—overdoses, hepatitis, and jail—the threat of dying from AIDS seems, to many, merely redundant" (Goode, 2005).

■ Experiences in Becoming a Drug Abuser

Contrary to popular belief, it is not the drug peddler, "the merchant of death," who pushes drugs on the innocent youth. It is instead their friends who introduce them to drug use. This is particularly true of those who smoke marijuana, the most widely used illicit drug. As shown by one national survey, an overwhelming majority (nearly 90%) of pot smokers obtain their marijuana from a friend or relative (Caulkins and Liccardo, 2006).

Once they have tried the drug, would-be users usually go through a learning process—with instruction from drug-introducing friends—to end up becoming hooked on the drug. Howard Becker (1963) has identified three kinds of experiences in the process of becoming a marijuana user.

The first experience involves learning the *technique* to get high. Because beginners tend to smoke marijuana like an ordinary cigarette, they may fail to achieve the desired drug effects. Thus they may watch their experienced friends smoke or they may receive direct coaching from them on the proper way of smoking the drug. They may eventually learn to hold the smoke in their lungs long enough for the bloodstream to absorb the psychoactive substance of marijuana.

The second experience is learning to *recognize* the drug effects. After learning the proper technique of smoking marijuana, new users may feel that they still do not get high. So they have to learn from friends that having cold feet, rubbery legs, intense hunger, and unawareness of the passage of time are some of the signs of a marijuana high.

The third experience requires learning to *enjoy* the drug effects. While high, novices may have such feelings as dizziness, thirst, and tingling of the scalp; they may misjudge time and distance or feel themselves to be simultaneously at two places; and they may hear strange sounds and other sensations. These experiences may be unpleasant or even frightening to beginning drug users. They must learn to redefine these sensations as pleasurable; otherwise, they will not use the drug again. New marijuana users usually learn to enjoy these experiences only after receiving encouragement and reassurances from experienced friends. These friends may tell them such things as, "You sure are lucky; I'd give anything to get that high myself. I haven't been that high in years."

With the use of cocaine, heroin, and other illegal drugs, the beginner may also have to learn the first experience—the technique of using the drug. But it may not be necessary for them to go through the second and third experiences by recognizing and enjoying the drug effects because the effects are more clear-cut and predictable than the effects of marijuana. In virtually all cases of initial cocaine use, for example, the user feels its effect as extremely pleasurable, which makes it unnecessary to learn to recognize and enjoy the drug effects. This may explain why cocaine is highly addictive; however, this positive experience does not mean everybody who uses cocaine—or other highly addictive drugs like heroin—will become addicted (see **Box 9.4**).

BOX 9.4   WHAT RESEARCH REVEALS

Addiction Does Discriminate

It is widely believed that if a person uses drugs he or she will most likely end up being addicted. This is because, as the popular belief suggests, "Drug abuse is an equal opportunity destroyer; drug addiction is a bipartisan illness; addiction does not discriminate; it doesn't care if you are rich or poor, famous or unknown, a man or woman, or even a child." Everybody who uses drugs, then, is supposed to become addicted, no matter who they are.

The democratization of addiction may sound persuasive, but it doesn't reflect reality. For one thing, most drug users and abusers eventually extricate themselves from addiction. Research has found that from 60% to 80% of people who have been addicted in their teens and twenties stop being heavy, problem users in their thirties. Large national surveys have also revealed that those who kept using were much more likely than those who got clean to be women who have been sexually abused as children, truant and aggressive young men, children of addicts, people diagnosed with depression and bipolar illnesses, and poor or Native Americans. Other studies found that people who continue to use drugs until they become addicted "are bad at delaying gratification and gauging consequences, are impulsive, think they have little to lose, have few competing interests, or are willing to lie to a spouse" (Satel, 2008). In short, addiction does discriminate, much more likely to victimize people with certain characteristics and experiences.

■ The War on Drugs

Punitive approach
Using law enforcement to stop the supply of drugs and punish drug sellers and users.

Supportive approach
Using drug prevention (or education) and treatment to reduce the demand for drugs and help drug addicts.

The war on drugs consists of two approaches: The **punitive approach** involves using law enforcement to stop the supply of drugs and punish drug sellers and users. The **supportive approach** requires using drug prevention (or education) and treatment to reduce the demand for drugs and help drug addicts. The U.S. war on drugs is mostly punitive, because the government devotes most of its antidrug budget to law enforcement. In 2008, for example, about $8.3 billion was spent on enforcing drug laws while only $4.6 billion went toward drug prevention and treatment (Kalb, 2008). This approach has caused a sharp increase in the incarceration of drug offenders.

The law enforcement approach has failed to reduce the general level of drug use, and this has led to calls for the legalization of drugs. Supporters of legalization contend that, like Prohibition (of alcohol) in the 1920s, current drug laws do more harm than good. They are said to generate many crimes, including homicides, and to encourage police corruption. By legalizing drugs, supporters argue, the government can take away obscene profits from drug traffickers, end police corruption, and reduce crime drastically. Finally, legalizers believe that with legalization, the huge amount of money currently spent on law enforcement can be used for drug treatment and education, which will dramatically reduce abuse of and demand for drugs (Moskos, 2008).

Those who oppose legalization respond that if drugs are legalized, drug use and addiction will skyrocket. As William Bennett (1989), a former national drug control policy director, points out, "After the repeal of Prohibition, consumption of alcohol soared by 350%." Most Americans are also viscerally opposed to the legalization of drugs. They particularly do not want to see heroin, cocaine, and other hard drugs as easily available as tobacco, alcoholic beverages, and other legal drugs (Bennett, 2001; Brown, 2008).

Today, a third approach has emerged to deal with the drug problems. It is opposed to both strict criminal punishment and outright legalization. It involves striking a middle ground between punishment and legalization with the aim of *reducing the harm* from drugs. This requires the use of treatment programs to help drug addicts and abusers reduce their drug use, commit less crime, and live longer, healthier lives. Other, similar programs such as providing clean needles can also be used to reduce harm, specifically by lowering the rates of human immunodeficiency virus transmission (Goode, 2004).

■ Sociological Theories of Drug Use

The three sociological theories can help us understand drug use. According to functionalist theory, drug use occurs because it serves a useful function in various ways. Conflict theory focuses on how the powerful use the war on drugs to oppress the powerless, such as the minorities. And symbolic interaction theory emphasizes the meaning attached to drug use as the cause of the problem.

Functionalist Theory

To functionalist theory, drug use serves a number of positive functions. Some of these functions are obvious. The use of tobacco, alcohol, or marijuana, for example, can relieve tension and enhance social interaction. Profit can be made from growing, distributing, and selling these drugs. But it is also obvious that the illegal hard drugs such as heroin and crack are dysfunctional, causing sickness, crimes, broken homes, poverty, and many other problems. Why then do some people still abuse these drugs? The reason is that although the drugs may appear dysfunctional to people who do not abuse them, they are functional to those who do abuse the drugs. It is noteworthy that those drug abusers are mostly poor. Elliott Currie (1993) found the following from reviewing numerous studies on drug abuse since the early 1950s: "The link between drug abuse and deprivation is one of the strongest in 40 years of careful research . . . in Europe as in the United States . . . among poor whites and Hispanics as well as inner-city blacks."

For these people, drugs can serve several latent functions. First, drugs can fulfill the need for *status*. In the larger, conventional society, the poor are denied legitimate avenues of attaining esteem, a sense of respect, or even a sense of community. Consequently, there has developed in the poor neighborhood a drug culture that serves as an alternative source of esteem and respect. As Currie finds, "Being in the drug culture is just like being a movie star. So many people depend on you, want to stop you in the street. The police are always on you. . . . You are a very important person." Another function of drugs involves helping the user *cope* with the harsh, oppressive realities of poverty. As Currie observes, "Drugs become a way of getting away from daily problems, medicating emotional anguish, relieving stress, escaping pain." Finally, drugs serve the third function of providing a sense of *structure* to shattered lives. Deprived of steady work or a stable family life, the poor cannot find the sense of structure that the nonpoor have. As a substitute, drug use helps relieve monotony and purposelessness among the poor.

Conflict Theory

While the functionalist theory points to the functions of drugs as the causes of drug use, conflict theory focuses on powerful people using law enforcement to oppress the powerless, particularly minorities, who use drugs. The first attempt to launch this oppression against the powerless appeared as a city ordinance against opium dens in San Francisco in 1875. The custom of opium smoking had earlier been introduced to the United States by Chinese laborers who were imported to work on railroad construction crews. Initially their opium dens were tolerated, but soon the Chinese laborers were seen as a threat to the white labor market because they were hired to work long hours for low wages. The white workers started a campaign against the Chinese and their opium dens, describing how the Chinese enticed little white boys and girls into becoming "opium fiends." Consequently, many cities followed San Francisco in passing ordinances against opium dens, which provided a legal basis for unrestrained and arbitrary police raids and searches of Chinese premises.

Around 1900, many state laws and municipal ordinances were enacted against the use of cocaine. These anticocaine laws were effectively intended to oppress blacks. In those days, cocaine was widely used by blacks, but whites fearfully believed that a cocaine high could spur blacks to violence against whites, stimulate sexual assaults by black men on white women, improve blacks' pistol marksmanship, give blacks superhuman strength, and make them cunning and efficient. The anticocaine laws, then, were aimed at controlling blacks and keeping them in their place.

In 1937 Congress passed the Marijuana Tax Act to turn marijuana use into a criminal offense. It was actually intended to drive Mexican migrant workers in the West and Southwest back across the border; they were known to smoke marijuana while being seen as a threat for taking jobs away from Anglo-American workers. However, since the late 1960s, large numbers of conventional, middle-class whites have used marijuana. The drug has stopped being associated with the powerless minority. Consequently, affluent and respectable marijuana users are more likely to go free or receive light sentences. Nevertheless, minorities, especially African Americans, continue to suffer the brunt of antidrug law enforcement. African Americans, for example, are more severely punished with longer sentences for using crack—the cheap form of cocaine—than are whites for using the more expensive cocaine.

Symbolic Interaction Theory

According to symbolic interaction theory, whether a certain drug constitutes a social problem is a subjective phenomenon. This theory may explain why some drugs are illegal in some societies but not in others or why they are illegal today but not in the past. Marijuana, for example, is regarded as harmful and therefore illegal in many societies today, but it was treated as a sacred and useful drug in many societies in ancient times. Similarly, cocaine is widely seen as dangerous and illegal today, but before 1900 it was a major ingredient in numerous patent medicines and in many soft drinks, such as Coca-Cola. In 1885 it was widely known as a wonder drug, endorsed by Pope Leo XIII, Pope Pius X, President McKinley, the kings of four countries, and many famous writers and artists (Goode, 2005).

Symbolic interaction theory also can help us understand why people use and abuse drugs from how they perceive the drugs. Basically, they use a certain drug because they see that they can get some benefits from the drug although society may condemn it as harmful. This can be illustrated by a few examples. First, the use of alcohol and tobacco is popular because these drugs are widely viewed as means of easing physical aches and pains, relieving psychological stresses and strains, reducing a sense of social incompetence and awkwardness, or providing quiet companionship or lively conversation. These positive meanings of the drugs are part of the legal drug culture propagated by the alcohol and tobacco industries spending billions of dollars on advertising—coaxing and seducing people to use the drugs.

Second, people with a certain type of personal problem tend to use one particular drug regularly because they find it helpful in relieving their specific problem. Thus people who are restless, aggressive, or given to violent eruptions tend to use heroin regularly. They find the drug helpful in feeling calm, soothed, and relaxed. Those who often feel depressed, fatigued, bored, or shy are inclined to choose cocaine because they feel it helps make them energetic, self-assured, and sociable.

Third, people can become addicted to a drug if they suffer from withdrawal sickness and perceive their continuing to use the drug as effective in getting rid of the withdrawal sickness. The cause of addiction, then, is the drug user's *cognitive association* between withdrawal distress and the discontinuous use of the drug. This association may explain why the mentally challenged, young children, and animals usually are immune to addiction; they cannot understand the meaning of withdrawal symptoms even if it is explained to them. However, normal people with average intelligence can easily get hooked on drugs once they experience withdrawal distress and know the cause of it (Lindesmith, 1968).

For a summary of this symbolic interaction theory of drug use along with the conflict and functionalist theories, see **Box 9.5**.

QUESTIONS TO EXPLORE

1. Consider a national drug-related problem that has been getting some media attention, such as the problem involving the use of methamphetamine. From a functionalist perspective, do you see any latent or manifest functions being served in your community by this problem? Please explain.

2. Employ a conflict theory to discuss who might directly benefit from fighting a given drug problem. Who stands to profit the most?

3. Please visit the Al-Anon Web site at http://www.al-anon.alateen.org/. After reading the description of the organization, its purpose, and the services provided, state which one of the major theories most directly reflects its views? Why so?

BOX 9.5   THEORETICAL THUMBNAIL

Explaining Drug Use

Theory	Focus	Insights
Functionalist Theory	Positive functions of drug use	Drug use occurs because it serves various functions.
Conflict Theory	The powerful oppress the powerless by criminalizing their drug use	The criminalization of opium, cocaine, and marijuana has involved oppressing the minorities.
Symbolic Interaction Theory	Whether drug use is harmful is subjective, and why people use drugs depends on how they perceive the drug	The perceived harm of drugs varies across time and space, and drug use results from the user's perception.

Review

SUMMARY

1. The abuse of prescription drugs is mostly a middle-class phenomenon. There are three reasons for the prevalence of prescription-drug abuse: The drug is easily available, it is widely assumed to be safe, and its users are under the influence of peer pressure and other social factors.

2. Despite the widely reported hazards of smoking, 25% of Americans continue to smoke. They do so because they find the benefits of smoking outweigh the costs, and they are more inclined to take risks than nonsmokers. Globally, Americans are moderate drinkers. Still, they consume more alcohol than all legal and illegal drugs, and alcoholism is one of America's biggest health problems.

3. A large minority (44%) of American college students are binge drinkers. The reasons include the stress from studying hard, social pressure to get drunk to fit in, regarding partying as an important part of college life, and the popular belief that binge drinking is very common. Supporters of the law that bans young people younger than 21 years of age from drinking argue that the law saves many lives by reducing drunken driving and car crashes. Opponents contend that the drinking age law encourages binge drinking by causing underage youth to drink in secrecy.

4. According to popular myths about alcohol abuse, most alcoholics are homeless, mixing different kinds of alcoholic drinks makes one get drunk faster, drinking black coffee can sober up the intoxicated person, drinking beer only is unlikely to make one an alcoholic, and sex becomes more exciting after several drinks.

5. Men are more likely than women to get drunk, and young men are more likely than older men to drink heavily. African Americans are less likely than whites to drink but are more likely to become alcoholics. Hispanics are also more likely to become alcoholics than are whites, largely because of their high rates of poverty. Native Americans have the highest incidence of alcoholism, while Italian and Chinese Americans have the lowest, though they often drink. Conservative Protestants are less likely than other Protestants to drink but more likely to become problem drinkers. People of the lower classes drink less than those of higher classes but are more likely to have drinking problems. Alcohol consumption is the highest in the Northeast and the lowest in the South.

6. There is more drinking in affluent societies than poorer ones. Of the developed countries, Russia drinks the most. Excessive drinking can bring about high rates of automobile accidents, criminal offenses, and violent crimes. To become alcoholic, individuals go through four stages: drinking to seek relief from tension, being psychologically addicted, being physically addicted, and becoming isolated and withdrawn from friends and relatives while totally dependent on alcohol. An effective way to deal with alcoholism is to battle isolation and withdrawal by seeking social support—via joining AA.

7. Legal drugs such as alcohol and tobacco are more dangerous than illegal ones such as heroin and cocaine because they are more prevalent and cause more social problems. The United States has the highest rate of drug use in the world, but most of the drug problems are confined to the lower classes. Marijuana is widely known to be harmful, but critics do not consider it so. Only if used to the point of intoxication, it can impair judgment and memory—in the same way as alcohol. Heroin can be highly addictive because it can deliver an intense high, but most heroin users do not become addicted because they quit after the high diminishes. Cocaine can be extremely dangerous if used frequently for a long time, and crack is even more powerful. Meth is said to produce a high that lasts much longer than cocaine, but it is also likely to lead to depression and paranoia. Roofies are a depressant that often cause blackouts. Ecstasy is a psychedelic drug that can make the user happier but is deadly if used in high doses.

8. Users of marijuana and cocaine are more likely to be relatively affluent, while users of heroin and crack are more likely to be poor. Users of meth and roofies are largely working class and young. Ecstasy users are mostly students and young professionals. People who abuse drugs are much more likely to commit crime and contract AIDS than those who do not. To become a drug abuser, the individual usually goes through three experiences: learning the technique to get high, recognizing the drug effects, and enjoying the drug effects. Research has shown that most drug users do not get addicted to the drug.

9. The U.S. war on drugs is mostly punitive, using law enforcement to stop the supply of drugs and punish drug sellers and users. This approach has failed to significantly reduce drug use, leading to calls for legalizing the drugs. Opponents of legalization argue that drug use and addiction will skyrocket. A third proposal is to focus on reducing the harm from drugs.

10. To the functionalists, drug use occurs because it serves some positive functions. To conflict theorists, the powerful oppress the powerless by criminalizing the latter's drug use. And to the symbolic interaction theorists, whether drug use is harmful is subjective, and its use can be explained by how the user perceives the drug.

CRITICAL THINKING QUESTIONS

1. How have the drugs of preference in your own community changed throughout your life? To what do you attribute these changes? Could it be media, pop culture, some unique local phenomenon? Explain why this is the case.

2. Because drug users continue to consume illegal drugs to get "high" or pleasure from taking the drugs, what social rewards might they get from taking illegal drugs?

3. Which side of the binge drinking argument do you support? With 44% of college students engaging in drinking while the legal age is 21 years, will lowering the drinking age only make a bad problem worse? Explain your response.

⌨ INTERNET RESOURCES

Al-Anon (http://www.al-anon.alateen.org/) groups are comprised of relatives and friends of alcoholics who share their experience, strength, and hope in order to solve their common problems. Al-Anon seeks to give comfort to families of alcoholics, while giving understanding and encouragement to the alcoholic. Al-Anon promotes the position that alcoholism is a family illness and that changed attitudes can aid recovery. Al-Anon is not associated with any political party or cause and is self-supporting through voluntary contributions.

Drug Abuse Resistance Education (D.A.R.E.) (http://www.dare.com/home/default.asp) is a police officer–led lecture series for students ranging in grade level from kindergarten through 12th grade.

The mission of the Drug Enforcement Administration (DEA) (http://www.justice.gov/dea/index.htm) is to regulate controlled substances by enforcing the drug laws of the United States and to proactively seek to build cooperative relationships with internal and outside groups and agencies dedicated to "reducing the availability of illicit controlled substances on the domestic and international markets."

Mothers Against Drunk Driving (MADD) (http://www.madd.org/) was created in 1980. MADD was intended to increase public awareness and continues to provide educational services and public service announcements, with a mission to "stop drunk driving, support the victims of this violent crime, and prevent underage drinking."

The mission of the National Drug Intelligence Center (NDIC) of the U.S. Department of Justice (http://www.justice.gov/ndic/) is to provide strategic drug-related intelligence, computer support, and training assistance to the drug control, public health, law enforcement, and intelligence communities of the United States (in order to reduce the adverse effects of drug trafficking, drug abuse, and other drug-related criminal activity).

The principal purpose of the Office of National Drug Control Policy (ONDCP) (http://www.whitehousedrugpolicy.gov/) is to establish policies, priorities, and objectives for the nation's drug control program. The goals of the program are to reduce illicit drug use, manufacturing, and trafficking; drug-related crime and violence; and drug-related health consequences.

Problems of Institutions

IV

Family Problems

About 1 million American children go through this experience every year. Their parents get them together and break the news that they are divorcing. But not to worry, they say, because they are parting amicably and sharing joint custody. The scene might play out like this:

"We're splitting up the week, alternating days," explains the dad.

"How are you splitting up seven days?" says the son, reeling and confused.

"I've got Tuesday, Wednesday, and Saturday, and every other Thursday," the dad says reassuringly.

"That was your father's idea," the mom chimes in proudly.

"Well," the son asks anxiously, "what about the cat?"

A pause. "We haven't discussed the cat," the mom says with consternation.

This scene appears in the movie *The Squid and the Whale*. It illustrates the director's take on his own parents' divorce when he was a teen. It captures the emotional havoc experienced by children although their parents believe that as long as they divorce amicably and stay involved with the kids everything will be fine. In fact, research has found that after the ending of those marriages, the children typically struggle with such symptoms as anxiety, depression, and problems in school (Marquardt, 2005). We will discuss these and other problems of the family in this chapter. But first we will put the American family in perspective by comparing it with other families around the world.

■ Varieties of Marriage and the Family

Marriage and the family vary in form from one society to another. So does who has authority in the family. These variations are determined by the different norms of societies.

Types of Marriage

The norms of societies differ in specifying who chooses the partners for marriage. In many traditional societies, **arranged marriages**—in which the partners are chosen by the couple's parents—are the norm. The young couple may not know each other until the wedding day, but they are expected to learn to love each other during the marriage. They are assumed to be too emotional to choose compatible mates. Usually, the parents base their choice of a husband for their daughter on how financially secure his family is, how agreeable the prospective daughter-in-law is to the young man's mother, and how compatible the couple's personalities are. In arranged marriages, the brides are usually very young, aged 15 to 19 years. Such marriages are most prevalent in relatively poor and traditional societies, where marrying off a young daughter often means having one fewer mouth to feed and avoiding the dishonor of her bearing illegitimate children. In the United States and other affluent and modern societies, women marry at an older age and make their own decisions about whom to marry.

Everywhere, the choice of a partner depends on society's norms regarding which partners are appropriate. In most societies, people are required to practice **exogamy** (literally, "marrying outward"), the act of marrying someone from outside one's group, such as the clan, tribe, or village. Contrasted with exogamy is **endogamy** ("marrying within"), the act of marrying someone from within one's own group. Endogamy stops short, though, of violating the incest taboo because endogamous societies do not encourage marriage between close relatives.

Other norms govern the number of spouses a person may have. **Monogamy**—the marriage of one man to one woman—is the most common form in the world. It is also very popular in the United States (see **Box 10.1**). However, many societies, especially Muslim and small, preindustrial ones, approve of **polygamy**, the marriage of one person to two or more people of the opposite sex. It is rare for society to allow the practice of **polyandry**, marriage of one woman to two or more men, but many societies permit **polygyny**, marriage of one man to two or more women. A new variant of polygamy has become increasingly common in the United States. Rather than having several spouses at the same time, many Americans have one spouse at a time, going through a succession of marriage, divorce, and remarriage. Such practice is not really polygamy but **serial monogamy**, the marriage of one person to two or more people but only one at a time.

Types of Family

When it comes to who should make up a family, society's definitions of a family can be divided into two basic types. In the United States, a family has long been defined as a **nuclear family**, comprising two parents and their unmarried children. It is also called a *conjugal family* because

A nuclear family comprises two parents and their unmarried children. This type of family is quite common in Western industrial societies.

its members are related through the marriage between the parents. This type of family is quite common in Western industrial societies.

Arranged marriage
A marriage in which the partners are chosen by the couple's parents.

Exogamy
The practice of marrying someone from outside one's group.

Endogamy
The practice of marrying someone from within one's own group.

Monogamy
The marriage of one man to one woman.

Polygamy
The marriage of one person to two or more people of the opposite sex.

Polyandry
The marriage of one woman to two or more men.

Polygyny
The marriage of one man to two or more women.

Serial monogamy
The marriage of one person to two or more people, but only one at a time.

Nuclear family
A family comprised of two parents and their unmarried children.

BOX 10.1   WHAT RESEARCH REVEALS

The Dark Side of Successful Marriages

In analyzing two national surveys, sociologists Naomi Gerstel and Natalia Sarkisian (2006) discovered something ironical about successful monogamy—the most popular form of marriage in the world that involves the union of one man and one woman. It is not surprising for them to find that when such marriages are good, happy, or successful they become "greedy" by demanding total and undivided commitment. However, by demanding total commitment, successful marriages weaken the social ties outside the marital bond. More specifically, the married couples are less involved with their parents and siblings when compared with singles. The married are less likely to visit, call, or write these relatives. They are also less likely to give the relatives emotional support and practical help such as offering concern and affection, doing household chores, and providing transportation. In addition, they are less likely to socialize with neighbors or hang out with friends.

Why do successfully married couples stay away from relatives, neighbors, and friends? There are at least three reasons. One is economic in nature. The married have more money than the unmarried so they need less help from family and friends. The second reason is emotional. Since a successful marriage requires intense emotional involvement, the newlyweds are so wrapped up with each other that they have little time left for others. Even older couples have little time to spend with others. Since these spouses depend on each other as confidants and as the main source of emotional support, they are less likely than singles to "call a sibling, parent, or friend to recount their day at work or their problems with kids" (Gerstel and Sarkisian, 2006). And the third reason is the culture of self-sufficiency: Americans take for granted that married people should be able to support and care for themselves.

The other type of family is more prevalent in less industrialized or more traditional societies. It includes not only the nuclear family but also grandparents, uncles, aunts, and cousins. All these people constitute an **extended family**, consisting of two parents, their unmarried children, and other relatives. This kind of family is also called a *consanguine family* because the blood tie among relatives is considered more important than the marital bond. In traditional Chinese extended families, for example, the tie between a married man and his mother is much stronger than his bond to his wife. In fact, if a mother does not like her son's wife, she can force him to divorce the wife.

Authority in the Family

Societies differ in defining who has authority in the family. In most societies, authority rests with the oldest male. Thus, the **patriarchal family**, in which the dominant figure is the oldest male, is the most prevalent around the world. In such a family, the oldest male dominates everyone else. He allocates tasks, settles disputes, and makes other important decisions that affect family members.

In a few societies there is the **matriarchal family**, in which the dominant figure is the oldest female. There is also an **egalitarian family**, in which authority is equally distributed between husband and wife. Globally, these two types of family are rare. A variant to the matriarchal family, however, has appeared in many industrial countries. In the United States, for example, many poor families are matriarchal by default. Either the father is not present or has lost his dominant status because of chronic unemployment. Many

---

Extended family
A family that consists of two parents, their unmarried children, and other relatives.

Patriarchal family
A family in which the dominant figure is the oldest male.

Matriarchal family
A family in which the dominant figure is the oldest female.

Egalitarian family
A family in which the authority is equally distributed between husband and wife.

other U.S. families, though still dominated by husbands, are also becoming increasingly egalitarian because of wives' relatively high professional status and income.

■ Problems of American Families

Most American couples are relatively happy with their marriages, but many do have serious problems. Two of the most serious are divorce and violence. Also serious, though less so, are the sharp decline in marriages among African Americans and the spreading of high divorce rates around the world because of the widespread belief in love-based marriages.

Divorce

Divorce is very common in the United States. Nearly half of the Americans who marry now will eventually get a divorce. The U.S. divorce rate is the highest in the world. Why do so many marriages end in divorce? A cross-cultural analysis suggests at least four social forces behind the current divorce rate in American society.

1. *The disappearing of the stigma of divorce.* In many traditional societies, unhappily married couples stay married because of the stigma attached to divorce. But in the United States, there is virtually no such stigma anymore. Divorce has gained wide acceptance as a solution to marital unhappiness, and it has become easier to obtain from the courts. Under the no-fault divorce law, anybody may end a marriage without getting his or her spouse's consent.

2. *Greater availability of services and opportunities for the divorced.* In traditional societies, men depend heavily on marriage for sexual gratification and housekeeping, and women look to it for financial security. Such services and opportunities are more easily available to U.S. adults without the need for marriage. After all, men can find sexual gratification outside marriage, and women can become financially independent without husbands. In addition, the high divorce rate today has expanded the pool of eligible new partners. All this has made divorce more attractive to unhappily married couples.

3. *High expectations about the quality of the marital relationship.* Young people in traditional societies do not expect exciting romantic experiences with their spouses, especially if their marriages are arranged by their parents. In contrast, young people in the United States expect a lot, including an intense love relationship. Such experiences are difficult to fulfill year after year, and the chances of disillusionment with the partner are therefore great. Because young people have higher expectations than older ones, it is not surprising that most divorces occur within the first 4 years of marriage.

4. *The importance of individualism.* The rights of individuals are considered much more important in the United States than in traditional societies. Individualism encourages people to put their own needs and desires ahead of those of others, including their spouses, and to feel that if they want a divorce, they are entitled to get one. In traditional societies, people are more likely to subordinate their needs to those of the kinship group and thus to feel that they have no right to seek a divorce (Cherlin, 2010).

The high divorce rate in the United States does not mean, as common sense would suggest, that marriage is no longer popular. On the contrary, Americans apparently continue to love marriage too much. Thus they not only divorce more, they also marry more, as shown by several pieces of evidence. First, American society has the highest rate of marriage in the industrial world despite having the highest rate of divorce. Second, in the United States, most of the southern, southwestern, and western states have higher divorce rates than the national average, but they also have higher marriage rates. Third, the majority of those who divorce eventually marry once or more again. Why the simultaneous but conflicting popularity of marriage and divorce in the United States? American culture emphasizes the importance of marriage for those who want to commit themselves to a marriage but also the importance of divorce for those who are unhappy with their marriage (Cherlin, 2010).

Divorce usually makes the couples happier for having left behind the unhappy marriage, but it is likely to cause problems for the children. When researchers compared children in divorced families with those in intact families, they found the former more likely to have problems such as having sexual intercourse at an earlier age, to have a first child outside of marriage, and to have lower levels of happiness. Studies in other countries have produced similar results. Most children are not seriously damaged by divorce, but divorce does raise the risk that a child will have problems (Cherlin, 2010; Marquardt, 2005). For thoughts on avoiding divorce, see **Box 10.2**.

Violence

Family violence is very common in the United States. Its exact incidence is difficult to pin down because various researchers do not define family violence in the same way. Some researchers consider spanking, for example, an act of violence, whereas others do not. Thus, there have been different estimates of the extent of family violence in the United States. The ones on the proportion of families in which violence occurs at least once a year range from 10% to 20%. According to another estimate, anywhere between 25% and 50% of all couples have experienced serious family violence at least once during their marriage (Waltermaurer, Ortega, and McNutt, 2003). These findings may make family violence appear to be an enormous problem. After all, the family is supposed to be a source of love and support.

Why does violence occur in so many families? A major reason seems to be stress. As research has found, the incidence of violence is highest among groups most likely to feel stressed, such as the urban poor, families with a jobless husband, and those with four to six children. However, stress by itself does not necessarily cause violence. It is the culture of violence in U.S. society that encourages people to resort to violence as a way of relieving their stress. The violence on television, corporal punishment in schools, and the death penalty, for example, all convey the idea that violence is an acceptable solution to problems (Linsky, Bachman, and Straus, 1995).

Many women who have been abused do not leave their husbands. One reason is that they are *the most socially and economically isolated* of all women because they have too little education and are not able to earn enough to support themselves or their children. Another reason is their *fear that their husbands will retaliate* by stalking

BOX 10.2 USING SOCIOLOGICAL INSIGHTS

How to Turn Unhappy Marriages Around

For many years, marriage counselors have not been very successful: Only half of their clients reported significant increases in marital happiness. This is because the counselors focused on *changing behavior*. Suppose a couple had reached an impasse because the wife couldn't get her husband to do any housework and he couldn't get her to make time for just the two of them. Faced with this problem, the counselor usually would try to change the behavior of both the husband and wife. Thus the counselor would advise the husband to agree to do some housework, the wife to agree to one night out per month, and both to agree to stop yelling at each other. But this effort at change was much easier said than done. Although the couple agreed to change, in actuality they could not pull it off.

A better approach is called *acceptance therapy*, which involves encouraging the spouses to accept each other's weaknesses. This is better than telling the couple to change the annoying things about each other that most likely cannot be changed. Instead, the couple should learn to tolerate and live with those annoyances, much in the same way one learns to live with a bad back. This approach is similar to what some researchers have called the *marital endurance ethic*, which requires couples to endure and outlast their problems rather than trying to solve them (Christensen and Jacobson, 2000).

In acceptance therapy, marriage counselors encourage the spouses to accept each other's weaknesses. This requires the spouses to endure and outlast their problems rather than trying to solve them.

A study of 20 unhappy couples has found that after 6 months of acceptance therapy, 90% reported dramatic increases in satisfaction. One of these couples had come for therapy because the wife complained of recurrent bouts of stomach pain after three decades of constant criticisms by her husband. Now, after 1 year of acceptance therapy, the couple says they are happier than ever. "I still tell her it's ridiculous to spend $500 on a coat that's really just a scarf," the husband says, but his anger about her overspending is gone. As for the wife, she is pleased with her new cashmere stole, while she has learned not to be bothered by his criticism (Schrof, 1998; Waite et al., 2002).

Acceptance therapy
A marriage counseling approach that encourages the spouses to accept each other's weaknesses.

them to inflict more serious violence if they leave. By staying, however, these women are more likely to end up getting killed or to struggle desperately to survive by killing their husbands (Anderson et al., 2003; Mann, 1996).

Sharp Decline in Black Marriage

Over the last five decades, African Americans have suffered a sharp decline in marriage that is far greater than all the other groups in the United States. In the 1950s, about 90% of African American women married at some point in their lives. Since then, their chances of marrying have plummeted. Today only about 67% will marry during their lifetimes. Among those who do marry, a large majority (70%) are projected to have their marriage break up (Cherlin, 2010).

Why the sharp decline in marriage? One reason is economic in nature. For one thing, globalization has transferred overseas most of the low-skilled jobs. Another thing is that automation has taken over from men most of their routine jobs. These economic forces have drastically reduced the earning prospects of numerous African Americans without college educations. It is thus much more difficult today for black men to earn the steady income that they need for marriage.

However, the terrible job market alone cannot totally discourage African Americans from marrying. Hispanic young adults are even less likely to have college degrees, yet they are much more likely to marry. There is, therefore, another reason for the sharp decline in marriage for African Americans. It is cultural in nature. Compared to European American culture, African American culture has always treated the marriage-based nuclear family as less important and kinship-based extended family as more important. Over the last 50 years, the importance of the extended family has further greatly increased in response to the problems of the job market. Within this enlarged family, marriage has lost its importance, replaced by ties among such women as mothers, grandmothers, aunts, and sisters (Cherlin, 2010).

Many other countries have also suffered a sharp decline in marriage but for a different reason: marrying for love (see Box 10.3).

BOX 10.3   GLOBAL PERSPECTIVE

How Love Kills Marriage

For thousands of years, throughout most of the world, marriage has been a stable social institution because it had little to do with love. It was, instead, a practical affair. Upper- and middle-class families arranged marriages for their children for political and business gain. In the lower classes, marriage was employed as a means of expanding the family's financial resources. Only 200 years ago did the Americans begin to believe that young people should be allowed to choose their spouses, and to do so for love. Once marriage was based on love, people began to think it was better to be single than to marry or stay married to someone they didn't love. Consequently, the divorce rates in the United States began to rise (Coontz, 2006).

Nowadays, the love craze is spreading like wildfire around the globe. Even in rural areas of Africa and Asia, where parents still negotiate the number of cows or goats demanded by the young woman's family, many young people look up newspaper personal ads to find their "true love." Although arranged marriages continue to be the norm in India, its young people are having the final say over whether to marry someone whom the parents have chosen. Even deeply conservative Saudi Arabia has recently passed a law to prohibit a father from forcing his daughter into marriage. As the belief in love becomes more and more popular, it gets harder and harder to discourage people from remaining single or getting a divorce when love fails to blossom (Coontz, 2006).

As a result, divorce rates are rising and marriage rates are falling all over the world. In China, divorce rates are soaring. In Japan, South Korea, Italy, and Hong Kong, the numbers of marriages have fallen so much that the authorities are fearful that their birth rates will sharply decline and their populations will drastically shrink. Singapore's government has started to sponsor singles' nights in an attempt to raise marriage rates. In Japan, a magazine has encouraged singles to get married, pleading, "Young people, don't hate sex" (Coontz, 2006).

■ Changes in American Families

There have been many challenging changes in the American family. Let us begin by examining the traditional nuclear family, the earliest form of family in the United States.

Nuclear Families

Before the United States was industrialized in the 19th century, the family had long consisted of a husband, wife, and children, with no other relatives. One reason for the popularity of this nuclear family in those days was that few people lived long enough to form an extended three-generation family. Another reason was the *impartible* inheritance practices, which allowed only one heir to inherit all the family property, consequently forcing sons who did not inherit their family's farm to leave and set up their own households.

On colonial farms, members of the nuclear family worked together to produce its livelihood. The wife was typically an essential economic partner to the husband. If her husband was a farmer, she would run the household; make the clothes; raise cows, pigs, and poultry; tend a garden; and sell milk, vegetables, chickens, and eggs. If her husband was a skilled craftsman, she would work with him. Thus, weavers' wives spun yarn, cutlers' wives polished metal, tailors' wives sewed buttonholes, and shoemakers' wives waxed shoes.

As the United States became industrialized in the 19th century, production was moved out of the home. Initially husbands, wives, and children worked for wages in factories and workshops to contribute to the common family budget. However, because of the difficulty of combining paid employment with the domestic tasks imposed on them, married women tended to work for wages irregularly. As wages rose, growing numbers of families could earn enough without the wife's paid work. Then, increasingly, the home was seen as the emotional center of life and a private refuge from the competitive public world. The women's role became emotional and moral rather than economic. Women were expected to rear their children and comfort their husbands. This turned into the stereotype of a typical and ideal U.S. family.

After industrialization was in full swing, women lost their status as their husbands' economic partners and acquired a subordinate status as homemakers. However, over the last few decades, there have been significant increases in gender equality, female independence through paid employment, and personal freedom for everybody. As a result, various forms of family have emerged, each being confronted with its own challenges.

Two-Career Families

Today, in most families with married couples and children, both parents work (see **Figure 10.1**). With children or not, more married women than ever have entered the workforce, doubling in number since 1970. Especially for women with children, employment has made it difficult to care for children while going to work. They have solved the problem by turning to others, which has spawned a huge industry for child care. The employment of married women has increased family income significantly. The income of two-career families is now much higher than that for one-career families.

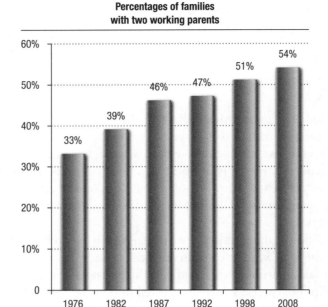

FIGURE 10.1 Two-Career Families Dominate U.S. Households

Since 1998, both parents work outside of the home in the majority of traditional families with married couples and children.

Critical Thinking: *Although marital happiness is generally higher with increases in average household income, what kinds of problems could result from both parents working outside of the home? Why?*

Source: U.S. Census Bureau, *2006–2008 American Community Survey.*

But does this economic gain bring marital happiness? Apparently, it does for *most* two-career couples. Such couples have also been found to be happier than couples in one-career families. There is, however, more strain in a two-career marriage if the wife is still expected to be a homemaker rather than a career seeker. The strain is much heavier for the employed wife than for the husband because she does most of the housework and child care. The resulting fatigue of the overworked wife has helped create a new demographic group, DINS (dual-income, no-sex couples), who still have sex but only about once a month or less (Deveny, 2003).

The impact of a wife's employment seems to depend on how much support she gets from her husband. Some husbands still find it difficult to render total support to their wives' careers, particularly if their wives earn more than they do. Consequently, in cases where the wife outperforms the husband in earnings, sex lives are more likely to suffer, feelings of love are more likely to diminish, and marriages are more likely to end in divorce. On the other hand, in cases where the husbands fully support their wives' employment by doing their share of house cleaning and child care, the couples head off marital stress and achieve marital happiness. Generally, supportive husbands have long been exposed to egalitarian ideologies and lifestyles. They have accepted the value of gender equality. They have also seen their mothers as competent and influential individuals who shared equal status with their fathers (Barnett and Rivers, 1996).

Interestingly, as sociologist Arlie Hochschild (1997) has found, increasing numbers of married career women are discovering the "great male secret" that work can be a great escape from the pressures of traditional home life. They find that the work environment has become more employee friendly and the home life more hectic. As a result, many working women choose to work long hours, as their husbands do. Unfortunately, this makes it difficult for both parents to spend enough time with their children.

Single-Parent Families

Nearly one out of three American families with children younger than 18 years of age has only one parent in the household. Most (over 80%) of these families are headed by women. It has been estimated that more than half of all children born in the 1990s will live with their mothers alone before they reach age 18 (U.S. Census Bureau, 2010).

The majority of the unmarried mothers are 20 years of age and older. They have been divorced, separated, widowed, or abandoned by their husbands. Most live below or near the poverty level. Among them, African American mothers are more likely to reside with the children's grandmothers, who provide free child care. Since the early 1990s, the number of teenagers who are unmarried mothers has declined sharply, thanks to an increase in birth control and a reduction in sexual activity. But states with higher poverty rates, such as those in the South, continue to have higher teenage birth rates than other states (McKay and Carrns, 2004).

Compared to two-parent families, female-headed families are more likely to experience social and psychological stress, such as unemployment, job change, lack of social support, negative self-image, and pessimism about the future. Children from single-parent families also have a larger share of such problems as juvenile delinquency, truancy, and poor schoolwork. Some researchers argue that these problems do not result directly from the absence of a father in a female-headed home, but from other factors that characterize the two-parent family with problem children, such as low income, poor living conditions, and lack of parental supervision. Without these factors, many children from single-parent families are said to do just fine (Kantrowitz and Wingert, 2001). However, studies by Sara McLanahan and Gary Sandefur (1994) show that children who grow up with a single mom are worse off, on average, than their peers who grow up with both parents, regardless of the parents' income and educational background.

Blended Families

Because of the high rates of divorce and remarriage, blended families (or stepfamilies) have become very common. About one-third of all Americans are members of a blended family. Because women usually get custody of children in divorce cases, most blended families consist of mothers, their biological children, and stepfathers (U.S. Census Bureau, 2010).

The happiness of blended families depends largely on how well the stepfather gets along with the children. It is difficult to be a stepfather because society has not yet provided a script for performing the stepfather role, as it has for the father role. Thus, it is more difficult for stepfathers to develop intimate and durable bonds with their stepchildren than for other fathers to do so with their biological children.

Having grown accustomed to living with their biological fathers, children tend to regard their stepfathers as interlopers or as distant, unwanted relatives overstaying their visits. They may resent having to change their lifestyle. As a 15-year-old girl sobbed to her mother, "I can't stand it. I have to put on my bathrobe at 10 o'clock at night in 'our' own house to go downstairs to get an apple from the refrigerator because he's there in 'our' living room." Aside from running into such conflicts over territoriality, stepfathers are likely to have problems with discipline. If they tell a 13-year-old that he should not watch an R-rated cable movie, he may retort, "My dad lets me watch them. Besides, it's Mom's television set" (Herbert, 1999; Nordheimer, 1990).

Conflicts over territoriality and discipline are especially likely to erupt with teenagers. Younger children can quickly get along with a stepfather because of their physical and emotional dependence on adults. However, teenagers are striving to break free of adult authority, as they are preoccupied with schoolwork, friends, sports, and their developing sexuality. Thus, during an argument, they are likely to shout at their stepfathers, "You're not my real father!" Not surprisingly, the presence of stepchildren has been found to be a major reason why second marriages fail at a higher rate than first marriages (Strong et al., 2005).

Surrogate Motherhood

Surrogate motherhood
The arrangement for a woman to carry and bear a child for a couple.

In some families the wife cannot conceive and carry a baby; she and her husband may therefore turn to **surrogate motherhood**, an arrangement for another woman to carry and bear a child for the couple. Such families first appeared in the late 1980s, and today their number has grown to over 25,000. In most of the surrogacies involving these families, the egg comes from the wife—or from the surrogate herself in a few cases where the couple is gay. The egg is then fertilized with sperm from the intended father, and the embryo is implanted in the surrogate's womb. When the baby is born, it is handed over to the intended parents.

Most surrogates are 20 to 40 years old, married, and have their own children. More than a dozen states, including Pennsylvania, Massachusetts, and California, have legalized surrogacy. But the practice is expensive, with the intended parents paying the surrogate between $20,000 and $25,000. If the medical and legal bills are included, the entire cost runs from $40,000 to $120,000. Moreover, surrogacy challenges our profound belief in the unbreakable bond between mother and child. Many feminists also liken the surrogates to prostitutes for degrading themselves by renting out their bodies. Other critics see surrogacy as an exploitation of poor women.

Most surrogates deny being in it only for the money. They insist that their motive is mostly altruistic. They feel emotionally rewarded by the experience of helping an infertile couple realize their dream of becoming parents. As one surrogate puts it, "Being a surrogate is like giving an organ transplant to someone—only before you die, and you actually get to see their joy" (Ali and Kelley, 2008). But don't they feel such a strong motherly bond to the baby that they would find it impossible to give the baby up to the intended couples? This is unlikely to occur because the baby usually is not biologically related to the surrogate, as the egg does not belong to her but to the intended mother.

International Adoptions

It is less controversial for parents to adopt children from other countries than to bring home the babies from the surrogate. Thus international adoptions are more popular than the practice of surrogacy. Today there are many countries that provide American families with children for adoption, the largest providers being China, Ethiopia, and Russia (see **Figure 10.2**). Virtually all of these children are orphans. The majority grow up to be normal and happy in their new American families. This is largely because most of the children are adopted at a very young age, before they are 1 year old. A few cause problems for the adoptive parents because when they are adopted they are already 4 or 5 years old. As an adoption attorney says, "Violent outbursts and detachment in older children adopted internationally are very familiar to those of us in the field, as sad as it may be" (Pickert, 2010).

This problem has apparently driven the American woman Torry Hansen to send her 7-year-old adopted son back to his native Russia. The boy arrived in Moscow alone with a note from Hansen saying that he was "mentally unstable." She also said, "I no longer wish to parent this child." The boy's adoptive grandmother, who put the boy on his flight to Russia, said that he was violent, threatening to burn his adoptive mother's house down. Russia's president called Hansen's act "a monstrous deed," and his foreign minister called for a halt to all foreign adoptions.

In addition to this problem with the Russians, there are problems with other countries that make it more difficult for American families to adopt foreign children. Ukraine and South Korea, for example, are faced with declining birthrates and are therefore encouraging domestic adoptions and discouraging foreign adoptions. The increased prosperity in China has resulted in fewer abandoned children, prompting

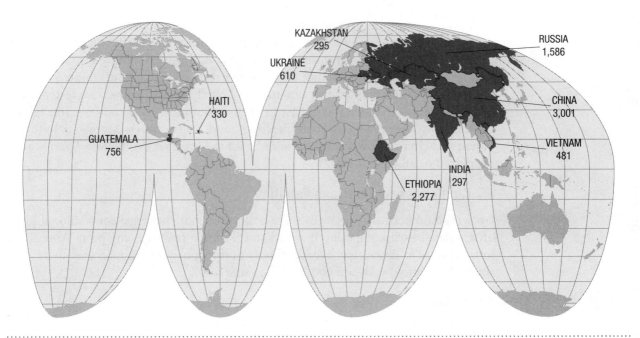

FIGURE 10.2 U.S. Adoptions of Children from Abroad

International adoptions are relatively popular, and many countries provide American families with children for adoption, the largest providers being China, Ethiopia, and Russia. However, problems can crop up with these adoptions, as dramatically illustrated by the experience of the adoptive mother Torry Hansen.

Critical Thinking: *What kind of help can Hansen and other adoptive parents receive from adoption agencies to avoid problems?*

Source: U.S. Department of State, 2010.

the country to scale back foreign adoptions with stricter regulations. Adoptive parents are now required to be married, be younger than 50 years old, not be obese, not have taken antidepressant medications in the past 2 years, and not have any facial deformities (Webley, 2009).

Children of War

About 900,000 U.S. soldiers with children have deployed to the wars in Iraq and Afghanistan since 2001. In its survey of the effects of war on the military children, the

According to various studies, many children of U.S. soldiers who have deployed to the wars in Iraq and Afghanistan are showing fear, anxiety, and behavioral problems.

Pentagon found that most are showing more fear, anxiety, and behavioral problems. More than half of the children have coped well or very well when their parent has gone to war. However, one in four has coped poorly or very poorly, and one in three has had poor grades and behavioral problems in school. Another study shows that a year after a parent returned from combat, 30% of the children exhibited clinical levels of anxiety that required possible treatment (Zoroya, 2009b).

One study further suggests that military children suffer more when a soldier-parent is deployed for a combat tour in Iraq or Afghanistan. After the parent left home, the rates of child abuse and neglect rose more than 40% at the hands of the parent who stayed behind. The problem seems to stem from the considerable stress experienced by both the stay-at-home parent and children. As the researcher explains, older children are stuck with increased family responsibilities, from yard work to taking care of younger siblings to offering emotional support to the remaining parent. Other children struggle academically when their parent who used to help them with homework is deployed. The remaining parent finds it harder to keep up with the usual routines, like taking the kids to soccer practices, scout meetings, and ballet classes. Moreover, both the parent and children are constantly seized with the fear that the deployed parent may be injured or killed (Au, 2007).

■ Challenges to American Families

Growing numbers of Americans pursue lifestyles that challenge conventional ideas of families. Instead of getting married and having a family, many more Americans today choose to stay single, live together with someone without marrying them, and share a household with somebody of the same sex.

Staying Single

Of the various lifestyles that differ from conventional marriage, staying single is by far the most prevalent. Today unmarried adults account for nearly 30% of all U.S. households, compared to only 10% in the 1950s. Some of these people are in their thirties and forties, but most are younger adults who postpone marriage into their late twenties. More significantly, an increasing number of young adults live with their parents and stay single for some time (U.S. Census Bureau, 2010).

Most singles actually expect to be married sooner or later. One reason they often give for their current singlehood is that they have not met the right person. But growing numbers of men and women choose to stay single. Some studies have found them to be generally happier than their married peers (Harayda, 1986; Janus and Janus, 1993). There are two sociological reasons for the increase in committed singlehood.

First is the sharp decline in the social pressure to get married. This is especially true for city dwellers, who face far less pressure to marry than small-town residents. The second reason is the expansion of the opportunity for singles to have a good life. This is particularly true for women. As educational and career opportunities open up for them, along with the freedom to choose to be a single mother, marriage is no longer the only avenue to economic security, emotional support, social respectability, and meaningful work (Edwards, 2000). Thus, some argue that it is no longer important to get married, but others hold on to the conventional idea that marriage does matter (see Box 10.4).

BOX 10.4 DIVERGENT VIEWS

Is It Really Important to Be Married?

In her essay, "Why Marriage Matters," Caitlin Flanagan (2009) argues that it is extremely important for adults to get married. The main reason, according to her, is that there is no other single force causing as much hardship and misery as the collapse of marriage. It hurts children, it reduces mothers' financial security, and it devastates the underclass—who can bear it least.

The vast majority of unmarried women having babies are poor and uneducated. Three U.S. Presidents in a row have tried to convince them that having babies before marriage is a catastrophic way to live. Bill Clinton's welfare-to-work program encouraged marriage, George W. Bush spent millions to promote marriage, and Barack Obama has urged men to stay with their children, saying "What makes you a man is not the ability to have a child but the courage to raise one." The reason for these appeals to marriage is that, as research has shown, children from intact, two-parent families outperform those from single-parent households. They live longer, are less likely to abuse drugs, get better grades in school, have lower dropout rates, and are less likely to get pregnant as a teenager, commit crime, and go to prison (Flanagan, 2009).

On the other hand, in their essay "'I Don't': The Case Against Marriage," Jessica Bennett and Jesse Ellison (2010) contend that given the sweeping changes in American marriage and family, it is no longer important to get married. Fifty years ago, marriage made sense. That was how women could get their financial security and encourage the fathers of their children to stick around. But today women make up a majority of the workforce, being breadwinners or co-breadwinners in two-thirds of American families. They are more educated, live longer, and have vacuum cleaners and washing machines to make domestic life easier. Besides, Americans have the highest divorce rate in the world, making it risky to get married. That's why fewer and fewer Americans have married since the 1950s, and the number of unmarried-but-cohabiting partners has soared 1,000% over the last 40 years. It is not true that only marriage between parents is good for children. A study of the Scandinavian countries, where most children are born out of wedlock, found that they actually spend more time with their parents than American children do (Bennett and Ellison, 2010).

Cohabitation

Cohabitation
The practice of living with a partner without having a formal wedding ceremony or obtaining a marriage license.

More than 30 years ago, very few couples were involved in **cohabitation**, living together with a partner without having a formal wedding ceremony or obtaining a marriage license. These couples were said to be "shacking up" or "living in sin." They were mostly the very rich, who could afford to ignore society's rules, and the very poor, who had little to lose by ignoring them. Today, cohabitation has spread to other sectors of U.S. society, including college students and young working adults. The result is a dramatic rise in cohabitation, so that now the majority (about two-thirds) of couples who marry have lived together first. Social disapproval has vastly diminished, and courts have stepped in to protect couples' rights as if they were legally married (Jayson, 2010a).

Because the incidence of cohabitation continues to rise, some fear it may undermine the institution of marriage. However, most cohabitants live like married couples and intend to marry eventually. To them, cohabitation is a temporary arrangement, not a permanent substitute for marriage. It is a modern extension of the courtship process, comparable to the traditional custom of going steady (Brown, 2005; Smock, 2000). But does living together lead to more marital failures than the traditional courtship? Thirty years ago, studies often showed that if a couple had cohabited before they married, their marriage was more likely to dissolve and end in divorce. Today researchers are more likely to find that cohabitation does not increase the risk of divorce (Jayson, 2008).

Gay Families

Since the early 1990s same-sex marriages have been legalized in a dozen or so countries, such as Canada, Denmark, and the Netherlands. They are legally recognized in only about six states within the United States. Without legal marriage, gay couples do not have the same legal protections and financial benefits as heterosexual couples, such as tax exemptions and Social Security survivor's benefits. A number of cities have, however, granted unmarried couples, no matter what their sexual orientation,

Most gay men and women have the same desire to get married as do heterosexuals. As many as 31% of same-sex couples, compared to 43% of different-sex couples, are raising children.

a legal document called a *domestic partnership agreement*. Some gay couples have used it to gain family benefits from employers, insurance companies, health clubs, and other commercial establishments.

Most gay men and lesbians have the same desire to get married as do heterosexuals. Even though they are denied the legal right to marry, they tie the knot in about the same way as their heterosexual counterparts. Gay weddings range from simply exchanging rings in private to having an elaborate ceremony. The wedding serves the sociological function of strengthening the couple's relationship. By expressing their vows and love for each other in the presence of their significant others, the same-sex partners tend to feel a stronger sense of commitment and security.

Also, as many as 31% of same-sex couples (compared to 43% of heterosexual couples) are raising children. Most of these children come from earlier heterosexual relationships, but an increasing number of children are adopted or born through artificial insemination. The American Academy of Pediatrics (AAP) has found that children who grow up in gay families fare as well in emotional, cognitive, social, and sexual functioning as do children in heterosexual families. The AAP has further noted that the key to children's optimal development is the quality of parental care, not whether the parents are gay or straight. Many other researchers have also found that children of same-sex parents do not significantly differ from those of heterosexual parents. They do not show an increased incidence of psychiatric disorders. They are just as popular at school and also have as many friends (Belkin, 2009; Robison, 2003).

However, same-sex parents are generally far more egalitarian toward each other than are heterosexual parents. Heterosexual men and women usually have been socialized in childhood to play different gender roles, with the men expected to do "masculine" things, such as fixing the family car, and the women "feminine" things, such as preparing the family meals. Such gender-role differences often make men dominant over women. By contrast, gay partners have been socialized to the same gender role, and they therefore tend to have an egalitarian relationship. If both partners in a gay or lesbian couple are employed—as most are—both do about the same amount of housework. One does not do more housework than the other, as is often the case with heterosexual couples (Belkin, 2009).

◼ Sociological Theories of Family Problems

The three major theories in sociology shed light on different causes of family problems. Functionalist theory attributes family problems to some social change that makes it difficult for the family to perform its traditional functions. Conflict theory blames family problems on the family being a violent institution and a place for men to exploit women. And symbolic interaction theory traces family problems to certain forms of interaction between husband and wife.

Functionalist Theory

According to functionalist theory, the family contributes to the stability of society by performing certain functions. These functions include sexual regulation, reproduction, socialization, division of labor, and providing emotional security. In the past, our society regulated sex by encouraging people to wait until they are married to have sex. People were also encouraged to have babies within marriage rather than outside, to take care of their own children rather than taking them to day-care centers, to let the husband be the breadwinner and the wife be the homemaker, and to give emotional support to their spouses and children.

Traditionally, the family has performed these functions relatively well, and the rates of divorce, teenage pregnancies, single parenthood, cohabitation, and other family problems were quite low. Today they are much higher because the society has changed from being traditional to modern, which in turn makes it difficult for the family to perform its traditional functions. The sexual revolution, a hallmark of modern society, for example, makes it hard for society to regulate sexual practices because sex has become easily available outside marriage. This change in sexual behavior is likely to lead many people to divorce, become pregnant before marriage, turn into single parents, cohabit with the intimate other without marriage, and develop other problems that challenge the institution of marriage, as suggested by the fact that all these problems are more common in sexually free modern societies than in sexually restrictive traditional societies. In short, when the family fails to perform its traditional functions, it experiences many problems.

Conflict Theory

There are at least two major points in conflict theory about why family problems exist. First, the family, because of the strong feelings it generates, is a powerful source not just of love and care but also of pain and conflict. As researchers have found, the family is the most violent institution in U.S. society, except the military in time of war. In most families, there are instances of conflict and violence, such as anger, spanking of children, and spouses slapping each other. In fact, the family is one of the few groups in society empowered by tradition to hit its members. It is socially acceptable, for example, for parents to spank their children as a form of punishment. Moreover, many husbands who strike their wives are not arrested, prosecuted, or imprisoned (Barnett, Miller-Perrin, and Perrin, 2005).

Second, the family is a mechanism for men's exploitation of women. Homemakers and mothers have greatly contributed to the rise and maintenance of capitalism with such forms of labor as reproduction and care of children, food preparation, daily health care, and emotional support. Without this *household production*, men would not have been free to go to work. Yet while men are paid for their work outside the home, women are not paid for their work inside the home. Ironically, women's household work is, on average, worth more than men's paid employment. If a woman were paid for her services as a mother and homemaker according to the wage scale for chauffeurs, cooks, and therapists, she would earn more than most men do. By devaluing women's housework, however, the family serves the interests of male domination. Even in families where both spouses are gainfully employed, wives still do most of the housework.

In sum, according to conflict theory, the family is far from a "haven in a heartless world." It is instead an extension of that world, full of violence and exploitation of women.

Symbolic Interaction Theory

In a family, symbolic interaction can be observed between husband and wife, between parent and child, between one sibling and another, and among all of these individuals. Using the symbolic interaction theory as a guide, we can focus on any of these interactions and learn how they affect the group.

In his studies of marital interaction, John Gottman (1994, 2002) has observed many couples in his lab, concentrating on what the spouses say to each other as well as on the tone of voice they use. He found three different types of interaction. The first is *validating* interaction, in which the partners compromise, showing mutual respect and accepting their differences. The second is *conflict-avoiding* interaction, in which the partners agree to disagree, making light of their differences rather than trying to confront them. The third is *volatile* interaction, in which conflict erupts, resulting in a vehement, loud dispute. The validating interaction contributes most to marital happiness. The conflict-avoiding interaction also brings some marital happiness but less than the validating interaction. It is the third type—volatile interaction—that causes marital unhappiness.

Gottman has also found that marital interactions can be either *positive* or *negative*. Positive interactions involve acts of *thoughtful friendliness*, such as touching, smiling, and paying compliments. Negative interactions involve acts of *thoughtless nastiness*, such as ignoring, criticizing, and calling names. Among happy couples, there are at least five positive interactions for every one negative interaction. Among unhappy couples, there is more than one negative interaction for each positive interaction. Thus, if a partner commits just one negative act, he or she must make up for it by committing more than five positive acts to bring about marital happiness. However, if a partner commits fewer than five positive acts for each negative act, he or she will encounter marital unhappiness and experience marriage problems.

For a quick review of the three theories on family problems, see **Box 10.5**.

QUESTIONS TO EXPLORE

1. Do you agree with Gottman that in marital interaction one negative action carries more weight than one positive act—that is, if a partner commits just one negative act, he or she must commit more than five positive acts to ensure marital happiness? Why do you agree or disagree?

2. In today's American society, what are supposed to be the functions of the modern family?

3. Visit the Child Trends Web site at http://www.childtrends.org. Note that its mission seeks to "improve outcomes of children" by providing relevant research to the "people" and "institutions" that affect the quality of life of others. Which of the sociological theories discussed here is most relevant to the mission of Child Trends?

BOX 10.5   THEORETICAL THUMBNAIL

Explaining Family Problems

Theory	Focus	Insights
Functionalist Theory	The family's failure to perform its traditional functions	Social change makes it hard for the family to perform its functions, thereby causing family problems.
Conflict Theory	The family as a place for violence and female exploitation	The violent and exploitative nature of the family causes family problems.
Symbolic Interaction Theory	The interaction between husband and wife	Volatile interaction and thoughtless nastiness lead to marital unhappiness.

Review

SUMMARY

1. There are different forms of marriages, including arranged marriages, exogamies, endogamies, monogamies, polygamies, polygynies, and serial monogamies. Successful monogamies demand total commitment from the spouses, thereby weakening their social bond to relatives, neighbors, and friends. There are different types of families, including nuclear and extended families, and patriarchal, matriarchal, and egalitarian families.

2. The United States has the highest divorce rate in the world. The causes are the disappearance of the stigma of divorce, greater availability of services and opportunities for the divorced, higher expectations for marital love and happiness, and the increased importance of individualism. One way to prevent divorce is the use of acceptance therapy, learning to accept and tolerate the other spouse's weaknesses. Family violence is also common in the United States because Americans tend to use violence to deal with stress.

3. Since the 1950s, the rate of marriage among African Americans has dropped sharply, as a result of the rise of their economic problems and kinship-based extended families. Ironically, as the American belief in romantic love spreads all over the world, many countries are experiencing significant increases in divorce.

4. Before the United States became industrialized in the 19th century, the nuclear family involved the wife working side by side with the husband at home. After industrialization, the wife lost her status as her husband's economic partner and acquired the subordinate status as the homemaker. Two-career families have increased their income, but the employed wife still does most of the housework and child care. Single-parent families suffer more stress than two-parent families, resulting in more problems for their children. Stepfathers often encounter conflicts of territoriality and discipline with their stepchildren. Most surrogates insist that they are doing it for altruistic reasons, not money alone. International adoptions have become relatively popular with American parents, but the adoptive parents may run into problems with their adopted children. Children whose parents are fighting the wars overseas tend to experience considerable stress.

5. Most singles expect to be married sooner or later, but growing numbers are committed to staying single, because there is less social pressure today to get married, while there are more opportunities for singles to have a good life. Some argue that it is important for adults to be married, but others contend that marriage is no longer important. In the past, cohabitors were more likely to end up divorced after they got married, but today cohabitation does not increase the risk of divorce. Most same-sex couples have the same desire as their heterosexual peers to get married, and same-sex couples are more egalitarian toward each other than heterosexual couples are.

6. According to functionalist theory, families are more likely to have problems today than in the past because social change has made it difficult for families to perform their traditional functions. Conflict theory blames the family for being a source of domestic violence and female exploitation. And symbolic interaction theory attributes marital unhappiness to hostile interaction between the spouses and their acts of thoughtless nastiness toward each other.

CRITICAL THINKING QUESTIONS

1. Of these three social institutions—media, education, and religion—which has the most influence in shaping family as a social institution? Explain your response.

2. Explore the pros and cons of surrogate motherhood. Are there any special issues that need to be taken into consideration?

3. Will the egalitarian family model eventually become dominant in the United States? Why or why not? Be specific.

INTERNET RESOURCES

The *Journal of Marriage and Family* (http://www.wiley.com/bw/journal. asp?ref=0022-2445) offers insights on all aspects of family, marriage, and close, interpersonal relationships, through the sharing of original research and related discussions.

The National Council on Family Relations (NCFR) (http://www.ncfr.org/) is an educational forum where educators, medical/clinical professionals, and family-related scholars share ideas and research findings about family topics. The NCFR is also proactive in establishing professional standards and promoting family well-being.

The National Marriage Project (http://www.virginia.edu/marriageproject/) is concerned with collecting research results aimed at understanding cultural and social influences that impact relationships, and identifying and recommending "strategies to improve marital quality and stability."

Planned Parenthood (http://www.plannedparenthood.org/) is an organization of over 840 health centers and more than 80 locally governed affiliates. It seeks to promote sexual health and provide reliable, safe health care to families. Planned Parenthood also attempts to educate beyond the local community level by being active in foreign policy related to global reproductive health and rights initiatives.

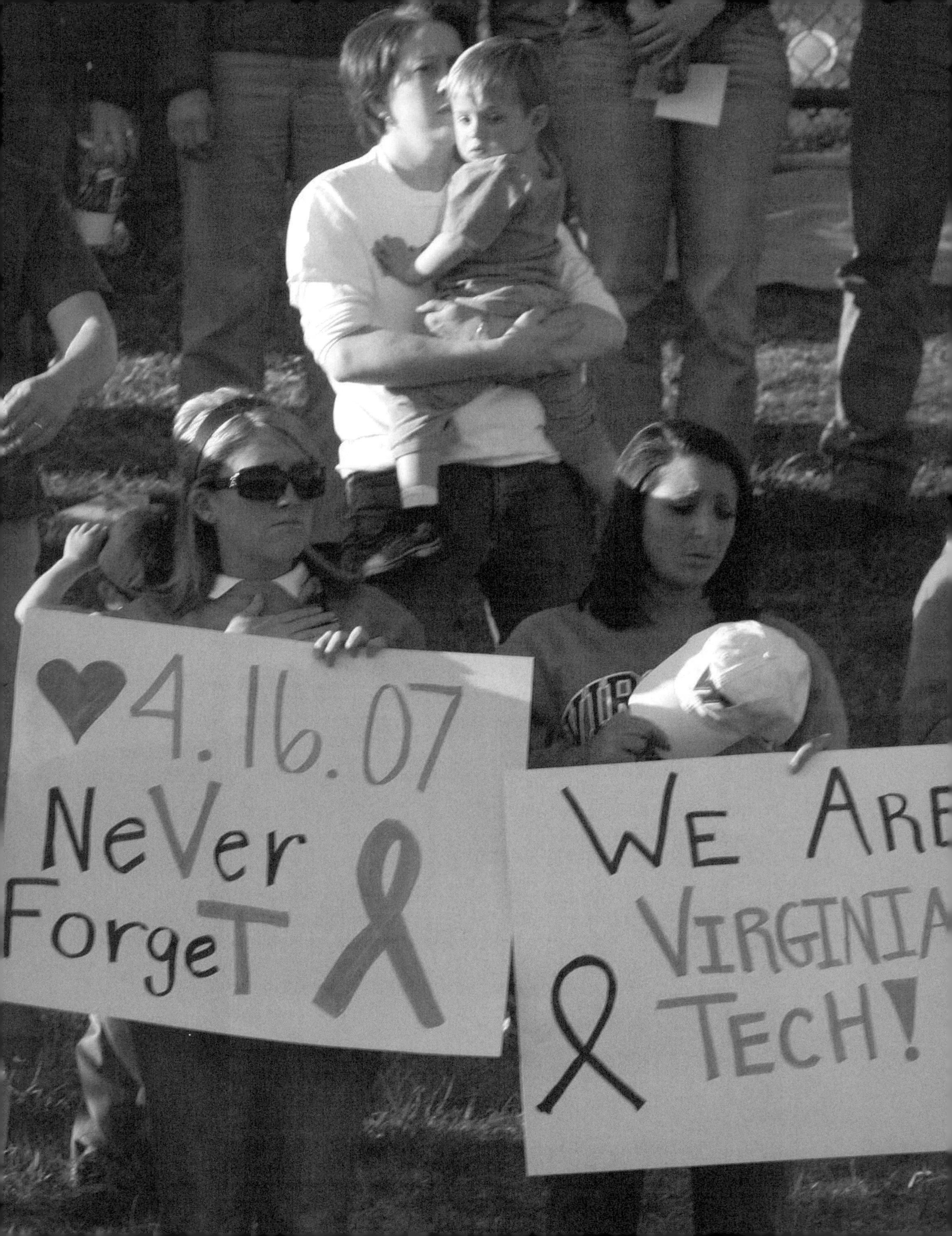
4.16.07
NeVer ForgeT
WE ARE
VIRGINIA
TECH!

Educational Problems

Fifteen-year-old Phoebe Prince apparently had a bright future. Pretty and smart, she wanted to be a journalist. In the fall of 2009, she and her family had just moved from Ireland to South Hadley, Massachusetts. Phoebe enrolled as a freshman at South Hadley High School. She soon caught the attention of the school's football star Sean Mulveyhill. Phoebe and Sean dated briefly, angering Kayla Narey, who considered Sean her boyfriend. Kayla and her friend Sharon Velazquez warned Phoebe to stay away. Phoebe apologized. Later, in December 2009, Phoebe briefly dated Austin Renaud, only to learn that another girl also considered Austin to be her boyfriend. This girl joined forces with the other girls and their friends to attack Phoebe. They taunted her, calling her names and challenging her to fight. They harassed her in the library and screamed at her as she walked home. On January 14, Phoebe endured a particularly rough day of harassment, which included having a can of sports drink thrown at her. When she went home after school, she hanged herself (*Current Events,* 2010).

Phoebe's suicide has shocked everybody. School bullying that led to her death is one of the most serious educational problems. In this chapter, we will discuss school bullying and other educational problems. We will also take a look at various attempts to improve the American education.

■ Educational Problems

The institution of education in the United States is faced with many problems. We will here analyze just a few. First, it is important to note that virtually all U.S. educational problems involve public schools, and they differ from private schools. Then we will examine a series of school problems including the high dropout rate, school shootings, and school bullying.

Public Versus Private Schools

Public schools differ from private schools in a number of ways. Public schools receive their funds from the local, state, and federal governments, while private schools receive theirs from private sources such as donations and organizations. Most public schools are administered by local governments, but private schools are under the control of a private body or charitable trust.

Public school education is much more common than private education. About 90% of children attend public schools. Public and private schools are similar in offering three stages of schooling: primary or elementary school (kindergarten to 5th grade), middle school or junior high school (6th to 8th grade), and high school (9th to 12th grade).

The most common educational problem of public schools is the larger school size. Most public schools are on average twice as large as private schools. Public schools have an average of 16 students per teacher, compared to 13 students for the private school teacher. Public school students consequently receive less individual attention.

Public schools admit all students who apply for admission, regardless of the applicants' behavior and talent. However, private schools can reject a student who is considered not up to the mark. Thus, public schools often perform more poorly in standardized achievement tests while having a higher rate of violence and student dropout. In the following sections, we will discuss these and other problems that challenge public schools. Still, public schools do offer certain advantages. Since the student demographics in public schools are much more diverse than in private schools, students are able to learn to get along with people regardless of their socioeconomic backgrounds (Buzzle.com, 2010).

Falling in Test Scores

For some time now, many critics of education in the United States have documented a decline in student test scores compared with the past and with many other countries. Scores on Scholastic Aptitude Tests (SATs) taken by college-bound high school seniors fell sharply and continuously from the 1960s to the 1980s. Although SAT scores have continued to move upward since the 1980s, today they still remain below those in the 1960s (see Figure 11.1). In addition, compared with their peers in such countries as Singapore, South Korea, Hong Kong,

Since the 1960s, many critics of education in the United States have documented a decline in student test scores compared with the past and with many other countries.

Japan, and the Czech Republic, American high school students have continued to score lower on science and math. As shown by recent international test results, U.S. 10th-graders ranked just 17th in science among their peers from 30 countries, while in math they placed in the bottom five (Wallis, 2008). As a result, the media, along with many national task forces on education, have raised the alarm about a crisis in U.S. schools. Is American education really in a crisis? If we put the discouraging data in proper perspective, the answer is probably no.

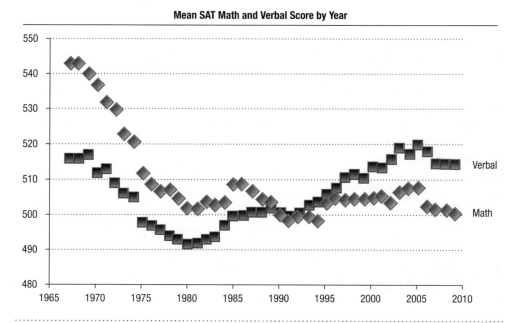

FIGURE 11.1 Declining SAT Scores Among U.S. Students

Scores on Scholastic Aptitude Tests (SATs) taken by U.S. college-bound high school seniors fell sharply and continuously from the 1960s to the 1980s. Although SAT scores have continued to move upward since the 1980s, they remain below those in the 1960s.

Critical Thinking: *What could have caused the verbal and math test scores to drop following their peak in 2005?*

Source: 2010 College-Bound Seniors. Copyright © 2010. The College Board. www.collegeboard.com. Reproduced with permission.

First, the decline of SAT scores may have resulted partly from the increasing democratization of U.S. education. In contrast to the continued elitism of foreign educational systems, the U.S. system has included growing numbers of poor, minority, and immigrant students. As a result of inadequate academic preparation or the tests' cultural bias, or both, the socially disadvantaged students do not do as well on the SAT as the socially advantaged, helping to bring down the average score for the entire group. However, the investment in equal education has paid off. Since 1999, national SAT averages have been rising, partly as a result of the steady improvement in test scores among African American, Hispanic, and other minority students. Nonetheless, the U.S. students' poor performance on international science and math tests calls for more training and support for science and math teachers.

Second, the United States is not alone in having educational problems. Japan, which is often touted as a world leader in science and technology, has serious problems with its higher education. Although Japanese schoolchildren are under enormous pressure to study hard, university students are allowed to take it easy, as if to be rewarded for having worked so hard before college. As Robert Christopher (1983) has observed, "The great majority of Japanese universities are extraordinarily permissive; once you get into one, it takes real effort to get kicked out. . . . Japanese authorities do not regard a student's failure to attend classes or even to pass courses as a ground for dismissal."

Dropout
The quitting of high school before graduation.

The Dropout Crisis

The U.S. rate of high school **dropout**—quitting high school before graduation—was once the lowest in the developed world, but now it is among the highest. Leading researchers estimate that 15% to 30% of the students who attend high school in the United States fail to graduate. The dropout problem is much worse in many of the largest urban school districts, such as Detroit, Cleveland, and Indianapolis, where as high as 60% of high school students fail to graduate. Similar problems plague many rural areas. The high dropout rate has led President Obama to declare in his first address to Congress that "dropping out of high school is no longer an option. It's not just quitting on yourself, it's quitting on your country—and this country needs and values the talents of every American" (Colvin, 2010).

Indeed, it costs the individual a great deal to quit high school, because the dropout is much more likely than the high school graduate to be unemployed, to fall into poverty, to use drugs, and to be arrested for criminal behavior. It also costs the larger society in multiple ways. First is the high cost of incarcerating dropouts, who make up a huge majority of the prison population. Second is the high cost of providing unemployment benefits, food stamps, and other aid to the dropouts. And third is the high cost of losing tax revenues because dropouts earn less and therefore pay less in taxes than high school graduates (Dillon, 2009).

There are various reasons for the high dropout rate. Many of the dropouts learn English as a second language, are already busy as parents, and have to work to help support their families. Researchers have found ways to prevent dropout, including the hiring of graduation coaches from whom students with poor attendance and test scores could receive a lot of tutoring (Aarons and Sawchuk, 2010).

School Shootings

Boys as young as 11 years old have gunned down classmates or teachers in the public schools of many little-known places such as Littleton, Colorado, and West Paducah, Kentucky. It appears that school violence, long known as a phenomenon of large and noisy cities, has now spread to small and tranquil towns, suburbs, and rural areas. Most recently, similar violence has taken place at Virginia Tech University and Northern Illinois University.

Following the massacre of 32 students and professors at Virginia Tech in 2007, many people wondered what had brought about such a violent act. The media tried to explain the carnage largely by focusing on the killer's mental problems (Gibbs, 2007).

It is true that mental illness plays a role in school shootings, because more than half of the shooters have experienced severe depression, but only an extremely small number of even the most depressed persons turn into mass murderers. Depression, then, cannot by itself cause the killing. Other factors are also likely to be implicated, such as having been abused by parents and rejected, taunted, or ostracized by peers. All these personal experiences are especially likely to lead to violence if they occur under the influence of some larger social forces. One is the easy availability of *guns*, without which depressed and angry young men would have difficulty acting out violent tendencies. Another social force is the glamorization of violence in such *media* as movies, television, and video games. Media violence cannot cause actual violence among the overwhelming majority of young men, but it is likely to turn a few susceptible, violence-prone young men to violence. A third social force is the *culture* of violence, which favors the possession of firearms and accepts the use of force for settling interpersonal conflict (Newman, 2004).

School Bullying

As has been suggested, bullying may lead its victims to shoot their fellow students. According to a study by the U.S. Secret Service, 71% of the shooters felt "bullied, persecuted, threatened, attacked, or injured by others." This is particularly true of the shooters at the middle and high schools, though not in college (Toppo and Elias, 2009). The high incidence of shooters being victimized by bullies should not be surprising because bullying is apparently a popular choice for students, especially in middle schools, where bullying often peaks. A survey by KidsHealth found that 40% of children aged 9 to 13 years admitted to bullying. Another study prepared for the American Psychological Association indicated that 80% of middle school students said they had bullied somebody in the prior 30 days (Turley, 2008).

Today, bullying seems to have acquired a new face. The perpetrators no longer resemble the stereotypical bully of the past: "a swaggering schoolyard lout, low on self-esteem, quick to lash out, easy to identify." Instead, they are "attractive, athletic, and academically accomplished—and comfortable enough around adults to know what they can and can't get away with" (Hampson, 2010).

Today researchers suggest that one reason for bullying is the proliferation of electronic communication, which makes it difficult for young people to develop social skills for face-to-face encounters.

In the past, bullying was often blamed on low self-esteem, which was assumed to cause the perpetrator to use bullying as a way of feeling powerful and important. Today, researchers have suggested different reasons for bullying: First, there is less playtime in kindergarten and preschool. Kids used to spend much time playing with, and learning to get along with, other children, but now they spend more time on academics and tests. The second reason is the proliferation of electronic communication. By using text or instant messaging to ask someone out or break up with someone, children need not develop social skills for face-to-face encounters. Thirdly, children are bombarded by TV and movies with the message that teenage meanness is cool. Fourthly, many parents do not supervise their children's online activity and therefore cannot stop their kids from bullying when it occurs (Hampson, 2010). Finally, researchers found that bullying stems from the perpetrator's desire to seek peer approval and affection (see **Box 11.1**).

■ Inequalities in Educational Attainment

In the United States, various racial or ethnic groups do not attain the same amount of education. Instead, educational attainment varies from one group to another. According to the latest U.S. Census Bureau's Current Population Survey (2001b), Asian Americans have the highest proportion with a college degree, followed by whites, blacks, Hispanics, and Native Americans. Here we will focus on the educational experiences of four groups to see why they have different academic achievements.

BOX 11.1   WHAT RESEARCH REVEALS

Bullying for Love

According to a nationwide survey of students in grades 6 through 10, the amount of parental support and the number of friends that adolescents have can have an impact on whether they bully others or are themselves bullied. More specifically, both the amount of parental support and the number of friends have the same impact on preventing adolescents from becoming victims of bullying. This is simply because youngsters can obtain protection directly from parents and friends against being bullied. When it comes to bullying, parents and friends exert their influence differently. The greater the parental support adolescents have, the *less* likely they are to bully others, but the more friends adolescents have, the *more* likely they are to bully others. Why the difference? Because parents normally discourage their children from bullying other kids, but friends tend to encourage bullying as a manly activity (Wang, Iannotti, and Nansel, 2009).

Another study dug into the bullies' motivation and feelings, finding a deeper reason why they went along with their friends' expectation that they bully other youngsters: They are looking for approval and affection from their friends. They want to make sure their friends will give them the emotional support they are seeking (Paul, 2010).

Asian American Education

Not only at the top U.S. universities are Asian Americans overrepresented, comprising more than 10% of the freshman classes, despite making up merely about 4% of the U.S. population; in high school, they are also overrepresented among students who excel in math and science, particularly as winners of the annual national science competition, the Westinghouse Science Talent Search. These factors have served to reinforce the popular stereotype of Asian Americans as naturally gifted in math and science.

The reality is that not all Asians are scientifically competent. Many, especially immigrants not yet proficient in English, often have low grades and high dropout rates. More importantly, the Asians who score high on math and science do so because of hard work rather than natural talent. Asian students actually spend more time studying and less time on after-school sports or part-time jobs. Compared to their non-Asian peers, they spend twice as much time on homework, a habit fostered by their parents placing a tremendous emphasis on doing well in school (Abboud and Kim, 2006). This emphasis on the importance of education is particularly strong in the Chinese American families, which can be traced to their ancestral culture in China (see **Box 11.2**).

African American Education

For many years until the mid-20th century, black and white children attended separate schools, with the former receiving inferior education. This prompted the U.S. Supreme Court in 1954 to declare segregated public schools unconstitutional and to order them desegregated "with all deliberate speed." This attempt to achieve integration ran into the roadblock of residential segregation: Because they lived in different neighborhoods, black and white children typically attended different schools. Thus, the courts ordered that pupils be bused to schools away from their own neighborhoods. In the 1980s and 1990s,

BOX 11.2   GLOBAL PERSPECTIVE

The Obsession with Education

On a Saturday afternoon, at a fancy restaurant in Shanghai, China, Liu Zhihe sat fidgeting at the table, knowing it was about time for him to leave. All around him were many relatives, there to celebrate the 90th birthday of Liu's great-grandmother. But Liu knew he had to leave because it was time for him to go to school. This Saturday, as he does every Saturday, he had two special classes to attend. One was a math tutorial, and the other English. Liu's study habits might have been impressive at any age, but he was only 7 years old!

To many foreigners, the obsession with education in China is overdone. After several decades of investment in its educational system, the country's literacy rate has now reached 90%, compared to 86% in the United States. Chinese children are already proficient in reading at a young age. They are also ahead of American kids in math and science. The kids in China study extremely hard. In the United States, 37% of 10th-graders in 2002 spent more than 10 hours on homework each week. That's not bad at all. However, Chinese students spend twice as many hours doing homework as do their American peers. A major reason is family involvement. Consider Liu, the 7-year-old who had to leave a birthday party to attend classes on Saturday. Both his parents work, but when he goes home every day, his grandparents are there to spend hours with him on his homework. "This is normal," his mother says. "All his classmates work like this after school" (Powell, 2009).

most white parents did not want their children transported to predominantly black schools, but many black parents agreed to let their children be bused to mostly white schools. As a result, today both black and white children throughout the United States are more likely to attend integrated schools than before. In fact, the schools in the South, which were once the most segregated in the country, are now the most integrated.

Mandatory, court-ordered busing has also led to some "white flight" from the cities (where many blacks live) to the suburbs (where there are fewer blacks). Even prior to forced busing, however, many whites had already moved from the city to the suburbs as part of the larger demographic trend. Due to this residential segregation, schools in the central city have become predominantly black while those in suburban periphery have become mostly white. Moreover, since 1989, the courts have helped slow school integration by rescinding some mandatory busing and other past desegregation orders. A certain amount of school segregation, then, contributes to the lower academic performance among black students, when compared to their white peers.

Black students do better at the college level, as most black students attend predominantly white institutions. There is no real integration, though, on such campuses, where African American students usually form their own social networks, separate from white networks, because they do not feel part of the white campus life. Historically, at black colleges, where most black faculty members teach, black students feel more at home. As a consequence, African American students are more likely to succeed in earning a bachelor's degree at a black college than at a white school (Feagin and Feagin, 2003).

Hispanic American Education

Educational attainment is lower among Hispanic Americans than most other groups. Hispanic students are also much more likely than most other groups to drop out of school. Their higher poverty rate is a major factor, but there are at least two school-related factors that contribute more directly to the problem.

One is the lack of multicultural sensitivity on the part of school administrators and teachers. Most Hispanic children attend predominantly minority schools in the city, where educational resources are generally less adequate than those of Anglo suburban schools. Although the majority of the students in these schools are Hispanic, most teachers and administrators are European Americans, and they tend to be insensitive to Hispanic history and culture. Thus European American teachers treat Hispanic students less well than their white peers: Hispanics are praised less often, are asked fewer questions, and have their ideas accepted less frequently. These factors contribute to their lower academic achievement and higher dropout rate (Feagin and Feagin, 2003).

Another contributor to the poor academic problem among Hispanics is the lack of bilingual programs for many Hispanic children with limited English proficiency. Research has generally suggested that children learn English faster and get better grades when taught academic subjects in their native language for several years while gradually learning English as a second language. However, many schools do not have bilingual classes. In fact, nearly half of the U.S. population, especially conservative politicians, are opposed to bilingual schooling. When instructed entirely in English, many Hispanic pupils with limited English proficiency become discouraged, feel less self-confident, and fall behind their English-speaking counterparts (Feagin and Feagin, 2003).

Native American Education

For over 100 years, Native American children were subjected to forced assimilation into the European American culture. They were sent away to boarding schools that the U.S. Bureau of Indian Affairs (BIA) operated with the intent to civilize the "wild Indians." At these schools, the children were forbidden to speak their native languages, indoctrinated with white values, and compelled to dress and act like whites. Since the 1960s, Native Americans have often pressed for the inclusion in BIA-operated schools of classes in native languages, art, and other aspects of Native American cultures. Many of these schools have consequently included Native American cultures in the curriculum. Even so, they generally have very low academic standards and poorly trained teachers.

Most Native American children are now enrolled in local public schools, which usually fail to meet these students' needs. The problem stems from the absence of a Native American perspective in the curricula, the loss of native language ability, the abandonment of native spiritual values, and the racism of white teachers and administrators (Feagin and Feagin, 2003). Consequently, Native American students have more problems than their peers of any other ethnic group. As the director of the Native American Scholarship Fund has said, "We got the worse of everything: the lowest test scores, lowest rate of reading books, highest dropout rate, and lowest rate of entering college" (Belluck, 2000).

■ Attempts to Improve Education

There are always ideas about how to improve U.S. education. On the surface, it sometimes appears as if these ideas change like fashions. These shifts are often more than fads, though. They frequently reflect changing problems and changing needs. In the 1960s, people awoke to the problem of educational inequalities, but by the 1980s a decline in academic performance became a pressing problem. Here we will analyze various attempts to improve education in response to a variety of educational problems and needs. We will first zero in on whether or not children should spend more time in school (see **Box 11.3**).

Head Start

In the 1960s, sociologists often found that equalizing the quality of the nation's schools and educational opportunities did not produce educational equality because some children's family backgrounds handicapped them from the very start of school. Some youngsters never saw a book at home and were never encouraged to do well at school. There was apparently a need for **compensatory education**, a school program for improving the academic performance of socially and educationally disadvantaged children. So in the mid-1960s, the federal government began funding **Head Start**, a compensatory education program for disadvantaged preschoolers across the nation. It was run mostly by pediatricians and child psychologists working for poverty agencies. The goal was to prepare poor children ages 3 and 4 for kindergarten. These children were taught the skills and vocabulary that many of their middle-class peers learn at home. Their parents were also brought in to learn about child care, health care, and nutrition.

Early results were not encouraging. They showed that although the training did raise children's IQ scores and scholastic achievement, the benefits were temporary. In the first grade, disadvantaged pupils who had undergone preschool training might perform better than those who had not, but by the third grade this difference tended

Compensatory education
A school program for improving the academic performance of socially and educationally disadvantaged children.

Head Start
A compensatory education program for disadvantaged preschoolers across the nation.

BOX 11.3   DIVERGENT VIEWS

More School Time?

Some Americans argue that children can learn more by spending more time in school. They insist that today's school schedule simply does not work because it was developed in a vastly different era of more than a hundred years ago. As the U.S. Education Secretary Arne Duncan says, "Our school calendar is based upon the agrarian economy and not too many of our kids are working the fields today" (Associated Press, 2009). When they had to work long hours on the farm in the old days, it made sense for young people to spend little time in school. Nowadays, it seems foolhardy to do so, not only because there is no farm work to do but particularly because today's complex society and high-skills economy require long hours of learning in school. In fact, expanding learning time has been proven to help school children perform better. At 66 charter public schools in 19 states, which use considerably more learning time than conventional schools, students show much better academic performance than their peers at other schools (Gabrieli, 2009).

However, there are Americans who argue that it is a bad idea to simply add more time to the school day. They contend that more school time is a good idea only if there are "talented and impassioned faculty, firm discipline, a powerful school culture, and students who have chosen to be there" (Hess, 2009). They observe that those 66 charter public schools are successful not because they simply add more school time but because they also have better teachers and other characteristics of a high-quality school. Adding more learning time at a mediocre or lousy school doesn't work. It is better to also focus on improving the school.

to disappear (Stearns, 1971). This is the kind of evidence that conservative politicians in the 1990s often pointed to in their call for the elimination of Head Start.

Why did the benefits disappear, and why did students not respond better to remedial programs? In the 1970s, researchers were unable to find a definitive answer. Most argued that the continuing influence of a poor family environment simply overwhelmed the influence that any educational program could have. Others contended that the preschool programs had been doomed to failure because of inadequate funding. A few argued that the programs had been unfairly evaluated before they had time to prove their effectiveness. The last argument turned out to be the one that hit the nail on the head.

Over the last two decades, many studies have shown that the preschool programs do benefit low-income students in the long run. When poor youngsters who were in the preschool programs reach ages 9 to 19 years, they do better in school than peers who were not. They have higher reading scores, are less likely to be held back a grade, and are more likely to graduate from high school, attend college, and have higher rates of employment. They are also less likely to go on welfare or get involved in delinquency and crime (Sebelius, 2010; Vinci, 2010; Zigler, 2000).

School Vouchers

In the late 1960s, a new idea began to attract considerable publicity. It was vintage American: If there were more competition among the schools, perhaps the schools would be pressured to do better. After all, people were entitled to more freedom in choosing where they could send their children to be educated. This idea inspired proposals for voucher plans. Public schools had a virtual monopoly on public funds for education, and which school children attended depended, for the most part, on there they lived. A voucher plan could change this situation. With a **school voucher**, parents, not schools, would receive public money in the form of a voucher, which they would use to pay for their children's attendance at the schools of their choice. The greater the number of parents who chose a particular school, the more money it would receive. The idea was to force the public schools to compete with each other, and with private and parochial schools, for customers. Presumably, good schools would attract plenty of students, and poor schools would be forced to improve in order to compete effectively. More importantly, by using the vouchers for their children to attend better schools, parents would improve their children's education.

In the 1990s, popular support for vouchers grew significantly because many schools continued to face such problems as overcrowding, violence, and poor test scores. The voucher program was particularly popular among poor parents because they were anxious to pull their children out of failing public schools and put them in better schools. In 1998, the U.S. Supreme Court even upheld a Wisconsin law that provided low-income students with public money to attend private or parochial schools.

Then, in 2002, the U.S. Supreme Court ruled that the voucher program in Cleveland did not violate the constitutional separation of church and state, even though most of the parents who received the tax dollars chose to send their children to religious schools. The key reason the Court cited for its decision was that the government did not promote one religion over another while providing a "true private choice" by letting the individual decide where the public money should go (Anrig, 2009).

School voucher
A plan that allows parents, not schools, to receive public money, which they use to pay for their children's attendance at the schools of their choice.

But do vouchers improve poor schools and raise students' academic performance, as its advocates believe? So far, the evidence is inconclusive: Some studies have shown higher test scores among voucher students than among their public school peers, but other studies have found no such differences between the two groups. As for the public schools, they generally continue to do poorly because most suburban, middle-class parents are opposed to vouchers for fear that many poor and minority students would attend their children's private schools (Anrig, 2009; Greene, 2003).

Charter School

Charter school
A privately run but publicly funded school.

One way to improve the public school is to turn it into a **charter school**, a privately run but publicly funded school. Charter schools are supported by public funds just like traditional public schools so that they are free for students to attend; however, they are operated like a private school because they do not have to answer to the local school board. Freed of this outside control and red tape, they are believed capable of forging new and creative approaches to help students learn much more than in traditional public schools. The first charter school appeared in 1991 when Minnesota passed the law to create the school. Now, 20 years later, the number of such schools has soared to about 5,000. They have received strong support from local political leaders, financial backing from philanthropic giants like the Bill & Melinda Gates Foundation, and even the support of President Obama.

However, research on the performance of charter schools in 15 states and the District of Columbia has shown disappointing results. According to a study by Stanford University's Center for Research on Educational Outcomes, only 17% of charter schools perform significantly better than public schools, while 37% do worse. The Stanford researchers also find that students at charters do not, on average, learn as much as their traditional public school peers. There is, however, considerable variation across states. In Arizona and Ohio, charter school students perform worse than their public school peers, but in Massachusetts and Louisiana, charter students show stronger academic gains than their public school peers (Raymond, 2010; Thomas and Wingert, 2010b). Studies on successful charter schools reveal that the secret of their success includes longer school days, high standards, lots of tutoring, and even school uniforms (Clark, 2010).

Home Schooling

The number of children who receive their formal education at home has grown from only 0.3 million in 1990 to 1.5 million in 2007. Before 1994, most home-schooling parents were fundamentalist Christians who believed that religion was either abused or ignored in the public school. Today, three-quarters of home-schooling families reject public education for secular reasons: poor teaching, crowded classrooms, and lack of safety. Many of the older children, however, enroll in public schools part-time, for a math class or a chemistry lab, or for after-school activities, such as football, soccer, and other sports. Compared to parents whose children attend public schools, home-schooling parents are more likely to be white and college educated (Cloud and Morse, 2001; Toppo, 2009).

There are three types of home-based curricula. The first one is the *back-to-basic* approach, which emphasizes the three Rs (reading, writing, and arithmetic), American patriots, and Bible studies. It excludes sex education, drug abuse programs, education about acquired immune deficiency syndrome, self-esteem exercises, and other non-academic programs that are often provided in public schools. Most back-to-basic programs teach reading phonetically; use fact-rich history, geography, and science texts; and emphasize simple repetition and drill exercises.

The second type of home teaching is the *unschooling* approach, which offers children the freedom to pursue their interests but with parental guidance. The children are provided with various educational resources such as encyclopedias, dictionaries, atlases, and computers—supported by the Internet and new educational software. The parent also teaches concepts related to the activities the children have chosen (Kilborn, 2000).

The third type of home curriculum emphasizes *classical learning*. Children are taught to read great books, to memorize important facts, and to think logically and express their ideas effectively. They study not only classical literature but also history, geography, and Latin or some other foreign language in the early grades. This kind of curriculum has long been popular with missionary and diplomatic families stationed abroad. Famous figures of the past such as Abraham Lincoln, Thomas Edison, Leo Tolstoy, and John Stuart Mill went through this kind of home schooling during childhood (Seuffert, 1990).

Home schooling has been criticized for depriving children of the opportunity to interact with their peers. Such criticism is based on the popular assumption that children need to socialize with their peers to learn how to get along with people. However, many home schoolers develop social skills by associating with people of different ages and backgrounds rather than mostly with their peers. Moreover, home-schooled children are not isolated at home all day. They participate in various outside activities, including Scouting, ballet, church activities, sports, and 4-H clubs (Farris, 1997).

What about the quality of home education? Research has shown that compared to students in public schools, home schoolers score much higher on standardized tests and have a better chance of getting admitted to top universities. Undoubtedly, some home schools turn out to be disasters, but their advocates argue that public schools are no better, because they already are disasters (Cogan, 2010).

Lifelong Learning

An innovative way of improving the education for American citizens is not aimed at children and adolescents but at adults who have been out of school for some time. The appeal of *lifelong learning* has led many adults to return to the classroom, often for formal college credits. Most of these lifelong learners attend 2-year community colleges. Seeing the popularity of adult education in community colleges, many 4-year colleges and universities have

The appeal of lifelong learning has led many adults to return to the classroom, often for formal college credits.

offered their own continuing education programs. Today, adults aged 25 years and older make up over 38% of total enrollment, twice the figure of 20 years ago (Levine, 1993; NCES, 2009).

The remarkable growth of continuing education owes much to changing economic forces, such as the loss of blue-collar jobs that used to pay middle-class wages and the demands imposed on workers by new technology. Not surprisingly, many non-traditional students are adult workers seeking retraining, additional training, or new careers. There are many others, including homemakers preparing to enter the job market at middle age, retired people seeking to pursue interests postponed or dormant during their working years, and people wanting to enrich the quality of their personal, family, and social lives. Most of these adults are serious students, much more likely than younger students to earn A's and B's (Francese, 2002). However, regular, younger students can also succeed in college (see **Box 11.4**).

To accommodate their students' diverse responsibilities and interests, continuing education courses tend to be flexible. The courses are usually offered in the evenings or

---

BOX 11.4   USING SOCIOLOGICAL INSIGHTS

The Secret of Doing Well in College

After 10 years of studying 1,600 Harvard students, Richard Light (2001) has discovered the secret to success and happiness in college:

- *Find a faculty mentor.* At the beginning of each semester or quarter, get to know just one professor reasonably well and get that professor to know you reasonably well. If you do that, at the end of 4 years, you will have 8 or 12 professors to choose from to write a recommendation letter for you when you apply for jobs. Even more important than this practical, opportunistic reason for seeking out faculty mentors, you will do better academically. In Light's study, freshmen who asked for help with academic problems improved their grades; those who did not, got worse.
- *Take a smorgasbord of courses.* Your well-meaning parents may have told you to take required courses during the first year, to choose a major during the second, to take advanced courses for your major during the third, and to save fun electives for the last. But Light advises that you avoid taking only required courses during the early years. Instead, you should *also* take a variety of other courses that seem interesting to you. Afterward, you will know for sure what you really want to major in or whether your chosen major interests you as much as expected.
- *Manage your time effectively.* Don't study the way you might have in high school, squeezing in 25 minutes in study hall, 35 minutes after some social or physical activity, and 45 minutes after dinner. Rather than study in short bursts like these, set aside a long uninterrupted block of several hours. You will accomplish much more.
- *Study in groups.* It's important to do homework, but make sure you do it in a way that helps you understand the material. Thus, after studying on your own, discuss your work with a group of four to six classmates. By doing so even just once a week, you will comprehend the material better and feel more engaged with your classes. This method is particularly helpful with science courses, which have complicated concepts and require a great deal of solitary study.
- *Get involved in extracurriculars.* According to Light, students who have worked hard to get into college tend to say, "Academic work is my priority, and doing other things will hurt that." But Light's research found otherwise: Students who worked long hours at jobs had the same grades as those who worked a few hours or not at all. More importantly, students who worked or got involved in extracurricular activities, such as athletics, band, or volunteer work, were the happiest on campus.

on weekends, and sometimes outside conventional classrooms, in various community facilities such as public libraries. Their requirements are flexible, too. Some programs allow students to earn college credits without taking a course, by passing an examination or by proving their competency through their life experiences in political work, retail management, corporate administration, writing, and even travel (Aviv, 2008). Many courses offered on the campus are shorter and more focused than typical college courses. Although most of the nontraditional students are older than 35 years of age and employed full-time, most of the courses currently designed for lifelong learners may well become the standard curricula at most colleges and universities (Johnson, 1995; Rimer, 2000).

Recruiting Good Teachers

Research suggests that a good teacher is the most important factor in boosting student achievement. It is more important than class size, the amount of money spent per student, or the quality of textbooks and other teaching materials. Now, across the United States, hundreds of school districts are struggling to attract, reward, and keep good teachers. But what makes a good teacher? The general consensus among the recruiters is that good teachers must possess three fundamental qualifications.

First, they must have an unshakable belief in children's ability to learn; such belief can be found in virtually all teachers. Second, they must have a deep knowledge of the subject they teach. Unfortunately, many teachers have not developed this knowledge. Nationally, in about 30% of middle- and high school classes in math, English, science, and social studies, the teachers did not major in the subject they teach. It is worse for classes in the physical sciences, because 68% of the teachers did not major in this subject. And third, it takes a number of years of practice to become a good teacher: At least 2 years are required to master the basics of classroom management, and 6 to 7 years to become fully proficient in teaching. However, large numbers of public school teachers give up before getting there, because 25% to 33% of them quit within the first 3 years on the job. The biggest reason for quitting is low pay. Thus the solution is to offer higher pay. But to ensure the high quality of teachers, the higher pay should be based on better performance.

There is, however, disagreement over what constitutes good performance. School reformers generally believe that the students' test scores at the end of the year are a good indicator of the teacher performance for that year, but many teachers and their unions do not agree (Thomas and Wingert, 2010a; Wallis, 2008). This difficulty assessing the quality of a teacher may explain why it is extremely difficult to fire bad teachers. In the 2006–2007 school year, for example, only 8 out of 55,000 (or 0.01%) teachers in New York City were fired for incompetence. Each of these firings took 25 days of hearings and 150 hours of the principal's time, costing a total of $225,000 to get rid of each bad teacher (Thomas and Wingert, 2010a).

Money for Learning

In recent years, hundreds of U.S. schools have experimented with the program of paying children with cash for showing up at classes or getting good grades. Virtually all the children like this program. But adults find it greatly uncomfortable. Teachers complain that kids should not be rewarded for doing what they should be doing on their own; they should learn for the love of learning rather than for money. Psychologists are afraid that the cash can actually make kids perform worse by cheapening the act of learning. Parents predict there will be widespread slacking once schools stop paying children with money.

But does this cash-for-learning program work? To find out, Harvard professor Roland Fryer conducted a randomized experiment in hundreds of classrooms in four cities: New York City, Chicago, Washington, and Dallas. Fryer and his research team persuaded 143 schools to participate in the study. About half of the children were randomly selected as a control group, who were not paid. In the other half, students earned money for passing 10 routine tests given throughout the year. The experiment produced different results: In New York City, paying kids for good test scores did not lead to more learning or better grades. In Chicago, the kids who earned money for grades cut fewer classes and got slightly better grades, but failed to do better on their standardized tests at the end of the year. In Washington, getting paid for small accomplishments such as class attendance and good behavior seemed to improve reading skills. And in Dallas, paying second-graders to read books greatly raised their reading-comprehension scores.

How could cash payment motivate students in one city but not in another? The researchers discovered that students respond better to the financial incentive if they can control the task for which they are paid, such as attending class, as in Washington. However, getting paid for good test scores, as in New York City, is less likely to improve learning because the students are less able to control their test scores. It is no wonder that KIPP (the Knowledge Is Power Program) has become one of the most successful charter-school networks in the United States. For the last 15 years, KIPP students have been paid for actions they can control, which include getting to school on time, participating in class, and having a positive attitude (Ripley, 2010).

Stopping the Summer Slide

Summer slide
A student's loss of a great deal of what he or she learned during the school year because of the summer vacation.

As researchers have been documenting for more than a century, millions of low-income children suffer the "summer slide," losing a great deal of what they learn during the school year by having the summer vacation. This further widens the achievement gap between lower-income and higher-income students in America's schools. During the summer, higher-income children are able to "keep exercising their minds and bodies at sleepaway camps, on family vacations, in museums and libraries, and enrichment classes" (von Drehle, 2010). But lower-income children lack resources and end up spending too much time on street corners and in front of the TV. At the start of a new school year, the poorer children have significantly fallen behind. A recent study concludes that all students lose, on average, about a month of progress in math skills each summer, while lower-income students slip about 3 months in reading comprehension, with no loss of progress among middle-income students.

A majority of these poor American kids do not attend any kind of summer enrichment program. Leaders in a number of states have tried to offer such programs through the public schools, but in the current bad economy, state and local governments are shrinking, not enlarging, their school budgets. Consequently, many summer learning initiatives fall into the hands of educational entrepreneurs. Every year in Indianapolis, for example, 11 charitable organizations—ranging from United Way to small family foundations—raise about $3 million to support nearly 200 summer programs. Not all of the programs are completely educational, but their emphasis is. The funds support everything from busing children to the Chicago aquarium to paying salaries to certified teachers to funding day-camp visits by professional artists and musicians to offering gardens where students explore plant science.

A similar program run by an education entrepreneur is Summer Advantage. It is operating at a dozen sites throughout Indiana, serving some 3,100 students, and its goal is to enroll 100,000 students 5 years from now. Among its supporters is the U.S. Department of Education. All its students are in economic and academic need. From kindergarten to eighth grade, they are offered 5 weeks of intensive, all-day education. They study a wide range of subjects, from math, reading, and writ-

A school program called Summer Advantage provides students from kindergarten to eighth grade with 5 weeks of intensive, all-day education. In the program a competent teacher works with a small group of excited students.

ing to cooking, dance, and music. The consistent pattern of the program is competent teachers working in small groups with excited students (von Drehle, 2010).

Sociological Theories of Educational Problems

The three sociological theories can help us understand how education creates social problems. From functionalist theory, we can learn that social problems arise from the failure of education to perform its functions adequately. From conflict theory, we can see how education reinforces social inequality. And from symbolic interaction theory, we can discern how low teacher expectations lead to poor student performance.

Functionalist Theory

According to functionalist theory, education performs many functions for society. The most important are teaching of knowledge and skills, enhancing social mobility (see **Figure 11.2**), promoting national unity, and providing custodial care of youngsters. If education fails to perform each of these functions adequately, certain problems will occur.

First, if education does a poor job of teaching knowledge and skills, many people in the near future will have a hard time getting employed. This will in turn bring about

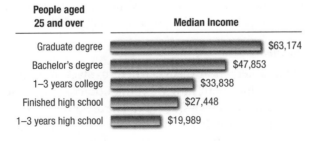

People aged 25 and over   **Median Income**

Graduate degree	$63,174
Bachelor's degree	$47,853
1–3 years college	$33,838
Finished high school	$27,448
1–3 years high school	$19,989

FIGURE 11.2 Income Rises with Education

The knowledge and intellectual skills learned in school can be translated into good jobs and money. Not surprisingly, then, the more education people have, the bigger their earnings. The value of college education, in particular, has risen most significantly.

Critical Thinking: *With an increased emphasis on the value of education, and the widespread message that "everyone should go to college," will college degrees retain their monetary value? Why or why not?*

Source: U.S. Census Bureau, *American Community Survey, 2006–2008.*

a high rate of unemployment and poverty. Even if there were full employment, the workers would be less competitive globally—less knowledgeable and skillful than their peers in other parts of the world. Second, if education fails to enhance social mobility by creating a well-educated and prosperous society, many people will not be able to obtain a good job to achieve upward mobility to improve their lives. Third, if education fails to promote national unity, social conflict and chaos will ensue. And fourth, if education fails to satisfactorily provide custodial care of youngsters as students, juvenile delinquency and youthful violence will run rampant.

Conflict Theory

Viewed through the eye of conflict theory, education in the United States supports the capitalist system by producing an array of skills and attitudes appropriate for maintaining social inequality. In elementary and secondary schools, lower-class children are trained to respect authority and follow orders—characteristics that employers require in manual laborers. In high school, higher-income youths are usually channeled into college-preparatory courses, thereby eventually into higher-status jobs, while lower-income students are typically guided into vocational courses, which lead to lower-status jobs. After graduating from high school, higher-income students are more likely to attend college than are lower-income students. Those in elite universities learn independent thinking and decision-making skills, which are useful for leadership positions. Meanwhile, in average universities and colleges, middle-class youths are taught responsibility, dependability, and the ability to work without close supervision—qualities that are needed for middle-level professions and occupations. In short, seen through conflict theory, education teaches youths to know their place and to fill it (Lee and Smith, 2001).

Tracking
The system of sorting students into different groups according to past academic achievement.

Support for conflict theory can be found in the practice of tracking in many elementary and secondary schools. Tracking is the system of sorting students into different groups according to past academic achievement. Higher-income students tend to be in higher-track (higher-ability) classes, and lower-class and minority students in lower-track classes. Higher-track students are taught independent thinking, which emphasizes self-direction, creativity, critical thinking, pursuing individual assignments, and active involvement in learning. By contrast, lower-track students are taught a more conforming type of classroom behavior—working quietly, punctuality, cooperation, improving study habits, obeying rules, and getting along with others. Higher-income students are, in effect, taught to be high-paid professionals, while lower-class and minority students are taught to become low-paid manual workers (Goodlad, 1984).

Symbolic Interaction Theory

According to symbolic interaction theory, when involved in social interaction, we tend to behave in accordance with how we think others see us. Thus, in classroom interaction, how the teacher defines a student can have powerful consequences for the student's academic performance. If a student is viewed as intelligent, the student will likely perform well. If another student is considered less intelligent, that student will likely perform less well. Such power held by the teacher reflects the Pygmalion effect, the impact of a teacher's expectations on student performance.

Pygmalion effect
The impact of a teacher's expectations on student performance.

In Greek mythology, Pygmalion was a sculptor who created Galatea, an ivory statue of a beautiful woman. Pygmalion fell in love with his creation and prayed to the goddess of love, who brought the statue of Galatea to life. In a sense, teachers can be compared to Pygmalion and their students to Galatea: Teachers can bring their expectations to life. If a teacher expects certain students to fail, then these students are likely to fail. If a teacher expects them to succeed, then they are likely to succeed.

How does the Pygmalion effect work? The teacher's expectations do not affect the student's performance *directly*, but they do influence the teacher's behavior, which in turn directly affects the student's performance. Teachers tend to give attention, praise, and encouragement to students they consider bright. If the students fail to perform as well as expected, the teachers will work extra hard to help them live up to expectations. Teachers tend to be uninterested in, critical toward, and even impatient with those they expect to do poorly in school. When these students have some difficulty, teachers are likely to think it will be a waste of time trying to help them. As a result of this disparate treatment, the differences in students' performances tend to match teachers' expectations: The presumably bright students do better than the presumably poor ones, which becomes an educational problem because teachers are supposed to treat all students equally (Harris and Rosenthal, 1985; Rosenthal, 1973).

For a quick summary of how the three sociological theories explain educational problems, see **Box 11.5**.

BOX 11.5   THEORETICAL THUMBNAIL

Explaining Educational Problems

Theory	Focus	Insights
Functionalist Theory	Failure of schools to perform their functions adequately	Social problems arise from schools' failures to perform their functions adequately.
Conflict Theory	Disparity in how high- and low-income students are taught	Schools reinforce inequality by teaching high- and low-income students differently.
Symbolic Interaction Theory	Teachers' failure to help students who are expected to do poorly	Low teacher expectation leads to poor student performance.

QUESTIONS TO EXPLORE

1. Functionalists state that one of the essential functions of education is promoting national unity. But education also promotes social diversity, emphasizing the importance of many different cultures. How do you simultaneously promote national unity and social diversity?

2. Is it possible for an institution of learning to meet the demands of a democratic society by practicing a form of tracking that teaches some groups of students to get better jobs than others? Why or why not?

3. Visit the Web site of the Educational Testing Service at http://www.ets.org/. Which theoretical perspective do its mission and services reflect? Explain your response.

Review

SUMMARY

1. Public schools differ from private schools in a number of ways, including being larger in size and admitting all students who apply for admission.

2. American students have lower test scores when compared with the past and with many other countries. Part of the reason is the democratization of the U.S. educational system. The United States is not unique in having educational problems; Japan, whose students score higher than their American peers, has a worse problem with its college education.

3. The United States has a very high dropout rate among its high school students. Reasons include many students being immigrants, being parents, and having to work to help support families.

4. School shootings often involve emotionally troubled students who resort to violence because of the easy availability of guns, the media glamorization of violence, and the culture of violence. Many school shooters are victims of school bullying. Today's school bullies are doing well academically, but they belong to groups that encourage them to seek peer approval through bullying.

5. Educational attainment varies from one racial or ethnic group to another, with Asian Americans having the highest level of attainment, followed by whites, African Americans, Hispanics, and Native Americans. Asians' high educational achievement has to do with their emphasis on the importance of education and heavy family involvement in children's education.

6. Various attempts have been made to improve education. Some Americans argue that schools can improve by expanding school time, but others disagree. Head Start is designed to help disadvantaged preschoolers perform better when they attend school years later. School vouchers enable parents to receive public money for paying the school they choose for their children. Charter schools are publicly funded but privately operated. Home schooling is carried out by parents who believe they can do a better job teaching their children than do public schools. Lifelong learning enables adults to return to school for more education. The secret of doing well in college includes finding a faculty mentor and managing time effectively. Other ways to improve education include recruiting good teachers, using money to motivate student learning, and stopping the summer slide.

7. According to functionalist theory, social problems stem from the failure of schools to perform their functions properly. Conflict theory blames education for reinforcing social inequality. And symbolic interaction theory points out that teachers' low expectations for some students cause them to do poorly in school.

CRITICAL THINKING QUESTIONS

1. The current economic downturn has caused a high number of jobless people to return to college. Could this lead to a stronger economy in the long run? Explain your answer.

2. Throughout your educational career, how has the Pygmalion effect affected your life and those around you?

3. Discuss the advantages and disadvantages of the summer vacation. Be specific.

INTERNET RESOURCES

The American Educational Research Association (AERA) (http://www.aera.net/) encourages the conducting and sharing of research related to educational advancement and its direct, practical application. The organization caters to educators, administrators, directors of research, state and federal and local program evaluators, counselors, graduate students, and behavioral scientists.

Educational Testing Service (ETS) (http://www.ets.org/) is a nonprofit organization that develops and administers a variety of educational assessment tests, such as the Graduate Record Exam (GRE) and Praxis, in addition to academic research and policy evaluation.

The Institute of Education Sciences (IES) (http://ies.ed.gov/) is the research division of the U.S. Department of Education. Research conducted and shared by the institute is intended to provide a foundation for educational practice and policy, and improve student outcomes—especially for high-risk students.

The National Board for Education Sciences (http://ies.ed.gov/director/board/index.asp) is comprised of 15 voting members who are selected by the President of the United States "by and with the advice and consent of the Senate." The duties of the National Board for Education Sciences are to consider and approve priorities, policies, funding, research agendas, and program evaluation pertaining to the U.S. Department of Education.

The National Center for Education Statistics (NCES) (http://nces.ed.gov) is the "primary federal entity for collecting and analyzing data related to education."

The United Negro College Fund (http://www.uncf.org/) is the nation's largest minority education organization, overseeing scholarships and internships for students at close to 1,000 institutions, in addition to faculty and administrators.

The U.S. Department of Education (DOE) (http://www.ed.gov/) promotes student achievement and success in order to meet global competition. The DOE works to ensure equal access to services, which span the following four areas: (1) establishment of policies pertaining to federal education spending; (2) data collection and research on U.S. schools; (3) identification of problem areas; and (4) enforcement of federal discrimination laws involving education programs that receive federal funding.

Economic Problems

CHAPTER OUTLINE

N owadays, in the midst of a recession, many Americans believe it is no longer possible to achieve the American Dream. However, it will take more than a recession to threaten the Dream for Greek immigrants Christos Koskiniotis, 46, and his mother, 67, who own a dry-cleaning business. They came to the United States in the 1970s after the political turmoil in Greece forced Christos's father to close the cafés he owned. They are confident that the recession will eventually end. As Christos says, "For the long term, this is the best place to be. You're going to hit rough spots no matter where you're at . . . I don't think the American Dream is ever going to die. To think that would be like giving up hope" (Keen, 2009).

Is Christos right that the United States will eventually recover from the recession? In this chapter, we will find the answers to this and many other questions about the U.S. economy. But first we will put the U.S. economy in perspective by analyzing the global economy, of which it is a part.

Capitalism
An economic system that allows private ownership of property and encourages competition in producing and selling goods and services.

Socialism
An economic system that requires public ownership of property and government control of the economy.

Mixed economy
An economy having some elements of both capitalism and socialism.

■ The Economic Systems in the World

Economic systems vary from one society to another. Some societies are mainly capitalist, operating on **capitalism**, an economic system that allows private ownership of property and encourages competition in producing and selling goods and services. Other societies are mostly socialist, operating on **socialism**, an economic system that requires public ownership of property and government control of the economy. Many societies have a **mixed economy**, having some elements of both capitalism and socialism. Societies, then, differ in degree, ranging on an economic continuum from the most capitalist at one end to the most socialist at the other end, with some having mixed economies located somewhere in the middle.

The Economic Continuum

The United States is situated at the capitalist end of the continuum and is among the world's most capitalist societies. It is not completely capitalistic, though. Elements of socialism exist, such as the government managing the economy by levying taxes, controlling the supply of money, regulating such industries as banking and car manufacturing, supporting clean energy with grants and loans, and running healthcare, pensions, and other social programs (Freedman, 2009). Still, to all intents and purposes, the United States is one of the most capitalist nations.

Also capitalist but less so than the United States are the European democracies, which are located near the middle of the continuum. From time to time, several of these democracies have had socialist governments. In general, these nations have combined capitalist enterprises with wide-ranging governmental control—and high taxes. They set stricter controls on business and offer more extensive social services than the United States. They provide, for example, a national system of health insurance and generous jobless benefits (see Box 12.1). Over the years, their governments have owned and managed many industries. In Great Britain, for example, the coal, steel, automobile, and television industries have been under government control at various times. Nevertheless, these European democracies are so much more capitalist than socialist that they are usually considered capitalist.

At the socialist end of the continuum, we find so-called communist countries such as North Korea, China, Vietnam, and Cuba. They are far from economically free, because their governments control the economy by restricting free enterprise

---

BOX 12.1   GLOBAL PERSPECTIVE

Better Jobless Benefits in Germany

In the United States, Dylan DeRoberts lost his job at a Chrysler assembly plant. Several months later he also lost his medical insurance. He cannot afford to pay the insurance premiums on his own. "It's scary being without insurance," he says. While working, he earned around $5,000 per month, and now he gets only $1,426 per month in jobless benefits, which is equal to about 29% of his old salary. His girlfriend, an elementary school teacher, makes slightly more. Their combined income is enough to cover rent for their two-bedroom apartment, electricity, groceries, car insurance, and gasoline, but little else. The couple rarely eats out and usually waits for a $5 discount to see a movie.

In Germany, Alfred Butt lost a similar job, but it does not stop him and his wife from taking a 1-week vacation in Cyprus. He says being out of work has not changed his life that much. This is because he receives generous jobless benefits. Every month he gets 80% of his old salary, a 51% improvement over his American counterpart. In addition, his wife is employed as a nurse at a rheumatism clinic. She and her husband no longer go as often to their favorite Greek restaurant, but other than that, he can still afford his lifestyle, he says. The German economy is expected to get worse, but his biggest worry is not surviving while jobless; it is finding another job, because employers frown on applicants who have been unemployed for more than a year, thinking they do not want to work. Now he constantly searches online for jobs in sales, purchasing, or administration at all kinds of companies. But so far he still has not found one (Walker and Thurow, 2009).

and private ownership of property. Some communist countries, however, have tried to introduce a new economic arrangement in which centralized direction of the nation's economy is reduced. China, for example, has adopted some free enterprise practices, granted state-owned enterprises wide autonomy in running their businesses, and opened up some industries to foreign investors. Still, the economies of China and other officially socialist countries remain largely unfree.

Also economically unfree are a number of countries whose governments do not consider themselves socialist, such as Kenya and Angola in Africa, Pakistan and Bangladesh in Asia, and Bolivia and Peru in Latin America. These countries do not restrict private ownership and free enterprise in the same way as their socialist counterparts, but their governments do severely control their economies by imposing heavy taxes, setting wages and prices, and excessively regulating various industries (O'Grady, 2008).

Economic Performance

Socialist or unfree economies have decidedly poor records. Their total wealth is generally far below that of capitalist or economically free countries. True, under socialism, nations such as Cuba and China had improved the standard of living for vast numbers of people who had been destitute before their governments became socialist. In general, socialist nations have reduced the extremes of poverty, inflation, and unemployment that occasionally affect capitalist countries. But the central planning of socialist states, especially in North Korea, often creates inefficiencies, causing, among other things, severe shortages of food and products. Similar problems plague a number of countries in Africa, Asia, and Latin America that are not socialist but are economically unfree (O'Grady, 2008; O'Grady et al., 2005).

In the meantime, capitalist economies in the West have little trouble producing ample quantities of goods. Moreover, their social peace has depended to a great extent on economic growth, which gives even the poor some hope of improving their standard of living. Their ability to sustain this growth may not be certain all the time. Sometimes their productivity goes down, ratcheting up unemployment (as it does now, in 2010), but sooner or later recovery will follow, as it did in 1991 and 2001.

Despite the ups and downs of their economic conditions, capitalist countries tend to remain considerably more productive than their socialist counterparts—as well as many nonsocialist but economically unfree countries. The capitalist system is much more efficient because it allows the freedom to pursue personal gain and minimizes government control of the economy. In fact, a study of 156 countries shows that those with more economic freedom are generally more prosperous than those with less freedom. Economic freedom, then, is the key to prosperity (O'Grady, 2008; O'Grady et al., 2005).

However, in the current economic crisis, the socialist system in China performs better than the capitalist system in the United States and other developed countries. While the production of capitalist countries has slowed, the production by the Chinese state-owned companies continues to grow. As China's prime minister recently said, "The socialist system's advantages enable us to make decisions efficiently, organize effectively, and concentrate resources to accomplish large undertakings" (Wines, 2010).

The Global Economy

Modern transportation and communication have created a **global economy**, in which many countries from all over the world trade with each other. In the past, the international trade was confined to the importing of raw materials such as food, fuels, and minerals from poor countries and a few industrial products such as clothes and shoes from rich countries. Today, all kinds of products and services, as well as stocks, bonds, and other investments, flow from one country to another. Over the last decade, world trade has increased ninefold in value, from $6.4 trillion in 2002 to $58 trillion today (Elliott, 2010; Samuelson, 2003b).

The global economy seems to work relatively well. Some poor countries sell inexpensive labor-intensive products (such as clothes, shoes, and toys) to rich nations and buy from rich nations sophisticated knowledge-intensive goods and services (such as aircraft, medical equipment, banking, and insurance). In rich countries, importing the low-cost merchandise enables consumers to live better. While low-wage workers may temporarily lose their jobs, they will eventually get reemployed in trade-competitive, stronger industries. The international trade, in turn, helps those in poor countries to prosper (Samuelson, 2003a).

However, the global economy is not completely free. In the large majority of developing countries, the government heavily supports businesses by, for example, having state-owned banks lend them money at extremely low interest rates. Such government support has alarmed the United States and other rich countries. They fear that given the huge number of developing countries with government-subsidized companies, the rich countries will be swamped with extremely cheap imports, which will bankrupt many of their own companies and cause a widespread loss of jobs. Rich countries have therefore demanded "a level playing field," pressuring the developing countries to abandon government support if they want to participate in world trade. But complying with this demand will effectively dash those poor countries' hopes of becoming prosperous. For their part, rich countries have promised to reduce their farm subsidies (Amsden, 2007; Lynch, 2008).

Globalization: Unfounded Fears

By shipping jobs to poor, low-wage countries in order to build factories there, globalization has created unfounded fears in many Americans. One fear is that outsourcing can cause a lot of job loss in the United States. Americans tend to believe that if Asians manufacture our cars, American auto workers will lose their jobs, and that foreigners and poor countries will increasingly produce many other things we need, until there are no more jobs left for us. However, evidence suggests just the opposite. Since outsourcing began in the mid-1970s, far more jobs have been created in the United States than have been lost to foreign countries. Moreover, most of the new jobs pay well, often better than the old ones. This is because they come from more innovative, more efficient, and more profitable industries and businesses (Norberg, 2004; Weidenbaum, 2001).

Another fear is that, by encouraging free trade, globalization can impoverish our economy because it opens our market to cheap foreign goods that outsell ours. However, evidence shows a strong connection between free trade and economic

Global economy
An economic system in which many countries from all over the world trade with each other.

growth. Among developed countries such as the United States, the free traders have seen their economies grow much more than those of the protectionists, who close their markets to foreign goods. This growth is because foreign competition forces our companies to make their products as good and cheap as possible or to specialize so they can produce their unique merchandise to sell not only in our domestic market but also in foreign markets.

There are other signs of the United States having benefited enormously from globalization. American companies have been dominating the new global economic order. The standard of living has risen significantly for the masses of Americans because they pay very low prices for goods from China and other developing countries. The U.S. economy has grown faster than the economy of any other large industrial nation over the last two decades. The unemployment rate in the United States has stood lower than that in many large European economies (Zakaria, 2007).

Nonetheless, those Americans who temporarily lose their jobs to global competition do need help from the U.S. government. First, like their unemployed counterparts in other rich countries, they should not lose their health care and pension, as they do now after being laid off. And second, they should be retrained or further educated for a new job or career in the current global economy (Zakaria, 2007).

■ U.S. Economic Problems

There are many economic problems in the United States. Here we will discuss only a few: the recession that still goes on in 2010, the effects of unemployment, the inability of baby boomers to retire, and the loss of summer jobs among teenagers.

The Great Recession

The collapse of the U.S. housing market led the country into a severe economic downturn called the Great Recession. Since the early 2000s, reckless heavy investing by home buyers, banks, Wall Street investment houses, and insurance companies had greatly driven up the prices of houses every year. Then, in 2008, houses began to get so expensive that it was difficult to sell them. As a result, sales and prices of new and existing homes started to fall and continue to do so today. This problem hit the banking industry the hardest. At least 176 banks failed in 2009 alone, and most of the banks still in business have stopped lending for fear that potential borrowers would not pay them back. Consequently, many businesses cannot borrow the money to buy inventory or pay their workers, let alone hire new ones.

The recession has hurt Americans in a number of ways. First is the huge job loss at 10%, the worst since the early 1940s. The groups that suffer the highest unemployment rate are the young, the unskilled, and blacks. Second is the pay cuts, which affect a quarter of workers. And third is the loss of housing and stock market wealth by higher-income Americans. The recession also has changed the lives of many Americans. According to a study by the Pew Research Center, Americans have become more frugal: 71% say they are buying less expensive brands and 57% say they have eliminated vacations. Other Americans have changed their life plans: 11% have postponed marriage or having children and 9% have moved in with parents. But the Pew researchers found that most Americans are still optimistic, believing that the recession is temporary and the country will sooner or later recover from it (Havemann, 2010; Samuelson, 2010).

The Effects of Unemployment

When a company lays off employees, the result is usually lowered morale and increased fear in the workplace. According to a survey by the American Management Association, 88% of the companies that have downsized say that morale has declined. Because of the layoffs, the remaining employees tend to distrust management, become unhappy and stressed out, and steal from their employers, which explains why for retailers employee theft typically exceeds shoplifting losses (Pfeffer, 2010).

Losing a job is devastating to the employee. It can literally kill people. In the United States, when individuals are laid off, they lose their health insurance. And not having health insurance has been related to high mortality rates. Getting laid off can also cause people to get angry and depressed, which increases the likelihood of violent behavior, as is often suggested by the news coverage of the fired employee returning to the workplace with a gun to wound or kill people. In fact, research has shown that people without any history of violent behavior are six times more likely to exhibit violent behavior after a layoff when compared to similar people who remain employed. Getting laid off further increases the likelihood of suicide, mental health problems, alcoholism, drug abuse, and smoking.

It is widely believed that layoffs benefit the companies by increasing their stock prices, productivity, and profits. However, a study of 141 layoff announcements between 1979 and 1997 shows that the companies suffered a decline in their stock prices. Another study in the 1980s did find that labor costs went down after downsizing, but the firms did not become "lean and mean" because sales per employee, and therefore company profits, also fell. Layoffs are indeed generally bad for companies. Consider now-defunct Circuit City, the electronic retailer. It got rid of its 3,400 highest-paid sales associates to cut its costs. The resulting fewer employees with fewer skills in the Circuit City stores enabled competitors such as Best Buy to gain ground. Eventually Circuit City could not compete and filed for bankruptcy, closing its doors in 2009.

With many companies laying off employees, as is occurring now in the Great Recession, the economy is getting worse. By losing jobs, people also lose incomes, so they spend less. Workers who do not lose their jobs are fearful of layoffs, so they are likely to cut back on spending, too. With less combined demand in the economy, sales are bound to fall. With smaller sales, companies lay off more employees, and the vicious cycle with fewer employees, less income, lower sales, and more layoffs continues, driving the economy into a deep recession (Pfeffer, 2010).

To avoid being unemployed, you may want to consider some ways of finding a job (see **Box 12.2**).

Boomers Can't Retire

Even before the financial crisis in early 2008, many baby boomers had not saved enough for retirement. The boomers are mostly 46 to 64 years old, born between 1946 and 1964, the years when the U.S. birth rates were the highest. Now, after the stock market has plummeted, and hit with the Great Recession, the boomers have seen

BOX 12.2   USING SOCIOLOGICAL INSIGHTS

How to Land a Job—Even in a Down Economy

Using sociological insights into how people interact, Penelope Trunk (2006) offers what she considers some of the best tips to land a job:

- *Use proactive recommendations.* Tell your references not to wait for calls from a would-be employer. If a job really interests you, have your references go ahead and call the employer on your behalf. This is likely to work better if you have exceptional or noteworthy references, such as business leaders. However, professors or even coaches who have worked with you and know you well could also have a positive impact on the employer's decision to interview or hire you.
- *Use social networking sites.* You are not the only one out there looking for a job, or unhappy with your current employer. Sites like LinkedIn have been created to make it easier for job seekers to find one another, share work histories and profiles, post job opportunities, reveal employment needs, and dish out advice on how to deal with employers. Those tidbits of information are already there, usually free, and waiting for you. You will have a leg up on the competition because most people get their job through networking.
- *Turn a nonjob into a job.* Don't be afraid to start with a temporary employment agency, or offer working as an intern. Employers often use interns and also employment agencies for filling positions—especially those requiring little skill—frequently listing positions as "temp to perm." Once you get a foot in the door, you never know what might materialize when you demonstrate your abilities and let the employer know that you are interested in a full-time position.
- *Use U.S. mail.* Even in less-competitive markets, employers and hiring managers are flooded with resumes and feelers via e-mail and automated job posting sites. Most of them receive more e-mail than they can sift through in a given day. But they receive relatively light loads of "snail" or paper mail. If you have the name of the company's chief executive officer (CEO) or hiring personnel, go ahead and mail them a nice, high-quality copy of your cover letter and resume directly. Doing so will increase your odds of having your materials reviewed, especially within smaller companies.
- *Be nice.* As elementary and obvious as it may sound, the people whom employers find to be the most pleasant and nice get most of the jobs. So either work to be nice or at least convince them that you are. The problem is, how do you know if you are really nice? If you are applying for dozens of jobs and are never hearing back from anyone, this could mean that you are not seen as nice enough. You may be the nicest person in the room, but if others are not picking up on this before they get to know you, then you might need to rethink your tactics and presentation. Think like a fisherman and use more obvious and alluring bait.

There are ways to land a job even in the current down economy. It helps to use sociological insights into how people interact, such as using social networking sites and presenting yourself as a nice and pleasant person.

their retirement savings shrink considerably. They have to delay retirement, having to work longer and harder than they had planned.

Usually, when many older people retire, they will help smooth the recession. This is because as they quit working, they spend their pensions and savings, which helps to stimulate the economy. In addition, they make room for younger workers, which helps reduce the unemployment rate. Presently, however, with the horde of older workers continuing to work, the younger generation will have a hard time finding employment. Already, according to a study at Northeastern University, employment rates for teenagers and twenty-somethings have fallen, while the number of people 55 years of age and older who have jobs has gone up (Gandel, 2009).

It is tough for those boomers who have been laid off. The experience of 66-year-old Gilbert Brooks is typical. When he lost his job at a trucking company in 2008, he was forced into early retirement. He had worked in transportation sales and marketing for 35 years. "I am highly qualified," he says. But 2 years and 12 job interviews later, he still cannot land a job. Adding to his misery, his wife has also lost her job as a secretary and receptionist for real estate lawyers. Unemployed boomers find it hard to get a new job because they have had higher salaries, they are rusty about applying for a job, and their skills are out of date (Dugas, 2010).

After losing his job at a trucking company in 2008, Gilbert Brooks was forced to retire early. After 2 years and 12 job interviews later, he still cannot find a job. Now his wife has also lost her job as a secretary and receptionist.

Teens Losing Summer Jobs

Teenagers across the United States need summer jobs for car insurance, college funds, and spending money, but it is getting harder for them to find employment. According to the U.S. Bureau of Labor Statistics, in the summer of 2000, 45% of teens worked, but for the same period in 2009 the employment rate went down to 32.7%. The economic downturn has apparently made the hunt for summer work brutal for teens. Seventeen-year-old Stephanie Russo, for example, applied for jobs at a grocery store, a clothing retailer, a pet store, a kennel, an ice cream parlor, and even a Minor League baseball team, but she failed to get hired. Her boyfriend also had applied for various jobs at local businesses but could only find one at fast-food restaurant Arby's, the last place he wanted to be working.

Nowadays, because of the economic downturn, many more teenagers have failed to find summer jobs than before, even though they still need the jobs for car insurance, college funds, and spending money.

The current economic downturn has created new competition in the job market for teens. This competition comes from adults seeking teen-friendly jobs such as babysitter, valet car parker, amusement park worker, and grocery store cashier.

Compared to adults, teens find it harder to get hired. The reason is simply that most employers will choose more mature adults over teenagers, because there is no need to spend any time training them. The number of such adults has increased significantly. They include retirees, people who have been laid off, and low-paid workers looking for a second income. All this competition makes it more difficult for teens to find jobs.

The American Recovery and Reinvestment Act has allocated $1.2 billion to stimulate the job market for young people ages 14 to 24 years by helping them find employment, with much of the money supporting summer job opportunities. However, most of the stimulus money is directed to lower-income and disadvantaged teens, not middle-class youngsters. As a result, most teenagers are having a hard time finding employment in their summer job search. Youth experts are concerned that without the experience of a summer job, the teens will continue to have a hard time finding employment when they become adults (Petrecca, 2009).

■ The Dominance of Big Corporations

The competitive market system in which business companies operate has an inherent contradiction. The more efficient it is, the more it threatens to destroy itself. Through free competition, the most successful companies gain more resources, which gives them an edge on their competitors. They may use this edge to drive their competitors out of business or to buy them out. As a result, there will be fewer companies left. Eventually, just one firm dominates the entire market, achieving a **monopoly**—the situation in which one firm controls the market. In today's society, however, it is more likely that a handful of big companies control a certain market, forming an **oligopoly**—the situation in which only a few companies control the market. Indeed, only a small number of corporations, all of which are big, dominate the economy in many countries. These corporations not only reduce competition in the marketplace but also create other problems.

Monopoly
The situation in which one firm controls the market.

Oligopoly
The situation in which only a few companies control the market.

How Big Corporations Operate

A big corporation does not have a single owner. Instead, it has thousands or even hundreds of thousands of stockholders, who own shares in the corporation and its profits. Stockholders do not communicate with one another, much less organize to control the corporation. But they can exercise their right to vote and elect a board of directors to run the corporation. The directors make overall plans for the company. They may decide how to raise money, how to expand the company, and what dividends to pay shareholders. The directors also appoint the president, vice president, and other officers to conduct the company's day-to-day operations. In corporations, then, ownership and control are separated.

The big corporation is a far cry from what Adam Smith, the proponent of capitalism, expected. To him, a typical company was supposed to be small, started by one or a few individuals with their personal savings. These entrepreneurs were expected to personally manage the company and reap the profits or suffer the losses, depending on how well they performed in a competitive market. The rise of big corporations today, then, can have serious consequences that Smith did not anticipate.

First, the few big corporations, relatively free from competitive challenges, can force consumers to pay high prices for their products. Or they may slow down production and then increase the prices for their supposedly scarce goods. Price hikes can generate inflation, and production slowdown can cause unemployment, both of which can throw society into an economic crisis.

Moreover, given their control over large shares of the market, big corporations usually do not feel competitive. So they have little incentive to build new plants, increase research and development of new products, make themselves more efficient, and offer consumers better goods and services. This may explain why several decades ago some big U.S. corporations—especially in the car and steel industries—sat back complacently and did not compete with Japanese and other foreign firms until their shrinking market share and falling profits spurred them back into action.

Welfare for the Rich

As discussed in Chapter 2, two welfare systems exist in the United States. One is for the poor, and the other for the rich. In the welfare for the rich, the government provides big corporations and wealthy individuals with special tax breaks often called tax credits, tax deductions, and other loopholes in the tax law. Some of the government help for corporations may also be in the form of direct payments or loans, usually called subsidies. Welfare for big corporations—and rich individuals—is far more generous than welfare for the poor.

Big corporations receive the greatest amount of government benefits. The income taxes paid by corporations have always been proportionately smaller than those paid by individuals. Over the past 50 years, the corporate income tax as a fraction of federal government revenue has steadily declined, from over 20% in the 1960s to less than 10% today. The government also supplies big business with more dollars in direct loans and loan guarantees than all the commercial and industrial loans provided by private banks. Every year, the government further pays an enormous sum for research and development projects in such areas as the military, space exploration, and atomic energy. After developing the technology at taxpayers' expense, big corporations are allowed to use it to earn a profit. The government even annually gives about $100 million to food and beverage companies to advertise their products abroad, such as Miller beer, Campbell's soup, and McDonald's burgers (Browning, 2004; Nader and Weissman, 2001).

Multinational Corporations

In many big corporate mergers, a corporation buys others that operate different kinds of business to form a **conglomerate**, a corporation that owns companies in various unrelated industries. An example is General Electric, the largest conglomerate in the United States. It operates in at least 14 different businesses, such as lighting, appliances, health care, electronics, aviation, media and entertainment, and oil and gas. Most conglomerates have further expanded by becoming **multinational corporations**, with subsidiaries in many countries. Many multinationals have more economic power than a medium-sized nation. Exxon, for example, is more powerful than Israel, Jordan, the Philippines, and Guatemala combined, because the value of the corporation's annual sales exceeds the gross national product of those nations (Chimerine, 1995; Tolentino, 2000).

In search of lower labor costs, lower taxes, and larger markets, many multinational corporations have shifted their assets out of their industrial birthplaces into

Conglomerate
A corporation that owns companies in various unrelated industries.

Multinational corporations
Corporations with subsidiaries in many countries.

the developing world. From these foreign investments, U.S. corporations can earn as much as 70% of their total profits. For these profits, multinational corporations pay very little in taxes because of the much lower tax rates in foreign countries. In recent years, the growing affluence of many developing countries such as India and China has led multinational corporations to change from pursuing cheap labor to directly selling U.S. consumer goods (Benjamin, 2003).

Multinational corporations can have far-reaching effects on developing nations. They can generate social conflict by bringing in elements of a foreign culture. They can promote dangerous practices such as smoking. They can control a small nation's most important industry such as copper production. Despite these dangers, however, most developing countries still welcome multinationals. They often try to attract more foreign investment with a wide array of incentives, ranging from extensive tax benefits to subsidized labor, even the elimination of trade unions (Luo, 2000).

■ Harmful Corporate Practices

Because they dominate the business world, big corporations tend to engage in practices harmful to employees, consumers, the government, and the environment.

Harming Employees

The law requires corporations to ensure that their employees remain free from known hazards in the work environment. Yet many workers are still exposed to various kinds of pollutants such as coal dust, cotton dust, and radiation. Although these substances have been found to cause cancer, leukemia, and other serious illnesses, corporations tend to ignore or deny the problem rather than take corrective action to make their workplaces safer. Three reasons have been proposed for corporations' tendencies to be negligent about their employees' health and safety (Ermann and Lundman, 2002).

First is corporate concern with profit maximization. Corporate executives are inclined to ignore health hazards in their plants because elimination of these hazards will eat into their companies' profits.

Second is the corporate culture that judges employees' worth impersonally, focusing only on their contribution to production. As a result, employees tend to be treated as if they were machines, easily replaceable. If some workers become disabled or die, others can be found to take their place. Such a callous attitude toward employees can lead corporate executives to disregard employee health and safety.

Third is the government's reluctance to take action against offending corporations. Instead of using threats or penalties to deter offenses, the Occupational Safety and Health Administration often relies on negotiation and persuasion to obtain compliance. In cases where citations and fines are used as a last resort, the corporations are allowed to have their penalties reduced if they correct their "deficiencies."

Exploiting Consumers

Corporate abuses may involve selling dangerous foods and unsafe products as well as violating antitrust laws.

The food industry has been known to seek greater profits by selling contaminated or adulterated foods. Meat-packing companies often sell their products without being certain that the meat is safe for human consumption. That's why health experts advise consumers to make sure their hamburgers are fully cooked; otherwise, one may be stricken with *E. coli*, a dangerous colon bacterial infection. However, other foods may also be contaminated with salmonella bacteria, causing diarrhea and abdominal cramping. Moreover, it is customary for the food industry to use all kinds of chemical additives in its products, although government scientists suspect that some of them may cause cancer and other diseases. The apparent purpose is not only to keep the foods from spoiling, as the food industry claims, but to make them look fresh and appealing so that the companies can sell huge quantities of them to make a huge profit. As a food marketer says, "The profit margin on food additives is fantastically good, much better than the profit margins on basic, traditional foods" (Simon, 2008).

The profit motive is also behind the manufacturing and selling of unsafe products by car, drug, tobacco, and other industries. Tobacco companies, for example, have long known that smoking is addictive and causes cancer, but they continue to make and sell cigarettes. Dealing in unsafe products also appears frequently in the pharmaceutical industry. Drug companies are often found committing such product-safety offenses as the sale of impure, overstrength, expired, or unsterile products (Gorman, 1992a).

Big corporations may further take advantage of consumers by violating antitrust laws. These laws prohibit companies from conspiring to reduce or eliminate competition. If there is little or no competition, prices will go up and consumers will have no choice but to pay them. To break the antitrust laws, corporations selling the same kind of products usually get together to fix prices that are abnormally high. Sometimes corporations prevent new competition from entering the market, as the two largest credit-card companies Visa and MasterCard once did, barring banks from issuing American Express and Discover cards. If not prosecuted, antitrust violations can produce enormous profits. Although profit is an obvious motive behind antitrust violations, at least three subtle forces may be at work also: (1) a history of cooperation among corporations, (2) an oligopolistic market, dominated by only a few companies, which makes cooperation easy, and (3) a lack of public awareness of antitrust violations (Ermann and Lundman, 2002).

Corrupting the Government

Big corporations often give huge sums of campaign donations to both political parties to influence legislation toward favoring their business interests. Also, in today's global economy, giant U.S. corporations may even bribe foreign governments or engage in other activities abroad that are forbidden by U.S. law. An example is Baxter International, Inc., the world's largest hospital-supply company, which pleaded guilty to a felony charge of violating the U.S. law that prohibits cooperating with the Arab boycott of Israel. For many years Baxter had tried to enter the vast, lucrative market of the Arab world. Arab boycott authorities would not cooperate unless Baxter first ceased its business in Israel, which Baxter finally did. Most of the illegal activities engaged in by U.S. companies involve giving bribes worth millions of dollars to foreign officials.

Actually, compared to their European and Asian counterparts, U.S. corporations are much less likely to use payoffs to do business abroad, an extremely common practice in the global economy. In 2007, for example, the giant German technology corporation Siemens was found to have paid millions in bribes to government officials in Nigeria, Russia, and Libya in order to win lucrative contracts for its telecommunication equipment (Crawford et al., 2007).

Polluting the Environment

Most corporations tend to dump their wastes onto the land and into the air and water because they find it too costly to develop ecologically safer alternatives or antipollution devices. They are also unwilling to clean up the mess or to assume liability for the health of citizens affected by it; to do so would cut into their profits. Big corporations in the petrochemical, metals, electrical, and transportation industries are most likely to pollute the environment.

Environmental pollution affects practically all of us in some way. As Ralph Nader (1970) said, "The efflux from motor vehicles, plants, and incineration of sulfur oxides, hydrocarbons, carbon monoxide, oxides of nitrogen, particulates, and many more contaminants amounts to compulsory consumption of violence by most Americans. There is no full escape from such violent ingestions, for breathing is required."

The federal government had tried to combat environmental pollution from the early 1970s to 1980 but with little success. Then, in 1980, Congress passed a law called the Comprehensive Environmental Response Commission and Liability Act, popularly known as the Superfund program. It was intended to clean up some of the worst hazardous waste sites in the nation. In the early 1980s the Superfund got off to a shaky start because the Environmental Protection Agency (EPA) was soft on environmental offenses. Many corporations that polluted the environment were left alone, and the few corporations found guilty were given every opportunity to negotiate cleanup settlements with the EPA. However, in the late 1980s, the EPA began aggressively enforcing the Superfund law against guilty corporations. Since then, such corporations have been under a great deal of EPA pressure to pay for the cleanup (Parenti, 2010). The EPA's action raises the larger question of whether the government should control the economy by preventing environmental pollution and other harmful corporate activities. See **Box 12.3**.

Since the late 1980s the U.S. Environmental Protection Agency has put a great deal of pressure on corporations that pollute the environment to pay for the cleanup. But this raises the question of whether the government should control the economy by preventing harmful corporate activities.

■ The Problems with Work

When we meet a stranger, one of our first questions is likely to be "What do you do?" The person may answer "I'm a salesperson" or "I'm a teacher" or a cabdriver or a lawyer. Work is not just a way to make enough money to pay the bills. For many of us, work allows us to enjoy our lives. Unfortunately, most of the work we do today is unpleasant, and many workers are dissatisfied with their work.

BOX 12.3   DIVERGENT VIEWS

Should Government Control the Economy?

Eliot Spitzer and Andrew Celli (2004) argue that government is needed to protect society against various harmful business practices. However, John Stossel (2001) contends that government regulations do more harm than good to Americans.

Spitzer and Celli show how government can prevent air pollution by forcing corporations to pay for the costs of pollution they have caused. Consider the air pollution in the Northeast caused by coal-burning power plants in the Midwest. (Plant owners had purposely built smokestacks tall enough for pollutants to fall not on their consumers nearby but on farther-away northeastern areas.) The costs were devastating effects on human health, with thousands of children in the Northeast suffering from asthma. Plant owners got away with it until the victimized states and citizens went to court and successfully forced them to pay for the costs of the pollution, which stopped the problem.

Spitzer and Celli also show how government stopped predatory lending—"the practice of imposing inflated interest rates, fees, charges, and other onerous terms on home mortgage loans." Many victims of predatory lending were low-income people and racial minorities. Government had to step in to curb this unfair and discriminatory practice. Such regulating is part of the government's larger attempt to safeguard core American values, which includes having instituted antidiscrimination laws, child-labor laws, and minimum wage laws.

Finally, Spitzer and Celli argue that government is best suited to protect against corporate corruption and abuse by requiring *integrity* and *transparency* in the financial market. Integrity is the idea that "those who are entrusted with protecting shareholders do so, rather than enriching themselves at shareholders' expenses." Transparency is the idea that "information in a free market must be accurate and truthful, freely flowing, and available to all." Without integrity and transparency, fraud is likely to occur. A financial analyst, for example, may hype a banking stock to clients while telling his colleagues that the stock is "a piece of junk."

Stossel argues that instead of protecting us, government regulations make things worse, not better. He points out, among other things, that the Food and Drug Administration (FDA), a government agency, has grown 10 times larger over the last 30 years, yet it now does more harm than good. For example, to get a new drug approved today, it costs about $500 million and takes about 10 years. This means that many new drugs would improve or even save lives, but they are being withheld from Americans just because there could be a tiny chance of dangerous side effects. Some years ago, the FDA held a press conference to announce its long-awaited approval of a new medication, predicting that it would save 14,000 American lives each year. Stossel asks, "Why didn't anybody stand up at the time and say, 'Excuse me, doesn't that mean you killed 14,000 people last year by not approving it?'" (Stossel, 2001).

Working Odd Hours

Most U.S. employees no longer work from 9 to 5, Monday through Friday. Instead, they work odd hours—evenings, weekends, rotating shifts, and when the rest of the world sleeps. Such employees now make up more than half (53%) of the workforce, with one-third working weekends and one-fifth working nights or rotating shifts. The demand for these employees to work late or weekends comes from changes in the U.S. economy, demography, and technology (Presser, 2003; Rivas, 2006).

Over the last 40 years the economy has changed from emphasizing the production of goods (cars, refrigerators, and other things) to focusing on providing services (nursing, airlines, restaurants, and the like). In the 1960s there were many more jobs in production than in service, but today it is just the opposite, with twice as many workers in service as in production. Many of the services we purchase, such as hospital care, airline travels, and restaurant dinners, must be provided in the evenings or on weekends. The increased demand for these services, then, has spurred the demand for employees to work odd hours.

The increased demand for those services has in turn originated from a significant change in the U.S. demography. For one thing, the population has aged considerably, with many more elderly people today than in the past. This has raised the demand for medical services around the clock. Young people have more time for recreation, entertainment, and travel during evenings, nights, and weekends. The rising demand for these services further gets a boost from the increase in family income that has been fueled by the growth of two-earner couples.

Finally, advances in transportation, communication, and other technologies, such as airliners, computers, the Internet, and cell phones, have brought us a global 24-hour economy. We can now work after midnight in the United States providing services to people in other parts of the world during their daytime. This has created employment opportunities in financial, investment, and other highly skilled professions. However, most of the demand for employment in late hours involves jobs in low-skilled, low-paying occupations in local markets. The most common of these jobs include cashiers, truck drivers, restaurant servers, cooks, janitors and cleaners, nurses and other hospital workers, and hotel managers and workers.

A few late-night or weekend workers like their jobs because they find them interesting, requiring little supervision or offering better camaraderie with coworkers. But the majority accept the jobs out of necessity rather than preference. According to one study, about 63% of the workers said they could not get any other job, the late hours were mandated by employers, and the nature of the job required the odd hours. Moreover, these workers are paid less than their peers who work during standard daytime hours. If they are married and have children, they are also more likely to experience marital unhappiness and divorce (Presser, 2003; Rivas, 2006).

Unhappy Workers

Many workers are dissatisfied with their jobs, especially in the current economic downturn (see Box 12.4). However, job dissatisfaction does vary from one group to

---

BOX 12.4   WHAT RESEARCH REVEALS

Job Dissatisfaction Hits New High

According to a survey by the Conference Board, a research firm funded by about 2,000 corporations around the world, 55% of American workers are dissatisfied with their jobs. It is the highest rate in 22 years. Given the current high unemployment, wouldn't the workers be happy just to have a job? No, they would not, for at least three reasons (Cohan, 2010):

- Fewer workers find their job interesting at all.
- Workers' incomes have not kept up with inflation. They have fallen when adjusted for inflation.
- The rising cost of health insurance has reduced workers' take-home pay.

The most unhappy workers are relatively young, younger than 25 years old. Of this demographic, 64% are not happy in their jobs.

another. Generally, younger workers are more dissatisfied with their jobs than older workers. One reason is that younger workers are more likely to expect their jobs to be highly interesting and stimulating and hence are more likely to be dissatisfied because of the difficulty in realizing their high aspirations. Older workers are happier because they are more advanced in their careers, have better jobs, are more likely to have found a field they do well in, and are given more autonomy to do their work.

Blue-collar workers are also more likely than their white-collar peers to be unhappy in their jobs. Among blue-collar workers, labor union members are significantly less happy when compared to nonmembers, which may suggest job dissatisfaction as the primary reason for joining unions in the first place.

In today's fiercely competitive global economy, many U.S. companies have begun to minimize production costs by paying their employees low wages, comparable to those received by skilled but low-paid workers in the fast-developing economies in Asia and Eastern Europe. A popular way to keep payroll costs low involves hiring temporary, contingent, part-time, and contract workers. In fact, since 1982, temporary employment has soared by nearly 250% compared with less than a 20% increase in all employment. Temporary workers now compose at least one-third of the U.S. labor force, and their ranks are still growing. Temporary workers are generally less happy than their full-time peers (Kirk and Belovics, 2008; Larson, 1996; Thottam, 2003).

Temporary workers normally do not join labor unions, but as has been suggested, unhappy full-time workers do. They expect to get higher pay and better working conditions. However, over the last three decades, the proportion of the workers in unions has declined continuously, from about 20% in 1983 to nearly 13% in 2004 (see **Figure 12.1**). One reason for the decline is the loss of unionized jobs in the

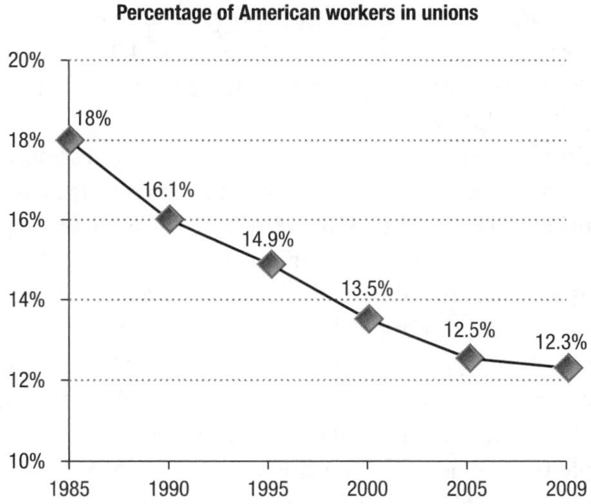

Percentage of American workers in unions

FIGURE 12.1 Decline of U.S. Labor Unions

Although the rate of decline has slowed a little since 2005, American union membership has been in a constant state of decline for the past three decades. The increase in demand and availability of high-tech and other service industries requiring more specialized training and college degrees is partially to blame. Another reason is increased reliance on outsourcing expensive, unionized manufacturing positions to foreign countries with cheaper labor.

Critical Thinking: *What factors would influence your decision to seek employment in a unionized versus a nonunionized shop?*

Source: U.S. Bureau of Labor Statistics, 2010.

manufacturing industry. Another is the lack of union appeal in fast-growing service and technological industries, where employees are relatively well educated.

■ Sociological Theories of Capitalism

No factory functions on its own. It must buy raw materials and sell its products. It is enmeshed in a complicated network of exchanges. This network must be organized in some way. One way is through markets. A market economy is driven by the countless decisions individuals make to buy and sell. This is how capitalism works. But is it good for society? To functionalists, the answer is yes, because it brings about a prosperous and stable social order. To conflict theorists, capitalism is harmful to society because it produces extremes of inequality by encouraging a powerful wealthy class to exploit a weak lower class. Finally, the symbolic interactionists focus on how people's definition of their world creates and supports capitalism.

Functionalist Theory

Functionalist ideas about the contributions of capitalism to a prosperous society can be traced to Adam Smith (1732–1790). Although Smith was an economist, his theory of capitalism has become part of economic sociology. At the core of the theory lies a belief about the psychology of human beings: We are inherently selfish and act to serve our own interests. Capitalism works by allowing this pursuit of self-interest to flourish. It does so through two key characteristics: (1) *private ownership* of property and (2) *free competition* in buying and selling goods and services.

Private ownership is considered functional for society's economic health because it motivates people to be efficient and productive. This may explain why, for example, Federal Express and other private delivery companies in the United States are generally more financially successful than the U.S. Postal Service. Private ownership may also explain why private lands in China are more productive than state-owned farms. In that country, the private plots once constituted only 4% of all cultivated land, but they produced 50% of the country's potatoes and 33% of its meat and dairy products (Naisbitt and Aburdene, 1990).

Free competition is also considered beneficial to society's economic health because it compels businesses to make the most efficient use of resources, to produce the best possible goods and services, and to sell them at the lowest price possible. Only by doing so can businesses expect to beat their competitors. Competition, then, acts—in Smith's terminology—as an "invisible hand," bringing profits to the efficient producers and putting the inefficient ones out of business.

Doesn't the pursuit of self-interest reduce society to a jungle and harm the public good? On the contrary, Smith argued; because of free competition, the self-serving decisions of individuals to buy and sell end up promoting the public good. Competition forces people to take account of others' interests in order to serve their own. If Apple Computer does not meet your needs, you can buy a product from Dell or Gateway—and Apple knows it. It is in *their* interest to serve *your* interests. Because many businesses strive to serve their own interests by serving those of the public, the whole society will benefit. There will be an abundance of high-quality, low-priced goods and services, which will entice many people to buy. Businesses will then produce more to meet consumers' increased demand, which will create more jobs and raise wages. The result will be a prosperous economy for the society as a whole.

Conflict Theory

According to Karl Marx (1818–1883), capitalism is harmful to society. He saw it as inevitable that private property owners would exploit their laborers by paying them as little as possible. Marx also disagreed with Smith on the specialized division of labor in industrial capitalism. To Smith, specialization enhances efficiency in the generation of wealth, but when Marx looked at specialization, he saw **alienation of labor**, laborers' loss of control over their work process. Because workers own neither their tools nor the products they make, and because they cannot exercise all their capacities as they choose but are forced to perform an isolated, specific task like a robot, their work is no longer their own. Instead, Marx contended, it becomes a separate, alien thing, making the workers feel as if somebody else did their work.

Alienation of labor
Laborers' loss of satisfaction in their work because of the loss of control over their work process.

Marx further saw severe contradictions within the capitalist system, contradictions that would serve as "its own gravediggers." One such contradiction grows from capitalism's devotion to individualism. As Robert Heilbroner (1972) said, "Capitalism had become so complex that it needed direction, but capitalists insisted on ruinous freedom," especially the freedom to overcharge customers. Marx saw another contradiction as well: Capitalists depend on profit, but their profit comes from the fact workers put more value into products than they are given in the form of wages. To increase their profits, capitalists often hold down wages and, whenever possible, also substitute machines for human labor. As a result, the workers get poorer from lower wages or job loss. With less income, the workers are forced to reduce the demand for the capitalists' products, thereby decreasing their profits. The economy can work itself out of this crisis, but such crises will recur, argued Marx, with each one getting worse until the workers revolt.

Ultimately, Marx believed, the contradictions of capitalism would lead to **communism**, a classless society that operates on the principle of "from each according to his ability, to each according to his need." In this society, the state would wither away. First, however, the destruction of capitalism would be followed by a temporary era of socialism. No state, including so-called communist countries such as China and the former Soviet Union, has ever reached full-blown communism, but many have tried socialism. In a socialist economy, as discussed previously, the state owns and operates much of the means of production and distribution, such as land, factories, railroads, airlines, and banks. It determines what the nation's economic needs are and develops plans to meet these needs. It also sets wages and prices. Individual interests are subordinate to those of society.

Communism
A classless society that operates on Marx's principle of "from each according to his ability, to each according to his need."

Symbolic Interaction Theory

As a symbolic interactionist, Max Weber (1864–1920) concentrated on how subjective meanings affect economic action. To Weber, subjective meanings come from interacting with others, which, in turn, leads the individual to engage in certain activities. Weber then saw how the early Protestants in Europe acquired from their interactions with each other some shared beliefs about their religion that gave rise to capitalist activities.

First, the Protestants defined hard work as a sign that God would send them to heaven rather than hell. In effect, they equated toil with God's work. By working hard, they ended up producing wealth. Second, they defined play as the devil's temptation. They were thus afraid to spend the fruit of their labor on amusements and other worldly pleasures. The wealth, then, was used as capital to be put into business. The continuing accumulation of capital led to the development of capitalism.

After capitalism emerged, it continued to operate for a long time because the early Protestants learned to behave in a rational or responsible—namely, what they considered a godly—manner. Early Protestantism effectively helped discipline what used to be an unruly working class, restraining its members from consuming alcohol, from engaging in disorderly conduct, and even from taking breaks or walking off their jobs, thus transforming them into a docile labor force. Simultaneously, these capitalists developed bureaucracy as a rational form of organization to perpetuate capitalism.

In short, the meanings imputed by the early Protestants to hard work and play helped create capitalism. Moreover, the continuing existence of capitalism is further supported by the Protestant values of self-restraint and rationality.

For a quick review of the three sociological theories about capitalism, see **Box 12.5.**

BOX 12.5   THEORETICAL THUMBNAIL

Explaining Capitalism

Theory	Focus	Insights
Functionalist Theory	How capitalism benefits society	Capitalism brings prosperity to society as a whole.
Conflict Theory	How capitalism harms society	Capitalism enables the rich to exploit the poor.
Symbolic Interaction Theory	How shared beliefs create and sustain capitalism	The belief that it is God's command to live a hard-working life gives rise to capitalism.

QUESTIONS TO EXPLORE

1. What functional role might the "invisible hand" play amid today's corporate climate of excessive greed, massive government bailouts, and CEOs in scandal?

2. Do you see evidence of Weber's "protestant work ethic" or Marx's "ruinous freedom" in modern businesses? Explain your answer.

3. Visit the Web site for the U.S. Economic Development Administration at http://www.eda. gov/. After reviewing its mission statement, do you agree with the current initiatives and focus, or would you recommend changes? Explain your response.

Review

SUMMARY

1. The United States is among the world's most capitalist societies. Also capitalist but less so than the United States are the European democracies. The socialist elements of Germany bring better benefits to its unemployed workers. The so-called communist countries are the most socialist in the world. Socialist countries are generally poor, but capitalist countries are far more prosperous. Global economy works relatively well, but the governments of many developed countries support their economy so that they can swamp developing countries with cheap imports. Globalization has generated unfounded fears in many Americans, especially the fear of losing jobs to poor countries.

2. One economic problem in the United States is the Great Recession, which has driven the country into a severe economic crisis. The recession has caused a high unemployment rate, widespread pay cuts, and a sharp drop in housing and stock market values. Unemployment is devastating to employees, while it lowers stock prices, productivity, and profits. It further worsens the recession. There are ways, though, to find a job in this recession.

3. Many baby boomers cannot retire because they have not saved enough. They have to work longer and harder than they had planned, but it is difficult for them to get jobs. It is also difficult for teenagers to find summer employment.

4. The numerous shareholders who own the big corporation do not run it. Only a small group of directors and managers do. Big corporations tend to become less competitive in the marketplace. They can raise the prices of their products and services, and the price hikes can lead to inflation and other economic problems. Big corporations often receive special tax breaks and direct payment from the government. Multinational corporations reap huge profits from abroad and can create problems for foreign countries.

5. Corporations often harm their employees by ignoring their health and safety, exploit their customers by selling them dangerous foods and unsafe products and violating antitrust laws, use campaign donations to buy influence and use bribes to gain favor from foreign governments, and pollute the environment without bearing the cost of the pollution. But should government control the economy by forcing corporations to refrain from these harmful practices? One view says yes; another says no.

6. Nowadays, most Americans work odd hours—evenings, weekends, rotating shifts, and when the rest of the world sleeps. This work schedule results from changes in the U.S. economy, demography, and technology. Many workers are not satisfied with their jobs, especially in the current recession. Job dissatisfaction has reached a new high, but some workers are more dissatisfied with their jobs than are others. Younger workers, for example, are more dissatisfied than their older peers.

7. According to functionalist theory, capitalism benefits society by making it prosperous. Conflict theory views capitalism as harmful for allowing the rich to exploit the poor. And symbolic interaction theory attributes the emergence of capitalism to the early Protestants' belief in working hard as a sign that God would send them to heaven rather than hell.

CRITICAL THINKING QUESTIONS

1. What are two or three of the primary economic issues facing U.S. citizens today? From your observations, are we making progress in these areas? Explain your response.

2. Is the United States moving toward more of a "mixed economy" or will capitalism always be favored more highly than socialism? Why so?

3. In what ways have you been directly influenced by the global economy?

INTERNET RESOURCES

The Bureau of Labor Statistics (BLS) (http://www.bls.gov/) is an agency within the federal government that oversees the gathering and dissemination of statistical data on labor.

The U.S. Economic Development Administration (EDA) (http://www.eda.gov/) is an agency housed within the U.S. Department of Commerce that is dedicated to identifying and assisting high-risk and "distressed" communities with an eye toward reinvigorating job markets.

The United States Department of Labor (DOL) (http://www.dol.gov/index.htm) strives to advance better working condition for employees, retirees, active job seekers, and even employers through ever-improving working environments and opportunities pertaining to labor. The DOL also serves as a dispute arbitrator, while administering a variety of federal labor laws—particularly in the areas of health, safety, protection, and related legal rights.

The Wall Street Journal (www.wallstreetjournal.com) is the premier economy-related newspaper, providing up-to-date information on stock market analyses, along with business, political, social, and legal developments that influence the U.S. and global economies.

Political Problems

In late 2008, right after Barack Obama won the presidential election, the governor of Illinois, Rod Blagojevich, was arrested for political corruption. In recorded conversations with advisors, he brazenly talked about how he was going to sell Obama's seat in the U.S. Senate. On one recording, he said, "I've got this thing, and it's [expletive] golden. And I'm just not giving it up for [expletive] nothing. I'm not going to do it. And I can always use it. I can parachute me there." The gold he sought included a cabinet post in the White House. A year later, he was tried on 24 charges, including attempted extortion and soliciting bribes, but the jury found him guilty on just one lesser charge of making false statements to the Federal Bureau of Investigation (FBI). Apparently his lawyers convinced the jury that he was only talking too much and that no money or jobs ever changed hands (Bury et al., 2010).

Political corruption is one of the many problems that involve public officials and politicians. In this chapter, we will discuss this and other political problems, including political inconsistency, voting behavior, political parties, special-interest groups, political deviance, and the tortuous attempts by public officials and politicians to deal with their deviant acts.

■ Political Inconsistency

Americans are politically inconsistent, being conservative and liberal at the same time. There is also an inconsistency between politicians and voters, with the former being extreme and the latter moderate. These inconsistencies reflect a uniquely American political character.

Simultaneously Conservative and Liberal

Although Americans are divided by social class, they tend to share the same political characteristic of being simultaneously conservative and liberal. Consider members of the working class. They are generally liberal on economic issues, such as supporting intervention in the economy by the government, but they are at the same time conservative on social issues, such as opposing gay rights. On the other hand, higher-income Americans tend to be economically conservative, opposing government intervention, but socially liberal, supporting gay rights.

Americans of all classes are also politically inconsistent in other ways. Surveys have shown all classes to be liberal for supporting many kinds of government spending, including cleaning up the environment, bettering the nation's health, combating crime, strengthening the educational system, improving the situation of minorities, and providing medical care and legal assistance for the poor. However, while virtually everybody supports these government services, they are conservative for being highly critical of the government, which they believe to have become too powerful, too intrusive, and too wasteful—spending too much of taxpayers' money (NORC, 2010).

Their dislike of big government suggests that they are **ideological conservatives**, who oppose big government because they believe in free enterprise, rugged individualism, and capitalism. Simultaneously, the same people can be said to be **operational liberals**, who, in effect, support big government by backing government programs that render services to the public. Such mixed, ambivalent attitudes pertain not only to economic issues but also to social issues. Many conservatives, for example, want to "get government off our backs," but at the same time, they support school prayer and antiabortion laws, which effectively represent the liberal position that allows government to intervene in private lives (Lakoff, 2002; Thomas and Taylor, 2010).

Extreme Politicians and Moderate Voters

In the 1950s and 1960s, liberal and conservative politicians generally treated each other with civility during working hours, while many drank, played poker, and golfed together after hours. That culture of friendliness is long gone. Now politicians of the right and the left have become fiercely contentious over social issues such as abortion and immigration. They have become more extreme, apparently egged on by powerful interest groups and the attack-mode spirit of radio talk shows and cable TV.

The proportion of Republican delegates to nominating conventions who identify themselves as "very conservative" has risen from about 12% in 1972 to more than 30% today, and the share of Democrats self-identified as "very liberal" has climbed from about 8% to nearly 20%. By contrast, the general public hardly shows any change in "very conservative" and "very liberal" percentages. Thus, there are now many more extreme politicians, but the voters remain moderate. Understandably, Capitol Hill has become disturbingly nasty, uncivil, and polarized, while the more moderate citizens have been turned off by the rigid, angry arguments between conservative and liberal politicians.

In the past, when those politicians were more civil and friendly toward each other, it was relatively easy to get bipartisan support for the passage of important legislation. When Democrats introduced Social Security during the New Deal, large majorities of Republicans in both the House and Senate voted for it, even though Democrats controlled Congress. The same bipartisan support ensured the passage of civil-rights

Ideological conservatives
People who oppose big government because they believe in free enterprise, rugged individualism, and capitalism.

Operational liberals
People who support big government by backing government programs that render services to the public.

legislation in the 1960s. Today fierce partisanship makes it extremely difficult to pass those kinds of legislation (Thomas and Taylor, 2010).

■ Political Involvement

People can get involved in politics in many ways. They can attend a rally, run for office, form an interest group, send money to a candidate, write to their representatives, or work to promote the agendas of the opposition to incumbent representatives. But most Americans do not go beyond taking the simple action of voting during an election. Even in voting, Americans are far from enthusiastic. Here we will see which groups of Americans are more, or less, likely to vote, how they go about deciding whom to vote for, and why the voter turnout is low.

Voter Demographics

Voting varies from one group to another. As indicated by the data from the 2008 election as well as the survey by the Pew Research Center, some groups are significantly more likely than others to vote:

- Older people are more likely than younger persons to vote.
- Whites show higher voter turnout than Asians and Hispanics, but not blacks—who are just as likely as whites to vote.
- The more affluent are more likely to vote.
- The more educated are more likely to vote. In 2008, for example, 79% of college graduates voted, while only 55% of high school graduates did.
- The more religiously involved Americans are more likely to vote. More specifically, those who frequently go to church are more likely to vote when compared to those who seldom or never attend church.
- There is no significant gender difference in voting. Men are just as likely as women to go to the polls.

People who stay away from the voting booth are less likely to be married and more distrustful of others. They are also more likely to say that voting does not make much of a difference (File and Crissey, 2010; Pew Research Center, 2006).

Emotional Voting

Most voters know nothing about the important records or positions of politicians who are running for office. In the 1992 election, nearly every voter knew that the presidential candidate George H. W. Bush didn't like broccoli or that the name of his dog was Millie. But when it came to Bush's and his opponent Bill Clinton's positions on important issues, very few voters knew them. Just 15%, for example, knew that both candidates supported the death penalty.

Since they have no idea about candidates' positions, how do most voters decide which candidate to support? According to researchers, voters rely on how they feel about the candidate and whom they identify with to decide which candidate to vote for. They hardly use reason or logic to make their voting decision. In other words, voting is mostly an emotional act rather than a rational one (Begley, 2008; Lee, 2009). Consider how

President Gerald Ford lost Texas to Ronald Reagan in the 1976 Republican primaries. While campaigning in Texas, Ford nearly choked from trying to eat a tamale without first removing its corn-husk wrapper. This led Mexican American voters to feel that Ford didn't know much about them or their culture. It was thus difficult or impossible for them to identify with him. As a result, they did not vote for him but instead overwhelmingly pulled the lever for Reagan. Similarly, in the 1992 campaign, George H. W. Bush kept looking at his watch during a TV debate with Bill Clinton, making many Americans feel that "He just doesn't understand the country anymore."

But what emotions influence voting behavior the most? In every election, the emotions that successful candidates stir up in voters are most likely to include "fear and the yearning for security, hope and a desire for inspiration, and a wish for a certain level of comfort with a candidate" (Begley, 2008).

Low Voter Turnout

The percentage of people who vote is lower in the United States than in other Western democracies. Usually, only about half of all eligible voters in the United States go to the polls compared with over 75% in other countries. As a consequence, U.S. officials are routinely put into office by a minority of citizens. In the 2008 presidential election, Barack Obama was officially reported to receive 52% of all eligible votes but actually obtained only 32% because only 61.6% of eligible voters went to the polls. In the 2004 presidential election, George W. Bush was reported to have won 51% of the votes cast, but only 26% of the eligible electorate voted for him because close to half didn't bother to register to vote. In the 1980 election, Ronald Reagan's victory was often called a landslide because he beat Jimmy Carter by a wide margin. However, most eligible voters did not vote; only about 20% voted for Reagan.

What's behind these low turnouts? There are at least four reasons. First, large numbers of U.S. citizens simply get tired of voting because many more elections are held here than in other countries. Second, many regard political campaigns as mean-spirited and lacking in substance. The profusion of negative political advertising launched by two candidates against each other makes *both* look like liars and crooks. Third, even in regard to substantive issues such as jobs and taxes, voters see little or no difference between candidates, who are equally inclined to promise the same things that voters like to hear. And fourth, the longstanding political stability of the United States makes it seem unnecessary to vote. Thus, Americans can usually forget about politics and focus on the serious business of living—education, jobs, families, and the like.

Most political scientists hold the view that the low voter turnout poses a threat to democracy. They assume that a true democracy requires citizens' full participation because the people are supposed to rule. Without adequate support from its citizens, the government lacks legitimacy and therefore tends to be unstable.

The percentage of people who vote is relatively low in the United States. Reasons include too many elections, too much negative political advertising, no difference between candidates, and the longstanding political stability of the United States.

BOX 13.1   USING SOCIOLOGICAL INSIGHTS

How to Increase Voter Turnout

For modern campaigns, it is very common to use phone calls to encourage citizens to vote. But is there a way to make more people go to the polls? Prior to the presidential election in 2008, David Nickerson and Todd Rogers (2010) wanted to find the answer. They conducted an experiment on 287,228 would-be voters in Pennsylvania.

Nickerson and Rogers divided the sample into four groups, with three groups receiving different kinds of phone calls (these are the experimental groups), while the fourth one is the control group, which received no phone calls. One experimental group was *encouraged* to vote, but with no success, as they later were no more likely than the control group to vote. The second experimental group was asked whether they *intended* to vote; this group was no more likely than the control group to vote. The third group was asked *more detailed questions*, such as what time they planned to vote, where they would come from prior to voting, and what they would do before going to the polls. This third group was found to be significantly more likely to vote. The reason is that answering more detailed questions helped the voters develop a concrete voting plan, creating the effect of a self-fulfilling prophecy—doing something the individual has predicted he or she will do.

Nickerson and Rogers further unexpectedly discovered that if there were more than one eligible voter in the household, voter turnout was more likely to occur than if there was only a single eligible voter. The researchers explained that "eligible voters who live together may be more likely to make voting plans than those who live alone."

It is clear from the findings of this research that if you want to increase voter turnout, you should work harder with single eligible voters and discuss their voting plans by asking more rather than few questions.

The government is also likely to ride roughshod over the people. But there is a contrary view: The low voter turnout means that people are relatively contented with their lives. They "see politics as quite marginal to their lives, as neither salvation nor ruin" (Krauthammer, 1990). At any rate, if you feel strongly that the voter turnout should be raised, you will be interested in a research study that has suggested a simple strategy to do so (see Box 13.1).

■ Political Parties

Political party
A group of people organized for the purpose of gaining government offices.

A **political party** is a group of people organized for the purpose of gaining government offices. By seeking this goal for themselves, political parties perform several functions vital to the operation of a democracy. First, parties recruit members, nominate candidates, and raise campaign money to support their choices for public office. Without the parties, the process of electing officials would be chaotic, because hundreds of people might offer themselves as candidates for each office. Second, parties formulate and promote policies. The desire to seek voters' support ensures that these policies reflect public opinion. This is one way for the parties to serve as a link between the people and their government. Finally, the parties help organize the main institutions of government. Leadership positions in the legislature and its committees, for example, are parceled out on the basis of which party holds the allegiance of the most members of Congress.

Democrats and Republicans

There are two major parties, Democrats and Republicans. For more than a century, these two parties have held unquestioned dominance over the U.S. political system. Of course, there are many other parties, which are collectively called *third parties*. Occasionally, a third-party candidate wins a local or even a state election, as some Socialist party candidates have done. But no third party has had much of a chance of winning the presidency. No third party has any influence in Congress either.

Generally, Republicans are more conservative than Democrats. Republicans tend to advocate tax breaks for the wealthy, reduction in government spending, more local control, and less government interference with the economy. Consequently, the Republican Party usually gets more support from the economically advantaged, whites, members of major Protestant churches, and suburban and small-town residents. Democrats, on the other hand, are inclined to emphasize the government's role in promoting social welfare, and to institute programs to combat unemployment and relieve poverty. Therefore, the Democratic Party tends to gain more support from the economically disadvantaged, minority groups, and residents of the central-city areas in large metropolitan regions.

Republicans are generally more conservative than Democrats. They tend to advocate tax breaks for the wealthy, reduction in government spending, more local control, and less government interference with the economy.

The two-party system requires that each party represent as many citizens as possible if it is to win election or reelection. Thus, both parties usually aim for the center of public opinion, trying to appeal to everyone and offend no one. They represent a broad coalition of politicians with many different viewpoints. We can find such "strange bedfellows" as conservatives and liberals in each party. When it's time to nominate presidential candidates, each party usually looks to its center. This has led to the charge that there is "not a dime's worth of difference" between them. Yet if the Republican Party overemphasizes its conservatism and the Democratic Party its liberalism, either is certain to turn off many voters and get a severe beating at the polls. This is what happened when the conservative wing seized control of the Republican Party and nominated ultraconservative Barry Goldwater for president in 1964; the Democratic liberals did the same with ultraliberal George McGovern in 1972. Both choices led to landslide defeats in the general election.

Declining Party Influence

Since the late 1960s, U.S. political parties have suffered a decline in influence. More and more voters identify themselves as independent rather than as Democrats or Republicans. Today the independents make up the largest proportion (39%) of voters, compared to 33% for Democrats and 28% for Republicans (Brinkley, 2008). Even those who say they are Democrats or Republicans often split their vote, choosing some candidates from one party and some from the other. Most politicians still call themselves Democrats or Republicans, but they often act like independents, refusing to follow the direction of party leaders in Congress or even the president from their party. A number of factors seem to have caused this party decline.

The first two are television and the Internet, which enable candidates to reach voters directly rather than through an organized army of volunteers and party activists knocking on doors. A third factor is the large spread of party primaries, which put the choice of candidates in the hand of voters rather than party leaders and activists. A fourth factor is the rise of political action committees (PACs) as a big source of campaign money. **PACs** are political organizations that funnel money from business, labor, and other special-interest groups into election campaigns to help elect or defeat candidates. PACs act independently of the parties, so party leaders can no longer keep straying members in line by threatening to cut off their campaign funds. Finally, politicians have largely turned to pollsters and political consultants rather than local or state party leaders for data on what the public is thinking and feeling.

In short, whatever the parties can offer, politicians can find elsewhere. The parties have fewer carrots and sticks to control politicians. If politicians do not follow a party's position, then the party labels mean less, and voters have little reason to pay attention to them. Without the support of parties, however, elected officials often find themselves without the allies they need to deal with their problems. This may explain the low success rate of recent presidents. Since 1968, one president has been driven from office, two presidents discredited and defeated after single terms, and two others badly weakened by scandals, with one of them impeached. And the last president ended his term as one of the most unpopular leaders in our history (Brinkley, 2008).

■ Special-Interest Groups

For people who find neither the Democratic nor Republican Party to be an effective representative of their concerns, there is another alternative: special-interest groups. A **special-interest group** is an organized collection of people who attempt to influence government policies. If you are a hog farmer interested in keeping the price of hogs high, there is a group for you. If you are a hunter interested in preventing the regulation of firearms or a baseball bat manufacturer interested in breaking into the Japanese market, there are groups for you, too. There are business groups like the U.S. Chamber of Commerce and the National Association of Manufacturers; labor groups like the American Federation of Labor and Congress of Industrial Organizations; professional groups like the American Medical Association; and civil rights groups, civil liberties groups, environmental groups, consumer groups, religious groups, and more. All these are special-interest groups.

What They Do

All special-interest groups use the same basic methods in trying to influence the government's policies. First, they try to influence public opinion. They advertise in the media, collect petitions, and send out letters urging people to write or call their legislators. Second, they help elect sympathetic candidates by endorsing them, urging their members to support those candidates, and donating money to their campaigns. Third, special-interest groups frequently file lawsuits to further their goals. Finally, they hire lobbyists, people who deal directly with government officials and attempt to influence them on behalf of the groups. There are more than 11,500 lobbyists in

PACs
Political Action Committees; political organizations that funnel money from business, labor, and other special-interest groups into election campaigns to help elect or defeat candidates.

Special-interest group
An organized collection of people who attempt to influence government policies.

Washington, DC, which means there is an average of 23 lobbyists working on each member of Congress for his or her votes (Brill, 2010; Mayberry, 2006).

Special-interest groups, through their lobbyists, serve some useful functions. First, they provide a way for millions of citizens to make their voices heard. Civil rights, environmental issues, and term limits for political officeholders are but a few examples of issues that were first put on the political agenda by special-interest groups. To the political parties and the politicians in office, these issues were either unimportant or too controversial to warrant action until special-interest groups forced the politicians to address them. Being masters of their subject, lobbyists, in effect, become technical advisers to legislators and their staffs, supplying them with information vital to wise decision making and to the writing of workable laws. Of course, lobbyists are likely to slant the information they present to favor their special-interest group, so lawmakers rely on a multitude of lobbyists with different views that balance one another (Barone, 2008).

Problems with Lobbying

If special-interest groups appear so useful, why do so many people fear and criticize them and their lobbyists? Why do Democrats and Republicans, along with the general public, rail against special interests? One concern is that through relentless pursuit of their narrow goals, some special-interest groups are thwarting the will of the majority and harming the public good. Although polls have consistently shown broad support for gun control, for example, the National Rifle Association has often successfully persuaded Congress to reject gun-control bills. Another concern is that as the power of special-interest groups grows, the government may end up being for sale to whatever group has the most money to contribute. Federal tax policy, for instance, favors business more than labor because business donates much more money to legislators (see **Figure 13.1**). To stop this kind of monetary influence on government policy, Congress has passed a law banning unregulated, unlimited contributions to any political group and candidate (Brill, 2010).

For a discussion of why some Americans see lobbying as good for America but others view it as bad, see **Box 13.2**.

Contributions in millions of dollars

FIGURE 13.1 Distribution of Political Campaign Contributions

Compared to labor unions, big business contributes far more to political candidates—and, consequently, to current and future law makers. This could, in part, explain why tax laws typically benefit business more than labor. In order to impede this sort of corrupt influence, law makers have endeavored to pass a series of restrictions on unlimited campaign contributions by the very wealthy, big business, and labor unions.

Critical Thinking: *Will the government's attempt to limit the amount of campaign contributions reduce the opportunity for political influence and corruption? Why?*

Source: Data from Center for Responsive Politics, 2010.

■ Political Deviance

Most of us seem ambivalent about our political leaders. On the one hand, we expect them to break the law every now and then and we may, when seeing one of them get caught, remark, "There goes another crook." Mark Twain expressed this popular sentiment well when he said way back in 1894, "It could probably be shown with facts and figures that there is no distinctly American criminal class except Congress." On the other hand, we respect and admire them for being our leaders, often so much that we would scramble in a crowd to get their autographs or shake their hands with a sense of pride and honor. Given these conflicting feelings of revulsion and respect, political deviance—wrongdoing committed by our political leaders—is different from the offenses carried out by less privileged people. This type of deviance essentially involves the abuse of power by government officials or politicians running for elected office.

We expect our political leaders to break the law now and then, and when seeing one of them get caught we may protest and say "There goes another crook."

Political corruption
The abuse of official power for personal gain.

Political Corruption

Political corruption, which involves the abuse of official power for personal gain, is common around the world (see **Box 13.3**). Here we will discuss political corruption in the United States.

Causes of Political Corruption

Research in various countries has found at least three major causes of political corruption:

- The first is *poverty*, as suggested by the finding that corruption is much more common in developing than in developed countries. This is because the governments in poor countries do not have enough tax revenues to pay their public officials adequately on a regular basis.
- The second cause of corruption is *a large population*, which makes surveillance on a massive number of public officials difficult. This may explain why the world's largest country, China, and the fourth largest country, Indonesia, are among the most corrupt on earth while the tiny city-state of Singapore is one of the least corrupt.
- The third cause of corruption is *the lack of democracy*. This may explain the higher frequency of corruption in authoritarian countries, which generally do not have what democracies have: the anticorruption surveillance by citizen groups, the press, and reform-minded politicians (Cheung and Chan, 2008; Xin and Rudel, 2004).

It may take the form of committing sexual improprieties, receiving an outright bribe, and abusing public funds.

COMMITTING SEXUAL TRANSGRESSIONS. There is a variety of sexual transgressions that politicians are known to have committed. In 2008 New York Governor Eliot Spitzer, who was married, bought sex from a high-priced prostitute in one of Washington, DC's grandest hotels. He later resigned from his governorship. In 2006 Florida Congressman Mark Foley resigned after he was confronted for sending sexually explicit e-mails to teenage boys who worked as congressional pages. In 2005 Pennsylvania Congressman Don Sherwood lost his seat after the media reported that he, a married man, paid a $500,000 settlement to his mistress for choking her (Moore, 2006).

Political leaders are known to have committed a variety of sexual transgressions, such as the former New York Governor Eliot Spitzer, who bought sex from a prostitute in Washington, DC.

RECEIVING AN OUTRIGHT BRIBE. The federal government spends an enormous sum of taxpayer money on goods and services supplied by various businesses. The officials in charge of purchasing these goods and services sometimes receive kickbacks from the companies they are dealing with. To receive kickbacks, the officials will allow businesses to send the government outrageous bills. Repair contractors and suppliers, for example, have been known to bill the government for work that was never done and for materials that were never delivered. Officials in the U.S. Defense Department are also known to have paid hundreds of dollars for a hammer and hundreds more for a toilet seat.

Moreover, there are always some U.S. Congress members who receive bribes from companies for helping them get lucrative contracts and other favors from the government. In 2006, for example, Duke Cunningham, Republican Congressman from California, was sentenced to prison for accepting $2.4 million in bribes from defense contractors in exchange for government contracts. Other Congress members are known to receive bribes from various businesses. In 2006, for example, Ohio Congressman Bob Ney was convicted for performing official acts for lobbyists in exchange for campaign contributions, expensive meals, luxury travel, and skybox sports tickets, while taking thousands of dollars in gambling chips from a foreign businessman who sought his help with the State Department. In 2009 Louisiana Congressman William Jefferson was convicted for getting bribes from businessmen who needed his help with doing business in Africa. He was caught with a freezer full of $90,000 in FBI-marked bills at his Washington home (Broder, 2006; Brush, 2005).

ABUSING PUBLIC FUNDS. The access to public funds is a potential source of political corruption. Whether they work for the city, state, or federal governments, public officials can be tempted to misuse the millions of dollars for personal gain, especially because there are many subtle, unprosecutable ways to do it. In deciding which bank to deposit an enormous sum of public money into, government officials may base their decision on whether it will profit themselves financially and politically. Thus, they may choose a bank of which they are shareholders; or a bank that will give their family members or business associates loans at low interest rates; or a bank that has promised to contribute substantially to their political campaigns. Some officials may divert public funds to their private bank accounts or use the funds to repair or remodel their homes (Hunnicutt, 2010).

Election Improprieties

Our representative democracy requires that we, the masses, have the right to choose our leaders. This right, however, often has little meaning to politicians who want to be our leaders. Therefore, various devious means are often used to win elections.

DENIAL OF VOTING RIGHT. The masses of citizenry are encouraged to participate in the presidential election, but in reality it is the electoral college—consisting of political leaders, not the populace—that selects the president. This should largely be blamed on the writers of the Constitution rather than on current political leaders, but it is important to realize that the "voters" are in a way bypassed to let political leaders decide who should be president (Simon, 2008).

POLITICAL DIRTY TRICKS. Dirty tricks are often employed to ensure victory in an election. They include spreading rumors about the opponent's strange character, kinky sex life, or association with drug kingpins; having individuals in the audience at the opponent's rally heckle or ask embarrassing questions; defacing an opponent's billboards; and stealing the opponent's campaign mail. A more sophisticated form of dirty trick is the "telephone sleaze" in which campaign workers call voters, say they are conducting a nonpartisan survey, then ask loaded questions, such as, "Did you know Senator Jones wants to vote against the banning of child pornography?" (Sabato and Simpson, 1996).

CAMPAIGN FINANCE ABUSES. Candidates for elected office often solicit and receive huge campaign contributions from moneyed interests (large corporations and wealthy individuals), and the donors expect the politicians to return the favor if elected. Incumbent legislators running *unopposed* also receive large contributions from the rich with the same expectation. As a result, the rich can gain access to the White House and Congress that ordinary citizens cannot. All this, in effect, involves the buying and selling of political influence or access to elected officials. When Bill Clinton was president, for example, prominent bankers who had contributed heavily to his reelection campaign were invited to the White House to discuss banking regulations with him and the nation's senior banking regulator, while executives of the giant tobacco company Philip Morris, a huge contributor to the Republicans, were able to discuss their concerns with Republican congressional leaders (van Natta and Fritsch, 1997; Wertheimer, 1996).

■ The Ritual of Wiggle

Politicians and public officials take great care to distance themselves from their deviant activities. They rarely admit their guilt. Instead, they automatically resort to a tortuous attempt to neutralize their deviance—to make it appear as if they have done nothing wrong. Such an attempt has been called "the ritual of wiggle." It comprises different ways to wiggle out of the morass of their deviance (Lieberman, 1973).

Denying the Obvious

Politicians and public officials seem naturally inclined to deny having done anything wrong, no matter how strong the suspicion or how clear the reality. The denial is as frequently repeated as possible. Even a popular president like Ronald Reagan found it hard to tell the truth. In 1986, when the secret arms deal with Iran shocked the nation, he insisted that he did not know about it, although it was clear to many Americans that he did. In a nationwide poll, 47% of the respondents said he was "lying" while only 37% said he was telling the truth (Church, 1986). More recently, President Clinton denied that there was anything wrong with him having coffees or lunches in the White House with his wealthy contributors. He said, "I think it is an appropriate thing and can be a good thing for the President and for the Secretary of the Treasury to meet with a group of banks and listen to them and listen to their concerns" (Mitchell, 1997a). Most recently, President Bush, along with his vice president and other members of his administration, was reluctant to admit making some mistakes in starting or executing the war in Iraq. The prevalence of this official denial of wrongdoing has led a political observer to conclude, "No one in politics can ever admit to a mistake these days. In real life, none of us is perfect. But in politics, strangely enough, mistakes almost never happen" (Borger, 2006).

Ignoring the Wrongdoing

If politicians and public officials commit a wrongful act, they tend to ignore it by disconnecting their phones, going into hiding or a trip away from the press, or simply saying "no comment." If the government is supposed to take action against its officials for some lawbreaking, it may resort to evasive responses by insisting that the facts do not conclusively and absolutely warrant governmental intervention. The government, for example, has never addressed itself adequately regarding the legality of U.S. involvement in the Vietnam War. Even if they have been found guilty, politicians

BOX 13.4   WHAT RESEARCH REVEALS

Supporting Wayward Politicians

There are many cases where politicians have won public office in the United States even though they are known to have done something wrong. Here we will discuss only a few of them.

During his 2000 presidential campaign, George W. Bush openly admitted that in his youth he often drank too much. Just before Election Day, news broke that he had been arrested in 1976 for driving under the influence of alcohol. He admitted that the news was true, but he went on to become the President (Romero, 2010).

During Bill Clinton's 1992 presidential campaign, Gennifer Flowers showed the media taped conversations between her and the candidate, claiming they had maintained an affair for more than 12 years. Still, Clinton went on to win the election. Rumors of Clinton's womanizing continued over the next few years, but he was reelected by an even wider margin in 1996 (Suddath, 2010).

When Arnold Schwarzenegger ran for governor of California in 2003, he was asked about an earlier interview in which he said he had participated in an orgy and admitted to smoking pot, in addition to using a gay slur. He said his previous statements were true. "I never lived my life to be a politician," he said. "Obviously, I've made statements that were ludicrous and crazy and outrageous and all those things, because that's the way I always was." But he went on to win the governorship (Fitzpatrick, 2010).

When he was campaigning for president in 2008, Barack Obama was often criticized for his youth and inexperience. But one indiscretion that received little attention was his past drug use. In his 1995 book *Dreams from My Father*, he admitted to using marijuana and cocaine as a teenager. This obviously did not bother most Americans, as he was elected President (Webley, 2010).

still tend to act as if their wrongful act is not really wrongful. In 1997, for example, after House Speaker Newt Gingrich was reprimanded and fined $300,000 for years of unethical conduct, he dismissed his misdeeds as only comparable to jaywalking (Weisman, 1997). Yet, the general public often still supports such wayward politicians (see **Box 13.4**).

Accusing the Accuser

In the case of private offenses, the politician and public officials may threaten or actually file a libel suit against the reporter who publicizes the offense. Although it is almost impossible to prove libel, the politician hopes that the suit will divert public attention from his or her own wrongdoing. In 1992, when Senator Brock Adams of Washington State was accused by a woman of sexually molesting her, he claimed she was mentally ill, though eight other women had independently alleged similar sexual harassment by him (Trost and Thomas, 1993). More recently, in 2006, the FBI videotaped Congressman William Jefferson of Louisiana receiving a $100,000 bribe and then executed a search warrant of his home and found $90,000 of that money in his freezer. Later the FBI searched his office, also with a warrant from a federal judge. His lawyer called the search "outrageous," and congressional leaders accused the federal agents of violating the separation of powers between the legislative and executive branches of government (Isikoff et al., 2006).

Promising to Take Action

When politicians and public officials are under intense pressure to do something about a certain incident, they will publicly promise to take action to deal with it. Yet, behind the scenes, the promised action is not seriously carried out. In the 1970s, when the Watergate scandal broke, the Attorney General promised to make the Justice Department's investigation of the scandal "the most extensive, thorough and comprehensive investigation since the assassination of President Kennedy." But nothing came out of this promise. In the 1980s, when confronted with the scandal of selling arms to Iran, President Reagan kept repeating that he wanted all the facts to come out. Yet he did not try very hard to get the facts out. He did not even demand from his aides, who were the key figures in the scandal, an accounting of what they did (Church, 1986). More recently, President Clinton repeatedly announced his intent to help clean up the system that effectively encourages politicians to sell access or influence for large campaign contributions. He then continued to raise funds for his political party by soliciting huge donations from big corporations and wealthy individuals (Mitchell, 1997a). Similarly, in 2006 the U.S. Congress promised to pass reform bills to crack down on corrupt lawmakers, but it was widely seen as mere window dressing and thus was not expected to change business as usual (Continetti, 2006; Knight, 2006).

Justifying the Deviance

Politicians and public officials often rationalize that it is necessary for them to commit the deviant act they are accused of committing. This rationalization should not be surprising; it is supported by the popular belief that the end sometimes justifies the means. Thus, many politicians and public officials justify the use of unlawful wiretapping on the grounds that the danger of not using it against suspected criminals or terrorists is too great. In the early 1970s, President Nixon, the Central Intelligence Agency, and the FBI even justified domestic surveillance of U.S. citizens as being in the interest of national security. In the 1950s and 1960s, following reports of Soviet success at mind control, top U.S. military and intelligence officials insisted it was necessary to use unsuspecting Americans as guinea pigs for mind-control experiments by sneaking powerful mind-altering drugs into their drinks (Budiansky et al., 1994). In 2004 the Secretary of Defense effectively approved torturing captured terrorists when he declared that they should not get all the rights and privileges accorded prisoners of war under the Geneva Convention because they were unlawful combatants (Barry et al., 2004).

■ Sociological Theories of "Who Really Governs?"

The emergence of political parties and special-interest groups in the United States has brought Americans a long way from the government envisioned by James Madison, U.S. president from 1809 to 1817. It was his hope to exclude interests and factions from the government. Legislators were to represent and vote for the public good, not one interest or another.

The opposite view is that interest groups and political parties are merely mechanisms through which the people gain more effective control of government; the people actually have not lost control. Who then really governs the country? According to functionalist theory, the people do—by using the service of many diverse interest groups.

According to conflict theory, a small group of powerful individuals do—by serving their self-interests.

Functionalist Theory

In looking at the U.S. government, functionalists see many centers of power as well as many competing interest groups. Government reflects the outcome of their competition. In this view, the interest groups are central to U.S. democracy. Together, they create a mutually restraining influence. No one group can always prevail. Thus, through their competition, the interests of the public are reflected in government policy.

However, as we have seen in earlier chapters, there are large inequalities of wealth, power, and prestige. How, in the face of such inequalities, can pluralism be maintained? Cannot one group marshal its resources to dominate others? Why doesn't one group or one coalition of groups gradually achieve a concentration of power?

The reason, as Robert Dahl (1981) explains, is that inequalities are *dispersed*, not cumulative. Inequalities would be cumulative if a group rich in one resource (wealth, for example) were also better off than other groups in almost every other resource—political power, social standing, prestige, legitimacy, knowledge, and control over religious, educational, and other institutions. In the United States, however, one group may hold most of one of these resources, but other groups may have the lion's share of the others. What the upper-middle class lacks in wealth, for example, it makes up for in knowledge and legitimacy. Power over economic institutions may be concentrated in the hands of corporations, but U.S. religious institutions elude their grasp.

This dispersal of power in U.S. society is reflected in a dispersal of political clout. The country's many competing groups vie for control over government policy and end up dominating different spheres. Corporations may dominate the government's decisions on taxes but not on crime. Even tax policy is not dictated solely by corporations because labor unions and other groups fight with the corporations to influence politicians and votes. The structure of the government, with its separation of powers, promotes this pluralism. What civil rights groups could not win in Congress in the 1950s, they sometimes won in the courts. A corporation that has lost a battle in Congress may win the war by influencing regulations issued by the executive branch. In the end, in Dahl's view, competing groups usually compromise and share power. Thus, there is no ruling group in the United States. Instead, a pluralist democracy exists, dominated by many different sets of leaders.

David Riesman (1950) and Arnold Rose (1967) have developed a somewhat different analysis. In their views, the United States has become so pluralistic that various interest groups constitute *veto groups*, which are powerful enough to block each other's actions. To get anything done, the veto groups must seek support from the unorganized public. The masses, then, have the ultimate power to ensure that their interests and concerns will be protected. The bottom line is that the overall leadership is weak, stalemate is frequent, and no single elite can emerge to dominate the others.

Conflict Theory

There are many competing groups in the United States. But does their competition actually determine how policy is made? Is the government merely the neutral arbitrator among these different interests? According to conflict theory, the answer is no.

Many years ago, Italian sociologists Vilfredo Pareto (1848–1823) and Gaetano Mosca (1858–1941) argued that a small elite governs the masses in all societies. Why is this so? If a nation is set up along truly democratic lines, isn't control by an elite avoidable? According to German sociologist Robert Michels (1915), there is an "iron law of oligarchy" by which even a democracy inevitably degenerates into an *oligarchy*— rule by a few. A democracy is an organization, and according to Michels, "whoever says organization says oligarchy."

In Michels's view, three characteristics of organizations eventually produce rule by the elite. First, to work efficiently, even a democratic organization must allow a few leaders to make the decisions. Second, through these positions of leadership, the leaders accumulate skills and knowledge that make them indispensable to the rank and file. Third, the rank and file lack the time, inclination, and knowledge to master the complex tasks of government, and they become politically apathetic. Thus, in time, even a democracy yields to rule by an elite.

Michel's view explains what has happened to the United States, a democracy ruled by an elite. According to C. Wright Mills (1916–1962), there are three levels of power in this country. At the bottom are ordinary people—powerless, unorganized, fragmented, and manipulated by the mass media into believing in democracy. In the middle are Congress, political parties, and interest groups as well as most political leaders. At this level, pluralism reigns. The middle groups form "a drifting set of stalemated, balancing forces." Above them is an elite, which Mills calls the *power elite*, that makes the most important decisions. This elite consists of the top leaders in three institutions—the federal government, the military, and the large corporations. These leaders cooperate with one another in controlling the nation. Government leaders can allocate billions of dollars to defense to strengthen the military and enrich the corporations from which the weapons are purchased. Big business can support political leaders with campaign money. The politicians can aid business with favorable legislation.

If Mills is correct, all the hoopla of political campaigns and debates is but so much sound and fury because the power elite determines who gets elected and how the government is run. There is some evidence to support Mills's view that a cohesive elite exists. Time and again, the top officials in both Democratic and Republican administrations previously held high positions in corporations, and they return to those corporations after leaving the government. It is also significant that members of the elite come disproportionately from upper-class backgrounds.

However, according to the Marxist view, the members of the power elite—the top governmental, political, and military leaders—are not free to act in their own interests. They are instead merely agents of the capitalist class, commonly known as big business. To control the state, the capitalists use the same methods employed by interest groups, such as lobbying and supporting sympathetic candidates. In using these tools, however, the capitalists have a great advantage over the run-of-the-mill interest group: they have more money. The capitalists also use the media, schools, churches, and other institutions to permeate society with their values, such as free enterprise, economic growth, and competition. Violations of these capitalist values are often taken to be un-American, giving capitalist interests a potent weapon against unsympathetic politicians. Understandably, few U.S. politicians want to be branded antigrowth, antibusiness, or socialist. In addition, if the government acts against the capitalists' interests, big business can refuse to put its capital to work. It may close plants or stop investing in the United States or send its money and investments abroad (Szymanski, 1978).

For a quick summary of the functionalist and conflict theories, see Box 13.5.

BOX 13.5   THEORETICAL THUMBNAIL

Explaining "Who Really Governs?"

Theory	Focus	Insights
Functionalist Theory	Rule by many interest groups	Many groups compete for and share power in governing the country.
Conflict Theory	Rule by a few powerful leaders	Power elite and capitalists run the country.

QUESTIONS TO EXPLORE

1. From the conflict perspective, do you buy into Mills's argument that a "power elite" made up of governmental, political, and military leaders calls the shots, or Marx's position that each of these three entities is a puppet controlled by a handful of powerful capitalists? Please explain.

2. What are the primary functions of politics in the United States today? How has this changed in your lifetime?

3. According to a September 2010 Gallup poll (http://www.gallup.com/poll/143051/Americans-Renew-Call-Third-Party.aspx), 60% of Americans are unhappy with both major political parties and are calling for the establishment of a third major party. According to conflict theory, why will a third party mean little change in terms of a power shift and just give us more of the same?

Review

SUMMARY

1. Americans are politically inconsistent, conservative and liberal at the same time. If they are liberal on economic issues, they may be conservative on social issues. They tend to be ideological conservatives and operational liberals. There is also an inconsistency between politicians and voters, with the former being extreme and the latter moderate.

2. Americans who are older, white, more affluent, better educated, and more religious are more likely than others to vote. There is no gender difference in the likelihood of voting. Voting is largely emotional rather than rational. Voter turnout is lower in the United States than in other Western democracies because U.S. voters are tired of being confronted with too many elections, political campaigns are mean-spirited, there is little difference between candidates, and the country is already politically stable.

3. There are two major political parties—Democrats and Republicans. Democrats are generally more liberal than Republicans, but actually there is little difference between them. Today the two parties have lost much of their influence, and more voters identify themselves as independent rather than either Democrat or Republican.

4. Special-interest groups serve such useful functions as enabling citizens to make their voices heard and helping legislators make wise, workable laws. One problem with special-interest groups or their lobbyists is that some special interests can harm the public good. Another problem is that the government may end up being for sale to whatever group has the most money.

5. Public officials and politicians tend to engage in political deviance. One example is political corruption, the abuse of official power for personal gain. This includes committing sexual transgression, receiving outright bribes, and abusing public funds. Another example of political deviance involves using devious means to win elections, such as denying citizens their right to vote, playing political dirty tricks, and abusing campaign finance.

6. After getting caught for engaging in deviance, public officials and politicians usually try to extricate themselves from the morass of their deviance. They may deny that they have done anything wrong, ignore their wrongdoing, accuse the accuser of committing improper acts, promise to take action to solve the problem, and justify their wrongdoing by arguing that the end justifies the means.

7. According to functionalist theory, the country is governed by the masses, but according to conflict theory, the country is run by a few powerful leaders.

CRITICAL THINKING QUESTIONS

1. What groups have the most power and influence in U.S. politics today?
2. Why have third-party candidates, such as the Tea Party members, had such difficulty competing with Democratic and Republican candidates on a national level?
3. What factors have led to a steady decline in party loyalty among both Democrats and Republicans since the 1960s? Be specific.

INTERNET RESOURCES

The Democratic Party (http://www.democrats.org/) has been one of the dominant political parties in the United States for over 200 years. Democrats are commonly associated with the struggle for equal rights and fighting for working families.

When diplomacy and other peaceful means of crisis management and arbitration fail, the North Atlantic Treaty Organization (NATO) (http://www.nato.int/), which represents an international political and military alliance, is able to use military force on its own or in concert with a variety of participating countries and international organizations in seeking conflict resolution.

The Republican National Committee oversees the fundraising and management for the Republicans, or GOP (Grand Old Party) (http://www.gop.com/), which is one of the two major political parties in the United States. It is known to support conservative values, smaller or decentralized government, deregulation, and efforts to avoid tax increases.

The Tea Party (http://www.teaparty.org/) began in 2009 as a politically conservative social movement, spearheading protests that center on tax increases and controversial federal relief or "bailouts." The name of the movement was borrowed from the famous Boston Tea Party of 1773, which involved, among other things, a revolt of American colonists against the British government for a controversial tax on imported goods, such as tea.

The United Nations (UN) (http://www.un.org/en/) was founded immediately following World War II, in 1945, as an international organization focused on proactively promoting and maintaining international peace, basic human rights, improved quality of living, and security, and brokering mutually beneficial relations among nations.

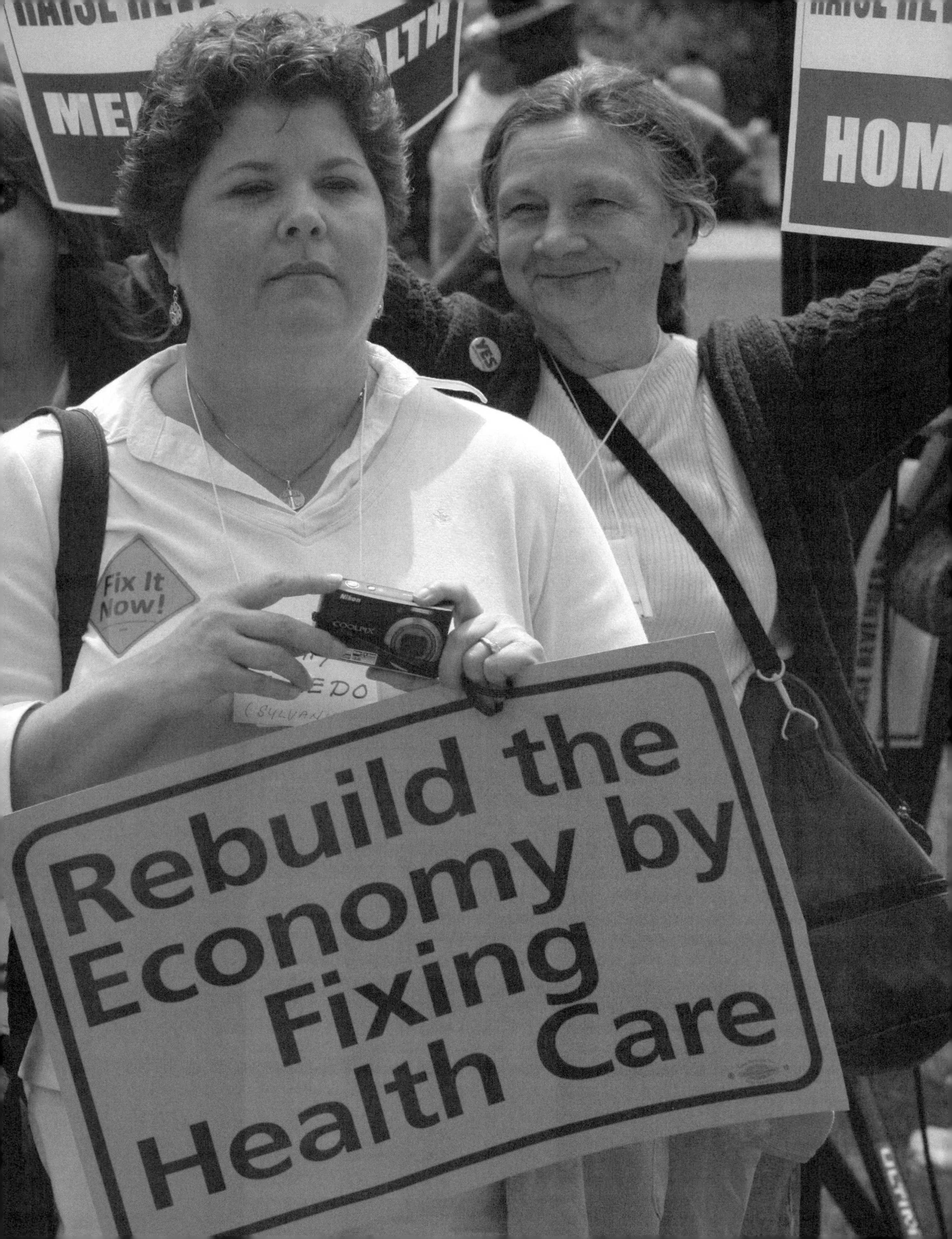
Fix It Now!
Rebuild the Economy by Fixing Health Care

Healthcare Problems

When movie actress Carrie Fisher suffered from bipolar disorder, she did not seek help for several years, primarily because of the stigma associated with mental illness. This reluctance nearly cost her life when she attempted suicide with an overdose of pills. Fortunately, she finally underwent a series of treatment and recovered from the mental problem. As she now says, "I have gotten to the point where I can live a normal life, where my daughter can rely on me for predictable behavior, and that's very important to me." She confesses, however, that the road to recovery through treatment has not been easy. She freely admits that she has not always stayed with the treatment, but she has never given up actively fighting the stigma of mental illness. Proclaiming herself "the poster child for mental illness," she champions the message that there is treatment for mental illness. As she says, "You can lead a normal life, whatever that is" (McDowell, 2006).

Mental illness like the one that afflicts Fisher is a healthcare problem. Despite the stigma attached to it, it requires treatment as much as physical illness. In this chapter, we discuss both mental and physical illnesses.

■ Social Aspects of Health

Health is a biological condition involving the individual, but it is also a social phenomenon that varies from one society to another and from one group to another within the same society. From these variations, we can see how social factors affect health and what consequences an outbreak of illness has for the entire society. We can also track the origin of a disease by examining all of its victims for something that they have in common as a social group.

Global Diversity in Health

Americans today are much healthier than ever before. Since 1900, their life expectancy has gone up by more than 50%, from about 49 years old in 1900 to 78 years old today. In other words, people born today can expect to live 29 more years than did people born in 1900. **Life expectancy** is thus the number of years people born in a specific year can expect to live. Another indicator of health is the **infant mortality rate**, the number of babies who die before 1 year of age for every 1,000 live births. This rate has shown even more dramatic improvement in the health of the United States. About 15% of all U.S. babies died during the first year of life at the turn of the 20th century, but less than 1% do today (U.S. Census Bureau, 2010). All this can be chalked up to healthier living conditions, better diet, immunization against various diseases, and penicillin and other antibiotics.

However, Americans' increasing life expectancy is far from impressive when compared with the life expectancies of people in other industrialized countries. As Table 14.1 shows, Americans live a shorter life than people in other industrialized countries. Also, proportionately more babies die in the United States than in other industrialized countries.

Why does the United States have such a lower rate of health? The reason is that our society is less egalitarian than other industrialized countries. Being in a less egalitarian society, relatively few Americans are at the top, enjoying power or domination

Life expectancy
The number of years people born in a specific year can expect to live.

Infant mortality rate
The number of babies who die before 1 year of age for every 1,000 live births.

TABLE 14.1 U.S. Health Status Among Industrialized Countries

The United States has the lowest life expectancy and the highest infant mortality in the industrialized world.

Country	Life Expectancy*	Country	Infant Mortality Rate**
1. Japan	82.1	1. United States	6.2
2. Australia	81.6	2. Italy	5.5
3. Canada	81.2	3. Germany	5.1
4. France	80.9	4. Canada	5.0
5. Switzerland	80.8	5. Britain	4.9
6. Italy	80.2	6. Australia	4.7
7. Spain	80.0	7. Switzerland	4.2
8. Germany	79.2	8. Spain	4.2
9. Britain	79.0	9. France	3.3
10. United States	78.1	10. Japan	2.8

*Number of years an infant at birth can be expected to live.

**Number of infant deaths per thousand live births.

Source: U.S. Census Bureau, International Data Base, 2009.

over others and therefore having better health. Many more people are at the bottom, feeling resigned, resentful, or submissive and therefore unhealthy. By contrast, in a more egalitarian society, most people enjoy the experiences that contribute to good health, such as social support, friendship, cooperation, and sociability (Bezruchka, 1997, 2001). By the way, this reasoning also explains why the United States has a much higher life expectancy and a considerably lower infant mortality rate than many poor, developing countries, which are generally less egalitarian.

U.S. Diversity in Health

Acute diseases
Serious illnesses that strike suddenly.
Chronic diseases
Illnesses that have been developing for a long time.

In the United States, age plays a significant role in health. Older people are less likely than young people to contract acute diseases, such as measles and pneumonia. **Acute diseases** are serious illnesses that strike suddenly. Older people are, however, more likely to fall victim to **chronic diseases**, illnesses that have been developing for a long time, such as arthritis, heart disease, and cancer. Cancer deaths, in particular, climb steeply and steadily among people 55 years of age and older.

Gender also influences our health. Women live longer than men—generally, 5 years longer. Part of the reason is biological, as evidenced by the fact that women's sex hormones protect them from the risk of cardiovascular disease up to the time of menopause. Most of the reason is sociological, though, as reflected in the cultural belief that taking risks is a badge of masculine toughness. Thus, men are more likely than women to put their health at risk by smoking, drinking, abusing drugs, and driving fast. Further, when sick, men are less likely than women to see a doctor (Parker-Pope, 2007b; David Williams, 2003).

Race and ethnicity further make a difference in health. African Americans, Hispanic Americans, and Native Americans all have lower life expectancies than whites. Minorities are far more likely to suffer or die from many diseases, such as influenza, pneumonia, and acquired immune deficiency syndrome (AIDS). Both Hispanic and Native Americans, however, are less likely than whites to die from heart disease and cancer, partly because whites live longer and the odds of developing these chronic illnesses typically increase with age (Cockerham, 2010).

These racial and ethnic differences may reflect another social factor that influences health: social class. The diseases that hit minority groups the hardest are those associated with poverty, such as acute diseases. Researchers have attributed the higher rates of disease among the lower classes to several related factors: toxic, hazardous, and unhygienic environments; stress resulting from such life changes as job loss and divorce; and inadequate medical care. Researchers have further found another problem: unhealthy eating habits. Poor people are much more likely than others to eat high-sugar, high-salt, and high-fat food (Berkman, 2004; Freedman, 1990; Shweder, 1997).

■ The Epidemic of Obesity

Americans are getting heavier, putting themselves at greater risk for developing diabetes, heart disease, and other health problems. Two out of three U.S. adults are now overweight. One-third are obese—severely or dangerously overweight. This rate of obesity is twice that of 20 years ago. Worse yet, over the same period, the rates of obesity among children and teenagers have tripled. Obesity has indeed become an

American **epidemic**, a health problem that afflicts many people throughout the entire population (Lemonick, 2004; Tumulty, 2006).

How We Got So Big

We got so big in two ways. One is by overeating, especially of high-fat, high-sugar, and high-salt foods. Another is through lack of physical exercise. All around us is our **culture of corpulence**, which encourages us to overeat and avoid exercise in the following ways.

First, American innovations in food and transportation may have been intended to improve, not corrupt, our lifestyles, but they end up making us eat more and exercise less. For example, fast food is meant to be a quick fix for hungry working families, and cars and buses are meant to get kids to school faster than sidewalks. But we have become so accustomed to a life of speed and convenience that we eat too much fast food and avoid walking.

One way to get heavy is through lack of exercise. Another way is by overeating.

Second, high-calorie, low-nutrient foods are easily available everywhere—at gas stations, at airports, and even at schools, where it matters most for children to eat healthy meals. School meals are subsidized by the government and subject to nutritional standards, but many schools do not serve fresh fruits or raw vegetables on a daily basis.

Third, school children often supplement, or substitute, their lunches with "competitive foods"—unhealthy foods such as cookies and sodas from vending machines. These vending machines can be found in 17% of elementary schools, 82% of middle schools, and 97% of high schools.

Fourth, many schools do not offer physical education. Although the Surgeon General recommends at least 60 minutes of moderate exercise per day most days of the week for young people, two-thirds of high school students fail to get it. Too many youngsters, from 8 to 18 years old, end up wired instead, spending an average of seven and a half hours each day in front of TVs, videogames, or computers. Most adults do not engage in physical activities, either. They live in subdivisions and drive to shopping centers and office parks. Biking and walking have been removed from their lives.

Fifth, the food industry spends an enormous amount of money ($1.6 billion) annually on advertising food and drinks to children. According to a recent Yale study, the product most aggressively and frequently advertised to children is the least nutritious cereals. Another study found that a large majority (72%) of the ads aimed at children and teenagers urge them to eat candy, snacks, sugary cereals, or fast food (Kalb, 2010).

War on Obesity

Efforts have been made to fight obesity by encouraging people to eat less and exercise more. Somerville, a city just outside Boston, has tried to combat childhood obesity in

Epidemic
A health problem that afflicts many people throughout the entire population.

Culture of corpulence
The culture that encourages us to overeat and avoid exercise.

a number of ways. Its restaurants have offered healthier meals, including low-fat milk, smaller portions, and fruits and vegetables as side dishes. Its schools have substantially increased the amount of fresh fruit and vegetables at lunch, and its teachers have encouraged children to be more active before, during, and after school. Its crosswalks have been repainted to get more people walking to school—or work. As a result, Somerville schoolchildren have gained less weight than their peers in two nearby communities, which, like most other places, have lacked an anti-obesity program (Parker-Pope, 2007a).

Another effort to combat childhood obesity has come from health officials and health-related groups such as the American Academy of Pediatrics and the U.S. Department of Health and Human Services. They have long warned that bombarding children with junk food commercials has contributed to the spread of childhood obesity. As a result, food companies have made various commitments to promote fitness and healthier foods. For example, 11 large companies, including PepsiCo, Kraft Foods, and McDonald's, have agreed to make healthier foods and healthier lifestyles

---

BOX 14.1   USING SOCIOLOGICAL INSIGHTS

How to Battle the Bulge

Everybody knows that if you want to lose weight, you should eat healthy food and exercise—or eat less and exercise more. But many overweight Americans still don't do it. As Claire McCarthy (2010), a Harvard professor of medicine, says, "Obesity comes down to a simple energy equation: if you eat too many calories, or you don't burn off enough, or both, you gain weight. People know this. So why is everyone getting fat?" After talking with a lot of overweight people, McCarthy has found four major reasons, which may help you lose weight.

The first reason is *denial*. Many people think they aren't overweight. This is probably because they are among so many overweight people that they don't stick out. Refusing to see themselves as overweight, they let themselves think that they don't eat too much, or that they have enough exercise from walking to the car from the store.

The second reason is *delaying*. They say they'll start the diet next week. There are too many things going on in their lives right now. They will join a gym next spring or summer. This can wait.

The third reason is *discouragement*. The hard truth is that losing weight is not easy. It takes work and time. It's easy to get discouraged when you see no results from dieting and exercising for a few days. You will start thinking, "Why should I make myself miserable eating carrots and going to the gym?"

The fourth reason is *difficulty*. For many people there are real obstacles to maintaining a good diet and joining a gym. Healthy foods are expensive and not easily available, and gym membership can be expensive.

There are ways to deal with those four reasons. To fight the denial, you need only to know the scary fact that obesity carries a higher risk of diabetes, heart disease, cancer, and orthopedic problems, along with social and emotional problems. To fight the delaying, you can take action immediately; for example, stop buying soda and start taking a daily walk. To fight the discouragement, you need to celebrate your adoption of a healthy lifestyle. If a diet or exercise idea doesn't work, try a different one. And to fight the difficulty, seek out community resources, such as low-cost exercise options or farmer's markets (McCarthy, 2010).

the subject of at least 50% of advertising aimed at children. The food industry has further introduced new and healthier "reformulated" products, which contain fewer calories, less sodium or sugar, and more whole grains (Olson, 2007).

The government has gotten into the act, treating obesity as a public health issue rather than merely a personal problem. Nearly every state has taken steps to fight obesity, mostly involving children. Arizona has set nutritional standards for all food and beverages sold on school grounds. California has banned the sale of junk food in schools. Kentucky has required students to engage in vigorous exercise for 30 minutes a day and prohibited schools from serving deep-fried foods. And many states have planned to include nutrition instruction in their school curricula (Tumulty, 2006).

We have discussed how schools, health officials, city governments, restaurants, and state governments are involved in combating obesity. Individuals like yourself can help them win the battle against obesity (see Box 14.1).

■ The Problem of AIDS

AIDS is a deadly disease that destroys the body's immune system, leaving the victim defenseless against other diseases. It is directly caused by a virus called *human immunodeficiency virus* (HIV). AIDS first came to the attention of U.S. physicians in early 1981. Since then, it has spread rapidly. Today, the risk for HIV remains high among certain groups of the population (Box 14.2).

BOX 14.2   WHAT RESEARCH REVEALS

HIV Risks Remain High

During the height of the AIDS scare in the mid-1980s, media were saturated with horror stories about the new disease. As coverage has waned today, the general public might have been lulled into a state of false security concerning the threat of the disease. But the risks for HIV have increased significantly or remain high for certain groups of people. The most notable high-risk groups are homosexual men who have sex with other men, racial and ethnic minorities, intravenous drug users, and prisoners. Consider the following statistics:

- Although the rate of new HIV infections among homosexual men dropped by 5.2% from 1996 to 2000, it rose steadily every year for a total increase of 16.5% from 2000 to 2005 (Hall et al., 2008).
- Although African Americans represent approximately 12% of the U.S. population, they account for about 46% of all known HIV cases (Centers for Disease Control and Prevention, 2009; Hall et al., 2008).
- Intravenous drug use–related HIV transmissions have continued to decline since the mid-1980s. However, the drug users remain at a significant risk, accounting for about 8% of new cases of HIV in 2009 (Centers for Disease Control and Prevention, 2009).
- HIV instances remain high among prison populations in the United States. The HIV rate in the general population is only 0.6%, but among prisoners, approximately 1.6% of male and 2.4% of female offenders incarcerated in federal and state facilities in 2006 were HIV positive (Maruschak, 2006).

Social Origins

Epidemiology
The study of the origin and spread of disease in a given population.

In analyzing the social forces behind illness, sociologists can track the causes of the disease. This task requires a kind of detective work called **epidemiology**, the study of the origin and spread of disease in a given population. In their role as epidemiologists, sociologists first seek out all the people who already have the disease. Then, they ask the victims where they were and what they did before they got sick. Epidemiologists also collect data on the victims' age, gender, marital status, occupation, and other characteristics. The aim is to find out what all the victims have in common besides the disease so that its cause can be identified and eliminated. Usually, the common factor that ties all the victims together provides the essential clue.

In searching for the origins of AIDS, epidemiologists have found clues in the social characteristics and behaviors of the victims. In the United States, the largest group of victims are gay men. The second largest group consists of intravenous drug users. The rest are non-drug-using heterosexuals. Most of these heterosexuals have caught the virus through sex, and a few have been infected through blood transfusions or by being born to mothers with HIV or AIDS.

New cases of HIV and AIDS among gay men declined in the late 1980s and the 1990s because of the increasing practice of safe sex, but now, both are on the rise again, a result of the return to unsafe sex (Healy, 2006). HIV and AIDS have also increased among non-drug-using heterosexuals as well as intravenous drug users. These drug users are mostly poor, African American, and Hispanic American heterosexuals in the inner city. They often share contaminated needles when shooting drugs, thus passing the virus that causes AIDS from one to another.

All these epidemiological facts clearly suggest that HIV and AIDS spread mostly through sexual intercourse with an infected person and through the sharing of a hypodermic needle that has been contaminated with the virus. Studies in other societies have found some similarities and differences between Africans with AIDS and their U.S. counterparts. Unlike Americans with AIDS, Africans with the same disease do not have histories of intravenous drug use, homosexuality, or blood transfusion. But like American gays with AIDS, African heterosexuals with the disease mostly live in large cities and have had sex with many different partners. Thus, AIDS has spread among Africans in the same way it has among gays in the United States: through sex with multiple partners. By itself, though, promiscuity is not the source of the AIDS virus. Rather, *unprotected sex* is what increases the risk of infection (Altman, 2005).

Social Consequences

Unlike such familiar killers as cancer and heart disease, AIDS is mysterious and has had an unusual impact on U.S. society. As we have seen, the dangerous disease can be transmitted through life's most basic human interaction—sex. Understandably, the general public is gripped with the fear of contagion. The initial appearance of AIDS among two groups of which the larger society disapproves—gays and drug addicts—has added to the fear because prejudice discourages understanding of "their" disease.

According to a series of surveys by the U.S. Public Health Service, many people have quickly learned the risk factors for HIV and AIDS, but misinformation about the virus's transmission remains a problem. Many still fear that they can get HIV by donating blood or through casual contact with an infected person. Such fears are particularly rampant in small towns and rural areas. While the fears are groundless, they have spawned strange, sad, and sometimes hostile actions against people with HIV and AIDS.

Many parents, for example, have demanded the mandatory testing of schoolchildren and segregation of those with HIV and AIDS. There have also been instances in which people with HIV and AIDS have been prevented from keeping jobs or getting housing, insurance coverage, and medical care. Those who care for AIDS patients are further likely to encounter discrimination. Still, most Americans today are sympathetic to AIDS victims (Jefferson, 2006).

▧ Mental Illness

To get a sense of what it is like to be mentally ill, we may want to take a look at the problem that plagues Bob Antonioni, a 48-year-old lawyer. He has struggled with depression for nearly a decade. In public he appears normal, as he does in court on behalf of his clients. However, in private he is irritable and short-tempered, and becomes easily frustrated by small things, such as deciding which television show to watch with his girlfriend. Working at his office, he often gets so exhausted by noon that he will go home and collapse on the couch, where he will stay for the rest of the day. When he decides to get help, he keeps it a secret from friends and family. He sees a therapist in secret, and he has his prescriptions for antidepressants filled at a pharmacy 20 miles away (Scelfo, 2007).

A Common Problem

Like Antonioni, millions of Americans suffer from depression. If other, less serious psychiatric problems are also taken into account, mental illness is indeed very prevalent. According to the latest national survey, about half of all adult Americans have experienced at least one episode of psychiatric disorder during their lifetime, and a quarter within the past year alone (Kessler et al., 20005a, 2005b; Sergo, 2008).

In fact, *all* of us have been mentally ill at one time or another in the same way as all of us have been physically ill. Of course, most of our mental illnesses are not serious at all, just as most of our physical illnesses are not. Nonetheless, just as we all have occasionally come down with a relatively minor physical ailment such as the flu, we all have occasionally come down with a relatively minor mental disorder such as mild depression. Indeed mild depression is so prevalent that it has been called "the common cold of mental illness."

Nevertheless, because of the stigma attached to mental illness, most people associate it with only severe forms of illness such as major depression and schizophrenia. Therefore, if we come down with the flu and call in sick, we would say to our boss, "I'm sick today," but if we are too depressed to go to work, we would be too afraid to tell our boss that we are mentally ill. If we say we are *physically* ill, most people would *not* automatically assume we are suffering from a serious illness such as heart disease, cancer, or AIDS. But if we say we are *mentally* ill, most people would jump to the conclusion that we need to be sent to a mental institution right away.

While the general public equates "mental illness" only with severe and uncommon forms of mental disorder, most of the mental illnesses that occur every day are far from severe. They are extremely common. They are basically problems of everyday life, ranging from being sad, anxious, irritable, or antisocial to being dependent on drugs, alcohol, or coffee to doing poorly in reading, writing, or math as a youngster. Psychiatrists define all such problems as mental disorders (APA, 1994; Ratey and Johnson, 1997), but we would not if we associate mental illness only with its relatively serious forms, such as being too depressed to function adequately in one's daily life (Horwitz and Wakefield, 2006; Kutchins and Kirk, 1997).

Popular Myths

The mentally ill are widely believed to be extremely weird. In fact, most are far from greatly disturbed. Contrary to common misconceptions, only a few mentally ill inmates in mental institutions spend their time cutting out paper dolls, screaming and yelling, talking to the air, or posing as kings or queens. Even among the most severely mentally ill—schizophrenics—the flamboyant symptoms of hallucinations and delusions are not the most important characteristics of their disorder. Instead, the less demonstrative symptoms of apathy and inertia constitute the core of schizophrenia. In fact, most patients resemble other members of society, "much more simply human than otherwise" (Boffey, 1986; Zimmerman, 2003).

A second popular belief is that mental illness is hopeless, essentially incurable. Even after people are discharged from a mental hospital as recovered, they are likely to be viewed with suspicion. In reality, the majority (some 70% to 80%) of hospitalized mental patients can recover and live relatively normal lives if their treatment has been adequate and received in time. Even many schizophrenics, whose illness is probably the most debilitating and devastating, can eventually recover. According to studies in the United States and Europe, about half of all schizophrenics *spontaneously* get better over the course of 20 years, and professional treatment with support from family and friends further makes the recovery easier and faster (Boffey, 1986; Kopelowicz and Bidder, 1992).

According to a popular myth, there is a sharp, clear distinction between being mentally ill and healthy. But it is difficult to differentiate the vast majority of the mentally ill from the healthy.

A third popular myth is that there is a sharp, clear distinction between "mentally ill" and "mentally healthy." This distinction is widely taken for granted, but it is true only if we compare the extremely few mentally ill persons who are extraordinarily disturbed with average "normal" people. Most of the time even a psychiatrist cannot clearly differentiate the vast majority of the mentally ill from the mentally healthy. Thus the dividing line between mental health and illness is mostly arbitrary. This is not only because the behavior of different individuals ranges by imperceptible degrees from normal to abnormal, but also because an individual may shift at different times to different positions along that range, appearing normal at one time and abnormal at another (APA, 1994; Brody, 1997).

A fourth popular myth is that the mentally ill are mostly crazed or violent, as often portrayed in news media, movies, and television programs. In fact, the

great majority (about 90%) of mental patients are not prone to violence and criminality. They are more likely to engage in behavior harmful to themselves rather than
to others. Most significantly, they are six or seven times more likely than others to
become *victims* of homicide (Cuvelier, 2002; Harris and Lurigio, 2007).

A fifth popular myth is about the "midwinter" depression, which psychiatrists
call seasonal affective disorder. Many people assume that we are likely to become
depressed in the middle of winter because of its coldness and lack of sunshine. Research
has shown otherwise: Depression is more likely to strike people in the summer than
winter (Christensen and Dowrick, 1983; Smyth and Thompson, 1990). Presumably,
the summer is more likely to give us the blues because we spend less time with our
loved ones than we do in the winter.

Most recently, a new popular myth has emerged that there is an epidemic of
autism—a disease characterized by serious problems with language and social bonding—among American children. According to the U.S. Department of Education,
the nationwide rate of autism had jumped 657% over the last decade, leading a
congressman to declare, "We have an epidemic on our hands." But many behavioral
scientists disagree. They point out that much of the startling rise in autism results
from a broader definition that includes many more children with mild symptoms
who would not have been considered autistic in the past. The sharp rise in autism
can also be traced to a school policy that causes any child with mental retardation
or learning disabilities to be labeled autistic (*Current Science*, 2008; Lilienfeld and
Arkowitz, 2007; Monastersky, 2007).

■ Social Factors in Mental Illness

Sociologists have long found a number of social factors in mental illness. They include
social class, gender, age, race and ethnicity, and urban environment. They are associated in one way or another with mental illness.

Social Class

Social class has been consistently found in various studies to be related to mental
illness. More specifically, people from the lower classes are more likely than those
from other classes to become mentally ill. This finding has prompted two conflicting
explanations. One, called *social causation*, suggests that lower-class people are more
prone to mental illness because they have a more stressful life. This means that being
lower class is a *cause* of mental illness. The other explanation, called *social selection* or
drift, suggests that mentally ill people from higher social classes often drift downward
into the lower-class neighborhood, which increases the rate of mental illness in that
neighborhood. This means that the lower-class position is a *consequence* of mental
illness among formerly higher-class people. Both explanations have been found to
have some basis in fact: Some lower-class people do become mentally ill because of
their stressful lives, and some middle-class people with emotional problems do drift
into the lower-class neighborhood (Rodgers and Mann, 1993).

Gender

There are conflicting findings on which gender is more likely to become mentally ill.
In most studies, women are found to have higher rates of mental illness, but in some

studies, men have higher rates. Still other studies fail to find any difference between the genders (Dohrenwend and Dohrenwend, 1976; Schwartz, 1991).

These conflicting findings, however, concern mental illness *in general*. Studies on *specific types* of disorder do indicate a gender difference. They usually show that women are more likely to suffer from depression, anxiety attacks, and post-traumatic stress disorder, while men are more likely to have antisocial personality, paranoia, and drug and alcohol abuse disorders (Norris et al., 2002; Yonkers and Gurguis, 1995).

Why this difference between men and women? The answer can be found in their gender roles. The female role is relatively restrictive and oppressive, likely to confine the woman to her inner self, so that she tends to internalize her problems (such as keeping her frustration and anger to herself) rather than externalize them (aggressively taking them out on others). Hence, women are more likely than men to fall victim to depression and anxiety attacks, which essentially involve the victims hurting themselves. In contrast, the male role is more liberating, more likely to encourage men to be assertive, bold, and aggressive in social relations. If frustrated and angry, they tend more to take it out on others, behaving like antisocial and paranoid individuals (Rescorla et al., 2007; Schwartz, 1991).

Age

Many studies before the mid-1980s suggested that in our society older persons were more likely than younger ones to suffer from mental illness. This was typically attributed to societal neglect of older persons: Older individuals are not given meaningful and satisfying roles to play in society, since these roles are largely allocated to the young, on whom industrial production depends heavily. Deprived of respect by others, older individuals become alienated or isolated. As they begin to develop psychopathological symptoms, their families and other close relatives do not bother taking them to a hospital or psychiatrist. By the time their psychopathology becomes hopelessly severe, they are brought to a mental institution where they will be kept out of their families' sight for a long time (Gallagher, 2002).

More recent studies in the 1980s and 1990s showed that the elderly were the least likely among all age groups to become mentally ill. According to a national survey, for example, relatively young people, aged 25 to 34 years, have the highest rate of mental illness (Kessler et al., 1994). Another study by a research team called the Cross-National Collaborative Group (1992) also found a significant increase in major depression among the younger generations. In countries as diverse as the United States, Taiwan, Lebanon, and New Zealand, each successive generation has been growing more vulnerable to depressive disorders. In those countries, people born after 1955 are more than three times as likely as their grandparents to have a major depression. Among Americans, about 6% of those born after 1955 have become severely depressed by 24 years of age, while only 1% of those born before 1905 have suffered similar depression by 75 years of age.

The increasingly greater prevalence of depression among young people can be attributed to changes in modern society—more specifically, to an increase in social stresses and a decrease in social resources for coping with the stresses. Most of the stresses come from family problems, such as divorce, child abuse, or parental indifference to children's needs for love and support. The difficulty in coping with these stresses comes largely from modern society's loss of the extended family and close-knit, village-like community.

Race and Ethnicity

Race and ethnicity, like gender, have not been consistently found to be related to mental illness in general. Many studies have shown higher rates of mental illness among blacks, Hispanics, and Asians than whites. The standard explanation for this finding is that minorities experience more social stresses stemming from discrimination, poverty, and cultural conflict (Kessler and Neighbors, 1986; Yamamoto et al., 1983). On the other hand, there are studies showing no significant difference in psychiatric problems between minorities and whites. An equally plausible reason has been given for this finding: The minorities' group identification, group solidarity, or social network protects them against those social stresses (Kessler et al., 1985; Kuo and Tsai, 1986).

More consistent data are available on the relationship between race or ethnicity and specific forms of mental disorder. Among the lower classes, Puerto Ricans and African Americans are more likely than Irish and Jewish Americans to have sociopathic inclinations ("I can easily make people afraid of me and sometimes do just that for the fun of it"), as well as paranoid tendencies ("Behind my back people say all kinds of things about me"). While African Americans are more likely to show paranoid disorders (viewed by researchers as anger expressed outwardly—against others), Jewish Americans tend more to manifest depressive disorders (anger turned inward—against oneself). Asian Americans, particularly those of Korean ancestry, also have more depressive symptoms than whites (Kuo, 1984; Ruiz, 1982).

Urban Environment

Many studies have shown the urban environment to be a major producer of mental illness. Surveys in the United States and the Netherlands, for example, indicate higher rates of mental disorders in urban areas, particularly the inner city, than in rural areas, including the suburbs and small towns (Peen et al., 2007; Robins et al., 1984). According to many sociologists and psychiatrists, the urban environment produces a lot of mental problems by generating an abundance of physical and social stresses. These stresses appear in the forms of traffic congestion, excessive noise, population density, tenuous social relations, loneliness, and lack of social support.

Some community studies further reveal a link between urban living and specific psychiatric problems. Generally, urban residents exhibit higher levels of neurotic and personality disorders while the more serious psychotic conditions, especially severe depression, are more prevalent among rural and small-town dwellers. Why? Perhaps rural and small-town residents are more likely to find their lives in nonurban areas too restrictive. They cannot freely express frustration and anger in the presence of relatives, friends, acquaintances, and even strangers—who can easily find out who the troublemakers are. By suppressing their frustration,

Generally, urban residents tend to exhibit higher levels of neurotic and personality disorders while rural and small-town residents are more likely to suffer from psychotic condition such as severe depression.

> **BOX 14.3   GLOBAL PERSPECTIVE**
>
> **How Their Mental Illness Is Different**
>
> Research has shown that modern industrialized societies such as the United States and France have more mental illness than traditional agricultural societies such as China and Nigeria. Why? A major reason is the culture of individualism and competitiveness in modern societies. In this kind of culture, individuals with personal problems often have to fend for themselves, doing without relatives and friends who are more readily available to offer support in group-oriented, traditional societies. It is no wonder that as the world's most individualistic and competitive society, the United States has the world's highest rate of mental illness. As indicated by a survey, over 26% of Americans suffer from mental illness, compared with 18% of French, 15% of Dutch, 9% of Chinese, and 5% of Nigerians (Demyttenaere et al., 2004; Kessler et al., 2004).
>
> Mental illness does not always appear in the same way in all societies. In Latin America, some people are tormented by *susto*, a pathological fear that their souls have left their bodies. In Malaysia, some people suffer from *latah*, which makes the victim scream, swear, or gesture for a prolonged period when startled by something like a loud noise or snake. These mental illnesses are unheard of in Western societies. In the United States, though, some women are afflicted with anorexia nervosa, the extreme fear of weight gain, which rarely or never occurs in third-world countries (Lemelson, 2001).
>
> The symptoms of mental illness may reflect the culture in which they occur. Depression often appears as a physical illness in many developing countries but as an emotional problem in the West. This is because it is shameful to admit to emotional distress in the culture of developing countries but not so in the West. In the United States, people suffering from obsessive-compulsive disorder often wash their hands over and over, because the U.S. culture places a high value on cleanliness and health. In Bali, Indonesia, a common symptom of a compulsive disorder is the uncontrollable urge to collect information about people. A Balinese man with the disorder would find out the name of every person who passes by his house, so that he could treat even strangers like friends. This is because the Balinese culture emphasizes the importance of extreme friendliness to everybody (Osborne, 2001).

the ruralites and small-towners may get deeper and deeper into themselves until they become psychotic, totally withdrawing into themselves, breaking the ties between themselves and others, or losing touch with conventional reality. In contrast, urban dwellers can more easily get away from family and friends and are freer to express frustration in the midst of strangers, who tend to tolerate unconventional behavior or antisocial outbursts. If they persist in doing so, the urbanites may become neurotics, who, unlike psychotics, retain their grip on conventional reality. Otherwise, they may develop an antisocial psychopathic personality, which essentially is an "acting out" disorder (Dohrenwend and Dohrenwend, 1974; Kringlen et al., 2006). In short, mental illness can reflect the impact of the urban environment, but it can also reflect the influence of the larger societies and cultures (see Box 14.3).

■ Providers and Users of Health Care

Before 1870, doctoring was a lowly profession. Many doctors were more like quacks than true medical scientists. They had little knowledge of how the human body worked and how diseases developed. In the face of such ignorance, doctors could be a menace. For many ailments, they bled patients; evacuated their bowels, often until they passed out; stuffed them with dangerous drugs; and tormented them with ghastly appliances. Sometimes, the patients survived despite all this "assistance," but more often, they died. In time, they developed a store of knowledge that eventually enabled them to practice a highly respectable profession (Blundell, 1986). Today, the medical profession has changed again, and we will see what it is like and what kinds of people use its services.

The Medical Profession Today

Over the last 30 years, significant changes have taken place in the medical profession. Today, doctors often find their autonomy eroded, their prestige reduced, and their competence challenged by everyone from insurance companies to patients (Hobson, 2005).

Before 1980, most doctors practiced alone. By 1983, the share of doctors in solo practice had dropped to only 41%, and later it fell even more—to 26% by 1997. Today, a large majority of doctors have become salaried employees, working in group practices, health maintenance organizations (HMOs), and other healthcare companies. One reason is that the cost of starting a private practice is too high for most young doctors, whose medical training has left them deeply in debt. Another reason is that doctors get most of their payments from the government and insurance companies, not from patients, as they did in the past. To be paid, doctors must fill out numerous forms to justify their fees, which often proves too burdensome for a private doctor to handle (Stolberg, 1998).

Efforts by employers, insurance companies, and the government to control rising medical costs have caused many doctors to complain about losing their professional autonomy. Doctors must get permission from outside regulators, such as government agencies and insurance companies, for major but nonemergency hospitalization and surgeries. If the regulators do not approve a case in advance, they will not pay the cost of treatment. They occasionally refuse to authorize a treatment that they consider too costly or unnecessary. While chafing at these outside regulators, doctors also complain of internal controls from their employers. HMOs routinely pass around lists ranking their physicians on the time spent with patients. This is intended to give the doctors the subtle but clear message that those highest on the list cause a financial drain on the organization (Belkin, 1990; Gorman, 1998).

The general public also seems to hold doctors in less esteem than before. Gallup polls often show that a majority (from 57% to 75%) of the people questioned agreed with these statements: "Doctors don't care about people as much as they used to," "Doctors are too interested in making money," and "Doctors keep patients waiting too long." One Gallup poll indicated that only 44% of Americans have "a great deal" or "quite a lot" of confidence in the medical system. Not fully trusting their doctors, people who are better educated often feel obliged to become as informed as possible about their illness so that they can get the best treatment. This has led many doctors to complain that some patients challenge their expertise after learning about medical advances only from the Internet and television or newspapers and magazines (Gorman, 1998; Mallory, 2003).

But today there is a significant increase in the numbers of women and minority-group members becoming doctors. These demographic changes make the medical profession more representative of and responsive to an increasingly diverse society. Moreover, today's medical students of diverse backgrounds have a lower income expectation and a greater sense of public duty than their elders, which should help them meet the increasingly cost-conscious need for health care in the near future. More importantly, patients are likely to see them as less authoritarian and more patient-friendly than traditional doctors of the past. Younger doctors, however, are less willing to be on call 24/7 and are therefore more likely to work as **hospitalists**, a new breed of doctors who focus on the general care of hospitalized patients (Eisenberg, 1999; Goldstein, 2008).

Hospitalists
A new breed of doctors who focus on the general care of hospitalized patients.

Diverse Users of Health Care

When feeling sick, people obviously want to get well again, but not everyone automatically goes to see a doctor. Some may simply shrug off their illness, thinking that it's not serious enough. The severity of the illness is only one factor that may motivate people to seek medical care. Social factors such as age, gender, ethnicity, and class, which reflect the social diversity of American society, also influence whether individuals see a doctor.

Generally, older people are ill more often than younger people are. It is therefore not surprising that the elderly are the most likely age group to seek medical care.

Women are more likely than men to seek health services, but women are less likely to obtain proper care. Under the influence of sexual prejudice, doctors tend to dismiss women's complaints with such thoughts as "overstress," "back strain," "could be just the heat," or "nothing to worry about." Even when a patient complains of chest pains and other symptoms of heart disease, the doctor is less likely to take the complaints seriously when they come from a woman. In fact, doctors are twice as likely to label women's chest pains as a psychiatric complaint or something other than a sign of heart disease. Among those who suffer from kidney failure, women are also less likely than men to receive kidney transplants. Still, when they feel ill, women are more likely than men to consult doctors (Jauhar, 2001).

Some ethnic groups visit doctors less often than others. When ill, Mexican Americans often see the doctor as a last resort, preferring to try Mexican folk medicine first. Their relatives, friends, neighbors, and *curanderos* (folk healers) are generally ready to provide certain patent medicines, herbs, and teas along with the performance of religious rituals. Native Americans have a similar system of folk medicine, which they believe to be capable of restoring health by bringing back a harmonious balance among various biological and spiritual forces in the sick person's life. Similar principles of harmonious balance can be found in traditional Chinese medicine, which is popular with residents in America's Chinatowns. According to the Chinese, illness results from an imbalance between *yin* (the female, cold force) and *yang* (the male, hot force). If illness results from an excess of yin (cold), certain herbs and foods that are classified as hot should be taken to restore the balance—and hence health. If illness results from too much yang (hot), cold herbs and foods should be taken (Cockerham, 2010).

African Americans lack the systems of folk medicine available to other minorities. Still, they are less likely than whites to utilize health care because they are less trusting of the healthcare system (Ozols, 2005). They are, however, more likely than other minorities to visit doctors, but the quality of the health care they receive tends to be lower than that received by whites. Blacks are also more likely than whites to receive treatment in hospital outpatient clinics and emergency rooms, which are more often public than private. Whites are more likely to go to a private doctor's office. This difference is largely the result of a greater proportion of African Americans being poor. The poor are more likely than the rich to get medical treatment in public clinics and emergency departments (Cockerham, 2010).

Poor blacks are apparently more reluctant than poor whites to seek treatment for AIDS and HIV because they distrust the government. This has resulted partly from the infamous Tuskegee experiments conducted by the U.S. government for 40 years from 1931 to 1972. For the experiments, 399 poor black men were recruited and led to believe they would receive free medical treatment for their so-called "bad blood"; in reality, they were left untreated for syphilis so that government health researchers could study the impact of the disease on them. To restore trust in government among African Americans, President Clinton publicly apologized to the few remaining survivors and to relatives of the 399 victims (Mitchell, 1997b).

■ The U.S. Healthcare System

There are problems with the U.S. healthcare system. The most important ones are the high cost and unequal distribution of medical care. We will take a close look at these problems, along with the new healthcare reform that is intended to fix some of these problems.

The High Cost of Health Care

In the last 50 years, healthcare costs in the United States have gone up sharply. In 1960 Americans spent only 5% of their total income on health care, but now it is about 17% (Samuelson, 2008).

Why have healthcare costs escalated so much? The aging of the U.S. population is one contributing factor, and proliferation of expensive medical technology is another. Significant advances also have been made in keeping coma and stroke victims alive, but these patients sometimes require extremely expensive medical care for years. Perhaps most important, Americans now visit doctors more often, spend more days in hospitals, swallow more pills, and seek ever-more costly treatments and prescription drugs.

The high cost of health care in the United States can also be attributed to the fact that medical care is organized as a business that is quite different from other businesses. Medical customers do not have much say about what they buy because they cannot judge what they need and how much they must pay. Meanwhile, consumers have little incentive to keep prices down. They pay only a small share (about 15%) of the bill. Most of it is passed on to third parties, including insurance companies, employers, and the government (Zuckerman, 2009).

These third parties have recently tried to reduce costs through managed health care: putting a squeeze on doctors' incomes, requiring patients to pay a larger share of the cost, and cutting back on treatment and hospital stays. These efforts to cut costs, however, may have forced doctors to be too stingy with care, causing many patients to complain and some to sue the managed care companies. Moreover, the cost of prescription drugs has gone up so much that some Americans are buying cheaper drugs in Mexico and Canada (Martinez, 2003).

Unequal Distribution of Health Care

Being opposed to big government in favor of greater personal liberty, the United States stands alone among rich industrialized countries for not having government-paid universal health insurance for all its citizens. We have instead a fee-for-service system, which requires patients to pay for the services they receive from doctors and hospitals. As has been suggested, though, most Americans pay out of their own pockets a portion rather than the entirety of the medical bill, with the rest paid by their insurance companies, employers, and the government.

A majority (about 60%) of Americans have private medical insurance. Most of them share the cost of that insurance with their employer, and about half receive their medical care from an HMO for a fixed fee. Another 25% of Americans are covered by one of two types of public, government-paid insurance: *Medicare*, which pays most of the medical bills for older, retired people, and *Medicaid*, which pays all of the medical expenses of the poor and the disabled. About 15% of the population—over 40 million

The United States has an unequal distribution of health care: Some Americans get more insurance coverage and better medial care than others, while some others do not even have insurance and medical care.

Americans who are mostly low-income but not poor enough to qualify for Medicaid—are left high and dry, without any insurance to protect them against illness or death. This is the group who will benefit the most from the new healthcare bill, as it will provide them with insurance coverage.

Thus, we have an unequal distribution of health care, with some Americans getting more insurance coverage and better medical care than others—and others having less or no insurance and medical care. As a result, about 22,000 Americans die each year due to lack of insurance and medical treatment, and 700,000 become bankrupt from having to pay high medical bills. By contrast, in all the other industrialized countries that guarantee health care for everybody, no one dies or goes broke when they get sick. It is true that these countries do a good job of providing free and prompt care to anyone suffering from an acute medical condition, but for less serious, nonemergency cases, they often provide nothing but a long wait. Still, people in those countries do not mind the long wait because they know that the rich wait just as long as the poor (Reid, 2009).

Five Myths in the Healthcare Debate

At least five myths have emerged in the debate about the new healthcare bill. Myth 1: You cannot choose your own health benefits; the government will decide what benefits you get. Actually, individuals are provided with a list of private insurers and one government plan from which they are free to choose what they like. The government requires only that no participating insurance plan may refuse people with preexisting conditions.

Myth 2: Chemotherapy will not be covered for older Medicare patients. In other words, Medicare will give cancer patients older than 70 years of age only end-of-life counseling and not chemotherapy. This is not true at all; older Medicare patients will get chemotherapy.

Myth 3: Illegal immigrants will get free health insurance. In fact, as the new healthcare bill says, "individuals who are not lawfully present in the United States" will not be allowed to receive government subsidies to buy health insurance.

Myth 4: Death panels will decide who lives. The new healthcare bill does offer end-of-life care as an *option* for any senior who requests it. But this does not mean that the law forces anyone to have the end-of-life care.

Myth 5: The government will determine doctors' wages. This is completely false because the physicians who choose to accept patients in the public insurance plan are not employees of the government just as your doctor is not an employee of your private insurance company. Since the doctors do not work for the government, they are free to set their own fees (Begley, 2009).

While the new healthcare bill has generated those five myths, it has also stirred up a debate over how to keep the country healthy. Some argue that a public health insurance plan (or the public option, for short) will do the trick, but others contend that letting a new government bureaucracy run a healthcare business will make the situation worse (see **Box 14.4**).

BOX 14.4   DIVERGENT VIEWS

For or Against Public Option?

A public option is a health insurance program run by the government. It is operated just like a private health insurance plan, except that the public option involves the government rather than a private company selling insurance. The public insurance is expected to be much less expensive than the private insurance, as it is designed to serve mostly low-income people who cannot afford the more expensive private insurance.

Generally, liberals support a public option. This is their argument: We need a public insurance program because our current healthcare system is broken. More than 45 million Americans lack health insurance and therefore usually do not receive adequate or high-quality health care. About 22,000 people die each year because they lack insurance. The uninsured live sicker and die younger than the insured. But the health insurance costs are so high that many people cannot afford to buy insurance. As a result, every year 57 million Americans have problems paying medical bills, and half of all personal bankruptcies happen because health expenses are too high. To solve all these problems, advocates argue, we need the government to offer the public option and thereby ensure that everyone has health insurance (Feder, 2009).

Conservatives usually oppose the public option. They argue that if the government gets involved in health care by providing the public option, the situation will get worse. Consider our two largest government-run health programs: Medicare and Medicaid. They are always in danger of going bankrupt without the constant steep benefit cuts and much higher taxes. Many doctors also resent the fact that politicians and government bureaucrats threaten their fees and meddle with their judgment. Moreover, it would be destructive to patients' health if more government bureaucrats are involved in their health care. As shown in other countries with the government-run healthcare system, patients face long and often deadly waiting (Gingrich, 2009).

■ Sociological Theories of Healthcare Problems

Through functionalist theory, we can see how healthcare problems bring together the patient's sick role and the doctor's healing role, which in turn jointly contribute to the social order of society. In contrast, conflict theory directs our attention to the negative aspects of the healthcare system in its task of combating healthcare problems. While these two theories deal with larger issues of how to deal with healthcare problems, symbolic interaction theory focuses on what goes on in the interaction between doctor and patient that affects how the two individuals feel and act toward each other.

Functionalist Theory

Sick role
A set of social expectations of how an ill person should behave.

To functionalist theory, healthcare problems involve doctors and patients playing roles that contribute to social order. In playing the sick role, patients are carrying out a set of social expectations of how an ill person should behave. In his classic definition of the sick role, Talcott Parsons (1964) laid out what *rights* the sick can claim and what *obligations* they should discharge.

The rights of the sick are as follows:

- The sick have the right to be taken care of by others because they do not choose to be sick and thus should not be blamed for their illness.
- They have the right to be exempted from certain social duties. They should not be forced to go to work. Students should be allowed to miss an exam and take it later.

The obligations of the sick are as follows:

- The sick are obligated to want to get well. They should not expect to remain ill and use the illness to take advantage of others' love, concern, and care for them or to shirk their work and other social responsibilities.
- They are obligated to seek technically competent help. In seeing a doctor, they must cooperate to help ensure their recovery.

Healing role
A set of social expectations of how a doctor should behave.

Doctors have their own rights and obligations in playing the healing role, a set of social expectations of how a doctor should behave. Basically, doctors are obligated to help the sick get well, as required by the Hippocratic oath, which they take when beginning their medical careers. At the same time, they have the right to receive appropriate compensation for their work. Because their work is widely regarded as highly important, they may expect to make a great deal of money and enjoy considerable respect.

Seen from functionalist theory, both the sick and the healing roles jointly serve a social control function. They help to prevent illnesses from disrupting economic production, family relations, and social activities. Moreover, functionalist theory suggests that the system of health care helps to maintain the health of society. Thus functionalists attribute an improvement in the nation's health to medicine, the doctor, the medical profession, and some new technology of treatment. Medical discoveries such as the germ theory and medical interventions such as vaccines and drugs are credited for the victory over infectious diseases.

Conflict Theory

As seen by conflict theorists, improvements in the social environment contribute far more than medical interventions to the reduction of illness and mortality. One study shows that only about 3.5% of the total decline in mortality from five infectious diseases (influenza, pneumonia, diphtheria, whooping cough, and poliomyelitis) since 1900 can be attributed to medical measures (McKinlay and McKinlay, 1994). In many instances, the new measures to combat those diseases were introduced several decades *after* a substantial decline in mortality from the diseases had occurred. This decline in mortality has been brought about mostly by several social and environmental factors: (1) a rising standard of living, (2) better sanitation and hygiene, and (3) improved housing and nutrition (Conrad, 2009).

But conflict theorists do not mean to suggest that modern clinical medicine does not alleviate pain or cure disease in *some individuals*. Their point is that the healthcare institution fails to improve the health of *the population as a whole*. Why, then, does U.S. society continue to spend such vast sums of money on health care? This, according to conflict theorists, has much to do with the pursuit of private profit in a capitalist society.

In analyzing the coronary care technology, for example, conflict theorist Howard Waitzkin (1994) found that soon after their introduction in the 1960s, the expensive coronary care units became so popular that they could be found in half of all acute-care hospitals in the United States. However, the intensive care provided by that medical technology had not been proven to be more effective than simple rest at home. Waitzkin argued that the proliferation of this expensive but ineffective form of treatment could be traced to the profit motive. He found that corporations such as Warner-Lambert Pharmaceutical and Hewlett-Packard had participated in every phase of the research, development, promotion, and dissemination of coronary care technology, which ultimately produced huge profits for them. Waitzkin also noted that the same profit motive had driven corporations to oversell many other expensive technological advances, such as computed tomography and fetal monitoring devices, even though they had not significantly improved the nation's health; they had benefited only a limited number of patients.

Symbolic Interaction Theory

By focusing on the interaction between doctor and patient, we can learn why those two individuals feel and act in a certain way toward each other. According to symbolic interaction theorists, patients tend to evaluate warm, friendly doctors favorably even when such doctors have failed to provide successful treatment. In contrast, patients are more likely to sue for malpractice those doctors who are the mostly highly trained and who practice in the most sophisticated hospitals. Although these doctors are not intentionally negligent, they are most likely to be viewed by their patients in general—not just the ones who sue them—as cold and bureaucratic. It is the friendly doctor's *affiliative* style of communication that enhances patient satisfaction, and it is the highly competent but bureaucratic doctor's *dominant* style that alienates patients. Affiliative style involves behaviors that show honesty, compassion, humor, and a nonjudgmental attitude. Dominant style involves the manifestation of power, authority, professional detachment, and status in the doctor's interaction with the patient (Buller and Buller, 1987; Fischman, 2005).

Why does the doctor's communication style affect patient satisfaction? Symbolic interaction theory assumes that in interacting with patients, friendly doctors are more likely than dominant doctors to take into account the views, feelings, and expectations the patients have about themselves, their illnesses, and their doctors. To the patients, their illness is unusual, as it does not happen to them every day, and their suffering is a highly intimate, emotional reality. Thus, they expect their doctors to show a great deal of concern. They obviously want a cure, but they also crave emotional support. If doctors attune themselves to these expectations, they can develop warm relationships with their patients. This is no easy task because doctors have been trained to take an objective, dispassionate approach to disease. They have learned to view patients unemotionally, especially when performing surgery, which involves inserting their hands into diseased strangers without flinching or losing their nerve (Konner, 2001).

Such an emotional detachment often intrudes into a typical doctor–patient encounter. The doctor tends to dominate with questions based on his or her technical understanding of the cause and treatment of the illness, thereby failing to pay attention to the patient's very personal sense of the illness. More specifically, after asking a patient "What brings you here today?" the doctor usually interrupts the reply within just 18 seconds. Many doctors also intimidate patients into silence by tapping a pencil impatiently or keeping one hand on the door handle. If patients are allowed to speak freely, doctors often respond merely with an "uh-huh," which indicates only minimal interest (Schrof, 1998).

This detached professionalism tends to exact a price by alienating patients, making them feel that they are being treated as mere cases of disease rather than as people. Such patients are also likely to suffer other consequences: As many as 60% of patients leave their doctors' offices confused about medication instructions, and more than half of new prescriptions are taken improperly or not at all (Schrof, 1998).

To review the three sociological theories of healthcare problems, see Box 14.5.

BOX 14.5   THEORETICAL THUMBNAIL

Explaining Healthcare Problems

Theory	Focus	Insights
Functionalist Theory	The rights and obligations in the patient's sick role and the doctor's healing role	The function of sick and healing roles is to keep illnesses from disrupting society.
Conflict Theory	The lack of success in combating healthcare problems	Costly medical technology brings huge profit but little decline in illness and mortality.
Symbolic Interaction Theory	How the doctor and patient behave when they interact in dealing with a healthcare problem	The doctor's objective professionalism increases patient dissatisfaction.

QUESTIONS TO EXPLORE

1. What experiences in your own life could you use to support or reject the notion of the "sick role"?

2. Do you agree with the conflict theorists that suppliers of medical technologies are more interested in reaping profits than curing patients?

3. If symbolic interactionists are correct in that the cold, impersonal, or sterile atmosphere of a doctor's office and examination room serves to drive a wedge between caregivers and patients, what can be done to solve the problem?

Review

SUMMARY

1. Americans live longer today than before. But when compared with other industrialized countries, the United States has lower life expectancy and higher infant mortality. Within the United States, older people are less likely to suffer from acute diseases but are more susceptible to chronic illnesses. Women live longer than men. Minority Americans have lower life expectancy than whites. The poor are more likely to get sick than higher-income Americans.

2. Two-thirds of Americans are overweight and one-third are obese because of overeating and lack of exercise, encouraged by the culture of corpulence. Cities, schools, health officials, and state governments have tried to fight obesity by encouraging people to eat less and exercise more. Individuals can lose weight by dealing with the reasons that prevent people from losing weight.

3. HIV and AIDS spread most commonly through sexual intercourse with an infected person and through using a contaminated hypodermic needle. Many people are misinformed about the diseases, afraid that they can get HIV or AIDS by donating blood or through casual contact with an infected person. Many people also discriminate against the victims.

4. Large numbers of Americans have experienced an episode of mental illness. In fact, all of us have been mentally ill in the same way as we have been physically ill, though most of these mental illnesses, like physical illnesses, are not serious. There are popular myths about mental illness, as follow: Mental patients are extremely weird, hopeless or incurable, crazed or violent; there is a sharp distinction between "mentally ill" and "mentally healthy"; depression is more common in the winter; and there is an epidemic of autism.

5. There is more mental illness in the lower classes than higher classes for two possible reasons: lower-class life is more stressful, and the mentally ill of the higher class tend to drift downward to the lower classes. Women are more likely than men to suffer from depression, anxiety attacks, and posttraumatic stress disorder, while men are more likely to suffer from antisocial personality, paranoia, and drug and alcohol abuse. Young people have higher rates of mental illness than the elderly. Puerto Ricans and African Americans are more likely than Irish and Jewish Americans to be sociopathic and paranoiac. Jewish and Asian Americans are more likely to suffer from depression. There is more mental illness in the city than in the suburb and small town because there are more physical and social stresses in the urban area. The rate of mental illness is higher in modern than in traditional societies, and some mental illnesses take place in some societies and cultures but not in others.

6. Today's doctors often find their autonomy eroded, their prestige reduced, and their competence challenged by everyone from insurance companies to patients. Now there are more women and minority doctors, making the medical profession

more representative of and responsive to the increasingly diverse population in the United States. Social factors such as age, gender, ethnicity, and class influence whether individuals will see a doctor. Older people, women, and African Americans are more likely than other minorities to seek medical care.

7. Healthcare costs in the United States have gone up sharply. The reasons include the aging of the population, the proliferation of expensive medical technology, doctors' freedom to charge high fees, and consumers' lack of incentive to keep prices down. Another problem with the healthcare system is the unequal distribution of health care, with some Americans getting more insurance coverage and better medical care than others. Five myths have emerged from the debate about the new healthcare bill: (1) The government will decide what health benefits a person gets, (2) no treatment will be offered for older Medicare patients, (3) illegal immigrants will get free health insurance, (4) death panels will decide who lives, and (5) the government will determine doctors' wages. Liberals support the public option, a health insurance program run by the government, but conservatives oppose it.

8. According to functionalist theory, a healthcare problem brings together the patient's sick role and the doctor's healing role, which jointly contribute to the social order of society. Conflict theory focuses on how the costly medical technology brings more profit to the healthcare system than it decreases illness and mortality. Symbolic interaction theory zeroes in on how the doctor and patient behave toward each other in dealing with a healthcare problem.

CRITICAL THINKING QUESTIONS

1. What will the current, prolonged economic downturn spell for the "culture of corpulence"? Will the problem of obesity escalate, or will the downturn whip us into shape? Explain your position.

2. What social factors have contributed most to the extreme disparity in health care for those with insurance and those without insurance?

3. In the debate over the new healthcare bill, why is it inaccurate to state that "the government sets the wages of physicians?"

INTERNET RESOURCES

The American Medical Association (AMA) (http://www.ama-assn.org/ama/home/index.shtml) was founded in 1847. The AMA's central mission is to advocate and champion medicine and health. By sharing best practices, research findings, and cutting-edge medical developments, the AMA "helps doctors help patients."

The Centers for Disease Control and Prevention (CDC) (http://www.cdc.gov/) serves the general public as a free, comprehensive online medical encyclopedia and resource center. The site seeks to offer reliable and valid health information on a breadth of health-related topics including causes, symptoms, and cures for diseases, disasters, injury prevention, workplace safety, travelers' health updates, environmental health, and workplace safety.

The U.S. Department of Health and Human Services (www.hhs.gov/) "is the United States government's principal agency for protecting the health of all Americans and providing essential human services—especially for those who are least able to help themselves."

The mission of the National Institutes of Health (http://www.nih.gov/) "is to seek fundamental knowledge about the nature and behavior of living systems and the application of that knowledge to enhance health, lengthen life, and reduce the burdens of illness and disability."

The Office on Women's Health (OWH) (http://www.womenshealth.gov/) was established in 1991, serving as a subsection of the U.S. Department of Health and Human Services. OWH's singular mission is to promote a better and more active sense of well-being among women and girls through the sharing of accurate and relevant gender- and sex-specific research findings among health professionals and consumers.

Problems of Globalization

Urbanization, Population, and Environment

Maggie Zhang, a secretary in China, appears obsessed with an online game called Happy Farm. "I play at least 10 times a day," she says. "My boss has warned me several times to stop playing. But he ended up joining the game." The rules of the game are simple. Each player acts as the owner of a virtual farm, cultivating, irrigating, fertilizing, and harvesting various kinds of vegetables, flowers, and fruit. Players sell their produce in exchange for virtual money, which they may use to buy better seeds and a more beautiful farm. Since the game debuted in 2008, all kinds of people including students, white-collar workers, children, and even government officials have apparently become hopelessly addicted. The popularity of Happy Farm is not only due to addiction, though. It stems from a desire to escape the fast-paced, crowded, and impersonal city life. As Zhang Lin, a college graduate, says, "Job pressure and the tall, cold buildings sometimes make me feel like I can't breathe. I have to turn to virtual nature, and own a virtual house and farm" (Fish, 2010; Huifeng, 2009).

The same kind of problems can be found in the United States and other countries. The problems involve being highly urbanized, having a large population, and the environment being polluted. We will discuss these problems in this chapter.

■ Cities: From Past to Present

Way back before the birth of the United States as a nation in 1693, William Penn wrote that "the country life is to be preferred for there we see the works of God, but in cities little else than the work of man." Most people at the time probably agreed with him. After all, less than 2% of the world's population then lived in cities. But today more than half live in urban areas.

While urban populations have grown, cities themselves have changed. We can identify the stages they have gone through, from the time they first appeared to today.

The Preindustrial City

For more than 99% of the time we humans have been on Earth, our ancestors have roamed about in search for food. They have gathered edible plants, hunted, and fished, but they have never found enough food in one place to sustain them for very long. They have had to move on, traveling in small bands from place to place.

Then, about 10,000 years ago, technological advances made it possible for people to stop their wandering. This was the dawn of what is called the *Neolithic period.* People now had the simple tools and the know-how to cultivate plants and domesticate animals. They could produce their food supplies in one locale, which enabled them to settle down and build villages. The villages were very small—with only about 200 to 400 residents in each. For the next 5,000 years, villagers produced just enough food to feed themselves.

Then, about 5,000 years ago, they developed more powerful technologies. Thanks to innovations like the ox-drawn plow, irrigation, and metallurgy, farmers could produce more food than they needed to sustain themselves and their families. Because of this food surplus, some people abandoned agriculture and made their living by weaving, making pottery, and practicing other specialized crafts. Methods of transporting and storing food were also improved. The result was the emergence of cities.

Cities first appeared on the fertile banks of such rivers as the Nile of Egypt, the Euphrates and Tigris in the Middle East, the Indus in Pakistan, and the Yellow River in China. Similar urban settlements later appeared in other parts of the world. These *preindustrial cities* were very small if compared with the cities today. Most had populations of 5,000 to 10,000 people. Only a few cities had more than 100,000 people, and even Rome never had more than several hundred thousand.

A number of factors prevented expansion of the preindustrial city. By modern standards, agricultural techniques were still primitive. It took at least 75 farmers to produce enough of a surplus to support just one city dweller. For transportation, people had to depend on their own muscle power or that of animals. It was difficult to carry food supplies from farms to cities and even more difficult to transport heavy materials for construction in the cities. Poor sanitation, lack of sewage facilities, and ineffective medicine kept the death rate high. Epidemics regularly killed as much as half of the city's population. Many families still had a strong attachment to the land, which discouraged immigration to cities. All these characteristics of the preindustrial society kept cities small (Davis, 1955).

The Industrial City

For the next 5,000 years, cities changed little. Then their growth, in size and number, was so rapid that it has been called an *urban revolution* or *explosion.* In 1700, less than 2% of the population of Great Britain lived in cities, but by 1900, the majority of the British did so. Other European countries and the United States soon achieved the same level of urbanization in an even shorter period. Today, these and other Western

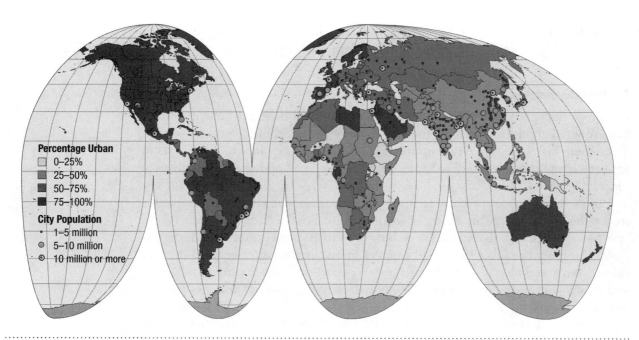

FIGURE 15.1 Various Levels of Urbanization Around the World

Western countries, such as the United States and European nations, are among the most urbanized in the world today. More recently, though, many Latin American countries have also become mostly urbanized.

Critical Thinking: *What is good or bad about urbanization?*

Source: United Nations, Department of Economic and Social Affairs, Population Division: *World Urbanization Prospects*, 2010.

nations are among the most urbanized in the world, along with many Latin American countries, which have become mostly urbanized in more recent years (**Figure 15.1**).

The major stimulus to the urban explosion came from the Industrial Revolution. It triggered a series of related events. Industrialization first caused a rise in production growth, as the mechanization of farming brought about an agricultural surplus. Fewer farmers were thus able to support more people—and larger urban populations. Meanwhile, workers no longer needed on the farms moved to cities, which led to a larger urban population. This urbanization further gained momentum from the development of other new technologies. Improved transportation, for example, sped the movement of food and other materials to urban centers.

The outcome of those events was the *industrial city*. Compared with the preindustrial city, the industrial city was larger, more densely settled, and more diverse. It was a place where large numbers of people—with a wide range of skills, interests, and cultural backgrounds—could live and work together in a limited space. Also, unlike the preindustrial city, which had served primarily as a religious or governmental center, the industrial city was a commercial hub. In fact, its abundant job opportunities attracted so many rural migrants that migration accounted for the largest share of its population growth. Without these migrants, cities would not have grown at all because of their high mortality rates brought on by extremely poor sanitary conditions (Hauser, 1981).

Metropolises and Megalopolises

Metropolis
A large urban area that includes a city and its surrounding suburbs.

Early in the 20th century, the large cities of the industrialized nations began to spread outward. They formed **metropolises**, large urban areas that include a city and its surrounding suburbs. Some of these suburbs are politically separate from their central cities, but socially, economically, and geographically, the suburbs and the city are tied together as a metropolis. Since 1990, most U.S. residents have been living in metropolitan areas with 1 million residents or more (Suro, 1991).

In the United States, it is the upper and middle classes that usually spark the expansion of cities outward. Typically, as migrants from rural areas moved into the central city, the wealthier classes in the city moved to the suburbs. The automobile greatly facilitated this development, encouraging people to leave the crowded inner city for the comfortable life of the suburbs. As the number of cars increased, so did the size of the suburbs and metropolises (Glaab and Brown, 1983).

Since 1950, virtually all the growth in metropolitan areas has taken place in the suburbs. During the 1960s, U.S. suburbs grew four times faster than inner cities, and stores and entertainment facilities followed the people there. Suburban jobs increased 44%, while inner-city employment dropped 7%. This pattern of suburban growth at the expense of the urban core continued in the 1970s and 1980s. Today suburbanites outnumber city residents three to two (U.S. Census Bureau, 2010).

As suburbs expand, they sometimes combine with the suburbs of adjacent metropolitan areas to form a **megalopolis**, a vast area in which many metropolises merge. For hundreds of miles from one major city to the next, suburbs and cities have merged with one another to form a continuous region in which distinctions between suburban, urban, and rural areas are blurred. The hundreds of miles from Boston to Washington, DC, form one such megalopolis; another stretches from Detroit through Chicago to Milwaukee in the Midwest; and a third spans from San Francisco to San Diego.

Megalopolis
A vast area in which many metropolises merge.

The World's Megacities

A megacity is a city with more than 5 million inhabitants. Today there are about 40 megacities in the world. This number is expected to reach 60 in 2015. Contrary to popular belief, most of these cities are not in the highly urbanized developed world. They are in the poorer, developing world (UNESCO, 2005).

Since the emergence of the preindustrial city 5,000 years ago, great cities have risen and fallen. The same is true today. One city that is collapsing is Kinshasa, the capital of the Democratic Republic of the Congo. Although the country is endowed with abundant natural resources, such as gold, diamonds, copper, and rich agricultural land, Kinshasa has produced massive miseries under the corrupt 30-year reign of former President Sese Mobutu. Government officials have routinely looted manufactured goods, fuel, food, and medical supplies, even most of the emergency food aid sent by foreign countries. As a result, the annual inflation rate often soared to more than 3,000% and the jobless rate to 80%, posing serious threats of starvation and epidemics. In contrast, the city of Curitiba in Brazil is a success story. The city is not rich, but its government makes the most of its scant resources. They light their parks with lamps made from soda bottles and build some government offices partly with old telephone poles. Their cities also deliver excellent services, including a highly efficient bus system and well-constructed housing projects for the poor (Zwingle, 2002).

Most megacities fit between these two contrasting types. They are saddled with serious problems but manage to cope reasonably well, usually in ways that reflect

The technologically advanced Japanese have developed an urban heating system that extracts heat from sewage and then use it to regulate the temperature in several buildings in Tokyo.

the nature of their societies. Consider Tokyo, the world's most densely populated metropolis. It faces enormous problems, such as overwhelming amounts of waste, traffic-choked streets, and sky-high housing costs. Yet the technologically advanced Japanese have, among other things, developed an urban heating system that extracts heat from sewage, which is then utilized to regulate the temperature in several of Tokyo's buildings. To reduce traffic jams, the city has used wireless communication to show drivers whose cars have a computerized navigation system where the congested streets are. And to lower housing costs, Tokyo has planned to build an underground city (Kuchment, 2003; Wehrfritz and Itoi, 2003). There are even signs that Japan is becoming a "post-car society" (see Box 15.1).

Turning Suburbs into Edge Cities

In the United States, most suburbs still offer better schools, more living space, less pollution, and less crime than the central city, so people continue to "vote with their feet" and head for suburbia. Up to the 1970s, most suburbs were largely bedroom communities and their residents commuted to the nearby cities to work. Since then, a new kind of suburbanization has taken place, transforming many suburbs into economic centers.

BOX 15.1   GLOBAL PERSPECTIVE

A Post-Car Society

Kimiyuki Suda, a Tokyo resident, should be an ideal customer for Japan's car companies. He is 34 years old, and as a successful executive at an Internet-services firm, he makes a lot of money. He used to own a nice sport utility vehicle, but now he uses mostly trains and subways. He says, "Having a car is so 20th century!"

Suda reflects a new trend in Japan. Young people have lost interest in cars. They prefer to spend their money on the latest electronic gadgets such as the coolest mobile phones and personal computers. In fact, the younger the Japanese consumers are, the less interested they are in having a car. This has caused car sales to decline steadily over time. Since 1990, the yearly new-car sales have dropped from 7.8 million to 5.4 million in 2007.

There are at least three reasons for the car's diminishing popularity. First, most city dwellers in Japan use mass transit, because the country has built one of the best systems in the world. Second, it costs too much to own and drive a car. The cost can run up to $500 per month, including parking fees, car insurance, toll roads, and various taxes. And third, automobiles are no longer a status symbol. In the past, cars represented a Western, modern lifestyle that young people aspired for, but today, as a young Japanese says, "Such thinking is completely gone" (Kashiwagi, 2008).

In these suburbs, new office buildings, factories, and warehouses have sprung up alongside the housing subdivisions and shopping malls. Developers have already accommodated vast clusters of big buildings, people, and cars. Thus, many suburbs have, in effect, become cities in their own right. Unlike the traditional U.S. city, where diverse businesses operate, the new suburban cities, also popularly called *edge cities*, are typically focused on a principal activity, such as a collection of computer companies, a large regional medical center, or a sports or recreation complex. The growth of edge cities, therefore, has taken away many jobs from the urban cores.

By turning into edge cities, many suburbs are now less suburban and more urban, faced with problems once considered the special burden of cities. Particularly in the larger, sprawling suburbs, the way of life has become much less centered on community and much more on work, entrepreneurship, and private life, with neighborhood grocers and gathering spots giving way to superstores and fast-food franchises. The potential for being lonely and friendless is therefore considerably greater (Firestone, 2001).

Many suburbs have also developed other characteristically urban problems, such as congestion, pollution, and crime. Rapid, unregulated growth has created some of these problems. When industry and stores move to the suburbs to be near people's homes, they often bring with them traffic, noise, and air and water pollution, not to mention landscape pollution. Although many suburbs are still prosperous, increasing numbers are not. The Los Angeles suburbs have more poor families than the city, and there is more substandard housing in the suburbs of Pittsburgh than in the city itself. In fact, some studies have shown more immigrants and poor people in the suburbs as a whole than in the cities (Firestone, 2001; Katz and Bradley, 2009).

Given these problems, at least 11 states have initiated the smart-growth policy of discouraging the development of suburbs while revitalizing the inner cities. Thus these states would refrain from funding the construction of infrastructure (such as water lines and highways) for the development of new edge cities. But they would subsidize the building of affordable homes for low- and moderate-income households in the urban core while enticing the middle class to the inner city with improved school quality and public safety (Cohen, 2002).

Latest Urban Trends

The latest U.S. census, taken in 2000, has revealed a number of significant changes in American cities (Roberts, 2007; U.S. Census Bureau, 2010):

- A majority of cities have grown rapidly, with those in the West and South expanding the most. Fueling this growth were the booming economy, the influx of immigrants, and the sharp decline in crime in the 1990s.

- Immigration has served as a brake against population decline in some major cities such as New York and Miami. Given a large influx of immigrants from countries such as India, China, the Philippines, and the Dominican Republic, those declining American cities have registered population gains rather than losses.

- Cities that have highly educated residents—such as Madison, Wisconsin, and Columbus, Ohio, both university towns—have gained in population. By contrast, cities with large numbers of poor people, such as St. Louis, have suffered losses in population.

- Most state capitals have grown, even though the states themselves have stagnated. North Dakota's population, for example, has shrunk a little, but the population of its capital, Bismarck, has grown.
- For the first time in U.S. history, nearly half of the 100 largest cities have more African Americans, Hispanics, Asians, and other minorities than whites. Of the total population of the 100 largest cities, the minorities outnumber the whites, thanks to increased immigration, higher birth rates among the foreign born, and white flight from the cities.

■ Urban Problems

Virtually all problems in the larger society—such as crime, drug abuse, racism, poverty, poor education, and environmental pollution—are more severe if they take place in the cities. This is because the cities have their own problems that make it difficult to deal with those societal problems. Here we will look at the more important problems confronting the cities.

Population Decline

Over the last 10 years, large cities such as Detroit, Buffalo, Pittsburgh, and St. Louis have lost population. On the surface, this decreasing population may look like good news for the cities. Fewer people should mean less demand for, and less spending on, police protection, fire protection, education, and other public services. In reality, however, population decreases have created serious problems.

As the years go by, a city must spend more to maintain its road, sewer, and water networks because they get old and their maintenance costs increase. Similarly, when families abandon the central city, the need for police and fire protection increases because abandoned homes can become magnets for vandalism and crime. They become fire hazards and finally must be torn down at the city's expense. Moreover, behind the statistics of declining populations lies the fact that those who move out of the cities are largely middle-class people, and with them go many businesses. Thus, the cities have fewer private-sector jobs and suffer declining revenues. Those who are left behind in the city are typically less educated, poorer, and older—the people most in need of government spending for education, housing, health services, and welfare (Wessel, 2004).

The revenues for solving urban problems have shrunk because the suburbs have drained off much of the city's tax base by attracting industries and stores, as well as middle- and upper-class people.

Fiscal Problems

Urban problems stem largely from the inability of city governments to generate sufficient income to provide various kinds of services to the public. Cities get most of their revenues from taxes on property, income, sales, and corporations. Some money comes from charging fees for services. All these sources of revenue have shrunk over the last decade, largely because the suburbs have drained off much of the cities' tax base by attracting industries and stores, as well as middle- and upper-class people.

There are other potential sources of revenue, but cities generally cannot tap them. In many states, cities are prohibited from raising as much in taxes as they wish. Cities are also deprived of other revenue-producing opportunities. When federal and state governments use city property, they are exempted from paying city taxes totaling billions of dollars. Suburbanites come into town, adding to traffic congestion, garbage, and wear and tear on roads and parks, while benefiting from police protection and other urban resources. But they pay no taxes to the city for these services.

Consequently, cities have increasingly depended on the state governments to help pay their bills. However, in recent years the economic downturn has shrunk the state aid and local tax revenues, while the cost of running the city government, such as the payment for employee wages and public safety, has increased. These fiscal woes hit most of the cities, making them less able than before to meet their financial needs (Smith, 2004).

Political Dilemma

Much of the cities' fiscal problem originates from elected officials' unwillingness to raise taxes even if they have the power to do so and their citizens have the ability to pay. Given the unpopularity of tax increases, politicians tend to avoid risking taxpayers' anger, even when taxes are low and an increase is necessary. Consequently, they resolve this political dilemma by having the cities rely on private enterprise to tackle urban problems. With their eyes on economic development, cities compete with one another to keep or attract businesses and industries. Low taxes and tax exemptions are used as lures. Although this strategy may undermine the current tax base, the cities hope to build a larger tax base, through an increase in jobs.

Some cities set up **empowerment zones** (also known as *enterprise zones*), economically depressed urban areas that businesses, with the help of government grants, low-interest loans, and tax breaks, try to revive by creating jobs. In these special zones, thousands of jobs have been created for poor residents. A similar effort to solve public ills with private cures has appeared in another way. Grass-roots entrepreneurs known as *community development corporations* have rehabilitated abandoned homes, creating commercial enterprises and organizing social services in various large cities. Their objective is to succeed where governments have failed—by reclaiming city streets from crime and economic decline (Healy, 2005).

Empowerment zones
Economically depressed urban areas that businesses, with the help of government grants, low-interest loans, and tax breaks, try to revive by creating jobs.

Housing Segregation

Billions of dollars are spent every year on housing in the United States. This money comes from the government offering tax deductions to landlords and homeowners. As a result, Americans are among the best-housed people in the world, with most families owning their own homes. But it is difficult financially for minorities to own or rent a home. For one thing, minorities, especially African Americans, make up a high percentage of the population of the inner cities, where good housing at reasonable prices is scarce. While most African Americans living in metropolitan areas are concentrated in the inner cities, most of the metropolitan whites are spread out in the surrounding suburbs. In both the inner cities and the suburbs, African Americans are frequently segregated from whites and relegated to inferior housing.

Economics is apparently a factor in housing segregation. Because African Americans tend to have lower incomes, they often cannot afford to move into more expensive white neighborhoods. But racial discrimination is an even bigger factor. Real estate agents

Real estate agents tend to steer potential African American buyers and renters away from white neighborhoods. This helps to perpetuate residential segregation between the races.

tend to steer potential African American buyers and renters away from white neighborhoods, perpetuating segregation, although this is an illegal practice. Banks are often more cautious in granting loans to African Americans than to whites, making it difficult for them to own or rehabilitate homes and thus encouraging the deterioration of African American neighborhoods. Many African Americans will not move into white neighborhoods because they want to avoid rejection by whites (Krysan and Farley, 2002).

■ Sociological Theories of Urbanization

Both the functionalist and conflict theories can be used to explain what causes urbanization. The theories can also be used to explain urban problems, because urban problems are intricately linked to urbanization; without urbanization, urban problems would not have existed. Thus, what causes urbanization can be said to cause urban problems. What, then, causes urbanization? To functionalists, urbanization stems from masses of people seeking better lives and opportunities in the cities. To conflict theorists, urbanization originates from big business pursuing profit by causing farm populations to leave for the cities where they become workers and consumers for big business. Symbolic interactionists are more interested in how people interact with one another in the city.

Functionalist Theory

According to the functionalists, the masses of ordinary people are the primary driving force behind urbanization. Let us take a closer look at how the masses spur urbanization.

First, technology increases agricultural production so much that considerably fewer people are needed to work on farms. So, seeking better job opportunities, throngs of people leave the farms for the cities, which leads to explosive urban growth. Since these former farmers are mostly manual laborers, their influx to the cities helps to expand the manufacturing industry, allowing the mass production of everything from shoes to clothes to cars and computers. Next, as cities become crowded, increasing numbers of people move to the outskirts to live. They can continue to work in the inner cities, however, thanks to the mass production of cars. Then, as the suburbs become increasingly populated, various businesses emerge to cater to the shopping needs of suburbanites, eventually leading to the proliferation of shopping malls. Finally, a cornucopia of jobs is created in the suburbs, and suburbanites do not need to commute to the central cities to work. At this late stage of urbanization, metropolises and megalopolises begin to emerge. Functionalists assume that all these social changes brought about by urbanization and suburbanization reflect what the masses need and seek to have a comfortable life (Rybczynski, 1995).

Conflict Theory

To conflict theorists, big business plays a key role in the growth and expansion of cities.

First, in pursuing profit, large corporations have bought up huge tracts of farmland and produced an enormous amount of food, driving many small family farms into bankruptcy and forcing huge numbers of farmers to leave for the city. In doing so, big business received considerable assistance from big government as a partner of the ruling elite. The assistance included direct subsidies to businesses, grants for research and development, low-interest loans, and support of farm-related education.

Second, big business has made a killing in the real estate, construction, and banking industries, enabling cities to expand into suburbs. Again, with considerable government subsidies and tax deductions, numerous single-family homes were built in the suburbs in the 1950s and 1960s. To induce people to buy these houses, the government guaranteed mortgages and provided tax deductions for interest payments. The result was massive suburbanization.

Third, from the 1970s to today, large corporations have helped turn many suburbs into edge cities by moving their businesses and factories there from central cities. This move has been motivated by profit. By building new plants in the suburbs, corporations have intended to avoid problems in central cities such as labor unrest, high city taxes, and other financial costs. Otherwise, corporations have expected to receive such benefits from the suburbs as cheap land, lower taxes, a local industry-friendly government, and the lack of organized labor (Gottdiener, 1985, 1994).

Symbolic Interaction Theory

We can learn much from symbolic interactionists about how strangers interact in cities.

First, city people tend to interact with one another in a superficial, impersonal way. Given the density of the urban population and hence the huge number of potential interpersonal contacts, urbanites have learned to protect themselves from *psychic overload* by shutting out as many sensations as possible, maybe even the call of a neighbor for help. Thus, most interactions with strangers are brief. An example is one person asking another person on the street for directions and the second person responding by pointing at a street and saying "over there."

Second, city people tend to interact through *civil inattention* as a way of respecting others' desire for privacy in public places. This involves avoiding eye or physical contact in an elevator, a bus, or some other public place. Conversations with strangers do occur but often under unusual circumstances, as when people are stuck in a stalled elevator or a traffic jam.

Third, city people tend to tolerate others' lifestyles, such as different sexual orientations and religious practices. When such people interact, they usually refrain from imposing their values on others or showing disapproval of others' behavior.

For a quick review of the three sociological theories on urbanization, see **Box 15.2**.

■ Population Problems

Demography is the scientific study of population. It is based on a large body of reasonably accurate data, more so than any other area of sociology. From these data we can track the problems of population change and their consequences.

Demography
The scientific study of population.

BOX 15.2 THEORETICAL THUMBNAIL

Explaining Urbanization

Theory	Focus	Insights
Functionalist Theory	How the masses trigger urbanization	The masses leave farms to seek better lives in cities and suburbs.
Conflict Theory	How big business fuels urbanization	Large corporations profit by causing farmers to leave for cities.
Symbolic Interaction Theory	How city people interact	City people interact with civil inattention and tolerance for others' lifestyles.

QUESTIONS TO EXPLORE

1. How do people in modern U.S. cities protect themselves from "psychic overload?" Explain your response.

2. According to symbolic interaction theory, increased urbanization ushers in a notable decrease of direct, face-to-face, intimate exchanges with strangers. From your own observations, do you see more or less direct, fact-to-face communication among strangers within your community? Take your college environment, for example. Please be specific.

3. Visit the Sierra Club Web site at http://www.sierraclub.org and determine which theory best fits their agenda. What evidence supports your conclusion?

Population Growth

Demographers have long known that the world's population is increasing enormously. Nearly 100 million new babies are born every year, which equals the entire size of Mexico's population. Moreover, given the same yearly growth rate, population does not increase *linearly*, with the same number of people added annually. Instead, it grows *exponentially*, with an increasingly larger number of new people appearing in each succeeding year. It works like a savings account, which earns an increasingly larger amount of interest, rather than the same interest, in each succeeding year because it builds on a large base (the previous year's savings *plus* that year's interest) each year.

Increases in population are therefore far more dramatic in modern times, with large populations, than in ancient times, with small populations. Before the year 1600, it took more than 500,000 years for the human population to reach about half a billion. Today, it takes only 5 or 6 years for the world to produce half a billion people. Figure 15.2 shows the remarkable rate of population growth in the modern era.

In general, populations are growing much faster in poor, developing countries than in rich, developed ones. Rich nations generally have an annual growth rate of less than 1%, but poor nations typically grow at a rate of more than 2%. The growth of a nation's population is determined by the number of births minus the number of deaths plus the *net immigration rate*—the excess of people moving into a country (*immigrants*) compared to those leaving it (*emigrants*).

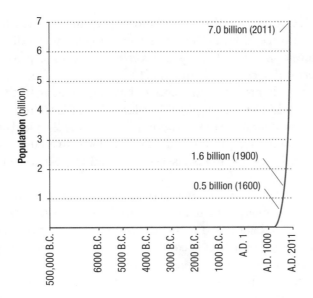

FIGURE 15.2 Human Population Growth Patterns

The world has experienced exponential population growth in recent history. At this point in human existence, the global population increases by another billion about every 12 years. However, before the modern era began in 1600, it had taken more than 500,000 years for the global population to reach only half a billion. But since 1600 it took only about 400 years for the population to explode to 7 billion today.

Critical Thinking: *Why does it only take a little over a decade now for the global population to grow remarkably larger than it did during the first several thousand years of human existence?*

Source: Population Reference Bureau, 2009.

Malthusian Warning

In 1798, English clergyman and economist Thomas Malthus (1766–1834) published a truly dismal portrait of population dynamics in *An Essay on the Principles of Population*. He warned that population grows much faster than the production of food supplies because a population *multiplies* but food production increases only by addition—through the cultivation of land. Thus, population typically increases geometrically (2, 4, 8, 16, . . .), but food supplies increase only arithmetically (2, 3, 4, 5, . . .). As a population outstrips its food supply, its growth will eventually be stopped by war, disease, and poverty.

People could stop this growth through what Malthus called "preventive checks"— that is, late marriage and sexual restraint, which would reduce the birth rate. But Malthus doubted that people, especially the lower classes, had the will to exercise

Great population growth can be stopped with lower birth rates through late marriage and sexual restraint, but in many poor, developing countries people lack the will to exercise such restraint.

such restraint. Instead, he warned, population growth would eventually be stopped by nature. Its tools would be what Malthus called "positive checks"—disease and famine.

Malthus failed to foresee three revolutions that undermined his warning: the revolutions in contraception, agricultural technology, and medicine. He did not anticipate the development of effective and convenient contraceptives such as the pill and the intrauterine device, nor did he expect birth control to become widespread. In the West, especially, the use of contraceptives has helped bring birth rates down to a point lower than Malthus thought possible. Meanwhile, the technological revolution has allowed farmers to increase food production by raising the yield of their land, not just by adding farmland. Finally, medical advances have given us an arsenal of effective weapons against the contagious diseases that Malthus expected would devastate overpopulated nations.

As result, disease and famine have failed to decimate the world's population, including most of the overpopulated nations in Asia, Latin America, and Africa. It can thus be concluded that the awful fate Malthus predicted has not come to pass for most of the world. His prediction is coming true only for some countries in Africa, where famine is common and acquired immune deficiency syndrome is killing over one-third of the population. Moreover, Malthus's theory serves as a valuable warning to all nations that populations cannot expand indefinitely; natural resources are finite.

Demographic Transition

Demographic transition
The movement of human populations through four demographic stages that are tied to economic development.

Most sociologists subscribe to the **demographic transition** theory, which states that human populations tend to go through four demographic stages that are tied to economic development, as shown in **Figure 15.3**.

In the first stage, both birth rates and death rates are high. Because the two rates more or less balance each other, the population is fairly stable, neither growing nor declining rapidly. This was the stage of the populations in Western Europe in 1650, before industrialization.

During the second stage, the birth rate remains high but the death rate declines sharply. This stage occurred in Western Europe after it became industrialized, and it is

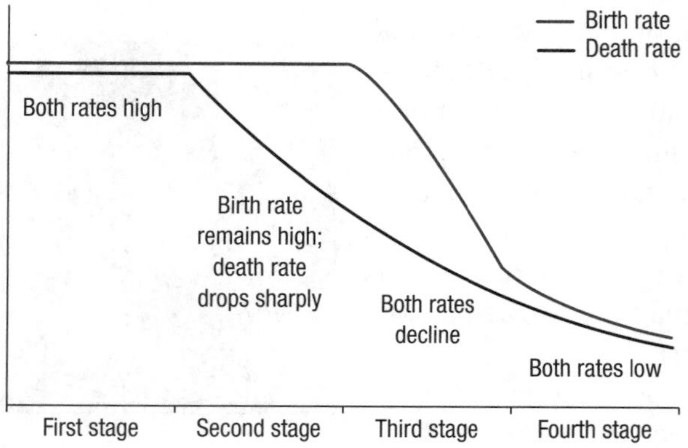

FIGURE 15.3 The Demographic Transition

According to demographic transition theory, human populations go through four stages. Each stage is tied to a specific social condition. In the fourth stage, for example, the birth and death rates are low. This is typical of today's highly industrialized societies, such as Germany and other European countries.

Critical Thinking: *The German population has continued to shrink because of its falling birth rate. Do you anticipate a similar fate for the United States? Why or why not?*

occurring today in many developing nations. The introduction of modern medicine, along with better hygiene and sanitation, has decreased the death rates in developing countries. However, because the economies and values of these countries are still essentially traditional, their birth rates remain high. As a result, their populations grow rapidly.

During the third stage, both birth rates and death rates decline. Western countries found themselves in this stage after they reached a rather high level of industrialization. Today, Taiwan, South Korea, and Argentina are among the developing nations that have reached this stage. The birth rates in these countries have declined significantly. In this stage, the population still grows because the birth rate continues to exceed the death rate, but growth is slower than during the second stage.

The fourth stage is marked by a low birth rate and a low death rate. Only the most industrialized nations of Western Europe, the United States, and Japan have reached this stage. They have fairly stable populations and are moving close to zero population growth. At least 40 countries, such as Italy, Spain, and Germany, have already fallen below zero growth, with birth rates lower than death rates. In other words, the fertility rate is less than the replacement level.

To proponents of the demographic transition theory, the future of human populations looks bright. They believe that developing countries will eventually join the industrialized world with a stable population. To critics of this theory, the future is far less certain. There is at least one major difference between the developing countries of today and European nations of 200 years ago. Thanks to modern medicine, death rates in developing countries have declined far more rapidly than they did in 19th-century Europe. While it took Europe 200 years to lower its mortality, it takes developing countries today only a year or so. That's why the population in the developing world today is exploding, a condition that could not possibly have occurred in 19th-century Europe.

Demographic Fallout

The population explosion has thrown many developing nations into oppressive poverty. Their cities are filled with people who live in overcrowded shacks and in such locations as the streets, sidewalks, vacant lots, rooftops, and cemeteries. In these poor countries, most people are undernourished, and malnutrition is devastating 163 million children younger than 5 years of age, weakening their bodies and minds. Some 15 million children die of starvation every year (United Nations, 2010).

The rapid population growth of developing nations seriously complicates their efforts to fight poverty. Instead of climbing up the economic ladder, these nations get stuck on a treadmill, constantly in danger of slipping backward into Malthusian famine. Economic investment can barely keep up with the rapid population growth. More than half of Africa's economic expansion, for example, has been used just to maintain the expanding population at a subsistence level. More than 40% of Africa's population is already living below the region's poverty line. Some African countries, such as Ethiopia, Somalia, and the Sudan, have experienced and will continue to face massive starvation (cozay.com, 2010).

■ Curbing Population Growth

Individuals have practiced birth control of various kinds for thousands of years, but many nations have sought to *increase* their populations because they believed that a large population brings great military power and national security. Moreover, religious, medical, and political authorities have often argued against birth control. Even the United States has passed laws to prohibit the mailing of contraceptive information and devices.

However, during the 1950s and 1960s, the United States along with many other countries began to see population growth as a social problem. By 1984, most countries, representing 95% of the world's population, had formulated official policies to curb population growth. These policies can be classified into two types: voluntary family planning and compulsory population control.

Voluntary Family Planning

Many countries make contraceptives available to anyone who wants them. They encourage the use of birth control, but they do not impose a limit on how many children a couple may have. For this voluntary family planning to work, however, people must prefer small families to large ones. Otherwise, they will not use birth control.

This may explain why many poor countries, such as those in sub-Saharan Africa, fail to use birth control. They still prefer large families, typical of agricultural societies. In these societies, having many children is a status enhancer, particularly for the less educated. Children are also considered a form of old-age pension because there is no social security like the one available to retirees in the United States. Because many children die young, parents are even more anxious to have large families to increase their chances of being looked after in their senior years. By contrast, people in more prosperous countries in the West are more likely to use birth control because they value small families.

Compulsory Population Control

In the early 1970s, India forced government employees who had more than two children to undergo sterilization. Some states in India also forced men to be sterilized after their second child was born. This program stirred up widespread opposition. Since then, India has returned to a voluntary program, but it has been difficult to control the relentless population growth because of low literacy and a dearth of sustained family-planning information and services. Thus, in 2001, the government began to encourage sterilization, but this time resorting to incentives rather than coercion. Poor people who are sterilized can now expect to get such benefits as houses, plots of land, wells, and loans. As a result, India's fertility rate has decreased from five children per woman in the 1980s to just three today (Naik et al., 2003).

China has had more success with its policy of encouraging parents to have only one child. The policy is carried out with a combination of rewards and punishments. For a couple with only one child, the rewards are substantial. The parents get a salary bonus, and the child receives free schooling, priority in medical care, admission to the best schools and universities, and preference in employment. By contrast, multichild parents are severely penalized. They have to pay higher income taxes and are often denied job promotion. Since this one-child family campaign started in 1979, China has sharply reduced its fertility, from six children per woman to only two today, a record unmatched by any other developing country (Chang, 2001; Rosenberg, 2010).

U.S. Population Policy

In the 1960s, the U.S. government began to recognize global population growth as a potential problem. By 1968, it had spent several hundred million dollars to help developing nations with their family-planning programs. During the conservative Reagan and Bush administrations in the 1980s and early 1990s, however, the U.S. government suspended aid to countries that advocated abortion as a family-planning operation. The more liberal Clinton administration restored the aid. Then the second conservative Bush administration refused to support family-planning programs that included the use of abortion. Now, the current Obama administration supports those programs.

BIRTH CONTROL. The federal government has been spending over $100 million a year to assist family-planning centers throughout the United States. However, the U.S. population growth has slowed not because of government action but because of social and economic factors, such as a widespread desire for small families and a high level of prosperity. Indeed, family planning has become very popular. Even the majority of U.S. Catholics use the pill and other birth-control methods forbidden by their church. Among the general population, sterilization is the most commonly used method of birth control, followed by the pill and the condom.

IMMIGRATION. Today, both legal and illegal immigration account for about 26% of the nation's population growth. That proportion is expected to rise to 50% in the first half of the 21st century, and then immigration will comprise the bulk of the nation's population growth in the second half of that century (U.S. Census Bureau, 2010). Knowing that immigration can contribute to the prosperity of this country, U.S. Congress has passed a law to admit larger numbers of highly educated and skilled immigrants, such as scientists, engineers, and medical technicians, as Canada and Australia have done for years.

However, opposition to the admission of poor and unskilled immigrants, especially illegals, has sharply increased today. California has denied illegal immigrants most government services, and the U.S. government has stopped providing legal immigrants with most federal benefits, such as food stamps and cash assistance for the poor and disabled. U.S. Congress has passed a law to prevent illegal aliens from getting state driver's licenses. Throughout the United States, there is rampant fear that immigrants take jobs from U.S. workers, particularly low-skilled workers. But supporters of immigration suspect that the anti-immigration sentiment is mere racism because most of the immigrants come from nonwhite countries rather than Europe (Samuelson, 2005). For more information on the impact of immigration, see Box 15.3.

■ Environmental Problems

The environment can be damaged in two ways: depleting the natural resources and polluting the environment. There are, however, ways of saving the environment.

Diminishing Resources

Although we Americans make up only about 4% of the world's population, we consume about 30% of the world's energy and raw materials each year. If this high level of

---

BOX 15.3   WHAT RESEARCH REVEALS

The Impact of Immigration

The stereotype of the hard-working immigrant turns out to be true. One bit of evidence is that immigrants are more likely to be employed and less likely to be unemployed when compared with native-born Americans. Male immigrants' employment rate is 81%, exceeding U.S.-born men's rate of 72%. Illegal immigrants' rate is even higher, around 94%. As for unemployment, the average rate for foreign-born workers is 4.6%, below the 5.2% for U.S.-born workers. Moreover, immigrants have contributed more than half of the U.S. labor force growth in the past decade, thanks to a high influx of immigrants and their desire to work (Orrenius, 2006).

But don't immigrants take jobs away from native-born workers as well as reduce their wages? The answer is no. Immigrants are more likely to compete with each other than with native-born workers. Immigrants typically lack the language skills, educational background, and institutional know-how to compete with U.S. workers. Immigrants also are likely to work in different occupations and industries, with many more employed in such backbreaking occupations as farming, fishing, and forestry than are native workers. Finally, due largely to their high productivity and low wages, immigrants benefit consumers by keeping prices down (Freeman, 2007).

What about the higher-paid and skilled immigrants such as scientists, engineers, doctors, nurses, and other professionals? Don't they threaten the jobs of native-born employees? The answer is no, because immigrant workers are needed to make up for a shortage of native professionals. When high-technology industries grew in the 1990s, for example, the need for highly skilled immigrants was so great that many firms had to lobby the government for increased worker visas to attract immigrant employees. Many companies still do today because of the continuing shortage of American professionals (Freeman, 2007).

---

consumption continues, the world will soon run out of resources. According to most environmentalists, the world's reserves of lead, silver, tungsten, mercury, and other precious resources will probably be depleted within 40 years. Even if new discoveries increase oil reserves fivefold, the global supply of oil will last for only 50 years. Developing countries fear that by the time they become fully industrialized, the resources they hope to enjoy will be gone. In short, we are fast running out of natural resources (Myerson, 1998; Wald, 1990).

However, a few environmentalists disagree. They argue that the future is likely to be better because our power to manage the environment has been increasing throughout human history. If nonrenewable resources such as minerals, metals, coal, and oil are used up, substitutes will be found through technology. Solar energy can be captured to replace coal and oil. We can also find substitutes for metals, such as plastics and aluminum for tin cans, and we can use satellites and fiberoptic lines instead of copper telephone wires. In fact, energy and other natural resources are more abundant today than they were in the past (Lomborg, 2001; Simon, 1990).

Environmental Pollution

To consume more, we must produce more and thereby create more waste. The by-products of our consumption must go somewhere. Nature has many cycles for transforming waste to be used in some other form, but we are overtaxing nature's recycling capacity. We put too much waste, such as automobile emissions, in one place at the same time, and we have created new toxic substances, such as dioxin, that cannot be recycled safely. The result is environmental pollution.

There are many kinds of pollution. The most common is *air pollution*. Throughout the world, power-generating plants, oil refineries, chemical plants, steel mills, and the like spew about 140 million tons of pollutants into the air every year. The heaviest polluter is the automobile, which accounts for at least 80% of air pollution. The pollutants irritate our eyes, noses, and throats; damage buildings; lower the productivity of the soil; and may cause serious illnesses, such as bronchitis, emphysema, and lung cancer. Air pollution is especially bad in Eastern Europe. As many as 10% of the deaths in Hungary are attributed directly to air pollution; the problem is even worse in parts of former Czechoslovakia, Poland, and the former East Germany (Jacobson, 2002; Nelson, 1990).

Throughout the world, the constant burning of coal, oil, and wood releases more and more industrial gases (such as carbon dioxide) into the atmosphere; the gases, in turn, trap an increasing amount of heat from the sun. This has significantly raised temperatures around the world, with the result that the 1990s was the hottest decade on record. This *global warming* has caused glaciers to melt, oceans to rise, floods and hurricanes to multiply, people to die from heat shock, and crops to wither. Moreover, some of the industrial gases used in refrigeration and air conditioning have already weakened the ozone layer in many areas of the globe. These weakened areas allow in more of the sun's ultraviolet light, which may cause skin cancer, harm the human immune system, and damage some crops and wild plants (Lemonick, 2001). Many Americans, however, doubt that global warming is for real (see **Box 15.4**).

Another kind of air pollution, called *acid rain*, has also aroused concern. When sulfur and nitrogen compounds are emitted by factories and automobiles, chemical reactions in the atmosphere may convert them to acidic compounds that can be carried hundreds of miles and then fall to the earth in rain and snow. Rain as acidic as vinegar has been recorded. This acid rain can kill fish and aquatic vegetation. It damages forests, crops, and soils. It corrodes buildings, water pipes, and tanks because it can erode limestone, marble, and even metal surfaces. Because of acid rain, thousands of lakes and rivers in North America and Europe are now dead, unable to support fish and plant life. Even worse is the acid rain in Russia's Siberia, which has ruined more than 1,500 square miles of timber, an area half as large as Rhode Island (Jacobson, 2002; Turco, 2002).

Saving the Environment

Various efforts have been made to bring environmental problems under control in the United States (Lemonick, 2001; Pianin, 2003).

First, many antipollution laws have been passed. The enforcement of these laws has significantly improved air quality throughout the United States.

Second, the federal and state governments have encouraged the conservation of energy and raw materials. This includes insulating homes, driving smaller cars at slower speeds, riding buses and trains, separating trash for recycling, and giving up plastic containers.

BOX 15.4 DIVERGENT VIEWS

Is Global Warming for Real?

For years, many scientists have concluded that global warming is for real, largely caused by the burning of gasoline and other fossil fuels. In 2006, 600 scientists from various organizations including governments, academia, environmental groups, and business firms in 40 countries issued a report to support that conclusion. In 2007, the United Nations' Intergovernmental Panel on Climate Change reported that, according to the research of nearly 1,000 scientists from 74 countries, global warming was already affecting the Earth and would lead to more severe and widespread drought and greater coastal and riverine flooding. On top of those two widely disseminated reports, in the summer of 2007, Texas was hit by exactly the kind of massive downpours and flooding the scientists had expected. In the same summer, Las Vegas and other cities broiled in record triple-digit temperatures (Begley, 2007a; Romm, 2010).

Despite such arguments from the scientific community, many Americans doubt that global warming really exists. They believe that if the Earth is getting hotter it is because the sun is putting out more energy, not because humans are burning up more fuel. In a 2006 poll, only 33% of Americans believed that global warming was "mainly caused by things people do." In a 2007 poll, only 38% identified climate change as the nation's gravest environmental threat. Similarly, in another poll in the same year, less than half were in favor of requiring high-mileage cars or energy-efficient appliances and buildings, which could reduce global warming. Finally, in November 2009, a hacker broke into the e-mail servers of a major climate research institute in England and found that scientists there had manipulated data to fit their preconceived conclusions. The release of these e-mails made it harder to believe that global warming is real (Begley, 2007a; Inhofe, 2010).

Third, industrialists have sought to develop new, alternative technology that is efficient, safe, and clean. They have, for example, increased the fuel efficiency of cars, reduced pollution by equipping cars with catalytic converters, and introduced hybrid gas-electric cars to boost mileage and cut pollution.

And fourth, various nations have tried to limit population growth, because nearly every environmental problem—be it acid rain, global warming, or ozone depletion—is driven by growth in the world's population. People are thus encouraged to use birth control while abandoning the traditional value that favors having many children. In addition to all these collective efforts to save the environment, there are some simple ways for you as an individual to do your part (see **Box 15.5**).

BOX 15.5 USING SOCIOLOGICAL INSIGHTS

Easy Ways to Go Green

Environmental problems affect billions of people around the world. You may think they are so overwhelming that there is no way you as an individual can make the environment better. But there are many simple ways you can make a difference. Here are a few examples:

- *Ride the bus.* Transportation produces more than 30% of the U.S. carbon dioxide emissions that pollute the air. We can reduce the problem by taking a bus as often as possible. Public transit saves an estimated 1.4 million gallons of gas annually and eliminates about 1.5 million tons of carbon emissions (Walsh, 2007).

- *Pay bills online.* By doing our banking and paying our bills online, we do more than save trees. We also help reduce fuel consumption by the trucks and planes that carry the paperwork. If every U.S. home paid its bills online, the switch would eliminate greenhouse-gas emissions by 2.1 million tons per year (Buechner, 2007a).

- *Open a window.* Most of the carbon emissions for which each American is responsible come from the home. Those emissions will go down by nearly 10%, if you do the following: During the summer, open a window rather than running the air conditioner. Adjust the thermostat a few degrees higher in summer and lower in winter. Weather-strip all your doors and windows. Wash clothes in warm or cold water (rather than hot water). Turn down the thermostat on your water heater (Sayre, 2007b).

- *Refrain from using plastic bags.* Every year, more than 500 billion plastic bags are distributed, but less than 3% of them are recycled. They usually end up in a landfill where they can take up to 1,000 years to biodegrade. In the meantime, the process emits harmful greenhouse gases. You can reduce your contribution to this problem by using a paper bag or, better, reusing a cloth bag (Sayre, 2007a).

- *Support your local farmer.* Whenever possible, buy your fruit, vegetables, meat, and milk at farmers' markets, greengrocers, and food co-ops in your local area. This will reduce the "petroleum miles" or gas consumption from transporting these foods across country to your table (Buechner, 2007b).

- *Check your tires.* Even if you own an old gas-guzzling car, you still can save gas. Just giving your engine a tune-up can give you 4% or more mileage for your gas. Replacing a clogged air filter can raise efficiency 10%. Keeping your tires properly inflated can boost gas mileage more than 3%. All these measures add up, saving the environment from the assault of about 200 pounds of carbon dioxide emissions (Bjerklie, 2007).

- *Live simply.* Live a simple life. Meditate more. Consume less. Think more. Spend more time with others. Borrow when you need to and lend when asked (Masters, 2007).

Review

SUMMARY

1. Preindustrial cities first appeared 5,000 years ago. They were small, and people lived where they worked. Industrial cities emerging after the Industrial Revolution triggered the mass movement of people from farms to cities. The industrial cities spread outward during the 20th century, causing the cities to merge with their suburbs, forming metropolises and megalopolises. Today megacities appear around the world, most located in developing countries. In Japan, there are signs that the country is becoming a carless society. In the United States, many suburbs have changed from residential communities to edge cities, which resemble central cities. Over the last decade, cities have changed in many ways, such as the largest cities having more minorities than whites.

2. Urban problems include the following: When large cities suffer a population decline, it costs more to maintain streets, services, and public buildings. It is difficult for cities to be financially independent because they cannot get tax revenues from suburbanites and other nonresidents who use the city services. Elected officials find it hard to run their cities because they are reluctant to raise taxes for fear of antagonizing voters. Urban housing remains segregated in many cities because of lower minority income and racial discrimination.

3. What causes urbanization can be said to cause urban problems. To functionalists, urbanization originates from masses of rural people seeking a better life in cities. To conflict theorists, urbanization stems from big business seeking profits by causing farm populations to leave for the cities. Symbolic interactionists reveal how people in the city interact with one another.

4. Population grows much faster in poor than in rich counties. According to Malthus, human populations grow faster than food supplies but will eventually be stopped from growing by war, disease, and poverty. According to the theory of demographic transition, human populations go through four stages, which are tied to economic development. The fallout from population explosion is oppressive poverty in many developing countries.

5. Governments can control population growth by encouraging voluntary family planning and setting up compulsory population programs. The U.S. government gives some aid to family-planning centers, but social and economic factors, not government action, keep birth rates low. Immigration contributes to population growth but does not take away jobs from native-born Americans.

6. There are two environmental problems: the depletion of natural resources and environmental pollution. While there is considerable evidence to show that global warming is real, many people still don't believe it. Efforts have been made to save the environment, such as passing antipollution laws, conserving energy and raw materials, developing more efficient technology, and encouraging the use of birth control to limit population growth. Individuals can improve the environment by doing such simple things as riding buses and paying bills online.

CRITICAL THINKING QUESTIONS

1. How committed is your community to environmental issues? Which issues are getting the most attention and response? What is being done to address these key issues?

2. In a world with a large population, why is population decline in places like Germany a matter of such concern to demographers?

3. If Americans make up only a small percentage (4%) of the global population, why is the United States among nations of chief concern in the matter of diminishing resources?

INTERNET RESOURCES

Among other services, the U.S. Department of Housing and Urban Development (HUD) (http://portal.hud.gov/portal/page/portal/HUD) seeks to influence and regulate social policy in such a way as to decrease homelessness and increase neighborhood equality, stability, safety, fair lending and leasing practices, and awareness of alternatives to and solutions for foreclosures.

The U.S. Environmental Protection Agency (EPA) (http://www.epa.gov/) promotes awareness, education, and the proactive creation and enforcement of laws created to improve human health through the quality of the physical environment.

The Population Resource Center (PRC) (http://www.prcdc.org/) has a history of funding and promoting the accurate collecting and sharing of data as an effort to guide and improve social policy and science pertaining to population issues.

Founded by John Muir in 1892, the Sierra Club (http://www.sierraclub.org), a grassroots organization boasting over 1 million members, concerns itself with raising awareness, guiding research, and educating the general public with any environmental issue concerning community members from around the world.

War and Terrorism

Sgt. Jacob Blaylock, 26 years old, was taping himself on a video camera at a military base in Iraq. "Hey, it's Jackie," he said. "It's the 20th of April. We go home in six days. I lost two good friends on the 14th. I'm having a hard time dealing with it." The two friends that Blaylock mentioned were fellow soldiers killed by a roadside bomb. Blaylock was close to them and felt especially shaken by their deaths. Sometime earlier, feeling the strain of riding the gunner position in the exposed front truck, he had switched places with them, moving to a Humvee at the rear. So he blamed himself for their deaths. "It was supposed to be me," he would tell others later. When he returned to his hometown in the United States, he was still wracked with guilt and grief, compounded by other stresses such as financial troubles and constant quarrels with his estranged wife. Several months later, during an argument with his girlfriend, he shot himself to death (Goode, 2009).

Such suicides among soldiers have become more and more common, to the extent that there are now as many service members killed by themselves as there are killed by the enemy. In this chapter, we will analyze these military suicides and other effects of **war**—the violent conflict between two nations. We will also take a deeper look at the causes of war, along with the nature of terrorism and its consequences.

War
Violent conflict between two nations.

■ The Causes of War

War is the most destructive force in the world. Still, we humans have more often been at war than we have lived in **peace**—the absence of war. In only 292 of the last 5,600 years has peace reigned in the world (Farley, 1987). This means that for 95% of that long history war has taken place somewhere in the world. What, then, causes war?

Peace
The absence of war.

According to the highly influential theory of war expounded by the 19th-century military strategist Karl von Clausewitz, "War is simply the continuation of state policy by other means." This means that if the policy of a totalitarian nation such as the former Soviet Union is to exercise total control over its citizens' lives, that nation is likely to wage war against another nation that refuses to submit to its domination. But war is a complex phenomenon. It cannot be attributed to totalitarianism alone. After all, as a democratic society, the United States has started many wars. There are many reasons for the United States—and other nations—to initiate wars. Sociologist Quincy Wright (1967) has identified the following five reasons as the most common:

1. *Perceived threats.* If a nation sees a dangerous threat from another, it will likely start a war in an attempt to eliminate the threat. This is primarily the reason why the United States started the war against Iraq in 2003. The United States believed that the Iraqi president Saddam Hussein possessed weapons of mass destruction and might use them against it. This belief led the United States to invade Iraq.

2. *Moral objectives.* Wars are often started to achieve some moral objectives such as saving the world for democracy, advancing peace, and protecting human rights. Thus the United States went to war in Vietnam to protect the democratic South against the communists in the North.

3. *Political objectives.* Wars are often used as a means of attaining some political objectives, which include enhancing the stature of being a world leader, acquiring land and other wealth, and getting rid of foreign domination. This is why in 1990 Iraq invaded Kuwait. The Iraqi wanted to get the Kuwaiti oil, but the United States drove out the Iraqi to demonstrate its leadership in the world.

4. *Unifying the nation.* Every now and then the government seeks to use wars to divert people's attention from some problems and unify the nation against a foreign enemy. In 1983, the United States invaded the Caribbean island of Grenada in order to turn the attention of Americans away from the terrorist bombing that had killed all the Marines in Beirut. The Grenada invasion further whipped up patriotic frenzy that greatly unified the nation.

5. *No peaceful alternatives.* A nation is most likely to fight back if invaded by another, as the United States did after Japan bombed Pearl Harbor. Also, often war becomes the only choice when diplomacy fails to prevent hostilities by a foreign country. After the U.S. ambassador in Iraq failed to persuade the Iraqi president against invading Kuwait, the United States had no choice but to resort to war to end the Iraqi occupation.

We have just presented the causes of war in broad strokes. We may have missed some specific details of what causes a particular war. To illustrate these details, we will now take a closer look at why the United States wages war in Iraq.

◾ Why We Are Fighting the War in Iraq

In 2003 the U.S. government under the George W. Bush administration initially argued that it was necessary to start the war in Iraq for these reasons: the threat posed by Iraq's **weapons of mass destruction** (weapons that can kill thousands of people at the same time), the regime's aid to international terrorists, and the U.S. government's expectation that the overthrow of Saddam Hussein's dictatorial rule would spread democracy throughout the Middle East. The U.S. government gradually backed down from

Weapons of mass destruction Weapons that can kill thousands of people at the same time.

One reason for the United States to invade Iraq was the alliance between religious and business conservatives within the Republican Party, both of which strongly supported the war.

these arguments because they turned out to be false. However, the Americans apparently believed these reasons, which might explain why the United States invaded Iraq.

Another reason for invading Iraq was the alliance between religious and business conservatives within the Republican Party. The religious right provided the votes while corporate conservatives delivered the cash to help the Republicans win elections. Both supported the war. Why? The rank and file of the religious right was deeply patriotic, quick to rally on behalf of a militaristic foreign policy. The business conservatives believed that they could use the administration's enhanced global power to advance their economic interests (Block, 2007).

The strongest reason for starting the war was the attacks of September 11, 2001. This event enabled the Republicans to gain enormous support for the war, portraying themselves as tough on terrorists while attacking the Democrats for their lack of determination to fight U.S. enemies in Iraq.

The Bush administration had envisioned a short, victorious war followed by a quick departure of most U.S. troops. Instead, the war has dragged on for years, longer than U.S. participation in World War II. The prolongation of the war has resulted from a number of mistakes made by the administration (Block, 2007). The most important ones include the following:

- Right after Saddam Hussein's fall, the United States lacked sufficient firepower to stop the looting of government offices. The looting took the Pentagon by surprise. The resulting chaos made it extremely difficult to rebuild the Iraq state.

- The U.S. authority in Iraq banned all former members of the country's ruling party from holding government offices. It also dissolved the Iraqi army. As a result, thousands of these unemployed people joined the anti-U.S. insurgency.

- Mass imprisonment, abuse of prisoners, and other heavy-handed tactics by the U.S. military during the first year of the war caused ordinary Iraqis to lose confidence in the occupying forces.

These mistakes of the U.S. occupation have brought chaos to Iraq, with anti-American insurgency and sectarian violence erupting frequently. As a consequence, most Americans are now opposed to the war. Nonetheless, these Americans (who include both mainstream Republicans and Democrats) do not favor an immediate withdrawal of all U.S. troops from Iraq. They fear that such an immediate and complete withdrawal will trigger more sectarian slaughter. They are also afraid that there will be widespread anarchy involving various political groups and various factions in every group seeking to impose their own agendas. Thus, most Americans favor a phased, gradual withdrawal: pulling out U.S. troops in stages within a certain period of time but leaving behind enough soldiers to go after terrorists, protect the U.S. embassy, and continue training the Iraqi army to secure their country.

Both Republicans and Democrats basically agree with this strategy, wanting to get out of Iraq sooner or later. But Democrats insist on "sooner" while Republicans "later." In the meantime, both sides play to their supporters. Democrats try to give the impression that they are all for getting out of Iraq, while Republicans try to portray themselves as determined to win the war while accusing Democrats of pursuing a defeatist, cut-and-run policy (Calabresi, 2007).

■ The Ripple Effects of War

The direct effect of war is the loss of many human lives. The number of U.S. war deaths has become increasingly larger. There were about 2 million war deaths in the Civil War, 9 million in the First World War, and 52 million in the Second World War. But there are also the indirect, ripple effects of war. They hit many more people. Consider the number of the wounded Americans as compared to the number of the dead in today's wars in Iraq and Afghanistan. For every one soldier who dies in these wars, 16 are wounded, while the ratio of the wounded to the dead was 2 to 1 in World War II and 3 to 1 in the Vietnam and Korean Wars. Many more soldiers—and their loved ones—also experience other ripple effects of war, such as suicides, war trauma, emotional stress, broken homes, joblessness, and homelessness (Ephron et al., 2007). Here we will discuss these ripple effects of war, but first let's take a quick look at how the war in Afghanistan affects the Afghan people (see Box 16.1).

Military Suicides

There is an epidemic of suicides in the U.S. military. Suicides have resulted in the deaths of about as many soldiers as combat operations in Iraq and Afghanistan combined. The

---

BOX 16.1 GLOBAL PERSPECTIVE

The View from Afghanistan

Fighting the war in Afghanistan, U.S. commanders emphasize that the goal is to win over civilians, not kill insurgents. But civilians have *mixed feelings* about the Americans in their country. More than 30 Afghan residents were asked this simple question: How has America influenced your life? They provided a mixture of both positive and negative answers, such as the following (Mohammad, 2010):

- **Zakia, 23, beautician:** "My Afghan sisters were robbed of their beauty during the harsh years of the Taliban regime. Teenage girls were suppressed and forced to wear burqas that made them look like ghosts. I was trained at the Kabul Beauty School, which was built and run by Americans."
- **Abdul Ali, 51, salesman:** "Americans have brought corruption to my city. My neighbor started working with American aid workers four years ago. . . . Now he gives bribes to get what he wants, and I'm still struggling to earn enough to feed my family."
- **Mohammad Yunus, 29, policeman:** "As far as the U.S. is concerned, let them run the country—at least I'll get paid well. They pay their employees lucrative salaries."
- **Najeeb Ullah, 27, security guard at an upscale hotel:** "Americans have influenced my life in an ironic way. My job would be much easier if Americans [a likely target of the insurgents] weren't staying at the hotel I work for. They pay me well but . . . I live in constant fear of being killed in an attack or bomb blast."

rate of these military suicides is now higher than that of civilians. These suicides are often attributed to the stress of repeated combat deployments. But evidence suggests otherwise. The fact is that the majority of soldiers who have committed suicide—about 80%—have had only one deployment or none at all (McKinley, 2010). This may appear surprising but it should not be. This is because the soldiers with relatively little experience of combat have not adjusted to the stressful environment as well as their more experienced comrades. Other factors may further explain the unusually high suicide rate among the soldiers.

First, it is noteworthy that the majority of the suicides have occurred *after* the soldiers return home to the United States (Gomez, 2009). This finding suggests that family problems may have compounded the stress from going through the horrible experiences of warfare. The family problems may have taken root while the soldiers were still in Iraq or Afghanistan. This is likely to occur because of the easy access to satellite phones and computers that allow troops to keep in touch with their loved ones but also get immersed in family problems while still at war.

Second, many soldiers who commit suicide are reluctant to seek professional help for their emotional problems because of the stigma attached to doing so. They have learned from the warrior culture that it is a sign of weakness for soldiers to seek help for emotional problems, although it should be as natural as seeking help for a sprained ankle (McKinley, 2010). Still, some behavioral scientists support the warrior culture for encouraging men to be masculine and tough (see **Box 16.2**).

Third, soldiers who are likely to commit suicide often keep their horrific experiences of war to themselves. An Army staff sergeant, for example, rarely spoke about the roadside bomb that hit his convoy in Iraq. He didn't share it with a chaplain, a counselor, or even his wife. Although he received the combat action badge for the bombing, he still barely spoke of it to his wife. Some other soldiers would not tell anybody even though they have gone through something as horrific as seeing a fellow

Warrior culture theory
The view that it is important for boys to grow up to be masculine and tough like a warrior.

Wounded-boy theory
The idea that boys are traumatized by the pressure of the warrior culture to separate from their mothers and hide their tender feelings.

BOX 16.2   DIVERGENT VIEWS

Should Boys Learn to be Tough?

Some behavioral scientists say yes, while others say no. Those who hold the positive view are said to embrace the warrior culture theory, and those who hold the negative view are said to espouse the wounded-boy theory. According to the **warrior culture theory**, it is important for boys to grow up to be masculine and tough like a warrior, especially now that Americans are faced with the threat of terrorism. As a behavioral scientist who supports this view says, "Recent events suggest we need to honor stoical, competitive, risk-taking males if we intend to survive." She further says, "The good news is that boys are not cooperating with the well-meaning politically correct efforts to liberate them from their masculinity." They still want to hang on to their G.I. Joe and other military toys, from which they learn to be masculine and tough (Tierney, 2001).

Those behavioral scientists who support the **wounded-boy theory** contend that boys are traumatized by the pressure of the warrior culture to separate from their mothers and hide their tender feelings. Moreover, the advocates of the wounded-boy theory argue that masculinity has proved worthless to men because it turns them into violent, insensitive, and patriarchal males (Tierney, 2001).

soldier cut in half by a bomb or seeing "his truck commander's head blown off and his severed head hit my head and knocked me out" (Gomez, 2009).

And fourth, there is some connection between the increased use of prescription drugs, mostly antidepressants, and the rising suicide rates in the Army. Nearly 40% of Army suicide victims in 2006 and 2007 had taken psychotropic drugs—overwhelmingly antidepressants like Prozac and Zoloft (Thompson, 2008).

Researchers have also found many other factors associated with military suicides, including relationship problems, financial pressures, and drug or alcohol abuse (Goode, 2009).

War Trauma in Female Soldiers

There are far fewer women than men in the U.S. military. In Iraq only 1 out of every 10 American soldiers is female. However, female soldiers are considerably more likely than their male peers to suffer the trauma of war that causes them to develop a mental problem called post-traumatic stress disorder (**PTSD**). In some studies, the percentage of female soldiers with PTSD is twice as high as men. The symptoms of PTSD include being anxious, depressed, irritable, and insomniac, and having nightmares (Corbett, 2007).

PTSD
Post-traumatic stress disorder is an anxiety disorder that results from exposure to any kind of terrifying event in which the threat of physical harm and death appears imminent.

There are two types of war trauma in military women. One springs from *combat exposure*. Women are traditionally supposed to support male soldiers in combat rather than get directly involved in combat themselves by killing the enemy. But, to all intents and purposes, the distinction between support and combat has blurred in Iraq.

The women in support are just as exposed as the men in combat to violence from roadside bombs and blind ambushes. "Frankly, one of the most dangerous things you can do in Iraq is drive a truck, and that's considered a support role," says Matthew Friedman, executive director of the National Center for PTSD. "You've got women that are in harm's way right up there with the men" (Corbett, 2007).

Another type of war trauma suffered by female soldiers comes from *sexual assault* by their male comrades in the military. This is worse than the trauma that originates from combat exposure, because research has found that women who endure sexual assault are more likely to develop PTSD than those who are exposed to combat. Being sexually assaulted by a fellow soldier is especially traumatic because it breaches the sacred code of military cohesion. As one woman says, "It's very disconcerting to have somebody who is supposed to save your life, to watch your back, turn on you and do something like that" (Corbett, 2007). Unfortunately, sexual assault against military women is relatively common: Nearly one-third of female veterans seeking health care through the Department of Veterans Affairs have experienced rape or attempted rape during their service. Why so common? Perhaps because the military has a macho culture, which encourages men to prove their manhood by sexually dominating women.

Veterans with PTSD

PTSD is a mental illness. Its symptoms include the abuse of alcohol and other drugs, an emotional numbness, outbursts of rage, severe depression, and recurring nightmares. In extreme cases, it can lead to suicide or homicide. The incidence of PTSD has been rising as the Iraq and Afghanistan wars drag on. Today, about 20% of military service members on combat tours return home with symptoms of PTSD. Nearly half

The wars in Iraq and Afghanistan have caused many U.S. soldiers to suffer from PTSD. Once, after coming home, a victim insisted on sleeping with a gun under his pillow. On another night, a nightmare caused him to wrap his fingers around his wife's neck until her face turned blue.

of these stricken veterans do not get treatment because of the stigma associated with mental disorders (McGirk, 2009).

Mark Waddell, a Navy commander, used to be one of them. Several years ago his wife and three children noticed that ordinary things like a whining vacuum cleaner could trigger his rage. Once, after coming home from a combat mission, he insisted on sleeping with a gun under his pillow. On another night, he had a nightmare that caused him to wrap his fingers around his wife's neck until her face turned blue. Every morning she had to change the sheets because of his night sweats.

Luckily for him, Waddell has received treatment that involved using drugs and psychological therapy to calm the storm of his wartime memories as well as his emotional reactions to them. He has also often spoken to church and community groups about his experience with PTSD, which helps him to keep its symptoms under control. Many studies show that veterans stricken with PTSD tend to bounce back to normal if they have a strong social network of family and friends. If stricken veterans do not have such a network, they still can recover from the illness by getting support from various groups of their community. These groups may include members of the clergy keeping an eye out for them, neighbors helping with babysitting to help them get reacquainted with their spouse after a long tour of duty, and healthy veterans helping them in any way they can (McGirk, 2009). For a systematic way to deal with PTSD, see **Box 16.3**. Some veterans with PTSD do complain, however, that what they get from the government is "mistreatment, maltreatment, and delay of treatment" (Gegax, 2004).

Broken Families

The long and multiple deployments of U.S. soldiers to Iraq and Afghanistan have taken their toll on their marriages and families. The divorce rate among soldiers is now higher than the civilian rate. Research has shown that in a recent year 6% of Army marriages ended in divorce and nearly 12% either became divorced or separated. Moreover, 33% of the troops in combat worry that their marriages might be breaking apart. The soldiers' tour of duty in Iraq or Afghanistan also generates severe problems for their spouses left at home raising their children by themselves. One soldier's wife, for example, grows weary of his absence in helping with their son's attention deficit disorder and their daughter's problems with not eating enough to keep her weight up (Zoroya, 2009b).

Most of the soldiers do not end up getting divorced, but they feel distant from their spouses, as if they are guests, tourists, or virtual strangers in their own homes. In talking with a researcher, Army Captain Mark Flitton and his wife Lynn explained how they live together only on a superficial level, because they no longer talk about what they are feeling as much as they used to. As Lynn said, "We've just become so comfortable in living separate lives," with her husband being a soldier at war and her being the spouse at home with the children. With each deployment, it becomes more difficult to get back together. Mark also feels estranged from his children. Once after

BOX 16.3   USING SOCIOLOGICAL INSIGHTS

How to Deal with PTSD

PTSD does not happen only to soldiers and veterans. It can also affect people like you if you have gone through a terribly frightening experience. It can hurt your close relationships and make it difficult for you to do well in college. But there are ways to deal effectively with the problem (Ruzek, 2010).

1. **See a therapist.** A mental health professional who specializes in the treatment of PTSD can help you control your problem with psychotherapy and medication.

2. **Join a support group.** When you are with people who have the same problem as you do, it will dawn on you that you are not the only one with PTSD. Besides, you can learn from others how to overcome the traumatic experience that has caused you to develop PTSD.

3. **Seek to improve your relationships with family and friends.** By increasing contact with your family and friends, you will control or diminish some of your PTSD symptoms such as emotional numbness, outbursts of rage, and severe depression.

4. **Change neighborhoods.** The traumatic experience that has led to your PTSD makes you feel that the world is a dangerous place and that you are likely to get hurt again. Thus, if you live in a high-crime area, you need to move to a safer and quieter neighborhood. Otherwise, you will be forced to go through a similar trauma repeatedly, which will make your PTSD worse

5. **Stop drinking.** Alcohol abuse is a common symptom of PTSD. If you keep drinking, your PTSD will get worse. Therefore, it is important for you to attend an alcohol treatment program. By teaming up with other trauma survivors in the program, you will likely quit drinking permanently.

6. **Start an exercise program.** You will benefit from exercising in moderation, such as walking, jogging, swimming, and weight lifting. This exercise program will not only reduce physical tension and thus the intensity of PTSD, but it will also distract you from painful memories.

7. **Volunteer in the community.** It is important to feel that you are making a contribution to your community. You can get such a feeling from helping with youth programs, medical services, literacy programs, community sporting activities, and so on.

an argument with him, his 15-year-old son Scott asked why his mother ever married "that man" (Zoroya, 2009b).

Ironically, the distance between the husband and wife seems to keep them together. Lynn feels sad about her husband going through his periods of depression, sleeping on the couch, and passing the weekend without asking her to go out on a husband-and-wife date. But she somehow looks forward to her husband going back to war. When he leaves for Iraq or Afghanistan, she will hear "I love you" from him on the phone, which delights her by bringing back a sense of intimacy to their relationship. Her husband also says life is less complicated when he goes to war. "What we do in war is clean. You get up, fight the war, and go to bed," he says. "You don't have to deal with the gas and the bills, and the kids, and the driving back and forth, and the school calling you up because the kids are late, and the paperwork and all the hustle and bustle." But his son Scott says he loves his father and is proud of his military service. He struggles to reconnect with his dad. On a recent Sunday, before his father left on a trip, Scott suddenly hugged him (Zoroya, 2009b).

Jobless Veterans

Unemployment among the veterans of the wars in Iraq and Afghanistan is relatively high. It is 15%, much higher than the 9.7% for the overall national jobless rate. "It makes you almost want to go out and rip off all the 'Support Your Troops' bumper stickers," says Joe Davis, a spokesman for the Veterans of Foreign Wars. "If you want to support your troops, give them a job" (Zoroya, 2010).

After they return home from the wars in Iraq and Afghanistan, U.S. veterans are more likely than other Americans to become jobless or homeless.

It may not be the fault of employers that many veterans cannot find employment. For one thing, veterans have a difficult time translating their military skills (such as initiative, leadership, and coolness under pressure) into language that civilian employers can grasp. Veterans also encounter a disadvantage from entering the civilian workforce. As Justin Brown, a specialist in veterans' economic issues, explains, "If you served in the military, you're disconnected from the civilian workforce, and you don't have contacts that a civilian person has" (Zoroya, 2009a).

But some employers do not understand combat-related illnesses, such as PTSD. The majority of Iraq and Afghanistan veterans do not have these illnesses, but their potential employers assume they do. According to a jobless veteran, the person who does the hiring is worried that the veterans will have PTSD and blow up on the job. Another unemployed veteran, a former paratrooper who served in Afghanistan, says that some employers consider a military record almost like having a felony. He further says, "People just frown upon us nowadays, thinking we're all flying-off-the-handle crazy guys. They don't even give us a chance" (Zoroya, 2009a).

Homeless Veterans

Veterans make up about 25% of the homeless people in the United States, although they constitute only 11% of the general population. There are many reasons for the high rate of homelessness among veterans. They include stress disorder, substance abuse, unemployment, and inability to get affordable housing. But the fundamental reason—more important than all these individual problems—is the failure of U.S. society to support the veterans. Most Americans would celebrate and honor troops upon their homecoming but would ultimately forget them. "It's a disgrace," says Jack Downing, who runs a homeless shelter for veterans. "You have served your country, you get damaged, and you come back, and we don't take care of you" (McClam, 2008).

Consider how Mike Lally, a veteran, ends up being homeless. After returning from Iraq, Lally thinks back to the long stretches in the stifling Iraq heat. He thinks about the day when insurgents killed the friendly shop owner who sold Pringles and candy bars to his battalion. He thinks about crouching in a Humvee watching bullets fly into fuel tanks during his first firefight. Of all these experiences, what finally cracked him was unloading bodies from ambulances and loading them onto helicopters. "I guess I loaded at least 20," he says. "Always a couple at a time. And you knew who it was." He began to wake up at night, sweating and screaming. During the days, he imagined

> ## BOX 16.4 WHAT RESEARCH REVEALS
>
> **Military Children Feel War Strain**
>
> We've already discussed how the wars in Iraq and Afghanistan have led to increases in suicide, mental health problems, alcohol abuse, and divorce. Now we can add troubled children to the list. According to the Pentagon's most sweeping survey of the effects of war, most of the U.S. combat troops' children are showing more fear, anxiety, and behavioral problems. More specifically, 60% of military parents told researchers that they had seen increased levels of fear and anxiety in their children when a parent is sent to war, while 57% reported increased behavioral problems at home.
>
> More than half of the parents say that generally their children have coped well or very well after a parent has gone to war. But one-fourth of the parents say their children have coped poorly or very poorly, and one-third say their children's behavior and grades in school have suffered. The researchers attribute these problems to multiple deployments. This may explain why children kept worrying that their parents might return to war. The researchers also point out that children have classmates who have lost a parent, which causes them to feel anxiously that "it could happen to me." Thus, "When the parent puts on the uniform, the child becomes distressed that they're not going to be coming back" (Zoroya, 2009a).

people in the shadows. Then he started drinking. Soon he was drunk on his job and finally got laid off. His wife kicked him out of their house. Now, unable to get help for all his problems, he becomes homeless (McClam, 2008). See also the impact of war on soldiers' children (Box 16.4).

■ Sociological Theories of War

The three sociological theories provide different views on what war is like. According to functionalist theory, war serves useful functions for society. To conflict theory, war reflects an exploitation of the masses by the ruling elite. And seen through symbolic interaction theory, war is the culmination of a series of interpretations that the leaders of two hostile nations impute to each other's actions.

Functionalist Theory

To functionalists, war serves a number of functions, including at least the following. First, war enhances social solidarity by focusing people's attention on fighting a common enemy. Consider the first Gulf War triggered by Iraq's invasion of Kuwait in 1991. The United States and its allies sought to drive Iraq out of Kuwait. But Arabs throughout the Middle East who supported Iraq became united against the United States and its allies. The United States, in turn, closed ranks with many other nations in waging the war against Iraq. That's why patriotism as a form of social solidarity among Americans increased significantly.

Second, war stimulates scientific and technological development. The Gulf War effectively served as a live laboratory for testing new high-tech weapons. Before the war, the U.S. military was not sure whether Tomahawk cruise missiles and stealth fighter-bombers could fly undetected and hit their targets with pinpoint accuracy.

The war provided the opportunity to test those weapons on the Iraqi. In addition, since the high-tech weapons were guided by computer systems, knowledge gained from their use in the war benefited the computer industry.

Third, war tends to bring about positive changes in society. The Gulf War, for example, brought pressures for democratic reforms in Kuwait, Saudi Arabia, and other Gulf states that had long been ruled with an iron hand by kings or sheiks. After the war, those countries became more democratic.

Conflict Theory

According to conflict theory, war involves the ruling elite exploiting the masses. Political leaders have been known to whip up war frenzy against some foreign enemy as a way of seeking popular support or diverting the citizenry's attention from domestic problems. Other members of the power elite also benefit, as the military brass become heroes and business tycoons reap profits from sales of military hardware. More important, members of the ruling elite do not have to suffer the heart-rending familial consequences of war. During the 1991 Gulf War, for example, no one in the president's cabinet had a son or daughter being sent to the front line. Of the 535 members of Congress, only 2 had sons involved in the war. It is mostly poor, working-class, and minority families whose children do the fighting and dying (Lacayo, 1990).

Symbolic Interaction Theory

According to symbolic interaction theory, the way the leaders of two hostile nations interpret each other's actions may lead to war. For example, consider how Presidents George H. W. Bush and Saddam Hussein interpreted each other's actions leading up to the Gulf War in 1991.

Before the Iraqi invasion of Kuwait, Bush regarded Saddam as a potential force for stability in the Middle East. Thus, Bush refrained from criticizing Saddam for using chemical weapons against Iran or for spreading poison gas on Iraq's Kurdish minority. A week before the Iraqi invasion of Kuwait, the U.S. ambassador in Iraq assured Saddam that Bush wanted to seek better relations with Iraq and that the United States would not intervene in Saddam's border dispute with Kuwait, but he urged that violence not be used. All this, however, was taken by Saddam as a green light to invade Kuwait.

The invasion outraged Bush, who threatened Saddam with war if he did not withdraw from Kuwait. Saddam shrugged off the threat, apparently believing that the United States' experience of losing the Vietnam War in the 1960s would deter it from going to war against Iraq. Even when he finally realized that Bush would carry out his threat, Saddam still did not want to pull out of Kuwait. He was hoping for a "victorious defeat."

As an Arab diplomat who had dealt personally with the Iraqi dictator on numerous occasions explained, "If there is no war and Saddam withdraws, then he looks like a coward, an idiot, who's lost everything. He is thinking, 'If I go to war, there is a chance that I will survive it, and at least I will be looked on by the Arabs as a hero who went against the whole world because of right and justice'" (Dickey, 1991). Thinking that Saddam did not appreciate the awesomeness of the military power arrayed against him, Bush finally decided to show it to him by starting the war. In short, a sequence

QUESTIONS TO EXPLORE

1. Aside from the three functions discussed here, what other functions of war are there?
2. How could conflict theory be used to explain the terrorist attacks waged against the United States on September 11, 2001?
3. How did the United States justify starting the wars in both Iraq and Afghanistan?

BOX 16.5 THEORETICAL THUMBNAIL

Explaining War

Theory	Focus	Insights
Functionalist Theory	The functions of war for society	War boosts patriotism, advances technology, and improves society.
Conflict Theory	The exploitation of the masses by the elite	War enables leaders to regain popular support, military brass to become heroes, and business tycoons to get richer.
Symbolic Interaction Theory	Hostile foreign leaders interpreting each other's actions	The decision to go to war is based on the interpretation of the hostile leader's actions.

of interpretations by the two national leaders of each other's actions culminated in the outbreak of the war.

For a quick review of the three sociological theories as they relate to war, see Box 16.5.

■ The Nature of Terrorism

Terrorism involves the use of terrifying, extreme violence to express dissatisfaction with a government. Those who carry out terrorism are basically powerless individuals futilely fighting a government. Some are international terrorists, who leave their country to attack a foreign government. An example is the Islamic radicals from the Middle East who used hijacked commercial planes to attack the United States on September 11, 2001. Other international terrorists, however, carry out the policies of their own governments. Examples of such governments are the militant regimes in Iran and North Korea, which have sent terrorists to foreign countries to assassinate their opponents. Other terrorists fight their own governments. Examples of these domestic terrorists include the bombers of the Murrah federal office building in Oklahoma City in 1995.

Terrorism
The use of terrifying, extreme violence to express dissatisfaction with a government.

The September 11 Attacks

On September 11, 2001, 19 Muslim terrorists from the Middle East hijacked four commercial passenger jet airliners. The terrorists intentionally crashed two of the airliners into the Twin Towers of the World Trade Center in New York City, killing everyone on board and many others in the buildings. The terrorists crashed a third airliner into the Pentagon in Arlington, Virginia, just outside Washington, DC. The fourth plane crashed into a field in rural Pennsylvania after some of its passengers and flight crew fought with the hijackers in an attempt to retake control of the plane, which was on its way to Washington, DC. There were no survivors from any of the flights. A total of about 3,000 people were killed. It was far and away the worst terrorist attack on U.S. soil, the most devastating terrorism in human history. Why did the terrorists commit this heinous crime with the certain knowledge that they would die, too? Were they mentally ill?

The suicide terrorists were far from mentally ill. They believed they were waging a holy war against the infidels, calling the United States "the Great Satan." Like the Palestinian suicide bombers who blow themselves up along with innocent Israeli citizens, the September 11 attackers were members of a terrorist organization. But unlike the Palestinians, who belong to local groups, the September 11 terrorists belonged to an international organization called al-Qaeda ("the base"), with members spread all over the world. The September 11 attacks were part of al-Qaeda's mission to destroy the United States and its interests abroad. The terrorists were following the orders of their organization's leader, Osama bin Laden.

According to bin Laden, the U.S. culture of secularism, materialism, and free immorality threatens the traditional Islamic way of life. Moreover, U.S. foreign policy—including support for Israel, the stationing of American troops in Saudi Arabia, and the war and blockade against Iraq—was believed to destroy Muslim lives and wound Muslim dignity as proud inheritors of a great religion. To redress these wrongs, bin Laden told his followers to engage in a holy war against the United States. He further mesmerized them with the seductive message that should they die as martyrs, they would go to heaven, where they each would be rewarded with 72 virgins (MacFarquhar, 2001). All this apparently resonated well with the young and unattached suicide terrorists who were already intensely religious and patriotic. It should not be surprising, then, that they carried out the horrendous crime on September 11, 2001.

The U.S. government fought the war against the terrorists with some success. The Taliban rulers of Afghanistan, who used to provide sanctuary to Islamic terrorists, have been eliminated. With cooperation from other governments, the United States has hacked into foreign banks' computer systems to find people who finance terrorist activities. The Americans also have obtained assistance from friendly Muslim countries such as Saudi Arabia and Pakistan in tracking down terrorists. Most Muslim communities express less support for terrorism than in the past, and fewer Muslims believe that suicide bombings are justified in the defense of Islam. Over half of al-Qaeda's key operational leaders have been killed or captured, along with some 3,000 of their associates. But al-Qaeda has changed from an organization to a movement, made up of a loosely affiliated network joined together by local terrorists in many different countries, the Internet, and a shared hatred of Western governments. Moreover, more than 4,000 U.S. soldiers have died in Iraq and more than 1,000 in Afghanistan. The insurgency continues to threaten U.S., Iraqi, and Afghan forces along with innocent civilians in those two countries, and nobody knows for sure when American troops can come home (Falkenrath, 2006; Kaplan and Whitelaw, 2004). Still, most Americans

(69%) believe the U.S. government is doing very or fairly well in reducing the threat of terrorism within the United States (Pew Research Center, 2010).

Suicide Bombers

Since the September 11 attacks, many Westerners have assumed that suicide bombers must be psychotic, or at least irrational, and that they must be poor and uneducated. But evidence suggests just the opposite. According to a study on the 149 Palestinian suicide bombers who tried to attack Israel between 1993 and 2002, the majority shared the same social profile as the September 11 terrorists. The suicide bombers in Iraq and Afghanistan who have frequently targeted U.S. troops also have the same social background as the September 11 terrorists. They are mostly young, male, and single. They come from relatively well-off, middle-class families. They are also better educated than most of their countrymen. Thus, they are apparently rational enough to know that they can only resort to suicide bombings as their ultimate, powerful weapon in an asymmetrical war with Israel or the United States. They know they can't fight a conventional war because they have no tanks, no artillery, and no air force, while their enemy has one of the world's most powerful and modern militaries (Nordland et al., 2007; Pape, 2005).

It should further be noted that, like the September 11 terrorists, the Palestinian, Iraqi, and Afghan suicide bombers consider themselves martyrs, rather than terrorists. They are also seen that way by their families and friends. Their parents are proud of them. After the Palestinian suicide bomber Saeed Hotari blew himself up, his father said, "I am very happy and proud of what my

The suicide bombers in the Middle East consider themselves martyrs, rather than terrorists. They are also seen that way by their families and friends. Their parents are proud of them.

son did. He has become a hero! What more could a father ask? My prayer is that Saeed's brothers and friends will sacrifice their lives too. There is no better way to show God you love him." The bombers also receive other, more concrete support. After they die carrying out a suicide mission, their family is rewarded with a permanent pension from the terrorist organization that sponsors the bombing. The suicide bombers achieve fame from the appearance of their pictures on posters throughout the area. Before departing on their suicide mission, they are filmed explaining what they are going to do, which will be broadcast on TV following the suicide bombings. Finally, they are assured that they will earn a special place in heaven (Begley, 2004; Weinberg, 2008).

Suicide attacks are not new; nor have they originated only from the Middle East. In 1911 in China, 72 pro-democracy revolutionaries, mostly students, sacrificed their lives by charging an overwhelming garrison of the Ching Dynasty in order to prod the apathetic Chinese masses to overthrow the tyrannical government. In 1945, toward the end of World War II, Japanese kamikaze pilots crashed their fighter planes into U.S. warships in the Pacific. Today in Sri Lanka, the separatist rebels known as the Tamil Tigers, who are fighting their government for an independent Tamil state, have launched about 200 suicide attacks (Gambetta, 2005). What do all these terrorists have in common that motivates them to engage in suicide bombing?

Altruistic suicide
Suicide committed by individuals who are so strongly tied to their group that they effectively lose their selves and stand ready to do what their group tells them to do.

The answer can be found in the sociological concept of altruistic suicide, which is likely to be committed by individuals who are so strongly tied to their group that they effectively lose their selves and stand ready to do whatever their group tells them to do (Pedahzur, Perliger, and Weinberg, 2003). Examples include elderly Eskimos and Hindu widows, who faithfully follow the tradition of their societies that encourage old people and widows to commit suicide. Such suicide was relatively common in some ancient societies, in which the group reigned supreme at the expense of the individual. Not surprisingly, the suicide bombers of today typically live in traditional societies that give priority to group conformity over individual freedom. Like the altruistic suicides of the past, the suicide bombers are too deeply integrated into their groups—terrorist organizations—and identify completely with them.

Terrorism in Cyberspace

Nowadays, members of the terrorist organization al-Qaeda use the Internet to plan and carry out their terrorist activities. They send some messages to each other by posting them in code on various Web sites. Other messages are transmitted electronically. After they are sent and read by the recipient, the whole communication and related files are deleted to maintain secrecy. Moreover, e-mail addresses are generally used only once or twice (Jehl and Rohde, 2004).

The terrorists are further able to launch a direct digital attack on the United States by hacking into its computer networks. The cyberattack could bring the country to its knees by disrupting or disabling its infrastructure. This infrastructure comprises many of the nation's vital facilities and services, including the power and water supply, gas and oil production and storage facilities, telecommunications and banking networks, air traffic control system, and transportation and emergency services (Hosenball, 2002; Mazzetti, 2004). Thus, a cyberterrorist can break into an air traffic control system, tamper with it, and cause jets to collide, so that hundreds of people die. Such cyberattacks have not taken place yet, but they can happen, as suggested by the success of some nonpolitical, recreational hackers to briefly disable Yahoo!, Amazon.com, and other online giants several years ago.

By using computers as a weapon of mass disruption, cyberterrorists can reach the United States more easily than intercontinental ballistic missiles, disregarding the physical barriers of two broad oceans (the Atlantic and the Pacific) and two large peaceful neighbors (Canada and Mexico) that have long enhanced America's sense of safety. In today's computer-driven world, the terrorists no longer have to physically invade the territory or the airspace of the United States in order to damage its resources and disrupt the lives of its people. Indeed, as a congressperson says, expressing the belief of most government officials, "Cyberterrorism presents a real and growing threat to American security. What I fear is the combination of a cyberattack coordinated with more traditional terrorism, undermining our ability to respond to an attack when lives are in danger" (Newton, 2004; Will, 2001).

Fortunately, the threat of cyberterrorism remains only a threat. Over the last 10 years, there has not been a single major cyberattack on the United States. But this does not mean that the terrorists have lost interest in attacking the United States—and other nations. After all, in those 10 years, there have been 1,813 international terrorist attacks and 217,394 computer hacking incidents, although none of these has knocked out the U.S. infrastructure or created nationwide panic (Lewis, 2005).

Myths About Terrorism

It is widely believed that two major social and political conditions give rise to terrorism. One is poverty or economic deprivation, and the other the absence of democracy. The reasoning behind these popular beliefs is that poor people find their lives so frustrating that they will turn to terrorist violence and that citizens will also turn to violence if they are denied the freedom to make themselves heard. This reasoning seems to make sense, but it does not jibe with reality (Weinberg, 2008).

Consider the poorest countries in the world, those in sub-Saharan Africa. They suffer from many problems, especially horrendous living conditions, but terrorist violence is rarely one of them. Terrorism is also rare in the impoverished regions of wealthier countries. In Italy, for example, when revolutionary activities were rampant during the 1970s, most of the terrorist operations took place in the prosperous northern cities, but rarely did terrorist attacks occur in the impoverished south of the country. The same can be said about the Basque militancy in Spain. Most of the militants come from the most prosperous parts of the country. There is virtually no terrorist violence in the poorest regions (Weinberg, 2008).

Evidence also fails to support the belief that the absence of democracy causes terrorism. In 1989, students in China were prevented from having the freedom to protest in Tiananmen Square, but terrorism did not occur. Similarly, in the Soviet Union between 1917 and 1991, virtually all forms of popular opposition to the government were suppressed, and yet terrorism did not occur. Only after the Soviet Union fell apart in 1991, enabling the states in Eastern Europe and Central Asia to become independent and free, did terrorism erupt in these states. A similar situation has occurred in Indonesia. For many years when the country was ruled by a military dictatorship, there was relatively little terrorism. But after the dictatorship was replaced by democracy, a series of terrorist incidents appeared, with the most dramatic being the nightclub bombings on the Indonesian island of Bali. All these findings suggest that democracy, rather than the absence of it, could well be a cause of terrorism (Weinberg, 2008).

▓ The Ripple Effects of Terrorism

Terrorism directly kills a number of people, but it indirectly affects many more. Here we will focus on some of the indirect, ripple effects of terrorism, namely, how terrorism causes millions of Americans to suffer a high level of stress, increase their anti-Muslim sentiment, and have their privacy invaded by their government.

A High Level of Stress

Virtually all Americans were shocked when terrorists attacked the World Trade Center in New York and the Pentagon in Washington, DC, on September 11, 2001. Since then, researchers have tried to determine the extent and severity of the damage to the American psyche.

A national survey of 560 randomly selected U.S. adults was conducted *3 to 5 days* after September 11. It shows that the terrorist attacks dealt a psychological blow to all Americans, not just those in New York and Washington. Many suffered a high level of stress, with about 44% of Americans experiencing serious symptoms of PTSD, such as difficulty sleeping, irritability, inability to concentrate, overvigilance, and exaggerated startle (Schuster et al., 2001). Another survey was taken of 1,008 adults living in Manhattan *5 to 9 weeks* after the attacks on the towers. This study shows that about 8% of the New Yorkers experienced symptoms of PTSD and 10% came down with symptoms of major depression. Those residing closest to the attack site were nearly three times as likely to suffer from PTSD as those living farther away (Galea et al., 2002).

The most comprehensive survey is the National Study of Americans' Reactions to September 11. It sought information from a representative sample of 2,273 adults throughout the United States *1 to 2 months* after the terrorist attacks. First, it found that geographic proximity to the World Trade Center was related to the prevalence of post-traumatic stress. More specifically, a significantly higher percentage of New Yorkers reported symptoms of PTSD than did the percentage of people in other parts of the nation. (The prevalence of PTSD was 11.2% in New York City, compared with 3.6% in other major U.S. cities, 2.7% in Washington, DC, and 4% in the rest of the country.) Second was the surprising finding that the rate of PTSD in Washington, DC, was lower than that in other parts of the United States. This is probably because the target was military, thereby reducing the Washington civilian residents' identification with the victims. A third finding was that the more hours people spent watching TV coverage of the attacks, the more they experienced post-traumatic stress (Schlenger et al., 2002).

To provide some perspective on these findings, the seriousness of the stress suffered by those 2.7% to 11.2% of Americans was comparable to that found among survivors of motor vehicle crashes and survivors of sexual assault. Thus, the stress resulting from the September 11 terrorist attacks could be considered a significant public health problem (Schlenger et al., 2002).

Anti-Muslim Sentiment

There has long been an anti-Muslim sentiment in U.S. society. This can be seen in the popular American stereotype of the Muslim as a "convenience store clerk who doesn't speak English, watches you like a hawk, and smells bad." There is also the stereotype of "the Middle Eastern cab driver who doesn't know where he's going, plays music that sounds like a cat being beaten to death with an out of tune violin, and tries to jack up your fare." Then there is the stereotype of "the Muslim religious zealot, with his funny hat and robe, mumbling some nonsense while he kneels on a carpet to pray to some strange god" (Yaeger, 2006). Now, since the September 11 terrorist attacks in 2001, the anti-Muslim sentiment has increased significantly. As an American Muslim says, "In the past few years or so . . . many times I've heard someone yell, 'Kill all them fuckin' ragheads!', seen t-shirts with mosques being destroyed or urinated on, or driven behind someone with an anti-Muslim bumper sticker" (Yaeger, 2006).

Apparently, Americans who are prejudiced against Muslims associate Islam with terrorism because the terrorists are mostly Muslim. That's why after the September 11 attacks, many American Muslims worked hard to improve relationships with non-Muslims, making it clear that they condemn terrorism, educating people about Islam, and participating in interfaith services. However, now they are concerned about widespread ignorance, suspicion, and even hatred of Muslims, as shown by many Americans' fierce opposition to the plan to build a mosque and Islamic cultural center near the former site of the World Trade Center towers. The opposition has unleashed a torrent of anti-Muslim sentiment and vandalism, including the knifing of a Muslim cab driver in New York City (Goodstein, 2010).

Invasion of Privacy

Since the September 11 attacks in 2001, the U.S. government has aggressively conducted the war on terrorism but in the process has threatened the civil rights and privacy of Americans. Six weeks after the attacks, the USA Patriot Act was enacted giving the government broad authority to track suspected terrorists. Thus, today, federal agents are allowed to eavesdrop on U.S. citizens without court orders, to listen in on overseas telephone conversations, to read U.S. citizens' e-mail, to force libraries and bookstores to divulge information about people interested in books advocating radical Islam, and so on. The majority (two out of three) of Americans believe that those antiterrorism activities are intruding on the privacy of their fellow citizens, but fewer than a third consider such intrusions unjustified. Most Americans (two in three) find it more important for the government to investigate terrorist threats than to protect individual privacy. Most American travelers feel the same way even when they have to go through the full-body scanner at the airport (Balz and Deane, 2006; McCartney, 2010).

The aggressive attempt to catch terrorists seems to have paid off. Since the September 11 attacks, the United States has not been hit again. Also, according to the Justice Department, in just one year after the Patriot Act was passed, hundreds of suspected terrorists were identified and tracked in the United States, and more than 1,000 international terrorists suspected of threatening national security were targeted by U.S. law enforcement authorities (*USA Today*, 2003).

Review

SUMMARY

1. The causes of war include perceived threats, moral objectives, political objectives, unifying the nation, and the absence of alternatives. The United States went to war against Iraq because of the belief that Iraq possessed weapons of mass destruction, Iraq provided aid to terrorists, and the United States could spread democracy throughout the Middle East. Another reason for invading Iraq was the joint support of the war by U.S. religious and business conservatives. The strongest reason was the September 11, 2001, attacks.

2. Afghan civilians have mixed feelings about the presence of Americans in their country. Suicides are about as common among U.S. service members as the deaths resulting from combat. Reasons for the suicides include family problems, reluctance to seek professional help for emotional problems, keeping horrific war experiences to oneself, and increased use of antidepressants. American female soldiers are much more likely than their male peers to suffer from the trauma of war that causes them to develop PTSD. Their war trauma stems from combat exposure and sexual assault.

3. Warrior culture theory suggests that boys should learn to be tough, but wounded-boy theory says that boys should not. There is a growing number of veterans with PTSD, but half of these veterans do not seek treatment. Effective ways to deal with PTSD include seeing a therapist, joining a support group, and improving relations with family and friends.

4. The wars in Iraq and Afghanistan have hurt soldiers' marriages and families. The soldiers' divorce rate is now higher than the civilian rate, and it is difficult for their spouses left at home to raise their children. Veterans have a much higher incidence of joblessness than other Americans. They also have a considerably higher rate of homelessness. Most of the U.S. combat troops' children exhibit an increased amount of fear, anxiety, and behavioral problems.

5. According to functionalist theory, war serves useful functions for society. To conflict theory, war reflects the exploitation of the masses by the ruling class. To symbolic interaction theory, war culminates from a series of interpretations imputed by the leaders of two nations to each other.

6. The terrorists that launched the suicide attacks on September 11, 2001, were not mentally ill. They believed they were waging a holy war on the United States. Since the September 11 attacks, many Westerners have assumed that suicide bombers must be psychotic and that they must be poor and uneducated, but evidence suggests just the opposite. Nowadays, terrorists use the Internet to plan and carry out their activities, but so far they have not launched a major cyberattack on the United States. There are two popular myths about terrorism, one attributing terrorism to poverty and the other to the absence of democracy.

7. Many Americans experienced emotional stress after the September 11, 2001, attacks. These attacks have also increased the anti-Muslim sentiment throughout

the United States. Furthermore, in its aggressive pursuit of terrorists, the U.S. government has invaded the privacy of American citizens.

CRITICAL THINKING QUESTIONS

1. How have you seen the "warrior culture" being promoted in your own community? Provide at least one example.
2. Is it possible to catch terrorists without having your privacy invaded at the airport? If so, what would you recommend for the government to do?
3. In what ways have war and terrorism influenced you the most? What specific changes have you noticed in your day-to-day life?

INTERNET RESOURCES

The Central Intelligence Agency (CIA) (https://www.cia.gov/news-information/ cia-the-war-on-terrorism/index.html) "is an independent U.S. Government agency responsible for providing national security intelligence to senior U.S. policymakers." At present, the CIA partners with law enforcement agencies around the globe, with its primary mission being the efforts to understand, predict, and prevent acts of terrorism.

The Department of Homeland Security (DHS) (http://www.dhs.gov/) comprises more than 87,000 separate governmental jurisdictions at the local, state, and federal levels. The goal of DHS is to create a "complementary system" by reducing the bureaucracy of crucial information flow and connecting all levels of government necessary to protect the American homeland from all internal and external threats.

The Federal Bureau of Investigation (FBI) (http://www.fbi.gov/) is an intelligence-driven security organization that exists to gather information on and assess all potential threats to American life and safety, and take steps necessary to alleviate and control real threats and hazards. At present, the FBI's top stated priority is to protect the citizens of the United States from the threat of terrorist attacks.

START is the National Consortium for the Study of Terrorism and Responses to Terrorism (http://www.start.umd.edu/start/), an extension of the DHS that is hosted by The University of Maryland. The consortium provides a variety of education, media, and public, accessible research and other information pertaining to global terrorism.

The Transportation Security Administration (http://www.tsa.gov) is a division of the DHS tasked with security and law-enforcement measures that help to ensure the safe passage and transportation of both passengers and commerce. Services range from the presence of Federal Air Marshals on flights and basic airport security screening, to the use of canines to detect drugs and explosives.

References

Aarons, Dakarai, and Stephen Sawchuk. 2010. "Data in action." *Education Week*, June 10, pp. 6–9.

Abboud, Soo Kim, and Jane Kim. 2006. *Top of the Class: How Asian Parents Raise High Achievers, and How You Can Too*. New York: Berkley Books.

Ackman, Dan. 2004. "A star is born." *Wall Street Journal*, August 27, p. W13.

Adams, Kathryn Betts. 2004. "Changing investment in activities and interests in elders' lives: Theory and measurement." *International Journal of Aging & Human Development*, 58, pp. 87–108.

Adams-Curtis, Leah E., and Gordon B. Forbes. 2004. "College women's experiences of sexual coercion: A review of cultural, perpetrator, victim, and situational variables." *Trauma, Violence, & Abuse*, 5, pp. 91–122.

Adler, Jerry. 1996. "Adultery: A new furor over an old sin." *Newsweek*, September 30, pp. 54–60.

Adler, Jerry. 2008. "The working-class smoker." *Newsweek*, March 31, p. 16.

Adler, Roy D., and Michael Summers. 2007. "Capital punishment works." *Wall Street Journal*, November 2, p. A13.

Aguilar-Millan, Stephen, et al. 2008. "Global crime case: The modern slave trade." *The Futurist*, November/December, p. 45.

Ahlstrom, Salme K., and Esa L. Osterberg. 2005. "International perspectives on adolescent and young adult drinking." *Alcohol Research & Health*, 28, pp. 258–268.

Ahmadu, Fuambai. 2000. "Rites and wrongs: An insider/outsider reflects on power and excision." In Bettina Shell-Duncan and Ylva Hernlund (eds.), *Female "Circumcision" in Africa*. Boulder, CO: Lynne Rienner.

Ali, Lorraine, and Raina Kelley. 2008. "The curious lives of surrogates." *Newsweek*, April 7, pp. 45–51.

Allan, Graham. 2004. "Being unfaithful: His and her affairs." In Jean Duncombe, et al., *The State of Affairs: Explorations in Infidelity and Commitment*, pp. 121–140. Mahwah, NJ: Lawrence Erlbaum Associates.

Altman, Lawrence K. 2005. "Study challenges abstinence as crucial to AIDS strategy." *New York Times*, February 24, p. A16.

Amsden, Alice H. 2007. *Escape from Empire: The Developing World's Journey Through Heaven and Hell*. Cambridge, MA: MIT Press.

Anderson, Curt. 2003. "States face growing prison population." July 27. Available online: www.story.news.yahoo.com

Anderson, David C. 1994. "The crime funnel." *New York Times Magazine*, June 12, pp. 57–58.

Anderson, Michael, et al., 2003. "'Why doesn't she just leave?' A descriptive study of victim reported impediments to her safety." *Journal of Family Violence*, 18, pp. 151–154.

Angier, Natalie. 2000. "Do races differ? Not really, genes show." *New York Times*, August 22, pp. D1, D6.

Anrig, Greg. 2009. "A failed experiment." *Christian Century*, January 27, pp. 20–23.

Ansberry, Clare. 2009. "Elderly emerge as a new class of workers—and the jobless." *Wall Street Journal*, February 23, pp. A1, A12.

APA (American Psychiatric Association). 1994. *Diagnostic and Statistical Manual of Mental Disorders*, 4th ed. Washington, DC: APA.

Associated Press. 2009. "More school: Obama says kids need longer school days, shorter summers." September 28. Available online: www.timesnews.net/article .php?id=9017201

Au, Ceri. 2007. "The new children of war." July 31. Available online: www.time.com

Audi, Tamara. 2006. "TV images skewing Americans' view of peaceful Islam, Muslim leaders say." *USA Today*, April 17, p. 14A.

Aviv, Rachel. 2008. "Strategy adult ad." *New York Times*, November 2, p. 06.

Bailey, William C. 1998. "Deterrence, brutalization, and the death penalty: Another examination of Oklahoma's return to capital punishment." *Criminology*, 36, pp. 711–733.

Baker, Al. 2007. "City homicides still dropping, to under 500." *New York Times*, November 23, p. 1.

Balkan, Sheila, Ronald, J. Berger, and Janet Schmidt. 1980. *Crime and Deviance in America: A Critical Approach*. Belmont, CA: Wadsworth.

Balz, Dan, and Claudia Deane. 2006. "Differing views on terrorism." *Washington Post*, January 11, p. A4.

Barnett, Ola W., Cindy, L. Miller-Perrin, and Robin D. Perrin. 2005. *Family Violence Across the Lifespan: An Introduction*, 2nd ed. Thousand Oaks, CA: Sage.

Barnett, Rosalind C., and Caryl Rivers. 1996. *She Works/He Works: How Two-Income Families Are Happier, Healthier, and Better-Off*. San Francisco: HarperCollins.

Baron, Beth. 2006. "Women, honour, and the state: Evidence from Egypt." *Middle Eastern Studies*, 42, pp. 1–20.

Barone, Michael. 2008. "In defense of lobbyists." *U.S. News & World Report*, June 23/ June 30, p. 22.

Barron, James. 2009. "Billionaires at play: Mike versus Mikhail." *New York Times*, September 25. Available online: www.nytimes.com

Barry, John, et al. 2004. "Abu Ghraib and beyond." *Newsweek*, May 17, pp. 32–37.

Barstow, Donald G. 2004. "Female genital mutilation." In Alex Thio and Thomas C. Calhoun (eds.), *Readings in Deviant Behavior*, 3rd ed. Boston: Allyn & Bacon.

Becker, Howard S. 1963. *Outsiders*. New York: Free Press.

Begley, Sharon. 2004. "Alternative peer groups may offer way to deter some suicide bombers." *Wall Street Journal*, October 8, p. B1.

Begley, Sharon. 2007a. "The truth about denial." *Newsweek*, August 13, pp. 20–29.

Begley, Sharon. 2007b. "The upside of aging." *Wall Street Journal*, February 16, pp. W1, W4.

Begley, Sharon. 2008. "When it's head versus heart, the heart wins." *Newsweek*, February 11, pp. 34–36.

Begley, Sharon. 2009. "The five biggest lies in the health care debate." *Newsweek*, September 7, pp. 42–43.

Belkin, Lisa. 1990. "Many in medicine are calling rules a professional malaise." *New York Times*, February 19, pp. A1, A9.

Belkin, Lisa. 2009. "What's good for the kids." *New York Times*, November 8, p. 9.

Belluck, Pam. 2000. "Indian schools, long failing, press for money and quality." *New York Times*, May 18, pp. A1, A22.

Benderly, Beryl Lieff. 1989. "Don't Believe Everything You Read." *Psychology Today*, November, pp. 67–69.

Benjamin, Matthew. 2003. "China conundrum." *U.S. News & World Report*, September 15, pp. 37–38.

Bennett, Jessica, and Jesse Ellison. 2010. "'I don't': The case against marriage." *Newsweek*, June 21, pp. 42–45.

Bennett, Trevor, et al. 2008. "The statistical association between drug misuse and crime: A meta-analysis." *Aggression & Violent Behavior*, 13, pp. 107–118.

Bennett, William J. 1989. "A response to Milton Friedman." *Wall Street Journal*, September 19, p. A32.

Bennett, William J. 2001. "The drug has worked once. It can again." *Wall Street Journal*, May 15, p. A26.

Bergen, Raquel Kennedy. 2006. "Marital rape: New research and directions." *Applied Research Forum*, February, pp. 1–13.

Berkman, Lisa F. 2004. "The health divide." *Contexts*, fall, pp. 38–43.

Bezruchka, Stephen. 1997. "Unhealthy societies: The afflictions of inequality." *New England Journal of Medicine*, 336, pp. 1616–1617.

Bezruchka, Stephen. 2001. "Is our society making you sick?" *Newsweek*, February 26, p. 14.

Birmingham Post. 2009. "Stereotyping commercials give children mixed messages." March 3, p. 15.

Bjerklie, David. 2007. "Check your tires." *Time*, April 9, p. 97.

Black, Jane A. 2008. "The not-so-golden years: Power of attorney, elder abuse, and why our laws are failing a vulnerable population." *St. John's Law Review*, 82, pp. 289–314.

Blizzard, Rick. 2004a. "Americans and alcohol: Drink, drank, drunk?" The Gallup Poll Tuesday Briefing, August 24. Available online: www.gallup.com

Blizzard, Rick. 2004b. "Smoking: Will education overpower addiction?" The Gallup Poll Tuesday Brief, August 31. Available online: www.gallup.com

Block, Fred. 2007. "Why is the U.S. fighting in Iraq?" *Contexts*, summer, pp. 33–37.

Block, Fred, Anna C. Korteweg, and Kerry Woodward. 2006. "The compassionate gap in American policy." *Contexts*, spring, pp. 13–20.

Blundell, William E. 1986. "Gripe session." *Wall Street Journal*, May 9, pp. 1, 9.

Boffey, Philip M. 1986. "Schizophrenia: Insights fail to halt rising toll." *New York Times*, March 16, p. 1.

Bogert, Carroll. 1994. "Good news on drugs from the inner city." *Newsweek*, February 14, pp. 28–29.

Borger, Gloria. 2006. "A real shot . . . in the foot." *U.S. News & World Report*, February 27, p. 32.

Bork, Robert H. 1996. *Slouching Towards Gomorrah: Modern Liberalism and American Decline*. New York: HarperCollins.

Brasch, Walter. 2008. "It's a welfare state . . . if you're rich." March 19. Available online: www.counterpunch.org

Breslow, Rosalind A., and Barbara Smothers. 2004. "Drinking patterns of older Americans: National health interview surveys, 1997–2001." *Journal of Studies on Alcohol*, 65, pp. 232–240.

Brill, Steven. 2010. "On sale: your government. Why lobbying is Washington's best bargain." *Time*, July 12, pp. 28–35.

Brinkley, Alan. 2008. "The party's over." *Wall Street Journal*, September 6–7, pp. w1, w6.

Broder, David S. 2006. "The seer and the scandals." *Washington Post*, June 1, p. A19.

Brody, Jane E. 1997. "Quirks, oddities may be illnesses." *New York Times*, February 4, pp. B9, B11.

Brooks, Arthur C. 2007. "The left's 'inequality' obsession." *Wall Street Journal*, July 19, p. A15.

Brown, Lee P. 2008. "End the demand, end the supply." *U.S. News & World Report*, August 4, p. 9.

Brown, Susan I. 2005. "How cohabitation is reshaping American families." *Contexts*, summer, pp. 33–37.

Browne, Angela. 1987. *Why Battered Women Kill*. New York: Free Press.

Browning, Lynnley. 2004. "Study finds accelerating decline in corporate taxes." *New York Times*, September 23, Section C, p. 3.

Brush, Silla. 2005. "Who's sorry now?" *U.S. News & World Report*, December 12, pp. 35–43.

Bryan, James H. 1966. "Occupational ideologies and individual attitudes of call girls." *Social Problems*, 13, pp. 441–450.

Buchwald, Emilie, et al. 2005. *Transforming a Rape Culture* (revised edition). Minneapolis, MN: Milkweed.

Budiansky, Stephen, et al. 1994. "How lawyers abuse the law." *U.S. News & World Report*, January 30, pp. 50–56.

Budig, Michelle J. 2002. "Male advantage and the gender composition of jobs: Who rides the glass escalator?" *Social Problems*, 49, pp. 258–277.

Buechner, Maryanne Murray. 2007a. "Pay your bills online." *Time*, April 9, p. 78.

Buechner, Maryanne Murray. 2007b. "Support your local farmer." *Time*, April 9, p. 84.

Buller, Mary Klein, and David B. Buller. 1987. "Physicians' communication style and patient satisfaction." *Journal of Health and Social Behavior*, 28, pp. 375–388.

Burch, Edmond. 2005. "Corporate crime vs. street crime: Interview with Robert Weissman, editor of *Multinational Monitor*." *Clamor*, July/August.

Bury, Chris, et al. 2010. "Rod Blagojevich's narrow escape: Ex-Illinois gov. guilty on 1 count." August 18. Available online: http://abcnews.go.com

Butler, Robert. 2001. "The myth of old age." *Newsweek*, fall/winter [special issue], p. 33.

Buzzle.com. 2010. "Educational Problems in Public Schools." Available online: www.buzzle.com/articles/education-problems-in-public-schools.html

Calabresi, Massimo. 2007. "The Iraq debate that wasn't." July 12. Available online: www.time.com

Calmes, Jackie. 2009. "U.S. forecasts smaller loss from bailout of banks." Available online: www.nytimes.com

Carlson, Eric Stener. 2006. "The hidden prevalence of male sexual assault during war: Observations on blunt trauma to the male genitals." *British Journal of Criminology*, 46, pp. 16–25.

Carter, Cynthia, and Linda Steiner. 2003. *Critical Readings: Media and Gender Issues in Cultural and Media Studies*. London: Open University Press.

Catalano, Ralph, et al. 1993. "Job loss and alcohol abuse: A test using data from the epidemiologic catchment area project." *Journal of Health and Social Behavior*, 34, pp. 215–225.

Caulkins, Jonathan P., et al. 2005. *How Goes the "War on Drugs"?* Santa Monica, CA: RAND.

Caulkins, Jonathan P., and Rosalie Liccardo. 2006. "Marijuana markets: Inferences from reports by the household population." *Journal of Drug Issues*, 36, pp. 173–200.

Centers for Disease Control and Prevention. 2009. HIV/AIDS Surveillance Report, Vol. 19. Atlanta, Georgia.

Chamlin, Mitchell B., and John K. Cochran. 2005. "Ascribed economic inequality and homicide among modern societies." *Homicide Studies*, 9, 3–29.

Chang, Leslie. 2001. "Parental discretion." *Wall Street Journal*, February 2, pp. A1, A6.

Charles, Susan T., and Laura L. Carstensen. 2007. "Emotion regulation and aging." In J. J. Gross (ed.), *Handbook of Emotion Regulation*, pp. 307–20. New York: Guilford.

Charles, Susan T., and Laura L. Carstensen. 2010. "Social and emotional aging." *Annual Review of Psychology*, pp. 383–409.

Chase, Marilyn. 1996. "Americans seem to drink a lot or hardly at all." *Wall Street Journal*, December 30, p. B1.

Chassin, Laurie, et al. 2010. "The association between membership in the sandwich generation and health behaviors: A longitudinal study." *Journal of Applied Developmental Psychology*, 31, pp. 36–46.

Chen, Kathy. 2005. "New relations: China's growth places strains on family's ties." *Wall Street Journal*, April 13, pp. A1, A15.

Cherlin, Andrew J. 2010. *The Marriage-Go-Round*. New York: Vintage Books.

Cheung, Hoi Yan, and Alex W. H. Chan. 2008. "Corruption across countries: Impacts from education and cultural dimensions." *Social Science Journal*, 45, pp. 223–239.

Chimerine, Lawrence. 1995. *Multinational Corporations and the U.S. Economy*. Washington, DC: Economic Strategy Institute.

Christensen, Andrew, and Neil Jacobson. 2000. *Reconcilable Differences*. New York: Guilford.

Christensen, Russ, and Peter W. Dowrick. 1983. "Myths of mid-winder depression." *Community Mental Health Journal*, 19, pp. 177–186.

Christopher, Robert C. 1983. *The Japanese Mind: The Goliath Explained*. New York: Simon & Schuster.

Chu, Kathy. 2009. "Credit card debt rises faster for seniors." *USA Today*, July 28, p. 1B.

Church, George. 1986. "What he needs to know." *Time*, December 22, pp. 17–18.

Clark, Kim. 2010. "Can school reform ever really work?" *U.S. News & World Report*, January, pp. 23–31.

Clary, Mike. 2009. "Life begins in a homeless shelter." *Los Angeles Times*, July 31, p. 22.

Clemmitt, Marcia. 2009. "Women in the military." *CQ Researcher*, November 13, pp. 1–13.

Cloud, John, and Jodie Morse. 2001. "Home sweet school." *Time*, August 27, pp. 47–54.

Cockerham, William. 2010. *Medical Sociology*, 11th ed. Upper Saddle River, NJ: Prentice Hall.

Cogan, Michael F. 2010. "Exploring academic outcomes of home-schooled students." *Journal of College Admission*, 208, pp. 18–25.

Cohan, Peter. 2010. "Americans' job dissatisfaction hits 22-year high." January 5. Available online: www.dailyfinance.com

Cohen, James R. 2002. "Maryland's 'smart growth': Using incentives to combat sprawl." In Gregory D. Squires (ed.), *Urban Sprawl: Causes, Consequences and Policy Responses*, pp. 293–324. Washington, DC: Urban Institute Press.

Cohen, Jeffrey E. 2009. "Perceptions of anti-semitism among American Jews, 2000–2005: A survey analysis." *Political Psychology*, Nov. 23. Available online: www3.interscience.wiley.com

Coleman, James William. 2006. *The Criminal Elite: The Sociology of White Collar Crime*, 5th ed. New York: St. Martin's.

Collins, Randall. 1975. *Conflict Sociology*. New York: Academic Press.

Colvin, Richard Lee. 2010. "Introduction." *Washington Monthly*, July/August, pp. A2–A4.

Comiteau, Jennifer. 2005. "From Rosie to real." September 12. Available online: www.adweek.com

Compton, Wilson M., and Nora D. Volkow. 2006. "Abuse of prescription drugs and the risk of addiction." *Drugs and Alcohol Dependence*, 83, pp. 54–57.

Conant, Eve. 2010. "The conscience of a conservative." *Newsweek*, January 18, pp. 46–54.

Conklin, John E. 2003. *Why Crime Rates Fell*. Boston: Allyn & Bacon.

Conklin, John E. 2007. *Criminology*, 9th ed. Boston: Allyn & Bacon.

Connell, R. W. 2000. *The Men and the Boys*. Los Angeles, CA: University of California Press.

Conrad, Peter. 2009. *Sociology of Health and Illness: Critical Perspectives*. New York: Worth.

Continetti, Matthew. 2006. *The K Street Gang: The Rise and Fall of the Republican Machine*. New York: Doubleday.

Coontz, Stephanie. 2006. "Do you take this man? No thanks . . .," *The Observer*, December 31, p. 25.

Corbett, Sara. 2007. "The women's war." *New York Times Magazine*, March 18, pp. 40–72.

Corliss, Richard. 2006. "How the west was won over." *Time*, January 30, pp. 60–63.

Cornwell, Benjamin, et al. 2008. "The social connectedness of older adults: a national profile." *American Sociological Review*, 73, pp. 185–203.

cozay.com. 2010. "Extreme poverty in Africa." Available online: http://cozay.com

Crawford, David, et al. 2007. "Siemens ruling details bribery across the globe." *Wall Street Journal*, November 16, pp. A1, A17.

Cross-National Collaborative Group. 1992. "The changing rate of major depression: Cross-national comparisons." *Journal of the American Medical Association*, 268, pp. 3098–3105.

Current Events. 2010. "A teen tragedy." May 3, Vol. 109, Issue 24.

Current Science. 2008. "Autism epidemic a myth." March 28, p. 14.

Currie, Elliott. 1993. *Reckoning: Drugs, the Cities, and the American Future*. New York: Hill and Wang.

Cuvelier, Monique. 2002. "Victim, not villain." *Psychology Today*, May/June, p. 23.

Dahl, Robert. 1981. *Democracy in the United States: Promise and Performance*, 4th ed. Boston: Houghton Mifflin.

Das, Aniruddha. 2009. "Sexual harassment at work in the United States." *Archives of Sexual Behavior*, December, pp. 909–921.

Davis, Kingsley. 1955. "The origin and growth of urbanization in the world." *American Journal of Sociology*, 60, pp. 429–437.

Davis, Kingsley. 1971. "Sexual behavior." *American Sociological Review*, 10, pp. 242–249.

Davis, Kingsley, and Wilbert E. Moore. 1945. "Some principles of stratification." *American Sociological Review*, 10, pp. 242–249.

DEA (Drug Enforcement Administration). 2010. "Successes in the fight against drugs." DEA Office of Public Affairs, January 2010.

Deam, Jenny. 2009. "Homeless in the suburbs." *Parenting*, July, pp. 68–73.

Dean-Mooney, Laura. 2008. "A lower age would be unsafe." *U.S. News & World Report*, September 15, p. 10.

Demyttenaere, K., et al. 2004. "Prevalence of mental disorders in Europe: Results from the European Study of the Epidemiology of Mental Disorders project." *Acta Psychiatrica Scandinavica*, 109, pp. 21–27.

Denfield, Duane. 1974. "Dropouts from swinging." *The Family Coordinator*, January, pp. 45–49.

Denzin, Norman. 1991. "The AA group." In David J. Pittman and Helene Raskin White (eds.), *Society, Culture, and Drinking Patterns Reexamined*. New Brunswick, NJ: Rutgers Center of Alcohol Studies.

de Seve, Karen. 2006. "The perils of ecstasy." *Current Health*, February, pp. 26–29.

DeSimone, Jeff. 2007. "Fraternity membership and binge drinking." *Journal of Health Economics*, 26, pp. 950–967.

Deveny, Kathleen. 2003. "We're not in the mood." *Newsweek*, June 30, pp. 40–46.

De Visser, Richard, and Dee McDonald. 2007. "Swings and roundabouts: Management of jealousy in heterosexual 'swinging' couples." *British Journal of Social Psychology*, 46, pp. 459–476.

Diamond, Milton. 2009. "Pornography, public acceptance and sex related crime: A review." *International Journal of Law & Psychiatry*, September, pp. 304–314.

Dickey, Christopher. 1991. "Not just a case of trying to save face." *Newsweek*, January 21, p. 22.

Diken, Bulent, and Carsten Bagge Laustsen. 2005. "Becoming abject: Rape as a weapon of war." *Body & Society*, 11, pp. 111–128.

Dillon, Sam. 2009. "Study finds that about 10 percent of young male dropouts are in jail or detention." *New York Times*, October 9, p. A12.

Dohrenwend, Bruce, and Barbara Dohrenwend. 1974. "Psychiatric disorders in urban settings." In S. Arietti and G. Caplan (eds.), *American Handbook of Psychiatry*. New York: Basic Books.

Dohrenwend, Bruce P., and Barbara Snell Dohrenwend. 1976. "Sex differences and psychiatric disorders." *American Journal of Sociology*, 81, pp. 1447–1454.

Dokoupil, Tony. 2008. "Why I am leaving guyland." *Newsweek*, September 8, pp. 70–71.

Donnerstein, Edward, et al. 1987. *The Question of Pornography: Research Findings and Policy Implications*. New York: Free Press.

Dresser, Norine. 2005. *Multicultural Manners: Essential Rules of Etiquette for the 21st Century*. Hoboken, NJ: John Wiley & Sons.

Dugas, Christine. 2008. "More consumers, workers shoplift as economy slows." *USA Today*, June 19, p. 1B.

Dugas, Christine. 2010. "For boomers, retirement jobs can be a tough fit . . . ." *USA Today*, August 10, p. 1A.

Dugger, Celia W. 1996. "African ritual pain: Genital cutting." *New York Times*, October 5, pp. 1, 4–5.

Duncombe, Jean, et al. (eds.). 2004. *The State of Affairs: Explorations in Infidelity and Commitment*. Mahwah, NJ: Lawrence Erlbaum Associates.

Dunn, Jennifer L. 2010. "'Everyone knows who the sluts are': How young women get around the stigma." In Alex Thio et al., *Readings in Deviant Behavior*, 6th ed, pp. 207–210. Boston: Allyn & Bacon.

Durkheim, Emile. 1915/1966. *The Elementary Forms of the Religious Life*. New York: Free Press.

Dychtwald, Ken. 1989. *Age Wave: The Challenges and Opportunities of an Aging America*. Los Angeles: Jeremy Tarcher.

Ebenkamp, Becky. 2001. "Dancing 'round the gay poll." *Brandweek*, June 11, p. 23.

Edwards, Tamala M. 2000. "Flying solo." *Time*, August 28, pp. 47–53.

Egan, Timothy. 2000. "Technology sent Wall Street into market for pornography." *New York Times*, October 23, pp. A1, A20.

Ehrenreich, Barbara. 2001. *Nickel and Dined: On (Not) Getting By in America*. New York: Henry Holt.

Eisenberg, Anne. 1999. "Female M.D.'s more open with options, patients say." *New York Times*, August 17, p. D8.

Elias, Sean. 2008. "Investigating the aspen elite." *Contexts*, fall, pp. 62–64.

Elliott, Diana M., et al. 2004. "Adult sexual assault: Prevalence, symptomatology, and sex differences in the general population." *Journal of Traumatic Stress*, 17, pp. 203–211.

Elliott, Michael. 2010. "The world economy." *Time*, July 12, pp. G1–G3.

Elwert, Felix, and Nicholas Christakis. 2006. "Widowhood and race." *American Sociological Review*, 71, pp. 16–41.

Engs, Ruth C., and David J. Hanson. 1994. "Boozing and brawling on campus: A national study of violent problems associated with drinking over the last decade." *Journal of Criminal Justice*, 22, pp. 171–180.

Ephron, Dan, et al. 2007. "Forgotten heroes." *Newsweek*, March 5, p. 28.

Epstein, Cynthia Fuchs. 1976. "Sex roles." In Robert K. Merton and Robert Nisbet (eds.), *Contemporary Social Problems*. New York: Harcourt Brace Jovanovich.

Ermann, M. David, and Richard J. Lundman (eds.). 2002. *Corporate and Governmental Deviance*, 6th ed. New York: Oxford University Press.

Erofeyev, Victor. 2002. "The Russian god." *New Yorker*, December 16, pp. 56–63.

Evans, Kelly. 2009. "Recession drives more women into the work force." *Wall Street Journal*, November 12, p. A21.

Fahim, Kareem, and Nate Schweber. 2008. "Three youths in Montclair are charged in sex attack." *New York Times*, March 12, p. A3.

Falkenrath, Richard A. 2006. "Grading the war on terrorism." *Foreign Affairs*, 85, pp. 122–128.

Farley, John E. 1984. *American Social Problems*. Englewood Cliffs, NJ: Prentice Hall.

Farris, Michael P. 1997. "Solid evidence to support home schooling." *Wall Street Journal*, March 5, p. A18.

Farwell, Nancy. 2004. "War rape: New conceptualizations and responses." *Affilia*, 19, pp. 389–403.

FBI (Federal Bureau of Investigation). 2010. *Uniform Crime Reports*. Washington, DC: U.S. Government Printing Office.

Feagin, Joe R., and Clairece Booher Feagin. 2003. *Racial and Ethnic Relations*, 7th ed. Englewood Cliffs, NJ: Prentice Hall.

Feder, Judy. 2009. "Federal action is required." *U.S. News & World Report*, February, p. 6.

Fergusson, David M. 2006. "Cannabis use and other illicit drug use: Testing the cannabis gateway hypothesis." *Addiction*, 101, pp. 556–569.

Ferro, Christine, et al. 2008. "Current perceptions of marital rape: Some good and not-so-good news." *Journal of Interpersonal Violence*, 23, pp. 764–779.

Feyerick, Deborah, and Sheila Steffen. 2009. "'Sexting' lands teen on sex offender list." April 8. Available online: www.cnn.com

File, Thom, and Sarah Crissey. 2010. "Voting and registration in the election of November. 2008." *Current Population Reports*, pp. 1–20.

Firestone, David. 2001. "The new-look suburbs: Denser or more far-flung?" *New York Times*, April 17, pp. A1, A14.

Fischman, Josh. 2005. "Who will take care of you?" *U.S. News & World Report*, January 31/February 7, p. 46.

Fish, Isaac Stone. 2010. "Back to the Land." *Newsweek*, April 19, p. 1.

Fisher, Bonnie S., Francis T. Cullen, and Leah E. Daigle. 2005. "The discovery of acquaintance rape: The salience of methodological innovation and rigor." *Journal of Interpersonal Violence*, 20, pp. 493–500.

Fisher, Helen E. 1994. *Anatomy of Love: The Natural History of Monogamy, Adultery, and Divorce*. New York: Norton.

Fitzpatrick, Laura. 2010. "Arnold Schwarzenegger." Available online: www.time.com/time/specials/packages/article/

Fitzpatrick, Maureen, and Barbara McPherson. 2010. "Coloring within the lines: Gender stereotypes in contemporary coloring books." *Sex Roles*, January, pp. 127–137.

Flanagan, Caitlin. 2009. "Why marriage matters." *Time*, July 13, pp. 45–49.

Flexner, Eleanor, and Ellen F. Fitzpatrick. 1996. *Century of Struggle: The Women's Rights Movement in the United States*. Cambridge, MA: Harvard University Press.

Ford, Clellan S., and Frank A. Beach. 1970. *Patterns of Sexual Behavior*. New York: Harper & Row.

Fox, James Alan, and Jack Levin. 2005. *Extreme Killing: Understanding Serial and Mass Murder*. Thousand Oaks, CA: Sage.

Fox, James Alan, Jack Levin, and Kenna Quinet. 2007. *The Will to Kill*, 3rd ed. Boston: Allyn & Bacon.

Fram, Leslie. 2003. *How to Marry a Divorced Man*. New York: Regan Books.

Francese, Peter. 2002. "Continuing education." *Demographics*, April, pp. 46–47.

Freedman, Alix M. 1990. "Deadly diet." *Wall Street Journal*, December 18, pp. A1, A4.

Freedman, Michael. 2009. "Big government is back—big time." *Newsweek*, February 16, pp. 24–27.

Freeman, Richard B. 2007. "Immigration's economic impact." *Encyclopaedia Britannica Book of the Year*, pp. 486–487.

Fried, Wendy. 2008. "Slow road to wealth, with no shortcuts." *New York Times*, October 12, p. 2.

Fukuyama, Francis. 2009. "How to re-moralize America." *Wilson Quarterly*, Vol. 23, Issue 3, pp. 32–44.

Fussell, Paul. 1992. *Class: A Guide Through the American Status System*. New York: Touchstone.

Gabrieli, Chris. 2009. "Expand hours, expand learning." *U.S. News & World Report*, May, p. 12.

Galea, S., et al. 2002. "Psychological sequelae of the September 11 terrorist attacks in New York City." *New England Journal of Medicine*, 346, pp. 982–987.

Galen, Luke W., and William M. Rogers. 2004. "Religiosity, alcohol expectancies, drinking motives and their interaction in the prediction of drinking among college students." *Journal of Studies on Alcohol, 65*, pp. 469–476.

Gallagher, Bernard. 2002. *The Sociology of Mental Illness*, 4th ed. Upper Saddle River, NJ: Prentice Hall.

Gambetta, Diego (ed.). 2005. *Making Sense of Suicide Missions*. New York: Oxford University Press.

Gandel, Stephen. 2009. "Why boomers can't quit." *Time*, May 25, p. 46.

Gans, Herbert J. 1971. "The uses of poverty: The poor pay all." *Social Policy*, 2, pp. 20–24.

Gauthier, DeAnn K., and William B. Bankston. 2004. "'Who kills whom' revisited: A sociological study of variation in the sex ratio of spouse killings." *Homicide Studies*, 8, pp. 96–122.

Gearan, Ann. 2006. "U.S. cites countries for human trafficking." June 5, 2006. Available online: www.yahoo.com

Gegax, T. Trent. 2004. "The second war." *Newsweek*, March 12, p. 1.

Gerber, Gwendolyn L. 1989. "The more positive evaluation of men than women on the gender-stereotyped traits." *Psychological Reports*, 65, pp. 275–286.

Gerstel, Naomi, and Natalia Sarkisian. 2006. "Marriage: The good, the bad, and the greedy." *Contexts*, fall, pp. 16–21.

Gezari, Vanessa. 2009. "Where to now?" *The Washington Post*, March 15, p. W8.

Gibbs, Nancy. 2007. "Darkness falls: One troubled student rains down death on a quiet campus." *Time*, April 30, pp. 37–53.

Gibbs, Nancy. 2009. "Thrift nation." *Time*, April 27, pp. 20–23.

Gilligan, Carol. 2006. "Mommy, I know you." *Newsweek*, January 30, p. 53.

Gilman, Hank. 1986. "Marketers court older consumers as balance of buying power shifts." *Wall Street Journal*, April 23, p. A37.

Gilmartin, Brian G. 1975. "That swinging couple down the block." *Psychology Today*, February, pp. 54–58.

Gingrich, Newt. 2009. "The market can fix the problem." *U.S. News & World Report*, February, p. 7.

Giordano, Peggy C., Monica A. Longmore, and Wendy D. Manning. 2006. "Gender and the meanings of adolescent romantic relationships: A focus on boys." *American Sociological Review*, 71, pp. 260–287.

Girard, Chris. 1993. "Age, gender, and suicide: A cross-national analysis." *American Sociological Review*, 58, pp. 553–574.

Glaab, Charles N., and A. Theodore Brown. 1983. *A History of Urban America*, 3rd ed. New York: Macmillan.

Goldstein, Jacob. 2008. "As doctors get a life, strains show." *Wall Street Journal*, April 29, pp. A1, A14.

Goldstein, Melvyn C., and Cynthia M. Beall. 1982. "Indirect modernization and the status of the elderly in a rural third-world setting." *Journal of Gerontology*, 37, pp. 743–748.

Goleman, Daniel. 1990. "Stereotypes of the sexes said to persist in therapy." *New York Times*, April 10, pp. B1, B7.

Gomez, Alan. 2009. "Military focuses on 'internal insurgents' in suicides." *USA Today*, March 25, p. 1a.

Goode, Erica. 2009. "After combat, victims of an inner war." *New York Times*, August 2, p. 1.

Goode, Erich. 1981. "Drugs and crime." In Abraham S. Blumberg (ed.), *Current Perspective on Criminal Behavior*. New York: Knopf.

Goode, Erich. 2004. "Legalize it? A bulletin from the war on drugs." *Contexts*, summer, pp. 19–25.

Goode, Erich. 2005. *Drugs in American Society*, 6th ed. New York: McGraw-Hill.

Goodlad, John I. 1984. *A Place Called School: Prospects for the Future*. New York: McGraw-Hill.

Goodstein, Laurie. 2009. "Poll finds U.S. Muslims thriving, but not content." *New York Times*, March 2, p. 11.

Goodstein, Laurie. 2010. "American Muslims ask, will we ever belong?" *New York Times*, September 6, p. 1.

Gorman, Christine. 1992a. "Can drug firms be trusted?" *Time*, February 10, p. 43.

Gorman, Christine. 1992b. "Sizing up the sexes." *Time*, January 20, pp. 42–51.

Gorman, Christine. 1998. "Playing the HMO game." *Time*, July 13, pp. 22–32.

Gottdiener, Mark. 1985. *The Social Production of Urban Space*. Austin: University of Texas Press.

Gottdiener, Mark. 1994. *The New Urban Sociology*. New York: McGraw-Hill.

Gottlieb, Annie. 1971. "Female human beings." *New York Times Book Review*, February 21, p. 2.

Gottman, John. 1994. *Why Marriages Succeed or Fail*. New York: Simon & Schuster.

Gottman, John. 2002. *The Mathematics of Marriage: Dynamic Nonlinear Models*. Cambridge, MA: MIT Press.

Götz, Ignacio. 1999. *The Culture of Sexism*. Westport, CT: Praeger.

Gould, Terry. 2000. *The Lifestyle: A Look at the Erotic Rites of Swingers*. Buffalo, NY: Firefly Books.

Gray, Paul. 1995. "The Catholic paradox." *Time*, October 9, pp. 64–68.

Greenberg, David F. (ed.) 1981. *Crime and Capitalism: Readings in Marxist Criminology*. Palo Alto, CA: Mayfield.

Greene, Jay P. 2003. "An unfair grade for vouchers." *Wall Street Journal*, May 16, p. A8.

Greene, Kelly. 2009. "There goes retirement." *Wall Street Journal*, February 14, pp. R1, R4.

Greenhouse, Steven. 1994. "State department finds widespread abuse of world's women." *New York Times*, February 3, pp. A1, A6.

Gregory, Raymond F. 2004. *Unwelcome and Unlawful: Sexual Harassment in the American Workplace*. Ithaca, NY: Cornell University Press.

Gross, Jane. 2007. "Prevalence of Alzheimer's rises 10% in 5 years." *New York Times*, March 21, p. 14.

Gruenbaum, Ellen. 2001. *The Female Circumcision Controversy: An Anthropological Perspective*. Philadelphia: University of Pennsylvania Press.

Guttmacher Institute. 2010. "Facts on American teens' sexual and reproductive health." Available online: www. Guttmacher.org/pubs/FB-ATSRH.html

Hacker, Andrew. 1992. *Two Nations: Black and White, Separate, Hostile, Unequal*. New York: Scribner's.

Hall, Irene H., et al. 2008. "Estimation of HIV incidence in the United States." *Journal of the American Medical Association*, 300, pp. 520–529.

Hamill, Heathe, and Diego Gambetta. 2006. "Who do taxi drivers trust?" *Contexts*, summer, pp. 29–33.

Hammond, D. Corydon, and Gary Q. Jorgenson. 1981. "Alcohol and sex: A volatile cocktail." *USA Today*, July, pp. 44–46.

Hampson, Rick. 2010. "A 'watershed' case in school bullying?" *USA Today*, April 5, p. 1A.

Hannon, Lance E. 2005. "Extremely poor neighborhoods and homicide." *Social Science Quarterly*, 86, pp. 1418–1434.

Hansen, Brian. 2004. "The proliferation of cybercrimes." In Alex Thio and Thomas Calhoun (eds.), *Readings in Deviant Behavior*, 3rd ed. Boston: Allyn & Bacon.

Hanson, David J. 1995. "The United States of America." In Dwight B. Heath (ed.), *International Handbook on Alcohol and Culture*. Westport, CT: Greenwood.

Harayda, Janice. 1986. *The Joy of Being Single*. Garden City, NY: Doubleday.

Harned, Melanie S. 2005. "Understanding women's labeling of unwanted sexual experiences with dating partners: A qualitative analysis." *Violence Against Women*, 11, pp. 374–413.

Harper, Dee Wood, and Lydia Voigt. 2007. "Homicide followed by suicide: An integrated theoretical perspective." *Homicide Studies*, 11, pp. 295–318.

Harris, Andrew, and Arthur J. Lurigio. 2007. "Mental illness and violence: A brief review of research and assessment strategies." *Aggression and Violent Behavior*, 12, pp. 542–552.

Harris, Anthony R., and Lisa R. Meidlinger. 1995. "Criminal behavior: Race and class." In Joseph F. Sheley (ed.), *Criminology: A Contemporary Handbook*. Belmont, CA: Wadsworth.

Harris, Marvin. 1995. *Cultural Anthropology*, 4th ed. New York: HarperCollins.

Harris, Monica J., and Robert Rosenthal. 1985. "Mediation of interpersonal expectancy effects: 31 meta-analyses." *Psychological Bulletin*, 97, pp. 363–386.

Hartmann, Heidi. 2009. "Women, the recession, and the stimulus package." *Dissent*, fall, pp. 42–47.

Hassanin, Ibrahim, et al. 2008. "Prevalence of female genital cutting in Upper Egypt: 6 years after enforcement of prohibition law." *Reproductive BioMedicine Online*, 16, pp. 27–31.

Hauffe, Sarah, and Louise Porter. 2009. "An interpersonal comparison of lone and group rape offenses." *Psychology, Crime & Law*, June, pp. 469–491.

Hauser, Philip M. 1981. "Chicago—Urban crisis exemplar." In John Palen (ed.), *City Scenes*, 2nd ed. Boston: Little, Brown.

Havemann, Joel. 2010. "The great recession." *Encyclopedia Britannica: 2010 Book of the Year*, pp. 170–173. Encyclopedia Britannica, Inc.

Hayden, Thomas. 2004. "A modern life." *U.S. News & World Report*, October 4, pp. 45–50.

Healy, Bernadine. 2006. "AIDS: We're not there yet." *U.S. News & World Report*, December 11, p. 86.

Healy, Patrick O'Gilfoil. 2005. "Once derelict, now desirable." *New York Times*, July 23, Section 11, pp. 1, 8.

Hechinger, John. 2002. "Easy money." *Wall Street Journal*, October 8, pp. A1, A18.

Heilbroner, Robert L. 1972. *The Worldly Philosophers: The Lives, Times, and Ideas of the Great Economic Thinkers*, 4th ed. New York: Simon & Schuster.

Hendrie, Caroline. 2004. "Report examining sexual misconduct taps some nerves." *Education Week*, July 14, pp. 1–2.

Henry, Andrew, and James Short. 1954. *Suicide and Homicide*. New York: Free Press.

Hensley, Christopher, and Richard Tewksbury. 2005. "Wardens' perceptions of prison sex." *The Prison Journal*, 85, pp. 186–197.

Herbert, Wray. 1999. "When strangers become family." *U.S News & World Report*, November 29, pp. 58–67.

Herd, Denise. 1991. "Drinking patterns in the black population." In Walter B. Clark and Michael E. Hilton (eds.), *Alcohol in America*. Albany, NY: State University of New York Press.

Hernlund, Ylva, and Bettina Shell-Duncan. 2007. *Transcultural Bodies: Female Genital Cutting in Global Context*. New Brunswick, NJ: Rutgers University Press.

Hess, Frederick M. 2009. "Time needs to be better spent." *U.S. News & World Report*, May, p. 13.

Hildreth, Carolyn J. 2009. "Elder abuse." *Journal of the American Medical Association*, August 5, p. 588.

Hilton, Michael E. 1991. "Regional diversity in U.S. drinking practices." In Walter B. Clark and Michael E. Hilton (eds.), *Alcohol in America: Drinking Practices and problems*. Albany, NY: State University of New York Press.

Hirschi, Travis. 1962. "The professional prostitute." *Berkeley Journal of Sociology*, 7, pp. 44–45.

Hirschi, Travis. 1969. *Causes of Delinquency*. Berkeley: University of California Press.

Hobson, Katherine. 2005. "Doctors vanish from view." *U.S. News & World Report*, January 31/February 7, pp. 48–53.

Hochschild, Arlie Russell. 1997. *The Time Bind: When Work Becomes Home and Home Becomes Work*. New York: Metropolitan Books.

Hoover, Eric. 2004. "Studies find 'social norms' strategy reduces drinking at colleges." *Chronicle of Higher Education*, August 13, p. A32.

Horwitz, Allan V., and Jerome C. Wakefield. 2006. "The epidemic in mental illness: Clinical fact or survey artifact?" *Contexts*, 5, pp. 19–23.

Hosenball, Mark. 2002. "Islamic cyberterror." *Newsweek*, May 20, p. 10.

Hraba, Joseph. 1979. *American Ethnicity*. Itasca, IL: Peacock.

HUD (U.S. Department of Housing and Urban Development). 2009. "The 2008 annual homeless assessment report to congress, July, 2009."

Huifeng, He. 2009. "Stealing of cyber veggies thrives in a lonely world." *South China Morning Post*, p. 5.

Human Rights Campaign. 2008. "Answers to questions about marriage equality." In Kurt Finsterbusch, *Taking Sides: Clashing Views on Social Issues*, 14th ed. Dubuque, IA: McGraw-Hill.

Humphreys, Laud. 1970. *Tearoom Trade: Impersonal Sex in Public Places*. Chicago: Aldine.

Hunnicutt, Trevor. 2010. "CSU rebuts report that it mismanaged public funds." August 26. Available online: http://boston.com

Huselid, Rebecca Farmer, and M. Lynne Cooper. 1992. "Gender roles as mediators of sex differences in adolescent alcohol use and abuse." *Journal of Health and Social Behavior*, 33, pp. 348–362.

Hutson, Matthew. 2008. "Vice or virtue?" *Psychology Today*, February, p. 18.

Hymowitz, Kay S. 2004. "Our changing culture: Abandoning the sixties." *Current*, June, pp. 12–18.

Ilesanmi, Olufemi. 2010. "Sexual offenses in a Muslim world." *International Journal of Human Rights*, April, pp. 215–231.

Inhofe, James. 2010. "'Consensus' is no such thing." *U.S. News & World Report*, April, p. 20.

Isikoff, Michael, et al. 2006. "How the Jefferson search put Bush in a bind." *Newsweek*, June 5, p. 6.

Jacobs, Jerry A, 2003. Detours on the road to equality: Women, work and higher education." *Contexts*, winter, pp. 32–41.

Jacobson, Mark Z. 2002. *Atmospheric Pollution: History, Science, and Regulation*. New York: Cambridge University Press.

Janus, Samuel S., and Cynthia L. Janus. 1993. *The Janus Report on Sexual Behavior*. New York: Wiley.

Jauhar, Sandeep. 2001. "Hidden in the world of medicine, discrimination and stereotypes." *New York Times*, June 19, p. D6.

Jayson, Sharon. 2006. "Colorblind." *USA Today*, February 8, p. 1A.

Jayson, Sharon. 2008. "Living together isn't just 'playing house.'" *USA Today*, July 29, p. D6.

Jayson, Sharon. 2009. "Gender roles see a 'conflict' shift." *USA Today*, March 26, p. A1.

Jayson, Sharon. 2010a. "Living together first has little effect on marriage success." *USA Today*, March 3, p. D7.

Jayson, Sharon. 2010b. "Teen pregnancies, abortions rise—some find link to abstinence focus." *USA Today*, January 26, p. A1.

Jefferson, David J. 2005. "America's most dangerous drug." *Newsweek*, August 8, pp. 41–48.

Jefferson, David J. 2006. "How AIDS changed America." *Newsweek*, May 15, pp. 36–41.

Jehl, Douglas. 1999. "Arab honor's price: A woman's blood." *New York Times*, June 20, pp. 1, 9.

Jehl, Douglas, and David Rohde. 2004. "Captured Queda figure led way to information behind warning." *New York Times*, August 2, p. A1.

Jellinek, E. M. 1952. "Phases of alcohol addiction." *Quarterly Journal of Studies on Alcohol*, 13, pp. 673–684.

Jencks, Christopher. 2002. "Does inequality matter?" *Daedalus*, winter, pp. 49–65.

Jenks, Richard J. 1998. "Swinging: A review of the literature." *Archives of Sexual Behavior*, 27, pp. 507–521.

Jenness, Valerie. 1990. "From sex as sin to sex as work: COYOTE and the reorganization of prostitution as a social problem." *Social Problems*, 37, pp. 403–420.

Johnson, Dirk. 2004. "Policing a rural plague." *Newsweek*, March 8, p. 41.

Johnson, Sally. 1995. "Continuing education: College à la carte." *New York Times*, December 6, pp. 22–24.

Johnson, Sally. 2005. "Continuing education: College à la carte." *New York Times: Education Life*, August 6, pp. 22–24.

Jones, Jeffrey M. 2009. "Majority of Americans continue to oppose gay marriage." *Gallup Poll*, May 27, 2009.

Jost, Kenneth. 2008. "Women in politics." *CQ Researcher*, March 21, pp. 1–33.

Joyner, Chris. 2008. "Bank robberies increase around USA." *USA Today*, June 16, p. 3A.

Joyner, Kara, and Grace Kao. 2005. "Interracial relationship and the transition to adulthood." *American Sociological Review*, 70, pp. 563–581.

Jukkala, Tanya, et al. 2008. "Economic strain, social relations, gender, and binge drinking in Moscow." *Social Science & Medicine*, 66, pp. 663–674.

Kalb, Claudia, 2001. "Playing with painkillers." *Newsweek*, April 9, pp. 45–48.

Kalb, Claudia. 2008. "And now, back in the real world. . . ." *Newsweek*, March 3, p. 41.

Kalb, Claudia. 2010. "Culture of Corpulence." *Newsweek*, March 22, pp. 42–48.

Kantrowitz, Barbara, and Pat Wingert. 2001. "Unmarried, with children." *Newsweek*, May 28, pp. 46–54.

Kaplan, David E., and Kevin Whitelaw. 2004. "Terror's new soldiers." *U.S. News & World Report*, November 1, pp. 34–35.

Karp, David A., and William C. Yoels. 1998. *Sociology in Everyday Life*. Prospect Height, IL: Waveland.

Kashiwagi, Akiko. 2008. "A post-car society." *Newsweek*, February 25, p. 10.

Katchadourian, Herant. 1989. *Fundamentals of Human Sexuality*, 5th ed. New York: Holt, Rinehart and Winston.

Katz, Bruce, and Jennifer Bradley. 2009. "The suburban challenge." *Newsweek*, January 26, p. 57.

Keen, Judy. 2009. "For immigrants, living the dream is getting tougher. . . ." *USA Today*, June 16, p. 1A.

Kenworthy, Lane. 2009. "Tax myths." *Contexts*, summer, pp. 28–32.

Kessler, Ronald C., et al. 1985. "Social factors in psychopathology: Stress, social support, and coping processes." *Annual Review of Psychology*, 36, pp. 560–561.

Kessler, Ronald C., et al. 1994. "Lifetime and 12-month prevalence of *DSM-III*-psychiatric disorders in the United States." *Archives of General Psychiatry*, 51, pp. 8–19.

Kessler, Ronald C., et al. 2004. "Prevalence, severity, and unmet need for treatment of mental disorders in the World Health Organization world mental health surveys." *Journal of the American Medical Association*, pp. 2581–2590.

Kessler, Ronald C., et al. 2005a. "Lifetime prevalence and age-of-onset distribution of *DSM* disorders in the national comorbidity survey replication." *Archives of General Psychiatry*, 62, pp. 593–602.

Kessler, Ronald C., et al. 2005b. "Prevalence, severity, and comorbidity of 12-month *DSM-IV* disorders in the national comorbidity survey replication." *Archives of General Psychiatry*, 62, pp. 617–627.

Kessler, Ronald C., and Harold W. Neighbors. 1986. "A new perspective on the relationships among race, social class, and psychological distress." *Journal of Health and Social Behavior*, 27, pp. 107–115.

Kilborn, Peter T. 2000. "Learning at home, students take the lead." *New York Times*, December 5, pp. 4–5.

Kimball, Meredith M. 1989. "A new perspective on women's math achievement." *Psychological Bulletin*, 105, pp. 198–214.

Kimmel, Michael. 2008. *Guyland: The Perilous World Where Boys Become Men*. New York: HarperCollins.

Kingsbury, Alex. 2006. "The great campus divide." *U.S. News & World Report*, May 15, pp. 31–32.

Kingsbury, Alex. 2007. "The ex-con next door." *U.S. News & World Report*, December 17, pp. 38–40.

Kingston, Anne. 2010. "The birth of botox feminism." *Maclean's*, January 18, p. 42.

Kingston, Drew A., et al. 2008. "Pornography use and sexual aggression: The impact of frequency and type of pornography use on recidivism among sexual offenders." *Aggressive Behavior*, 34, pp. 341–351.

Kinsey, Alfred C., et al. 1948. *Sexual Behavior in the Human Male*. Philadelphia: Saunders.

Kinsey, Afred C., et al. 1953. *Sexual Behavior in the Human Female*. Philadelphia: Saunders.

Kirk, James, and Robert Belovics. 2008. "A look into the temporary employment industry and its workers." *Journal of Employment Counseling*, September, pp. 131–142.

Klam, Matthew. 2001. "Experiencing Ecstasy." *New York Times Magazine*, January 21, pp. 38–43, 64–79.

Klemke, Lloyd W. 1992. *The Sociology of Shoplifting: Boosters and Snitches Today.* Westport, CT: Praeger.

Kliff, Sarah. 2008. "No glass ceiling here." *Newsweek*, June 22, p. 17.

Klinger, David A. 2001. "Suicidal intent in victim-precipitated homicide." *Homicide Studies*, 5, pp. 206–226.

Knight, Danielle. 2006. "Ethically challenged." *U.S. News & World Report*, May 22, pp. 24–25.

Koch, Wendy. 2008. "Ban on child porn web forums affects few." *USA Today*, June 13, p. 3A.

Konner, Melvin. 2001. "Have we lost the healing touch?" *Newsweek*, June 25, p. 77.

Konty, Mark. 2005. "Microanomie: The cognitive foundations of the relationship between anomie and deviance." *Criminology*, 43, pp. 107–131.

Kopelowicz, Alex, and T. George Bidder. 1992. "Outcomes of schizophrenia." *American Journal of Psychiatry*, 149, p. 426.

Kosova, Weston. 2007. "The power that was." *Newsweek*, April 23, pp. 24–31.

Koss, Mary P. 1995. "Hidden rape: Sexual aggression and victimization in a national sample of students in higher education." In Patricia Searles and Ronald J. Berger (eds.), *Rape and Society*. Boulder, CO: Westview.

Kotkin, Joel. 2009. "The end of upward mobility?" *Newsweek*, January 26, p. 64.

Kotz, Deborah. 2009. "5 common myths about aging." February 20. Available online: www.usnews.com

Krauthammer, Charles. 1990. "In praise of low voter turnout." *Time*, May 21, p. 88.

Kringlen, Einas, et al. 2006. "Mental illness in a rural area." *Social Psychiatry & Psychiatric Epidemiology*, 41, pp. 713–719.

Krysan, Maria, and Reynolds Farley. 2002. "The residential preferences of blacks: Do they explain persistent segregation?" *Social Forces*, 80, pp. 937–981.

Kuchment, Anna. 2003. "Get a move on." *Newsweek*, October 20, p. E28.

Kuczynski, Alex. 1999. "Enough about feminism. Should I wear lipstick?" *New York Times*, March 28, p. 4.

Kuo, Michelle. 2001. "Asia's dirty secret." *Harvard International Review*, 22 (summer), pp. 42–45.

Kuo, Wen H. 1984. "Prevalence of depression among Asian-Americans." *Journal of Nervous and Mental Disease*, 172, pp. 449–457.

Kuo, Wen H., and Yung-Mei Tsai. 1986. "Social networking, hardiness, and immigrant's mental health." *Journal of Health and Social Behavior*, 27, pp. 133–149.

Kutchins, Herb, and Stuart A. Kirk. 1997. *Making Us Crazy*. New York: Free Press.

Lacayo, Richard. 1990. "Why no blue blood will flow." *Time*, November 26, p. 34.

Lacayo, Richard. 2004. "For better or for worse?" *Time*, March 8, pp. 26–33.

Lacey, Marc. 2004. "Amnesty says Sudan militias use rape as weapon." *New York Times*, July 19, p. 9.

Lakoff, George. 2002. *Moral Politics: How Liberals and Conservatives Think*. Chicago: University of Chicago Press.

Larson, Jan. 1996. "Temps are here to stay." *American Demographics*, February, pp. 26–31.

Laumann, Edward O., et al. 1994. *The Social Organization of Sexuality: Sexual Practices in the United States*. Chicago: University of Chicago Press.

Laumann, Edward O., and Robert T. Michael (eds). 2001. *Sex, Love, and Health in America: Private Choices and Public Policies*. Chicago: University of Chicago Press.

Lauritsen, Janet L., et al. 2009. "Trends in the gender gap in violent offending: New evidence from the national crime victimization survey." *Criminology*, 47, pp. 361–399.

Lawson, Annette. 1988. *Adultery: An Analysis of Love and Betrayal*. New York: Basic Books.

Lee, Jongho. 2009. "Variation in the significance of emotional response as a guide to the voting decision." Paper presented at the annual meeting of Southern Political Science Association. January 7, 2009, New Orleans, LA.

Lee, Louise. 2006. "Kick out the kids, bring in the sales." *Business Week*, April 17, p. 42.

Lee, Matthew R., et al. 2007. "Revisiting the southern culture of violence." *Sociological Quarterly*, 48, pp. 253–275.

Lee, Matthew R., Timothy C. Hayes, and Shaun A. Thomas. 2008. "Regional variation in the effect of structural factors on homicide in rural areas." *Social Science Journal*, 45, pp. 76–94.

Lee, Valerie, and Julia Smith. 2001. *Restructuring High Schools for Equity and Excellence: What Works?* New York: Teachers College Press.

Lehrer, Eli. 2001. "Hell behind bars." *National Review*, February 5, pp. 24–25.

Leinwand, Donna. 2009. "Half of men arrested test 'positive' for drugs; 10-city study shows need to offer treatment." *USA Today*, May 28, p. 3A.

Leland, John. 1995. "Bisexuality." *Newsweek*, July 17, pp. 44–50.

Leland, John. 1996. "The fear of heroin is shooting up." *Newsweek*, August 26, pp. 55–56.

Leland, John. 2000. "Shades of gay." *Newsweek*, March 20, pp. 46–49.

Lemelson, Robert. 2001. "Strange maladies." *Psychology Today*, December, pp. 60–64.

Lemonick, Michael D. 2001. "Life in the greenhouse." *Time*, June 7, pp. 24–29.

Lemonick, Michael D. 2004. "How we grew so big." *Time*, June 7, pp. 66–74.

Leslie, Leigh A. 1996. "Sexism in family therapy: Does training in gender roles make a difference?" *Journal of Marital and Family Therapy*, 22, pp. 253–269.

LeVay, Simon, and Elisabeth Nonas. 1995. *City of Friends: A Portrait of the Gay and Lesbian Community in America*. Cambridge, MA: MIT Press.

Levine, Daniel S. 1993. "Adult students, adult needs." *New York Times*, April 4. Sect. 4A, pp. 32–33.

Levy, Ariel. 1999. "Sex clubs." *New York*, May 3, p. 72.

Lewin, Tamar. 2008. "Girls' gains have not cost boys, report says." *New York Times*, May 20. Available online: www.nytimes.com

Lewis, James. 2005. "The threat of cyberterrorism is exaggerated." In James D. Torr (ed.), *The Internet: Opposing Viewpoints*, pp. 101–109. Detroit, MI: Greenhaven Press.

Lewis, Janet V. 2001. *Sexual Harassment: Issues and Analyses*. Huntington, NY: Nova Science.

Lieberman, Jethro K. 1973. *How the Government Breaks the Law*. Baltimore, MD: Penguin.

Light, Richard J. 2001. *Making the Most of College: Students Speak Their Minds*. Cambridge, MA: Harvard University Press.

Lilienfeld, Scott O., and Hal Arkowitz. 2007. "Is there really an autism epidemic?" *Scientific American Special Edition*, Vol. 17, Issue 4, pp. 58–61.

Lindesmith, Alfred R. 1968. *Addiction and Opiates*. Chicago: Aldine.

Linsky, Arnold, Ronet Bachman, and Murray Straus. 1995. *Stress, Culture, and Aggression*. New Haven, CT: Yale University Press.

Linz, Daniel, and Neil Malamuth. 1993. *Pornography*. Newbury Park, CA: Sage.

Liptak, Adam. 2007. "Does death penalty save lives? A new debate." *New York Times*, November 18, pp. 1, 32.

Liptak, Adam. 2008. "Inmate count in U.S. dwarfs other nations.'" *New York Times*, April 23, p. A1.

Listwan, Shelley Johnson, Francis T. Cullen, and Edward J. Latessa. 2006. "How to prevent prisoner re-entry programs from failing: Insights from evidence-based corrections." *Federal Probation*, 70, pp. 19–25.

Lithwick, Dahlia. 2009. "Women: Truly the fairer sex." *Newsweek*, April 20, p. 13.

Liu, Melinda. 2008. "China's new empty nest." *Newsweek*, March 10, p. 41.

Logan, Samuel. 2009. *This is for the Mara Salvatrucha: Inside the MS-13, America's Most Violent Gang*. New York: Hyperion.

Lomborg, Bjorn. 2001. *The Skeptical Environmentalist: Measuring the Real State of the World*. New York: Cambridge University Press.

Luckenbill, David F. 1985. "Entering male prostitution." *Urban Life*, 14, pp. 131–153.

Luo, Yadong. 2000. *Multinational Corporations in China: Benefiting from Structural Transformation*. Herndon, VA: Books International.

Lynch, David J. 2008. "Global trade talks fall apart." *USA Today*, July 30, p. 1b.

Lynch, Sarah N. 2008. "An American pastime: Smoking pot." *Time*, July 11. Available online: www.time.com/time/health/article/0,8599,1821697,00.html

MacArthur Foundation (Research Network on an Aging Society). 2009. "Facts and fictions about an aging America." *Contexts*, fall, pp. 16–21.

MacArthur Foundation (Research Network on an Aging Society). 2010. "Policies and politics for an aging America." *Contexts*, winter, pp. 22–27.

MacDonald, Heather. 2010. "A crime theory demolished." *Wall Street Journal*, January 5, p. A17.

MacFarquhar, Neil. 2001. "Bin Laden and his followers adhere to an austere, stringent form of Islam." *New York Times*, October 7, p. B7.

Mahbubani, Kishore. 2008. "Tibet through Chinese eyes." *Newsweek*, May 5.

Mallory, Larry. 2003. "Confidence in medical system climbs." August 19. Available online: www.gallup.com

Manegold, Catherine A. 1994. "Bill seeks equality of sexes in school." *New York Times*, February 13, p. 14.

Mann, Coramae Richey. 1996. *Why Women Kill*. Albany, NY: State University of New York Press.

Mann, Joseph. 2006. "Internet use increases the risk of identity theft." In Lisa Yount (ed.), *Does the Internet Increase the Risk of Crime?* pp. 66–72. Detroit, MI: Greenhaven Press.

Marino, Anthony. 2009. "Bosnia v. Serbia and the status of rape as genocide under international law." Available online: www.heinonlinebackup.com

Markon, Jerry. 2010. "Sentence in Bernanke identity theft case." *Washington Post*, January 26, p. B3.

Markon, Jerry, and Neil Irwin. 2009. "ID-theft ring ensnares even the fed chairman." *Washington Post*, August 28, p. A22.

Marquardt, Elizabeth. 2005. "Just whom is this divorce 'good' for?" *The Washington Post*, November 6, p. B1.

Martin, M. Kay, and Barbara Voorhies. 1975. *Female of the Species.* New York: Columbia University Press.

Martin, Michel. 2009. "Economic hardship nothing new for many native Americans." *National Public Radio*, June 9, 9 a.m.

Martin, Patricia Yancey, and Robert A. Hummer. 1995. "Fraternities and rape on campus." In Alex Thio and Thomas C. Calhoun (eds.), *Readings in Deviant Behavior*. New York: HarperCollins.

Martinez, Barbara. 2003. "With medical costs climbing, workers are asked to pay more." *Wall Street Journal*, June 16, pp. A1, A6.

Maruschak, L. M. 2006. *HIV in Prisons.* Washington, DC: Department of Justice.

Masters, Coco. 2007. "Consume less, share more, live simply." *Time*, April 9, p. 100.

Mayberry, Debra. 2006. "32,000? 39,402? 11,500? Just how many lobbyists are there in Washington, anyway?" *The Washington Post*, January 29.

Mazzetti, Mark. 2004. "Rethinking the next wars." *U.S. News & World Report*, January 5, p. 70.

McCardell, John. 2008. "The status quo has bombed." *U.S. News & World Report*, September 15–22, p. 11.

McCarthy, Claire. 2010. "Strong medicine." *Newsweek*, March 22, p. 49.

McCartney, Scott. 2010. "Time to rethink airport security?" November 18. Available online: http://blogs.wsj.com/

McClam, Erin. 2008. "Next wave of homeless vets emerges." *Associated Press*, January 19.

McDowell, Jeanne. 2006. "Q&A: Carrie Fisher." December 7. Available online: www.time.com

McGirk, Tim. 2002. "Lifting the veil on sex slavery." *Time*, February 18, p. 8.

McGirk, Tim. 2009. "The hell of PTSD." *Time*, November 30, pp. 40–43.

McGlone, Matthew. 1998. "Sounds true to me." *Psychology Today*, October, pp. 12–13.

McKay, Betsy, and Ann Carrns. 2004. "As teen births drop, experts are asking why." *Wall Street Journal*, November 17, pp. B1, B2.

McKinlay, John B., and Sonja M. McKinlay. 1994. "Medical measures and the decline of mortality." In Howard D. Schwartz (ed.), *Dominant Issues in Medical Sociology*, 3rd ed. New York: McGraw-Hill.

McKinley, James C. 2010. "Despite army efforts, soldier suicides continue." *New York Times*, October 11, p. A11.

McLanahan, Sara, and Gary D. Sandefur. 1994. *Growing Up with a Single Parent: What Hurts, What Helps*. Cambridge, MA: Harvard University Press.

McMurray, Coleen. 2004. "Number of teen smokers holding steady." The Gallup Poll Tuesday Briefing. Available online: www.gallup.com

Mead, Margaret. 1935. *Sex and Temperament in Three Primitive Societies*. New York: Morrow.

Meloy, J. Reid, et al. 2004. "A comparative analysis of North American adolescent and adult mass murderers." *Behavioral Sciences and the Law*, 22, pp. 291–309.

Mendenhall, Preston. 2009. "Sold as a sex slave in Europe." Available online: www.msnbc.msn.com

Merton, Robert K. 1938. "Social structure and anomie." *American Sociological Review*, 3, pp. 672–682.

Messner, Steven F., and Richard Rosenfeld. 2007. *Crime and the American Dream*, 4th ed. Belmont, CA: Thomson/Wadsworth.

Michael, Robert T., et al. 1994. *Sex in America: A Definitive Survey*. Boston: Little, Brown.

Michels, Robert. 1915. *Political Parties*. Glencoe, IL: Free Press.

Miethe, Terance D., and Wendy C. Regoeczi, with Kriss A. Drass. 2004. *Rethinking Homicide: Exploring the Structure and Process Underlying Deadly Situations*. New York: Cambridge University Press.

Mitchell, Alison. 1997a. "President regrets top U.S. regulator met with bankers." *New York Times*, January 29, pp. A1, A12.

Mitchell, Alison. 1997b. "Survivors of Tuskegee study get apology from Clinton." *New York Times*, May 17, p. 9.

Mohammad, Asef Ali. 2010. "The view from Afghanistan." *Newsweek*, March 8, pp. 40–43.

Monastersky, Richard. 2007. "Is there an autism epidemic?" *Chronicle of Higher Education*, May 11, p. 19.

Moore, Martha. 2006. "Sex and money scandals figure into some House races." *USA Today*, November 8, p. 7A.

Morning, Ann. 2005. "Race." *Contexts*, fall, pp. 44–46.

Moskos, Peter. 2008. "Too dangerous not to regulate." *U.S. News & World Report*, August 4, p. 8.

Mulia, Nina, et al. 2008. "Stress, social support, and problem drinking among women in poverty." *Addiction*, 103, pp. 1283–1293.

Mullins, Christopher W. 2006. *Holding Your Square: Masculinities, Streetlife, and Violence*. Portland, OR: Willan.

Myerson, Allen R. 1998. "Energy addicted in America." *New York Times*, November 1, p. 5.

Nader, Ralph. 1970. "'Foreword' to John C. Esposito," p. viii, *Vanishing Air*. New York: Grossman.

Nader, Ralph, and Robert Weissman. 2001. "Ending corporate welfare as we know it." *Wall Street Journal*, March 7, p. A22.

Naik, Gautam, et al. 2003. "Global baby bust." *Wall Street Journal*, January 24, pp. B1, B4.

Naisbitt, John, and Patricia Aburdene. 1990. *Megatrends 2000: The next ten years—major changes in your life and world.* London: Pan Books.

National Institute on Aging. 2007. "Growing older in America: The health and retirement study." Publication No. 07-5757, March 2007.

Nation's Health. 2008. "UN agencies unite against female genital mutilation." April, p. 10.

NCES (National Center for Education Statistics). 2009. *Digest of Education Statistics.* Available online: http://nces.ed.gov/programs/digest/

Nelson, Mark M. 1990. "Darkness at noon." *Wall Street Journal,* March 1, pp. A1, A13.

New Internationalist. 2010. "Ageing—7 myths." January/February, p. 9.

Newman, Katherine S. 2004. *Rampage: The Social Roots of School Shootings.* New York: Basic Books.

Newman, Rick. 2008. "More welfare for really rich guys." December 30. Available online: www.usnews.com

Newport, Frank. 2009. "Extramarital affairs, like Sanford's, morally taboo." *Gallup Poll,* May 7–10, 2009.

Newton, Michael. 2004. *The Encyclopedia of High-Tech Crime and Crime-Fighting.* New York: Facts on File.

NHSDA (National Household Survey on Drug Abuse). 2008. *National Household Survey on Drug Abuse.* Washington, DC: U.S. Government Printing Office.

Nickerson, David W., and Todd Rogers. 2010. "Do you have a voting plan? Implementation intentions, voter turnout, and organic plan making." *Psychological Science,* 21, pp. 194–199.

Niebuhr, Gustav. 1992. "The lord's name." *Wall Street Journal,* April 27, pp. A1, A4.

Noonan, Erica. 2008. "Watertown center helps survivors tell their stories to following generations." *Boston Globe,* April 20, p. 1.

Norberg, Johan. 2004. "Three cheers for global capitalism." *American Enterprise,* June, pp. 20–27.

NORC (National Opinion Research Center). 2010. *General Social Survey.* Chicago: University of Chicago Press.

Nordheimer, Jon. 1990. "Stepfathers: The shoes rarely fit." *New York Times,* October 18, p. B6.

Nordland, Rod, et al. 2007. "Surge of suicide bombers." *Newsweek,* August 13, pp. 30–32.

Norman, Michael. 1998. "Getting serious about adultery." *New York Times,* July 4, pp. A13, A15.

Norris, Frank H., et al. 2002. "The epidemiology of sex differences in PTSD across developmental, societal, and research contextrs." In Rachel Kimerling, Paige Ouimette, and Jessica Wolfe (eds.), *Gender and PTSD.* New York: Guilford.

NSDUH (National Survey on Drug Use & Health). 2006. "SAMHSA's Latest National Survey on Drug Use & Health." Available online: http://oas.samhsa.gov/NSDUHLatest.htm

Nuland, Sherwin B. 1994. *How We Die: Reflections on Life's Final Chapter.* New York: Knopf.

O'Grady, Mary Anastasia, et al. 2005. *The 2005 Index of Economic Freedom.* Washington, DC: Heritage Foundation.

O'Grady, Mary Anastasia. 2008. "The real key to development." *Wall Street Journal,* January 15, p. A13.

Ohlemacher, Stephen. 2007. "Welfare state growing despite overhauls." February 25. Available online: http://news.yahoo.com

Olson, Elizabeth. 2007. "Study says junk food still dominates youth TV." *New York Times*, March 29, p. C10.

Olson, Theodore B. 2010. "The conservative case for gay marriage." *Newsweek*, January 18, pp. 48–54.

ONDCP (Office of National Drug Control Policy). 2008. "Prescription drug abuse." Available online: www.whitehousedrugpolicy.gov/

Orrenius, Pia. 2006. "The impact of immigration." *Wall Street Journal*, April 25, p. A18.

Osborne, Lawrence. 2001. "Regional disturbances." *New York Times Magazine*, May 6, pp. 100–102.

O'Shaughnessy, Lynn. 2008. "Rising prices hammer seniors on fixed incomes." *USA Today*, July 2, p. 1B.

Overall, Christine. 1992. "What's wrong with prostitution? Evaluating sex work." *Signs*, 17, pp. 705–724.

Ozols, Jennifer Barrett. 2005. "Health isn't color-blind." *Newsweek*, February 3, p. 10.

Page, Susan, and William Risser. 2008. "Poll: Racial divide narrowing but persists." *USA Today*, July 24, p. 6A.

Pager, Devah. 2003. "The mark of a criminal record." *American Journal of Sociology*, 108, pp. 937–975.

Pager, Devah. 2007. *Marked: Race, Crime, and Finding Work in an Era of Mass Incarceration*. Chicago: University of Chicago Press.

Pan, Philip P. 2008. "In Russia, a grisly message marks rise in hate crimes." *Washington Post*, December 14, p. A31.

Pape, Robert. 2005. *Dying to Win: The Strategic Logic of Suicide Terrorism*. New York: Random House.

Parenti, Christian. 2010. "The case for EPA action." *Nation*, May 3, pp. 14–17.

Park, Andrew. 2005. "Between a rocker and a high chair." *BusinessWeek*, February 21, pp. 86–88.

Parker, Robert Nash, with Linda-Anne Rebhun. 1995. *Alcohol and Homicide: A Deadly Combination of Two American Traditions*. Albany, NY: State University of New York Press.

Parker-Pope, Tara. 2007a. "As child obesity surges, one town finds way to slim." *Wall Street Journal*, May 10, pp. A1, A15.

Parker-Pope, Tara. 2007b. "The man problem." *Wall Street Journal*, April 24, pp. D1, D3.

Parker-Pope, Tara. 2008. "Love, sex and the changing landscape of infidelity." *New York Times*, October 28, p. D1.

Parker-Pope, Tara. 2010. "She works. They are happy." *New York Times*, January 24, p. 1.

Parsons, Talcott. 1964. *The Social System*. Glencoe, IL: Free Press.

Parsons, Talcott, and Robert F. Bales. 1953. *Family, Socialization, and Interaction Process*. Glencoe, IL: Free Press.

Paul, Pamela. 2004. "The porn factor." *Time*, January 19, pp. 99–100.

Paul, Pamela. 2010. "Maybe bullies just want to be loved." *New York Times*, May 23, p. 7.

Paxton, Pamela. 2005. "Trust in Decline?" *Contexts*, winter, pp. 40–46.

Pedahzur, Ami, Arie Perliger, and Leonard Weinberg. 2003. "Altruism and fatalism: The characteristics of Palestinian suicide terrorists." *Deviant Behavior*, 24, pp. 405–423.

Peen, Jaap, et al. 2007. "Is the prevalence of psychiatric disorders associated with urbanization?" *Social Psychiatry & Psychiatric Epidemiology*, 42, pp. 984–989.

Peplau, Letitia Anne, and Susan D. Cochran. 1990. "A relationship perspective on homosexuality." In David P. McWhirter et al. (eds.), *Homosexuality/Heterosexuality*. New York: Oxford University Press.

Peplau, Letitia Anne, and Adam W. Fingerhut. 2007. "The close relationships of lesbians and gay men." *Annual Review of Psychology*, 58, pp. 405–424.

Peralta, Robert L. 2005. "Race and the culture of college drinking." In Wilson R. Palacios (ed.), *Cocktails & Dreams: Perspectives on Drug and Alcohol Use*, pp. 127–141. Upper Saddle River, NJ: Prentice Hall.

Perkins, Roberta. 1991. *Working Girls: Prostitutes, Their Life and Social Control*. Canberra: Australian Institute of Criminology.

Petrecca, Laura. 2009. "Teens compete with laid-off adults for summer jobs." *USA Today*, May 7, p. 1A.

Pew Research Center. 2006. "Who votes, who doesn't, and why?" October 16, pp. 1–4.

Pew Research Center. 2010. "Continued positive marks for government anti-terror efforts." October 22.

Pfeffer, Jeffrey. 2010. "Lay off the layoffs." *Newsweek*, February 15, pp. 32–37.

Pianin, Eric. 2003. "Study finds net gain from pollution rules." September 27. Available online: www.washingtonpost.com

Pickert, Kate. 2010. "Spotlight: Russian adoption." *Time*, April 26, p. 14.

Pittman, Frank III. 1993. "Beyond betrayal: Life after infidelity." *Psychology Today*, May/June, p. 36.

Ponse, Barbara. 1984. "The problematic meanings of 'lesbian.'" In Jack D. Douglas (ed.), *The Sociology of Deviance*. Boston: Allyn & Bacon.

Pope, Victoria. 1994. "To be young and pretty in Moscow." *U.S. News & World Report*, March 28, p. 56.

Porter, Eduardo. 2006. "Study finds wealth inequality is widening worldwide." *New York Times*, December 6, p. C3.

Potterat, John J., et al. 1990. "Estimating the prevalence and career longevity of prostitute women." *Journal of Sex Research*, 27, pp. 233–243.

Powell, Bill. 2009. "Five things the U.S. can learn from China." *Time*, November 23, pp. 28–35.

Pratt, Timothy. 2001. "Sex slavery packet: A growing concern in Latin America." *Christian Science Monitor*, January 11, p. 7.

Presser, Harriet B. 2003. *Working in a 24/7 Economy*. New York: Russell Sage Foundation.

Pridemore, William Alex. 2008. "A methodological addition to the cross-national empirical literature on social structure and homicide: A first test of the poverty-homicide thesis." *Criminology*, 46, pp. 133–154.

Pristina, Andrew Purvis, and Jan Stojaspal Chisinau. 2001. "Human slavery." *Time Europe*, February 18, pp. 18–21.

Procida, Richard, and Rita J. Simon. 2003. *Global Perspectives on Social Issues: Pornography*. Lanham, MD: Lexington.

Putnam, Robert. 2006. "You gotta have friends." *Times*, July 3, p. 36.

Quenqua, Douglas. 2009. "Recklessly seeking sex on Craigslist." *New York Times*, April 18, p. S1.

Quindlen, Anna. 2006. "The failed experiment." *Newsweek*, June 26, p. 64.

Rank, Mark R. 2003. "As American as apple pie: Poverty and welfare." *Contexts*, summer, pp. 41–49.

Ratey, John J., and Catherine Johnson. 1997. *Shadow Syndromes*. New York: Pantheon Books.

Raymond, Margaret E. 2010. "Be careful on the charter school bandwagon. . . ." *Los Angeles Times*, February 1, p. 19.

Read, Jen'nan Ghazal. 2008. "Muslims in America." *Contexts*, pp. 39–43.

Reid, Scott A., Jonathan Epstein, and D. E. Benson. 1995. "Does exotic dancing pay well but cost dearly?" In Alex Thio and Thomas C. Calhoun (eds.), *Readings in Deviant Behavior*. New York: HarperCollins.

Reid, T. R. 2009. "No country for sick men." *Newsweek*, September 21, pp. 42–45.

Reiss, Ira L. 1986. *Journey into Sexuality: An Exploratory Voyage*. Englewood Cliffs, NJ: Prentice Hall.

Rescorla, L., et al. 2007. "Epidemiological comparisons of problems and positive qualities reported by adolescents in 24 countries." *Journal of Consulting and Clinical Psychology*, 75, pp. 351–358.

Reuters. 2009. "Iceland: Nordic countries lead in gender equality, report says." *New York Times*, October 28, p. 13.

Richardson, Laurel. 1988. *The Dynamics of Sex and Gender: A Sociological Perspective*. New York: Harper & Row.

Riesman, David. 1950. *The Lonely Crowd*. New Haven, CT: Yale University Press.

Riley, Matilda White. 1982. "Aging and health in modern communities." *Ekistics*, 196, pp. 381–383.

Rimer, Sara. 1993. "Campus lesbians step into unfamiliar light." *New York Times*, June 5, p. 6.

Rimer, Sara. 2000. "A lost moment recaptured." *New York Times: Educational Life*, January 9, pp. 21–24.

Ripley, Amanda. 2005. "Who Says Women Can't Be Einstein." *Time*, March 7, pp. 51–60.

Ripley, Amanda. 2010. "Is cash the answer?" *Time*, April 19, pp. 40–47.

Rivara, Frederick, et al. 2004. "Mortality attributable to harmful drinking in the United States, 2000." *Journal of Studies on Alcohol*, 65, pp. 530–536.

Rivas, Teresa. 2006. "Atypical workdays becoming routine." *Wall Street Journal*, April 4, p. A19.

Roberts, Sam. 2007. "Biggest urban growth is in South and West." *New York Times*, June 28, p. A14.

Robins, Lee N., et al. 1984. "Lifetime prevalence of specific psychiatric disorders in three sites." *Archives of General Psychiatry*, 41, pp. 949–958.

Robison, Jennifer. 2003. "Homosexual parenting evenly divides Americans." July 1. Available online: www.gallup.com

Rodgers, Bryan, and Susan L. Mann. 1993. "Rethinking the analysis of intergenerational social mobility: A comment on John W. Fox's 'Social class, mental illness, and social mobility.'" *Journal of Health and Social Behavior*, 34, pp. 165–172.

Rohter, Larry. 2008. "Social Security too hot to touch? Not in 2008." *New York Times*, August 14, p. 20.

Roldan, Kenneth Arroyo, and Gary M. Stern. 2006. *Minority Rules: Turn Your Ethnicity into a Competitive Edge*. New York: HarperCollins.

Romero, Frances. 2010. "George W. Bush." Available online: www.time.com/time/specials/packages/article/

Romm, Joseph. 2010. "Big oil keeps blowing smoke." *U.S. News & World Report*, p. 24.

Roscigno, Vincent J. 2010. "Ageism in the American workplace." *Contexts*, winter, pp. 16–21.

Rose, Arnold. 1967. *The Power Structure*. New York: Oxford University Press.

Rosen, Ruth. 2000. *The World Split Open*. New York: Viking.

Rosenberg, Debra. 2004. "The *Will & Grace* effect." *Newsweek*, May 24, pp. 38–39.

Rosenberg, Matt. 2010. "China's one child policy." Available online: http://geography.about.com

Rosenblatt, Roger. 1994. "A killer in the eye." *New York Times Magazine*, June 5, pp. 38–47.

Rosenthal, Robert. 1973. "The Pygmalion effect lives." *Psychology Today*, February, pp. 56–63.

Rossi, Alice S. 1984. "Gender and Parenthood." *American Sociological Review*, 49, pp. 1–19.

Rother, John. 2009. "Stop age discrimination." *USA Today*, October 23, p. 12a.

Rother, John. 2010. "Let's not kill the golden goose." *U.S. News & World Report*, February, p. 14.

Rowe, Paul M. 1995. "Alcoholism in U.S.A." *Lancet*, 345, April 1, p. 860.

Rubin, Arline M., and James R. Adams. 1986. "Outcomes of sexually open marriages." *Journal of Sex Research*, 22, pp. 311–319.

Ruiz, Dorothy S. 1982. "Epidemiology of schizophrenia: Some diagnostic and sociocultural considerations." *Phylon*, 43, pp. 315–326.

Rumney, Philip N. S. 2008. "Policing male rape and sexual assault." *Journal of Criminal Law*, 72, pp. 67–86.

Rust, Paula C. 1995. *Bisexuality and the Challenge to Lesbian Politics: Sex, Loyalty, and Revolution*. New York: New York University Press.

Rutherford, Megan. 2000. "Catching their second wind." *Time*, January 31, pp. E5–E7.

Ruzek, Joe. 2010. "Coping with PTSD." National Center for PTSD. November 15. Available online: www.hiddenhurt.co.uk/

Rybczynski, Witold. 1995. *City Life: Urban Expectations in a New World*. New York: Scribner's.

Sabato, Larry J., and Glenn R. Simpson. 1996. *Dirty Little Secrets*. New York: Times Books.

Sadker, Myra, and David Sadker. 1995. *Failing at Fairness: How Our Schools Cheat Girls*. New York: Touchstone.

SAMHSA (Substance Abuse and Mental Health Services Administration). 2002. Annual Household Survey. Available online: www.hhs.gov/news

Samuelson, Robert J. 2003a. "A crackup for world trade?" *Newsweek*, August 25, p. 55.

Samuelson, Robert J. 2003b. "Globalization goes to war." *Newsweek*, February 24, p. 41.

Samuelson, Robert J. 2005. "The hard truth of immigration." *Newsweek*, June 13, pp. 64–65.

Samuelson, Robert J. 2008. "Getting real about health care." *Newsweek*, September 15, p. 73.

Samuelson, Robert J. 2010. "Insecurity goes upscale." *Newsweek*, July 19, p. 24.

Sanday, Peggy Reeves. 1996. "Rape-prone versus rape-free campus cultures." *Violence Against Women*, 2, pp. 191–208.

Sanday, Peggy Reeves. 2007. *Fraternity Gang Rape: Sex, Brotherhood, and Privilege on Campus*, 2nd ed. New York: New York University Press.

Sapp, M., et al. 1999. "Attitudes toward rape among African American male and female college students." *Journal of Counseling and Development*, 77, pp. 204–208.

Satel, Sally. 2008. "Addiction doesn't discriminate? Wrong." *New York Times*, September 2, p. F6.

Savin-Williams, Ritch C. 2005. "Who's gay? Does it matter?" *Current Directions in Psychological Science*, 15, pp. 40–44.

Sayre, Carolyn. 2007a. "Just say no to plastic bags." *Time*, April 9, p. 82.

Sayre, Carolyn. 2007b. "Open a window." *Time*, April 9, p. 78.

Scarce, Michael. 1997. *Male on Male Rape: The Hidden Toll of Stigma and Shame*. New York: Insight Books.

Scelfo, Julie. 2007. "Men & depression: facing darkness." *Newsweek*, February 26, pp. 43–49.

Schaefer, Richard T. 2008. *Racial and Ethnic Groups*. Upper Saddle River, NJ: Pearson.

Schepis, Ty S., and Suchitra Krishnan-Sarin. 2008. "Characterizing adolescent prescription misusers: A population-based study." *Journal of the American Academy of Child & Adolescent Psychiatry*, 47, pp. 745–754.

Schiff, Frederick. 1999. "Nude dancing: Scenes of sexual celebration in a contested culture." *Journal of American Culture*, winter, pp. 9–16.

Schlenger, William, et al. 2002. "Psychological reactions to terrorist attacks: Findings from the National Study of Americans' Reactions to September 11." *Journal of the American Medical Association*, 288, pp. 581–588.

Schlosser, Eric. 1997. "The business of pornography." *U.S. News & World Report*, February 10, pp. 42–50.

Schmid, Randolph E. 2010. "Girls may learn math anxiety from female teachers." January 25. Available online: http://news.yahoo.com

Schnittker, Jason, Jeremy Freese, and Brian Powell. 2003. "Who are feminists and what do they believe? The role of generations." *American Sociological Review*, 68, pp. 607–622.

Schreiber, Mordecai, Alvin Schiff, and Leon Klenicki. 2003. *The Shengold Jewish Encyclopedia*. Rockville, MD: Schreiber Publishing.

Schrof, Joannie M. 1998. "Required course: Bedside manner 101." *U.S. News & World Report*, December 21, p. 66.

Schuster, Mark, et al. 2001. "National survey of stress reactions after the September 11, 2001 terrorist attacks." *New England Journal of Medicine*, 345, pp. 1507–1512.

Schutt, Russell. 2009. *Investigating the Social World: The Process and Practice of Research*, 6th ed. Thousand Oaks, CA: Pine Forge.

Schwartz, Sharon. 1991. "Women and depression: A Durkheimian perspective." *Social Science and Medicine*, 32, p. 127.

Seager, Joni. 2003. *The Penguin Atlas of Women in the World*. New York: Penguin.

Seaman, Barrett. 2005. *Binge: What Your College Student Won't Tell You*. Hoboken, NJ: Wiley & Sons.

Sebelius, Kathleen. 2010. "Administration already has started improving Head Start." *USA Today*, July 20, p. 8a.

Seligmann, Jean. 1994. "The death of a spouse." *Newsweek*, May 9, p. 57.

Sergo, Peter. 2008. "Mental illness in America." *Scientific American Mind*, Vol. 19, Issue 1, p. 15.

Seuffert, Virginia. 1990. "Home remedy." *Policy Review*, 52, pp. 70–75.

Shellenbarger, Sue. 2006. "Work and family." *Wall Street Journal*, February 28, p. B1.

Shweder, Richard A. 1997. "It's called poor health for a reason." *New York Times*, March 9, p. E5.

Siegel, Robert. 2006. "Memoir of Rwanda's genocide." *National Public Radio*, April 24, 9 am.

Simon, David R. 2008. *Elite Deviance*, 9th ed. Boston: Allyn & Bacon.

Simon, Julian L. 1990. *Population Matters: People, Resources, Environment, and Immigration*. New Brunswick, NJ: Transaction.

Skinner, B. F. 1983. "Creativity in old age." *Psychology Today*, September, pp. 28–29.

Sloan, Allan. 1997. "A sexy new loophole." *Newsweek*, February 3, pp. 37–38.

Smith, Ray A. 2004. "U.S. cities are mired in fiscal woes." *Wall Street Journal*, September 21, p. A6.

Smock, Pamela J. 2000. "Cohabitation in the United States: An appraisal of research themes, findings, and implications." *Annual Review of Sociology*, 26, pp. 1–20.

Smyth, Angela, and Chris Thompson. 1990. *SAD: Seasonal Affective Disorder*. New York: Unwin.

Snow, David A., and Leon Anderson. 2003. "Street people." *Contexts*, winter, pp. 12–17.

Sommers, Christina Hoff. 2000. *The War Against Boys*. New York: Simon & Schuster.

Spencer, Jennifer, et al. 2002. "Self-esteem as a predictor of initiation of coitus in early adolescents." *Pediatrics*, 109, pp. 581–584.

Spitzer, Eliot, and Andrew G. Celli, Jr. 2004. "Bull run: capitalism with a democratic face." *The New Republic*, March 22, pp. 18–21.

Spivey, Sue E. 2005. "Distancing and solidarity as resistance to sexual objectification in a nude dancing bar." *Deviant Behavior*, 26, pp. 417–437.

Sprigg, Peter. 2008. "Questions and answers: What's wrong with letting same-sex couples 'marry'?" In Kurt Finsterbusch (ed.), *Taking Sides: Clashing Views on Social Issues*, 14th ed. Dubuque, IA: McGraw-Hill.

St. John, Warren. 2004. "Today's bank robber might look like a neighbor." *New York Times*, July 3, pp. A1, A16.

Stanley, Thomas J., and William D. Danko. 1998. *The Millionaire Next Door: The Surprising Secrets of America's Wealthy*. New York: Pocket Books.

Stearns, Marion S. 1971. *Report on Preschool Programs*. Washington, DC: U.S. Government Printing Office.

Steffensmeier, Darrell, and Emilie Allan. 1995. "Criminal behavior: Gender and age." In Joseph F. Sheley (ed.), *Criminology: A Contemporary Handbook*. Belmont, CA: Wadsworth.

Stewart, Jay. 2006. "Male nonworkers: Who are they and who supports them?" *Demography*, August, pp. 537–552.

Stolberg, Sheryl Gay. 1998. "As doctors trade shingle for marquee, cries of woe." *New York Times*, August 3, pp. A1, A14.

Stossel, John. 2001. "The real cost of regulation." *Imprimis*, May, pp. 1–5.

Strate, John M., et al. 2009. "Sexual harassment." *Public Integrity*, winter, pp. 61–75.

Strom, Kevin J., and John M. MacDonald. 2007. "The influence of social and economic disadvantage on racial patterns in youth homicide over time." *Homicide Studies*, 11, pp. 50–69.

Strong, Bryan, et al. 2005. *The Marriage and Family Experience: Intimate Relationships in a Changing Society*, 9th ed. Belmont, CA: Wadsworth.

Suddath, Claire. 2010. "Bill Clinton." Available online: www.time.com/time/specials/packages/article/

Suro, Roberto. 1991. "Where America is growing: The suburban cities." *New York Times*, February 23, pp. 1, 10.

Sutherland, Edwin H. 1939. *Principles of Criminology*, 3rd ed. Philadelphia: Lippincott.

Sutton, John R. 2004. "The political economy of imprisonment in affluent Western democracies, 1960–1990." *American Sociological Review*, 69, pp. 170–189.

Szabo, Liz. 2009. "Painkillers lead to abuse: Prescriptions are now the biggest cause of fatal drug overdoses." *USA Today*, October 1, p, 1D.

Szymanski, Albert. 1978. *The Capitalist State and the Politics of Class*. Cambridge, MA: Winthrop.

Tannen, Deborah. 2001. *Talking from 9 to 5: Women and Men at Work*. New York: Quill.

Tannenbaum, Frank. 1938. *Crime and the Community*. New York: Columbia University Press.

ter Bogt, Tom, et al. 2006. "Economic and cultural correlates of cannabis use among mid-adolescents in 31 countries." *Addiction*, 101, pp. 241–251.

Terkel, Studs. 1992. *Race: How Blacks and Whites Think and Feel About the American Obsession*. New York: New Press.

Testa, Maria, and Jennifer A. Livingston. 2009. "Alcohol consumption and women's vulnerability to sexual victimization: Can reducing women's drinking prevent rape?" *Substance Use & Misuse*. 44, pp. 1349–1376.

Tewksbury, Richard. 2007. "Effects of sexual assaults on men: Physical mental and sexual consequences." *International Journal of Men's Health*, 6, pp. 22–35.

Thibault, Marie. 2009. "Recipe for riches." *Forbes*, October 19, pp. 36–37.

Thio, Alex. 2010. *Deviant Behavior*, 10th ed. Boston: Allyn & Bacon.

Thomas, Evan, and Stuart Taylor. 2010. "Fight club." *Newsweek*, January 11, pp. 48–49.

Thomas, Evan, and Pat Wingert. 2010a. "Schoolyard brawl." *Newsweek*, March 15, pp. 30–32.

Thomas, Evan, and Pat Wingert. 2010b. "Understanding charter schools." *Newsweek*, June 21, p. 46.

Thompson, Mark. 2008. "America's Medicated Army." June 5. Available online: www.time.com

Thorne, Barrie. 1993. *Gender Play: Girls and Boys in School*. New Brunswick, NJ: Rutgers University Press.

Thottam, Jyoti. 2003. "Where the good jobs are going." *Time*, August 4, pp. 36–39.

Tierney, John. 2001. "The big city: G.I. stands tall again (12 inches)." *New York Times*, December 11, p. D1.

Tolentino, Paz Estrella. 2000. *Multinational Corporations: Emergence and Evolution*. London: Routledge.

Tolson, Jay. 2007. "An ugly truth." *U.S. News & World Report*, October 29, pp. 35–37.

Toppo, Greg. 2009. "Profound shift in home schooling: Numbers, parents' income are growing." *USA Today*, May 29, p. 1a.

Toppo, Greg, and Marilyn Elias. 2009. "Lessons from Columbine." *USA Today*, April 14, p. 1d.

Toufexis, Anastasia. 1992. "Bisexuality: What is it?" *Time*, August 17, p. 49.

Toumanoff, Peter. 2005. "The effects of gender on salary-at-hire in the academic labor market." *Economics of Education Review*, 24, pp. 179–188.

Trost, Cathy, and Paulette Thomas. 1993. "Sexual politics." *Wall Street Journal*, March 10, p. A6.

Trotter, Robert J. 1987. "Mathematics: A male advantage?" *Psychology Today*, January, pp. 66–67.

Trunk, Penelope. 2006. "Ten tips to help you find work." *The Boston Globe*, October 29. Available online: www.boston.com

Tumin, Melvin M. 1953. "Some principles of stratification: A critical analysis." *American Sociological Review*, 18, pp. 387–393.

Tumulty, Karen. 2006. "The politics of fat." *Time*, March 27, pp. 40–43.

Turco, Richard P. 2002. *Earth Under Siege: From Air Pollution to Global Change*. New York: Oxford University Press.

Turley, Jonathan. 2008. "Bullying's day in court. . . ." *USA Today*, July 15, p. 13A.

Twenge, Jean M. 2010. "Entitled Americans don't get it." *U.S. News & World Report*, February, p. 12.

Uggen, Christopher, and Amy Blackstone. 2004. "Sexual harassment as a gendered expression of power." *American Sociological Review*, 69, pp. 64–92.

UNESCO. 2005. "Megacities—our global urban future." Leiden, Netherlands: Earth Sciences for Society Foundation.

United Nations. 2010. *Human Development Report 2010*. New York: Oxford University Press.

Unnever, James D., et al. 2008. "Public support for getting tough on corporate crime: Racial and political divides." *Journal of Research in Crime and Delinquency*, 45, pp. 163–190.

U.S. Bureau of Labor Statistics. 2010. "Economic news release." February 5, 2010.

U.S. Census Bureau. 2001a. *Current Population Survey*. "Educational attainment in the U.S.: 2009." Available online: www.census.gov/cps/

U.S. Census Bureau. 2001b. *Statistical Abstract of the United States*. Washington, DC: U.S. Government Printing Office.

U.S. Census Bureau. 2009a. *Statistical Abstract of the United States*. Washington, DC: U.S. Government Printing Office.

U.S. Census Bureau. 2009b. *Current Population Survey*. "2009 Annual Social and Economic Supplement." Available online: www.census.gov/cps/

U.S. Census Bureau. 2010. *Statistical Abstract of the United States*. Washington, DC: U.S. Government Printing Office.

USA Today. 2003. "Don't deny government useful anti-terror tools." September 23, p. 22A.

Van Biema, David. 1995. "Bury my heart in committee." *Time*, September 18, pp. 48–51.

Van den Hoonaard, Deborah K. 2009. "Experiences of living alone: Widows' and widowers' perspectives." *Housing Studies*, 24, pp. 737–753.

Van Der Poel, Agnes, and Dike Van De Mheen. 2006. "Young people using crack and the process of marginalization." *Drugs: Education, Prevention & Policy*, 13, pp. 45–59.

Van Leeuwen, Mary Stewart. 1990. "Life after Eden." *Christianity Today*, July 16, pp. 19–21.

van Natta, Don Jr., and Jane Fritsch. 1997. "$250,000 buys donors' best access to Congress." *New York Times*, January 27, pp. A1, A10.

Vassallo, Suzanne, et al. 2009. "The roles that parents play in the lives of their young adult children." *Family Matters*, 82, pp. 8–14.

Vinci, Yasmina. 2010. "Significant dividends." *USA Today*, July 13, p. 10a.

Viscusi, W. Kip. 1992. *Smoking: Making the Risky Decision*. New York: Oxford University Press.

Voeller, Bruce. 1990. "Some uses and abuses of the Kinsey scale." In David P. McWhirter, Stephanie A. Sanders, and June Machover Reinisch (eds.), *Homosexuality/Heterosexuality*. New York: Oxford University Press.

Volpato, Chiara. 2009. "Italian women rise up." *New York Times*, August 27, p. A31.

von Drehle, David. 2010. "The case against summer vacation." *Time*, August 2, pp. 36–42.

von Drehle, David, and Sam Jewler. 2010. "Why crime went away." *Time*, February 22, pp. 32–35.

Waite, Linda J., et al. 2002. *Does Divorce Make People Happy? Findings from a Study of Unhappy Marriages*. New York: Institute for American Values.

Waitzkin, Howard. 1994. "A Marxian interpretation of the growth and development of coronary care technology." In Howard D. Schwartz (ed.), *Dominant Issues in Medical Sociology*, 3rd ed. New York: McGraw-Hill.

Wald, Matthew L. 1990. "Guarding environment: A world of challenges." *New York Times*, April 22, pp. 1, 16–17.

Walker, Jayne, John Archer, and Michelle Davies. 2005. "Effects of rape on men: A descriptive analysis." *Archives of Sexual Behavior*, 34, pp. 69–80.

Walker, Marcus, and Roger Thurow. 2009. "U.S., Europe are ocean apart on human toll of joblessness." *Wall Street Journal*, May 7, pp. A1, A14.

Wallis, Claudia. 2008. "How to make great teachers." *Time*, February 25, pp. 28–34.

Walsh, Brian. 2007. "Ride the bus." *Time*, April 8, p. 77.

Waltermaurer, Eve, Christina Ortega, and Louise-Anne McNutt. 2003. "Issues in estimating the prevalence of intimate partner violence." *Journal of Interpersonal Violence*, 18, pp. 959–974.

Wang, Jing, Ronald J. Iannotti, and Tonja R. Nansel. 2009. "School bullying among adolescents in the United States: Physical, verbal, relational, and cyber." *Journal of Adolescent Health*, 45, pp. 368–375.

Webley, Kayla. 2009. "Why Americans are adopting fewer kids from China." April 28. Available online: www.time.com

Webley, Kayla. 2010. "Top 10 embarrassing things that didn't stop people from getting elected: Barack Obama." January 21. Available online: www.time.com/time/specials/packages/article/

Wechsler, Henry, et al. 2002. "Trends in college binge drinking during a period of increased prevention efforts." *Journal of American College Health*, 50, pp. 203–217.

Wehrfritz, George, and Kay Itoi. 2003. Subterranean city." *Newsweek*, October 20, pp. E14–E16.

Weidenbaum, Murray. 2001. "Globalization is not a dirty word." *Vital Speeches of the Day*, May 1, pp. 296–300.

Weinberg, Leonard. 2008. *Global Terrorism*. Oxford, England: Oneworld.

Weisman, Steven R. 1997. "Spin nation." *New York Times*, January 26, p. 12.

Weiss, Robert S. 2004. "In their own words: Making the most of qualitative interviews." *Contexts*, fall, pp. 44–51.

Weitzer, Ronald. 1991. "Prostitutes' rights in the United States: The failure of a movement." *Sociological Quarterly*, 32, pp. 23–41.

Weitzer, Ronald. 2005. "Flawed theory and method in studies of prostitution." *Violence Against Women*, 11, pp. 934–949.

Wertheimer, Fred. 1996. "Stop soft money now." *New York Times Magazine*, December 22, pp. 38–39.

Wessel, David. 2004. "If a city isn't sunny—and air conditioned—it should be smart." *Wall Street Journal*, February 26, p. A2.

Wheeler, John, and Peter R. Kilmann. 1983. "Comarital sexual behavior: Individual and relationship variables." *Archives of Sexual Behavior*, 12, pp. 304–310.

Whittier, Nancy. 1995. *Feminist Generations: The Persistence of Radical Women's Movement*. Philadelphia: Temple University Press.

Wilke, John. 2004. "Price-fixing investigations sweep chemical industry." *Wall Street Journal*, June 22, pp. A1, A6.

Wilkinson, Kenneth P. 1984. "A research note on homicide and rurality." *Social Forces*, 63, pp. 445–452.

Wilkinson, Richard, and Kate Pickett. 2009. *The Spirit Level: Why More Equal Societies Almost Always Do Better*. London: Penguin Books.

Will, George. 2001. "Now, weapons of mass disruption?" *Newsweek*, October 29, p. 76.

Williams, David R. 2003. "The health of men: Structured inequalities and opportunities." *American Journal of Public Health*, 93, pp. 724–732.

Williams, Mary E. 2003. *Marijuana*. San Diego, CA: Greenhaven Press.

Wines, Michael. 2010. "China fortifies state businesses to fuel growth." *New York Times*, August 29. Available online: www.nytimes.com

Wolf, Richard. 2010. "Social Security races to 'negative.'" *USA Today*, February 6, p. 1a.

Wolfgang, Marvin E. 1958. *Patterns in Criminal Homicide*. Philadelphia: University of Pennsylvania Press.

Wood, Elizabeth Anne. 2001. "Strip club dancers: Working in the fantasy factory." In Alex Thio and Thomas C. Calhoun (eds.), *Readings in Deviant Behavior*, 2nd ed. Boston: Allyn & Bacon.

Wren, Christopher S. 1999. "Study compares U.S. and English drug crimes." *New York Times*, May 14, p. A10.

Wright, Bradley R. Entner, and C. Wesley Younts. 2009. "Reconsidering the relationship between race and crime." *Journal of Research in Crime and Delinquency*, 46, pp. 327–352.

Wright, Quincy. 1967. *A Study of War*, 2nd ed. Chicago: University of Chicago Press.

Xin, Niaohui, and Thomas K. Rudel. 2004. "The context for political corruption: A cross-national analysis." *Social Science Quarterly*, 85, pp. 294–309.

Yabroff, Jennie. 2008. "The myths of teen sex." *Newsweek*, June 9, p. 55.

Yaeger, Mark. 2006. "Anti-Arab sentiment in post-9/11 America." October 31. Available online: www.associatedcontent.com/

Yamamoto, J., et al. 1983. "Symptom checklist of normal subjects from Asian-Pacific islander population." *Pacific/Asian American Mental Health Research Center Review*, 2, pp. 6–8.

Yen, Hope. 2010. "Poverty formula revised: New method doubles number of elderly poor." *Washington Post*, March 3. Available online: www.washingtonpost.com

Yonkers, Kimberly A., and George Gurguis. 1995. "Gender differences in the prevalence and expression of anxiety disorders." In Mary V. Seeman (ed.), *Gender and Psychopathology*. Washington, DC: American Psychiatric Press.

Young, Cathy. 2007. "Assault behind bars." *Reason*, May, pp. 17–18.

Young, Gay, and Bette J. Dickerson (eds.). 1994. *Color, Class, and Country: Experiences of Gender*. London: Zed Books.

Zakaria, Fareed. 2007. "The Democrats' trade troubles." *Newsweek*, May 21, p. 38.

Zaslow, Jeffrey. 2003a. "Staying in touch. . . ." *Wall Street Journal*, June 24, p. D1.

Zaslow, Jeffrey. 2003b. "Will you still need me . . . ?" *Wall Street Journal*, June 17, p. D1.

Zeller, Tom., Jr. 2006. "Cyberthieves silently copy as you type." *New York Times*, February 27, pp. A1, A16.

Zezima, Katie. 2004. "Girl, 17, was raped by a group of teenagers, Boston police say." *New York Times*, December 10, p. 27A.

Zigler, Edward. 2000. "The wrong read on Head Start." *New York Times*, December 23, p. A13.

Zimmerman, Jacqueline Noll. 2003. *People Like Ourselves: Portrayals of Mental Illness in the Movies.* Lanham, MD: Scarecrow Press.

Zimring, Franklin E., et al. 2009. "Executions, deterrence, and homicide: A tale of two cities." UC Berkeley: Center for the Study of Law and Society Jurisprudence and Social Policy Program.

Zoroya, Gregg. 2009a. "Jobless rate hits 11.2% for veterans." *USA Today*, March 20, p. 1a.

Zoroya, Gregg. 2009b. "Troops' kids feel war toll: 6 of 10 parents see signs of fear, anxiety." *USA Today*, June 25, p. 1A.

Zoroya, Gregg. 2010. "Joblessness hits male vets of current wars." *USA Today*, April 6, p. 1.

Zuckerman, Mortimer. 2009. "Hard choices on healthcare reform." *U.S. News & World Report*, August, pp. 136–138.

Zwingle, Erla. 2002. "Cities: Where's everybody going?" *National Geographic*, November, pp. 70–99.

Glossary

Absolute poverty The lack of minimal food and shelter necessary for maintaining life.

Acceptance therapy A marriage counseling approach that encourages the spouses to accept each other's weaknesses.

Acute diseases Serious illnesses that strike suddenly.

Affirmative action A policy that requires employers and colleges to make special efforts to recruit qualified minorities and women for jobs, promotions, and educational opportunities.

Ageism Prejudice and discrimination against older people.

Alcoholics Persons who have lost control over drinking and consequently have problems with health, work, or personal relationships.

Alienation of labor Laborers' loss of satisfaction in their work because of the loss of control over their work process.

Altruistic suicide Suicide committed by individuals who are so strongly tied to their group that they effectively lose their selves and stand ready to do what their group tells them to do.

Alzheimer's disease A disease of the brain characterized by progressive loss of memory and other mental abilities.

Amalgamation The process by which various groups blend their subcultures to form a new culture.

American dilemma The discrepancy between the ideal of equality and the reality of inequality in the United States.

Anomie A social condition in which norms are absent, weak, or in conflict.

Anti-Semitism Prejudice or discrimination against Jews.

Arranged marriage A marriage in which the partners are chosen by the couple's parents.

Assimilation The process by which a minority adopts the culture of the larger society.

Binge drinkers Men who consume five or more drinks in a row, and women who consume four or more.

Bisexuals Individuals who are sexually attracted to members of both sexes.

Blackout An attack of memory loss, different from passing out.

Boosters Professional criminals who shoplift for large profit.

Bourgeoisie The capitalists who own the means of production such as factories and machineries.

Capitalism An economic system that allows private ownership of property and encourages competition in producing and selling goods and services.

Charter school A privately run but publicly funded school.

Chronic diseases Illnesses that have been developing for a long time.

Class conflict Marx's term for the struggle between capitalists, who own the means of production such as factories and machineries, and laborers, who do not.

Cohabitation The practice of living with a partner without having a formal wedding ceremony or obtaining a marriage license.

Communism A classless society that operates on Marx's principle of "from each according to his ability, to each according to his need."

Compensatory education A school program for improving the academic performance of socially and educationally disadvantaged children.

Conglomerate A corporation that owns companies in various unrelated industries.

Content analysis Searching for specific words or ideas and then turning them into numbers.

Corporate crime A crime that is carried out by the executive of a company for the company's benefit rather than for personal gain.

Crack A less pure form of cocaine that is still capable of producing an intense high because users typically smoke rather than snort it.

Crystalline intelligence Wisdom and insight into the human condition, as shown by one's skills in language, philosophy, music, or painting.

Cultural pluralism The peaceful coexistence among various racial and ethnic groups while allowing each group to retain its own subculture.

Culture of corpulence The culture that encourages us to overeat and avoid exercise.

De facto segregation Segregation that results from tradition and custom.

De jure segregation Segregation sanctioned by law.

Demographic transition The movement of human populations through four demographic stages that are tied to economic development.

Demography The scientific study of population.

Detached observation A method of observation in which the researcher observes as an outsider, from a distance, without getting involved.

Discrimination An unfavorable action against individuals that is taken because they are members of a certain category.

Double sexual standard The social norm that allows males, but not females, to have certain sexual experiences.

Dropout The quitting of high school before graduation.

Dysfunction The failure of some parts of society to perform their functions and the resulting disruption of the network of interdependence among all parts.

Egalitarian family A family in which the authority is equally distributed between husband and wife.

Empowerment zones Economically depressed urban areas that businesses, with the help of government grants, low-interest loans, and tax breaks, try to revive by creating jobs.

Endogamy The practice of marrying someone from within one's own group.

Epidemic A health problem that afflicts many people throughout the entire population.

Epidemiology The study of the origin and spread of disease in a given population.

Ethnic group A collection of people who share a distinctive cultural heritage.

Ethnography An analysis of people's lives from their own perspectives.

Exogamy The practice of marrying someone from outside one's group.

Experiment A research operation in which the researcher manipulates variables so their influence can be determined.

Expressive role A role that requires taking care of personal relationships.

Expulsion An act that involves the dominant group expelling a minority from certain areas or even from the country entirely.

Extended family A family that consists of two parents, their unmarried children, and other relatives.

External restraint The social control imposed on people to limit their freedom and range of behaviors.

Female genital cutting Female circumcision that involves removing some of the female genitalia such as the clitoris, its foreskin, or the labia.

Feminism The belief that women and men should be equal in various aspects of their lives.

Feminization of poverty The persistent and pervasive phenomenon of women experiencing poverty at higher rates than men.

Fluid intelligence The ability to grasp abstract relationships, as in mathematics, physics, or other sciences.

Freebasing Purifying a drug with ether and then smoking it.

Gays Exclusively homosexual men.

Gender inequality The difference in the amount of rewards that males and females are socially expected to get.

Gender roles The patterns of attitude and behavior that a society expects of its members as females and males.

Gender-neutral socialization The socialization of children into egalitarian gender roles.

Genocide The wholesale killing of members of a specific racial or ethnic group.

Glass ceiling The prejudiced belief that keeps minority professionals from holding leadership positions.

Global economy An economic system in which many countries from all over the world trade with each other.

Hate crime An offense committed because of the victim's race, religion, national origin, or sexual orientation.

Head Start A compensatory education program for disadvantaged preschoolers across the nation.

Healing role A set of social expectations of how a doctor should behave.

Heterosexuals Individuals who are sexually attracted to members of the opposite sex.

Homicide The killing of a person by another.

Homophobia Antihomosexual attitude.

Homosexuals Individuals who are sexually attracted to members of the same sex.

Hospitalists A new breed of doctors who focus on the general care of hospitalized patients.

Ideological conservatives People who oppose big government because they believe in free enterprise, rugged individualism, and capitalism.

Income The amount of money one earns from employment, business, investments, and other economic activities.

Infant mortality rate The number of babies who die before 1 year of age for every 1,000 live births.

Institutionalized discrimination The persistence of discrimination in social institutions that is not necessarily recognized by everyone as discrimination.

Instrumental role A role that requires performance of a task.

Jim Crow laws A set of laws that segregated blacks from whites in all kinds of public and private facilities, from restrooms to schools.

Latent function A function that is unintended and unrecognized.

Lesbians Exclusively homosexual women.

Life expectancy The number of years people born in a specific year can expect to live.

Manifest function A function that is intended and widely recognized.

Marginal surplus population People who are superfluous or useless to the economy.

Matriarchal family A family in which the dominant figure is the oldest female.

Means testing The system of determining whether a person is qualified for help from the government, which effectively refuses Social Security benefits to the wealthy.

Megalopolis A vast area in which many metropolises merge.

Metropolis A large urban area that includes a city and its surrounding suburbs.

Minority A racial or ethnic group that is victimized by prejudice and discrimination.

Mixed economy An economy having some elements of both capitalism and socialism.

Monogamy The marriage of one man to one woman.

Monopoly The situation in which one firm controls the market.

Multinational corporations Corporations with subsidiaries in many countries.

Nuclear family A family comprised of two parents and their unmarried children.

Oligopoly The situation in which only a few companies control the market.

Operational liberals People who support big government by backing government programs that render services to the public.

Opportunists Heterosexuals who engage in same-sex acts in situations where the opportunity presents itself.

PACs Political Action Committees; political organizations that funnel money from business, labor, and other special-interest groups into election campaigns to help elect or defeat candidates.

Participant observation A method of observation in which the researcher takes part in the activities of the group being studied.

Patriarchal family A family in which the dominant figure is the oldest male.

Patriarchy A system of domination in which men exercise power over women.

Peace The absence of war.

Physical addiction Having such a strong craving for alcohol or other drugs that the user suffers chills, shakes, and other withdrawal distresses when discontinuing use of the drugs.

Political corruption The abuse of official power for personal gain.

Political party A group of people organized for the purpose of gaining government offices.

Polyandry The marriage of one woman to two or more men.

Polygamy The marriage of one person to two or more people of the opposite sex.

Polygyny The marriage of one man to two or more women.

Population The entire group of people to be studied.

Pornography Sexually explicit material including pictures or words.

Prejudice A negative attitude toward a certain category of people.

Progressive taxation Government's attempt to reduce economic inequality by taxing the rich more than the poor.

Proletariat The laborers who do not own the means of production.

Prostitution The selling of sexual services.

Psychological addiction Having a strong craving for alcohol or other drugs.

PTSD Post-traumatic stress disorder, an anxiety disorder that results from exposure to any kind of terrifying event in which the threat of physical harm and death appears imminent.

Punitive approach Using law enforcement to stop the supply of drugs and punish drug sellers and users.

Pygmalion effect The impact of a teacher's expectations on student performance.

Race A group of people who are *perceived* by a given society to be biologically different from others.

Racism The belief that one's own race or ethnicity is superior to that of others.

Random sample A sample drawn in such a way that all members of a population must have the same chance of being selected.

Rape The use of force to get a person to do something sexual against his or her will.

Rape-free societies Societies that have a culture that discourages sexual aggression.

Rape-prone societies Societies that have a culture that encourages sexual aggression.

Relative deprivation The seeming inability to achieve a relatively high aspiration.

Relative poverty A state of deprivation resulting from an individual having less than the majority of the people in their society.

Roleless role Being assigned no role in society's division of labor.

Sample A relatively small number of people selected from a large population.

School voucher A plan that allows parents, not schools, to receive public money, which they use to pay for their children's attendance at the schools of their choice.

Secondary analysis Searching for new knowledge in the data collected earlier by another researcher.

Senescence The natural physical process of aging.

Senility An abnormal condition characterized by serious memory loss, confusion, and loss of the ability to reason.

Serial monogamy The marriage of one person to two or more people, but only one at a time.

Sexism Prejudice and discrimination based on one's sex.

Sexting Sending nude or seminude photos electronically.

Sexual harassment An unwelcome act of a sexual nature.

Showy masculinity A cultural characteristic that encourages males to show off their toughness and conceal their tenderness, to act like a "man" and avoid acting like a "woman."

Sick role A set of social expectations of how an ill person should behave.

Snitches Amateurs who steal articles of small value for personal use.

Social forces Forces that arise from the society of which we are a part.

Social problem A social condition that is perceived to be harmful to more than just a few people.

Socialism An economic system that requires public ownership of property and government control of the economy.

Sociological imagination Mills's term for the ability to see the impact of social forces on individuals, especially on their private lives.

Special-interest group An organized collection of people who attempt to influence government policies.

Stereotype An oversimplified, inaccurate mental picture of others.

Street hustlers Male heterosexuals whose sexual feelings are predominantly heterosexual but who engage in a greater volume of same-sex activities than trades.

Structured interview An interview in which the researcher asks standardized questions that require respondents to choose from several standardized options.

Summer slide A student's loss of a great deal of what he or she learned during the school year because of the summer vacation.

Supportive approach Using drug prevention (or education) and treatment to reduce the demand for drugs and help drug addicts.

Surrogate motherhood The arrangement for a woman to carry and bear a child for a couple.

Survey A research method that involves asking people questions about their opinions, beliefs, or behaviors.

Swinging The exchange of spouses for sex only by married couples.

Teetotalers Persons who completely abstain from drinking.

Terrorism The use of terrifying, extreme violence to express dissatisfaction with a government.

Tracking The system of sorting students into different groups according to past academic achievement.

Trades Male heterosexuals whose sexual feelings are predominantly heterosexual but who engage in same-sex activities.

Unstructured interview An interview in which open-ended questions are asked and respondents are allowed to answer freely, in their own words.

War Violent conflict between two nations.

Warrior culture theory The view that it is important for boys to grow up to be masculine and tough like a warrior.

Wealth The value of all assets one owns subtracted by the debts one owes.

Weapons of mass destruction Weapons that can kill thousands of people at the same time.

White-collar crime A crime that is *occupationally* related, carried out in the course of the offender's occupation, and the occupation involved is *white collar* as opposed to blue collar.

Working poor Individuals who are poor because they work for a wage that makes them fall below the official poverty line.

Wounded-boy theory The idea that boys are traumatized by the pressure of the warrior culture to separate from their mothers and hide their tender feelings.

Subject Index

Author Index

Photo Credits

ShutterStock, Inc.; **page 271** © Monkey Business Images/ShutterStock, Inc.; **page 275** © ImageSource/age fotostock

CHAPTER 12
Opener © Jim West/age fotostock; **page 288** © Rmarmion/Dreamstime.com; **page 289 (top)** © @erics/ShutterStock, Inc.; **page 289 (bottom)** © Elena Elisseeva/ShutterStock, Inc.; **page 294** © Lane V. Erickson/ShutterStock, Inc.

CHAPTER 13
Opener © EPA/Tannen Maury/Landov; **page 309** © Dennis MacDonald/age fotostock; **page 311** © Frontpage/ShutterStock, Inc.; **page 314** © CREATISTA/ShutterStock, Inc.; **page 315** © Newsday/MCT/Landov

CHAPTER 14
Opener © Robert J. Daveant/ShutterStock, Inc.; **page 331** © olly/ShutterStock, Inc.; **page 336** © David Buffington/Photodisc/

Getty Images; **page 339** © John Wollwerth/ShutterStock, Inc.; **page 344** © Corbis/age fotostock

CHAPTER 15
Opener © RexRover/ShutterStock, Inc.; **page 360** © mypokcik/ShutterStock, Inc.; **page 362** © Yury Asotov/ShutterStock, Inc.; **page 364** © rSnapshotPhotos/ShutterStock, Inc.; **page 367** © JeremyRichards/ShutterStock, Inc.

CHAPTER 16
Opener © Geoff Green/Landov; **page 382** © Matt McClain/ShutterStock, Inc.; **page 386** © Reuters/Jessica Rinaldi/Landov; **page 388** © VStock/Alamy Images; **page 393** © UPI Photo/HO/Landov